A

NEW

DICTIONARY OF QUOTATIONS

FROM THE

GREEK, LATIN, AND MODERN LANGUAGES.

Translated into English,

AND

OCCASIONALLY ACCOMPANIED WITH ILLUSTRATIONS, HISTORICAL, POETICAL, AND ANECDOTICAL.

WITH

An Extensive Index,

REFERRING TO EVERY IMPORTANT WORD.

BY THE AUTHOR OF

"LIVE AND LEARN," "THE NEWSPAPER AND GENERAL READER'S POCKET COMPANION," ETC.

From The Last London Edition.

PHILADELPHIA:
J. B. LIPPINCOTT & CO.
1869.

PREFACE.

THE advantages of Books of Reference are now so universally acknowledged that it would be wholly superfluous to endeavor to recommend the present work by dwelling on its peculiar merits.

To give a more copious amount of information than has hitherto appeared in any work of the kind has been the design of the present publication; and, unless its author be greatly deceived as to its execution, it can hardly fail to be useful to individuals of all ranks and conditions,—to the man of business and the man of pleasure, the student and the superficial reader, the busy and the idle. Every one who takes any share in conversation, or who dips, however cursorily, into any newspaper or other publication, will every now and then find the advantage of having access to the "New Dictionary of Quotations."

The author has not restricted himself to purely Classical Quotations, but, as his object is to supply the need of the unlearned as well as to refresh the memory of the scholar, isolated words, expressions in frequent use but imperfectly understood, and terms which have wandered far from their original import, have been freely incorporated in the work.

The value of this Dictionary is greatly enhanced by the complete and voluminous Index which is appended, by the aid of which a passage may be readily found where only two or three words of a quotation have been caught by the ear or remain upon the memory. Without this addition the utility of such a work is limited to the occasions on which an entire quotation is sought for.

The abbreviations *Gr. Lat. Fr. Ital. Ger. Span. Port.* and *Prov.* stand respectively for *Greek, Latin, French, Italian, German, Spanish, Portuguese,* and *Proverb.*

A

NEW DICTIONARY OF QUOTATIONS,

&c.

A.

A barbe de fou, on apprend à raire. Fr.—"Men learn to shave on the chin of a fool."—They like to make experiments at the expense of others.

"By trimming fools about the gill,
A barber's 'prentice learns his skill."

A bas. Fr.—"Down, down with." "With audacious and fearful sincerity do these hungry hordes inscribe on their banners two watchwords, destructive alike of domestic and political society, '*A bas la famille,* Down with family! and *La propriété est un vol,* Property is robbery!"

A beau jour beau retour. Fr.—"One good turn deserves another." N.B. This must be understood ironically in English, as the French proverb is said when one has, has had, or is likely to have, an opportunity of resenting an injury.

A beau mentir qui vient de loin. Fr. prov.—"Travelers have the privilege of lying." "It would be difficult to find a more striking proof of the truth of this proverb, '*A beau mentir qui vient de loin:* that is to say, *He who comes from afar may lie with impunity, without fear of contradiction, as he is sure of being listened to with the utmost attention.* Travelers, they say, often *draw the long bow* [indulge in exaggeration]."

A bis et à blanc. Fr. prov.—"By fits and starts."

A bolza vazia, e a casa acabada, faz o home sesudo, mas tarde. Port. prov.—"An empty purse, and a new house, make a man wise, but too late."

A bon appetit il ne faut point de sauce. Fr. prov.—"A good appetite needs no sauce; hunger, or a good stomach, is the best sauce."

A bon chat bon rat. Fr.—"To a good cat a good rat; tit for tat; set a thief to catch a thief." The parties are well matched, well met.

A bon chien il ne vient jamais un bon os. Fr. prov.—"A good bone does not always come to a good dog." Merit seldom meets with its reward.

1*

A bon demandeur bon refuseur. Fr. prov.—"Shameless craving must have shameful nay."

A bon entendeur il ne faut que demie parole. Fr. prov.—"A word is enough to the wise;" literally, "To one of quick apprehension half a word is sufficient." The Italians say, "*A buon intenditor poche parole,*" which has about the same meaning.

A bon entendeur peu de paroles, *or*, **A bon entendeur salut.** Fr. prov.—"To a good, an attentive, hearer, but few words are necessary." A word to the wise.

A bon vin il ne faut point de bouchon. Fr. prov.—"Good wine needs no bush."

A brebis tondue, Dieu mesure le vent. Fr.—"God tempers the wind to the shorn lamb."

A cade va, chi troppo alto sale. Ital. prov.—"Hasty climbers have sudden falls."

A capite ad calcem. Lat.—"From head to foot." Thoroughly, completely. From the beginning to the end.

A causa persa parole assai. Ital. prov.—"When the cause, law-suit, is lost, there has been enough of words, enough has been said." Do not discuss what has already been decided—settled.

A chaque oiseau
Son nid est beau. } Fr. prov.—

"Every bird thinks its own nest, finds its own nest, beautiful." See "*Ad ogni uccello,*" *&c.*

A chi consiglia, non duole il capo. Ital. prov.—"He who gives advice is not often troubled with a headache."

A cœur jeûn. Fr.—"Fasting."

A cœur ouvert. Fr.—"Openly; open-heartedly; with the most perfect candor, or unreservedness."

A contre cœur. Fr.—"Against the grain; against one's will; with a bad grace."

A cuspide corona. Lat.—"A crown from the spear." *Honor!* earned by military exploits: in other words, by *legally* blowing one's fellow-creatures' brains out, *or* running them through. "If Christian nations," said SOAME JENYNS, "were nations of Christians, there would be no wars."

"War is a game, which, were their subjects wise,
Kings could not play at."—COWPER.

"The worse the man, the better the soldier; if soldiers be not corrupt, they ought to be made so."—BONAPARTE.

"I abominate war as unchristian. I hold it the greatest of human crimes. I deem it to involve all others—violence, blood, rapine, fraud; every thing that can deform the character, alter the nature, and debase the name of man."—LORD BROUGHAM.

On the subject of *Honor* there is more philosophy in FALSTAFF's soliloquy, than many casual readers have discovered:

"Well, 'tis no matter; Honor pricks me on. Yea, but how if Honor prick me off, when I come on? how then? Can Honor set a leg? No. Or an arm? No. Or take away the grief of a wound? No. Honor hath no skill in surgery, then? No. What is Honor? A word. What is that word Honor? Air. A trim reckoning! Who hath it? He that died o' Wednesday. Doth he feel it? No. Doth he hear it? No. Is it insensible, then? Yea, to the dead. But will it not live with the living? No. Why? Detraction will not suffer it—therefore, I'll none of it! Honor is a mere scutcheon; and so ends my catechism."—*First Part of Henry IV.*

A facto ad jus non datur consequentia. Lat. Law maxim.—"The inference from the fact to the law is not allowed." A general law is not to be trammeled by a specific or particular precedent.

A fome he boa mostarda. Port. prov.—"Hunger is the best sauce." Literally, "Hunger is capital, good, mustard."

A fortiori. Lat.—"With stronger or greater reason." If a weak man be dangerous, it follows, *a fortiori*, that a weak and bad man must be more dangerous.

A fronte praecipitium, a tergo lupi. Lat. prov.—"A precipice in front of you, and wolves behind you, in your rear." Go forward, and fall: go backward, and mar all.

À gorge déployée. Fr.—"Immoderately, to or in an immoderate degree." "A poor pleasantry, by the help of some ludicrous turn, or expression, or association of ideas, may provoke cachinnation [*roars of laughter*] *à gorge déployée*," that is, *sufficient to split the sides.*

À goupil endormi rien ne tombe en la gueule. Old Fr. prov.—"A close mouth catcheth no flies."

À grands frais. Fr.—"At great expense; very expensively." Sumptuously.

À grand seigneur peu de paroles. Fr. prov.—"In addressing a man of distinguished rank, express yourself in few words, as briefly as possible."

A gusto. Ital.—"To one's heart's content."

À haute voix. Fr.—"Loudly, openly."

À l'abri. Fr.—"Sheltered, under cover."

À l'aise marche à pied qui mène son cheval par la bride. Fr. prov.—"'Tis good to go on foot when a man hath a horse in his hand."

À l'antique. Fr.—"After or according to the old way or fashion."

À l'impossible nul n'est tenu. Fr. prov.—"There is no flying without wings; there is no doing impossibilities."

À l'improviste. Fr.—"Unawares; on a sudden; unexpectedly."

A l'ongle on connait le lion. Fr.—"The lion is known by his paw."

A la barba de pazzi, il barbier impara a radere. Ital. prov.—"A barber learns to shave by shaving fools."

À la belle étoile. Fr.—"In the street, in the open air."

À la bonne heure! Fr.—"Well and good; very well; so be it; be it so!"

À la dérobée. Fr.—"By stealth; stealthily; on the sly; secretly; privately."

À la faim il n'y a point de mauvais pain. Fr. prov.—"With hunger no bread is nasty." Hungry dogs will eat dirty puddings.

À la française. Fr.—"After or according to the French fashion."

A la immortalidad el alma asida. Span. LOPE DE VEGA.—"The soul aspires to immortality."

À la lettre. Fr.—"Word for word, literally."

À loisir. Fr.—"At leisure; leisurely; at one's own convenience."

À la mode. Fr.—"In fashion; in the fashion; fashionably."

À longue corde tire qui d'autrui mort désire. Fr. prov.—"He who is anxious for the death of another has a long rope to pull." He that waits for dead men's shoes may go long enough barefoot.

A los osados ayuda la fortuna. Span. prov.—"Fortune helps, assists, the daring." Faint heart never won fair lady.

À main armée. Fr.—"Armed; in arms; with open force; by force of arms."

A mensa et thoro. Lat.—"*From table and bed*, or, as we say in English, *from bed and board*." A sentence of divorce, or separation of man and wife, issuing from the Consistorial Court, on account of acts of adultery which may have been substantiated against either party.

À merveille. Fr.—"Admirably well; wonderfully well; wondrous well." He executed his part *à merveille.*

À mon avis. Fr.—"In my opinion."

A multo fortiori. Lat.—"On much stronger grounds; with much stronger or greater reason."

A numine salus. Lat.—"Salvation, health of body or mind, protection, is from the Deity, from on high." LORD MANSFIELD, being told of the above motto on the carriage of a very noted quack, thus translated it: "*GOD help the patient!*"

À outrance. Fr.—"To the utmost; with tooth and nail; with might and main; out and out; with desperation." "A champion has started up, not only to avouch the purity of her general morals, but also to maintain *à outrance* her innocence of the great offense:" that is to say, *to the utmost, in the strongest terms, the most decided terms or manner*, her innocence, &c. N.B. Instead of *à outrance*, as above, or, *à toute outrance*, which is a stronger form, the *incorrect* form *à l'outrance* is nearly always used by English writers.

À pas de géant. Fr.—"With a giant's stride." This is a phrase of exaggeration not uncommon with our continental neighbors. They will say, for instance, "We have hitherto advanced with a slow pace, but slowly; but now we shall proceed *à pas de géant* [with gigantic steps], and come sturdily and fairly to the purpose."

À peu près. Fr.—"Very nearly; almost; thereabouts." "The produce is *à peu près* a seventh less."

À pied. Fr.—"On foot."

À la portée de tout le monde. Fr.—"Within reach of every one, attainable by everybody." "We may be laughed at for our passion for these old etiquettes, but, like MILTON, we cannot separate the *monarchy* from its *trappings;* the hoop was, it is true, a mere court ceremony,—useless, expensive, inconvenient, as an ordinary dress,—but is it not the essence of a *ceremony* to be all that? If a thing be useful, economical, and convenient, it is for every-day wear,—ceremonies ought not to be quite *à la portée de tout le monde:* if hoops are abolished for the ladies, why are men obliged to wear bags, and laced coats, and swords—all much more useless, if there can be degrees in inutility—than the prohibited hoops? But it is idle to dwell on such trifles: we observe them merely as tokens and harbingers; the leaves fall before the tree dies!"

N.B. The phrase is often used to signify, *comprehensible; understandable by everybody, every one; intelligible to every one.*

A posteriori. Lat.—"From the latter."

A priori. Lat.—"From the former, in the first instance." "I have demonstrably proved that the argument *a priori* and the argument *a posteriori* are one and the same process of ratiocination [reasoning]." "*A priori*" means, *from the former*, from the cause to the effect: "*A posteriori*" means, *from the latter*, from the effect to the cause. These are phrases, which are used in logical argument, to denote a reference to its different modes. The schoolmen distinguished them into the *propter quod* [on account of which], wherein an effect is proved from the next cause—as when it is proved that the moon is eclipsed, because the earth is then between the sun and the moon. The second is the *quia* [because], wherein the cause is proved from a remote effect—as that plants do not breathe because they are not animals; or, that there is a GOD from the works of the creation. The former of these is called demonstration *a priori*—the latter, demonstration *a posteriori.*

À propos. Fr.—"To the purpose; opportunely; seasonably; pertinently."

À propos de bottes. Fr.—"Without reason, for nothing." A phrase used proverbially, when, in the course of conversation, one passes from one subject to another that has no reference to it. It is then equivalent to our "*By-the-bye; now I think on't; now you put me in mind of it.*" *À propos de bottes, comment se porte monsieur votre père? By-the-bye, how is your father?*

À quelque chose malheur est bon. Fr. prov.—"Misfortune is good for something, is not always an evil, is not always thrown away." 'Tis an ill wind that blows nobody luck.

À qui chapon mange, chapon lui vient. Fr. prov.—"Capon comes to him who eats capon."—Spend, and GOD will send.

À quoi bon tant barguigner, et tant tourner autour du pot? Fr.—"To what purpose is, of what use is, so much humming and hawing, and beating about the bush?"

A tavola rotonda non si contende del luogo. Ital. prov.—"At a round table there's no dispute about place."

A tergo. Lat.—"Behind; at one's back; in the rear."

À tort et à droit. Fr.—"Right or wrong."

À tort et à travers. Fr.—"At random; without discretion; without due consideration; making a mull of a thing."

À tort ou à droit. Fr.—"Reason or none."

À tort ou à raison. Fr.—"Reason or none."

À tous oiseaux leurs nids sont beaux. Fr. prov.—"All birds like their own nests."

À tout propos. Fr.—"At every turn, ever and anon."

À toutes jambes. Fr.—"As fast as one's legs can carry one."

A tutiori. Lat.—"The safer side to take."

A vieux comptes nouvelles disputes. Fr. prov.—"Old reckonings cause new disputes, fresh strife." The English proverb is, "Short reckonings make long friends. Even reckoning keeps long friends."

A verbis legis non est recedendum. Lat. Law maxim.—"There is no departing from the words of the law." The judges are not to make any interpretation contrary to the express words of the statute.

A vinculo matrimonii. Lat.—"From the chain, bond, bonds, or tie of marriage, matrimony."

Aad jold, aad hae, aad brae, stiel ien wol to stae. Frisian.—

"Old gold, old bread, and fine old hay
Are well indeed by one to stay."

Ab actu ad posse valet consecutio. Lat.—"The induction is good, from what has been to what may be." By this logical maxim it is meant to state that when a thing has once happened it is but just to infer that such a matter may again occur.

Ab alio expectes alteri quod feceris. Lat. LABERIUS.—"You may expect from one person that which you have done to another."—Your conduct to others will form the measure of your own expectations.

Ab ante. Lat.—"Beforehand."

Ab asino lanam. Lat. prov.—"Wool from an ass." An impossibility.

Ab equinis pedibus procul recede. Lat. prov.—"Keep at a good distance from horses' feet." Trust not a horse's heel, nor a dog's tooth.

Ab equis ad asinos. Lat. prov.—"From horses to asses." To come from little good to stark naught.

Ab extra. Lat.—"From without."

Ab inconvenienti. Lat. phrase.—"From the inconvenience." *Argumentum ab inconvenienti*, An argument to show that the result of a proposed measure will prove inconvenient or unsuited to circumstances.

Ab incunabulis. Lat.—"From the very cradle."

Ab initio. Lat. phrase.—"From the beginning; from the very beginning; the very first." "His proceedings were ill founded *ab initio*."

Ab integro. Lat.—"Afresh, anew." N.B. We may also say "*de integro*," to express the same idea.

Ab irato. Lat.—"From an angry man." "A measure *ab irato*," that is, a measure proceeding *from*, or taken *by*, *an angry man*. "It is not safe in private life, and still less amongst nations, to accustom unreasonable and hot-tempered people to feel that they can obtain whatever they happen to wish for, by flying into a passion. England has shown—we trust, to the satisfaction of Europe—assuredly to the approbation of her own conscience—how well we can keep our temper, under severe provocation; but for the future quiet of our lives, we must endeavor to convince our irascible neighbors that wanton provocations and appeals '*ab irato*,' as M. de Valmy calls them, are not the modes by which any thing can be obtained from us; and that honor as well as policy will be best consulted by civiler manners and a more friendly spirit."

Ab officio et beneficio. Lat.—"From his office [*the discharge of his* *clerical functions*] and his benefice." "The Bishop suspended him for five years *ab officio et beneficio*."

Ab origine. Lat.—"From the very first."

Ab ovo usque ad mala. Lat. HORACE.—N.B. "*Ab ovo*," which is often used to signify "*at or from the beginning*," is the former portion of the expression "*ab ovo usque ad mala*," which literally means, *From the egg to the apples*, in allusion to the custom among the Romans of beginning their dinner or supper with eggs, and finishing with apples. WE use the expression to signify, *From the beginning to the end of any thing.*

Ab uno disce omnes. Lat. VIRGIL.—"From this, or a single instance, you may learn the nature of the whole, may form an estimate of the whole."

Ab urbe condita. Lat.—"From the building of the city."—In general thus abridged: A. U. C., in the chronology of the Romans.

Abad. Hindostanee.—"Built by." In the names of Indian towns, the concluding syllable usually affords some clew to their past history: thus, "*Abad*" signifies "*built by*," as, Ahmed-abad, a city built by AHMED SHAH; Aurung-abad, Hyder-abad, &c.

Abbé. Fr.—"An abbot, a ruler of an abbey." N.B. The word "*Abbé*" properly means *Father;* it is the title or designation of every French clergyman of the Roman Catholic Church.

Aberrare a scopo, *or*, **non attingere scopum.** Lat. prov. "To miss one's mark."

Abietibus juvenes patriis et montibus aequi. Lat. VIRGIL.—

"Youths, of height and size
Like firs, that on their mother-mountain rise."

May be applied to the Life-guards and Grenadiers.

Abnormis sapiens. Lat. HORACE.—"A person whose wisdom is not derived either from instruction or merely from books; one who is intuitively knowing." HORACE uses the expression to denote one who was a follower of no sect, and derived his doctrines and precepts from no rules of philosophizing, as laid down by others; but who drew them all from his own breast, and was guided by his own convictions respecting the fitness or unfitness of things.

Aborigines. Lat.—The original inhabitants of a country, equivalent to the Greek *Autochthones.*

Absens heres non erit. Lat. prov.—"The absent one has little chance of being the heir." Out of sight, out of mind.

Absentem laedit, cum ebrio qui litigat. Lat. PUBLIUS SYRUS. "He who quarrels with a drunken man hurts, injures, the absent." You should consider your adversary as absent, when his senses have left him.

Absit invidia. Lat.—"All envy apart." Without being supposed to speak invidiously, enviously. N.B. The *full* expression, which occurs in LIVY, is, "*Absit verbo invidia*," that is, *Take it not ill, amiss. Without disparagement to anybody, any one.*

**Abstineas igitur damnandis; hujus enim vel
Una potens ratio est, ne crimina nostra sequantur
Ex nobis geniti, quoniam dociles imitandis
Turpibus ac pravis omnes sumus.** Lat. JUVENAL.—

"Refrain from all that merits reprobation. *One* powerful motive, at least, there is to this, lest our children copy our crimes. For we are all of us too quick at learning to imitate base and depraved examples."

"O fatal guides! this reason should suffice
To win you from the slippery route of vice,
This powerful reason; lest your sons pursue
The guilty track, thus plainly marked by you!
For youth is facile, and its yielding will
Receives, with fatal ease, the imprint of ill."

Abundans cautela non nocet. Lat. prov.—"Plenty of caution can do no hurt, harm." We cannot be too cautious. "Take heed is a good reed." "Sure bind, sure find."

Abundat dulcibus vitiis. Lat. QUINTILIAN.—"He abounds with luscious faults." Spoken of an author even in whose errors something pleasing is to be found. "Modern ears are absolutely *debauched* by such poetry as DARWIN's, which marks the decline of simplicity and true taste in this country. It is to England what SENECA's prose was to Rome, *Abundat dulcibus vitiis.*"

Ac etiam. Law Lat.—"And also." A clause added by recent custom to a complaint of trespass, in the Court of King's Bench, which adds "and also" a plea of debt. The plea of trespass, by fiction, gives cognizance to the court, and the plea of debt authorizes the arrest.

Ac veluti MAGNO **in populo quum saepe coorta est**
Seditio, saevitque animis ignobile vulgus,
Jamque faces et saxa volant, furor arma ministrat;
Tum PIETATE **gravem ac meritis si forte virum quem**
Conspexere, silent, arrectisque auribus adstant,
Ille regit dictis animos, et pectora mulcet. Lat. VIRGIL.—

"And as when a sedition has perchance arisen among a *mighty* multitude, and the minds of the ignoble vulgar rage, now firebrands, now stones fly, fury supplies them with arms; if then, by chance, they espy a man revered in *piety* and worth, they are hushed, and stand with ears erect; he, by eloquence, rules their passions, and calms their breasts."

"As when sedition fires the ignoble crowd,
And the wild rabble storms, and thirsts for blood,
Of stones and brands a mingled tempest flies,
And all those arms that sudden rage supplies;
If some grave sire appears amid the strife,
In morals strict and sanctity of life,
All stand attentive, while the sage controls
Their wrath, and calms the tumult of their souls."

Accedas ad curiam. Law Lat.—"You may approach the court." This name is given to a writ by which proceedings may be removed from an inferior to a superior court.

Acceptissima semper munera sunt, auctor quæ pretiosa facit. Lat. OVID.—"Those gifts are ever the most acceptable which the giver has made precious." They frequently derive their value from our estimation of the donor. It may also allude to the *manner* of giving, as in SHAKSPEARE—

"You gave, with words of so sweet breath composed,
As made the things more rich."

Accipe, per longos tibi qui deserviat annos:
Accipe, qui pura norit amare fide.
Est nulli cessura fides: sine crimine mores:
Nudaque simplicitas, purpureusque pudor.
Non mihi mille placent: non sum desultor amoris:
Tu mihi si qua fides cura perennis eris. Lat. OVID.—
"Scorn me not, Chloe: me, whose faith well tried,
Long years approve, and honest passions guide:
My hopeless soul no foul affections move,
But chaste simplicity and modest love:
Nor I, like shallow fops, from fair to fair
Roving at random, faithless passion swear,
But thou alone shalt be my constant care."

Accusare nemo se debet nisi coram Deo. Lat. Law maxim.—"No man is bound to accuse himself, unless it be before God." No oath is to be administered, whereby any person may be compelled to confess a crime, or accuse himself. The law will not force any man to say or show that which is against him.

Acerrima proximorum odia. Lat. TACITUS.—"The hatred of those who are near to us is most violent." A contest between relatives is generally conducted with more acrimony than a dispute between strangers. The phrase may also be applied to that violence of rage which generally belongs to a civil war.

Acme. Gr.—"The highest point, the highest degree." "His fame was now supposed to have reached its *acme*."

Acquérir méchamment et dépenser sottement. Fr. prov.—"To acquire wickedly and spend foolishly." Ill got, ill spent.

Acribus initiis, incurioso fine. Lat. TACITUS.—"Alert in the beginning, but negligent in the end." Applied to a business vigorously conducted in the first instance, but where the exertion falls off as the affair draws nearer to a conclusion.

Acta exteriora indicant interiora secreta. Lat. Law maxim.—"By the outward acts we are to judge of the inward secrets." We can only decide on men's intentions from their conduct.

Actio personalis moritur cum persona. Lat. Law maxim.—"A personal action dies with the person." In case of a trespass or battery, the death of one or other of the parties puts an end to the action.

Actis aevum implet, non segnibus annis. Lat. OVID.—"He fills his space with deeds, and not with lingering years." Applied to a character distinguished for a number of brilliant actions accomplished in the course of a short life.

Actum est de Republica. Lat.—"It is all over with the Republic" A phrase used to intimate that the constitution is in extreme danger.

Actum ne agas. Lat. TERENCE.—"Do not overdo what has been already done." The work which is finished may be endangered by the touches of a superfluous anxiety.

Actus Dei nemini facit injuriam. Lat. Law maxim.—"No one shall be injured through the act of God." As, if a house be set on fire by lightning, the tenant shall not be responsible for the damage.

Actus legis nulli facit injuriam. Lat. Law maxim.—"The act of the law does injury to no man." If land, for instance, out of which a rent-charge is granted, be recovered by elder title, the grantee shall have a writ of annuity, because the rent-charge is made void by course of law.

Actus me invito factus, non est meus actus. Lat. Law maxim.—"An act done against my will is not my act." If a person be compelled, for instance, through fear or duress [imprisonment], to give a bond, or other writing, the deed is rendered void by the compulsion.

Actus non facit reum, nisi mens sit rea. Lat. Law maxim.—"The act does not make a man guilty, unless the mind be also guilty." Unless the intent be criminal, the deed cannot be attainted of criminality.

Acumen. Lat.—"The point or edge of any thing:" but metaphorically used to signify "sharpness, shrewdness, smartness, subtilty, cunning, sharpness of intellect, skill, accuracy of discrimination."

Ad absurdum. Lat.—"To an absurdity." "This is certainly reducing Protestantism *ad absurdum.*"

Ad aperturam libri. Lat.—"At the opening of the book, *or* opening the book at random."

Ad calamitatem quilibet rumor valet. Lat.—"Any rumor is sufficient against calamity." When a man is distressed, a breath may complete his ruin.

Ad arca aperta il giusto pecca. Ital. prov.—"The just man may sin with an open chest of gold before him." Opportunity makes the thief.

Ad captandum vulgus. Lat.—"To insnare the vulgar, to captivate the masses."—A lure thrown out to captivate the mobility.

N.B. Often used in an *abridged* form, thus, *Ad captandum.*

Ad eundem. Lat.—"To the same." In passing from one university or law society to another, it is said that he was admitted *ad eundem,* to the same precise rank which he held in the association or corporation of which he was previously a member.

Ad finem. Lat.—"At, or towards the end, conclusion." "See the 3d chapter, *ad finem.*"

Ad Graecas Kalendas. Lat.—"At the Greek Kalends." The Kalends formed a division of the Roman month which had no place in the Greek reckoning of time. The phrase was therefore used by the former to denote that the thing could never happen.

Ad humum moerore gravi deducit et angit. Lat. HORACE.—"Nature oft sinks us under a load of woe."

"Deep grief dejects, and wrings the tortured soul."

Or:—

[She] "wrings the sad soul, and bends it down to earth."

Ad hoc. Lat.—"For this purpose, thing, matter, object."

Ad infinitum. Lat.—"Without end." "Errors in reasoning on morals and on mind go on multiplying each other *ad infinitum.*"

Ad interim. Lat.—"For the mean time." "They hold their own opinions as *ad interim* truths."

Ad internecionem. Lat.—"To universal slaughter—e'en to the death." "The Ministers proposed to tax Cape wine *ad internecionem,*" that is, *to an extent amounting to an absolute prohibition.*

Ad invidiam. Lat.—"Invidiously; enviously; spitefully; maliciously."

Ad libitum. Lat.—"At one's pleasure, at pleasure." In music it is used to signify those ornamental graces which are left to the taste of the performer.

Ad nauseam. Lat.—"Enough to make one sick."—"The same ideas re-appear *ad nauseam,*" that is, *till they are absolutely sickening or nauseating.*

Ad ogni cosa è rimedio fuora ch'alla morte. Ital. prov.—"For every thing there's a remedy but death." There's a salve for every sore.

Ad ogni uccello il suo nido è bello. Ital. prov.—"With every bird its own nest is charming." This may mean either "the natural affection for home," or the preference bestowed on "the place of our nativity."

Ad omnia alia aetate sapimus rectius:
Solum unum hoc vitium senectus adfert hominibus—
Attentiores sumus ad rem omnes, quam sat est.
Lat. TERENCE.—

"In every thing else we are made wiser by age: but this one vice is inseparable from it, that we are all apt to be more worldly, more fond of money-making, more close-fisted, more grasping, than is either needful or becoming."

Ad perditam securim manubrium adjicere. Lat. prov.—"To throw the helve after the hatchet." Over shoes, over boots. To be in despair.

Ad populum phaleras. Ego te intus et in cute novi. Lat. PERSIUS.—"Away with those trappings to the vulgar; I know thee both inwardly and outwardly." I know the man too well to be deceived by appearances.

"Away! these trappings to the rabble show:
Me they deceive not; for thy soul I know,
Within, without."

Ad poenitendum properat, cito qui judicat. Lat.—"He who comes too speedily to a decision [and acts on the impulse of the moment] is not long ere he repents of it."

Ad quaestionem juris respondeant judices, ad quaestionem facti respondeant juratores. Lat. Law maxim.—"Let the judges answer to the question of law, and the jurors to the matter of fact."

Ad quod damnum. Lat.—"To what damage." A writ, which ought to be issued before the king grants certain liberties, such as a fair or market, ordering the sheriff to inquire what damage the county is liable to suffer by such grant. The same writ is also issued for a similar inquiry with respect to lands granted to religious houses or corporations, for turning highways, &c.

Ad referendum. Lat.—"To be left for future consideration, to be further considered." "The French and English Ministers took notice of the request, *ad referendum.*" N.B. "*Ad referendum*" is a phrase that was introduced into diplomacy by the Dutch, and is now become proverbial, to express slowness in deliberation, and a want of promptitude in decision.

Ad rem. Lat.—"To the purpose." "The arguments were not *ad rem.*"

Ad summam. Lat. HORACE.—"In short; in a word; in conclusion; to sum up the matter."

Ad tristem partem strenua est suspicio. Lat. PUBLIUS SYRUS. —"Suspicion is ever strong on the suffering side." When we play a losing game, we are apt to suspect all those who are around us of treachery.

Ad unguem. Lat. HORACE.—"With perfect accuracy; *literally*, to the [*pared*] nail." "He did not think it necessary to write *ad unguem.*" HORACE describes one of his characters as "*ad unguem factus homo,*" that is to say, as "*a man of the most polished manners.*" A metaphor, taken from workers in marble, who try the smoothness of the marble, and the exactness of the joinings, by drawing the nail over them. WE should say, in our own idiom, "*a perfect gentleman.*"

Ad usum fidelium. Lat.—"For the use of the faithful, of the Roman Catholics." N.B. The Church of England as well as the Church of Rome designates her sons and daughters as "THE FAITHFUL." See the Church Catechism.

Ad valorem. Lat.—"According to the value."

Ad vivum. Lat.—"To the life." "We have a picture of him *ad vivum*, by a master."

Adawlut. Hindostanee. "Justice; equity; a court of justice in India."

Adde parum parvo magnus acervus erit. Lat. prov.—"Add, keep adding, little to little, and soon will you have a good hoard." A good motto for the SAVINGS' BANKS.

Addenda. Lat.—"Additions; things to be added; additional matter appended to the body of a work [literary composition, book]."

Addictus, *or*, **addicti jurare in verba magistri.** Lat. HORACE. —"A person, or persons, blindly addicted to the tenets, opinions, of his or their master, teacher [*literally*, bound or compelled to swear to the opinions of a teacher]."

"Sworn to no master, of no sect, am I;
As drives the storm, at any door I knock,
And house with MONTAIGNE now, and now with LOCKE."

N.B. "*Addicti*" were properly those debtors whom the Praetor [a legal officer of ancient Rome] adjudged to their creditors, to be committed to prison, or otherwise secured, until satisfaction was made. Soldiers, however, were also called "*addicti,*" in allusion to the military oath, which they took when enrolled. We have a pleasant use of the word in SHAKSPEARE: *Leave off all thin potations*, says Falstaff, *and* addict *thyself unto sack.*

Adeo in teneris consuescere multum est. Lat. VIRGIL.—"Of so much value, of such avail, is custom [*the practice of good habits, the initiation into good habits*] in the tender years of childhood; of such importance is it to be accustomed to what is right and proper from the very dawn of existence." "Train up a child," says Solomon, "in the way he should go; and when he is old, he will not depart from it." Compare POPE:—

"Just as the twig is bent, the tree's inclined."

Adeon' homines immutari ex amore, ut non cognoscas eundem esse? Lat. TERENCE.—"Is it possible that man should be so perfectly changed by love, that you cannot know him to be the same individual?"

Adhuc sub judice lis est. Lat. HORACE.—"The contest is still before the judge." The matter in question, the point, is even yet, as yet, undecided.

Adieu. Fr.—"Good-bye, farewell." "There is something beautifully pious and tender in that word of sad import, '*Adieu!*'" that is to say, *may GOD guard you! to GOD I commit you:* literally, "*to GOD,*" "*A DIEU.*

Adieu pour toujours. Fr.—"Farewell forever."

Adieu jusqu'au revoir. Fr.—"Farewell, good-bye, till I see you again, till we meet again."

Adieu paniers, vendanges sont faites. Fr.—"Farewell basket, the grapes are gathered; 'tis all over, there's an end of it." A proverbial phrase, applicable to means or implements which have become useless through failure, or from our having been anticipated or disappointed in our views.

Adjutant. "One who assists the major of a regiment, and hence formerly called *aid-major.*"

Admiranda tibi levium spectacula rerum. Lat. VIRGIL.—
"A mighty pomp, though made of little things."

Adolescentem verecundum esse decet. Lat. PLAUTUS.—"It becomes a young man to be modest." Reserve and modesty are the flowers with which youth should be decorated.

———Adulandi gens prudentissima laudat
Sermonem indocti, faciem deformis amici. Lat. JUVENAL.—
"A certain class of individuals, most deeply versed in flattery, the arts of flattery, praise the discourse, conversation, of an ignorant friend, and the face, countenance, of a hideously ugly one." They attack each man on his weak side.

"For lo! where versed in every soothing art,
The sycophant assails his patron's heart—
Finds in each dull harangue an air, a grace,
And all ADONIS in a gorgon face."

Advenae. Lat.—"Settlers in a country," *literally,* strangers, foreigners, comers to a place or country.

Aedepol, nae nos aeque sumus omnes invisae viris,
Propter paucas, quae omnes faciunt dignae ut videamur malo. Lat. TERENCE.—
"In troth, we wives are all equally obnoxious to, slighted by, our husbands, and very unjustly, because of the faults of a few, on account of the faults of some few, of our sex, who make the world judge hardly, harshly, of us all, who make us all appear undeserving of their esteem." The ordinary complaint of wives.

Aegritudinem laudare, unam rem maxime detestabilem, quorum est tandem philosophorum? Lat. CICERO.—"What kind of philosophy is it to extol melancholy, the most detestable thing in nature?"

Aequalem uxorem quaere. Lat.—"Look out for a wife in your own sphere, in a position similar to your own." Like blood, like good, and like age, make the happiest marriage.

Aere ciere viros, Martemque accendere cantu. Lat. VIRGIL.—"[A man, who has the power of] rousing, stirring up, men by the sound of the trumpet, and thereby inflaming their martial or warlike spirit, of rousing fools and making slaughter." The character of MISENUS, the companion and trumpeter of AENEAS, the Trojan hero. "VIRGIL'S trumpeter never wants a successor, who is equally fortunate in his trade, *Aere ciere viros, &c.*"

Αεροβατων. Gr.—"One who affects to raise himself above the vulgar." *Literally*, "One who travels in the air." "The worthy Doctor loved neither high nor aerial standards in morals or in religion. Visionaries, who encouraged such notions, he viewed [to express it by a learned word] as αεροβατουντες [the *plural* form], and as fit subjects for the chastisement of the secular arm."

Aesopi ingenio statuam posuere Attici,
Certumque collocarunt aeterna in basi,
Patere honori scirent ut cuncti viam,
Nec generi tribui, sed virtuti gloriam. Lat. PHAEDRUS.—

"The Athenians raised, erected, a statue in honor of Æsop's genius, and placed him, though a slave, on a lasting, ever-during pedestal, to show that the way to honor lay open indifferently to all, and that glory, fame, renown, was due to, was to be the reward, not of mere family, not of high birth, not of mere ancestry, but of unsullied virtue, but of a thoroughly virtuous career."

Aesthetics. "The philosophy of taste." "*Æsthetic* philosophy," that is, "*Perceptive* philosophy," signifies, in the creative and somewhat fanciful language of the Germans, "*the philosophy of the sublime and beautiful, the theory of the fine arts and of poetry.*" N.B. "*Æsthetics*" comes from the Greek word αισθητικος, "sensitive, possessing the faculty of, or aptitude for, perception," and this from αισθανομαῖ, "to feel, perceive, comprehend." The word "*Æsthetics*" was introduced by BAUMGARTEN, above a century ago, to express generally the *Science of the Fine Arts*, and is now in universal use among the Germans. Perhaps WE also might as well adopt it; at least if any such *science* should ever arise among us.

——————— **Aestuat ingens**
Imo in corde pudor, mixtoque insania luctu,
Et furiis agitatus amor, et conscia virtus. Lat. VIRGIL.—

"Rage boiling from the bottom of his breast,
And sorrow mixed with shame, his soul oppressed;
And conscious worth lay laboring in his thought,
And love by jealousy to madness wrought."

A description of the rise and sorrow of jealousy.

Aethiopem lavare, *or*, dealbare. Lat.—"To wash a blackamoor white." Labor in vain.

Africa semper aliquid novi offert. Lat.—"Africa always offers to our notice something new; of the interior we are in almost perfect ignorance " "Africa may be said to possess a stronger attraction than most other regions of the globe, from its having been less explored; and consequently affording a more fertile and extensive source of novelty for the gratification of curiosity and adventure. It was said of old, and the saying holds good at the present day, '*Africa semper aliquid novi offert*;' and this very circumstance is a sufficient spur to a daring and inquisitive mind. Great as the progress has been in our day in the development of geographical information relative to this great continent, consequent on the exertions and zeal of Hornemann, Park, Oudney, Denham, Clapperton, Laing, and many other travelers, not forgetting the last, and by no means the least, the modest, unpretending, and straightforward Lander, much still remains to be done to complete the geography even of Northern Africa; and as to the southern part of this continent, it continues to exhibit almost a blank on our maps."

Afflatus. Lat.—"Inspiration." "The divine *afflatus* failing him, he ascended from poetry to politics."

Afflavit Deus, et dissipantur! Lat.—"GOD sent forth his breath, and they are [*were*] at once dispersed." N.B. In the reign of Queen Elizabeth, a medal was struck, bearing the above inscription, for the purpose of recording the dispersion and destruction of the Spanish Armada. The same quotation is sometimes used to express the divine interference in overthrowing a hostile army by disease, or otherwise in defeating their designs. "ELIZABETH of England had warmly espoused the cause of the revolted Netherlands, and her admiral, Sir Francis Drake, had taken some of the Spanish settlements in America. To avenge these injuries, the Invincible Armada of 150 ships of war, 27,000 men, and 3000 pieces of cannon, was equipped by Philip for the invasion of England. The English fleet of 108 ships attacked them in the night, and burnt and destroyed a great part of the squadron. A storm, which drove them on the rocks and sands of Zealand, completed their discomfiture, and only 50 shattered vessels, with 6000 men, returned to Spain, 1588."—*Tytler's General History.*

Aga. Turkish and Persian.—Equivalent to "*gentleman*" in English, and used when the person addressed is not noble, neither *khan, bey,* nor *meerza* [which see], neither in the civil nor military service of the court.

——————Age, libertate Decembri,
Quando ita majores voluerunt, utere. Lat. HORACE.—"Well, then, since our ancestors would have it so, take the liberty, make use of the customary liberty, of the month of December."

"Come, let us, like our jovial sires of old,
With gambols and mince-pies our Christmas hold."

N.B. The reference in the above passage is to the festival of the SATURNALIA, [which see].

Agent de change. Fr.—"A stockbroker."

Αγευστοι καλλιστου και γονιμωτατου λογων ναματος, την ελευθεριαν λεγω, ουδεν ότι μη κολακες εκβαινομεν μεγαλοφυεις. Gr. LONGINUS.—"Never tasting of that most fair and genial fountain of all eloquence, I speak of liberty, we can become no other than *splendid sycophants*." "HORACE lived in a servile age; and though he cheated himself with an imaginary independence, his life was servile, his *tongue* was servile. Nobly and well is it said by LONGINUS, *Αγευστοι*, &c."

Agiotage. Fr.—"Gambling in commercial shares, stocks, and government securities."

Αγωνιαι, δοξαι, φιλοτιμιαι, νομοι,
'Απαντα ταυτ' επιθετα τη φυσει κακα. Gr. MENANDER.—
"Our contentions, disputes, our opinions, our feelings of ambition, ambitious promptings, our laws, are all evils, which we ourselves have superadded to Nature."

Αἱ δ' ελπιδες βοσκουσι φυγαδας, ὡς λογος
Καλως βλεπουσιν ὀμμασι, μελλουσιν δε. Gr. EURIPIDES.—
"Exiles, the proverb says, subsist on hope,
Delusive hope still points to distant good,
To good, that mocks approach."

Ai ricchi non mancano parenti. Ital. prov.—"The rich have never relations to seek, to hunt after." Land was never lost for want of an heir.

Aide toi, et le ciel t'aidera. Fr. LA FONTAINE.—"Help thyself, and Heaven will help thee." Depend rather on your own exertions than your prayers. The allusion is to the wagoner in Æsop, who, when his wagon was overturned in a ditch, prayed stoutly for the aid of Hercules.

Aide-de-camp. Fr.—"An officer who attends a general to carry orders."

Αιδως του καλλους και αρετης πολις. Gr. DEMADES.—"Modesty is the citadel of beauty and virtue."

Αιει κολοιος προς κολοιον ἱζανει. Gr. prov.—"A jackdaw always gets alongside of another jackdaw." Birds of a feather flock together.

Αιει μεν κακοδαιμονα αναγκα τον κακον, αιτε εχοι ὑλαν [κακως τε γαρ αυτα χρεεται] αιτε σπανιζοι. Gr. ARCHYTAS [a philosopher of the Pythagorean school].—"The bad man must needs be at all times miserable, whether he have, or whether he want, the materials of external fortune; for if he have them, he will employ them ill."

Αιεν αριστευειν. Gr.—"Always, ever, to excel, *in any manner;* to be of surpassing excellence."

——————— Αιων δ' ασφαλης
Ουκ εγενετ', ουτ' Αιακιδα παρα Πηλει,
Ουτε παρ' αντιθεῳ
Καδμῳ λεγονται γε μαν βροτων
Ολβον ὑπερτατον οἱ
Σχειν.———— Gr. PINDAR.—
"For not the brave, or wise, or great,
E'er yet had happiness complete:
Nor PELEUS, grandson of the sky,
Nor CADMUS, 'scaped the shafts of Spain,
Though favored by the powers on high
With every bliss that man could gain."

From the above lines we learn that Happiness is not complete in any state, position of life. See "*Nihil est ab omni, &c.*"

Air de fête. Fr.—"A festive or joyous appearance."

Air distingué. Fr.—"A distinguished appearance, the appearance of a person of distinction."

Air distrait. Fr.—"An absent look, a look expressive of abstraction, or expressive of absence of mind."

Air noble. Fr.—"A noble, distinguished, patrician air [a distinguished position in society]."

Al amico cura gli il fico, al inimico il persico. Ital. prov.—"Pull a fig for your friend, and a peach for your enemy."

Al canto si conosce l'uccello;
Ed al parlar, il cervello. Ital. prov.—
"We know a bird by its song, and the man by his words, speech [whether he be a wise man or a fool]."

Al confessor, medico, ed avocato, non side tener il vero celato. Ital. prov.—"Hide nothing from thy minister, physician, and lawyer."

Al finir del gioco, si vede che ha guadagnato. Ital. prov.—"At the end of the game one may see who hath won."

Al fresco. Ital.—"In the open air." "An *al fresco* ball."

Al molino, ed alla sposa
Sempre manca qualche cosa. Ital. prov.—
"A mill and a woman are always in want of something:" the former from the complexity of its machinery, and the latter from the influences of her caprice.

Al pobre no es provechoso,
Acompañarse con el poderoso. Span. prov.—
"The poor man gains naught by allying himself with, by forming an alliance with, a powerful man." See "*Nunquam est fidelis, &c.*"

Al Rey, en viendolo; a DIOS, en oyendolo. Span. prov.—"External homage is due to the king upon seeing him; and to God [that is, the host, preceded by its never-failing appendage, the bell] the very moment you hear him." GOD and the king are so coupled in the language of Spain, that the same title of MAJESTY is applied to both; you hear, from the pulpit, the duties that men owe to BOTH MAJESTIES; and a foreigner is often surprised at the hopes expressed by the people that HIS MAJESTY will be pleased to grant them life and health for some years more.

Alba ligustra cadunt, vaccinia nigra leguntur. Lat. VIRGIL.—"Privets, prime-prints, though white, are suffered to lie untouched, while hyacinths, though black, of a dark hue, are speedily gathered."

"Snow is white, and lies in the dike,
And every man lets it lie:
Pepper is black, and hath a good smack,
And every man doth it buy."

Albumen, and, **Alburnum.** Lat.—"On the contact of corrosive sublimate with any vegetable juice containing *albumen*, a new combination, a *tertium quid*, results:" that is to say, a *third something* results. Struck out by the collision [knocking together] of two opposite forces or principles. N.B. "*Albumen*," in animal and in vegetable substances, is the main element of physical vitality, and consequently of fermentation and putrefaction. Every *tiro* [novice, beginner of any particular study] who walks an hospital knows that "*albumen*" [the white of an egg] is the simplest antidote [counter-poison, thing given to counteract poison] to corrosive sublimate; and, in like manner, when a solution of sublimate is applied to timber, it at once penetrates the "*alburnum*" [outer wood, sappy part of trees on the outside next the bark, subject to rot and be worm-eaten], and then flies to the heart-wood, combining with the "*albumen*," whether in an active or a dormant [sleeping, inactive] state, and *killing* it.

Alcinoö poma dare. Lat. prov.—"To give tree-fruit [such as apples, pears, oranges, &c.] to ALCINOUS." To carry coals to Newcastle. ALCINOUS was king of the island Corcyra [now Corfu], much commended for his strict justice by the poet ORPHEUS. His orchard was so famed for choice fruit of all kinds, that it gave occasion to the above proverb.

Alea sequa vorax species certissima furti
Non contenta bonis, animum quoque perfida mergit;
Furca, furax—infamis, iners, furiosa, ruina.
Lat. PETRONIUS.—

"Gaming, that direst felon of the breast,
Steals more than fortune from its wretched thrall,
Spreads o'er the soul the inert devouring pest,
And gnaws, and rots, and taints, and ruins all."

Aleator quantum in arte melior tanto est nequior. Lat. PUBLIUS SYRUS.—"The gambler, dice-player, gamester, is more wicked according as he is a greater proficient in his art." His demerits keep pace with his acquirements.

Alere flammam. Lat.—"To feed, cherish, nourish, the flame, ardor, love [of learning]." N.B. A motto sometimes printed on the title-pages of literary works.

Alia res sceptrum, alia plectrum. Lat. prov.—"A scepter is one thing, a quill [with which to play upon the strings of musical instruments] another." A scepter is one thing, a ladle another.

[Alia] tentanda via est. Lat. *Altered* from VIRGIL.—"Another way must be tried." We must diversify our means, change our plans if need be, to attain our end. The original passage runs thus:—

———Tentanda via est, qua me quoque possim,
Tollere humo.

"I too [I, the poet VIRGIL] must attempt a way, must strike out into a path, method, by which I may raise myself from the ground, by which I may rise into celebrity [as other poets have done], by which I may soar aloft."

Alias. Lat.—"Otherwise, at another time." A law term used when one changes his name, or assumes a different one; as, Jackson *alias* Johnson. The plural is *aliases*, "different names." An *alias* is also a name given to a second writ issuing from the courts of Westminster, after a first writ has been sued out without effect.

Alibi. Lat.—"Elsewhere, in another place." A law term used when one, charged with an offense, alleges that he was elsewhere when it was committed.

———Aliena negotia centum
Per caput, et circa saliunt latus. Lat. HORACE.—"A hundred affairs of other people leap through my head and around my side," that is, "beset me on every side." Compare the form which the

same idea would assume in our vulgar idiom, "I am over head and ears in the affairs of others." The above quotation may be applied to the situation of a Minister of state.

"A hundred men's affairs confound
My senses, and besiege me round."

Aliena negotia curo, excussus propriis. Lat. HORACE.—"I attend to other men's business, having none of my own to occupy me." PUBLIUS SYRUS.—The quotation is used to mark an idle obtruder.

Aliena nobis, nostra plus aliis placent. Lat. PUBLIUS SYRUS.—"The things which belong to others please us more, and that which is our own is more pleasing to others." This maxim is applicable in a variety of cases.

Aliena optimum frui insania. Lat.—"It is of the highest advantage to be able to derive instruction from the madness of another." It is true practical wisdom to make the faults of others serve as so many beacons to warn us from the rocks and shoals on which they have been wrecked.

Alieni appetens, sui profusus. Lat. SALLUST.—"Coveting the property of others, and lavish or profuse in the expenditure of his own." This, which was the historian's description of *Catiline* [a conspirator of Rome], has since been justly applied to other political adventurers.

Alieno in loco haud stabile regnum est. Lat. SENECA.—"The sovereignty which is held over strange or remote territories is precarious."

Alii sementem faciunt, alii metentem. Lat. prov.—"Some do the sowing, and others the reaping or mowing." One beats the bush, and another catcheth the bird. The Italian proverb is—*I picciol cani trovano, ma i grandi hanno la lepre.* "The little dogs find, hunt out, but the great ones seize the hare."

Aliis, quia defit quod amant, aegre'st: tibi, quia superest dolet. Lat. TERENCE.—"Some persons grieve, take it to heart, because they cannot have what they love: you, on the contrary, complain, because you have too much."

Alio sub sole. Lat.—"Under another sun;" in another climate, region. "Those who have seen earth and ocean *alio sub sole*, know how much larger an element color is in the landscape there than in middle or northern Europe. Nature in those countries has a brighter complexion, though men and women have not."

Aliorum medicus ipse ulceribus scates. Lat. prov.—"Though the physician of others, yet thou thyself art full of sores." Physician, heal thyself.

Aliquando praestat morte jungi, quam vita distrahi. Lat. VALERIUS MAXIMUS.—"It is sometimes, under certain circumstances, better to be joined, united, in death, than to be separated in or during life."

**———Aliquis de gente hircosa centurionum
Dicat: 'Quod sapio, satis est mihi; non ego curo
Esse quod Arcesilas, aerumnosique Solones.'**

Lat. PERSIUS.-

"And now, some captain of the land or fleet,
Stout of his hands, but of a soldier's wit,
Cries, 'I have sense to serve my turn in store,
And he's a humbug who pretends to more:
Care I whate'er those book-learned blockheads say?
Solon's the veriest fool—can one say nay?'"

Aliquis malo sit usus ab illo. Lat.—"Some use or benefit may possibly be derived from that evil." There are some mischiefs which have a tendency not only to rectify themselves, but also to produce an opposite result.

Aliquis non debet esse judex in propria causa. Lat. Law maxim.—"No man should be a judge in his own cause." A lord of the manor, though having cognizance of all kinds of pleas, cannot hold plea where he himself is a party.

Aliquid inane. Lat.—"An indescribable, unaccountable, kind or degree of silliness; trifling; folly."

Alitur vitium, vivitque tegendo. Lat. VIRGIL.—"Vice thrives and lives by concealment." It is in the nature of foul deeds to delight in darkness. The above translation, however, does not convey the meaning of the passage in the original, which has reference to the disease in sheep, called the *scab:* "This distemper is nourished, and continues to live, continues in a state of vitality, by being covered [instead of being brought to a head by the lancet, according to the suggestion of Virgil]."

Aliud et idem. Lat.—"One and the same thing, though under different aspects." "We never have returned from abroad after having *feasted* a month or two on the bread and water called '*potage*,' and the exhausted rags denominated '*bouilli*,' and all the *aliud et idem* hash and trash of the common French *cuisine*, without enjoying, as a great luxury, the natural flavor of beef, mutton, and pork, peas, beans, and potatoes, tasting *of themselves*, and not of one general clammy stock-pot."

Alium silere quod valeas, primus sile. Lat. SENECA.—"To make another person hold his tongue, be you first silent, do you first hold your peace." Do not irritate an idle dispute by fruitless perseverance.

Aliunde. Lat.—"From some other quarter, person."

All the Russias.—The expression of "*All the Russias*" is founded on the ancient division of Russia, which comprehended the provinces of Great or Black Russia, Little or Red Russia, and White Russia. St. Petersburg, the capital of Russia, took its name from having been built by PETER THE GREAT.

Allah. The name given by the Mohammedans of all classes, to the Almighty.

Allevato nella bambagia. Ital.—"Brought up very tenderly." To be nursed in cotton.

Αλλων ιατρος, αυτος ἑλκεσι βρυων. Gr. PLUTARCH.—"The physician of others, whilst he himself teems with ulcers." Applied to a man who pretends to cure the faults of others, whilst he has abundance of his own.

ALMA MATER. Lat.—"A mild, gentle, benign mother." A term used by students to designate the University in which they were educated.

It is also applied to nature, and to the earth, which affords us every thing we enjoy.

Almans frioun is almans gick. Frisian prov.—"All men's friend is all men's fool."

Alter ego. Lat. CICERO.—"The duplicate, double, second impersonation, counterpart, deputy, representative [*should be* representive]." "The *alter ego* of the Sovereign," a phrase applied by LORD CAMPBELL to PRINCE ALBERT.

Alter in obsequium plus aequo pronus:
Alter rixatur de lana saepe caprina,
Propugnat nugis armatus. Lat. HORACE.—
"One man carries his obsequious complaisance to excess [*the toad-eater*]: another wrangles eternally about trifles, things of no consequence whatever, and, armed with jargon, combats every thing you say [the man of rude and blunt manners]." The application of "*Alter rixatur, &c.*" is to those who are always contending for objects, things, of no moment.

"He strives for trifles, and for toys contends,
And then, in earnest, what he says defends."

N.B. The expression "*de lana caprina rixari*" is a proverbial one, and is well explained by the scholiast [commentator]: "To dispute about goat's wool," that is, about nothing, since a goat is covered with hair, and not with wool. On the subject of the man of rude and blunt manners, compare SHAKSPEARE:—

————————"This is some fellow
Who, having been praised for bluntness, doth affect
A saucy roughness; and constrains the garb,
Quite from his nature: He cannot flatter, he!—
An honest mind and plain,—he must speak truth:
An they will take it, so; if not, he's plain."

King Lear, Act 2, sc. 2.

Alter remus aquas, alter mihi radat arenas. Lat. PROPERTIUS.—"Let me strike the water with one oar, and with the other scrape the sands." Let me never hazard my safety by getting out of my depth.

————————**Alterius** [sic]
Altera poscit opem res, et conjurat amice. Lat. HORACE.—"Each [Art and Genius] demands the aid of the other, and conspires amicably to the same end." This is applied by the poet to the alliance which should exist between Art and Genius. It is sometimes used, however, to describe combinations of a different nature.

Alterum lumen Angliæ. Lat.—"The other light, luminary, of England." A phrase at one time applied to the University of OXFORD. "We do not go farther back into times when Oxford was recognized by all as the '*alterum lumen Angliæ*,' and the glory of the Church; times, in which all her goodness might be traced to herself; and whenever studies declined or corruptions crept in, it was through some external interference."

Αλυτοι αποριαι. Gr.—"Difficulties of hard solution, inexplicable difficulties, problematical questions of hard solution." "The lovers of wisdom [*philosophers*], in the best ages of Athens and of Rome, always discoursed with reverence and submission to the Author and Governor of the world.

3

They considered of whom they spoke. If they turned to the origin of evil, or to any dark and unfathomable question, they *first* called upon man to consider the limits of his understanding. They warned him, with most peculiar emphasis, to beware of those αλυτοι αποριαι, which are but increased by defenses or arguments ill constructed. They implored him affectionately to avoid all that tends to overthrow, to trouble or disturb, those principles which conduct to peace and to right action. Their advice was to strengthen the intellect, and to compose the passions, not by braving and insulting the all-powerful, all-wise, and all-merciful Creator, but by an humble, patient inquiry into his works, and by submission to his dispensations. They seemed to be well aware that, to him who understood all the bearings and relations of the word, RESIGNATION TO THE WILL OF GOD was the whole of piety."

Alum, si sit stalum, non est malum,
Beerum, si sit clearum, est sincerum.
Dog Latin of the *Hudibrastic* cast.—"If ale be stale, old, it is not bad. If beer be clear, it is pure, unadulterated."

Alumnus. Lat.—"Pupil, one who receives literary food, mental nourishment, food for the mind." An *alumnus* of University College, King's College.

Amabilis insania. Lat. HORACE.—"A fond enthusiasm, an amiable madness, a pleasing frenzy, illusion, infatuation, delirium, a delightful insanity."

Αμαθια μεν θρασος, λογισμος δ' οκνον φερει. Gr. prov.—"Ignorance, stupidity, want of education, begets boldness, audacity of speech; but reflection [the result of good training], diffidence, hesitation in giving one's opinion." Who so bold as blind BAYARD?

Amantium irae. Lat. TERENCE.—"Lovers' quarrels."

Amantium irae amoris integratio 'st. Lat. TERENCE.—"The quarrels, falling-out, of lovers, is the renewal, renewing, revival, revivification, resuscitation, of love." The disputes of lovers generally end in a warm reconciliation.

Amanuensis. Lat.—"A secretary, scribe, clerk, a person who writes what another dictates."

Amarae mulieres sunt, non facile ferunt. Lat. TERENCE.—"Women resent strongly, and do not easily put up with affronts." Compare Menander: Φυσει γυνη δυσηνιον εστι και πικρον: "Woman is naturally difficult to rein in, unrestrainable, unguidable, intractable, undrawable, unleadable, and harsh, bitter, sour, austere, implacable."

Amaranth. From the Gr. word αμαραντος [amarantos], "unfading." A flower incorruptible. The "*Celosia cristata.*" "*Amaranth,*" says CLELAND, "is a name given to the *flower-gentle*, from its *never withering:* it is currently derived from *a*, signifying *not*, and μαραινω [maraino], *to fade, wither;* a derivation so agreeable to sense seems to fix it there: but there occurs to me a still more plausible one; the termination *anth* is so obviously the Gr. ανθος [anthos], *flower*, that I rather suspect the etymology to stand thus:—

a, privative [that is, signifying *not*],
μαρ [mar], the Celtic word for death;

whence μαραινω, *a fading*, or *tending to death.*
ανθος, *flower: un-dying-flower, a-mar-anth:*—
That the one was taken from the other, there can be no doubt.

Amateur. Fr.—"A lover of any particular pursuit or system." "It must always be, to those who are the greatest *amateurs* or even professors of revolutions, a matter very hard to prove, that the late French government was so bad, that nothing worse, in the infinite devices of men, could come in its place."—BURKE.

Ambigendi locus. "Reason for doubt, doubting."

Ambiguum pactum contra venditorem interpretandum est. Lat. Law maxim.—"An ambiguous deed or contract is to be expounded against the seller or grantor." Thus if a man has a warren in his lands, and grants the same land for life, without mentioning the warren, the grantee will have it with the land.

Ambizione di primeggiare. Ital.—"Personal ambition; desire to attain a position of eminence, a distinguished position."

Ambulances. Fr.—"Itinerant or movable military hospitals."

Âme damnée. Fr.—"A tool, drudge, one who will do any dirty work." "The [*late*] DUKE OF WELLINGTON is not the man to compromise the interests of his glory to the paltry ends of any; nor will he allow himself, we are assured, to be played as their puppet, their *âme damnée*, by such a body as the Oxford Heads."

Âme de bouc. Fr.—"A soul of mud." A debased, degraded, creature.

Ameer [or Emir]. "A nobleman." The term is Asiatic and African. Its origin is Moslem.

Ami du peuple. Fr.—"A friend to the people [*at large*]; the people's friend."

Amici vitium ni eras, prodis tuum. Lat. PUBLIUS SYRUS.—"Unless you bear with the faults of a friend, you betray your own." If you do not concede a little, you disclose your want of temper or of friendship.

Amicitia semper prodest, amor et nocet. Lat. LABERIUS.—"Friendship is always profitable, and love is [frequently] injurious."

Amicum ita habeas posse ut fieri hunc inimicum scias. Lat. LABERIUS.—"Be on such terms with your friend as if you knew that he might one day become your enemy."

Amicum perdere est damnorum maximum. Lat. PUBLIUS SYRUS.—"To lose a friend is the greatest of all losses."

Amicus certus in re incerta cernitur. Lat. ENNIUS.—"A sure friend is discovered, discerned, in a doubtful matter, when you are on your beam-ends; or, to use a LONDONISM, when you are hard up." It is only in situations of hazard that we can prove the sincerity of friendship.

Amicus curiae. Lat.—"A friend of the court." This appellation is given in Courts of Law to the person who gives his advice, or opinion, when not immediately concerned in the cause.

Amicus humani generis. Lat.—"The friend of the human race." The most glorious title that man can obtain, and which but few HOWARDS and FRANKLINS are found to claim.

Amicus Plato, amicus Socrates, sed magis amica veritas.

Lat.—"Plato is my friend, Socrates is my friend, but Truth is more my friend." By this quotation the speaker or writer intimates that he is not without his personal feelings and attachments, but that nothing can make him swerve from the sacred interests of truth.

Amicus usque ad aras. Lat.—"A friend even to the altar." One who will sustain his friendship even to the last extremity.

Amittit merito proprium qui alienum adpetit. Lat. PHAEDRUS.—"He deservedly loses his own property who covets, keenly endeavors to get for himself, that of another."

Amme brea is swieter az memme koeke. Frisian prov.—"Nurses' bread is sweeter than mothers' cake." A warning to mothers who do not nurse their children, that the affections of the infant will be transferred to those who have the care of them.

Amoebaéan. From αμοιβαιος. Gr.—"Alternately responsive." "*Amoebaean* verses."

Amor a nullo amato amar perdona. Ital. DANTE.—

"True love permits no loved one not to love."

Amor al cor gentil ratto s' apprende. Ital. DANTE.—"True love in gentle heart is quickly learnt, or, True love the gentle, noble, high-souled heart soon apprehends."

Amor e signoria non vogliono compagnia. Ital. prov.—"Love and lordship like no fellowship." The French proverb is, "*Amour et seigneurie ne se tinrent jamais compagnie,*" which has the same meaning.

Amor et deliciae. Lat. CICERO.—"The loved one and the darling favorite." "ANACREON was the favorite, the *amor et deliciae,* of his own age, and he has had the singular fortune to preserve to our days, not only his fame, but even his popularity, in the verses of imitators whose very names are long since lost."

Amor gignit amorem. Lat.—"Love begets, or gives rise to, love."

Amor nummi. Lat. JUVENAL.—"The love of money."

Amor omnibus idem. Lat. VIRGIL.—"Love is lord of all, and is in all the same."

Amor patriae. Lat.—"The love of our country, native soil, native land, the land of our birth."

Amor soli. Lat.—The meaning the same as "*amor patriae.*"

Amor tussisque non celantur. Lat.—"Love and a cough cannot be hidden, concealed."

Amoto quaeramus seria ludo. Lat. HORACE.—"Setting raillery aside, let us now attend to serious matters. Laying aside mirth, let us reason seriously."

Amour fait beaucoup, mais argent fait tout. Fr. prov.—"Love does much, but money does every thing." Beauty is potent, but money is OMNIPOTENT. Talk is but talk; but 'tis money that buys land.

Amour fait rage, mais argent fait mariage. Fr. prov.—"Love causes raging, but money marriaging."

Amour-propre. Fr.—"Self-love." The true meaning, however, of the term is "*a modification of pride.*"

Amphibious.—"Having two modes of existence, living:" applied, though not, *strictly* speaking, correctly, to animals that can live both on land and in water. The *true* meaning of *αμφιβιος*, amphibious, is "partaking of both sexes."

————————**Amphora coepit**
Institui; currente rota cur urceus exit? Lat. HORACE.—"A large jar was begun to be formed: why, as the wheel goes round, does it turn out to be an insignificant, paltry pitcher or water-pot?" The metaphor [an implied comparison, the use of a word in a sense different from its ordinary import, meaning] is taken from the potter's wheel. The quotation is applied to those who, having promised a magnificent work, produced in the end something inadequate, and perhaps contemptible.

Ampliat aetatis spatium sibi vir bonus. Hoc est
Vivere bis, vita posse priori frui. Lat. MARTIAL.—"A good man enlarges the term of his own existence. It is living twice to be enabled to enjoy one's former life." He lives the preceding years over again in pleasing recollection.

————————*Αμφι δ' ανθρω-*
πων φρασιν αμπλακιαι
αναριθμητοι κρεμανται,
τουτο δ' αμαχανον εὑρειν,
ὁ τι νυν εν και τελευτᾳ φερτατον ανδρι τυχειν. Gr. PINDAR.—
"Deep wrapt in error is the human mind,
And human bliss is ever insecure:
Know we what fortune yet remains behind?
Know we how long the present will endure?"

Αμφοτεροι κλωπες, και ὁ δεξαμενος και ὁ κλεψας. Gr. prov.—PHOCYLIDES. "Both are thieves, the receiver and the thief." The receiver is as bad as the thief.

————**An haec animos aerugo et cura peculi**
Quum semel imbuerit, speramus carmina fingi
Posse linenda cedro, et levi servanda cupresso?
Lat. HORACE.—
"When once this rust and love of gain has taken hold of the soul, got possession of the soul, can we imagine it capable of noble thoughts, or of poems worthy to be kept in cases of cypress and cedar?"—
"But when the rust of wealth pollutes the soul,
And moneyed cares the genius thus control,
How shall we dare to hope that distant times
With honor should preserve our lifeless rhymes?"

N.B. The ancients, for the better preservation of their manuscripts, rubbed them with oil of cedar and kept them in cases of cypress.

An nescis longas regibus esse manus? Lat. OVID.—"Do you not know that kings have long hands?" "It were to be wished," says SWIFT, "that they had as long ears."

An praeter esse reale actualis essentiae sit aliud esse necessarium, quo res actualiter existat? MARTINUS SCRIBLERUS.—"Whether, besides the *real being* of *actual being*, there be any other *being* necessary to cause a thing to *be?*" A question humorously put to ridicule the absurdity of metaphysics run mad.

**An quisquam est alius liber, nisi ducere vitam
Cui licet, ut voluit?** Lat. PERSIUS.—
"Is any man free, a freeman, but he that may live as he pleases?"

Anachronism. "A transposition of dates." "Major R. was once riding near a building which presented to his admiring gaze a fine specimen of antique Saxon architecture. Desirous of learning something respecting it, he made some inquiries of a man, who, as it turned out, was the *cobbler* of the village. This learned wight informed the inquisitive stranger that the building in question was reckoned a noble specimen of *Gothic* architecture, and was built by the *Romans*, who came over with JULIUS CÆSAR. 'Friend,' said the Major, 'you make anachronisms.' 'No, no, sir,' replied the man, 'indeed I don't make *anachronisms*, for I never made any thing but *shoes* in all my life.'"

Anagrammatism, *or*, **Metagrammatism.** The latter is the *correct* term. *Anagrammatism* means, literally, the art of writing backwards—in which sense *Amor* [Love] is an anagram of *Roma* [Rome], and *evil* of *live:* but *metagrammatism* implies a transposition of letters, which has become the popular sense of *anagrammatism.* A *metagram,* then, is the transposition of the letters in one or more words to form a new word, or new words. "Father Finardi, with great felicity, said of Magliabecchi, the celebrated librarian of the Grand Duke of Tuscany, *Is unus bibliotheca magna,* that being the metagram [transposition of letters] of his Latinized name, *Antonius Magliabbechius:*" that is to say, *He alone,* or *in himself, is a great library,* that being, &c. There seems to be a secret meaning in the very letters of a name, which only require to be decompounded and newly arranged, to reveal the life and character of the wearer. Let those who may be disposed to laugh at this theory, as fanciful, remember that they might in this manner have read the history of the battle of the Nile at the christening of HORATIO NELSON: "*Honor est a Nilo*" [a sentence composed of the letters of Lord Nelson's Christian name and surname—a metagram]: "*Honor est a Nilo*" means *Honor is from the Nile.* The metagram is said to have been made by a SCHOOL-BOY.

Anakim. Hebrew.—"Giants."

Ancien régime. Fr.—"The former, old, government, old form of government, former administration."

Ancienne noblesse. Fr.—The "old nobility" [of France], nobility prior to the Revolution of the last century.

Andare stretto. Ital.—"To go about a business in a miserly manner." To lose a sheep for a halfpenny-worth of tar.

Ανδρος δικαιου καρπος ουκ απολλυται. Gr.—"The good deeds [*literally,* fruit] of a righteous, just, upright, man perish not."

Ανδρος κακως πρασσοντος εκποδων φιλοι. Gr. prov.—"When a man is in difficulties, is ill to do in the world, his friends stand aloof, keep out of the way." A friend is never known till one have need. See "*Donec eris felix, &c.*"

Ανδρων ἡρωων τεκνα πηματα. Gr. prov.—"The children of brave men are often a disgrace to them." Many a good cow hath but a bad calf.

Ανηρ ατυχων σωζεται ταις ελπισι. Gr. prov.—"The man who is in adversity is supported, sustained, buoyed up, by hope." If it were not for hope, the heart would break.

Ανηρ δικαιος εστιν, ουχ ὁ μη αδικων,
Αλλ' ὁστις αδικειν δυναμενος, ου βουλεται. Gr.—

"Just, upright, righteous, is the man, not merely he who abstains from acting iniquitously, unjustly, but he who, having it in his power, having full scope, to indulge in every kind of wickedness, has no wish whatever to do so."

Anglice. Lat.—"In English, according to the English fashion."

Anguillam cauda tenes. Lat. prov.—"You hold an eel by the tail." You are engaged with an active and slippery opponent.

Anguis in herba. Lat. VIRGIL.—"A snake in the grass." "A lurking danger, or one not actually foreseen."

Angulus terrae. Lat. HORACE.—"A corner of the earth, some snug spot in the land." "When I leave the Temple, hopeless to find another spot consecrated by so much valor and so much wisdom, it should be for some *angulus terrae*, some wood-girt corner, which the foot of soldier or of lawyer has never yet been known to press."

Aniles fabulae. Lat. QUINTILIAN.—"Old wives' stories, humdrum prosings."

Aniliana. Lat. The same meaning as the preceding example.

Animal implume, bipes. Lat.—"An animal without feathers, and walking on two legs." This is PLATO's imperfect definition of a man, which was so successfully ridiculed by DIOGENES, who brought a *plucked cock* into the school, and scornfully asked "if that was PLATO's man?"

Animal propter convivia natum. Lat. JUVENAL.—"An animal created, called into existence, to feast a whole company." Applied to the porcine, piggish or hoggish family. "Of all the delicacies in the whole *mundus edibilis* [eatable world, world of things good to eat], says CHARLES LAMB, I will maintain roast pig to be the most delicate, *princeps obsoniorum* [the very prince of dishes, articles of food]. I speak not of your grown porkers, things between pig and pork, those hobbydehoys, but a young and tender suckling, under a moon old, guiltless as yet of the sty, with no original speck of the *amor immunditiae* [love of nastiness, uncleanness, filthiness], the hereditary failing of the first parent, yet manifest; his voice as yet not broken, but something between a childish treble and a grumble, the mild forerunner or *praeludium* [essay, proof, trial beforehand, preamble] of a grunt."

Animal risibile. Lat.—"An animal which can laugh." One of the definitions of man, given or suggested by the philosophers of the schools.

Animalcula. Lat.—"Very small, minute animals, living creatures." Usually, though *incorrectly*, written "*Animalculæ*," as there is no such word. "*Animalculum*," the singular of "*Animalcula*," is a word not sanctioned by the *ancient* Latin writers.

Animi cultus quasi quidam humanitatis cibus. Lat. CICERO.—"Cultivation is as necessary to the mind, as food is to the body."

Animo et facto. Lat.—"Verily and indeed; really and truly."

Animo vidit; ingenio complexus est; eloquentia illuminavit. Lat. VELLEIUS PATERCULUS concerning CICERO.—"These subjects he saw by the power of his mind; he comprehended them by his understanding; and by his eloquence he enlightened them, cast a brightness upon them." This quotation has been applied to BURKE.

——————Animoque supersunt
Jam prope post animam. Lat. SIDONIUS APOLLINARIS.—"Their spirit seems even to survive their breath." Compare the exquisitely beautiful lines of GRAY:—

"On some fond breast the parting soul relies,
Some pious drops the closing eye requires;
E'en from the tomb the voice of nature cries,
E'en in our ashes live their wonted fires."

Animula, vagula, blandula,
Hospes, comesque corporis!
Quae nunc abibis in loca,
Pallidula, frigida, nudula,
Nec, ut soles, dabis joca?

The celebrated verses of the Roman Emperor, HADRIAN, addressed to his soul. "Alas! my soul! thou pleasing companion of this body, thou fleeting thing, that art now deserting it? whither art thou flying? To what unknown region? Thou art all trembling, fearful, and pensive. Now, what is become of thy former wit and humor? Thou shalt jest and be gay no more."

Animum nunc huc celerem, nunc dividit illuc. Lat. VIRGIL.—"This way and that he turns his anxious mind." A picture of an active mind, always bent on exertion.

Animum pictura pascit inani. Lat. VIRGIL.—"He fills his mind with a vain or idle picture; or, He feeds his mind with empty representations." He dwells with eagerness upon the painted semblance. This is sometimes applied in ridicule to *dilettanti*, or picture-fanciers.

Animum rege, qui, nisi paret, imperat. Lat. HORACE.—"Subdue your passion, or it will subdue you." Study to acquire that self-control which will prevent your being hurried away by the force of your passions.

Animus. Lat.—"The feeling, disposition." "The *animus* of his charges," that is, the *feeling that prompted him to make* his charges.

Animus furandi. Lat. Law.—"The intention of stealing." He took the goods *animo furandi*, with a felonious design.

Animus in pedes decidit. Lat.—"His heart fell down to his hose, his heels."

Animus lucis contemtor. Lat. VIRGIL.—"A mind regardless of life [if sacrificed in a good cause]."

——————**Animus, quod perdidit, optat**
Atque in praeterita se totus imagine versat.
Lat. PETRONIUS ARBITER.—"Oft does the mind wish for, desiderate, what it has missed, and loses itself in the retrospective contemplation." Most men have occasion to look back with regret on their lost opportunities. Compare SHAKSPEARE:

"There is a tide in the affairs of men,
Which, taken at the flood, leads on to fortune;

Omitted, all the voyage of their life
Is bound in shallows and in miseries."

Anno aetatis. Lat.—"In the year of his, or her, age."

Anno di neve, anno di bene. Ital. prov.—"A snow year, a rich year."

Anno Domini. Lat.—"In the year of our Lord."

Annonce. Fr.—"Notice; intimation; advertisement."

Annosa vulpes non capitur laqueo. Lat. prov.—"An old fox is not caught in a snare, trap." You can't catch old birds with chaff.

Annus mirabilis. Lat.—"A wonderful year, year of wonders." N.B. A poem of DRYDEN's was so called in commemoration of the great fire of London.

Ante barbam doces senes. Lat. prov.—"You teach old persons before you yourself have a beard, while you are but a boy." Jack Sprat would teach his grandame, his granny.

Ante litem motam. Lat.—"Before the case is mooted; before the mooting of the case; before the commencement of the action, or trial."

Ante lucem. Lat.—"Before daybreak."

Ante omnia. Lat.—"Before every thing else; first and foremost; in the first place."

Ante tubam trepidat. Lat.—"He trembles, quakes for fear, before the trumpet or charge is sounded." His fears anticipate the danger.

Ante victoriam ne canas triumphum. Lat. prov.—"Do not triumph, exult, before you have gained the victory." Count not your chickens before they be hatched.

Ανϑρωπος εστι πνευμα και σκια μονον. Gr. EURIPIDES.—"Man is but a breath and a shadow." Compare HORACE:—

Pulvis et umbra sumus.
Quis scit an adjiciant hodiernae crastina summae
Tempora Di superi?

"We are naught but shade and dust. Who knows whether the gods above will add, intend to add, to-morrow to the days already passed?" Compare also this passage from the General Epistle of James:—*Ατμις προς ολιγον φαινομενη, και επειτα αφανιζομενη.*—[Your life is even] "a vapor, that appeareth for a little time, and then vanisheth away."

Antipodes. Gr.—"People on the opposite sides of the globe:" *literally*, "those who have their feet opposite to the feet of others."

Antiquarian.—"Relative to antiquities." "We must venerate Leland's undigested researches, as the first-fruits of *antiquarian* science among us." GOUGH.

N.B. GOUGH is one of the few authors who uniformly use this word as an adjective, which it is; and never as a substantive, which it is not. *Antiquarian* for *antiquary* is a downright confusion of speech, though SHENSTONE, BLACKSTONE, WALPOLE, BURKE, Professor REID, and even [that avower of his own studied correctness] Lord CHESTERFIELD, are guilty of it. No such blemish defaces the purer styles of LYTTELTON, ROBERTSON, or BRYANT.

Antiseptic. From the Greek.—"Good against putrefaction."

Antithesis. Gr.—"Opposition, contrast." "The wicked flee when no man pursueth; but the righteous are bold as a lion." "We are not more ingenious in searching out bad motives for good actions, when performed by others, than good motives for bad actions, when performed by ourselves."

Ανυπευθυνοι. Gr.—"Men who render no account, exempt from rendering an account of their conduct in the exercise of public functions, irresponsible, absolute, uncircumscribed individuals, men not to be called to account." "There is no autocrat [uncontrolled ruler, emperor, one who possesses independent sovereignty] so complete, not even the Czar of all the Russias, as the captain of a king's ship, and the head master of a grammar-school. Both of them are *ανυπευθυνοι* in the utmost degree."

Απ' ουρας την εγχελυν εχεις. Gr. prov.—"You hold the eel by the tail." There is as much hold of his word as of a wet eel by the tail. He is a slippery fellow.

Apathy. From the Greek.—"Without feeling, inertness, sluggish insensibility, avoidance of passion, folding of the hands to sleep."

Aperto mala cum est mulier, tum demum est bona. Lat. prov. —"When a woman is openly bad, she is then at the best." Her avowal is preferable to her hypocrisy.

Aperto vivere voto. Lat. PERSIUS.—"To live with undisguised prayers, to offer no prayer that you would fear to divulge." Compare PYTHAGORAS: *Μετα φωνης ευχεο*, "Pray with your voice," that is, "aloud," so that men may judge whether you "ask amiss," or not. Compare also SENECA: *Sic vive cum hominibus tanquam Deus videat: sic loquere cum Deo tanquam homines audiant,* that is, "So live with men as though GOD saw you: and so commune with the Deity as though men heard you, heard all you uttered."

Apocryphal. From the Greek.—Properly "concealed, surreptitious," but often used in reference to something of uncertain credit. "This is *apocryphal;* I may choose whether I believe it or not."

Απολοιτο πρωτυς αυτος
'Ο τον αργυρον φιλησας·
Δια τουτον ουκ αδελφος,
Δια τουτον ου τοκηες·
Πολεμοι, φονοι δι' αυτον. Gr. ANACREON.—

"Accurst be he who first of yore
Discovered the pernicious ore [gold]!
This sets a brother's heart on fire,
And arms the son against the sire."

Απορια ψαλτου βηξ. Gr. prov.—"A cough sometimes indicates the embarrassment of a harper, musician, sometimes shows that he is at a loss how to go on, that he is in a fix."

"When a musician hath forgot his note,
He makes as though a crumb stuck in his throat."

Apparent rari nantes in gurgite vasto. Lat. VIRGIL.—"They appear thinly scattered and swimming in the vast deep." This phrase, originally used to describe the mariners surviving a shipwreck, is now critically applied to a literary work in which the few thoughts of value are nearly overwhelmed in a mass of baser matter.

Appartement. Fr.—"Two or more rooms." The French word for a "single room" is *chambre.*

Appetito non vuol salse. Ital. prov.—"Hunger is the best sauce."

Appetitus rationi pareat. Lat.—"Let the appetite or desire be obedient to reason."

Apple of the eye. "According to our method," says LEMON, "of writing this word [*apple*], any person would suppose that, by *the apple of the eye*, we meant *the ball of the eye:* but, notwithstanding the apparent connection between these two ideas, the *apple of the eye* means quite another thing; at least, the derivation points out a different meaning; for the Gr. and Lat. words, from which we have taken our expression, do really signify quite a different thing from *the ball of the eye;* the Gr. words are *παρθενος* [parthenos], *κορη* [kore], and *παις* [pais], and the Lat. word is *pupilla;* all which signify what is commonly called *the bird of the eye:* that little opening, or round hole, that admits the rays of light, and through which is reflected from the bottom of the eye, *that little image, that little boy or girl, that puppet* [*pupilla*], which is discerned by every person who looks attentively into the eye."

Après la mort le medecin. Fr. prov.—"After death the doctor."

Après la pluie vient le beau temps. Fr. prov.—"After rain comes fine weather." After a storm comes a calm.

Après moi le déluge. Fr. prov.—"After me will come the deluge." This proverb is used when we wish to intimate that we give ourselves no trouble or concern about what will happen after our decease.

Après perdre perd on bien. Fr. prov.—"After losing we often continue to lose." Misfortunes seldom come alone.

Απροσικτων ερωτων οξυτεραι μανιαι. Gr. PINDAR.—"The rage after desires hard to be attained, inaccessible, unattainable, is increased by the difficulty."

Apud crepidam. Lat.—"At or near the [shoemaker's] last." "An *apud crepidam* discussion on Painting," that is, A discussion on Painting by one who is incompetent to speak on the subject. See "*Ne sutor ultra crepidam.*"

Aqua fortis. Lat.—"Strong water." "**Aqua regia,**" "Royal water." Two chemical preparations well known for their solution of metals. The latter is so called because it will dissolve gold, which has been termed a royal metal.

Aquam plorat, cum lavat, fundere. Lat. prov. PLAUTUS.—"He bewails the loss of the water, when he washes himself." He'll not lose the paring of his nails.

Aquellos son ricos, que tienen amigos. Span. prov.—"Rich are those who have [true] friends."

Aquila non capit muscas. Lat. prov.—"An eagle does not trouble himself to catch flies." A goss-hawk beateth not a bunting.

Aquila non mangia mosche. Ital. prov.—"An eagle does not feed upon flies." A great mind does not stoop to low or trifling pursuits.

Aquilam volare, delphinum natare doce. Lat. prov.—"Teach an eagle to fly, or a dolphin to swim." Teach your grandame, your granny, to suck eggs, to sup sour milk.

Aranearum telas texere. Lat.—"To weave spiders' webs." Metaphorically taken, to maintain sophistical arguments.

Arbiter elegantiarum. Lat.—"The arbitrator of the elegances, or elegancies, the master of the ceremonies." The person whose judgment decides on matters of taste and form. N.B. The *classic* term, used by TACITUS, is "*elegantiae arbiter.*"

Arbore dejecta quivis ligna colligit. Lat.—"When the tree is thrown down, any person may gather the wood." It is in the power of the meanest to triumph over fallen greatness.

———————————**Arcades ambo:**
Et cantare pares, et respondere parati. Lat. VIRGIL.—"Both Arcadians [natives of a country of ancient Greece, of Arcadia, the Switzerland of Greece; men who were passionately fond of music, and who cultivated it with success]; and both equally skilled in the opening song and in the response." The poet speaks of two contending shepherds. The quotation is applied, however, to disputants of another description, either to intimate that they are closely matched, or that they are playing, as the phrase is, into each other's hands.

Arcana imperii. Lat.—"State secrets." The mysteries of government.

Arcanum. Lat.—"A secret." The grand *arcanum,* the philosopher's stone.

Arcanum demens detegit ebrietas. Lat.—"Mad drunkenness discloses every secret." All reserve is laid aside in moments of intoxication.

Arcanum neque tu scrutaberis ullius unquam;
Commissumque teges, et vino tortus et ira.
Lat. HORACE.—"Never inquire into another man's secret; but conceal that which is intrusted to you, though tortured both by wine and by passion to reveal it."

Arcem ex cloaca facere, ex elephanto muscam. Lat. prov. CICERO.—"To make a castle, fort, stronghold, out of a common sewer, or an elephant from a fly," that is, to make a mountain of a mole-hill.

Αρχη ἡμισυ παντος. Gr. HESIOD.—"The beginning is the half of the whole." Of the tendency of this ancient saying, the best illustration is to be found in our own saying, "What's well begun is half done." See "*Dimidium facti,*" *&c.*

Αρχιλοχον πατεῖς. Gr.—"Thou tramplest upon, insultest, ARCHILOCHUS, treatest ARCHILOCHUS contumeliously—Thou, thoughtless mortal, presumest to trample upon, insult, ARCHILOCHUS, treat ARCHILOCHUS with contumely [and thou wilt repent of it, wilt rue thine egregious folly]." "ARCHILOCHUS is a famous name in the old world, and must surely have been deserving of it, for good or for evil of uncommon quality, there being scarcely half a dozen, amongst all the ancient classics, in whose works we may not trace some instance or record of his universal invention or exquisite skill, of his vigor of genius, or bitterness of spirit. Besides writing a man and his daughter who should have married him, into hanging themselves, he founded a colony, and then lampooned it; struck out a score of new metres, and, if we may judge by the diversity of the numerous but slender fragments of his poems still existing, was Grand master of Olympic odes, Bacchic hymns, warlike, moral, and consolatory elegies, *bird-and-beast* fables, love-songs, and libelous epigrams, throughout Greece and all her islands. 'Touch me who dare'—*Αρχιλοχον πατεῖς*—was his motto: which, nevertheless, he appears to have said once too often; for it is certainly not greatly improbable that the man who is said to have assassinated him, Calondas the Crow, had previously been hitched by him into the gripe of some fierce iambics, or exposed to ridicule in some tale of a fox and a crow."

Archipelago.—"An assemblage of islands." The Eastern Archipelago comprises the largest assemblage of islands on the globe.

Arcum intensio frangit, animum remissio. Lat. PUBLIUS SYRUS.—"Straining breaks the bow, and relaxation the mind." Our proverb has it that the bow, which is always bent, must break. This maxim properly adds that the mind will in time lose its powers, unless they are called into due activity.

Arcus nimis intensus rumpitur. Lat. prov.—"A bow too much bent, kept on the stretch, is soon broken." A bow long bent at last waxeth weak. See "*Cito rumpes arcum, &c.*"

Ardentia verba. Lat.—"Glowing words." Expressions of uncommon force and energy. One of our poets has carried the idea still further. He speaks of "thoughts that breathe, and words that burn."

Arena. Lat.—"Sand, grit." "The *arena* of battle," that is, the *field* of battle, or the battle-*field*. The clear open space in the center of the amphitheatre [a place in ancient Rome for the exhibition of public shows of combatants, wild beasts, and naval engagements] was called the *arena*, because it was covered with sand, or sawdust, to prevent the gladiators [men who fought with swords in the amphitheatre and other places, for the amusement of the Roman people] from slipping, and to absorb the blood.

Argent comptant. Fr.—"Ready money." For immediate payment, for cash. N.B. Instead of "*argent comptant*" we may use "*comptant*" alone, just as some persons speak of "*the ready*." We may also use "*argent sec*" [literally, *dry* money], *hard cash*, in the same sense as "*argent comptant*," or "*comptant*."

Argent reçu le bras rompu. Fr. prov.—"Borrowed money that you cannot repay, but must work out, is wellnigh having an arm broken." To work for a dead horse, or goose.

Argilla quidvis imitaberis uda. Lat. HORACE.—"You may mould the youth into any shape you please, at pleasure, like soft clay." This is one of the numerous apophthegms which insist on the advantage of early impressions.

Argumentum a particulari ad universale. Lat.—"An argument that attempts to show from a single instance that all other instances are the same, similar, alike." The practice of generalizing from individual instances.

Argumentum ad absurdum. Lat.—"An argument to prove the absurdity of any thing."

Argumentum ad hominem. Lat.—"An argument to the man." An argument which derives its strength from its personal application. An appeal to the practices, or professed principles, of one's adversary.

Argumentum ad ignorantiam. Lat.—An argument founded on the ignorance of facts, or circumstances, shown by your adversary.

Argumentum ad judicium. Lat.—"An argument to the judgment." An appeal made, according to LOCKE, to proofs drawn from any of the foundations of knowledge.

Argumentum ad verecundiam. Lat.—"An argument to the modesty." An appeal to the decency of your opponent.

Argumentum baculinum. Lat.—"The argument of the staff." Club law. Conviction per force, conviction enforced by drubbing.

Aria di finestra colpo di balestra. Ital. prov.—"The air of a window is as the stroke of a cross-bow."

Αριστον μετρον. Gr.—"A mean, a middle course, is best in every thing." This was the saying of CLEOBULUS, one of the seven wise men of Greece. On most occasions in common life it is most prudent to steer a middle course.

Arma tenenti omnia dat, qui justa negat. Lat. LUCAN.—"He who denies what is just grants every thing to those who have arms in their hands." A successful combatant will not be content with his naked right, but will insist on something more.

Armati terram exercent, semperque recentes
Convectare juvat praedas et vivere rapto. Lat. VIRGIL.—"In arms they ravage the earth, and it is ever their delight to collect the recent spoil, and live on plunder."

Armes blanches. Fr.—"Hand-weapons, cold steel."

Arrière-garde. Fr.—The "rear guard."

Arrière-pensée. Fr.—"Mental reservation, thought kept in reserve, kept to one's self."

Ars est celare artem. Lat.—"The art, the perfection of art, is to conceal art." In every practical science, as in painting or in acting, for instance, the great effort of the artist is to conceal from the spectator the means by which the effect is produced.

Ars est sine arte, cujus principium est mentiri, medium laborare, et finis mendicare. Lat.—This is a most happy definition of the business of alchemy, or the vain search after the philosopher's stone:—"It is an art without art, which has its beginning in falsehood, its middle in toil, and its end in poverty."

Arte perire sua. Lat. OVID.—"To perish, or fall, by their own machinations, to fall into the trap that they had prepared for others." "It is gratifying to man, and it seems the peculiar dispensation of GOD, that the malignant authors of mischief should themselves be the victims of their own contrivances."

Arts d'agrément. Fr.—"Accomplishments [in ladies' schools]."

Asinum tondes. Lat. prov.—"You are shearing an ass." "Here's a great cry, and but little wool," as the fellow said when he was shearing his hogs.

Asinus asino, sus sui pulcer, et suum cuique pulchrum. Lat. prov.—"To the ass, the sow, and every animal, their own offspring appears the fairest in the whole creation." The crow thinks her own bird fairest.

Asperae facetiae, ubi nimis ex vero traxere, acrem sui me-

moriam relinquunt. Lat. TACITUS.—"A bitter jest, when the satire comes too near the truth, leaves a sharp sting behind it." This experiment **is** always dangerous; but particularly when the shaft is leveled against high authorities.

Asperius nihil est humili cum surgit in altum. Lat. CLAUDIAN.—"Nothing is more harsh than a low man, when raised to a certain height."

Aspettare, e non venire,
Stare in letto, e non dormire,
Servire, e non gradire,
Son tre cose da far morire. Ital. prov.—
"To expect one who does not come, to lie in bed and not to sleep, to serve and not to be advanced, are three things enough to kill a man."

Assai ben balla a chi Fortuna suona. Ital. prov.—"He dances well, to whom Fortune pipes."

Assez y a, si trop n' y a. Old Fr. prov.—"There is enough, if there be not too much." Too much of one thing is good for nothing. Enough is as good as a feast.

Assidua stilla saxum excavat. Lat. prov.—"A continual dropping of water hollows out a stone." Compare OVID:—

Quid magis est durum saxo? Quid mollius unda?
Dura tamen molli saxa cavantur aqua.

That is, "What is harder than stone? what softer than water? and yet hard stones, stones hard though they are, are, in process of time, made hollow by the falling of water on them."

————————**Assiduo labuntur tempora motu**
Non secus ac flumen. Neque enim consistere flumen,
Nec levis hora potest: sed ut unda impellitur unda,
Urgeturque prior venienti, urgetque priorem,
Tempora sic fugiunt pariter, pariterque sequuntur;
Et nova sunt semper. Nam quod fuit ante, relictum est;
Fitque quod haud fuerat: momentaque cuncta novantur.
Lat. OVID.—

"With constant motion as the moments glide,
Behold in running life the rolling tide!
For none can stem by art, or stop by power,
The flowing ocean, or the fleeting hour;
But wave by wave pursued arrives on shore,
And each impelled behind impels before:
So time on time revolving we descry,
So minutes follow, and so minutes fly."

Assignat. Fr.—The paper money of France after the Revolution of the last century. "Is there a debt which presses them, issue *assignats*." BURKE.

Assistance obligée. Fr.—"Legal relief," to the poor.

Assisto divinis. Lat. HORACE.—"I stop [in the course of my morning walk] to observe the fortune-tellers in the pursuit of their craft, or, I stop to consult the itinerant diviners [who kept a kind of shop for the sale of oracles]." The Roman Catholics make use of an expression somewhat similar to the "*assisto divinis*" of Horace: they say that they "*assist* at mass," that is, they "*stand by* and look on at mass," when they attend the service of the Romish Church. CREECH, from whom better things might have been expected, most absurdly translated the expression, "I go to Church and pray:" thus raising ideas in the mind of the reader to which there was nothing correspondent in the religious services of Rome.

Assumpsit. Lat. Law term.—"He assumed, he took upon him to pay." An action on a verbal promise.

Astra regunt homines, sed regit astra Deus. Lat.—"The stars govern men, but GOD governs the stars." This forms a proper answer to the self-dubbed professors of judicial astrology.

Αθυμια. Gr.—"Dejection, sadness, despondency, melancholy, the exhaustion of all energy [*in-working, mental activity*], of all vitality of the soul; the exhaustion of the heart." "This feeling is melancholy, despondency, or, in the much more powerful expression of the Greek, it is *αθυμια*."

Attaché. Fr.—"One of the higher class of subordinates of an embassy, or representative mission." The plural is *attachés*.

Au contraire. Fr.—"On the contrary, on the other hand."

Au courant. Fr.—"Aware of, acquainted with, familiar with." "It is his office to keep the King *au courant* of all that appears in modern literature."

Au désespoir. Fr.—"Driven to despair, in a state of despondency."

Au fait. Fr.—"Up to the mark." "On these points he is quite *au fait*." "He is *au fait* in the whole matter."

Au fond. Fr.—"To the bottom." "I know the man *au fond*." I thoroughly understand his character.

Au jour la journée. Fr.—"From hand to mouth."

Au pied de la lettre. Fr.—"Literally."

Au pis aller. Fr.—"At the worst." Let the worst come to the worst.

Au plus debile la chandelle à la main. Fr. prov.—"He that is worst may still hold the candle."

Au regnard endormi rien ne cheut en la gueule. Old Fr. prov. —"When the fox is asleep, nothing falls into his mouth."

Au sérieux. Fr.—"Seriously, in a serious manner."

Au naturel. Fr.—"In its, or their, natural state."

Au reste. Fr.—"In addition to this, besides, moreover."

Au revoir. Fr.—"Good-bye, farewell."

Au royaume des aveugles les borgnes sont rois. Fr. prov.— "In blindmen's land those who are blessed with one eye are kings." N.B. This French proverb is very often quoted incorrectly, thus, *Dans le pays, &c.*, instead of as above.

Auch weiber wussten zu schweigen. German.—"Even the women knew how to be silent, to keep their tongues to themselves." "There is no instance upon record of any Tyrolian being induced to turn traitor for a bribe; and, says BARTHOLDY, '*Auch weiber, &c.*'"

Auctor pretiosa facit. Lat. OVID.—"The giver makes the gift more precious."

Aucune institution humaine ne peut subsister, si elle n'est

basée sur un sentiment, une vertu. Fr.—"No human institution can stand, unless grounded on some one feeling or virtue of our nature."

Audaces fortuna juvat, timidosque repellit. Lat.—"Fortune favors, or assists, the bold, but abandons, repels, the timid, the coward." Intrepidity will often succeed under circumstances in which timidity may produce a failure.

Audax omnia perpeti
Gens humana ruit per vetitum et nefas. Lat. HORACE.—"Daring to every extent of guilt, the human race rush onward in their mad career, setting at defiance all laws both human and divine." This often forms a motto to some discourse or invective against the wickedness of the age.

Aude aliquid brevibus Gyaris et carcere dignum
Si vis esse aliquis. Probitas laudatur et alget.
Lat. JUVENAL.—"Dare to do something worthy of transportation and imprisonment, if you mean to be of consequence. Honesty is praised, but starves." This is applied to the success of intrepid villainy, whilst virtue finds only a cold approbation.

"Dare nobly, man! if greatness be thy aim,
And practice what may chains and exile claim:
On Guilt's broad base thy towering fortunes raise,
For Virtue starves on universal praise!
[*While crimes, in scorn of niggard fate, afford*
The ivory couches, and the citron board,
The goblet, high-embossed, the antique plate,
The lordly mansion, and the fair estate.]"

The plain sober prose of these four lines is, "It is to their crimes that these *great men* [!] are indebted for their gardens, their palaces, their tables, their fine old plate, &c."—A sentence peculiarly pregnant with meaning at the present time [1857]. A pamphlet was published some time ago with the title, "*Whom shall we hang?*" A very appropriate one might *now* be written with a slight change in the title, "*Whom shall we trust?*"

Audendo magnus tegitur timor. Lat. LUCAN.—"Fear is often concealed by a show of daring." The coward blusters to disguise his terrors.

Audentes fortuna juvat. Lat. VIRGIL.—"Fortune assists the bold." Intrepidity will generally insure success.

Audi alteram partem. Lat.—"Hear the other party, hear the other side of the question, hear what the other disputant has to say for himself." Listen to what is said on both sides, and then judge impartially.

Audita querela. Law phrase.—"The complaint being heard." A writ, which lies where a person has any thing to plead, without having a day in court to make his plea.

Auditoria. Lat.—"Schools, professors' lecture-rooms, auditories, or assemblies of those that hear." N.B. "*Auditorium*" is the *singular* of "*Auditoria.*"

Auferre, trucidare, rapere, falsis nominibus imperium; atque ubi solitudinem faciunt, pacem appellant. Lat. TACITUS.—"To ravage, to murder, and to plunder is speciously called reigning, bearing kingly or imperial sway: and when monarchs through their bloodthirsty commanders desolate, lay waste, a country, they dignify their atrocity by calling it MAKING PEACE." See "*A cuspide corona.*" "There are crimes," says the DUKE DE LA ROCHEFOUCAULT, "which become innocent, and even glorious, through their splendor, number, and excess: hence it is that public theft is called address; and to seize unjustly on provinces is to make conquests."

Aufgeschoben ist nicht aufgehoben. Ger. prov.—"Delayed, deferred, put off [for a time], is not lost, rejected, denied." Putting one off does not necessarily imply refusal.

Augusta Trinobantum. Lat.—The designation of "LONDON" by the ancient Romans.

Aujourd'hui roi, demain rien. Fr. prov.—Literally, "To-day a king, to-morrow nothing." To-day me, to-morrow thee.

Aula regia. Lat.—"The Court; the Monarch's court; Court of the Sovereign."

Aula regis. Lat.—"The king's court." A court which in former times accompanied the king, wherever he traveled. This was the original of the present Court of King's Bench.

Aumônier du roi. Fr.—The "king's almoner [distributor of his charities, charitable gifts]."

Aunque seas prudente y viejo,
No desdeñes el consejo. Span. prov.—
"Old or young, wise or foolish, it matters not; disdain not [to take] advice."

Aunque vistays á la mona de seda, mona se queday. Span. prov.—

"An ape is an ape, a varlet's a varlet,
Though clothed in silk or clothed in scarlet."

Aurea mediocritas. Lat. HORACE.—"The golden mean." The happy intermediate state between pomp and poverty. See "Αριστον μετρον." "Give me," says AGUR, "neither poverty, nor riches:" PROVERBS xxx. 8. Compare also HESIOD: Καιρος επι πασιν αριστος: "Moderation is, under all circumstances, the best thing imaginable."

"AGUR's prayer," says COLTON, "will ever be the prayer of the wise. Our incomes should be like our shoes: if too small, they will gall and pinch us, but, if too large, they will cause us to stumble and to trip. But wealth, after all, is a relative thing: since he that has little, and wants less, is richer than he that has much, but wants more. True contentment depends not upon what we have, but upon what we would have; a tub was large enough for DIOGENES [the celebrated CYNIC philosopher]," "but a world was too little for ALEXANDER [the GREAT]."

Auream quisquis mediocritatem
Diligit, tutus caret obsoleti
Sordibus tecti, caret invidenda
Sobrius aula. Lat. HORACE.—
"Whoever makes choice of the golden mean, safe from all the ills of poverty, is not compelled to dwell amid the wretchedness of some miserable abode: while, on the other hand, moderate in his desires, he needs not the splendid palace, the object of envy."

"The man, within the golden mean
Who can his boldest wish restrain,
Securely views the ruined cell
Where sordid want and sorrow dwell,
And, in himself serenely great,
Declines an envied room of state."

Aureo hamo piscari. Lat. prov.—"To fish, angle, with a golden hook." With money one may do almost every thing.

Aureola. Lat.—" A halo [*circle*] of glory, rays of glory." "Around thine ample brow, oft as thy sweet countenance rises upon the darkness I fancy a *tiara* [a hat with a large high crown, turban, diadem, crown] of light or a gleaming *aureola* in token of thy premature intellectual *grandeur* [greatness, gorgeousness]." DE QUINCEY.

Auréole. Fr.—The same meaning as "*Aureola.*"

Auri sacra fames. Lat. VIRGIL.—"The accursed thirst for, or after, gold." See "*Quid non mortalia, &c.*"

Auribus tenemus lupum. Lat.—"We hold a wolf by the ears." "It is something beyond the ordinary necessity imposed on conquest which now impels us onward. *Auribus tenemus lupum.* We have got a powerful and ferocious beast in our clutches; which we have vainly tried to tame, and which we can neither conveniently hold nor safely let go." If we quit our hold, he will destroy us, yet we shall not be able long to retain him.

Aurora amica musarum. Lat. prov.—"The morning, early morning, is friendly to, favorable to, study, the cultivation of the intellect, of learning."

Aurora Borealis. Lat.—"The Northern lights." So called from being peculiar to the more *northern latitudes.* The appearances of the *Aurora* come under four different descriptions. 1st, A horizontal light, like the break of day. 2dly, Fine, slender, luminous beams of dense light. 3dly, Flashes pointing upward, or in the same direction with the beams, which they always succeed. 4thly, Arches, nearly in the form of a rainbow.

"The north pole is the holy mountain of the Eastern nations, the fabulous *Meru* of the Hindoos, the *Kaf* of the Arabian mythologists, and perhaps the real prototype of the Grecian Olympus."

Aurum e stercore. Lat.—"Gold from dung." Valuable knowledge extracted from literary rubbish.

Aurum omnes, victa pietate, colunt. Lat. PROPERTIUS.—"All men now worship gold, all other reverence being done away." So venal is the age become, that nothing is respected but wealth and its possessors.

Aurum per medios ire satellites,
Et perrumpere amat saxa potentius
Ictu fulmineo. Lat. HORACE.—

"Gold loves to make its way through the midst of guards and attendants, and, more powerful than thunder, it forces a passage through the strongest barriers, through the hardest rocks, through stone walls."

"Stronger than thunder's wingéd force
All-powerful gold can speed its course,
Through watchful guards its passage make,
And loves through solid walls to break."

Aurum potabile. Lat.—"Liquid or drinkable gold." Some quacks in ancient times pretended that they could form by a solution of this metal a *panacea,* or medicine which would cure all diseases. The phrase is now applied to *draughts* of a different kind, such as are generally prescribed by orthodox ministers for the cure of political heresies.

Auro pulsa fides, auro venalia jura,
Aurum lex sequitur, mox sine lege pudor.

Lat. PROPERTIUS.—"By gold all good faith has been banished; by gold our rights are abused; the law itself follows gold, and soon will there be an end of every modest restraint." The spirit of venality appears to have loosened all the bonds of society.

Auspicium melioris aevi. Lat.—"A pledge of better times."

Aussitôt meurt veau comme vache. Fr. prov.—"A calf dies as soon as a cow." As soon goes the young lamb's skin to the market as the old ewe's.

Ausum eum, quae nemo auderet bonus: perfecisse quae a nullo nisi fortissimo perfici possent. Lat. LIVY.—It was said of CINNA, the famous leader of the popular party during the absence of SULLA, the Roman dictator [*an extraordinary magistrate of ancient Rome*] in the East, "that he attempted those things which no good man durst have ventured on, and achieved those in which none but a valiant and great man could have succeeded." The same remark has been made in reference to the great NAPOLEON.

Aut amat, aut odit mulier; nil est tertium. Lat. PUBLIUS SYRUS.—"A woman either loves or hates; there is no intermediate course with her, no medium." Her passions are ever in extremes.

Aut Caesar, aut nullus. Lat.—"He will be a CAESAR, or a nobody, either cock of the walk, or nothing, or a mere cipher." N.B. "*Aut Caesar, aut nullus*" may also be translated, "I will attain the highest station, or position, or perish in the attempt."

Aut disce, aut discede; manet sors tertia, caedi. Lat.—"Either learn, or depart; a third course is open to you, and that is, submit to be flogged." The motto of the school-room of Winchester College.

Aut Erasmi aut Diaboli. Lat.—[The work] "either of ERASMUS or of the Devil." "Never, indeed, could the old formula [form, rule, maxim] of conviction, '*Aut Erasmi aut Diaboli,*' be better applied; the book is indubitably the production of *that lady or the Devil.*"

Aut insanit homo, aut versus facit. Lat. HORACE.—"The man is either mad, or he is making verses." The man has either lost his reason, or he is impressed with the idea that Nature designed him for a Poet; and he is now, in consequence, trying his hand at making verses.

Aut navis, aut galerus. Lat. prov.—"Either a ship or a fur cap, hat, beaver." Something, if you could but tell what. 'Tis either a hare or a brake-bush.

Aut nunquam tentes aut perfice [*better*, **perficias**]. Lat.—"Either never attempt any thing, or accomplish it, bring it to bear, determine to bring it to a successful issue."

——————————**Aut virtus nomen inane est,**
Aut decus et pretium recte petit experiens vir.
Lat. HORACE.—

"Either virtue is an empty name, or honor and recompense are due to the man who nobly enterprises."

"If virtue's aught beyond an empty name,
Rewards the daring may with justice claim."

Autant de têtes autant d'opinions. Fr. prov.—"So many men so many minds."

Autant en emporte le vent. Fr.—"So much does the wind carry away." This is all idle talk.

Autobiographia literaria. Lat.—"The literary account of one's own life, literary self-life writing."

Auto-da-fé. Spanish.—"An act of faith," in other words, *burning at the stake.* The name given in Spain and Portugal to the burning of Jews and heretics for the love of GOD! "If Cromwell had not braved death for Mr. Hallam and all the rest of us, Mr. Hallam's reason and philosophy might be skulking under a cassock, or flaming in an *auto-da-fé.*" N.B. An "*auto-da-fé*" was a judicial act of the Inquisition, or the judgment it gave in order to condemn those whom it thought worthy of punishment for having infringed religious laws. And also, "the execution of such judgments, or sentences, and particularly of those which condemned its victims to the flames."

Automaton. From a Greek word, signifying *self-moved, self-impelled.* Any piece of art that seems to move of itself, as a *clock, jack, &c.*

Αυτονομια. Gr.—"Self-government, the condition or privilege of being governed by one's own laws."

Autrefois acquit. Fr.—"Formerly acquitted." A plea, by which the culprit states that he has been tried for the same offense, and found *not guilty.*

Auxilia humilia firma consensus facit. Lat. LABERIUS.—"Union gives firmness and solidity to the humblest aids." When small states coalesce with unanimity, they are strong in their means. The most powerful coalitions will, on the contrary, moulder away from disunion.

Avalanche. Fr.—The large and increasing ball of snow, which frequently rolls destruction down the sides of the Alps and other high mountains.

Avant-coureur. Fr.—A "harbinger, forerunner." *Avant-courrière* has the same meaning.

Avant-garde. Fr.—The "van-guard."

Avant-propos. Fr.—The "preface, or introduction, to a book."

Avaritia senilis quid sibi velit, non intelligo; potest enim quidquam esse absurdius quam quo minus vitae restat, eo plus viatici quaerere? Lat. CICERO.—"What the avarice of old men means I certainly cannot comprehend; for can any thing, indeed, be more absurd than to be adding more and more to one's hoard, according as one's days are drawing nearer and nearer to their close?"

Avarus, nisi cum moritur, nil recte facit. Lat. prov.—"The miser does nothing right, except when he dies, gives up the ghost."

Avec de bon sens, le reste vient. Fr. prov.—"With good sense other things come as matters of course." Good sense will generally lead to a successful result.

Avec de la vertu, de la capacité, et une bonne conduite, on peut être insupportable ; les manières, que l'on néglige comme de petites choses, sont souvent ce qui fait que les hommes décident de vous en bien ou en mal. Fr.—"With virtue, capacity, and good conduct, a man may yet be insupportable; the manners, which one neglects as trifles, are often precisely that by which men decide on you favorably or the reverse; certain modes of behavior, which are often neglected as beneath notice, are frequently what make the world judge well or ill of you."

Avec nantissement. Fr.—"With security." "The sum is guaranteed *avec nantissement.*"

Aventurier. Fr.—An "adventurer," one who has every thing to win, and nothing to lose.

Aver la pera mondo. Ital. prov.—"To have one's pear ready pared." To be born with a silver spoon in his mouth.

Avere su la punta della lingua. Ital.—"To have a thing at one's tongue's end, or at the tip of one's tongue."

Avertissement. Fr.—An "admonition, caution, warning."

——————Avidos vicinum funus ut aegros
Exanimat, mortisque metu sibi parcere cogit;
Sic teneros animos aliena opprobria saepe
Absterrent vitiis. Lat. HORACE.—

"As the funeral of a neighbor, the death of an acquaintance, terrifies, almost frightens to death, the sick when eager after food, for food, and compels them, through fear of death, of the grim foe, to observe temperance and caution, to spare themselves, to curb their unruly appetites, and have a care for their health; in like manner do the miseries, which other men bring upon themselves by debauchery, often beget, in tender minds, a horror of vice."

"For, as when neighboring funerals affright
The patient, who indulged his appetite,
And bid him spare himself, we often find
Another's shame alarms a tender mind."

Aviendo pregonado vino, venden vinagre. Span. prov.—"After having cried up, vaunted, boasted of, their wine, they sell us vinegar." This proverb is strongly applicable to those who, having pre-excited attention, are the more ridiculous from their falling off in performance.

Avito viret honore. Lat.—"He flourishes with hereditary honors, with honors transmitted from his ancestors."

Avise la fin. Fr.—"Consider the end."

Avocat. Fr.—"A barrister." N.B. "*Avocat*" is sometimes confounded with "*avoué*," a very different word, meaning an *attorney.*

Avoir de la peine à joindre les deux bouts de l'an. Fr.—"To have some difficulty in making the two ends of the year to meet."

Avoir l'aller pour le venir. Fr. prov.—"To have one's going for one's coming," have one's journey in vain. To have nothing but one's labor for one's pains.

Avoir le cœur haut et la fortune basse. Fr.—"To have more spirit than fortune."

Αξια ἡ κυων του βρωματος. Gr. prov.—"The dog is worth his food, victuals." 'Tis an ill dog that deserves not a crust.

Axiomata. Gr.—"Admitted propositions, established principles [*in logic*], axioms; general rules, or maxims."

Ayah. A lady's maid in India. The Ayah has no innate taste for dressing, but can usually plait hair well, and contrives to fasten a hook, and to stick in a pin so that it shall soon come out again. She is often the wife of one of the khedmutgars [domestics, whose business in a full establishment is solely to lay the table, bring up the dinner, and wait during the meal], and then the double wages make the service valuable to the worthy couple. Frequently she is an Indo-Portuguese woman, and, though a sad and ugly drab, is in most respects superior to the Mussulman woman.

Ayn wera macket Hera. Frisian prov.—A proverb of great antiquity, which may be rendered, "Own land makes grand," betokening that family honor is represented by being lords of the soil.

Az dy bergen kealje, dan douset it wetter. Frisian prov.—"When the mountains bring forth, the waters dance," that is, One great event is followed by another.

Az ick wist dat myn himbd it wist, dan offere ick it oon't fjoer op. Frisian prov.—"If I knew that my shirt knew it, I would offer it to the fire," that is, If my secret were known even to my own shirt, I would burn it.

B.

Baba Logue. Hindostanee.—*Literally*, The "children people." It is the name by which the offspring of Europeans of the higher classes are called by the domestics.

Baboo.—"Master, Sir." A Hindoo title of respect paid to gentlemen. Merchants, head clerks, &c., in Bengal, are invariably called *Baboos.*

Bacchantes. Gr. in Roman letters.—Priestesses of Bacchus [the heathen god of wine], who, by wine and other exciting causes, worked themselves up to frenzy at the festivals of Bacchus: used also in French for *termagants, froward women.*

Badaud. Fr.—"Cockney." The *badauds* of Paris.

Badauderie. Fr.—"Silliness, doltishness, boobyism, a foolish admiration of any thing and every thing."

Badinage. Fr.—"Jocularity, mirth, gayety, merriment, pleasantry."

Bagatelle. Fr.—"Vive la bagatelle!" that is, "Long live trifling, or trifles!" "There is a pleasure arising from the perusal of the very *bagatelles* [literary *trifles*, light compositions] of men renowned for their knowledge and genius."

Bagne. Fr.—A place where galley-slaves or convicts are kept in chains, where galley-slaves or convicts are shut up after labor.

Bahadoor.—"A great person, a pompous fellow."

Βαια μεν, αλλα ῥοδα. Gr.—"Short [poems] in troth, but [all of them] roses;" compositions of the most exquisite character, of the very highest grade of excellence.

Bal abonné. Fr.—A "subscription ball."

Bal champêtre. Fr.—A "country ball."

Baliverne. Fr.—"Stuff, humbug, nonsense of any kind."

Ban. Slavonic.—"The *Ban* of Croatia is the third person of the realm of Hungary:" that is to say, The *Viceroy*, or *Lord-Lieutenant* of, &c. N.B. *Pan*, or *Ban*, in the Slavonic dialect, means *Lord*. The ruler of Croatia, in the days of CONSTANTINE PORPHYROGENITUS, was styled *Pan*.

Bande noire. Fr.—"The *beaux-esprits* of royalism now betook themselves to defending cathedrals, *donjons*, ruined towers, and feudal castles against the *bande noire*:" that is to say, The *wits*, *men of wit*, *geniuses*, *men of quick parts and ready at repartee* [reply], of royalism ...... against [those, whom they had the *particularly good taste!* to designate] the *black gang*, *black set of fellows*, the *bad lot* [an association of speculators, who bought large estates to sell them in lots, built villages with the materials of deserted mansions, and planted potatoes for human beings in the ancient domain of hares and foxes]. N.B. "*Donjon*" means the principal tower of a castle, which was usually raised on a natural or artificial mound, and situated in the innermost court. Its lower part was commonly used as a prison. It was sometimes called the *donjon-keep*, or *tower*.

Bandito. Ital.—An "outlaw, outlawed criminal, criminal who banishes himself from society at large." The plural is *banditi*, with only one *t*.

Barba bagnata mezza rasa. Ital. prov.—"A washed beard is half shaved." Well begun is half done. See Mr. Sheriff MECHI's "*Observations on Shaving*."

Barbara, celarent, darii, ferio, baralipton. Lat.—This line, which should close with the words *que prioris*, instead of *baralipton*, is a hexameter, consisting of words whose vowels indicate the moods in the First Figure of Logicians. Words full of sound, but quite devoid of sense. Applied to bombast.

Barbare loqui. Lat.—"To speak barbarously." "He insists on the distinction between *barbare loqui* and *incondite loque*:" that is to say, between *speaking barbarously* and *speaking confusedly*, or *in a disorderly, immethodical manner*. N.B. A man who writes in a piebald, hybrid [*mongrel*] diction, or style, made up of German, French, and Latin, for instance, may be said to write *barbare*, while he who writes without composition or digestion, without due regard to composition or digestion of his subject, may be said to write *incondite*.

Barbouillage. Fr.—"Scrawl; bad writing; rigmarole; confused discourse." "*On ne comprend rien à son barbouillage*:" "One can make nothing, neither head nor tail, of his rigmarole."

Bas bleu. Fr.—A "blue-stocking, literary lady." The *plural* is *bas bleus*.

Basis. Gr.—"Foundation, base." That on which any thing rests. "Now, so long as this work is made the *basis* [foundation] of any new edition, so long will it go on to be *rudis indigestaque moles*," that is to say, *a chaotic and undigested mass*, *a rude and unarranged mass* [a chaos of undigested matter]; a mazy labyrinth of valuable matter without system or arrangement.

Basis virtutum constantia. Lat.—"Steadiness is the foundation of all virtues."

Bassa.—A Turkish title of honor bestowed on governors of provinces and privy-councillors of the Grand Signor, the Sultan, or Sultaun, the sovereign of the Turkish empire, the acknowledged head of the Mohammedan religion.

Bastardus nullius est filius, aut filius populi. Lat. Law maxim.—"A bastard is the son of no man, or the son of the people." A bastard being born out of marriage, his father is not known by the law. He is, therefore, in law as no man's issue, it being regarded as uncertain from whom he is descended.

Baste pour cela. Fr.—"Well and good; well, so be it; mum for that."

Bastille. Fr.—The name of the castle, fort, citadel, stronghold, fortress, in which state-prisoners used to be confined at Paris, something like the Tower of London.

Bathos. Gr. in Roman letters.—"Profundity, depth." "Philosophy, that sounds all depths, has seldom approached a deeper *bathos* than the lines we have just quoted."

Batta. Hindostanee.—"Deficiency; discount; allowance." Also, allowance to troops in the field. "In the garrison, troops are allowed half-batta."

Battue. Fr.—"Slaughtering game on a large, gigantic scale." "The preserving of hares and pheasants in large numbers for *battues* is particularly injurious both to agriculture and to rural morality."

Bavarde. Fr.—A "chatterbox, silly woman, who talks at random, without discretion."

Beati possessores! Lat.—"Happy, lucky, fortunate, blessed, are the possessors, they who are in actual possession [of any thing, right, property, privilege, as possession is nine-tenths of the law]." "Henry VIII. silenced the professors of the Canon Law at the Universities, forbade the granting of degrees in it, and nominated a commission for its reform. But *beati possessores!* is a maxim of the law. Its masters of the science of defense have always been excellent in their own behalf."

Beau désordre. Fr. BOILEAU.—"Beautiful disorder,"—that sort of *lawless disorder* in verse-composition which has received the name of "*dithyrambic*," that is to say, "pertaining to, or resembling, hymns sung in honor of BACCHUS [see "*Bacchantes*"]: wildly enthusiastic, inflated, exaggerated."

Beau idéal. Fr.—The "very pink, or flower; true realization." "The *beau idéal* of a statesman."

Beau monde. Fr.—The "fashionable world, world of fashion."

Beauté et folie vont souvent de compagnie. Fr. prov.—"Beauty and folly often join company." Fair and sluttish [foolish], black and proud, long and lazy, short and loud.

Bed of justice.—This expression is a pure barbarism, into which we have been misled by the French, whose ancient language [the Gaulish, or

Celtic] being lost to them, the sense of this expression, "*un* lit *de justice*," among others, is now out of memory; hence that barbarous pleonasm [redundancy, the use of more words to express ideas than are necessary], *tenir une* lit *de justice* [as if the *lit* here were derived from *lectus*, *a bed*, instead of *loi, loit, lit*, law]: *to hold* a law *of justice, or a court of justice*, that is, *a court leet:* not *a bed* of justice, unless for her taking a nap on it. The ambiguity of the derivation is evident: the deception took its rise from the double construction of the Greek verb λεγω, and the Latin word *lectus;* λεγω, *I say*, gives origin to *lego*, *I read*, *legere;* whence we have *lex*, *law*, because the law is accustomed to be *read* and studied: the supines of *lego* are *lectum*, *lectu*, and the participle passive *lectus:* but *lectus* also signifies *a bed*, from λεγω, *I lie down*, whence we have λεχος, *lectus*, *a bed*, or *couch:* hence the barbarous pleonasm, and hideous ambiguity, are sufficiently manifest and plain.

Bedouins.—Arabs, who constantly live in tents. They wander over the whole of Turkey, Persia, Arabia, Egypt, and Syria. They recognize no government but that of their own sheikh or superior. See "*Sheikh.*"

Beef-eaters.—Can any word have degenerated more from the original idea than this now before us? the Queen's *beef-eaters!* and why not her *mutton-eaters* too? did our kings at first appoint them only to *eat beef* at their public entertainments merely for the diversion and amusement of their queens and their courtiers? History informs us that when the jealousies between the houses of York and Lancaster had scarcely subsided at the union of the two Roses under Henry the Seventh, that suspicious monarch instituted this company of *beef-eaters*, as his own body-guard, to attend him both *abroad* and at *board*, like the ancient *dapifers* [which see], that is, to go with him *abroad*, whenever he went from the palace; and to deck his *table*, and adorn his *board*, whenever he stayed at home: and even to this day, in their warrants, they are called *table-deckers*, that is, they were to place all *the vessels* belonging to the king's *board*, or were to be his *buffetiers* [degenerated into *beef-eaters*], the French term for "*side-board attendants, attendants at the side-board.*"

Begum.—A Hindoo lady, princess, woman of high rank.

Bel paese. Ital.—A "beautiful country, sunny land or clime."

Bella femina, che ride, vuol dir borsa, che piange. Ital. prov. —"The smiles of a pretty woman are the tears of the purse." The latter must be drained to insure the continuance of the former.

Bella gerant alii: tu, felix Austria, nube:
Nam quae Mars aliis, dat tibi regna Venus. Lat.—

"Let others, other nations, peoples, wage wars: do thou, O happy Austria, wed, think mainly of wedlock, be it thy care to form matrimonial alliances: for, inasmuch as, the kingdoms which Mars gives to others Venus gives to thee."

"Archdeacon Coxe, in the preface to his 'Memoirs of the House of Austria,' compares that House to the Danube of its native mountains, 'at first an inconsiderable rill, obscurely wandering amidst rocks and precipices, then swelling its volume by the accumulation of tributary streams, carrying plenty and fertility to numerous nations, and finally pouring its mighty waters by a hundred mouths into the Euxine Sea.' The peculiar policy to which it is principally indebted for its aggrandizement is indicated in the well-known lines—

'Bella gerant alii: tu, felix Austria, nube:
Nam quae Mars aliis, dat tibi regna Venus.'

"But it is beside our purpose to state by what alliances, conquests, or treaties the descendants of Rhodolph of Hapsburg contrived to mount the throne of the Caesars, and became possessed of two ancient independent kingdoms, besides archduchies, principalities, countships, and lordships without end. It is enough that the present emperor rules over more than thirty-five millions of subjects of all degrees of civilization and all modes of faith."

Bella, horrida bella. Lat. VIRGIL.—"Wars, horrid wars."

Bella matribus detestata. Lat. HORACE.—"Wars detested by mothers," by orphans, widows, &c., by all, in short, but ambitious ministers, commissaries, contractors, &c..

"Whose chief delight is blood, and bloody deeds."

Belle. Fr.—A "handsome, stylish, fashionably dressed lady." The *plural* is *belles*. N.B. "The word '*belle*,' (says LEMON,) has unluckily given our countrymen an opportunity of inventing one of the most nonsensical hieroglyphics that has ever yet appeared: the French have very properly applied their words '*belle sauvage*' to *a beautiful wild African woman*, and have as properly represented her as having been found in an African wood [if ever found]: but when an English painter would represent this incident, he draws us *a beautiful black woman standing near a bell!* and to this day there is a noted inn, called *the bell savage inn*, on Ludgate Hill, which formerly bore that enigmatical sign; but of late *the savage* has disappeared; and nothing now remains but a *large gilded bell in the yard*, to amuse us with that significant emblem of *beauty:* such poor conceits are fit only for a book of heraldry, or a new edition of 'QUARLES'S EMBLEMS.'"

Belle parole non pascon i gatti. Ital. prov.—"Fine words don't feed cats." Good words fill not a sack.

Belles conversations à la dérobée. Fr.—"Pleasant, interesting, agreeable, conversations by stealth, stealthily, on the sly."

Belles-lettres. Fr.—"Polite literature, learning."

Bellum internecinum. Lat.—"A war of extermination, of mutual destruction." A war to be continued until one or other of the contending parties be ruined or exterminated.

Bellum lethale. Lat.—"A deadly war." The meaning is nearly similar to that of the preceding phrase.

Bellum nec timendum, nec provocandum. Lat. PLINY.—"War is neither to be timidly shunned, nor is it to be unjustly provoked."

Bellum, pax rursum. Lat. TERENCE and HORACE.—"War, and again peace." Alternate warfare and reconciliation: applied by the authors to the contests between lovers.

Bellum plus quam civile. Lat.—"A war rather more, something more, than a merely civil one."

Bellum punitivum. Lat.—"A penal war, a war having for its object pain and punishment."

Bem sabe o gato cujas barbas lambe. Port. prov.—"The cat well knows whose lips she licks."

Ben' ti voglio. Ital.—"I wish thee well." "I wonder whether any one has ever adopted for a seal the beautiful head of Cardinal Bentivoglio, with the name for a motto, '*Ben' ti voglio;*' the conceit seems too obvious to have escaped notice."

Ben trovato. Ital.—"Well feigned, or invented." "When we are willing to be deceived, there is but small difference between the *vero* and the *ben trovato.*"

Ben vengas, si vengas solo. Span. prov.—"Thou comest well, if thou comest alone." Spoken of a misfortune.

Bene colligitur haec pueris et mulierculis et servis et servorum simillimis liberis esse grata: gravi vero homini et ea quae fiunt judicio certo ponderanti probari posse nullo modo. Lat. CICERO.—"It is rightly inferred that these things [frivolities] are pleasing to children, women, and slaves, and even to such freemen as greatly resemble slaves: but can by no means be approved by a man of figure, consideration, and character, and who forms a right judgment, estimate, of things."

Bene est cui Deus obtulit parca, quod satis est, manu. Lat. HORACE.—"Happy is the man, on whom the Deity has bestowed with a sparing hand what is sufficient for his wants."

"Oh! happy he whom Heaven hath fed
With frugal, but sufficient, bread."

See "*Auream quisquis, &c.,*" and "*Aurea mediocritas.*"

Bene est tentare. Lat.—"It is well, as well, to try," any thing that may turn out advantageously, to one's advantage.

Bene exeat. Lat.—"He may depart, take his departure, let him depart, creditably, without any fault attaching to him." "He brought a *bene exeat* from his last bishop."

Bene facit, qui ex aliorum erroribus sibi exemplum sumat. Lat. PUBLIUS SYRUS.—"Wisely does he act, who, from the errors, mistakes, of others, derives an instructive example for his own peculiar benefit, advantage."

Bene nummatum decorat Suadela, Venusque. Lat. HORACE.—"The goddesses of Beauty and Persuasion favor the suit of the rich man: Persuasion and Venus adorn the well-moneyed man." The rich man easily finds flatterers, to style him an eloquent and persuasive speaker, and a pleasing and agreeable companion:—

"The goddess of Persuasion forms his train,
And Venus decks the well-bemoneyed swain."

Bene qui latuit, bene vixit. Lat. OVID.—"Well has he lived, who has passed all his days in the bosom of obscurity:—"

"He lives not ill, who lives and dies unknown."

Compare EPICURUS [the Athenian philosopher], Λαθε βιωσας, "Pass thy days in a state of [comparative] obscurity."

Bene si amico feceris, ne pigeat fecisse,
Ut potius pudeat, si non feceris. Lat. PLAUTUS.—

"If you have acted kindly to your friend, do not regret that you have done so, as you should rather be ashamed of having acted otherwise."

Beneficia dare qui nescit, injuste petit. Lat. prov.—"He who knows not how to confer a kindness, must ask for one unjustly."

Beneficia usque eo laeta sunt, dum videntur exsolvi posse; ubi multum antevenere, pro gratia odium redditur. Lat. TACITUS. —"Benefits are so far acceptable, as the receiver thinks he may make an adequate return; but, once exceeding that, hatred is returned instead of thanks." A man hates to be indebted for a favor which he knows he cannot repay.

Bénéficiaire. Fr.—"One who has a benefit at a theater."

Beneficium accipere libertatem vendere est. Lat. LABERIUS. —"To receive a benefit is to sell your liberty." This is a phrase very often used; it is, however, but partially and circumstantially just. The sense of obligation is, however, not rarely a painful tie on the feeling mind.

Benigno numine. Lat.—"By the favor of Providence."

Benignus etiam dandi causam cogitat. Lat. prov.—"Even the benevolent man reflects on the cause of giving." There is but little merit in inconsiderate bounty.

Bête. Fr.—A "silly, foolish, stupid creature, a dolt, blockhead."

Bête noire. Fr.—Literally, "black beast," but often used to signify a person who is one's *aversion*. "He was long their idol, but is now their *bête noire*." N.B. "*Bêtes noires*" means *black game, or wild beasts of a dark color*.

Bêtise. Fr.—A "piece of nonsense, nonsense."

Bey.—A Turkish title of nobility.

Bibliomania. From the Greek.—"A rage for possessing books, book-madness."

Bibliomaniacs. From the Greek.—"Persons who are book-mad, mad for the possession of books."

Bien-aimé. Fr.—The "Beloved, well-loved." An epithet applied at one period of his life to LEWIS THE FIFTEENTH of France.

Bien attaqué, bien défendu. Fr. prov.—"Set a thief to catch a thief; they are well matched."

Bien perdu, bien connu. Fr. prov.—"Once lost, then prized." The worth of a thing is best known by the want. Compare SHAKSPEARE:—

"That which we have we prize not to the worth
While we enjoy it; but being lacked and lost,
Why then we rack the value; then we find
The virtue that possession would not give us."

Bien vengas, mal, si vienes solo. Span. prov.—"Welcome, mischief, if thou comest alone."

Biendar sin cuyo freno el hombre se queda a solas con su naturaleza. Sp. SOLIS.—[The curb of moral and religious discipline] "those reins, without whose restraint man is left all alone with his nature."

Bienséances. Fr.—The "decencies, proprieties, of life."

Bigarrer ses ouvrages de citations. Fr.—"To belard, interlard, one's work with quotations."

Billet-doux. Fr.—A "love-letter."

Billet d'état. Fr.—"Government paper, bank-notes."

Bis dat, qui cito dat. Lat. prov.—"He gives twice who gives soon." He who gives at once, and without any fuss, in a great measure doubles his gift. A promptitude in giving heightens a favor, which may be depreciated by delay.

Bis est gratum, quod opus est, si ultro offeras. Lat. prov.—"That which is necessary is doubly grateful if you offer it of your own accord." Spontaneous bounty is ever most acceptable.

Bis peccare in bello non licet. Lat. prov.—"It is not permitted to err twice in war." In hostile operations an error is to be prevented by as much caution as if it were irretrievable.

Bis vincit, qui se vincit in victoria. Lat. Publius Syrus.—"He conquers twice who conquers himself in victory." He conquers his enemy by his valor, and subdues himself by his moderation.

Bismillah! Persian.—"In the name of GOD!" An exclamation constantly in the mouths of Mohammedans, who pronounce it on all occasions before commencing even the most common operations of life: it is prayer, invocation, blessing.

Bisogna fa trottar la vecchia. Ital. prov.—"Need makes the old wife trot." The French say, "*Besoin fait vieille trotter,*" which has the same meaning.

Bissextile. From the Latin.—The name given to leap-year, because in that year *two* successive days were both denominated the *sixth* before the Calends of March. The Calends were the first day of the Roman month, on which day the people used anciently to be called together for particular purposes.

Bizarre. Fr.—"Whimsical, fantastical."

Bizarrerie. Fr.—"Whimsicalness, strangeness of fancy."

Boca de mel, coraçon de fel. Port. prov.—"A honey tongue, a heart of gall."

Bocado comido no gana amigo. Span. prov.—"A morsel eaten gains no friend."

Bocca truciata mosca non ci entra. Ital. prov.—"A close mouth catcheth no flies."

Boeotum in crasso jurares aëre natum. Lat. Horace.—"Thou wouldst swear that he had been born in the thick air of the Boeotians," that is, "was as stupid as any Boeotian." Boeotian dullness was proverbial, but how justly, the names of Pindar, Epaminondas, Plutarch, and other natives of this country, will sufficiently prove. Much of this sarcasm on the national character of the Boeotians is no doubt to be ascribed to the malignant wit of their Attic neighbors. "The genius," says Dr. Patrick, "depends much on the climate where a man is born. The people of Boeotia were the most gross and clownish of all Greece, because of the thickness and fogginess of the air there. Cicero, in his book *De Fato*, says, 'Athenis tenue coelum, ex quo acutiores etiam putantur Attici; crassum Thebis, itaque pingues Thebani et valentes;' that is, 'The climate of Athens is pure, and the air serene; whence the inhabitants have quicker parts, and a more piercing apprehension, than the rest of the Greeks. The heaven, on the contrary, at Thebes, is thick and foggy, its inhabitants dull and of slow capacities.' But experience shows that this remark does not hold good in all cases, and that sometimes the worst climates produce the finest geniuses: witness Pindar, who breathed the unpromising air of Thebes, and yet rose to be the prince of Lyrick Poets."

Bois ont oreilles et champs oeillets. Fr. prov.—"Fields have eyes, and woods have ears."

Bombalio, clangor, stridor, taratantara, murmur.
Lat. FARN. RHET.—
"Rend with tremendous sounds your ears asunder,
With gun, drum, trumpet, blunderbuss, and thunder."
Applied to any noisy assemblage.

Bon avocat, mauvais voisin. Fr. prov.—"A good lawyer is a bad neighbor." One of the popular satires on the professors of the law.

Bon bourgeois. Fr.—A "substantial, rich, citizen."

Bon diable. Fr.—A "good, jolly, fellow."

Bon fait avoir ami en cour, car le procès en est plus court. Fr. prov.—"'Tis a good thing to have a friend in court, as it shortens the process." A friend in court is worth a penny in a man's purse.

Bon gré, mal gré. Fr.—"With a good or ill grace." Whether the individual wills it or not.

Bon guet chasse mal aventure. Fr. prov.—"A good watch, good watching, keeps off ugly customers [thieves, &c.]." Sure bind, sure find. See "*Abundans cautela, &c.*"

Bon jour, bonne oeuvre. Fr. prov.—"A good day, a good work." This corresponds with the English proverb, "The better day, the better deed."

Bon marché tire l'argent hors de la bourse. Fr. prov.—"A good bargain draws the money from the purse." A good bargain is a pick-purse.

Bon naturel. Fr.—"Good temper, naturally good disposition."

Bon pays, mauvais chemin. Fr. prov.—"A good country, a bad road, way." The worse for the rider, the better for the bider.

Bon poëte, mauvais homme. Fr. prov.—"A good poet, a bad man." The better workman, the worse husband.

Bon soir. Fr.—"Good evening."

Bon vivant. Fr.—A "high feeder, liver; one who can play a good knife and fork, a good trencher-man." The *plural* is "*bons vivants.*"

Bon voyage. Fr.—"A pleasant journey [if by *land*]:" a "pleasant voyage [if by *water*]."

Bona fide. Lat.—"In good faith." Actually, in reality.

Bona fides. Lat.—"Good faith, integrity."

Bona malis paria non sunt, etiam pari numero; nec laetitia ulla minimo moerore pensanda. Lat. PLINY.—"The enjoyments of this life are not equal to its evils, even in number; and no joy can be weighed against the smallest degree of grief or pain." This is the sentiment of a melancholy man. It must, however, be generally admitted that the "compunctious visitings" of human life are such as to outweigh its most valued enjoyments.

Bonarum rerum consuetudo pessima est. Lat. PUBLIUS SYRUS.—"The too constant use even of good things is a very bad thing, a disadvantage, is hurtful, injurious." We should restrain ourselves so as to *use*, but not to *abuse*, our enjoyments.

Bonhommie. Fr.—"Good nature, easy humor, simplicity, credulity."

Boni pastoris est tondere pecus, non deglubere. Lat. The Roman emperor Tiberius.—"It is the part, duty, of a good shepherd to shear his flock, but not to flay them."

Boni principii finis bonus. Lat. prov.—"A good beginning makes a good ending."

Bonis nocet, quisquis pepercerit malis. Lat. Publius Syrus.—"He who spares the bad, hurts, injures, the good."

Bonis quod benefit, haud perit. Lat. Plautus.—"The kindness which is bestowed on the good is never lost."

Bonne. Fr.—A "nurse-maid, nursery-maid."

Bonne bête. Fr.—A "silly, foolish, stupid creature, good-natured fool."

Bonne bête s'échauffe en mangeant. Fr. prov.—"A good beast gets heated in eating." Quick at meat, quick at work.

Bonne-bouche. Fr.—A "dainty dish, morsel, delicate bit." Something reserved as a special gratification.

Bonne-chère. Fr.—"Good cheer, entertainment, fare."

Bonne foi. Fr.—"Good faith, sincerity, honesty, plain-dealing."

Bonne fortune. Fr.—"Good fortune."

Bonne la maille qui sauve le denier. Fr. prov.—"Well spent is the halfpenny that saves a penny." That penny is well spent that saves a groat. A penny saved is a penny got.

Bonne renommée vaut mieux que ceinture dorée. Fr. prov.—"A good name is above wealth, better than riches, better than a girdle of gold."

Bonne table. Fr.—A "good table, good dinners, good spreads."

Bonnes gens. Fr.—"Civilized beings, men of the right sort, stamp, good sort of persons."

Bonnet de nuit. Fr.—A "nightcap."

Bonnet rouge. Fr.—The "cap of liberty," literally, the "red cap."

Bons esprits. Fr.—"Sensible minds."

Bons-mots. Fr.—"Witticisms, jests, jokes." The *singular* is "*bon-mot.*"

Bonum est fugienda aspicere in alieno malo. Lat. Publius Syrus.—"It is well for those who can see, in the misfortunes of others, the things which they themselves should especially avoid, shun." In this case, without suffering adversity, a reverse of fortune, they acquire that prudence which it inculcates. See "*Bene facit, qui, &c.*"

Bonum magis carendo quam fruendo cernitur. Lat. prov.—"That which is good is descried more strongly in its absence than in its enjoyment." Compare Shakspeare:—

"That which we have we prize not to the worth,
But being lacked and lost, why, then we rate its value."

Bonum summum, quo tendimus omnes. Lat. Lucretius.—"That supreme good, to which we all aspire."

Bonus. Lat.—"The portion of *surplus* capital distributed at certain periodical intervals among the assurers is usually called a *bonus*, a term which is well understood, from the Chancellor of the Exchequer to the broker of 'Change Alley, to mean a *good thing*, so very good, we suppose, that, setting at utter defiance the time-honored rule of grammar, it has been thought entitled to the honor of appearing in 'the most worthy gender:'" that is to say, of capital *over and above what may be necessary to satisfy forthcoming claims, expenses of management*, &c. N.B. "*Surplus*" is a word compounded of two Latin words, super, *over*, or *above*, and plus, *more*, and means *what remains over after accomplishing a purpose* or *object*. "BONUS" means *a good* MAN: the *right* word for *a good* THING is BONUM.

Bonus atque fidus judex per obstantes catervas explicat sua victor arma. Lat. HORACE.—"A good and faithful judge, armed with an upright mind, triumphs over the crowd of enemies, who are always opposed to virtue."

"Perpetual magistrate is he,
Who keeps strict justice full in sight;
Who bids the crowd at awful distance gaze,
And virtue's arms victoriously displays."

Bonus dux bonum reddit comitem. Lat. prov.—"A good leader makes a good follower." A good *Jack* makes a good *Jill*.

Boreas. Gr. in Roman letters.—"The north or northwest wind, the north."

Bos alienus subinde prospectat foras. Lat. prov.—"A strange ox often, ever and anon, looks out for his former quarters,—for the home he has left." Home is home, though it be never so homely.

Bos lassus fortius figit pedem. Lat. prov.—"The ox when weariest treads heaviest."

Bostandgis.—The body-guard of the Sultan. They superintend his gardens and palaces, and attend him on his aquatic excursions. They are expert in the use of the oar, and invariably row the Sultan's caïque [a light bark, much used on the Bosphorus].

Bourbons. Fr.—The *legitimate* Royal Family of France.

Bourgeois. Fr.—A "citizen." N.B. Our English word "*burgess*" is derived from "bourgeois."

Bourgeoisie. Fr.—"The body of citizens, civic body, citizens, burgesses."

Bourse. Fr.—The "Exchange." N.B. The term "*Bourse*" takes its origin from a Mr. *Vander Burse*, whose house at Bruges was near the place where the merchants assembled for the transaction of business.

Βουστροφηδον. Gr.—Turning like plowing oxen; writing after the manner so called, namely, *from the left to the right, and continuing the writing from the right to the left uninterruptedly, resembling furrows traced by a plow*.

Boutade. Fr.—A "sally, invective."

Boute-feu. Fr.—An "incendiary, fire-brand."

Brahm.—According to the Hindoos, "the almighty, infinite, eternal, incomprehensible, self-existent being; he who sees every thing, though never seen; he who is beyond the limits of human conception; he from whom the universal world proceeds; whose name is too sacred to be pronounced, and whose power is too infinite to be imagined."

Brahma.—At the present day the least important deity of the Hindoo Triad. He is termed the creator, or the grandfather of gods and men.

Brahmuns [commonly written **Brahmins**].—The Brahmuns are the first and most distinguished race of the Hindoos, mythologically [fabulously] described to have sprung from the head of Brahma.

Breveté. Fr.—"Patented."

Brevi manu. Lat.—Literally, "With a short hand." "He released the man from duress *brevi manu*," that is, *in double quick time, without the slightest delay.* "He witnessed the *brevi manu* execution of a robber," that is, the *summary* execution, &c.

Brevis esse laboro, obscurus fio. Lat. HORACE.—"I labor, strive, to be short, brief, concise [*in my style*], but I become obscure." An expression applied to authors who, aiming at too great brevity, leave so much unexplained as to become obscure to their readers. Quintilian tells us that *Nimium corripientes omnia sequitur obscuritas*, that is, *Obscurity of expression*, or *want of perspicuity, follows* [is the necessary consequence, result, to] *those writers who aim at too great conciseness in their compositions.*

Βριαρεως φαινεται ων λαγως. Gr. prov.—"Though a hare, he would forsooth wish to be considered a BRIAREUS," that is, "a giant." "BRIAREUS" was a huge and powerful giant, whom the poets represent to have had a hundred arms and fifty heads.

Bride-cake.—This word takes its origin from the ancient Roman custom of *Confarreation*, a marriage ceremony in token of the most firm alliance between man and wife, in the common participation of *a cake of wheat* or barley: "this ceremony," says BLOUNT, "is still retained in part with us by that which we call *the bride-cake*, used at many weddings:" but whatever were the ingredients of the ancient *bride-cakes*, the modern are made of such costly articles, that the wealthy now-a-days seem to vie with each other more in the extravagance of the composition than in a knowledge of the institution.

Brochure. Fr.—A "pamphlet."

Brogues.—"This," says LEMON, "is another instance how strangely the sense of words will alter in course of time: thus, all our dictionaries tell us that *brogues* signify *Irish wooden shoes:* but SHERING tells us that there was a Danish king who acquired the surname of *Loth-brocus*, ita Regnerus, a *vestibus hirsutis*, quibus indutus, duos inusitatae magnitudinis serpentes occidit, ut Saxo refert, agnominatus est; nominis vero rationem ita explicat Stephanius; ab *hirsutis Braccis* dictus est *Lodbrog*, quasi *Loden-brog* [that is, he was surnamed *Loth-brocus*, on account of *the leather breeches* his Majesty wore]; *brog* enim *braccas*, sive *femoralia*, nostra lingua denotat:" and SAMMES calls them his *fur-leather breeches;* because perhaps dressed with *the fur or hair on: brog*, therefore, signifying *femoralia*, seems to have been contracted from *bracca, quasi brog-ga;* but now, *brog*, and *brogue*, appear so very much alike, that they seem to be one and the same.

Brusquerie. Fr.—"Bluntness, abruptness, sharpness, gruffness, roughness."

Brusquerie républicaine. Fr.—A "republican display of bluntness, roughness, republican rough procedure."

Brutum fulmen. Lat.—"A harmless, insignificant, thunderbolt, a mere bugbear." A loud but ineffectual menace, threat. A law which is neither respected nor obeyed. "His discourse was a mere *brutum fulmen;* it was 'full of sound and fury, signifying nothing.'"

Buccae noscenda est mensura tuae, spectandaque rebus in summis, minimis. Lat. JUVENAL.—"One must know one's own measure, and keep it in view, in the greatest and in the most trifling matters."

"Yes, KNOW THYSELF, in great concerns, in small,
Be this thy care; for this, my friend, is all."

Budha.—The founder of the religion of the Singhalese, Burmese, &c.

Buey viejo sulco derecho. Span. prov.—"An old ox makes a straight furrow."

Bukshish, *or* **Buxis.**—A term used to denote presents of money. The practice of making presents, either as a matter of compliment or in requital of service, is so very common in India and the East generally, that the natives lose no opportunity of asking for *bukshish.* In Egypt, perhaps more than anywhere else, the usage is a perfect nuisance. Half-naked Arabs, donkey-boys, boatmen, &c., if left alone with an Englishman, or getting near enough to him not to be heard by his fellows, will invariably whisper "bukshish!" whether he has or has not rendered any service. The word "boxes," as applied to our Christmas gifts, has probably taken its origin in the Oriental term.

Bulbul.—The nightingale of the East, often alluded to in the poems of Hafiz. The Oriental bulbul has prettier plumage than the Philomel of European groves, but does not boast so sweet a melody.

Bungalows.—Indian houses or villas of a single floor. They are either thatched or tiled.

Bureau. Fr.—An "office, public office." The *plural* is *bureaux.*

Bureau de conciliation. Fr.—The "Conciliation committee, or committee for making up matters, or settling disputes."

Bureau de la guerre. Fr.—The "War office, office of war."

Bureaucratie. Fr.—"Bureaucracy, clerkocracy, clerk-section, clerical section of the people, or community." N.B. This new word is seldom employed except in conversation, in order to express the undue influence of the clerks in the administration.

Burnoose.—Part of a Turk's or Arab's clothing, a cloak.

C.

Caaba.—The temple or mosque [place of religious adoration among the Mohammedans] at Mecca, towards which all good Mussulmans turn their faces at the time of prayer.

Cabala, or rather **Cabbala.**—A mysterious doctrine among the Jews, received by oral tradition from their fathers, and not committed to writing, but at last compiled into a body, called their *Talmud:* these two words are of Hebrew origin.

Caballero. Span.—A "gentleman."

Cacoëthes. Lat. from the Gr.—Literally, an evil habit, custom. It is never quoted alone, but always in combination with some other word, as in the two following instances.

Cacoëthes loquendi. Lat.—"A rage, itch, propensity, for speaking." An anxiety to speak in public.

Cacoëthes scribendi. Lat.—From JUVENAL, whose expression is, "*Scribendi cacoëthes.*" "A rage, itch, propensity, for writing." "He has the *Cacoëthes scribendi.*" He is an arrant scribbler.

Cada gallo canta en su muladar. Span. prov.—"Every cock is proud on his own dunghill." The French proverb is, *Chien sur son fumier est hardi.* "A dog is bold on his own dunghill."

Cada hum em sua casa e rey. Port. prov.—"Every one is a king in his own house." A man's house is his castle.

Cada hum folga com o seu igual. Port. prov.—"Every Jack must have his Jill."

Cada ovelha com sua parelha. Port. prov.—"Like will to like," as the scabbed squire said to the mangy knight, when they both met over a dish of buttered fish. The French proverb is, *Chacun cherche son semblable.*

Cada uno en su casa, y Dios en la de todas. Span. prov.—"Every one in his own house, and GOD in all of them." Every man for himself, and GOD for us all.

Cada uno sabe adonde la aprieta el capito. Span. prov.—"The wearer best knows where the shoe wrings, pinches, him."

Cader dalla padella nelle bragie. Ital. prov.—"Out of the frying-pan into the fire."

Cadit quaestio. Lat.—"The question, case, matter, falls, drops, to the ground." "If matters be as stated, *cadet quaestio*; the point at issue will not admit of further discussion."

Caeca invidia est, nec quidquam aliud scit quam detrectare virtutes. Lat. LIVY.—"Envy is blind, and she has no other quality than that of detracting from virtue."

Caftan.—A quilted or thick outer cloak, worn by the Turks, Persians, and Arab Sheikhs.

Cahier des charges. Fr.—A schedule of the clauses and conditions on which any public work is to be contracted for.

Caisse d'amortissement. Fr.—The "sinking fund."

Calamitosus est animus futuri anxius. Lat. SENECA.—"Dreadful is the state of that mind which is deeply concerned for the future."

"Incessant fears the anxious mind molest."

Callida junctura. Lat. HORACE.—"Skillful or judicious arrangement [of words in literary compositions]." "*Junctura,*" observes HURD, "as employed by HORACE, is a word of large and general import, and the same in expression as order or disposition in a subject. The poet would say: Instead of framing new words, I recommend to you any kind of artful management, by which you may be able to give a new air and cast to old ones."

Calumniare fortiter, et aliquid adhaerebit. Lat. prov.—"Slander stoutly, and some injury, damage, to the slandered is sure to result." Throw plenty of mud, and some of it will be sure to stick. Slander leaves a score behind it.

Calumniari si quis voluerit,
Quod arbores loquantur, non tantum ferae,
Fictis jocari nos meminerit fabulis. Lat. PHAEDRUS.—
"Let those, whom folly prompts to sneer,
Be told we sport with fable here;
Be told that brutes can morals teach,
And trees like soundest casuists preach."

Cambridge.—From the common appearance of this word, it seems to be derived from *a bridge built over the Cam*, as is currently believed; but, if we attend to the derivation of CLELAND, we shall find an etymology far more consonant to the institution of that place of learning as a University; he says then that "*Cambridge* is only a contraction of *Cantalbureich; cant* signifies *head; al*, a *school*, or *college*; and *bureich*, or *reich*, a *borough*, or *bury; the head precinct of a college*, or *principal college-borough:* there are many reasons," adds he, "to believe that *Cantalbury*, *Cambray*, or *Cambridge*, existed in the state of *a head collegiate borough* for ages before the Roman invasion."

Camerlingue. Fr.—"Camerlingo," Ital. One of the highest officers of the Roman Court, who is always a cardinal: he is perpetual president of the Apostolic chambers, and administers the civil government when the see [of Rome, the Papacy] is vacant.

Can scottato d'acqua calda ha paura, poi della fredda. Ital. prov.—"The scalded dog fears hot water, and afterwards cold." The burnt child dreads the fire.

Canada.—"The name of Canada has been long a matter of dispute among the etymologists. It has been supposed to have arisen from an exclamation of some of the early Portuguese navigators, who, observing the desolation of the country, either cried out, or wrote on their maps, *Aca-Nada, aca-Nada*, '*there is nothing here:*' [*nothing worth mentioning*]. It has also been supposed to have taken its name from the Spanish *Canada*, a canal, from the shape of the country, forming the blank banks of the St. Lawrence; but the more received explanation is the Indian one, *Canata*, a collection of huts."

Canaille. Fr.—"Rabble, mob, mobility, rascality, scum of the earth, snobocracy." "Mr. G. Dundas defended the conduct of the police in driving back the *canaille* from the carriage-way, and suggested the use of a six-pounder on the next occasion of a similar demonstration." While on this subject of "*canaille*" [a word so often in the mouths of those who ought to know better], the following anecdote may not be uninteresting: "François de Clermont Tonnerre, Bishop of Noyon, under Lewis the Fourteenth, a prelate so often mentioned by Madame de Sévigné, La Bruyère, and other contemporary writers, carried the vanity of birth to such an excess as to become the object of universal ridicule and sarcasm, even in that age. An epigram describes this meek and lowly successor of the apostles as disdaining to associate with the ignoble inmates of heaven; it ends thus:—

'On dit qu'entrant en paradis
Il fut reçu vaille que vaille,
Et qu'il en sortit par mépris,
N'y trouvant que de la CANAILLE.'"

Candida pax homines, trux decet ira feras. Lat. OVID.—"Fair, honorable, peace becomes men, ferocious anger should belong to beasts."

Candida perpetuo reside, Concordia, lecto,
Tamque pari semper sit Venus aequa jugo.
Diligat illa senem quondam, sed et ipsa marito,
Tunc quoque cum fuerit, non videatur, anus.
Lat. MARTIAL.—

"Perpetual harmony their bed attend,
And VENUS still the well-matched pair befriend!
May she, when time has sunk him into years,
Love her old man, and cherish his white hairs:
Nor he perceive her charms through age decay,
But think each happy sun his bridal day!"

Candor dat viribus alas. Lat.—"Truth gives wings to strength."

Cane, che abbaia, non morde. Ital. prov.—"The dog that barks does not bite." The greatest barkers bite not sorest. Dogs that bark at a distance bite not at hand.

Cane vecchio non baia indarno. Ital. prov.—"If the old dog barks, he gives counsel."

Canes timidi vehementius latrant. Lat. prov.—"Timid dogs bark the loudest."

Canis in praesepi. Lat. prov.—"The dog in the manger." To play the dog in the manger,—not eat yourself, nor let any one else. N.B. "*Manger*" is a French word, signifying "*to eat;*" hence, that part of a stable from which horses feed.

Cantabile. Ital.—"Something to be sung." A term applied to movements intended to be performed in a graceful, elegant, and melodious style.

Cantabit vacuus coram latrone viator. Lat. JUVENAL.—"The empty traveler will sing before the robber." The traveler with empty pockets will sing e'en in the robber's face:—

"Now, void of care, the beggar trips along,
And, in the spoiler's presence, trolls his song."

If poverty has its inconveniences, it has also its independence and security. Compare OVID:—

"Sic timet insidias qui scit se ferre viator
Cur timeat: tutum carpit inanis iter:"

that is, "Thus does the rich traveler fear a surprise, an attack, while the one with empty pockets, the one who has naught to lose, pursues his journey in perfect safety." Compare also SENECA: "Nudum latro transmittit," that is, "The robber passes by the man whose appearance bespeaks poverty."

Cantaro que muchas vezes va à la fuente alguna vez se ha de quebrar. Span. prov.—"The pitcher doth not go so often to the water but it comes home broken at last."

Capias. Law Lat.—"You may take." A writ to authorize the capture or taking of the defendant. It is divided into two sorts, namely:—

Capias ad respondendum.—"You take to answer." A writ issuing to take the defendant for the purpose of making him answerable to the plaintiff; and

Capias ad satisfaciendum.—"You take to satisfy." A writ of execution after judgment, empowering the officer to take and detain the body of the defendant until satisfaction be made to the plaintiff. "To act honorably is for an imprisoned and impoverished debtor out of the question; dishonesty is forced on him. He is compelled, when he should work, to remain utterly supine and inert, and to consume uselessly in prison the time and money which are the property of his creditors. By the Roman law a debtor was brought to his creditor bound in chains to work like a slave: by the wise English law he is entombed alive and debarred all power of exertion. The writ directs '*capias ad satisfaciendum*,' or, in the bailiff's very sensible translation, 'take him for your satisfaction;' and this being done, no other satisfaction is by law required or expected. In colloquial phrase, he may 'snap his fingers' at all pecuniary demands, except those incurred within his prison-walls, and for the rest of his life sit with his arms crossed. As to professional income, he may have been in receipt of £500 or £5000 per annum, and the proceedings of any one exasperated or malevolent creditor will cut it off irretrievably, for it is not by petitioning the Insolvency Court that he can be restored to his former station. With regard to estates and resources, beyond mere goods, chattels, and equipages, the present law, as we have seen, affords no power whatever. The conduct of those debtors, who possess means of payment, is quite optional. [Written in 1837.]"

Capiat, qui capere possit. Lat.—"Let him take it [the property] who can."

Capidgi. Persian and Turkish.—A porter or door-keeper; a chamberlain. The *Capidgi-Bashee* are a higher class of officers, and are exclusively employed to use the bowstring.

Capitan Pasha.—The Turkish High Admiral.

Captum te nidore suae putat ille culinae. Lat. JUVENAL.—"He thinks that you are taken with the smell of his kitchen; he looks upon you as one caught by the savor, savory smell, of his kitchen." He is inclined to regard you as a parasite [one who flatters another in order to live at his expense].

Caput mortuum. Lat.—"The dead head." In chemistry, "the ashes remaining in the crucible." Figuratively, "the worthless remains, rubbish, useless details."

Caput scabere. Lat. HORACE.—"To scratch one's head." A sportive mode of conveying the idea that one intends to bestow the greatest care and attention on one's literary compositions.

Car tel est notre plaisir. Fr.—"For such is our pleasure." This was anciently the form of a regal ordinance, under the Norman line. It is now happily used only in an ironical sense to mark some act of despotic uthority.

Caravan. Persian.—Merchants traveling together in companies, by troops.

Carbonaro. Ital.—*Literally*, a "charcoal-burner." A member of a secret society of Italy; it is applied by analogy to the extreme partisans of pure democracy, an ultra-democrat. The *plural* is *carbonari*. N.B. In the wooded districts of the Abruzzi, a secluded and romantic region of Italy, the manufacture of charcoal goes on; and from the name of the charcoal-burners, the noted sect of the CARBONARI took their appellation, originating here and in Calabria.

Carebant quia vate sacro. Lat. HORACE.—"[The names of these illustrious men are unknown to posterity] because they were without—they were not blessed with—a sacred or divine poet to hand them down to posterity; *in other words*, because they had no poet to perpetuate them, or because

'No bard had they to make all time their own.'

"The public mind is sometimes highly sensible of philological propriety, and has, therefore, endeavored to designate the *Pseudo*-gentleman [the GENT] by some other title than *gentleman;* which latter it saw was an abuse of terms; hence the words *dandy*, *Corinthian*, *swell*, *exquisite*, *&c.* But some high literary authority was wanted to record the change in lasting print; and, in the absence of such authority, no one of these words has been universally adopted, *carebant quia vate sacro*." N.B. A *gentleman* may be defined as a *man of unimpeachable honor and gallantry, of dignified carriage, spotless reputation, a high mind, liberal views, and a goodly education.*

Caret periculo, qui etiam tutus cavet. Lat. PUBLIUS SYRUS.—"He who, even when safe, is on his guard, is most free from danger." A proverb which well illustrates the advantages arising from vigilance, watchfulness, being "*wide awake*."

Caricature. From the Ital. *Caricatura*. A portrait made uglier than the natural figure.

Carior est illis homo quam sibi. Lat. JUVENAL.—"Man is dearer to them [the gods] than to himself." "To talk of the omnipotence of prayer, and of mocking or being mocked, unless we expect an answer to our prayers, is changing places, and putting GOD into the hands of man, instead of leaving ourselves, with pious confidence, in the hands of GOD. It might be expected of the Christian that he should feel at least as solemnly as the Roman satirist, *Carior est illis homo quam sibi*."

Carpe diem, quam minimum credula postero. Lat. HORACE.—"Enjoy the present day, as distrusting that which is to follow." This is one of the maxims of the *Epicurean* school, which recommended, but no doubt unwisely, the immediate enjoyment of pleasure in preference to remote speculation. N.B. Addressed by the poet to a *woman*, which accounts for "credul*a*." "Enjoy the present, whatsoever it be, and be not solicitous for the future; for if you take your foot from the present standing, and thrust it forward towards to-morrow's event, you are in a restless condition: it is like refusing to quench your present thirst by fearing you shall want drink the next day. If it be well to-day, it is madness to make the present miserable by fearing it may be ill to-morrow: when your belly is full of to-day's dinner, to fear you shall want the next day's supper; for it may be you shall not, and then to what purpose was this day's affliction? But if to-morrow you shall want, your sorrow will come time enough, though you do not hasten it: let your trouble tarry till its own day comes. But if it chance to be ill to-day, do not increase it by the care of to-morrow. Enjoy the blessings of this day, if God send them, and the evils of it bear patiently and sweetly; for this day is only ours: we are dead to yesterday, and we are not yet born to the morrow. He, therefore, that enjoys the present if it be good, enjoys as much as possible; and if only that day's trouble leans upon him, it is singular and finite. 'Sufficient to the day (said Christ) is the evil thereof:' sufficient but not intolerable. But if we look abroad, and bring into one day's thought the evil of many, certain and uncertain, what will be and what will never be, our load will be as intolerable as it is unreasonable."—*Jeremy Taylor.*

"Let to-morrow take care of to-morrow,
Leave the things of the future to fate:
What's the use to anticipate sorrow?
Life's troubles come never too late.
If to hope overmuch be an error,
'Tis one that the wise have preferred;
And how often have hearts been in terror
Of evils—that never occurred!

"Have faith, and thy faith shall sustain thee—
Permit not suspicion and care
With invisible bonds to enchain thee,
But bear what God gives thee to bear;
By His Spirit supported and gladdened,
Be ne'er by 'forebodings' deterred;
But think how oft hearts have been saddened
By fear of—what never occurred!

"Let to-morrow take care of to-morrow;
Short and dark as our life may appear,
We may make it still darker by sorrow—
Still shorter by folly and fear!
Half our troubles are half our invention,
And often from blessings conferred
Have we shrunk in the wild apprehension
Of evils—that never occurred!" C. SWAIN.

Carte. Fr.—The "bill of fare."

Carte blanche. Fr.—"Every department of the Government had a *carte blanche* for every thing that might be thought necessary for the apprehended war:" that is to say, had *power to act according to their own discretion, unlimited power* for every thing, &c. N.B. "*Carte blanche*" means *a blank sheet of paper, paper unwritten on.*

Carte du pays. Fr.—The "map of the country."

Cartel. Fr.—A "*cartel*" is a writing, or agreement, between states at war, for the exchange of prisoners, or for some mutual advantage; also, a vessel employed to convey the messenger on such occasions.

Cartesian.—A follower of the philosopher DES CARTES: also, relating to DES CARTES, as, "The *Cartesian* system has a tendency to spiritualize body and its qualities."

Casa de pupilos. Span.—A "boarding-house."

Cashier.—From the Fr. "*casser*," to render void. Hence *cashier*, to discard, dismiss from an office. This word must not be confounded with *cashier*, one who has charge of cash. From the same root JOHNSON derives *quash*, when it signifies to annul.

Casta ad virum matrona parendo imperat. Lat. PUBLIUS SYRUS.—

"How gently glides the marriage life away,
When she who rules still seems but to obey!"

Or— "Obey your husband at whatever cost,
And he will ne'er suspect you rule the roast."

Caste.—Tribe, breed, from the Portuguese word *casta*, a breed. The Hindoo religion divides the people into *castes*.

Castrant alios, ut libros suos, per se graciles, alieno adipe suffarciant. Lat. JOVIUS.—"They castrate the books of other men, in order that with the fat of their works they may lard their own lean volumes." Applied to plagiarists, in whose works whatever is good is found to be stolen.

Casus belli. Lat.—"A plea for going to war."

Casus foederis. Lat.—"A case of conspiracy."

Casus interventionis. Lat.—"A case calling for intervention [coming between parties], plea for interference."

Casus necessitatis. Lat.—"A case of necessity, desperate extremity."

Casus provisus. Lat.—"A case for which provision has been made,—case that has been foreseen, anticipated."

Casus, quem saepe transit, aliquando invenit. Lat. prov.—"Him whom chance frequently passes over, it at some time finds." The continuance of good fortune forms no ground for ultimate security.

Catalogue raisonné. Fr.—A catalogue with proofs, illustrations, or literary notices. N.B. "*Raisonné*" is nearly always spelt with *two* e's instead of *one* by English persons who use the above expression; this is incorrect, as the French word "*catalogue*" is of the *masculine* gender.

Catamaran.—A small boat, or rather a log of wood, on which some of the natives of the Coromandel coast traverse the sea. There is much communication between the shipping and the shore at Madras by means of these small craft.

Cattiva è quella lana, che non si puo tingere. Ital. prov.—"'Tis a bad cloth, indeed, that will take no color."

Caucus.—An American slang term, signifying an assembly of some of the members of Congress.

Caudae pilos equinae paulatim vellere. Lat. prov.—"To pluck out the hairs of a horse's tail by little and little, by degrees." "Pull hair and hair, and you'll make the carle bald."

Causa causans. Lat.—"The Great First Cause: the Supreme Being." "Whether we look to our own consciousness, or to our acquaintance with the opinions of others, we feel and witness no revolt against the possible existence of a superior power, the *causa causans*, by whose extraordinary interposition the old laws of nature may be either temporarily suspended, or permanently changed."

Causa et origo est materia negotii. Lat. Law maxim.—"The cause and beginning is the matter of the business." Every man has a right to enter into a tavern, and every lord to distrain his tenants' beasts; but if in the former case a riot ensues, or if in the latter the landlord kills the distress, the law will infer that they entered for these purposes, and deem them trespassers from the beginning.

Causa latet, vis est notissima. Lat. OVID.—"The cause is secret, but the effect is known."

————Causam hanc justam esse animum inducite,
Ut aliqua pars laboris minuatur mihi. Lat. TERENCE.—
"Write, correspondents, write, whene'er you will;
'Twill save me trouble, and my paper fill."

A suggestion to correspondents of newspapers, and contributors to periodicals.

Cause célèbre. Fr.—"A celebrated or remarkable trial in a Court of Justice."

Causeries. Fr.—"Familiar conversations, chat, chit-chat."

Cautus enim metuit foveam lupus, accipiterque
Suspectos laqueos, et opertum milvius hamum.
Lat. HORACE.—

"The wolf once cautioned by experience dreads the pitfall, the hawk suspects the snare, and the kite the covered hook." Even animals learn to avoid that by which they retain a sense of having been injured. N.B. In using the word "*milvius*" [a kite] in this passage, the poet alludes to a species of fish, living on prey, and sometimes, for the sake of obtaining food, darting up from the water like the flying-fish when pursued by its foe.

Caval non morire, che erba de venire. Ital. prov.—"While the grass grows, the steed starves."

Cavallo corriente sepoltura aperta. Ital. prov.—"A running horse is an open sepulcher."

Cavallo que bueta, no quiere espuela. Span. prov.—"Do not spur a free horse."

Cavar un chiodo e piantar una cavicchia. Ital. prov.—"To dig up a nail, and plant a pin." To cut down an oak, and set up a strawberry.

Cave tibi cane muto et aqua silente. Lat. prov.—"Be on your guard against a silent dog and still water."

Caveat actor. Lat. Law maxim.—"Let the actor or doer beware." Let him look to the consequences of his own conduct. If a landlord gives an acquittance to his tenant for the rent which is last due, the presumption is that all rent in arrear has been duly discharged.

Caveat creditor. Lat.—"Let the creditor beware, be on his guard."

Caveat emtor. Lat.—"Let the buyer, purchaser, beware, be on his guard."

Cavendo tutus. Lat.—"Safe by taking heed, proper care, safe by caution." The motto of the House of CAVENDISH.

Cavendum est ne major poena, quam culpa, sit; et ne iisdem

de causis alii plectantur, alii ne appellentur quidem. Lat. CICERO. —"Care should in all cases be taken that the punishment do not exceed the guilt; and also that some men may not suffer for offenses which, when committed by others, are allowed to pass with impunity."

Caxa de consolidacion. Span.—"The sinking fund."

C'è da fare pur tutto, diceva colui, che ferrava l'occa. Ital. prov.—"That's doing something, as the man said who was shoeing a goose." He that will meddle with all things, may go shoe the goslings.

C'est à dire. Fr.—"That is to say,—namely,"

C'est bonnet blanc et blanc bonnet. Fr.—"'Tis six of one and half a dozen of the other."

C'est de l'argent en barre. Fr.—"'Tis as good as ready money."

C'est du blé en grenier. Fr.—"'Tis as good as money in one's pocket."

C'est du neuf, du tout neuf, qu'il faut créer. Fr.—"'Tis from what is altogether new that we must originate something new."

C'est égal. Fr.—"No matter, 'tis all the same."

C'est folie de béer contre un four. Fr. prov.—"Tis folly to be gaping near an oven." He that gapeth until he be fed, well may he gape until he be dead.

C'est le chemin des passions, qui m'a conduit à la philosophie. Fr. ROUSSEAU.—"It is the path of the passions, which has conducted me to philosophy."

C'est le crime qui fait la honte, et non pas l'échafaud. Fr. CORNEILLE.—"It is the guilt, not the scaffold, which constitutes the shame." These were the last words of the heroine CORDAY, when, by depriving the miscreant MARAT of life, she had rid the earth of a monster.

C'est le fils de la poule blanche. Fr. prov.—"He was born with a silver spoon in his mouth."

C'est le mot de l'énigme. Fr.—"It is the meaning of the riddle [the key to the mystery]."

C'est le père aux écus. Fr.—"He is the father of the crowns." He is the moneyed man.

C'est le refrain de la ballade. Fr.—"The old story over again."

C'est le ton qui fait la musique. Fr.—"It is the tone that makes the music." By this it is intimated that as much depends on the *tone* and manner in which words are employed, on certain occasions, as on the words themselves.

C'est la plus belle rose de son chapeau. Fr.—"It is the best feather in his cap, the best spoke in his wheel, the best gem in his crown."

C'est la prospérité qui donne les amis, mais c'est l'adversité qui les épreuve. Fr.—"It is prosperity that gives us friends, but it is adversity that tries them, that shows us the worth of their professions."

C'est la source des combats des philosophes, dont les uns ont pris à tâche d'élever l'homme en découvrant ses grandeurs, et les autres de l'abaisser en représentant ses misères. Fr. PASCAL.—"The origin of the disputes between philosophers is, that one class of them have undertaken to raise man by displaying his greatness, and the other to debase him by showing his miseries."

C'est pour l'achever de peindre. Fr.—"This is to finish his picture." This is to complete his character.

C'est renouvelé des Grecs. Fr.—"The old thing over again!"

C'est son cheval de bataille. Fr.—"That is his *forte*," that is, "his ability, in which he shines most, in which his powers come out the strongest, his strong point."

C'est un balai neuf, il fait balai neuf. Fr.—"A new broom sweeps clean." Applied to servants, who discharge their duties well on entering on new situations.

C'est un beau venez-y voir. Fr.—"A fine thing, a very pretty thing indeed [sneeringly, meaning that the thing talked of is undeserving of notice, beneath our notice]."

C'est un homme qui biaise. Fr.—"He is a shuffler, plays fast and loose."

C'est un sot à vingt-quatre carats. Fr.—"He is a fool of twenty-four carats." His folly is absolutely without any *alloy*.

C'est un vrai bilboquet. Fr.—"He is a harum-scarum fellow, giddy-headed fellow."

C'est un vrai bleche. Fr.—"He is a regular milksop, spooney, a weak, poor, irresolute creature, one who has no resolution, no self-reliance,—one who would never set the Thames on fire."

C'est une autre chose. Fr.—"That is quite a different thing." The facts completely differ from the statement.

C'est une bibliothèque renversée. Fr.—"His notions are confused, in utter confusion."

C'est une grande folie de vouloir être sage tout seul. Fr. ROCHEFOUCAULT.—"It is a great folly to think of being wise alone." None but a fool can suppose that he has a monopoly of good sense.

C'est une grande habileté que de savoir cacher son habileté. Fr. ROCHEFOUCAULT.—"The greatest skill is shown in disguising our skill." The art of a painter or actor, for instance, is best shown when the art, by which he produces a strong effect, is completely concealed.

Ce monde est plein de fous, et qui n'en veut pas voir,
Doit se renfermer seul, et casser son miroir.

Fr. BOILEAU.—

"This world is full of fools, and he who would not wish to see one, must not only shut himself up alone, but must also break his looking-glass."

Ce n'est pas de sa juridiction. Fr.—"It is out of his latitude."

Ce n'est pas être bien aisé que de rire. Fr. ST. EVREMOND.—"Laughing is not always a proof that the mind is at ease, or in a state of composure."

Ce n'est pas merveille si ceux qui n'ont jamais mangé de bonnes choses, ne savent que c'est de bonnes viandes. Fr.—"It is not surprising that those who have never eaten of any delicacies, should be ignorant of the existence of such viands, articles of food." "It is natural that men should be inclined to soothe their vanity with the belief that what they do not themselves know is not worth knowing; and that they should find it easy to convert others, who are equally ignorant, to the same opinion, is what might also confidently be presumed, *Ce n'est pas merveille . . . . . de bonnes viandes.*"

Ce n'est qu'un centon. Fr.—"It is a mere cento, mere patchwork." Said of a work full of passages stolen from other authors.

Ce que l'enfant oit au foyer est bientôt connu jusqu'à Monstier. Fr. prov.—"What the child hears by the fire is soon known as far off as Monstier [a town in Savoy]." Little pitchers have great ears.

Ce qui fait qu'on n'est pas content de sa condition, c'est l'idée chimérique que l'on se forme du bonheur d'autrui. Fr. —"What makes many persons discontented with their own condition, is the absurd idea which they form of the happiness of others."

Ce qui manque aux orateurs en profondeur, ils vous la donnent en longueur. Fr. MONTESQUIEU.—"What orators want in *depth*, they give you in *length*."

Ce qui ne vaut pas la peine d'être dit, on le chante. Fr.—The solution that FIGARO gives of the quality of the words of songs in general, as there is too often a divorce between song and sense.

Ce qu'on nomme libéralité n'est souvent que la vanité de donner, que nous aimons mieux que ce que nous donnons. Fr. ROCHEFOUCAULT.—"That which is called liberality is frequently nothing more than the vanity of giving, of which we are more fond than of the thing given."

Ce sont balles perdues. Fr.—"Useless endeavors, useless shot."

Ce sont toujours les aventuriers qui font de grandes choses, et non pas les souverains des grandes empires. Fr. MONTESQUIEU. —"It is only adventurers that perform great actions, and not the sovereigns of large empires." A maxim which the commencement of the nineteenth century has elucidated, even beyond the expectation of its author.

Cedant arma togae, concedat laurea linguae. Lat. CICERO.— "Let arms yield, give place, to the gown [that is, to peace]; let war give way to civilianism, to the management of civil affairs, and the laurel to the tongue." The power of eloquence is sometimes superior to military force.

Cedat, uti conviva satur. Lat. HORACE.—"Let him depart, like a contented, well-satisfied, guest." A hint applicable to various characters and situations.

Cede Deo. Lat. VIRGIL.—"Yield to providence." Submit where all opposition must be vain.

Cede repugnanti, cedendo victor abibis. Lat. OVID.—"Yield to the opposer, by yielding you will obtain the victory." There are circumstances, under which a prudent concession is equal to an advantage gained over your opponent.

Cedite Romani scriptores, cedite Graii. Lat.—"Yield, ye Roman, and yield, ye Grecian writers." Yield to a competitor who outweighs you all. This is a quotation generally employed in an ironical sense.

Cedunt grammatici, vincuntur rhetores. Lat. JUVENAL.—"The grammarians yield, the rhetoricians are confuted [by the overwhelming eloquence of a would-be learned woman]."

"Full in the midst of Euclid dip at once,
And petrify a genius to a dunce."

Cela est bel et bon, mais de l'argent vaut mieux. Fr—"All that is very well, but I don't like it, or, but I must have my money." [Speaking to a debtor, or some such person, who gives us excuses, reasons, instead of the money we want.]

Cela n'est pas de mon bail. Fr.—"That is no concern of mine; I am not answerable, responsible, for that."

Cela saute aux yeux. Fr.—"That is quite obvious, can be seen at once."

Cela sert à faire bouillir la marmite. Fr.—"That helps to make the pot boil."

Cela viendra. Fr.—"That will come to pass some day or other: All in good time."

Cela vient comme marée en carême. Fr.—"That comes in the very nick of time; in pudding-time."

Celebrare domestica facta. Lat. HORACE.—[Those poets do well, who] seek a subject for their verse at home, find fit subjects for their, &c.

Celerius occidit festinata maturitas. Lat. QUINTILIAN.—"Precocious, premature, development of the powers of both mind and body leads to an early grave:" aptly rendered by the English proverb, "*Soon ripe, soon rotten.*"

Celsae graviore casu decidunt turres. Lat. HORACE.—"Stately towers tumble down with a heavier crash [than more lowly buildings]."—

"The palace, from its airy height,
Falls tumbling down with heavier weight."

The highest tree hath the greatest fall.

Celui gouverne bien mal le miel, qui n'en goûte, et ses doigts n'en leche. Fr. prov.—"He is a bad manager who tastes not the honey of which he has the charge, and also licks his fingers." He's an ill cook that cannot lick his own fingers.

Celui-là est le mieux servi, qui n'a pas besoin de mettre les mains des autres au bout de ses bras. Fr. ROUSSEAU.—"The man is best served, who has no occasion to put the hands of others at the end of his own arms." No maxim is more just or more useful in common life than this, that whatever a man can personally accomplish, he should never leave to be transacted by another person.

Celui peut hardiment nager à qui l'on soutient le menton. Fr. prov.—"He must needs swim that's held up by the chin."

Celui qui a trouvé un bon gendre a gagné un fils; mais celui, qui en a rencontré un mauvais, a perdu une fille. Fr.—"The man who has got a good son-in-law has gained a son; but he who has found a bad one has lost a daughter."

Celui qui dévore la substance du pauvre y trouve à la fin un os qui l'étrangle.—"He who devours the substance of the poor will find in it at length a bone to choke him."

Celui qui met un frein à la fureur des flots,
Sait aussi des méchants arrêter les complots.

Soumis avec respect à sa volonté sainte,
Je crains Dieu, cher Abner, et n'ai point d'autre crainte.
Fr. RACINE.—
"He who rules the raging of the sea knows also how to check the designs of the ungodly. Submitting myself with reverence to his holy will, I fear GOD, dear Abner, and I fear none but him."

Celui qui se défait de son bien avant que de mourir, se prépare à bien souffrir. Fr.—"He that parts with his property before his death, prepares himself for much suffering."

Cenotaph. From the Gr.—An empty monument, set up in honor of the dead; especially when they died abroad, and the body could not be conveyed home, but was buried in a foreign country. XENOPHON, in his Expedition of CYRUS, about the middle of the sixth book, says, "As for those whose bodies could not be found, they erected a large *cenotaph*, with a great funeral pile, which they crowned with garlands." On this passage Mr. SPELMAN observes, "In the same manner we find in THUCYDIDES that the Athenians in the funeral of the first of their countrymen who were killed in the Peloponnesian war, besides a coffin for every tribe, carried also *an empty one* in honor of the memory of those whose bodies could not be found." VIRGIL has translated the Greek word by *tumulus inanis*, where he says that ANDROMACHE had raised *an empty monument* to the manes [departed spirit] of HECTOR:

————————————Manesque vocabat
Hectoreum *ad tumulum*, viridi quem cespite *inanem*
Et geminas, causam lacrimis, sacraverat aras.

Censure littéraire. Fr.—"Literary censorship."

Censure politique. Fr.—"Political censorship."

Cent ans bannière, cent ans civière. Fr. prov.—Literally, "A hundred years a banner, a hundred years a hand-barrow." The same family that once hoisted a banner may in course of time handle a barrow.

Cento carre di pensieri non pagheranno un'oncia di debito. Ital. prov.—"A hundred wagon-loads of thoughts will not pay a single ounce of debt." A pound of care will not pay an ounce of debt.

Centuriae seniorum agitant expertia frugis:
Celsi praetereunt austera poëmata Ramnes,
Omne tulit punctum, qui miscuit utile dulci,
Lectorem delectando, pariterque monendo.
Lat. HORACE.—
"The centuries of the old," that is, "the old as a body, repudiate works that are devoid of instruction: the lofty Equites, knights, members of the equestrian order, disdain to notice poems of a severe character. That individual, however, has accomplished every thing, has carried every point, has gained universal applause, who has well blended the useful with the agreeable, amusing his reader at the same time that he instructs him."

"Grave age approves the solid and the wise:
Gay youth from too austere a drama flies:
Profit and pleasure, then, to mix with art,
T' inform the judgment, nor offend the heart,
Shall gain all votes."

Centurion.—"A captain over a hundred foot-soldiers."

Cereus in vitium flecti, monitoribus asper. Lat. HORACE.—"As pliable as wax in being bent towards vice, but rough, rude, bearish, to their tutors, instructors, counselors, advisers."

"[The youth] Yielding like wax, th' impressive folly bears,
Rough to reproof [and slow to future cares].

"The popular mind is like that of headstrong youth, *Cereus in vitium flecti, monitoribus asper.*" Pliant as wax in the direction to which its own bias inclines, but obstinate as oak when urged into a shape hostile to its own bent.

Cernit omnia Deus vindex. Lat.—"There is an avenging GOD, who sees all things, every thing."

Certamina divitiarum. Lat. HORACE.—"Unwearied struggles after wealth." An elegant expression to denote the striving to be richer than others.

Certiorari. Law Lat.—"To be made more certain." A writ issuing to order the record of a cause to be brought before a superior court.

Certum voto pete finem. Lat. HORACE.—"Learn to set bounds to your desires: To wishes fix an end."

Cervi, luporum praeda rapacium,
Sectamur ultro, quos opimus
Fallere et effugere est triumphus. Lat. HORACE.—

"We, like hinds destined to be the prey of rapacious wolves, of ourselves, of our own accord, seek after the Romans, whom it is the greatest triumph to deceive and avoid, whom to elude by flight is a glorious triumph."

"Like stags, of coward kind, the destined prey
Of ravening wolves, we unprovoked defy
Those whom to baffle is our fairest play,
The richest triumph we can boast, to fly."

"This eulogium of the Romans," says SANADON, "is in itself magnificent, but it becomes infinitely more valuable in the mouth of HANNIBAL [the celebrated commander-in-chief of the Carthaginians]." N.B. "Hannibal" was a common name among the Carthaginians, signifying "the grace or favor of BAAL;" the final syllable, *bal*, having reference to this tutelary deity of the Phoenicians.

Ces discours, il est vrai, sont fort beaux dans un livre. Fr. BOILEAU.—"All this would do very well for a book," that is, It is very showy in theory, but not reducible to practice.

Cessante causa, cessat et effectus. Lat. Law maxim.—"When the cause is removed, the effect must cease to follow." Thus, the release of a debt is a discharge also of the execution.

Cessio bonorum. Lat.—A Scottish law term. "A transference, cession, yielding-up, giving-up, of one's goods without reserve to one's creditors." "The Scottish legislature, a hundred and sixty years ago, gave insolvent debtors, by the right of applying for a *cessio bonorum*, a complete protection against the hardship of imprisonment, except in cases of fraudulent concealment of funds."

Cetera desiderantur. Lat.—Literally, "The rest is desiderated, wished for:" in other words, "The rest [of the poem, speech, &c.] is wanting, or wanted."

Cetera desunt. Lat.—Used in the same manner as "*Cetera desiderantur.*"

Cette nouvelle fut un baume pour moi. Fr.—"That news was life to me."

Ceux qui n'aiment pas ont rarement de grandes joies: ceux qui aiment ont souvent de grandes tristesses. Fr. prov.—"Those who do not love seldom feel great enjoyments: those who do are frequently liable to deep sorrows."

Ceux qui parlent beaucoup ne disent jamais rien. Fr. Boileau.—"Persons who talk much say nothing:" or as Terence expresses it: "*Nae ista hercle magno jam conatu magnas nugas dixerit,* In troth, with all these great efforts she is certainly going to be delivered of some mighty trifle."

Chacun a sa bête dans la figure. Fr.—"Every man looks more or less like a beast." "Conceiving *que chacun a sa bête dans la figure,* he insists that the strong animal likenesses, so distinctly traceable in men, are evidences of our having pre-existed in an inferior state of being:" that is to say, Conceiving *that every man looks more or less like a beast,* &c.

Chacun a sa manie, or, **sa marotte.** Fr.—"Every man has his own particular hobby."

Chacun à son goût. Fr.—"Every man to his taste." A proverbial remark in every language on the prevailing diversity of choice and opinion.

Chacun dit du bien de son coeur, et personne n'en ose dire de son esprit. Fr. Rochefoucault.—"Every man speaks of the goodness of his heart, but no man dares to speak in the same manner of his wit."

Chacun en particulier peut tromper et être trompé: personne n'a trompé tout le monde, et tout le monde n'a trompé personne. Fr. Bouhours.—"Every individual may deceive and be deceived: but no person has deceived the whole world, nor has the whole world ever deceived any person."

Chacun ira au moulin avec son propre sac. Fr. prov.—"Every one will go, must go, to the mill with his own sack." Let every tub stand on its own bottom.

Chacun joue au roi dépouillé. Fr. prov.—"Every one jeers at the king who has fallen from his high estate." Where the hedge is lowest, men commonly leap over.

Chacun porte sa croix. Fr. prov.—"Every one bears his cross." Each cross hath its inscription.

Χαιρ', ω πεδον αμφιαλον,
Καμ' ευπλοιᾳ πεμψον αμεμπτως,
ενθ' ἡ μεγαλη μοιρα κομιζει,
γνωμη τε φιλων, χω πανδαματωρ
Δαιμων, ὁς ταυτ' επεκρανεν. Gr. Sophocles.—

"Farewell, O sea-girt land, and send, waft, me by a prosperous voyage unrepiningly, uncomplainingly, to the spot where a mighty destiny, serious and responsible duty, transports me, together with the wishes of my friends, and the command of the Great Supreme, who subjects every thing to his will, and who decides on all such points, matters." N.B. The exclamation of Bishop Heber on leaving the shores of his native land for India.

Χαλεπα τα καλα. Gr. prov.—"The best things are worst to come by."

Chall.—The Turkish term for a shawl.

Chamade. Fr.—"A parley." "The drums of the garrison beat the *chamade*," that is, *sounded a parley*.

Champ clos. Fr.—"The lists." "He is prepared to maintain her peerless innocence, and to strive in *champ clos* against all gainsayers."

Champ mortel. Fr.—"A mortal combat."

Changer de note. Fr.—"To turn over a new leaf." To change one's line of conduct.

Changer son cheval borgne pour un aveugle. Fr.—"To change for the worse, make one's condition worse in endeavoring to amend it."

Chansonnette comique. Fr.—"A comic little song."

Chansonniers. Fr.—"Were all histories burned, the theatrical repertory could in no wise supply their places; whereas a collection of *chansonniers* would, as it is in the *chansons* of the epochs that you will find the true spirit and portraiture of each age:" that is to say, a collection of *song-writers*, or *ballad-writers*, would, . . . in the *songs*, or *ballads*, of the, &c.

Chansons à boire. Fr.—"Drinking-songs."

Chaos. Gr.—Properly, "A chasm, an abyss," especially the vast void, or the confused mass of elements floating in infinite space, from which, according to the notion of certain ancient philosophers, the world has been formed, namely, *Chaos*.

Chapeau bas. Fr.—"Off with your hat, hats off."

Chapeau de paille. Fr.—"A straw hat."

Chapelle ardente. Fr.—"The place where a dead person lies in state." "The Empress Dowager stood as chief mourner in the *chapelle ardente*, where the body of the Emperor Nicholas had been placed:" that is to say, in a *literal* translation, in the *burning chapel*, where, &c. This, however, does not convey the *correct* meaning of the phrase, as a "*chapelle ardente*" means the funeral paraphernalia, or appendages surrounding the bier or a representation of it, either in the choir of a church, a private chapel, or an apartment, lighted up for the occasion with a great number of wax-lights.

Chaque nation doit se gouverner selon le besoin de ses affaires, et la conservation du bien publique. Fr.—"Every nation ought to govern itself according to the necessity of its affairs, and the preservation of the public weal." These being best known to the nation concerned, no other country or government can with justice or propriety interfere, unless it finds its own interests endangered.

Chaque oiseau trouve son nid beau. Fr.—"Every bird thinks its own nest handsome." We are all strongly inclined to commend that which is our own. See "*Ad ogni uccello*," *&c.*

Char-à-bancs. Fr.—A "pleasure-car."

Charivari. Fr.—"Marrow-bones and cleavers." An unpopular person is treated in France with a *charivari*. This brings us to a class of newspapers, of which the *Charivari* may now be considered as the chief, a class reflecting little credit on the country, notwithstanding their cleverness. Their business is to laugh at everybody, and turn every thing into ridicule. If a celebrated man has a foible or defect, mental or physical, they point it out; if a celebrated woman has been suspected of a *faux pas*, they dwell upon it. Woe to the advocate who professes a fondness for rural amusements, and shame upon the deputy who squints! Nor do they confine themselves to words—

"Segnius irritant animos demissa per aurem
Quam quae sunt oculis subjecta fidelibus,"—[which see,]

and their most biting insinuations are illustrated by caricatures. The real or fancied resemblance of Louis Philippe's head to a pear was the discovery of Philipon, one of the illustrators of the *Charivari*, and gave the king more real annoyance than the attacks upon his life. Go where he would, this unlucky print haunted him; and it is thought that the famous laws of September, which extended to caricatures, were owing fully as much to the pear as to Fieschi.

Charlatan. Fr.—A "quack, quack-doctor, mountebank, empiric, juggler."

Charlatanerie. Fr.—"Quackery, empiricism," the *true* meaning of which latter word is, "practical or experimental physic," in opposition to "dogmatical physic," that is, "physic, or the practice of physic, founded on dogmas and established principles."

Charlatanisme. Fr.—The same meaning as "*charlatanerie*" [which see].

Charterhouse.—Scarcely any word has been more disfigured both in orthography and pronunciation than this: the beginning of which disfigurement came from the French language, with regard to etymology. Let any Englishman or literary Frenchman look at the original and its derivatives in both languages, and then give us any tolerable reason for their present appearance: it is generally agreed that the Carthusian order of monks was founded by CARTHUSIUS; they have, however, been so confounded, transposed, and transplanted as to their name by the French, that they wear at last the ridiculous appearance of CHARTREUX, which the English, by endeavoring to preserve something of the vitiated French pronunciation, have converted into CHARTER-HOUSE.

Chasse-cousin. Fr.—"Chase away, or drive away, cousin." Bad wine, such as is given for the purpose of driving away poor relations.

Chat échaudé craint l'eau froide. Fr. prov.—"A scalded cat dreads cold water." This is a saying rather more pregnant, more pithy, than the English, "A burnt child dreads the fire."

Château. Fr.—"A seat, country-seat." The plural is "*châteaux*." "They were found resting in the neighborhood of one of the huge old farm houses, which in that high-sounding land are called *châteaux*." N.B. The French *château* means any thing but a *castle;* and in a hundred instances for one to the contrary is little more than a large farm-house, gloomy as a dungeon, stuck upon the center of a huge field, naked of tree, shrub, or any other sign of the hand of man or the bounty of nature.

Châteaux en Espagne. Fr.—"Castles in the air:" *literally*, "Castles in Spain," a country in which "castles" are like angels' visits, "few and far between."

Chattah.—An Indian term for an umbrella or parasol.

Chattels, or rather, **Chattles.**—Personal property, particularly live stock, as cows, horses, hogs, and such like animals.

Che nasce bella nasce maritata. Ital. prov.—"She who is born handsome, is born married."

Che ne puo la gatta, se la massara è matta? Ital. prov.—"How can the cat help it, if the maid be such a fool [as not to put things out of her reach]?"

Che sarà sarà. Ital. prov.—"What will be, will be." This proverb, which so strongly supports the doctrine of *fatalism*, is the motto of the HOUSE of BEDFORD. N.B. The Italian is not correct: it should be, "*Sarà qual che sarà.*"

Che spezie! Ital.—"What arrogance, upstartishness!" What a deal of smoke!

Chef d'œuvre. Fr.—A "masterpiece." An unrivaled, unequaled, performance.

Chef de cuisine. Fr.—A "head cook, master cook."

Chef de mission. Fr.—The "head of an embassy, representative mission."

Chef de police. Fr.—The "head of the police, chief police official."

Cheval roigneux n'a cure qu'on l'estrille. Fr. prov.—"A galled horse will not endure the comb."

Chevalier. Fr.—A "knight." The plural is *chevaliers.*

Chevalier d'industrie. Fr.—A "knight of industry," swindler, sharper, shark. A man who lives by ingenious and persevering fraud.

Chevaux de frise. Fr. military term.—Literally, "Friesland horses." The name given to a military defense, consisting of a piece of timber with spikes of iron or pointed with iron: stakes sharpened at each end, and fastened by the middle across each other, to stop the progress of cavalry.

————————**Chi ama, qual chi muore,**
Non ha da gire al ciel dal mondo altr'ale.
Ital. MICHEL ANGELO.—

"Death and love are the two wings which bear man from earth to heaven."

Chi ben cena, ben dorme. Ital. prov.—"He who sups well sleeps well."

Chi bestia va a Roma bestia ritorna. Ital. prov.—"He who goes to Rome as a beast [an ignoramus] returns from it a beast." Send a fool to the market, and a fool he will return. See "*Coelum, non animum,*" *&c.*

Chi compra ha bisogna di cent'occhi, chi vende n'ha assai di uno. Ital. prov.—"He who buys, hath need of a hundred eyes; he who sells, hath enough of one."

Chi con l'occhio vede, col cuor crede. Ital. prov.—"He who sees with the eye, believes with the heart." Seeing is believing.

Chi da gatta nasce, sorici piglia. Ital. prov.—"That that comes of a cat, will catch mice."

Chi dice mal d'amore,
Dice la falsità. Ital. prov.—

"He who speaks ill of love, utters a falsehood, says what is false:"—

"The man, who ill doth speak of love,
Himself a liar thus doth prove."

Chi dona il suo inanzi il morire s'apparecchia assai patire. Ital. prov.—"He who gives away his goods, substance, before his death, prepares suffering enough for himself."

"Who gives away his goods before he's dead,
Take a beetle, and knock him on the head."

Chi fa conto senza l'oste, fa conto due volte. Ital. prov.—"He that reckons without his host, must reckon again."

Chi ferra, in chioda. Ital. prov.—"He that shoes a horse, pricks him." 'Tis a good horse that never stumbles, and a good wife that never grumbles.

Chi ha arte per tutto ha parte. Ital.—"He who has an art, has everywhere a part."

Chi ha cattivo vicino ha il mal mattino. Ital. prov.—"A good neighbor, a good morrow."

Chi ha la sanità è ricco, e non lo sa. Ital.—"He who enjoys good health is rich, though he knows it not."

Chi l'ha per natura fin alla fossa dura. Ital. prov.—"That which we have naturally, continues with us till death." What is bred in the bone will never out of the flesh.

Chi non ha cervello, abbia gambe. Ital. prov.—"He who has no brains, ought to have legs." Who has not a good tongue, ought to have good hands.

Chi non ha cuore, abbia gambe. Ital. prov.—"He who has no heart [courage] should have a good pair of legs." One pair of heels is often worth two pair of hands.

Chi non può fare come voglia, faccia come può. Ital. prov.—"He who cannot do as he would, must do as he can." They who cannot as they will, must will as they may.

Chi non sa niente, non dubita di niente. Ital. prov.—"He who knows nothing, doubts of nothing." Skepticism and curiosity are the great springs of knowledge; but ignorance, on the contrary, is found to go hand in hand with credulity.

Chi non s'arrischia non guadagna. Ital. prov.—"He who risks nothing, gains nothing." "Nothing venture, nothing have."

Chi paga inanzi è servito indietro. Ital. prov.—"He who pays beforehand, is served behindhand."

"Chi paga inanzi tratto,
Trova il lavor mal fatto"—

has the same meaning. To work for a dead horse, or goose.

Chi parla è mandato in galera; chi scrive è impiccato; chi sta quieto va al santo uffizio. Ital.—"He who speaks, presumes to speak, is sent to the galleys: he who writes, presumes to write any thing for publication, is hanged: while he who keeps himself quiet [abstains both from speaking and writing] goes, is marched off, to the holy office, the INQUISITION." A pasquinade, joke, in vogue at Rome about a hundred and seventy years ago.

Chi pecora si fa il lupo la mangia. Ital. prov.—"He that makes himself a sheep, shall be eaten by the wolf."

Chi per man d'altri s'imbocca, tardi satolla. Ital. prov.—"Who depends upon another man's table often dines late."

Chi perde moglie e un quattrino, ha gran perdita del quattrino. Ital. prov.—"He that loseth his wife and a farthing, hath a great loss of his farthing."

Chi prattica con lupi impara a urlar. Ital. prov.—"Who keeps company with a wolf will learn to howl."

Chi servigio fà, servigio aspetta. Ital. prov.—"He who does a service expects one in return." One good turn deserves another.

Chi sputa contra il vento si sputa contra il viso. Ital. prov.—"He that spits against the wind spits in his own face."

Chi tace confessa. Ital. prov.—"He who is silent confesses." Silence is consent, gives consent.

Chi te fa piu carezze che non vuoi, o ingannato t'ha, o ingannar te vuole. Ital. prov.—"He that caresses, flatters, you more than you desire, either has deceived you, or wishes to deceive." Full of courtesy, full of craft.

Chi t'ha offeso non ti perdona mai. Ital. prov.—"The man who has offended you will never forgive you." There are some men who can never be reconciled to a person whom they have knowingly injured.

Chi tutto abbraccia, nulla stringa. Ital. prov.—"He who grasps at every thing, catches nothing." Covetousness brings nothing home.

Chi va a letto senza cena, tutta notte si dimena. Ital. prov.—"Who goes to bed supperless, all night tumbles and tosses."

Chi va piano, va sano e anche lontano. Ital. prov.—"He that goes gently, steadily, goes safely, and also far." Fair and softly go far in a day.

Chi vive in corte, muore a paglia. Ital. prov.—"He who lives at court, dies in a hut, dies on straw." A young serving-man, an old beggar.

Chibouk.—A long Turkish pipe, the stem of which is formed of cherry-wood or ebony, the mouth-piece of amber, and the bowl of baked earthenware.

Chirurgeon.—The old way of spelling *surgeon:* the *correct* spelling, however, would be *cheirurgeon,* as the word is a compound of two Greek words, *χειρ* [cheir], the hand, and *εργον* [ergon], a work: a surgeon, then, is *literally* "a worker with the hand," one who performs medical operations by the hand, not by drugs or medicines.

Chit.—A corruption of the Hindoo term *Chit, hee* [loosely pronounced *Chitty*]. It means a letter, an epistle, a missive, whether the same be short or long.

Chop.—A Chinese word, indicating quality; *first chop* denotes superiority.

Chose qui plait est à demi vendue. Fr. prov.—"Pleasing ware is half sold."

Chouans.—"Insurgent Bretons." They were denominated "*Chouans,*" chiefly, as is supposed, from the circumstance of their movements being generally made, like those of owls [from which word the term may be derived], in the night.

Χρη και εν τοις ηθεσιν ὡσπερ και εν τῃ των πραγματων συστασει αει ζητειν

η τε αναγκαιον, η το εικος. Gr. ARISTOTLE.—"As well in the conduct of the manners as in the constitution of the fable we must always endeavor to produce either what is necessary, or what is probable." Probability, &c. is to be attended to in literary composition, in writing.

Χρειω παντ' εδιδαξε τι δ' ου χρειω κεν ανευροι; Gr.—From an ancient poet, quoted by STOBAEUS [a man of extensive reading, in the course of which he noted down the most interesting passages; to him we are indebted for a large proportion of the fragments that remain of the lost works of poets].

"Need all things taught: what cannot need invent?"

See "*Labor omnia vincit,*" and "*Haud facilem,*" *&c.*

Χρησις αρετης εν βιῳ τελειῳ. Gr. DIOGENES LAERTIUS.—"The use or exercise of virtue in a complete and perfect life." The idea of HAPPINESS, as entertained by the disciples of the Aristotelean, or Peripatetic, School. See "Το *ανθρωπινον αγαθον,*" &c.

Chronique scandaleuse. Fr.—"A chronicle of scandalous affairs, scandalous chronicle."

Χρυσῳ χρυσοτερα. Gr. SAPPHO.—[Poems] "more golden, lustrous, brilliant, resplendent, refulgent, than gold itself." "Out of nine books of lyric verse, besides an unspecified collection of epigrams, epithalamia [hymns in honor of a marriage], and other kinds of poetry, no more now remains than would lie on the extended palm of a lady's hand. Amongst these precious relics, which are all sweetness itself, there are two pieces, in SAPPHO'S own phrase, *χρυσῳ χρυσοτερα.* Those even to whose ears Greek is a jargon, know that we mean her odes to VENUS and to her Beloved, which last should be called by no other name than THE Fragment. There is no other such fragment in Greek, Latin, or English. It has made SAPPHO a name of power among men, a point of solitary glory in our backward view, the gage and boundary-mark of woman's genius to the world's end. To have shrouded the keenest appetite in the tenderest passion, and to have articulated the pulses of sensation in syllables that burn, and in a measure that breathes, and flutters, and swoons away,—to have done this, is to have written these immortal verses. The identical words are of the essence of the work: flashing the soul of the poet upon the reader in a hue of its own, they are not to be spelled out as mere grammatical signs. They are as echoes of unseen and unheard strokes, drops from the heart. They *are* very SAPPHO. You may render the sense, but you cannot translate the feeling: you cannot approach so near even as to PINDAR, who stands also aloof and inaccessible to modern touch: and all that ever yet has been done is little more than notice to the unlearned reader that some such thoughts, in some such order, were the production of a pagan poetess between two and three thousand years ago."

Ciborum ambitiosa fames, et lautae gloria mensae. Lat.—"The intense yearning for, ineffable aspiration after, the good things of this life, and the glories of a well-appointed table."

Cicada cicadae cara, formicae formica. Lat. prov.—"A balm-cricket is dear to a balm-cricket, and an ant to an ant." Like will to like. Birds of a feather flock together.

Cicerone. Ital.—"A guide, attendant."

Cicisbeo. Ital.—"A dangler after a lady, lady-dangler."

Ci-devant. Fr.—"Formerly." "*Ci-devant* philosophers," that is, "Philosophers *of other days*, *former* philosophers."

Cineres credis curare sepultos? Lat.—"Do you think that the ashes of the dead can by this be affected?" Do you think that they feel sensible of the regard or contempt of the living?

Circumduce.—In Scots law, to put a stop to, to render of no further avail.

Citius usura currit quam Heraclitus. Lat. prov.—"Usury runs quicker than Heraclitus." The pay-days come round before the borrower is aware. To borrow on usury brings sudden beggary.

Citius venit periculum cum contemnitur. Lat. LABERIUS.—"That danger which is despised arrives the sooner." The false contempt of an enemy naturally leads to insecurity.

Cito maturum cito putridum. Lat. prov.—"Soon ripe, soon rotten."

Cito pede praeterit aetas. Lat.—"Time fleeth away without delay."

Cito rumpes arcum, semper si tensum habueris;
At si laxaris, quum voles, erit utilis.
Sic ludus animo debet aliquando dari,
Ad cogitandum melior ut redeat tibi. Lat. PHAEDRUS.—

"You will soon break the bow, if you have it, keep it, always bent; but if you unbend it, keep it unbent, when not in use, it will be useful, usable, fit for use whenever you may want it. In like manner ought relaxation to be sometimes, occasionally, given to the mind, in order that it may return better qualified for thinking, for the exercise of the thinking power, the reflective faculties, in order that it may resume study with more vigor, more vigorously."

Civiliter mortuus. Lat.—"Civilly dead." "Before our monasteries were dissolved, if any one became a monk, he was accounted *civiliter mortuus:*" in other words, he was, as it were, *civilly put to death*, and executors were appointed, who administered all his effects.

Civisme. Fr.—"Civism, citizenism, patriotism, desire to bring every one under the designation of CITIZEN."

Civitas ea in libertate est posita, quae suis stat viribus, non ex alieno arbitrio pendet. Lat. LIVY.—"That state alone is free, which rests upon its own strength, and depends not on the arbitrary will of another." Whatever may be the internal constitution of a state, its freedom can be no more than a shadow, if it be subjected in any way to a foreign interference.

Civium ardor prava jubentium. Lat. HORACE.—"The wild fury of one's fellow-citizens ordering evil measures to be pursued." "He met these striking changes of feeling on the part of the people and the government with the honest intrepidity of a man equally disdainful of the *Civium ardor prava jubentium*, and the *Vultus instantis tyranni*. He disregarded both alike: his eye was fixed on immortality." Of such a man we may say—

"Unmoved he hears the crowd's tumultuous cries,
And the impetuous tyrant's angry brow defies."

See "*Vultus instantis tyranni.*"

Clairvoyance. Fr.—"Clear-sightedness, shrewdness, sharpness."

————————————**Clament periisse pudorem**
Cuncti pene patres, ea quum reprehendere coner,
Quae gravis Aesopus, quae doctus Roscius egit:
Vel, quia nil rectum, nisi quod placuit sibi, ducunt;
Vel, quia turpe putant parere minoribus, et quae
Imberbi didicere, senes perdenda fateri. Lat. HORACE.—

[Were I to question, call in question, the opinions of these old croakers] "almost the whole tribe of senators would exclaim that I was lost to all sense of shame, in daring to censure pieces dignified by the just action of grave AESOPUS, and learned ROSCIUS: either because they hold nothing good that has not before had the good fortune to please them, or because they think it shameful to submit to the judgment of those who are younger than themselves, and to own that they should forget in their old age what they had learnt in their infancy with so much care."

"[Should I presume their dogmas e'er to blame]
The Senate would pronounce me lost to shame.
What! criticize the scenes that charmed the age
When AESOP and when ROSCIUS trod the stage!
Whether too fond of their peculiar taste,
Or that they think their age may be disgraced,
Should they, with awkward modesty, submit
To younger judges in the cause of wit,
Or own that it were best—provoking truth!—
In age to unlearn the learning of their youth."

Thus imitated by POPE:—

"One tragic sentence if I dare deride,
Which Betterton's grave action dignified,
Or well-mouthed Booth with emphasis proclaims
[Though but, perhaps, a muster-roll of names],
How will our fathers rise up in a rage,
And swear all shame is lost in George's age!
You'd think no fools disgraced the former reign,
Did not some grave examples yet remain,
Who scorn a lad should teach his father skill,
And, having once been wrong, will be so still."

Aged persons make no allowance for juvenile opinion.

Clameur publique. Fr.—"Hue and cry."

Claqueur. Fr.—"A clapper, praiser, applauder, eulogizer."

Classes dangereuses. Fr.—"The dangerous classes, orders, of society."

[The] **Classics.** "What are the Classics?" is a question often asked. The great works, then, so designated [the literary compositions of those whose works have come down to us in Greek and in Latin] have earned the above epithet, and come recommended to the reverence of all mankind, solely in virtue of the scrupulous propriety of their language; and because they are fitted to serve as models of style to all succeeding generations. The purity of their diction, and nothing else, has been their passport to immortality.

Clausum fregit. Law Lat.—"He broke through the inclosure." A name, given by a fiction of law to an action for debt, in which such a trespass is supposed to have taken place.

Clavis regni. Lat.—"The key of the kingdom." Applied to the GREAT SEAL.

Climax. Gr. in Roman letters.—Properly, "a stair, winding staircase, ladder:" it is also a figure in Rhetoric [the art of oratory], by which the sense of the expressions rises gradually. WE use the word to signify "A gradation, conclusion, wind-up, finishing-stroke."

Clique. Fr.—"A set, party."

Coat-card.—What is now corrupted into *Court*-card: A pictured card.

Cobra capella.—The hooded snake of the East. Some medical men assert that the bite of a *cobra capella* in full vigor, and in possession of all its poisonous qualities, is as surely fatal as a pistol-ball; and that it is only when this poison is weakened by expenditure that medicine can be of any avail. "Where," says Mr. Charles Butler, in speaking of the authorship of JUNIUS, "do we find in the writing of Sir Philip Francis those thoughts that breathe, those words that burn, which JUNIUS scatters in every page? a single drop of the *cobra capella*, which falls from JUNIUS so often?"

Cockney.—Derived from the Greek word οικογενης [oikogenes], "one born in the family," as *opposed to purchased slaves*, "one born and brought up at home." "A thorough-paced, thorough-going, downright οικογενης" is, according to PLATO, "a genuine Athenian, who, having been born in the city, seldom, if ever, set foot beyond the bounds of it; one, moreover, utterly ignorant of every thing but city matters, and from want of experience and familiarity with the most ordinary things that everybody ought to know, things of daily occurrence, a foolish and gaping admirer of every, even the most trivial thing imaginable."

Coelum, non animum, mutant, qui trans mare currunt. Lat. HORACE.—"Those who cross the seas change their climate, but [in many instances] not their mind." This maxim of the poet is meant to enforce that weak minds can derive but little advantage from the survey of foreign countries; or, in another sense, that the guilty cannot leave *themselves* behind.

"Those wights who through the venturous ocean range,
Not their own passions, but—the climate, change."

Compare THOMAS MOORE:—

"Seasons may roll,
But the true soul
Burns the same where'er it goes."

See also "*Quid terras, &c.*," "*In culpa est, &c.*," and "*Longe fugit, &c.*"

**——————Coelumque tueri
Jussus, et erectos ad sidera tollere vultus.** Lat. OVID.—"When the negro," said George Canning, "is lifted from a level with the beast of the field, when he has been allowed to take his stand amongst the human race—

'Coelumque tueri
Jussus, et erectos ad sidera tollere vultus'—

then comes the fit opportunity for considering this most difficult subject" [the admissibility of the evidence of slaves in courts of justice]: that is to say, *and when he has received the gratifying command to raise his eyes to Heaven, and, feeling himself of the same flesh and blood as his fellow-mortals, to bear himself proudly as a man,* then, &c.

Coepisti melius quam desinis : ultima primis
Cedunt: dissimiles hic vir, et ille puer. Lat. OVID.—
"Succeeding years thy early fame destroy:
Thou, who began'st a man, wilt end a boy."

Cogenda mens est ut incipiat. Lat. SENECA.—"Compulsion must be used with the mind to impel it to exertion." This maxim should be inscribed over the study-door of every man who is subject to fits of indolence.

Cogi qui potest, nescit mori. Lat. SENECA.—"The man who can be compelled, knows not how to die." He who is fearless of death may smile at the menace of compulsion.

Cognovit actionem. Lat. Law maxim.—"He has acknowledged the action." This in law is where a defendant confesses the plaintiff's cause of action against him to be just and true, and, after issue, suffers judgment to be entered against him without trial.

Colubram sinu fovere. Lat. PHAEDRUS.—"To nurse, cherish, a snake in your bosom." To suffer a secret enemy to partake of your confidence.

Colluvies. Lat.—"A sink, an abominable mess." "A *colluvies* of publications."

Colluvies vitiorum. Lat.—"A sink, kennel of vices [of every kind and degree]."

Colossus. From the Gr.—"This word is used both by the Greeks and the Romans to signify a statue larger than life; but as such statues were very common, the word was more frequently applied to designate figures of gigantic dimensions. Such figures were first executed in Egypt, and were afterwards made by the Greeks and the Romans. Among the colossal statues of Greece, the most celebrated was the bronze *colossus* at Rhodes [the most easterly island of the Carpathian Sea], dedicated to the sun, the height of which was about ninety feet."—DR. WILLIAM SMITH. "RICHTER has been called an intellectual *Colossus.*"

Colui è il mio zio, che vuole il bene mio. Ital. prov.—"He is my uncle, who wishes my good." He is my friend, that grindeth at my mill.

Coma vigil. Lat.—An affection of the brain, when the principle of life is so reduced that all external objects appear to be passing in a dream; a sort of torpid, indistinct existence.

Comédie larmoyante. Fr.—"Distressing farces," literally, the "weeping comedy, comedy in tears."

Comer y rascar todo es empeçar. Span. prov.—"To eat, and to scratch, a man need but begin." Eating and drinking take away one's stomach.

Comes jucundus in via pro vehiculo est. Lat. PUBLIUS SYRUS.—"An agreeable companion upon the road is as good as a coach." His conversation will shorten, or seem to shorten, the way, and beguile the fatigue.

Comitas inter gentes. Lat.—"Politeness between nations." That mutual consideration which is due from one civilized nation to another; which interferes even in their conflicts, and mitigates the asperities of warfare.

Comité de Salut Public. Fr.—The "Committee of Public Safety." The butcher cabinet of France.

Comitia. Lat.—With the Romans "*comitia*" meant "the assembled people," and "*Comitium*" "the place of meeting." "*Comitia*" is used by English writers to signify "a gathering, assembling of friends and acquaintance."

Comitia tributa. Lat.—"The assembly of the people in tribes, the assembled multitudes."

Comme il faut. Fr.—"As it should be." It is done *comme il faut*, it is neatly or properly executed.

Commencement.—An academical act, a university act, on which the yearly account begins, and the computation, reckoning, of residence is entered. A time set apart for conferring degrees publicly at the University of Cambridge.

Commencement de la fin. Fr.—"The beginning of the end." "An old woman is quoted as having said on that occasion, *Voici le commencement de la fin.* Now, we had always heard this *mot* attributed to Monsieur de Talleyrand on the occasion of Bonaparte's invasion of Spain:" that is to say, *This is the beginning of the end.*

Commination.—"Threats, threatening." The "Commination" Service of the Church of England.

Commis. Fr.—"A commercial clerk."

Commis marchand. Fr.—"A merchant's clerk."

Commis voyageur. Fr.—"A commercial traveler."

Commissaire des guerres. Fr.—"If you only read one portion of these letters [the despatches of the Duke of Wellington], you might fancy the writer to have been bred in a merchant's counting-house; if another, you would say he was a *commissaire de guerre*, or a professed diplomatist, a financier, or a jurist, or that he had traveled all the world over to collect historical and geographical knowledge; he is the able counselor of his equals; the honest adviser of his superiors; the merciful chastiser of the erring; the warm friend of the brave, and the best practical politician and moralist of his time; he is throughout the true lover of his country, and if there is one quality more prominent than the rest, it is his inimitable singleness of heart and soul:" that is to say, if another, ... was a *muster-master* [literally, commissioner of war, or war commissioner], or a professed, &c. N.B. The very able author of the above brilliant passage should have used the term "*commissaire* des guerres," or *commissaire général.* This beautiful extract is from the pen of W. R. Hamilton, Esq., in his "Second Letter to the Earl of Elgin, on the Architecture of the New Houses of Parliament, p. 61. London, 1837."

Commissaire de police. Fr.—"A Commissioner of Police, Police Commissioner." N.B. "*Commissaire*" is often used alone in reference to the police, instead of the longer form.

Commissionnaire. Fr.—"A person *commissioned* to solicit travel-

8

ers for a preference for the inn or hotel that he represents," in other words, an "innkeeper's touter." The word is also used to signify an errand-boy, porter, messenger. N.B. Very often *incorrectly* written with *one* n, instead of with *two* as above.

Committée.—In law, One to whom the care of an idiot or lunatic, or of an idiot's or lunatic's estate, is committed.

"The Lord Chancellor usually commits the care of his person to some friend, who is then called his *committée.*"

"The heir is generally made the manager, or *committée*, of the estate."—BLACKSTONE.

N.B. In these senses the accent must always be placed on the *last* syllable of "*Committée*," and *not on the second.*

Commodius esse opinor duplici spe uti. Lat. TERENCE.—"I think it best to have two strings to my bow."

Common Law.—The *unwritten*, as opposed to the *written or statute, law.*

Commota fervet plebecula bile. Lat. PERSIUS.—"The populace is boiling with excited passion."

"Inspired by freedom and election ale,
The patriot mob at courts and placemen rail."

Applied to the ribaldry of Elections.

Commune bonum. Lat.—"A common good." A matter of mutual or general advantage.

Commune periculum concordiam paret. Lat.—"A common danger produces unanimity." The threats of a foreign foe in general put an end to civil dissensions.

Commune vitium in magnis liberisque civitatibus, ut invidia gloriae comes sit. Lat. CORN. NEPOS.—"It is a usual fault in great and free states that envy should always be the companion of glory." Turbulence and jealousy are as much the characteristics of free states as paralyzed quietude and implicit resignation are of despotic governments.

Communibus annis. Lat.—"One year with another." On the annual average.

Communis error. Lat.—"A common mistake, mistake common to every one."

Communitas Regni Angliae. Lat.—"The great council of the nation, Parliament."

Compagnia d'uno, compagnia di niuno. Ital. prov.—"One man's company is no company."

Compagno allegro per camino te serve per roncino. Ital. prov.—"A merry companion on the road is as good as a nag." See "*Comes jucundus, &c.*"

Compendia plerumque sunt dispendia. Lat. prov.—"Short cuts, the nearest ways, are for the most part the longest ways about." The farthest way about is the nearest way home.

Compendiaria res improbitas, virtusque tarda. Lat.—"Wickedness takes the shorter road, and virtue the longer." Bad men sometimes arrive at pre-eminence by a shorter, though less sure, road than those of a contrary description.

——————————**Componitur orbis**
Regis ad exemplum; nec sic inflectere sensus
Humanos edicta valent, quam vita regentis.

Lat. CLAUDIAN.—

"The people are fashioned according to the example of their king; and edicts are of less power than the model which his life exhibits." The fashions and models take their progress downward, and every thing depends on high example.

Compos mentis. Law Lat.—"A man of a sound and composed mind." A man in such a state of mind as to be legally qualified to execute a deed.

Compositum miraculi causa. Lat. TACITUS.—"A narrative made up only for the sake of the wonder which it may occasion." One of those fictions, the object of which is less to inform than to amaze the reader.

Compound.—Corrupted from the Portuguese word *campana*. The inclosure in which isolated houses or bungalows [which see] in India stand.

Compounder.—At the University of Oxford, one who, having a landed estate, takes a degree: when the estate amounts to a certain value, he is a *grand compounder*.

Comprar en neria, y vender en casa. Span. prov.—"Buy at a market, but sell at home."

Con amore. Ital.—"With love." "The author set to work *con amore:*" that is, *in good earnest, with his whole heart and soul, with earnest and particular zeal.*

Con arte ed inganno
Si vive mezzo l'anno:
Con inganne e con arte
Si vive l'altra parte. Ital.—

"They live, or one lives, one half of the year by art and deception, and by deception and art the other half is got over, got through."

This picture of a man of deceit is not ill translated in the following couplet:—

"You live one half year with deception and art;
With art and deception you live t'other part."

Con scienza. Ital.—"With learning, a thorough knowledge of the subject." "The book is written not only *con scienza*, but also *con amore*."

Con spirito. Ital.—"With spirit, spiritedly, in a spirited manner."

Concessis concedendis. Lat.—"Yielding, giving up, those points that ought to be yielded, given up, abandoned, conceded."

Concetto. Ital.—"A stroke of quick thought or wit; turn, or point." The *plural* is *concetti*. "In Butler's well-known comparison,

'When, like a lobster boiled the morn
From black to red began to turn,'

we discover a clever effort of wit, a *concetto*, associating the original idea with a thing to which, *in some view or other*, it bears a resemblance."

Conciergerie. Fr.—The name of one of the prisons of Paris.

Concordat. Lat.—"An agreement, convention, between the Pope and a temporal sovereign."

Concordia discors. Lat. LUCAN.—"Harmonious discord, discordant harmony, jarring sympathy, jarring concord, dissonant harmony." Applied to music badly played, also to an ill-suited junction of things or persons.

Concordia res parvae crescunt, discordia maximae dilabuntur. Lat. SALLUST.—"By union the smallest states thrive and flourish, by discord the greatest are wasted and destroyed, come to the dogs." This quotation is often and properly employed when stating the mischiefs which so frequently arise from civil dissensions.

Concours comparatif. Fr.—"The examination for government appointments, in which the candidates compete with each other."

Concours universel. Fr.—"The system of competitive examination, an examination open to all who choose to offer themselves as candidates for government appointments."

Concretam exemit labem, purumque relinquit
Aethereum sensum atque aurai simplicis ignem.

Lat. VIRGIL.—

"By length of time
The scurf is worn away of each committed crime;
No speck is left of their habitual stains,
But the pure ether of the soul remains."—DRYDEN.

Time obliterates remembrance of crimes.

Conditio sine qua non. Lat.—"An indispensable condition."

Condo et compono, quae mox depromere possim.

Lat. HORACE.—

"I bring together and digest my literary treasures, that they may be always ready when wanted."

And now I form my philosophic lore,
For all my future life a treasured store.

I range my knowledge under distinct heads, that I may know where to apply for it, when wanted.

Confiteor, si quid prodest delicta fateri. Lat. OVID.—"I confess my delinquencies, if confession be of any use, avail, benefit."

Congé. Fr.—"Leave of absence, dismissal."

Congé d'élire. Fr.—"A writ granting permission to choose a bishop." N.B. The term "*congé d'élire*" [French] is used in reference to the election of a bishop or a dean: in this country it is *a mere form*, as the electors are at liberty to elect only the nominee of [*person appointed by*] the Crown.

Connaisseur. Fr.—"A man who can thoroughly appreciate any thing, perfect judge in matters of taste," *literally*, a "knower, knowing one." N.B. "*Connaisseur*" is often spelt *connoisseur:* the former mode, however, is considered *preferable*, and more in unison with the practice of the *best* French writers.

Conocidos muchos, amigos pocos. Span. prov.—"Have but few friends, though many acquaintance."

Conoscenti. Ital.—The "scientific, those who are wide awake, those who keep their eyes and ears open and know HOW TO OBSERVE."

Conoscere il pel nel uovo. Ital. prov.—"To see, know where to find, the skin of an egg." He knows which side his bread is buttered on.

Conscia mens recti famae mendacia ridet. Lat. OVID.—"The mind, which is conscious of right, rectitude, undeviating integrity, despises, laughs at, treats with contempt, the lies of rumor, lying rumors." A maxim just in itself, but frequently abused. There are some species of calumny too dangerous to be overlooked.

Conseil de famille. Fr.—"A council of the nearest relations, of all the members of a family legally assembled to discuss matters relating to minors, management of property, &c."

Conseiller d'état. Fr.—"A Privy Counselor."

Conseils de Prud'hommes. Fr.—"A paper published by order of the House of Commons, on the motion of Sir G. Grey, supplies some interesting information respecting the *Conseils de Prud'hommes:*" that is to say, the *Councils of good and true men, of men well versed in any art or trade.* N.B. A "*Conseil de Prud'hommes*" is a mixed council of master tradesmen and workmen, for the decision of disputes between persons of both these denominations, for the decision of disputes between master and man. After the peace of 1815, councils of this description were established by law at several towns in Rhenish Prussia, where they are now called "*Tribunaux d'Industrie,*" that is to say, *Courts of Trade, Business, or Arts and Manufactures.*

Consensus facit legem. Law maxim.—"Consent makes the law." When the parties make an agreement, the terms are of their mutual willing, and are no longer a matter for legal consideration, if not against the law.

Consequitur quodcunque petit. Lat.—"He attains whatever he pursues, aims at."

Consilia qui dant prava cautis hominibus,
Et perdunt operam, et deridentur turpiter.

Lat. PHAEDRUS.—"They who give bad advice to prudent men, to men who are on their guard, who are *wide awake,* both lose their labor, both labor in vain, and are disgracefully exposed to ridicule, are basely derided, are shamefully jeered at."

Consiliis nox apta ducum, lux aptior armis. Lat. RABIRIUS.—"Night is adapted, suitable, for the deliberations of commanders, warriors; the day moreover is more suitable for warlike operations, for the tug of war."

Constans et lenis, ut res expostulet, esto. Lat. CATO.—"Be firm or mild as the occasion may require." Suit your conduct to the circumstances.

Consuetudo manerii et loci est observanda. Lat. Law maxim.—"The custom of the manor and of the place is to be observed."

Consuetudo pro lege servatur. Lat. Law maxim.—"Custom is to be held as a law." This and the preceding maxim only go to show the principle, that where customs have prevailed from time immemorial they have obtained the force of laws.

Consuetudinem benignitatis largitioni munerum longe antepono. Haec est gravium hominum atque magnorum; illa quasi assentatorum populi, multitudinis levitatem voluptate

quasi titillantium. Lat.—"I esteem, deem, a habit, the practice, of benignity greatly preferable to munificence. The former is peculiar to great and distinguished persons; the latter belongs to, is the peculiar characteristic of, flatterers of the people, who court the applause of the inconstant vulgar."

Contemni est gravius stultitiae, quam percuti. Lat.—"To folly it is more grievous to be despised than to be struck." Weak minds will sooner bear an injury than a reproach.

Conter fleurettes, conter des fleurettes. Fr.—"To say pretty, gallant, things to a lady, things that are purely complimentary."

Conti chiari amici cari. Ital. prov.—"Short reckonings make dear, long friends." Even reckoning keeps long friends.

Contra. Lat.—"Against."

Contra bonos mores. Lat.—"Contrary to, against, good manners, morals:" a breach of good manners. This quotation is generally used in legal discussions. If the act be not against law, it is an invasion upon morality.

Contra potentes nemo est munitus satis;
Si vero accessit consiliator maleficus,
Vis et nequitia quidquid oppugnant, ruit.

Lat. PHAEDRUS.—

"No one is sufficiently secure against the powerful, but if a mischievous counselor, adviser, be joined with such persons, be admitted as an adviser to such individuals, be associated with such persons as an adviser, then whatever person or object the might of the powerful, and the villainy, craft, knavery, of the evil counselor assail or attack, is inevitably ruined, comes to inevitable ruin, destruction."

Contra quoscunque. Lat.—"Against everybody, all persons whatsoever, all persons be they who they may." "Prussia," said Herzberg, the minister of the great Frederick, "is, by her geographical position as well as by her interest, specially called on to maintain the equilibrium of Germany, and consequently that of Europe herself, *contra quoscunque.*"

Contra torrentem niti. Lat. prov.—"To strive against the stream."

Contrabandista. Ital.—"A smuggler."

Contrada dei nobili. Ital.—"The quarter in Italian towns in which the nobles reside."

Contre fortune bon cœur. Fr.—"A good heart against fortune." A common phrase of admonition, to buoy up the spirits in case of disaster, reverse of fortune. Compare SHAKSPEARE:—

"In all emergencies play the man."

Again:—

"Vexations, duly borne,
Are but as trials, which Heaven's love to man
Sends for his good."

Again:—

"Be suffering what it may, time will bring Summer,
When briers shall have leaves as well as thorns,
And be as sweet as sharp."

Once more:—

"All may end well yet,
Though time seem most adverse, and means unfit."

See "*Nil desperandum*," and "*Tu ne cede malis, &c.*"

Contredire c'est quelquefois frapper à une porte, pour savoir s'il y a quelqu'un dans la maison. Fr.—"To contradict means sometimes to knock at a door, in order to know whether there is anybody at home." Contradiction does not always imply opposition. It is sometimes used to draw forth and to examine the weight of a man's opinions or arguments.

Contre-temps.—"A mischance, mishap."

Contribution foncière. Fr.—"The land-tax."

Conversazione. Ital.—"A conversational party of a literary or scientific cast." "It is," says COLTON, "a piece of pedantry to introduce foreign words into our language, when we have terms of legitimate English origin, that express all that these exotics convey, with the advantage of being intelligible to every one. Foreign sounds, like foreign servants, ought not to be introduced to the disadvantage of the natives, until these are found unworthy of trust. I was once asked at a party what was the difference between a *conversation* and a *conversazione;* I replied, that if there were any difference, I considered it must be this: In a *conversation*, if a blockhead talked nonsense you were not obliged to listen to him; but in a *conversazione* you were."

Copia fandi. Lat. VIRGIL.—In VIRGIL the meaning of the phrase is "permission to speak, opportunity for speaking:" modern writers, however, use the phrase in a different sense: "As an orator, Lord Melbourne wanted the *copia fandi*, which so eminently distinguishes his friend and contemporary, Lord Brougham:" that is to say, wanted the *abundance of expression*, the *power and fullness of diction*, which so, &c.

Copia vera. Lat.—Used by diplomatists to signify "a true copy" of any official document.

Coram domino Rege. Lat.—"Before our lord the King."

Coram nobis. Lat.—"Before us, before the Court of Law." The vulgar say, "He was on his *coram nobis*," that is, he was brought before persons in authority.

Coram non judice. Lat.—"Before one who is not a judge." The matter was *coram non judice*, it was before an improper tribunal.

Coram populo. Lat.—"Before the people:" often used to signify, "In newspapers or speeches."

Cordon. Fr. military term.—A "line," on which troops act and support each other.

Corduaner.—An Englishman at first sight [especially if he were unacquainted with the etymology of this word] would naturally suppose that *cordwainer*, as it is generally written, was a compound of *cord* and *wainer*, whatever he might understand by that termination: but it certainly is no compound, and therefore has not the least connection with the word *cord*, or any thing like it: but, by a strange perversion in writing, is derived and degenerated from *Corduba*, a city in Spain, from which comes the Flemish word, *kordewaen:* the French, *corduan:* the Italian, *cordouano:* the Spanish, *cordouan:* whence comes our *cord* *vain-er; Corium Hispanicum*, that is, *Cordubense; a corduaner, or worker in leather*, the finest sort of which was formerly made at *Corduba*. a *cordwainer* now signifies a *common shoemaker*. "If my feet," says SANCHO, when he is about to quit his government, "are not adorned with *pinked shoes of* Cordovan *leather*, they shall not want coarse sandals of cord or rushes."

Cornucopia. Lat.—It should be written *Cornucopiae*. "The horn of plenty," supposed to be borne by a goddess.

Coroner.—This word is not derived from *corona*, the Latin for *a crown*, but is purely a contraction of *corph-conner*, that is, a *corpse-inspector: corph* was the ancient British word for *corpse*, and *to ken*, and *to conn*, both signify *to know*, or *take cognizance of any thing*. In country places we may often hear the *coroner* spoken of as the *crowner*. There are, or were, in the city of London, certain officials, called *aleconners*, whose duty it was to visit the public-houses, and see what kind of malt-liquor the licensed victualers supplied the public with.

Corps d'armée. Fr.—"A military force."

Corps d'empire. Fr.—"A common political body."

Corps d'observation. Fr.—"A body of observation." A military term.

Corps de garde. Fr.—"A guard-house, guard-room."

Corps de logis. Fr.—"A main building."

Corps diplomatique. Fr.—"The diplomatic body." The ambassadors of several courts acting under the *diplomas* which invest them with that character. It is sometimes used, in a broader sense, to describe those men who are best acquainted with the diplomatic forms.

Corps dramatique. Fr.—"A dramatic body, or company."

Corpora lente augescunt, cito exstinguuntur. Lat. TACITUS.—"Bodies are slow of growth, but their dissolution is rapid."

Corporis et fortunae bonorum ut initium finis est. Omnia orta occidunt, et orta senescunt. Lat. SALLUST.—"The blessings of health and fortune, as they have a beginning, so they must also have an end. Every thing rises but to fall, and increases but to decay."

Corpus delicti. Lat. Law phrase.—"The body of the crime." The whole nature of the offense. The *corpus delicti* in many cases, as in that of a forged promissory note, is specially stated upon the record.

Corpus exsangue. Lat. VIRGIL.—"A lifeless, bloodless corpse." "They have produced, at the best, the mere *corpus exsangue* of the historical romance."

Corpus juris. Lat.—"The body of the law, of the laws, the whole mass of the law."

————————————Corpus onustum
Hesternis vitiis animum quoque praegravat una.

Lat. HORACE.—

"The body loaded, overcharged, with yesterday's excesses, weighs down the soul also along with it." The effect of dissipation is not only felt bodily, but also mentally.

"The body too, with yesterday's excess
Burdened and tired, shall the pure soul depress."

Corpus sine pectore. Lat. HORACE.—"A body without a soul, a mere body without a mind. A dull and inanimate being."

"A being formed of lifeless mold,
With breast inanimate and cold."

Corregidor. Span.—A "magistrate."

Correspondance particulière. Fr.—"Private correspondence," a "private communication," or "communication of a private nature"

Corrumpere et corrumpi seculum vocatur. Lat. TACITUS.—"To seduce, corrupt, others and be corrupt yourself is called LIFE."

Corrumpunt bonos mores colloquia prava. Lat. prov.—"Depraved conversation will corrupt the best morals." Or, as in the English maxim, "Evil communications," &c.

Corruptio optimi pessima. Lat.—"The corruption of the best is productive of the worst." The best and purest institutions, when once vitiated and gangrened, are found in the process of corruption to outdo the very worst. "Let us reconnect, to the shame of human nature, that *corruptio optimi pessima;* bribery, in some of its Proteus forms, seems to be a disease incident to every representative system:" that is to say, *the corruption, malversation, of the best things, is productive of, produces, the worst effects: the abuse of the best thing is the worst of all abuses.*

Corruptissima republica, plurimae leges. Lat. TACITUS.—"When the state is most corrupt, then are the laws most multiplied." The relaxed morals of a people may be estimated in some degree from the legal restraints which it is found necessary to impose.

Cortes. Span.—"The PARLIAMENT of Spain."

Corvée. Fr.—"Base service, statute labor, contribution in forced labor."

Coryphaeus. Gr. in Roman letters.—"A leader, chief." "He is the *Coryphaeus* of the ballot."

Cosa fatta capo ha. Ital. prov.—"A thing which is done has a head." There is, as it were, no *life* in a business until the main circumstance be completed. The statue may then be said to have gotten a *head,* and nothing is wanted but the finishing touches.

Cosas de España. Span.—"Spanish doings." "These are instances of *Cosas de España,* always odd and sometimes unintelligible."

Cosi tosto muore il capretto come capra. Ital. prov.—"The kid dies as soon as its mother." As soon goes the young lamb's skin to the market as the old ewe's.

Costumier. Fr.—"A dealer in costumes [dresses], particularly those of a *theatrical* character."

Coterie. Fr.—"A set, sociable set of acquaintance."

Cottage orné. Fr.—"A cottage-villa," literally, an "ornamented or adorned cottage." N.B. The expression "*cottage orné*" is nearly always *incorrectly* written: thus, *cottage ornée.*

Coudre le peau de regnard à celle du lion. Old Fr. prov.—"To sew the fox's skin to the lion's." If the lion's skin cannot, the fox's shall.

Couleur de rose. Fr.—Literally, "Rose-color:" but used to signify, "in a favorable point of view, brilliantly, favorably." "If the young paint too much *couleur de rose*, the old wash in their dark tints too freely."

Coup d'essai. Fr.—"A first essay, first production."

Coup d'état. Fr.—"A stroke, or measure, of state policy." N.B. A "*coup d'état*" is an extraordinary and violent measure taken by a government, when the safety of the state is in danger, or is supposed to be so.

Coup d'œil. Fr.—"A quick glance of the eye."

Coup de grâce. Fr.—"A stroke of mercy." The stroke which finished the sufferings of those who had been broken on the wheel. The "finishing stroke."

Coup de main. Fr.—"A bold effort, stroke." "A sudden assault." "An unexpected attack." "A sudden, bold, enterprise."

Coup de soleil. Fr.—"A sun-stroke, stroke of the sun."

Coup de théâtre. Fr.—"An unforeseen event."

Coupé. Fr.—"The front covered outside part" of the "*diligence*" [French stage-coach].

Coupe-gorge. Fr.—"A cut-throat place."

Coupon. Fr.—"A dividend-warrant."

Court-baron—"Is a court incident to every manor in the kingdom, and was holden by the steward within the said manor. This *court-baron* is of two natures: the one is a customary court, the other a court of common law."—BLACKSTONE.

Court-leet—"Is a court of record, held once in the year, and not oftener, within a particular hundred, lordship, or manor, before the steward of the leet."—BLACKSTONE.

Court of piepowder.—Such is the present corruption of the original and proper title of this court, of *piepoudre, curia pedis pulverizati*, so called from the dusty feet of the suitors; or, according to Sir Ed. Coke, because justice is there administered as speedily as dust falls from the foot; upon the same principle that justice among the Jews was administered in *porta civitatis;* that the proceedings might be more speedy as well as public. The etymology of a learned modern writer is, however, much more clear and evident (vide Barrington's Observations on the Stat. 337), it being derived, according to his opinion, from *pieds pul-dreaux*, a pedlar, in ancient French, and therefore signifying the court of such petty chapmen as resort to fairs or markets. It is a court of record incident to every fair and market, of which the steward of him who owns or has the toll of the market presides as judge. It was instituted to administer justice for all commercial injuries done in that very fair or market, and not in any preceding one: so that the injury must be done, complained of, heard, and determined during the continuance of the fair, and no longer. This court, which is the lowest, and at the same time the most expeditious, in England, was instituted for the purpose of doing immediate justice among the people who resort to fairs, &c., and the plaintiff must make oath that the cause of action arose there

Courtisanerie. Fr.—"Courtiership, the ways, practices, and habits of courtiers."

Coûte que coûte. Fr.—"He is evidently a special pleader, whose object is to serve his party, *coûte que coûte:*" that is to say, *cost what it*

may, at whatever cost, come what may or will, under all circumstances. N.B. The phrase "*coûte que coûte*" is nearly always incorrectly written by English persons: thus, "*coûte qui coûte.*"

Craignez honte. Fr.—"Fear, or dread, shame."

Craignez tout d'un auteur en courroux. Fr. BOILEAU.—"Fear every thing, the worst, from an enraged, incensed, author." The irritable temper of authors has long been a matter of notoriety. See "*Genus irritabile vatum.*"

Crambe bis cocta. Lat. prov.—"Colewort twice boiled, cooked." "To sing the same song, harp on the same string." The same story over again.

Cranium. Lat.—"The skull, brain-pan."

"He feared starvation, and his *cranium* ran
On want, with tens of thousands in his purse."

Cras credemus, hodie nihil. Lat. prov.—"To-morrow we will believe, but nothing to-day." Let us see what time may produce, for we cannot credit the present assertion.

Crassa Minerva. Lat. HORACE.—"A man of strong, rough, common sense." The full expression would be "*vir crassa Minerva.*" The phrase "*Crassa Minerva*" is meant to designate one who has no acquaintance with philosophical subtleties, or the precepts of art, but is swayed by the dictates and suggestions of plain, native sense.

Credat Judaeus. Lat. HORACE.—"He added that the Greeks were very ignorant of tactics, and that, *credat Judaeus!* he should rejoice to combat under the command of so distinguished a leader:" that is to say, *let a Jew believe it!* [I certainly do not.] N.B. The *full* expression is, *Credat Judaeus Apella, non ego:* that is, *Let the Jew Apella, or the Jew Apella may, believe it: I don't.* The expression is a contemptuous one, meaning that the thing was too absurd and improbable to obtain credence from a man of sense, but might possibly impose on the understanding of the superstitious Jew. The Jews were in those days treated pretty much as they are in our day, and were despised as the offscourings of the human race:—

"The silly Jew Apella may receive
The wondrous tale, which I can ne'er believe."

Crede Byron. Lat.—"The democratic principle in Upper Canada received a fatal wound. And why?—*Crede Byron!*—

'And why? Because a little—odd—*Old Man*,
Stripped to his shirt, had come to lead the van!'"

that is to say, *Believe what Lord Byron says on that point, in one of his poems.* N.B. "*Crede Byron*"—Trust Byron—is the motto of Lord Byron.

Crede quod habes, et habes. Lat.—"Believe that you have it, and you have it." Indulge your imagination, and it will gratify you in nearly an equal degree with the actual possession.

Credebant hoc grande nefas, et morte piandum,
Si juvenis vetulo non assurrexerat, et si
Barbato cuicunque puer, licet ipse videret
Plura domi fraga, et majores glandis acervos.

Lat. JUVENAL.—

"In days of old, men used to hold it as a heinous sin, that naught but death could expiate, if a young man had not risen from his seat to pay honor to an old one, or a boy to one whose beard was grown; even though he himself gloated over more strawberries at home. or a bigger pile of acorns."

"Then, had not men the hoary head revered,
And boys paid reverence when a man appeared,
Both must have died, though richer skins they wore,
And saw more heaps of acorns in their store."

Credenda. Lat.—"Things to be believed, tenets, creed." "The *credenda* must precede the *facienda*, but the two must not be separated by an interval."

——————————Creditur olim
Velificatus Athos, et quicquid Graecia mendax
Audet in historia. Lat. JUVENAL.—
"There was a canal in Greece, which proved a sad stumbling-block to the Roman satirist, Juvenal, whose unlucky accusation of 'lying Greece' is founded on his own ignorance of a fact recorded by Herodotus and Thucydides:—

——————————Creditur olim
Velificatus Athos, et quicquid Graecia mendax
Audet in historia:"

that is to say, *Men believe that Athos* [a mountain of Macedon, a province of ancient Greece] *was sailed through of yore, and all the bold assertions that lying Greece hazards in history.* See Colonel Leake's Travels in Northern Greece, vol. iii. p. 143.

Credo pudicitiam, Saturno rege, moratam
In terres. Lat. JUVENAL.—
"I believe that in the reign of SATURN [commonly called the Golden Age]" "chastity dwelt upon this earth." The satirist alludes to the relaxed manners of the Roman ladies in his time.

"In Saturn's time, at Nature's early birth,
There was that thing called chastity on earth."—DRYDEN.

Credula res amor est. Lat. OVID.—"Love is an affair of credulity."

"The man who loves is easy of belief."

Those who are in love believe every idle tale which flatters their expectations.

Cresce di, cresce 'l froddo, dice il pescatore. Ital. prov.—"As the days lengthen, the cold strengthens, says the fisherman."

Crescentem sequitur cura pecuniam,
Majorumque fames. Lat. HORACE.—
"Care ever follows after increasing riches, as well as the craving desire for more extensive possessions."

"Corroding care, and thirst of more,
Attends the still increasing store."

Crescit amor nummi quantum ipsa pecunia crescit.
Lat. JUVENAL.—
"The love of money, pelf, increases as much as, as fast as, the money itself increases." Compare OVID:—

"Creverunt et opes, et opum furiosa cupido,
Et, cum possideant plurima, plura volunt."

"Riches have also increased with them, and an unbridled desire after still greater wealth, and although they possess enough and more than enough, still do they yearn after more."

Crescit indulgens sibi dirus hydrops. Lat. HORACE.—"The fatal dropsy gains on the patient from his gratifying his thirst." The same inference belongs to this as to the preceding quotation.

Crescit sub pondere virtus. Lat.—"Virtue grows under the imposed weight." The idea is taken from the received opinion of the palm-tree, which is said to grow the faster in proportion to the incumbent weight.

Creta, an carbone notandi? Lat. HORACE.—"Are such outrageous individuals to be marked with chalk as sane, of sound mind, or with charcoal as insane? are they to be ranked with wise men, or with fools?" Among the Romans, white was considered lucky, black unlucky. Hence things of a favorable or auspicious nature were denoted by the former, and those of an opposite character by the latter.

Creverunt et opes et opum furiosa cupido,
Ut, quo possideant plurima, plura petant.
Sic quibus intumuit suffusa venter ab unda,
Quo plus sunt potae, plus sitiuntur aquae. Lat. OVID.—

"Riches also increased and the raging desire after more, so that, the more men possessed, the more they desired. In the same manner is it with those who suffer from dropsy—the more they drink, the more thirsty they are." Much would have more.

Cribro aquam haurire. Lat. prov.—"To draw water in a sieve." To lose one's time and pains, labor, trouble.

Crimen laesae majestatis. Lat.—"The crime of wronging or injuring majesty," that is, "The Sovereign." The guilt of high treason.

Crimina qui cernunt aliorum, non sua cernunt,
Hi sapiunt aliis, desipiuntque sibi. Lat.—

"There are those who can see the faults of others, but who cannot discern their own. Such men are wise for others, but fools to themselves."

Crimine ab uno disce omnes. Lat. VIRGIL.—"From a single offense, crime, you may form an estimate of the whole nation, people."

Crine ruber, niger ore, brevis pede, lumine laesus,
Rem magnam praestas, Zoile, si bonus es. Lat. MARTIAL.—

"Thy beard and head are of a different dye,
Short of one foot, distorted in an eye:
With all these tokens of a knave complete,
Shouldst thou be honest, thou'rt a roguish cheat."

An extraordinary physiognomy is sometimes supposed to be an indication of a knave.

Crise. Fr.—"A crisis, critical time, serious moment." A "crisis" in diseases of the human frame is, the decision of the conflict between nature and the disease. The *true* meaning of "*crisis*" is *judgment*.

Criterion. Gr.—A mark by which any thing is judged of. This Anglicized Greek word retains its Greek plural, *criteria*.

Critique. Fr.—"Criticism, piece of criticism."

Cruda viridisque senectus. Lat. VIRGIL.—"Tough, robust, and green old age."

Crudelem medicum intemperans aeger facit. Lat. PUBLIUS SYRUS.—"A disorderly patient makes the physician cruel." He compels him to use restraints which would otherwise be unnecessary.

Crudelis ubique luctus, ubique pavor, et plurima mortis imago. Lat. VIRGIL.—

"All parts resound with tumults, plaints, and fears,
And grisly death in sundry shapes appears."—DRYDEN.

Crux. Lat.—"A cross." Any thing particularly tormenting or vexatious: thus—

Crux criticorum, medicorum, mathematicorum, &c.—"The greatest difficulty that can occur to critics, physicians, mathematicians, &c."

Crux est si metuas quod vincere nequeas. Lat. AUSONIUS.—"It is a tormenting thing to fear what you cannot overcome."

Cubile ferarum. Lat.—"The den, lair, abode, of wild beasts, animals." "Names of English places ending in *den* always denoted *cubile ferarum*, or pasture, usually for swine."

Cucullus non facit monachum. Lat.—"The cowl does not make the man a monk, or a friar." We are not to judge of the man from his disguise, or assumed character.

Cui bono? Lat. CICERO.—What is the true rendering of the Latin phrase *Cui bono?* Most text-books say it means "For what good?" or, "What use was it?" But Francis Newman, in p. 316 of *Hebrew Monarchy*, says it means "who gained by (the crime)," and quotes *Cicero pro Milone*, xii. § 32, in favor of his meaning.

————————————————**Cui**
Gratia, fama, valetudo contingit abunde,
Et mundus victus, non deficiente crumena.

Lat. HORACE.—

"A man possessed of influence, reputation, and vigorous health, with decent fare, and money sufficient for all his wants, a purse not ill supplied." [The allusion is to ALBIUS TIBULLUS, a Roman Knight, and a celebrated elegiac poet.] Such, in the opinion of the poet, are the qualities and possessions which should form a man's content, if not his happiness.

We have no single term in our language capable of expressing the full force of *gratia*, as here employed. It is used, in the present instance, in what grammarians term both a passive and an active sense, denoting as well the favor of the powerful towards TIBULLUS, as that peculiar deportment on his own part by which he had conciliated the esteem and confidence of others.

Cui in manu sit quem esse dementem velit, quem sapere, quem sanari, quem in morbum injici, quem contra amari, quem arcessi, quem expeti. Lat. CAECILIUS.—"Who has it in her power to make any man mad, or in his senses; sick, or in health; and who can choose the object of her affections at pleasure." [Applied to an artful woman.]

Cui licet quod majus, non debet, quod minus est, non licere.

Lat. Law maxim.—"He to whom the greater thing is lawful, has certainly a right to do the lesser thing." Thus, if a man has an office for himself and his heirs, he may make an assignee, and, *a fortiori*, he may appoint a deputy.

——————Cui mens divinior atque os,
Magna sonaturum, des nominis hujus honorem.

Lat. HORACE.—"Honor with this illustrious name" [the title of poet] "the man who has a heaven-born soul, a mind soaring, or towering, above the average intellectual caliber, who has that enthusiasm, or poetic inspiration, which can alone give success to the votaries of the epic, tragic, or lyric muse; and a mouth fitted to speak great things, nobleness of style, eloquence that can give utterance to flashes of genius, eloquence pregnant with the celestial fire of genius."

"Is there a man whom real genius fires,
Whom the diviner soul of verse inspires,
Who talks true greatness? let him boldly claim
The sacred honors of a poet's name.—
——He alone can claim this name, who writes
With fancy high, and bold and daring flights."

Cui multum est piperis etiam oleribus immiscet. Lat. prov.—"He who has plenty of pepper can afford to season his cabbage well." They that have good store of butter may lay it thick on their bread, or put some in their shoes.

Cui non conveniet sua res, ut calceus olim,
Si pede major erit, subvertet; si minor, uret.

Lat. HORACE.—"When our fortune is not suited to our condition, it will oftentimes be like a shoe, which is apt to cause us to trip if too large, and pinches when too small."

"Our fortunes and our shoes are near allied:
We're pinched in strait, and stumble in the wide."

A fine practical lesson to induce us to adapt our minds to our circumstances.

Cui prodest scelus, is fecit. Lat. SENECA.—"He who has derived the profit, reaped the advantage, has committed the crime, has been the real author of the crime." This as a general maxim is true, but not without some exceptions.

Cui semper dederis, ubi negas, rapere imperas.

Lat. PUBLIUS SYRUS.-

"He, all whose wants you have, when asked, supplied,
Will learn to take as soon as he's denied."

Cuicunque aliquis quid concedit, concedere videtur et id, sine quo res ipsa esse non potest. Lat. Law maxim.—"To whomsoever a man grants a thing, he grants that without which the thing cannot be enjoyed." A person, for instance, selling the timber on his estate, the buyer may cut down the trees and convey them away without being responsible for the injury which the grass may sustain, from carts, &c., during the necessary time of conveyance.

Cuidaõ naõ he saber. Port. prov.—"Care's no cure."

Cuilibet in arte sua credendum est. Lat. prov.—"Every man is to be, should be, trusted in his own art, in the business or profession that he follows." We should *in general* give credit to men for superior skill in that art, or science, which they have made their peculiar study.

Cujus est dare, ejus est disponere. Lat. Law maxim.—"He who has the right to give, has also the right to dispose of his gift according as he may think fit, or proper, according to his own wish or fancy."

Cujus est solum, ejus usque ad coelum. Lat. Law maxim.—"He who has the property in the soil has the same up to the sky." His neighbor must not therefore offend by making any improper projections to impend over his land or tenement.

Cujus tu fidem in pecunia perspexeris,
Verere ei verba credere? Lat. TERENCE.—
"Can you fear to trust the word of a man whose probity you have experienced in pecuniary affairs?" There's no touchstone of a man's good faith beyond his punctuality in money-matters.

Cujuslibet rei simulator atque dissimulator. Lat. SALLUST, in his description of CATILINE.—"A man who could with equal skill pretend to be what he was not, and not to be what he really was." A person deeply versed in the arts of hypocrisy.

Cul-de-sac. Fr.—"The bottom of a bag." "Our Government makes it a rule, when it has appointed a consul, to appoint him to one place for life—a consulship being a *cul-de-sac:*" that is to say, a *blind alley*, an *alley blocked up at one end:* in other words, a *position leading to nothing else.*

Culprit.—BLACKSTONE supposes this word to be compounded of two abbreviations: *Cul* for culpable, which the clerk of arraigns declares the prisoner to be, and *prit* [corrupted from the French word *prêt*] for *ready* to prove him so.

——————Cum corpore mentem
Crescere sentimus pariterque senescere. Lat. LUCRETIUS.—
"We find that as the mind strengthens with the body, it decays with it in like manner." Whatever be the advantage derived from experience, we see that the mind is debilitated by age and infirmity.

Cum faciem videas, videtur esse quantivis preti.
Lat. TERENCE.—
"To look at him, you would take him for a man of consequence."

Cum fortuna manet, vultum servatis amici;
Cum cedit, turpi vertitis ora fuga. Lat. OVID.—
"Whilst fortune continues favorable, you have always the countenance of friends; but, when she changes, they then turn their backs in shameful flight."

Cum grano salis. Lat.—"The statement must be taken *cum grano salis:*" that is to say, *with some allowance, with due allowance, allowing for inaccuracies, intentional or otherwise;* literally, *with a grain of salt*, but, as the Latin word *sal*, which means *salt*, is used in a secondary sense to signify *natural ability, or wisdom*, we may interpret *cum grano salis*, "*with due discretion, with some little exercise of common sense.*"

Cum licet fugere, ne quaere litem. Lat. prov.—"Do not seek the quarrel, or the suit, which there is an opportunity of escaping."

——————————**Cum lux altera venit**
Jam cras hesternum consumsimus; ecce aliud cras
Egerit hos annos, et semper paulum erit ultra.

Lat. PERSIUS.—"When another day shall arrive, we shall find that we have consumed our yesterday's to-morrow: another morrow will arrive to propel our years, and still be a little beyond us." A strong reflection on the dilatory conduct of man, ever fixing for to-morrow that which he should do to-day, until his years have fled, and his opportunities are lost.

Cum magnis virtutibus affers grande supercilium. Lat. JUVENAL.—

"We own thy virtues; but we blame beside
Thy mind elate with insolence and pride."

Cum multis aliis, quae nunc perscribere longum est. Lat.—A line from the "*Propria, quae maribus,*" &c. of the Eton Latin Grammar. "With many other matters, which it would just now be tedious to state." A summary, which is generally placed at the end of a bead-roll of indifferent *items,* and in an ironical sense. N.B. Often quoted in an abridged form: thus, "*Cum multis aliis.*"

Cum notis variorum. Lat.—"With the notes of various editors." "We intend to prefix his testimony to our proposed critical edition of these works '*cum notis variorum.*'"

——————————**Cum prostrata sopore**
Urget membra quies, et mens sine pondere ludit.

Lat. PETRONIUS.—

"While sleep o'erwhelms the tired limbs, the mind
Plays without weight, and wantons unconfined."

The flights of the mind are extended by sleep.

Cum talis sis, utinam noster esses! Lat.—"As you are an individual of such worth, I would that you were one of us, or would that you were one of us!"

Cum tristibus severe, cum remissis jucunde, cum senibus graviter, cum juventute comiter vivere. Lat. CICERO, speaking of CATILINE.—"He was in the habit of living with the sorrowful, severely; with the cheerful, joyously, agreeably; with the aged, gravely; and with the young, pleasantly, jovially, companionably."

Cum volet illa dies, quae nil nisi corporis hujus
Jus habet, incerti spatium mihi finiat aevi. Lat. OVID.—

"Come, soon or late, death's undetermined day,
This mortal being only can decay."

Death destroys only the body.

Cumulatum usuris. Lat. LIVY.—[A debt] "increased by arrears of interest."

Cunctando restituit rem. Lat. ENNIUS.—"He restored his cause by delay." This praise was first given to FABIUS, who saved his country by avoiding the first onset of HANNIBAL. It is now generally applied to illustrate the advantages arising from caution, sagacity, and justifiable delay.

Cupias non placuisse nimis. Lat. MARTIAL.—"Don't be too anxious to please."

Cupido dominandi cunctis affectibus flagrantior est. Lat. TACITUS.—"The lust of power is the most flagrant of all the affections of the mind." Ambition may be termed the worst of vices, as it too often leads to the commission of every other crime.

Cur ante tubum tremor occupat artus? Lat. VIRGIL.—"Why does trembling seize the limbs before the trumpet sounds?" Wherefore those marks of trepidation before the danger is actually announced?

Cur moriatur homo cui salvia crescit in horto? Lat.—"Why should man die, who has sage growing in his garden?" "He that would live for aye, must eat sage in May."

Cur omnium fit culpa paucorum scelus? Lat.—"Why should the wickedness of a few be laid to the account of all?'

Cura pii Diis sunt. Lat. OVID.—

"The good are Heaven's peculiar care."

Curae leves loquuntur, ingentes stupent. Lat. SENECA.—

"Light griefs do speak, while sorrow's tongue is bound."

"Seneca has observed that *curae leves loquuntur, ingentes stupent:* and the silence that belongs to severe affliction is nowhere more beautifully described than by Shakspeare in Macbeth:

'The grief that does not speak
Whispers the o'er-fraught heart, and bids it break:'"

that is to say, Seneca has observed that *light griefs are loquacious, but that deep sorrow has no tongue:* in other words, that *those who have little to grumble about can bawl loud enough, while, on the other hand, those whose cup of sorrow is full to o'erflowing muse o'er their griefs and say not a word.*

Curae secundae. Lat.—"Further improvements" in a literary work.

Curatio funeris, conditio sepulturae, pompae exsequiarum, magis sunt vivorum solatia, quam subsidia mortuorum. Lat. AUGUSTUS.—"The care of the funeral, the place of burial, and the pomp of obsequies, are consolations to the living, but of no advantage to the dead."

Curé. Fr.—"A parson, incumbent of an ecclesiastical living, parish priest." N.B. The word "*curé*" never means a curate. The French for "*curate*" is "*vicaire*," a word derived from the Latin word "*vicarius*," which means, *one who performs or discharges the office of another, a deputy, a substitute.*

Curfew.—"As William had gained his crown by force, he was obliged to keep it by severe laws. Aware that those severe laws would cause discontent among his subjects, he began to fear that they would meet together at night in secret and concert measures against him. To prevent this, he made a law, that all persons should put out their fires and candles at eight o'clock every evening; and, that no one might excuse himself for having a light after the hour prescribed, a bellman was sent through the streets, ringing his bell, and calling out '*couvre feu! couvre feu!*' that is, 'cover,' or extinguish, 'the fire.' This order was announced in the Norman-French, because William desired that his new subjects should speak that language, so all public laws and notices were expressed in it. The term *couvre feu* was, by degrees, pronounced *curfew:* and you will find this word in your dictionary explained as *the evening or eight o'clock bell.*"—*True Stories from History of England.*

"Hark! from the dim church tower,
The deep slow curfew's chime!
A heavy sound unto hall and bower
In England's olden time!"

Curiosa felicitas. Lat.—"A lucky hit, clever or bright thought, happy idea."

Currente calamo. Lat.—"With a running pen, with great rapidity, off-hand." Applied to any thing written with fluency and expedition.

Curriculum. Lat.—Properly, "a place to run in, the lists." "A *curriculum* of vice," that is, an [academic] career of vice.

Currus bovem trahit. Lat. prov.—"The coach, chariot, draws the ox." To set the cart before the horse.

Curta supellex. Lat. PERSIUS.—"I knew as much of divinity," says Bishop Watson, "as could reasonably [?] be expected from a man, whose course of studies had been *fully* in other pursuits, but with this *curta supellex* in theology, to take possession of the first theological chair in Europe, seemed too daring an attempt even *for my intrepidity:*" that is, with this "scanty mental furnishing, or scanty furniture of the mind, slender mental provision" in theology, &c.

Curtae nescio quid semper abest rei. Lat. HORACE.—"A nameless, an indescribable, something is always wanting to our imperfect fortune: something or other is ever wanting to what seems an imperfect fortune in the eyes of its possessor." The most opulent and happy, in the eyes of the world, if brought to a frank confession, would acknowledge that they felt some want or deficiency.

"There's something wanting still to make him bless'd."

Custos morum. Lat.—"The guardian of morality, of morals." Every judge and magistrate is said, and ought, to be a *custos morum.*

Custos rotulorum. Lat.—The officer who has the charge, custody, safe-keeping, of the *rolls* and records of the sessions of peace.

Cynic. From the Gr.—"Doggish, impudent, snappish, a snarler, churl." "The *cynic* philosophers, or sect of the *cynics,*" of which DIOGENES was the well-known founder.

D.

D'accord, Fr.—"Agreed." In tune.

**D'un dévot souvent au chrétien véritable
La distance est deux fois plus longue, à mon avis,
Que du pôle antarctique au détroit de Davis.**

Fr. BOILEAU.—

"The distance between a devotee and a true Christian is often twice as great as that from the Southern Pole to Davis's Straits." The difference between hypocrisy and true devotion is almost immeasurable.

D'une fille deux gendres. Fr. prov.—"To get one's self two sons-in-law with one daughter." To stop two mouths with one morsel.

D'une pierre faire deux coups. Fr. prov.—"To kill two birds with one stone."

Da dextram misero. Lat.—"Give a lift, a helping hand, to the poor man."

Da locum melioribus. Lat. TERENCE.—"Give place to your betters." Let due reverence be shown to rank, to sex, and to superior station.

Da, Pater, augustam menti conscendere sedem:
Da fontem lustrare boni: da, luce reperta,
In te conspicuos animi defigere visus! Lat. BOETHIUS.—
"Give me, O Father, to thy throne access,
Unshaken seat of endless happiness!
Give me, unveiled, the source of good to see!
Give me thy light, and fix mine eyes on THEE!"

Da spatium tenuemque moram: male cuncta ministrat impetus. Lat. STATIUS.—"Allow time for deliberation: all things are done badly that are done with violence and precipitation." See "*Festina lente.*"

Dabit Deus his quoque finem. Lat. VIRGIL.—"GOD will also put an end to these things." Generally spoken of public calamities, or inflictions.

Dame de comptoir. Fr.—"A bar-woman, shop-woman."

Dames quêteuses. Fr.—"Money-gathering or collecting ladies." "There exists in France a species of charity entirely private, and which consists in seeking out and relieving the poor on the part of ladies in the higher and middle classes. These are called *les dames quêteuses*. They go about seeking relief for what each calls *mes pauvres:*" that is, "*my poor, needy ones.*"

Damnant quod non intelligunt. Lat. CICERO.—"They condemn what they do not understand." A phrase that may be justly applied to several of our modern critics.

Damnos quid non imminuit dies? Lat. HORACE.—"What has not wasting time impaired, or, what does not wasting time impair?"
"What feels not time's consuming rage?"
Every work of art and every production of nature is equally liable to injury in process of time.

Damnum absque injuria. Law Lat.—"A loss without an injury." Thus, the erection of a mill, or the establishment of a school, in any given place, may occasion a loss to others, but an action for the damage cannot be maintained.

Damnum appellandum est cum mala fama lucrum. Lat.—"The gain which is made at the expense of reputation should rather be set down as a loss."

Danari fanno danari. Ital. prov.—"Money begets money."

Danegelt.—A tribute, paid to the Danes by our ancestors, of twelve pence for every hide of land in the realm, for clearing the seas of pirates, who greatly infested the English sea-coasts in those days. King ETHELRED was the first who paid it, and it amounted to £48,000 yearly, exclusive of £113,000 at the first payment: this tribute was paid for thirty-one years, namely, from 1012 to 1043, when it was abolished by EDWARD THE CONFESSOR.

Dans l'art d'intéresser consiste l'art d'écrire Fr. DELILLE.

—"In the art of interesting consists the art of writing." The surest test of a writer of genius appears in arresting the feelings of the reader, and bearing them with him, through every scene, without diminution or relaxation to the end. Men of inferior minds may amuse by florid descriptions; these, however,

"Play round the head, but come not near the heart."

Dans les conseils d'un état il ne faut pas tant regarder ce qu'on doit faire que ce qu'on peut faire. Fr.—"In the councils of a state it is not so necessary to examine what *ought* to be done, as what *can* be done." The means are to be considered as well as the end.

Dans un pays libre on crie beaucoup quoiqu'on souffre peu; dans un pays de tyrannie on se plaint peu quoiqu'on souffre beaucoup. Fr. CARNOT.—"In a free country there is much clamor with little suffering; in a despotic state there is little complaint but much grievance." In a state of freedom men sometimes speak loudly upon slight occasions; under a tyranny they are compelled to silence, even under the severest inflictions.

Dapifer. Lat.—"The officer who carries up the first dish at a feast: a sewer."

Dar del naso dentro. Ital. prov.—"To thrust one's feet under another man's table." To live at another's expense; sponge on another; to be a smell-feast.

Dare in guardia la lattuga ai paperi. Ital. prov.—"To give the lettuce in charge, to the keeping, of the geese." To give the wolf the wether to keep.

Dare pondus idonea fumo. Lat. PERSIUS.—[A page, that is, a book] "fit only to give weight to smoke," that is, "to mere twaddle, stuff, matter of no importance whatever."

Dat Deus immiti cornua curta bovi. Lat.—"God gives short horns to the mischievous ox." Providence so curtails the means of the malicious, as to make them fall short of their end.

Dat veniam corvis, vexat censura columbas. Lat. JUVENAL.—"Male authors, like males of every other profession, have a kind of license to wear disguises, which has never been granted to the other sex:—

"Dat veniam corvis, vexat censura COLUMBAS:"

that is to say, *Censure grants pardon*, or *acquits the ravens, but falls foul of the doves:—*

"They, while with partial aim their censure moves,
Acquit the vultures, but condemn the doves!"

The above quotation is a phrase of general use and application. The censorious too often fasten on the innocent, whilst, in their misplaced malice, the guilty are suffered to escape; they

"Clip the dove's wings, but give the vulture course."

Data. Lat.—"Things granted, allowed premises" [*should be* "premisses"]. "He proceeds on certain *data*," on premises that have been previously admitted. N.B. The word is also used in its Latin singular number. "All the rules relating to purchases perpetually refer to this settled law of inheritance, as a *datum* or first principle." BLACKSTONE.

Date obolum Belisario. Lat.—"Give a farthing to BELISARIUS." This great general was in his old age reduced to beg. The phrase is therefore sometimes applied to fallen greatness.

Dawk.—In India, "the Post."

De alieno corio liberalis. Lat. prov.—"To cut large thongs from another man's leather." To be very liberal with what belongs to some one else. "The Spaniards express the same idea thus, *De piel agena larga la coréa.*"

De Bello Gallico. Lat. JULIUS CÆSAR.—"On the Gallic War, or the war with France." "Cabin-boys and drummers were then [1816] busy with their commentaries *de bello Gallico.*" N.B. "*De Bello Gallico*" is the title of one of the works of JULIUS CÆSAR.

De bon commencement bonne fin. Fr. prov.—"A good beginning makes a good end."

De bonne vie bonne fin. Fr. prov.—"A good life makes a good, happy death."

De Carthagine satius est silere quam parcius dicere. Lat.—"It is an old saying of any subject too vast or too sad to measure by hurried words, that *de Carthagine satius est silere quam parcius dicere:*" that is to say, that *it is better to be silent, to say nothing at all about Carthage, than to express one's self too sparingly, too scantily.*

De cauda equina. Lat.—"Of, about, or concerning, a horse's tail." "There is no magic in the words of Scripture: its virtue is in the meaning. The true meaning must depend on the whole words; on the limits, which the context may put on any single text. Old DONNE has applied to this effect the simile [comparison], *de cauda equina,* very quaintly. 'Sentences in Scripture, like hairs in horsetails, concur in one root of beauty and strength; but, being plucked out one by one, serve only for springes and snares.'"

De cette sorte. Fr.—"In this manner, in such a manner, thus, so." N.B. "*De la sorte*" and "*de telle sorte*" may be used to express the same idea.

De court plaisir long repentir. Fr. prov.—"Short pleasure, long lament."

De cualquier manera que vaya vestido, seré SANCHO PANZA. Span. CERVANTES.—"However I am dressed, I shall still be SANCHO PANZA." In rags or in finery, my merit, if I have any, will still be the same.

De die in diem. Lat.—"From day to day."

De facto. Lat. Law phrase.—"From the fact, in fact, actually."

De fide et officio judicis non recipitur quaestio. Lat. Law maxim.—"No question can be entertained respecting the good intention and duty of the judge." No presumption against him can be received in the first instance. There must be strong and full proof of malversation.

De fol juge brève sentence. Fr. prov.—"A foolish, stupid judge passes a hasty sentence." A fool's bolt is soon shot.

De fructu arborem cognosco. Lat. prov.—"I know the tree by its fruit." Such as the tree is, such is the fruit.

De fumo in flammam. Lat. prov.—"Out of the frying-pan into the fire."

De gaieté de cœur. Fr.—"From gayety of heart." Sportively, wantonly.

De gustibus non est disputandum. Lat.—"There is no disputing, we must not dispute, about tastes." They are too many, and too various, to be the objects of rational discussion.

De haeretico comburendo. Lat.—[A writ] "about the burning of heretics at the stake."

De haeretico relapso. Lat.—[A law] "about those who had originally been heretics returning to Protestantism, the Protestant faith." "Proselytism was busy at work, and the law *de haeretico relapso* inflicted severe penalties, among which was the loss of property, upon those converts to Catholicism who should return to their former religion."

De haute lutte. Fr.—"By a violent struggle." By main force.

De hoc multi multa, omnis aliquid, nemo satis. Lat.—"Of this many persons have said much, everybody something, and no man enough." This is often used to designate what, in the opinion of the author, are new observations, though on a trite subject.

De integro. Lat.—"Afresh, anew."

De jure. Law Lat.—"From the law." In some instances the penalty attaches on the offender at the instant when the *fact* is committed; in others, not until he is convicted by *law*. In the former case he is guilty *de facto;* in the latter *de jure.*

De l'audace, encore de l'audace, toujours de l'audace. Fr.—"They owe all their success, and their miraculous imposition of a Republic on the reluctant nation, to the maxim of one of their grand prototypes of 1793, '*de l'audace, encore de l'audace, toujours de l'audace:*'" that is to say, *unparalleled boldness and the most audacious assurance, again and again, and on all occasions;* literally, *audacity, audacity again, and audacity always.*

De la main à la bouche se perd souvent la soupe. Fr. prov.—"There's many a slip 'twixt the cup and the lip."

De lana caprina. Lat. HORACE.—"About goats' wool." "A dispute *de lana caprina,*" that is, *respecting a matter not worth discussion, a thing of no value, matter of no consequence* or *consideration.* See "*Alter rixatur.*"

De lunatico inquirendo. Lat.—[A commission appointed] "to inquire into the state of a man's mind."

De magnis majora loquuntur. Lat.—"The spirit of insubordination, indeed, as it has in too great a degree existed, so has it in a much greater degree been imputed: '*De magnis majora loquuntur:*'" that is to say, *about serious matters more serious things are uttered,* in other words, *bad as the matter certainly is, it has been grossly exaggerated.*

De mal en pis. Fr.—"From bad to worse."

De mal est venu l'agneau, et à mal retourne le peau. Fr. prov.—"Dishonestly came the lamb, and dishonestly goes the skin." Ill-gotten goods seldom prosper. Compare "*De male quaesitis vix gaudet tertius heres:*" "The third heir scarcely enjoys that which has been ill gotten, dishonestly acquired, obtained."

De mauvais corbeau, mauvais œuf. Fr. prov.—"From a bad crow you will have a bad egg." Like master, like man.

De minimis non curat lex. Lat. Law maxim.—"The law does not trouble itself about trifles, does not take cognizance of trivial matters." "The law itself, which professedly neglects trifles, [*de minimis non curat lex,*] and which, in criminal cases, will not entertain a charge where the injury is below a certain money amount, shows how essential to the moral estimate of acts is the quantity of the value in issue."

De mortuis nil nisi bonum. Lat.—"Of the dead, let nothing be said but what is *favorable.*" This long-received maxim is by some not improperly amended by substituting *verum* for *bonum.* "Let nothing be said but what is *true.*"

De muitos poucos se faz hum muito. Port. prov.—"Many littles make a much." The French say, "*De petit vient-on au grand,*" From small we arrive at great, and "*Les petits ruisseaux font les grandes rivières,*" Small streams make great rivers.

De non apparentibus et de non existentibus eadem est ratio. Lat.—"The reasoning must be the same with respect to things which do not *appear*, as to things which do not *exist;* or, Things non-apparent are to be considered as [*for logical purposes*] non-existent."

De nouveau seigneur nouvelle mesnie. Fr. prov.—"New lords, new laws."

De novo. Lat.—"Anew, afresh, over again."

De omni re scibili et quibusdam aliis. Lat.—"On, or about, every thing that may be known, knowable, and certain other matters; about every branch of knowledge, and certain other matters."

De omnibus rebus. Lat.—"On, or about, every thing, all kinds of matters." A treatise "*de omnibus rebus.*"

De omnibus rebus et quibusdam aliis. Lat.—"Hobbes prepared the way for Locke: an achievement of more lasting glory than if he had written a hundred treatises *De omnibus rebus et quibusdam aliis:*" that is to say, *On, or concerning, every thing in existence, and* SOME OTHER THINGS, *certain other things, or matters; On all kinds of matters, and sundry other things or subjects.*

De paupertate tacentes plus poscente ferent. Lat. HORACE.—"They who are silent on the subject of their poverty will receive more than those who are importunate."

"The man that's silent, nor proclaims his want,
Gets more than he who makes a loud complaint."

De propaganda fide et exstirpandis haereticis. Lat.—[A council held, a *congregation,* association, at Rome established] "for the propagation of the faith [POPERY], and the extirpation, rooting-out, of heretics [PROTESTANTS], the cutting-off of heretics, root and branch."

De quibus certus es, loquere opportune. Lat.—"Although '*de quibus ignoras tace*' is a maxim of profound wisdom, '*de quibus certus es, loquere opportune*' is an injunction of, perhaps, equal value:" that is to say, although "*hold your tongue about matters of which you know nothing,*" is, &c. . . . . "*speak to the purpose, and in season, about those you really do understand,*" is an injunction, &c.

De quo libelli in celeberrimis locis proponuntur, huic ne perire quidem tacite conceditur. Lat. CICERO.—"The man, whose conduct is publicly arraigned, is not suffered even to be ruined quietly."

De semaine. Fr.—"By the week." "TALLEYRAND contemptuously styled METTERNICH a politician *de semaine:*" that is, a politician who changed his aims and means every moment.

De son tort de mesme. Old Fr.—"As against Lord Durham the ministers may plead '*de son tort de mesme,*' that he is *in his own wrong.*" [Written in 1838.]

De te pendens, te respiciens amicus. Lat. HORACE.—"Your friend, whose whole dependence and hopes are in you." Said by HORACE of himself, in addressing his patron MAECENAS. It may, however, be applied to a parasite, toad-eater, lick-spittle:—

"Your flattering friend, your hanger-on, what not?
Your lackey, but without the shoulder-knot."

De trop. Fr.—"Out of place." "He found himself on that occasion *de trop,*" that is, "one too many, one whose room would have been more agreeable, acceptable, than his company."

De vita hominis nulla cunctatio longa est. Lat. Law maxim.—"When the life of a man is at stake, no delay, that is afforded, can be too long." By this humane maxim it is intimated that, as the effect of a rash sentence cannot be recalled, we should pause and deliberate before we consign a fellow-creature to death. This maxim could not be too strongly impressed, if we did not conceive it to be a mere fiction of the poet:

"Of wretches hanged that jurymen might dine!"

De vive voix. Fr.—"Orally, by word of mouth."

De vivis nil nisi bonum. Lat.—"Let nothing be said of *the living* but what is good, or favorable." "His cardinal maxim throughout [the converse of the old one] is, *De vivis,*" *&c.* See "*De mortuis,*" *&c.*

Deacon. From the Gr.—*Properly,* a servant; but used in England to signify "the lowest order of the clergy," and in Scotland, "an overseer of the poor," "a president of an incorporated trade."

Debito justitiae. Lat. Law phrase.—"By debt of justice." By a claim justly established.

Debitum naturae. Lat. CORNELIUS NEPOS.—"The debt of nature, death."

Débouchure. Fr. Military term.—"The mouth or opening of a strait or river."

Débris. Fr.—"Fragments, remains."

Début. Fr.—"Appearance in, entrance on, public life; appearance in public as a performer [actor], singer, opera-dancer, &c."

Débutant. Fr.—"An actor, performer, making his first appearance in public." "*Débutante*" is the corresponding *feminine term.*

Deceptio visus. Lat.—"A deceiving of the sight." An illusion practiced on the eye, a show without a substance.

Decet affectus animi neque se nimium erigere, nec subjacere serviliter. Lat. CICERO.—"We should keep our passions from being exalted above measure, or servilely depressed."

Decies repetita placebit. Lat. HORACE.—"It will continue to please, though ten times repeated." This complimentary phrase is often applied to modern dramatic works in particular: the event, however, has seldom confirmed the prediction.

Decipimur specie recti. Lat. HORACE.—"We are deluded, deceived, by the appearance of what is right, of rectitude, by a seeming excellence." Fair appearances are necessary to the purposes of deception.

Decipit exemplar vitiis imitabile. Lat. HORACE.—"An example, easy to be imitated in its faults, is sure to deceive the ignorant."—

"By such examples many a coxcomb's caught,
Whose utmost art can imitate a fault."

———————————————**Decipit**
Frons prima multos:—rara mens intelligit,
Quod interiore condidit cura angulo. Lat. PHAEDRUS.—"The first appearance deceives many. Our understandings seldom reach to that which has been carefully reposed in the inmost recesses of the mind." Those who attempt to judge at the first glance of the characters of men will be most frequently disappointed. The manners and conversation of men of the world are artificial. It is only by some severe ordeal, or by long experience, that their natural propensities are to be discovered.

Decolor, obscurus, vilis, non ille repexam
Caesariem regum, nec candida virginis ornat
Colla, nec insigni splendet per cingula morsu;
Sed nova si nigri videas miracula saxi,
Tunc superat pulcros cultus, et quicquid Eois,
Indus litoribus rubra scrutatur in alga. Lat. CLAUDIAN.—

"Obscure, unprized, and dark, the magnet lies,
Nor lures the search of avaricious eyes,
Nor binds the neck, nor sparkles in the hair,
Nor dignifies the great, nor decks the fair.
But search the wonders of the dusky stone,
And own all glories of the mine outdone,
Each grace of form, each ornament of state,
That decks the fair, or dignifies the great."

Decus et tutamen. Lat.—"The honor and defense, safeguard, protection." The words on the rim of the last crown-pieces that were issued.

Dedecus ille domus sciet ultimus. Lat. JUVENAL.—"The good man is the last to know what is amiss, going wrong, at home."

Dedimus potestatem. Lat.—"We have given power." A writ in law, whereby commission is given to one or more private persons to assist for the expedition of some act belonging to the judge. The words are used also to denote the commission of a justice of the peace, which begins in the same manner.

Dediscit animus sero quod didicit diu. Lat. SENECA.—"The mind unlearns with difficulty what it has long learned." Early impressions are not easily erased.

Deemster or **Dempster.** From the Saxon "*deman,*" or the Dutch "*doemen,*" to judge.—A judge; a word still used in this sense in the Isle of Man, and not many years ago applied in Scotland to the executioner, who used to repeat the sentence after the judge.

Deer de nuwt wol yte mot ze krecke. Frisian prov.—"He who will eat the nut must crack it."

Défaut de la cuirasse. Fr.—"The extremity or defective part of the armor." "He was taken *défaut de la cuirasse:* he was attacked on his weak side."

Défendez que personne, au milieu d'un banquet,
Ne vous vienne donner un avis indiscret:
Ecartez ce fâcheux, qui vers vous s'achemine,
Rien ne doit déranger l'honnête homme qui dine. Fr.—
"At meals no access to the indiscreet;
All are intruders on the wise who eat.
In that blest hour, your bore's the veriest sinner!
Naught must disturb a man of worth at dinner."

Deficit. Lat.—Part of a verb used as a noun to signify "a deficiency." "They make good the *deficit.*"

Deficiunt vires. Lat.—"Strength, power, is wanting; there is a deficiency, want, of strength, power, mental ability."

Degeneres animos timor arguit. Lat. VIRGIL.—"Fear is the proof of a degenerate mind." This is a universal mode of arraigning timidity, which, in every state and country, is stated as a falling-off from the valor of their ancestors.

Dehors. Law Fr.—"Foreign to; irrespective of." "The pleadings were matters *dehors* the award."

Δει φερειν τα των θεων. Gr. EURIPIDES.—"We must bear with patience, patiently submit to, whatever the gods impose on us:" in other words, "We must submit to the dispensations of Providence." See "*Durum! sed levius,*" *&c.*

Δεινα περι φακης. Gr.—Literally, "Frightful, dreadful, things about, or concerning, a lentil." "Much matter of a wooden platter." "Much ado about nothing."

Dejale, luego caerá. Span.—
"Never mind him, let him be;
By-and-by he'll follow thee."

"When a European arrives at Lima, in what is vulgarly called *rude health,*—and rude it does certainly appear to the effeminate Limenos [inhabitants of Lima],—they survey him with a smile and a '*dejale, luego caerá.*'"

Déjeûner. Fr.—"Breakfast."

Déjeûner à la fourchette. Fr.—"A meat breakfast." "Thither were the carriages wending their way, laden with the company invited to the *déjeûner à la fourchette.*" N.B. "*Déjeûner à la fourchette*" is *literally* "a fork breakfast," *a breakfast at which knives and forks are used.* It is a nondescript kind of expression, and, according to the time at which it is taken, may be considered either breakfast, lunch, or dinner, only under another name.

Déjeûner dinatoire. Fr.—"A breakfast serving as a dinner." "At five o'clock a *déjeûner dinatoire* was given by the Corporation."

Del cuoio d'altri si fanno le corregge larghe. Ital. prov.—"They cut large thongs for themselves from other persons' leather." See "*De alieno corio,*" *&c.*

Del dicho al hecho ay gran trecho. Span. prov.—"Great braggers, little doers."

Del mal el menos. Span. prov.—"Of two evils, choose the less."

Del mal pagador si quiera en paja. Span. prov.—"Of a bad paymaster get what you can, though it be but a straw."

Del senno di poi n'è pieno ogni fosso. Ital. prov.—"Every ditch is full of those who are wise when too late, when the time is past, is gone by."

Delectando pariterque monendo. Lat. HORACE.—"To give equal pleasure and instruction; amusing the reader at the same time that it [a book] instructs him." This best praise of an author, this great master has given elsewhere in other words, "*Miscuit utile dulci.*" He combined that which was *pleasurable* with what was *useful*. See "*Omne tulit,*" *&c.*

Delenda est Carthago. Lat.—"Carthage must be destroyed." The oft-repeated phrase of CATO, the Roman senator, tending to provoke the destruction of that rival city. It has often been used as a sort of war-whoop, to urge a "war of extermination."

Deliberandum est diu, quod statuendum semel. Lat. PUBLIUS SYRUS.—"That which can be decided but once, should be long considered, pondered on, reflected on." Every precaution is necessary where the deed is irrevocable.

Deliberat Roma, perit Saguntum. Lat.—"Rome deliberates, and Saguntum perishes." We are slow in resolving, coming to a decision, whilst our allies are in the extremity of danger.

Deliberare utilia mora utilissima est. Lat.—"To deliberate on things useful is the most useful delay."

Deliramenta doctrinae. Lat.—"The wild speculations or wanderings of learned men." The fantasies of those whom "too much learning hath made mad."

Delirant reges, plectuntur Achivi. Lat. HORACE.—"The monarchs err, the Greeks (*i.e.* the people) are punished." The people suffer for whatever folly their princes commit. The unhappy, unfortunate people always suffer for the faults of their leaders. The following poetical paraphrase will render the quotation still more intelligible:

———"When doting monarchs urge
Unsound resolves, their subjects feel the scourge."

Delirium tremens. Lat. Medical term.—"To the primitive apathy of the natives has succeeded a sort of exhibiting frenzy, which threatens to become a *delirium tremens:*" that is to say, a *kind of drunkards' insanity*. N.B. The *literal* meaning of "*delirium tremens*" is *trembling* or *shaking unsoundness of mind*. On this disease of the brain, Dr. Roots very judiciously makes the following interesting remarks: "The term, perhaps," says this accurate and close observer, "is one which we cannot regard as exactly correct, inasmuch as '*delirium tremens*' is a term which certainly implies a something which does not take place. The '*delirium*' itself cannot tremble. Other persons have variously christened it. Drs. PEARSON and ARMSTRONG called it '*brain fever*.' Dr. BLAKE called it the '*brain fever of drunkards*.' Dr. ELLIOTSON has called it much more properly '*delirium cum tremore*.' There is DELIRIUM [*withdrawal of reason*] and there is TREMBLING; therefore the latter, perhaps, is the better term. Still, if we distinctly understand by the term '*delirium tremens*' of what the disease really consists, there is no objection to that designation remaining."

Délit de la presse. Fr.—"A trial for libel."

Delle ingiurie il remedio è lo scordarsi. Ital. prov.—"To forget a wrong is the best revenge."

Delphinum silvis appingit, fluctibus aprum. Lat. HORACE.—"He paints a dolphin in the woods, and a boar in the waves." He introduces objects which are unsuited to the scene.

Demanda al osto s'egl'ha buon vino. Ital.—"Ask your host if he have good wine." Ask my *companion* if I be a thief.

Deme supercilio nubem. Lat. HORACE.—"Remove every cloud from thy brow;" that is, smooth thy forehead.

"Be every look serenely gay,
And drive all cloudy cares away."

The ancients called those wrinkles, which appear upon the forehead above the eyebrows when any thing displeases us, *clouds:* for, as clouds obscure the face of heaven, so do wrinkles obscure the forehead, and cause an appearance of sadness.

———————Demetri, teque, Tigelli,
Discipularum inter jubeo plorare cathedras.

Lat. HORACE.—

"As for you, DEMETRIUS and TIGELLIUS [men of an effeminate turn of mind, taken up only with love-verses, mere fools, in the estimation of the poet, and worthy only of his contempt], I leave you to lament and sigh amidst the circle of your female admirers:"—

"Demetrius and Tigellius, know your place:
Go hence, and whine among the school-girl race."

N.B. "*Jubeo plorare*" is an imitation of the Greek forms of expression, *οιμωζε* and *οιμωζειν λεγω σοι*, "*Go and indulge in wailing, bewailing, in continually uttering alas! alas!*" The more usual Latin phrases are, "*Pereas!*" "*Malum tibi sit!*" "*Abi in malam crucem!*" all of which expressions are equivalent to "*Go and be hanged, go and hang yourself.*"

Demise.—The only *decease* expressed by the word "*demise*" is that of a crowned head: and the word is much more frequently used of *the crown itself*, which suffers a *demise* or *transfer* by the death of the wearer of it. "When we say *the demise of the crown*, we mean only that, in consequence of the disunion of the king's body natural from his body politic, the kingdom is *transferred* or *demised* to his successor."—BLACKSTONE.

Demi-solde. Fr.—"Half-pay."

Demitto auriculas, ut iniquae mentis asellus. Lat. HORACE.—"I hang my ears, like an ass, meditating mischief," that is, contriving how to shake off his load, his usual burden. "I am taken quite aback." "*Demitto auriculas*" is a metaphor [the use of a word in a sense different from its ordinary import, meaning] taken from beasts; for the ears of men are immovable.

Democracy. From the Gr.—"The government of the people; popular or republican government; popular rule." ARISTOTLE defines Democracy to be an "Aristocracy of orators, sometimes interrupted by the monarchy of a single orator;" and the observation, based on a thorough knowledge of human nature as it appeared in the stormy forums [places where pleaders and orators harangued] of the Grecian commonwealths, has been abundantly verified by the experience of our own times.

Denoûment. Fr.—"Unraveling of a plot."

Dentro da un orecchio e fuora dal'altro. Ital.—"In at one ear, and out at the other."

Deo adjuvante, non timendum. Lat.—"With God's assistance, there is naught to be feared."

Deo favente. Lat.—"With God's favor."

Deo juvante. Lat.—"With God's help, assistance."

Deo volente. Lat.—"GOD willing; if the LORD will; or, with the Divine permission." N.B. "*Deo volente*" is *generally* used in the abridged form, thus: D.V.

Dépôt. Fr. military term.—A "store or magazine;" a "store-room, store-house."

Deprendi miserum est. Lat. HORACE.—"'Tis a wretched thing to be detected in the commission of crime, in doing wrong, or what is wrong."

Depressus extollor. Lat.—"Having been depressed, I am now exalted; having been on my beam-ends, I am now all right and tight."

Der ewige Jude. Ger.—"The everlasting Jew." "*Der ewige Jude* is the common German expression for *the wandering Jew*, and sublimer even than our own."

Derisor vero plus laudatore movetur. Lat. HORACE.—"The flatterer, who laughs at us in his sleeve, is, to all appearance, more worked upon, moved, affected, than he who praises in sincerity:"—

"So the false raptures of a flatterer's art
Exceed the praises of an honest heart."

Compare JUVENAL, Sat. 3, line 100, to which GIFFORD appends the following note, as applicable here:

"The character of the flatterer is touched with great force in these lines, which are, however, exceeded, at least in humor, by the following:—

Ham. Your bonnet to its right use: 'tis for the head.
Osr. I thank your lordship, 'tis very hot.
Ham. No, believe me, 'tis very cold; the wind is northerly.
Osr. It is indifferent cold, my lord, indeed.
Ham. But yet, methinks, it is very sultry and hot for my complexion.
Osr. Exceedingly, my lord; it is very sultry as it were; I can't tell how."

The difference between a friend and a flatterer is thus marked by PLUTARCH: "*You* laugh, I grant; but *I* kill myself with laughing."

Dernier ressort. Fr.—"They never resorted to it, except as the *dernier ressort:*" that is to say, as the *last resource, expedient*, or *shift*. N.B. "*Ressort*" is one of those French words which we nearly always see spelt incorrectly in English works, thus: *resort* instead of *ressort*.

Dervise, or **Dervish.**—A Turkish anchorite or fanatic.

**Desiderantem quod satis est, neque
Tumultuosum sollicitat mare,
Nec saevus Arcturi cadentis
Impetus, aut orientis Haedi.** Lat. HORACE.—

"He, who desires just what is enough, is not disturbed by the tumultuous ocean, nor by the violent influence of setting Arcturus [a constellation of fourteen stars], or of the rising Goat."

"Who nature's frugal dictates hears,
He nor the raging ocean fears,
Nor stars of power malign,
Whether in gloomy storms they rise,
Or swift descending through the skies
With angry luster shine."

According to the poet, the man "who desires merely what is sufficient for his wants" is free from all the cares that bring disquiet to those who are either already wealthy, or are eager in the pursuit of gain. His repose is neither disturbed by shipwrecks, nor by losses in agricultural pursuits.

N.B. "*Haedi*" is used by poetic license for "*Haedorum*," as there are two stars so called on the left hand of the Wain.

Desideratum. Lat.—"A thing desired, much wanted." "Such a work is a *desideratum* in that branch of literature." The plural of "*desideratum*" is "*desiderata*."

——————**Desinant Maledicere, malefacta ne noscant sua.** Lat. TERENCE.—"Let them cease to speak ill of others, lest they may hear of their own misdeeds." Advice to calumniators.

Desinit in piscem mulier formosa superne. Lat. HORACE.—"The poet is charged with making the Sirens [poetical monsters, partly maidens, partly birds or fishes], half fish, which Horace seems to have done before him, and Flaxman after:—

Desinit in piscem mulier formosa superne:"

that is to say, *A woman elegantly formed above, beautiful in the upper part of her body, ends in nothing but a fish, ends with the tail of a fish.* The idea is taken from the mermaid. The application is to literary works which give the fairest opening promise, but terminate in defect and deformity.

Despues de ydo el conejo, tomanos el consejo. Span. prov.—"When the steed is stolen, the stable-door shall be kept shut, shall be better looked to, after."

'Des't is attijd fet yn ien oormans schuyttel. Frisian prov.—"'Tis always fat in another man's platter."

Desunt cetera. Lat.—"The remainder, rest, is wanting." An observation placed at the end of an imperfect work.

Desunt inopiae multa, avaritiae omnia. Lat. PUBLIUS SYRUS.—"Poverty is in want of much, but avarice of every thing."

Détenus. Fr.—"Persons who were detained as prisoners in France during our war with that country." N.B. The *singular* is "*détenu*."

Deteriores omnes sumus licentia. Lat. TERENCE.—"We are all of us the worse for too much liberty [of action]." The heart is generally deteriorated in those, who can carry out their every wish without responsibility or restriction.

Détour. Fr. Military term.—"A circuitous march."

Detrahere aliquid alteri, et hominem hominis incommodo suum augere commodum, magis est contra naturam quam mors,

quam paupertas, quam dolor, quam cetera, quae possunt aut corpori accidere, aut rebus externis. Lat. CICERO.—"To deprive any one of what is his due, and for a man to increase his own property at the expense of his neighbor, is more contrary, contradictory, to human nature than death, poverty, pain, or grief, or any thing which can affect our bodies, happen to our person or external goods, circumstances."

Detras de la cruz esta el diablo. Span. prov.—"Behind the cross stands the devil." Where GOD has his church, the devil will have his chapel.

Detur aliquando otium quiesque fessis. Lat. SENECA.—"Let ease and rest be sometimes granted to the wearied." Let there be due alternations of labor and repose.

Detur digniori. Lat.—"Let it be given to the more worthy, to the one who is more worthy, deserving, of it than another, than any one else." "There is no rule better established respecting the disposal of every office, in which the public are concerned, than this, *detur digniori*. On principles of public policy, no money ought to influence the appointment to such offices." LORD KENYON, C. J.

Detur pulcriori. Lat.—"Let it be given to the fairest." This was the inscription on the apple which fable tells us was adjudged by PARIS to the goddess VENUS, to the mortification of JUNO and MINERVA. Let the prize be given to the most deserving.

Deum qui non summum putet,
Aut stultum, aut rerum esse imperitum existima.
Cui in manu sit quem esse dementem velit,
Quem sapere; quem sanari, quem in morbum injici;
Quem contra amari, quem arcessi, quem expeti.
Lat. CAECILIUS.—

"He who denies that there's a God supreme,
A fool, or ignorant, you well may deem:
As in his hand the power almighty lies
Who shall on earth be senseless or be wise,
Who shall be heal'd, and who by sickness proved,
Who amongst men regarded or beloved."

Deus avertat. Lat.—"If," said he, "a reasonable and honorable state provision for the Roman Catholic clergy of Ireland be not adopted, the Established Church of Ireland will be swept away by the irresistible pressure which our own folly and injustice will have accumulated against her. *Deus avertat!*" that is to say, *God forbid!* N.B. The *full* and correct form is *Quod Deus avertat!* that is, *Which may God forbid, avert, ward off, turn away, or aside!* An exclamation frequently used when any calamity is apprehended.

——————Deus haec fortasse benigna
Reducet in sedem vice. Lat. HORACE.—
"The Deity, Providence, will perhaps, by a kind, happy change, restore things to their former state, level:"—

"Prithee talk no more of sorrow;
To the gods belong to-morrow,
And, perhaps, with gracious power,
They may change the gloomy hour."

Deus nobis haec otia fecit. Lat. VIRGIL.—"GOD has given us this tranquillity, this peaceful state of things."

Deus sibi reservavit ex nihilo aliquid facere, et conscientiam regere. Lat.—"GOD reserved for himself the power of making something out of nothing, and also of ruling the consciences of men, the human conscience." The wise reply of BATHORI, King of Poland, on being asked which religion was the best, the Protestant or the Catholic.

Deus undecunque juvat modo propitius. Lat. ERASMUS.—"When GOD wills, all winds bring rain." "When GOD pleases, the most unlikely matters turn out well, turn to our benefit."

Deux ace non possunt et size-cinque solvere nolunt;
Est igitur notum quatre trey solvere votum.

Hudibrastic Lat.—"If *size-cinque* will not, *duce ace* cannot, then *quatre trey* must:" that is, The middle sort bear public burdens, taxes, &c. most.

Deux chiens ne s'accordent point à un os. Fr. prov.—"Two dogs never agree about a bone."

"Two cats and a mouse, two wives in one house,
Two dogs and a bone, never agree in one."

Deux hommes se rencontrent bien, mais jamais deux montagnes. Fr. prov.—"Two men meet on good terms, have a friendly meeting; but never two mountains." Friends may meet, but mountains never greet. Two proud fellows seldom agree, draw well together.

Deux yeux voient plus clair qu'un. Fr. prov.—"Two eyes see more clearly, see better, than one, than a single one." The Portuguese say, "*Mais vem dous olhos que hum.*"

Devenir d'évêque meûnier. Fr. prov.—"From a bishop to become a miller." From an elevated position to sink low in the scale of society.

Di badessa tornar conversa. Ital.—"From an abbess to become a lay-sister." To come down in the world, sink in the scale of society.

Di bene fecerunt inopis me quodque pusilli
Finxerunt animi, raro et perpauca loquentis.

Lat. HORACE.—"The gods have done well in enduing me with a modest and humble spirit, in having made me of a poor and humble mind, that inclines me to speak but little and seldom." The gods be praised for having made me what I am, a man of moderate powers and retiring character,

"Thank Heaven, that form'd me of an humble kind:
No wit, nor yet to prattling much inclined."

A commendation of mental humility. See "*Vir sapit,*" *&c.*, and "*Verborum multitudine,*" *&c.*

Di buona terra tò la vigna, di buon madre tò la figlia. Ital. prov.—"Take a vine of a good soil, and the daughter of a good mother."

Di giovani ne muoiono molti, di vecchi ne scampa nessuno. Ital. prov.—"Of young men die many, of old men escape not any."

Di natura aperto, e molto semplice. Ital.—"Naturally frank, and very simple."—The character given by GIANNONE, of SFORZA, who, born a peasant, raised himself by his abilities, political and military, to the rank of Lord High Constable of the kingdom of Naples, and, dying at the age of fifty-three, bequeathed to his natural son wealth, reputation, and troops, which, combined with hereditary talent, made him Duke of Milan.

Di un dono far duoi amici. Ital.—"With one gift to make two friends." To kill two birds with one stone.

Dia de dos cruces. Span.—"Two saints on one day."

Διαιρουμενα εις τα μερη τα αυτα μειζονα φαινεται. Gr. Aristotle.—"Few truisms are truer than the paradox" [something contrary to received opinions, notions, or belief] "of Aristotle, that to mankind in general, *the parts are greater than the whole.* Until we try to take in the particulars one after another, we do not discover how much is comprised in the universal."

Dias de uno ó dos cruces. Span.—"Saints' days."

Dicenda bona sunt bona verba die. Lat.—"Good words should be spoken on a good day." The better day, the better deed.

Dicenda tacendaque calles. Lat. Persius.—"Thou well knowest when to speak, and when to be silent, to hold thy tongue." A proof of wisdom.

————————Dicique beatus
Ante obitum nemo supremaque funera debet. Lat. Ovid.—"No one ought to be called, declared, happy before his death, and the completion of the funeral obsequies."

Dictum. Lat.—"A saying, assertion, expression." The *plural* is "*dicta.*"

Dictum sapienti sat est. Lat. Terence.—"A word to the wise is sufficient." N.B. Often quoted *incorrectly:* thus, "*Verbum sat sapienti.*"

Die Tugend ist das hochste Gut,
Das Laster weh dem Menschen thut! Ger. Goethe.—"Virtue is the highest, greatest good, blessing; while Vice brings grief, sorrow, woe, to men, man, mortals:"—

"Dear Christian people, one and all,
When will you cease your sinning?
Else can your comfort be but small,
Good hap scarce have beginning:
For vice is hurtful unto man;
In virtue lies his surest plan."

Dies adimit aegritudinem hominibus. Lat. Terence.—"Time allays human grief."

Dies datus. Lat. Law term.—"The day given." The day or time appointed for the answer of the tenant or defendant.

Dies faustus. Lat.—"A lucky day."

Dies infaustus. Lat.—"An unlucky day." These were marked by the superstitious Romans, the former with a *white* and the latter with a *black* stone.

Dies, nisi fallor, adest, quem semper acerbum,
Semper honoratum [sic Di voluistis] habebo.
Lat. Virgil.—

"And now the rising day renews the year,
A day forever sad, forever dear."

The anniversary of a remarkable day.

Dies non. Lat. Law phrase.—"*Dies non*" is a Law phrase, the word *juridicus* [of, *or*, pertaining to, the law] being understood, and means a *day on which no legal proceedings can take place.* Such days are, all Sundays in the year; the *Purification*, in Hilary term; the *Ascension*, in Easter term; the festival of St. *John* Baptist, in Trinity term; and those of *All Saints*, and *All Souls*, in Michaelmas term. "*Dies non*" is also often used in a general sense to signify "a day on which no business can be done, transacted."

Diet.—From the Latin word "*dies*," a day. The day fixed for a particular business. The word "*diet*," in this sense, seems to be a term peculiar to Scots law, being in no English dictionary; though the same notion is there assigned as one of the supposed origins of the name "*diet*," as applied to a convention of princes.

Dieu défend le droit. Fr.—"GOD defends the right."

Dieu donne le froid selon le drap. Fr. prov.—"GOD gives, sends, cold according to the cloth." GOD tempers the wind to the shorn lamb.

Dieu et mon droit. Fr.—"God and my right." The motto of the sovereigns of Great Britain.

Difficile est longum subito deponere amorem. Lat. CATULLUS. —"It is difficult at once, on a sudden, to relinquish, lay aside, a confirmed passion." The poet speaks of the passion of love, but it is the same with every other, when once strongly indulged in.

Difficile est plurimum virtutem revereri, qui semper secunda fortuna sit usus. Lat. CICERO.—"The man who has always been fortunate cannot easily have a great reverence, a high respect, for virtue."

Difficile est proprie communia dicere. Lat. HORACE.—"The proverbial difficulty of raising up such matters to the level of elegant composition—*proprie communia dicere*—was here pre-eminent:" that is to say, *to handle common topics in such a way as to make them appear our own property*, [to enter on subjects which every man can handle, in such a way as to make them appear our own property, from the manner in which we alone are able to treat them.] N.B. The *full* expression is, *Difficile est proprie communia dicere*, that is, *It is difficult, &c.*—

"'Tis hard a new-form'd fable to express,
And make it seem your own well-managed mess."

Difficile est satiram non scribere. Lat. JUVENAL.—"It is difficult not to write, difficult to abstain from writing, satire;" the times being such as to call for the severest correction.

Difficilem oportet aurem habere ad crimina. Lat. PUBLIUS SYRUS.—"One should not lend an easy ear, readily listen, to criminal charges." To attack is so much more easy than to repel, that an accuser should ever be listened to with distrust.

Difficili bile tumet jecur. Lat. HORACE.—"My liver swells with sharp bile, with bile difficult to be repressed."

"What gloomy spleen my bosom swells!"

An avowal of anger.

Difficilia quae pulcra. Lat. prov.—"The best things are the least attainable, accessible, come-at-able, are the worst to come by, get at."

Difficilis, facilis, jucundus, acerbus es idem
Nec tecum possum vivere nec sine te. Lat. MARTIAL.—

"Your manners are so harsh, yet so easy, so pleasant, and yet so severe, that I can neither live with you, nor without you:"

"In all thy humors, whether grave or mellow,
Thou'rt such a touchy, testy, pleasant fellow,
Hast so much wit, and mirth, and spleen about thee,
That there's no living with thee, nor without thee."

Difficilis, querulus, laudator temporis acti. Lat. HORACE.—"Harsh, morose, crabbed, surly, complaining, and the eulogist, praiser of the times that are past, of bygone days:"—

"Morose, complaining, and with tedious praise,
Talking the manners of their youthful days."

N.B. The feeling embodied in the expression "*Laudator temporis acti*" is as old as the time of the patriarch JACOB. "PHARAOH said unto JACOB, How old art thou? And JACOB said unto PHARAOH, The days of the years of my pilgrimage are a hundred and thirty years: few and evil have the days of the years of my life been, and have not attained unto the days of the years of the life of my fathers in the days of their pilgrimage." Genesis xlvii. 8, 9.

Digests.—A code or body of laws, so called by JULIAN [perhaps JUSTINIAN], who first regulated them. See "*Pandects.*"

Digito monstrari, et dicier: Hic est. Lat. PERSIUS.—[It is a nice thing] "to be pointed at by the finger, and have it said: 'There goes the man.'" Such is the ambition of many to be notorious, and such was one of the failings of the distinguished orator DEMOSTHENES.

Digna canis pabulo. Lat. prov.—"A dog that is worth his food, his keep." 'Tis an ill dog that deserves not a crust.

Dignum laude virum Musa vetat mori. Lat. HORACE.—"The Muse preserves the memory of a great and worthy man." She consecrates his name to immortality.

"The Muse forbids the virtuous man to die."

Dignus vindice nodus. Lat. HORACE.—"A knot worthy to be untied by such hands." A difficulty which calls for the highest interference. See "*Nec deus intersit,*" *&c.*, and "*E machina deus.*" "Where neither presumption nor proof of guilt exists, there all human means of ascertaining the truth seem to fail, and a *dignus vindice nodus* is conceived to arise:" that is to say, and a *difficulty worthy of a god's unraveling, &c.*, an *occasion on which the immediate interposition of Providence may be expected, &c.*

Dii laboribus omnia vendunt. Lat. prov.—"The gods sell us every thing in return for our labor, toils, exertions." "Without pains no gains." See "*Nil sine magno,*" *&c.*

Dii majores et minores. Lat.—"Denizens of clubs, crowders into coffee-houses, will you not elevate the directors and officials of the Submarine Telegraph Company by an immediate *apotheosis* into *dii majores et minores?*" that is to say, by an immediate *deification* [god-making], *raising to the rank of gods, raising into gods, some of a higher, and others of a lower grade, or degree.*

Dii penates. Lat.—"The household gods," among the ancients. Small images, which they worshiped at home. It is now sometimes used in an ironical sense. They were such a man's *dii penates;* they were the persons whom he caressed, entertained, and almost worshiped.

Dilationes in lege sunt odiosae. Lat. Law maxim.—"Delays in the law are odious." This is a maxim, it is to be feared, rather belied in the practice. It can now go merely to intimate that a dilatory plea cannot be received, unless the matter be supported by an *affidavit.*

Dilemma. Gr. in Roman letters.—An argument equally conclusive by contrary suppositions. · An argument containing two contradictory propositions, the choice of one of which is left to the opponent [opposing person], in order to bring thorough conviction to his mind, whichever side he may take up or espouse. "*Dilemma*" is often used in ordinary conversation to signify "*a difficulty, a fix.*" "An awkward *dilemma.*"

Dilettanti. Ital.—"Persons who take up art or science, devote themselves to art or science, merely for amusement, relaxation, recreation."

Diligence. Fr.—A French "stage-coach."

Diligitur nemo, nisi cui Fortuna secunda est,
Quae, simul intonuit, proxima quaeque fugat.

Lat. OVID.—

"When smiling Fortune spreads her golden ray,
All crowd around to flatter and obey:
But when she thunders from an angry sky,
Our friends, our flatterers, and our lovers fly."

Dimidium facti, qui coepit, habet. Lat. HORACE.—This is literally translated by our own proverb, "What's well begun is half done:"—

"Who sets about has half performed his deed."

Compare the Greek proverb, Αρχη ήμισυ παντος, "The beginning is the half of every thing, every deed, action."

Diminutio capitis. Lat.—"If this conceited sprig of nobility, who will not allow any one to be a '*gentleman*' who does not belong to what is called '*high life*,' will take some opportunity of properly disguising his aristocratic person, and trust himself for once to the interior of one of those Ark-like 'hacks' which now and then rattle even through Pimlico, every cook-maid they pick up shall be 'This here lady,' and the rival *cad*, that would fain have intercepted her, by summary *diminutio capitis*, proclaimed 'No gentleman:'" that is to say, by summary *deprivation of his dignity, of his reputed standing in society*, [ironically] proclaimed, &c. N.B. "*Diminutio capitis*" signified among the Romans *the losing, loss, of one's freedom.*

Dîners à la carte. Fr.—"Dinners from the bill of fare."

Dio ti guarda da mangiatore, che non beve! Ital. prov.—"May GOD keep, preserve, you from one who eats without drinking!" You eat and eat, but you do not drink to fill you.

Diplomate. Fr.—"A diplomatist."

Dire des fleurettes. Fr.—"To say pretty, or gallant, things." N.B. The French use the phrases "*conter fleurettes, conter des fleurettes,*" in the same sense as "*dire des fleurettes.*"

Diruit, aedificat, mutat quadrata rotundis. Lat. HORACE.—"He pulls down, he builds up [and is, upon the whole, a heap of contradictions], changing square for round, and round for square." He is perpetually changing, merely to gratify his own caprice.

Dis aliter visum. Lat. VIRGIL.—"It has seemed fit to the gods to ordain the matter otherwise; Providence ordained, has ordained, it otherwise." Providence has disposed of the matter in a different way.

Δις παιδες οἱ γεροντες. Gr. prov.—"Old men are twice children."

——————Dis proximus ille est,
Quem ratio, non ira movet: qui, facta rependens,
Consilio punire potest. Lat. CLAUDIAN.—

"He is next to the gods, whom reason, and not passion, impels; and who, after weighing the facts, can measure the punishment, can punish, with discretion." This is a pleasing picture of a mild governor.

Disce, docendus adhuc quae censet amiculus, ut si
Caecus iter monstrare velit: tamen adspice, si quid
Et nos, quod cures proprium fecisse, loquamur.
Lat. HORACE.—

"Now to th' instruction of an humble friend,
Who would himself be better taught, attend:
Though blind your guide, some precepts yet unknown
He may disclose, which you may make your own."

Something may be learned, even from the most unlettered individual.

Discenti assidue multa senecta venit. Lat.—"Old age steals on us while we are continually adding to, making additions to, our stores of knowledge." One may "live and learn."

Discere si quaeris, doceas, sic ipse doceris:
Nam studio tali tibi proficis atque sodali. Lat.—

"If you are anxious to learn, employ yourself in teaching, and thus will you yourself be taught; for, inasmuch as, by such means, practice, exercise, you equally benefit yourself and your companion, comrade."

Discipulus est prioris posterior dies. Lat. PUBLIUS SYRUS.—"Each succeeding day is the scholar of that which preceded." The errors that we commit on one day should teach us to conduct ourselves more wisely on those which follow. "Older and wiser."

Discit enim citius, meminitque libentius illud
Quod quis deridet, quam quod probat et veneratur.
Lat. HORACE.—

"Men learn sooner, and retain better, with greater pleasure, what is empty and ridiculous, than what they esteem and admire:"

——————"Quickly we discern,
With ease remember, and with pleasure learn,
Whate'er may ridicule and laughter move,
Not what deserves our best esteem and love."

Discite justitiam moniti, et non temnere divos.
Lat. VIRGIL.—

"Having been admonished, learn justice, and not to despise the gods:"—

"Beware, learn justice, and the gods revere."

Learn from infliction the sense of justice, and the respect which is due to Heaven.

Disjecta membra. Lat. HORACE.—"Disjointed portions, or parts."

Dispiccha l'impicchato, che impicchera poi te. Ital. prov.—"Save a thief from the gallows, and he'll be the first to cut your throat."

Disputandi pruritus ecclesiae scabies. Lat. SIR HENRY WOTTON.—"The itch for disputation, controversy, is the scab, the dirty spot, the disgrace, of the Church."

Distrahit animum librorum multitudo. Lat. SENECA.—"A multitude, great number, of books, distracts the mind." But little solid acquirement is to be expected from promiscuous, desultory reading.

Distringas. Lat. Law term.—"You may distrain." A writ to empower the sheriff to that effect.

Divan. Turkish.—The Sultan's privy council at Constantinople. Also a raised ground in a hall, or any other room in a house. It is likewise applied to a range of cushioned seats round a room.

Dives agris, dives positis in foenore nummis. Lat. HORACE.—"A person rich in lands, and money placed out, lent out, at usury, at interest." Used to describe a man of immense property.

Dives qui fieri vult, et cito vult fieri. Lat. JUVENAL.—"He who wishes to become rich also wishes to become so quickly, with as little delay as possible, in as short a time as possible."

Divide et impera. Lat.—"Divide and govern." This is the policy of almost all governments. By dividing a nation into parties, and poising them against each other, the people are deprived of their intrinsic weight, and their rulers incline the scale as suits their caprice or discretion.

Divieni tosto vecchio, se vuoi vivere lungamente vecchio. Ital. prov.—"You soon become old, if you wish to live long old, as an old person." "Old young, and old long."

Divitiarum et formae gloria fluxa atque fragilis; virtus clara, aeternaque habetur. Lat. SALLUST.—"The boast, so oft indulged in, of riches and of beauty, is frail and transitory; while virtue alone is worthy of renown, renowned, distinguished, patent to every one, and eternal."

Dixerit e multis aliquis, Quid virus in angues
Adjicis? et rabidae tradis ovile lupae? Lat. OVID.—
"But some exclaim, 'What frenzy rules your mind?
Would you increase the craft of womankind,
Teach them new wiles and arts?—As well you may
Instruct a snake to bite, or wolf to prey.'"

Dizeme com quem andas, dirte hei que manhas has. Port. prov.—"Tell me with whom thou goest, and I'll tell thee what thou doest." Compare the Ital. prov.—*La mala compagnia è quella che mena uomini a la furca*, "Bad company is that which leads, brings, men to the gallows."

Doce ut discas. Lat.—"Teach, that you may learn." Employ yourself in communicating what you know to others, and so will you improve yourself.

Dociles imitandis turpibus ac pravis omnes sumus. Lat. JUVENAL.—"We are all too apt, ready, to learn to imitate that which is base and depraved:"

"The mind of mortals, in perverseness strong,
Imbibes with dire docility the wrong."

Docti rationem artis intelligunt, indocti voluptatem. Lat.

QUINTILIAN.—"The learned understand the reason of the art, the unlearned feel the pleasure." This axiom serves to mark, and particularly in painting, the broad distinction between cultivated science and natural taste.

Doctrina sed vim promovet insitam,
Rectique cultus pectora roborant:
Utcunque defecere mores,
Indecorant bene nata culpae. Lat. HORACE.—

"It is education that improves the powers implanted in us by nature, and it is good culture that strengthens the heart: whenever moral principles are wanting, vice degrades the fair endowments of nature:"

"Yet sage instructions to refine the soul,
And raise the genius, wondrous aid impart,
Conveying inward, as they purely roll,
Strength to the mind, and vigor to the heart:
When morals fail, the stains of vice disgrace
The fairest honors of the noblest race."

Doctrinaire. Fr.—"This appears to us a fit moment to say a few words on a question which has often been put, and as variously replied to, of '*What is a Doctrinaire?*' The term has, of late years, been used as one of reproach. A politician of moderate, fixed, monarchical, and yet constitutional principles, is called a *Doctrinaire;* above all, if he be philosophical, moral, and religious. Before the first Revolution in France, the *Doctrinaires* existed as a corporation, whose business it was to instruct the youth of the country. Royer Collard was educated in a college of '*Doctrinaires;*' his brother was the '*Oratorien;*' and his uncle was at the head of a community of *Doctrinaires* at Arras. M. Royer Collard was denominated a '*Doctrinaire*' in the Chamber of Deputies, not, however, because he had been educated in a Doctrinaire college, but because, at the French tribune, his manner, logic, eloquence, were always severe, grave, and took that dogmatic form, that logical and rigorous deduction, which clearly announced a body of *doctrines* fully decided on and adopted. M. Royer Collard and his friends accepted, however, this term of reproach, accusing, in their turn, the ultra-Romanist portion of the monarchical party of marching blindly under the inspiration of their momentary passions and interests, without principles and without *doctrines* which could possibly secure the repose of the country, and the stability of the throne."—"We feel tempted to say a word or two upon the party designation *Doctrinaire*, respecting which, some of our readers may possibly be as much mistaken and perplexed as we ourselves were, French scholars as we fancy ourselves, until we were enlightened by a French friend. We had imagined that *doctrinaire* must answer to theorist; and there we were in the right, but even by that just conclusion were we misled, inasmuch as a French theorist is altogether different from an English theorist. We Britons are accustomed to call him a theorist who logically carries out his principles or opinions, unalloyed, to their impracticable extremes. Now, in France, such extremes are held to be what is most natural and simple; hence, in politics, despotism and republicanism are thought plain, natural opinions, whilst the theorist, the *doctrinaire*, is the philosophical politician, who endeavors to steer betwixt those extremes, taking the good, and shunning the evil of both. Should we then translate a *doctrinaire* a practical man?"

Doctus sermones utriusque linguae. Lat. HORACE.—"A man, learned in the antiquities of Greece and Rome." This is the meaning in the original passage: the reference is to MAECENAS, a Roman gentleman of extraordinary wit and eloquence, the patron of learning and learned men,—of VIRGIL and HORACE in particular. The expression is, however, often used to signify "a perfect master of both languages, Greek and Latin."—"Sermones" answers, in some respect, to the Greek *μυθοι*. In addressing his son, CICERO says—"*Ipse ad meam utilitatem semper cum Graecis Latina conjunxi; neque id in philosophia tantum, sed etiam in dicendi exercitatione feci: idem tibi censeo faciendum, ut par sis utriusque orationis facultate*"—that is, "I have always for my own especial benefit, advantage, combined the study of Greek and Latin; and this I have done not only in philosophical studies, but also in those of oratory and eloquence: I am consequently of opinion that you would do well in carrying out, in following, the same plan, that you may be thoroughly up to the mark in both tongues, languages."

Dogma. Gr. in Roman letters.—"An opinion, principle of belief, tenet."

Dolce cose a vedere, e dolci inganni. Ital. ARIOSTO.—"Things sweet to see, and sweet, pleasing, deceptions." A phrase frequently applied to specious, but deceitful, appearances.

Dolce far niente. Ital.—"He courts retirement, and the *dolce far niente*," that is, and the "exquisite pleasure of doing nothing but what he likes, chooses."

Doli, machinae, fallaciae, praestigiae, sine ratione esse non possunt. Lat. CICERO.—"Tricks, artful contrivances, dodges, frauds, and illusive practices, cannot be without a motive at the bottom of them."

Dolore affici, sed resistere tamen. Lat. PLINY.—"To be affected by grief, but still to resist it, bear up against it." This, that finished philosopher observes, is a duty incumbent on every one.

Dolus, an virtus, quis in hoste requirat? Lat. VIRGIL.—"Who shall ask of an enemy whether he succeeded by stratagem or by valor?" Either mode is to be adopted in cases of avowed hostility. The only question is, which is most likely to insure success? "If the lion's skin cannot, the fox's shall."

Dolus versatur in generalibus. Lat. Law maxim.—"Fraud lurks in loose generalities." It is in its nature to deal in broad and general statements, without coming to close and tangible assertions; or, in other terms, general propositions, without modification, often lead to very erroneous conclusions.

Dom, *and*, **Don.** Port. and Span.—"There is no doubt that *Dom* Miguel was the rightful sovereign of Portugal:" N.B. "*Dom*" [an abbreviation of "*dominus*," a master, who owns], as it is spelled by the Portuguese, and "*Don*," which has the same meaning in Spanish, are titles of honor and respect. At first they were applied only to princes and nobles; at the present day they are only a form of politeness. "*Don*" is generally applied by us ironically to one who thinks himself a great man.

Domat omnia virtus. Lat.—"Valor conquers all, every thing."

Domine, salvum fac Imperatorem. Lat.—"The *Domine, salvum fac Imperatorem* was sung by the musicians of the 94th Regiment:" that is to say, the [prayer] *O Lord, save the Emperor*, was sung, &c. N.B. A prayer in the breviary [prayer-book] of the Church of Rome, and also with "*Queen*" instead of "*Emperor*" in the prayer-book of the Church of England.

Dominium a possessione coepisse dicitur. Lat. Law maxim.—"Right is said to have its beginning from possession." This maxim goes to prevent the disturbance of titles to estates. But if there be proof of record established, it outweighs the memory of man, which, by the statute 32 Hen. VIII., is fixed at sixty years.

Dominus providebit. Lat.—"The Lord will provide."

Dominus videt plurimum in rebus suis. Lat. PHAEDRUS.—"The master is the most sharp-sighted in his own affairs." Compare the Ital. prov.—*Piu vide un occhio del patron che quatro de' servitori.* "One eye of the master sees more than four of the servants'."

Domum suam coërcuit, quod plerisque haud minus arduum est quam provinciam regere. Lat. TACITUS, speaking of his father-in-law, AGRICOLA, the Roman governor of Great Britain in the reign of DOMITIAN.—"He governed his family, which many find to be a harder task than to govern a province."

Domus, et placens uxor. Lat. HORACE.—"Your house and your beloved wife, pleasing consort."

Don de plaire. Fr.—"The art of pleasing, natural disposition to make one's self agreeable to every one."

Donde fuego se haze humo sale. Span. prov.—"There is no fire without some smoke."

Donde no se piensa, salta la liebre. Span.—"The hare springs out, when one thinks not on it, of it."

Donec eris felix multos numerabis amicos;
Tempora si fuerint nubila, solus eris. Lat. OVID.—

"So long as you are in good circumstances, you will number, reckon up, many friends; but, if the times change with you, if you get on your beam-ends, then will you find yourself alone in the world:"—

"The gale is favoring, numerous friends you'll find;
From th' adverse storm they fly before the wind."

Compare SHAKSPEARE:—

"Where you are liberal of your loves and counsels,
Be sure you be not loose: for those you make friends,
And give your hearts to, when they once perceive
The least rub in your fortunes, fall away
Like water from ye, never found again,
But where they mean to sink ye."

Donjon.—"*Donjon*" means the principal tower of a castle, which was usually raised on a natural or artificial mound, and situated in the innermost court. Its lower part was commonly used as a prison. It was sometimes called the *donjon-keep*, or *tower*.

Donna bruta è mal di stomaco, donna bella mal di teste.

Ital. prov.—"An ugly woman is a disease of the stomach, a handsome woman a disease of the head."

Donne, preti, e polli non son mai satolli. Ital. prov.—"Women, priests, and poultry never have enough."

Dono molto aspettato e vendato, non donato. Ital. prov.—"A gift long waited for is sold, and not given."

Dopo il cattivo ne vien il buon tempo. Ital. prov.—"After bad weather comes good." After a storm comes a calm.

Dormit aliquando jus, moritur nunquam. Lat. Law maxim.—"A right sometimes sleeps, but never dies." A right to land, for instance, it is understood, cannot die. If a man releases his right, it is extinguished for the time; but this is to be understood only of the right of the person making the release.

Dos d'âne. Fr.—"The ass's back." A military phrase used to describe a shelving ridge.

Dos est magna parentium virtus. Lat. HORACE.—"The virtue of parents is in itself a great portion, dowry." A rich dowry consists in the virtue instilled by parental instruction. No inheritance can be more valuable than that of a fair fame transmitted from our ancestors.

Dos sueños ay, el blando está compuesto
De plumas de aves; y el cruel vestido
De plomo, con que oprime, quando viene,
El pecho congojado que le tiene. Span. LOPE DE VEGA.—
"Two kind of dreams there be; of softest down
The gentle one is framed,—the sterner kind
Of lead, beneath whose painful weight the breast
Labors and struggles, fearfully oppress'd."

Double entendre. Fr.—"Some ladies," says the author of a very silly book that was published at Glasgow in 1837, "not only relish *double entendres*, but actually use them:" that is to say, not only relish *words that have a twofold, and often indelicate, meaning*, but, &c. N.B. "*Double entendres*" is bad French: the *right* and *full* expression is *mots à double entente*, words that have a twofold meaning: the singular is *mot à double entente*, a word that has a twofold meaning.

Douces, *or*, **belles paroles n'écorchent pas la langue.** Fr. prov.—"Soft words scald not the tongue." Soft words hurt not the mouth.

Douces promesses obligent les fols. Fr. prov.—"Fair promises gratify fools." "Fair words make fools fain, that is, glad."

Douceur. Fr.—"A present, bribe."

Doux yeux. Fr.—"Soft glances." To make the *doux yeux*, to interchange tender looks.

Dove l'oro parla, ogni lingua tace. Ital. prov.—"Where gold speaks, every tongue is silent."

Dove sono donne ed ocche non vi sono parole poche. Ital. prov.—"Where there are many women and geese, there is no lack of tittle-tattle and gabble."

Dragoman.—An interpreter of languages at the Court of the Sultan, and throughout Turkey. Several of them are attached to each European embassy.

Dragonnades. Fr.—"Dragoonings." N.B. The "*Dragonnades*" were expeditions of dragoons, in the reign of LEWIS THE FOURTEENTH, against the Protestants of France, to endeavor to force them to become Papists.

Drama. Gr. in Roman letters.—Properly, "An action, act, the representation of an action." A drama, stage-play proceedings.

Dramatis personae. Lat.—"Characters represented, representatives of characters, on the stage."

Drame. Fr.—"Dramatic parts."

Droit administratif. Fr.—"Administrative law."

Droit coutumier. Fr.—"Common law."

Droit d'aubaine. Fr.—"The right of escheat." By this law, which expired with the French monarchy of the last century, the personal property of every foreigner, dying within the king's dominions, escheated, fell, to the crown.

Droits d'auteur. Fr.—"Copyrights of authors."

Droits de seigneur. Fr.—"Lordly rights, or rights of the nobles."

Droits des gens. Fr.—"The law of nations."

Droits généraux. Fr.—"Government taxes."

Droits réunis. Fr.—"Assessed taxes."

Du dire au fait y a grand trait. Fr. prov.—"Saying and doing are very different things."

Du fort au faible. Fr.—"From the strong to the weak."

Duabus ancoris fultus. Lat.—

"Good riding at two anchors men have told;
For if one break, the other may hold."

Duabus niti ancoris. Lat. prov.—"To have two strings to one's bow."

Duabus sellis sedere. Lat. prov.—"To hold with the hare and run with the hounds. To be on both sides."

Dubiam salutem qui dat afflictis, negat. Lat. SENECA.—"He who holds out a doubtful safety to the afflicted denies all hope."

Duc me, Parens, celsique dominator poli,
Quocunque placuit: nulla parendi mora est:
Adsum impiger. Fac nolle: comitabor gemens,
Malusque patiar, quod bono licuit pati. Lat. SENECA.—

"Conduct me, Thou of beings Cause divine,
Where'er I'm destined in thy great design!
Active, I follow on: for should my will
Resist, I'm impious; but must follow still."

———————————**Ducimus autem**
Hos quoque felices, qui ferre incommoda vitae,
Nec jactare jugum via didicere magistra. Lat. JUVENAL.—"We also deem those happy, who from the experience of life have learned to bear its ills, and without descanting on their weight." That experience, which leads to resignation and composure, leads at the same time to comparative happiness.

———————————**Ducis ingenium res**
Adversae nudare solent, celare secundae. Lat. HORACE.—

"Misfortunes, untoward events, lay open, disclose, the skill of a general, while success conceals his weakness, his weak points." Success only serves to hide the abilities of a general, whereas Adversity often gives him an opportunity to discover, display them:—

"Good fortune hides, Adversity calls forth,
A landlord's genius, and a leader's worth."

It is less difficult to gain a battle than to conduct a retreat.

Ducit amor patriae. Lat.—"The love of my country leads me, spurs me on."

Due tordi ad una pania. Ital. prov.—"To stop two gaps with one bush."

Due visi sotto una beretta. Ital. prov.—"To carry two faces under one hood."

Duelos con pan son menos. Span. prov.—"Sorrows, troubles, with something to eat, are bearable, endurable." "A fat sorrow is better than a lean one."

Dulce est desipere in loco. Lat. HORACE.—"Though virtue and vice are always the same, decorum and propriety depend almost entirely upon the manners and observances exacted by the state of society. *Dulce est desipere in loco*, is a maxim which requires no illustration. The bravest men have had their fears, and the wisest their follies:" that is to say, *It is pleasant, or delightful, to play the fool, to come off one's high horse, to indulge in festive enjoyment, to unbend now and then, occasionally, or on fitting occasions.* N.B. The sentiment occurs in HORACE [the lyric poet and satirist], who took the idea from the comic writer MENANDER, who says, Ου πανταχου το φρονιμον ἁρμοττει παρον, και συμμανηναι δ' ενια δει, that is, "*it is not exactly the thing for a man* ALWAYS *to appear wise, but that a little innocent fun and frolic sit well on everybody.*"

"'Tis joyous folly that unbends the mind."

Dulce et decorum est pro patria mori. Lat. HORACE.—The memorable quotation of LORD LOVAT on the scaffold. "Sweet is it and glorious, honorable, to die for one's country:"—

"What joys, what glories, round him wait,
Who bravely for his country dies!"

The above is an apophthegm [a remarkable or wise saying, valuable maxim, oracular saying] cited in all wars, and in all ages. Sound philosophy, however, will confine its application to the single case of our country's being attacked. It is certainly honorable to die in repelling such an aggression.

Dulci animos novitate tenebo. Lat. OVID.—"I will engross your attention with sweet novelty."

**Dulcis inexpertis cultura potentis amici:
Expertus metuit.** Lat. HORACE.—
"The friendship of the great seems inviting to those that have never made trial; but he who has had experience of it is cautious." The pomp and splendor, with which great men are surrounded, makes us apt to think their friendship valuable; a little experience, however, soon convinces us that it is a most rigorous slavery.

"Untried, how sweet a court attendance!
When tried, how dreadful the dependence!"

Dulcis juventas. Lat.—"The bright days of one's youth."

Dum caput infestat, labor omnia membra molestat. Lat.—"When the head aches, all the body is the worse for it, feels the effects of it."

Dum deliberamus quando incipiendum, incipere jam serum fit. Lat. QUINTILIAN.—"Whilst we consider, are considering, when we are to begin, it is often too late to act." Deliberation protracted is, on some occasions, as dangerous as precipitancy.

Dum in dubio est animus, paulo momento huc illuc impellitur. Lat. TERENCE.—"Whilst the mind is in a state of uncertainty, the smallest impulse directs it to either side."

Dum lego, assentior. Lat.—"Whilst I am reading, I assent." I yield implicitly to the writer's opinions. This was used emphatically by *Cicero*, on reading *Plato's* arguments on the immortality of the soul.

Dum loquimur, fugerit invida aetas. Lat. HORACE.—"Whilst we are speaking, envious time speeds on."

"E'en while we talk, in careless ease,
Our envious minutes wing their flight."

Dum moliuntur, dum comuntur, annus est. Lat. TERENCE.—"Whilst they [the women] are absorbed in the all-engrossing, ever-important, business of rigging themselves out, business of the toilette, an age passes by, a terrific time elapses."

Dum potuit, solita gemitum virtute repressit. Lat. OVID.—

"With wonted fortitude she bore the smart,
And not a groan confessed her burning heart."

Dum quid superesset agendum. Lat. LUCAN.—"Adopting the noble maxim of considering nothing done *dum quid superesset agendum*, they would feel the very spires of our cathedrals an eyesore, and would never rest until they were overthrown:" that is to say, *whilst any thing remained to be done*, they would, &c.

Dum relego, scripsisse pudet. Lat.—"Whilst I am reading my compositions over again, I am ashamed of having written them." The motto prefixed by HURDIS to his first poem.

Dum spiro, spero. Lat.—"Whilst, or so long as, I breathe, I hope, indulge in hope."

Dum tacent, clamant. Lat. CICERO.—"Their silence speaks aloud." This is said by the great orator of antiquity of the people under certain circumstances, when their curses are "not loud but deep." That is the very aspect under which the despot or the advocate of terror should most dread the ebullition of their rage.

Dum te causidicum, dum te modo rhetora fingi
Et non decernis, Taure, quid esse velis,
Peleos et Priami transit vel Nestoris aetas,
Et serum fuerat jam tibi desinere—
Eja, age, rumpe moras, quo te spectabimus usque?
Dum quid sis dubitas, jam potes esse nihil.

Lat. MARTIAL.—

"To rhetoric now, and now to law inclined,
Uncertain where to fix thy changing mind;
Old Priam's age or Nestor's may be out,
And thou, O Taurus! still go on in doubt.
Come then, how long such wavering shall we see?
Thou may'st doubt on, thou now canst nothing be."

Mental wavering must ever be ruinous to our pursuits.

Dum vires annique sinunt tolerate laborem:
Jam veniet tacito curva senecta pede. Lat. OVID.—"Whilst your strength and years permit, endure and encounter labor: remember that crooked age will soon arrive with silent step, unperceivedly."

Dum vita est, spes est. Lat. CICERO.—"Whilst there is life, there is hope." The *full* expression is, "*Aegroto, dum vita est, spes est.*" "Whilst, or so long as, the sick man is alive, he may hope to recover." Compare SHAKSPEARE:—

"The miserable have no other medicine,
But only hope."

Again:—

"Have hope to live; but be prepared to die."

Dum vitant stulti vitia, in contraria currunt. Lat. HORACE.—"While fools strive to avoid, shun, one vice, they often fall into, run into, its contrary, opposite." They are ever in extremes.

Dum vivimus vivamus. Lat.—"Whilst we live, let us live." We only live whilst we enjoy life; let us, therefore, enjoy it as long as we can.

"'Live while you live,' the epicure would say,
'And seize the pleasures of the present day.'
'Live while you live,' the sacred preacher cries,
'And give to GOD each moment as it flies.'
Lord, in my views let both united be;
I live in *pleasure* when I live to THEE."—DODDRIDGE.

Duo cum faciunt idem, non est idem. Lat. prov.—"If a gamester, a bankrupt, no longer able to prolong his extravagant and worthless course of life, puts an end to it in a moment of despair, is he to be placed on a level with the Emperor Otho, and the philosophic Cato?" that is to say, *When two persons do the same thing, it is not* exactly *the same thing.*

Duos parietes de eadem fidelia dealbare. Lat. prov. —"To kill two birds with one stone. To do two things at once."

Duos qui sequitur lepores, neutrum capit. Lat. prov.—"He who follows two hares is sure to catch neither." When the attention of a man is divided between many objects, he rarely attains any of them. He has, according to the English proverb, "too many irons in the fire."

Dura messorum ilia. Lat. HORACE.—"The strong stomachs of the very hardiest of the working-classes." N.B. Garlic and wild-thyme pounded together were used by the Roman farmers to recruit the exhausted spirits of the reapers, and those who had labored in the heat. In the original passage, the poet expresses his surprise at their being able to endure such food.

Durans originis vis. Lat.—"We shall find, on the fiery banks of the Oronoco, Indians with skins inclining to white, *est durans originis* *vis:*" that is to say, *it is a lasting, or enduring, memorial of our common origin, or, The strong feature, or indication, of our common origin is, as it were, indelible, unblot-out-able, unroot-out-able.*

Durante bene placito. Lat.—"During our good pleasure." By this tenure the judges of this country once held their seats, at the will of the sovereign. They are now held, more properly, *quamdiu se bene gesserint:* "As long as they shall conduct themselves well;" that is to say, during life, unless a criminal charge shall be made and proved against them.

Durante vita. Lat.—"During life." A clause in letters-patent.

Durante, et vosmet rebus servate secundis. Lat. VIRGIL.—

"Endure the hardships of your present state:
Live, and reserve yourselves for better fate."

Compare SHAKSPEARE:—

"In all emergencies, play the man."

And—

"Vexations duly borne
Are but as trials, which Heaven's love to man
Sends for his good."

Again—

"Things at the worst will cease: or e'en climb upward
To what they were before."

Once more—

"If ills be necessary,
Then let us meet them like necessities."

Duro con duro non fa mai buon muro. Ital. prov.—"Hard with hard never makes a good wall." "Hard with hard," that is, stone without mortar or cement, "makes not the stone wall."

Duris urgens in rebus egestas. Lat. VIRGIL.—"The pressure of want, in the day of trouble, in hard times." The most powerful stimulus [motive, inducement, incentive] to industry and invention.

**Durum! sed levius fit patientia
Quidquid corrigere est nefas.** Lat. HORACE.—

"For some time I looked alternately at my widowed rod and my departed fish; which last were coursing it round and round the pool, pulling in opposite directions, like coupled dogs of dissenting opinions: *Durum! sed levius,*" &c., that is to say, *This is hard indeed! but whatever cannot possibly be amended becomes more light, is rendered more light, is made more easy* [to bear], *by patience, by bearing it patiently:*—

"'Tis hard! but patience must endure,
And soothe the woes it cannot cure."

N.B. Similar to the above sentiment is that of Seneca [a distinguished writer on philosophy]: *Optimum est pati quod emendare non possis,* that is to say, *It is the best thing you can do to bear patiently what you cannot amend, correct, or make better* [what cannot be cured must be endured]. Publius Syrus [a Syrian mimographer, writer of plays or farces] also tells us that *Miseriarum portus est patientia,* that is to say, *Patience is the asylum* [place of refuge] *of affliction.*

Durum telum necessitas. Lat. prov.—"Necessity is a hard wea-pou." It is dangerous to oppose those whom necessity has driven to extremes.

Dux femina facti. Lat. VIRGIL.—"A woman was the leader of the deed."—A quotation often used, as it frequently happens that female spirit takes the lead in the greatest enterprises.

Dyspepsy, or **Dyspepsia.** Gr. in Roman letters.—"Bad digestion, difficulty of digestion, indigestion."

E.

É bien asi como los marineros se guian en la noche oscura por el aguja, que les és medianera entre la piedra é la estrella, é les muestra por dō vayan, tambien en los malos tiempos, como en los buenos, otro si los que han de anconsejar al Rey deben siempre guiar por la justicia. Old Span.—"And as mariners guide themselves in the dark night by the *needle*, which is the medium between the magnet and the star, in like manner ought those who have to counsel the king always to guide themselves by justice." "It has been the fate of MARCO POLO not only to be charged with faults of commission and omission, but also to have other matters ascribed to him of which he makes no mention, and of which, indeed, he could have no knowledge. Thus, nothing is more common than to find it repeated from book to book, that gunpowder and the mariner's compass were first brought from China by this early traveler, though there can be very little doubt that both were known in Europe some time before his return. Indeed, there is good evidence that the use of the magnetic needle was familiar here long before he set out on his travels; for ALONZO EL SABIO, King of Castile, who, about the year 1260, promulgated the famous code of laws known by the title of '*Las siete Partidas*,' has [in the preamble of ley 28, titulo 9, partida 2] the following remarkable passage:—'*É bien asi*,' *&c.*"

E come il cane dell'ortolano, che non mangia de cavoli egli, e non ne lascia mangiar altri. Ital. prov.—"He is like the gardener's dog, who never eats coleworts himself, nor suffers others to eat them." To play the dog in the manger; not eat yourself, nor let anybody else.

E contra. Lat.—"On the other hand." "How, then, is it that, if the Parliament has a right to prohibit the publication of its own debates, because it is itself the *legal Public*, it should *e contra* imagine some other, and therefore illegal, Public, to whom it claims a right of communicating the proceedings of third parties?"

E flamma petere cibum. Lat. prov. TERENCE.—"To run any risk, to submit to any thing, however base." When the ancients burned the bodies of the dead, they commonly threw bread, &c. on the funeral pile, and the greatest affront that could be offered to any person, was to tell him that he was capable of snatching these from the middle of the flames. "*E flamma*" is therefore, in the above phrase, used instead of "*e rogo*." LUCILIUS [the Roman satirist, and the first to mold Roman satire into that form which afterwards received full development in the hands of HORACE, PERSIUS, and JUVENAL], endeavoring to give a character of one of the most contemptible wretches in nature, says, "*Mordicus petere aurum e coeno expediat, e flamma cibum:*" that is, "He could stoop to snatch with his teeth gold from dirt, mire, and meat from a funeral pile."

E meglio aver oggi un uovo, che dimani una gallina. Ital. prov.—"It is better to have an egg to-day than a hen to-morrow." A bird in the hand is worth two in the bush.

E meglio esser capo di cardella che coda di storione. Ital. prov.—"Better be the head of a sprat than the tail of a sturgeon."

E meglio esser fortunato che savio. Ital. prov.—"'Tis better to be lucky [in good circumstances] than wise."

E meglio esser mendicante che ignorante. Ital. prov.—"Better be a beggar than a fool, an ignorant fellow."

E meglio piegar che scavezzar. Ital. prov.—"Better to bow than break."

E meglio senza cibo restar che senz'onore. Ital. TRISSINO.—"Better be without food than without honor."

Ea animi elatio, quae cernitur in periculis, si justitia vacat pugnatque pro suis commodis, in vitio est. Lat. CICERO.—"That courage and intrepidity of mind, which distinguishes itself in dangers, is vicious, faulty, if it be void of all regard for justice, and support a man only in the pursuit of his own interest."

Ea sub oculis posita negligimus; proximorum incuriosi, longinqua sectamur. Lat. PLINY.—"We neglect the things that are placed before our eyes, and, regardless of what is within our reach, we pursue whatever is remote." This is frequently and properly applied to the rage for visiting foreign countries in those who are absolutely unacquainted with their own:—

"Abroad to see wonders the traveler goes,
And neglects the fine things which lie under his nose."

Eau sucrée. Fr.—"Sugared water," a favorite drink of the Parisians.

Ecce homo! Lat.—"Behold the man!"

Ecce iterum Crispinus! et est mihi saepe vocandus
Ad partes: monstrum, nulla virtute redemtum.

Lat. JUVENAL.—"Once more behold CRISPINUS! and often shall I have to call him on the stage: a monster, without a single virtue to redeem his vices:

"Again CRISPINUS comes! and yet again,
And oft, shall he be summoned to sustain
His dreadful part:—the monster of the times,
Without ONE virtue to redeem his crimes!"

[Applied by the author of "The Pursuits of Literature" to WILLIAM GODWIN.]

Ecce signum! Lat.—"Here is the proof." "India will soon be such another country as England. *Ecce signum!*"

Ecclesiae scabies. Lat. SIR HENRY WOTTON.—The scab, dirty spot, disgrace, of the Church, in reference to the "itch for disputation."

Εχθρος γαρ μοι κεινος ὁμως αϊδαο πυλῃσιν,
'Ο χ' ἑτερον μεν κευθει ενι φρεσιν, αλλο δε βαζει. Gr. HOMER.—

"Who dares think one thing, and another tell,
My heart detests him as the gates of hell."

Éclaircissement. Fr.—"An explanation," a "throwing light upon a subject."

Éclat Fr.—"The sports went off with great *éclat*," that is, with great *distinction;* went off *in grand style.*

Éclat de rire. Fr.—"A burst of laughter."

Εδιδαξα σε κυβισταν, και συ βυθισαι με θελεις. Gr. prov.—"I have taught you to dive, and you in return seek, wish, are anxious, to drown me." When I have thatched his house, he would needs throw me down.

Editio princeps. Lat.—"The first edition."

Editiones expurgatae. Lat.—"Editions of works [Greek and Latin works in particular] with the objectionable passages left out; purified editions of such works."

Effodiuntur opes, irritamenta malorum. Lat. OVID.—"Riches, the provocatives, incentives, to evil, are dug out of the bowels of the earth." Men seek with infinite toil that gold, which, being either coveted or misapplied, is productive of almost every sublunary mischief.

Egestas cupida rerum novarum. Lat.—"An eager desire of, ardent craving for, or after, a change of government, a revolution." "Just in proportion as this inflammable element [the democratic press] is scattered through society, is the *egestas cupida rerum novarum,* its natural tinder, at the same time, and from the same causes, extended."

Εγγυα, παρα δ' Ατη. Gr.—"Go, security, but ATE stands beside you," a proverbial expression. This was the saying of THALES, the Ionic philosopher, and of the Seven Sages [wise men] of Greece. "ATE" was an ancient Greek divinity, who visited men with misfortune: the personification of the folly, or improvidence, which brings men into calamity.

Egli m'ha dato un osso da rodere. Ital. prov.—"He has given me a bone to pick, to gnaw at." There's a bone for you to pick.

Ego de caseo loquor, tu de creta respondes. Lat. ERASMUS.—"I talk of chalk, and you of cheese." All the impertinence in *conversation, commerce,* or *business,* is reprehended by this saying, whenever the company do not harmonize in their *discourse,* or keep to the point in *question:* the English is a slightly altered version of the Latin.

Ego ero post principia. Lat. TERENCE.—"I'll take up my station in the rear." To be out of harm's way.

Ego hoc feci. Lat.—"*I* did this, *I* was the man to bring this about."

Ego meorum solus sum meus. Lat. TERENCE.—"I am myself the only friend I have at home."

——————**Ego nec studium sine divite vena,**
Nec rude, quid possit, video ingenium: alterius sic
Altera poscit opem res, et conjurat amice. Lat. HORACE.—"I neither see what art can do without a rich vein, or an uncultivated genius without the help of art: for each requires the other's aid, and conspires with it in a friendly manner, conspires amicably to the same end:"—

"Now art, if not enriched by nature's vein,
And a rude genius, of uncultured strain,

Are useless both; but when in friendship joined,
A mutual succor in each other find."

Again—

"Ah! what can application do,
Unless we have a genius too?
Or genius how have cultivation
Without due pains and application?"

Once more—

"Without a genius learning soars in vain:
And, without learning, genius sinks again:
Their force united crowns the sprightly reign."

————————**Ego, si risi, quod ineptus**
Pastillos Rufillus olet, Gorgonius hircum,
Lividus et mordax videor tibi? Lat. HORACE.—

"If I rally Rufillus for being perfumed, or Gorgonius for being nasty, offensive, must I, therefore, be regarded as envious or ill natured?" If, as a satirist, I lash the knave or coxcomb, shall my honest indignation be set down to the score of malice?

Ego spem pretio non emo. Lat. TERENCE.—"I do not buy hope with money." I do not purchase expectation at so dear a rate.

Εγω δ' ὑπελαβον χρησιμους ειναι Θεους
Τ' αργυριον ἡμιν και το χρυσιον μονον.
'Ιδρυσαμενος τουτους γαρ εις την οικιαν,
Ευξαι τι βουλει, παντα σοι γενησεται·
Αγρος, οικιαι, θεραποντες, αργυρωματα,
Φιλοι, δικασται, μαρτυρες. Gr.—

"I [in opposition to the opinion of some] am of opinion that gold and silver are our only powerful and propitious deities. For when once you have introduced these into your house, wish for what you will, and you will quickly obtain it: an estate, a habitation, servants, plate, friends, judges, witnesses."

Egomet mî ignosco. Lat. HORACE.—"Cant is the epidemic of periodical essayism; but, with an *Egomet mî ignosco*, it is very allowable:" that is, with a *disposition to be on the very best of terms with myself, and to be blind to my faults*, it is, &c. N.B. "*Egomet mî ignosco*" literally means, *I myself pardon myself*, I overlook my own faults.

Egregii mortalis altique silentî. Lat. HORACE.—"A man of uncommon silence and reserve."

Eheu fugaces, Postume, Postume,
Labuntur anni: nec pietas moram
Rugis et instanti senectae
Adferet, indomitaeque morti. Lat. HORACE.—

"Alas! POSTUMUS, POSTUMUS, the fleeting years glide away, swiftly by: nor will your piety bring any delay to wrinkles, to approaching, rapidly advancing, old age, or unconquerable death:"

"How swiftly glide our flying years!
Alas! nor piety nor tears
Can stop the fleeting day;

Deep-furrow'd wrinkles, posting age,
And death's unconquerable rage,
Are strangers to delay."

Compare MIMNERMUS [the celebrated elegiac poet of Smyrna, a city of Asia]:

Ολιγοχρονιον γιγνεται, ὥσπερ οναρ,
'Ηβη τιμηεσσα· το δ' αργαλεον και αμορφον
Γηρας ὑπερ κεφαλης αυτιχ' ὑπερκρεμαται.

"Honored youth, like a dream, lasts but a short time, and soon does distressing and deformed old age hang over one's head."

Eheu! quam brevibus pereunt ingentia causis! Lat. CLAUDIAN.—"Alas! by what slight means are great affairs brought to destruction!" What great events are sometimes brought about from trivial causes!

Eheu! quam temere in nosmet legem sancimus iniquam! Lat. HORACE.—"Alas! how rashly, inconsiderately, do we enact unjust and severe laws against ourselves!"—

"Alas! what laws, of how severe a strain,
Against ourselves we thoughtlessly ordain!"

Ει δειν' εδρασας, δειν' και παθειν σε δει. Gr. SOPHOCLES.—"If thou hast inflicted terrible calamities on others, thou thyself oughtest also to suffer in like manner." "The day will yet come [April, 1815], when an indignant nation will say to this monster [NAPOLEON BUONAPARTE] what ought to have been said on his first overthrow," "Ει δειν', &c."

Ein wörtlein kann ihn fallen. Ger.—"A single little word can strike him dead." Said by LUTHER of the Pope.

Εις το πυρ εκ του καπνου. Gr. prov.—"Out of the smoke into the fire." Out of the frying-pan into the fire.

Ejiciunda haec mollities animi. Lat. TERENCE.—"This weakness of mind must be got rid of; I must get the better of this weakness of mind."

Ejusdem farinae. Lat. prov.—Literally, "of the same meal, flour." Never a barrel the better herring. "This production has been the parent of some other pamphlets *ejusdem farinae*," that is, "of the same kidney."

Ejusdem generis. Lat.—"Of the same kind, description." "That is one instance, and very probably many other instances *ejusdem generis* might be put."

El ciégo mal juzgara de colores. Span. prov.—"The blind man is a bad judge of colors." Blind men can judge no colors.

El consejo de la muger es poco, y el, que no le toma, es loco. Span. prov.—"A woman's counsel is not worth much, but he that despises it is no wiser than he should be."

El dinero haze al hombre entero. Span. prov.—"Money makes the man complete, completes the man, puts the finishing-stroke to the man." God makes, and apparel shapes; but money makes the man.

El Dorado. Span.—Literally, "The Golden." "The *El Dorado* of fashion, that attractive region, into which so many of the middle classes are always struggling or hoping at some time or other to enter. The *El*

Dorado fictions of Raleigh. They indulged in their *El Dorado* anticipations."

El pan comido, la compañia deshecha. Span. prov.—"When good cheer is lacking, our friends will be packing. No longer foster, no longer friend."

El pie del dueño estiercol es para la herededad. Span. prov. —"The foot of the owner is the best manure for his land."

El vientre ayuno no oye a ninguno. Span. prov.—"The empty belly hears no one." The belly hath no ears.

El vino no trae bragas, ni de paño, ni de leño. Span. prov.— "Wine wears neither linen nor woolen breeches." When the wine is in, the wit is out.

El vino, que es bueno, no ha menester pregonero. Span. prov. —"Good wine needs no herald." Good wine needs no bush.

Élan. Fr.—"Enthusiasm, buoyancy."

Elchee. Persian.—"An ambassador, envoy."

Eleemosynary. From the Gr. word *ελεημοσυνη*.—"Alms, assistance, given to the unfortunate." "*Eleemosynary*" means "*relative to charitable donations.*" "The *eleemosynary* sort [of corporations] are such as are constituted for the perpetual distribution of free alms."—BLACKSTONE.

Elegit. Law Lat.—"He has chosen." A judicial writ directed to the sheriff, empowering him to seize for damages recovered.

Ελευθερους αφηκε παντας Θεος ουδενα δουλον ἡ φυσις πεποιηκε. Gr. ALCIDAMAS.—"GOD has sent forth all men free: nature has made no man a slave."

Elige eum, cujus tibi placuit et vita et oratio. Lat. SENECA. —"Choose that man, of whose *life*, as well as of whose *eloquence*, you can approve." Do not be misled by a specious harangue, but consider whether the conduct of the speaker through life has been such as to attach weight and respect to his opinions.

Élite. Fr.—"The best part, portion." "The flower." "The *élite* of the British army."

Elixir vitae. Lat.—"The marrow of existence; the prime of life; the flower of one's age." N.B. "*Elixir*" is an Arabic word, signifying *quintessence.*

Elle n'a que le bec. Fr. prov.—"She is all tongue, does nothing but prate."

Elle n'est plus l'époque de la grande épée. Fr. CHATEAUBRIAND.—"We no longer live in the days of chivalry; the days of chivalry are gone." Literally, "It is no longer the epoch, era, of the powerful sword."

Éloge. Fr.—"Commendation, praise, eulogium, encomium, panegyric."

Ελπιδες εν ζωοισιν, ανελπιστοι δε θανοντες. Gr. prov.—"In the living there are hopes, while the dying are [comparatively speaking] in total despair." The English proverb says, "While there is life, there is hope."

Embarras de richesses. Fr.—"An inexhaustible mine of wealth."

Embonpoint. Fr.—"Plumpness, fleshiness."

Embouchure. Fr.—"The mouth" of a river.

Embryo. From the Gr.—Literally, "That which grows within another body." "An *embryo* statesman," that is, "a statesman in progress of formation."

Emendatio pars studiorum longe utilissima. Lat. QUINTILIAN.—"Correction of one's writings is by far the most profitable part of one's studies."

Emeritus. Lat.—"An *emeritus* Professor of a University," that is, "A Professor who has retired from the duties of his office." N.B. "*Emeriti*," the plural of the above word, was the name given to those Roman soldiers who had served out their time, and had exemption from military service. At the end of their period of service they received a bounty or reward [*emeritum*], either in lands or money, or in both.

Emeute. Fr.—"A riot, disturbance."

Emeutier. Fr.—A new and expressive word, with which LOUIS PHILIPPE enriched his language, signifying a "rioter, rebel, disturber of the public peace, outbreaker."

Emigré. Fr.—"An emigrant." The plural is *émigrés*.

Emir. A title given to those Turks who claim to be of the race of MOHAMMED.

Emitur sola virtute potestas. Lat. CLAUDIAN.—"Power is rightly, properly, obtained by virtue alone, only by virtue:"—

"Virtue alone ennobles human kind,
And power should on her glorious footsteps wait."

Emollit mores, nec sinit esse feros. Lat. OVID.—[Learning, art, the polish of social life] "thoroughly softens men's manners, and prevents their being a pack of brutes, or unlicked cubs." N.B. The rule, however, so far as "learning" is concerned, admits of exceptions innumerable, as we may daily and hourly see.

Empire monstre. Fr.—"The monster empire," that is, the Russian empire.

Empiric. From the Gr.—"A quack, one who relies entirely on practice and experience, without regard to reason and sound philosophy."

Employé. Fr.—"A clerk under government." The plural is *employés*.

Empressement. Fr.—"Eagerness, earnestness."

En ancien camarade. Fr.—"As an old comrade."

En attendant. Fr.—"In the mean time."

En avant. Fr.—"Forward! Onward!" "Look not mournfully into the past: it comes not back again. Wisely improve the present: it is thine. Go forth to meet the shadowy future, without fear and with a manly heart."—LONGFELLOW.

En barbette. Fr. military term.—Said of a battery, when the cannon are higher than the breast-wall.

En beau. Fr.—"In a favorable light."

En bloc. Fr.—"In a lump." "The money will be paid *en bloc*."

En bocca cerrada no entra mosce. Span. prov.—"A close mouth catcheth no flies."

En bon train. Fr.—"In a fair way." "Things were now *en bon train*."

En buste. Fr.—"Half-length."

En cachette. Fr.—"In concealment."

En cavalier. Fr.—"As a gentleman."

En commandite. Fr.—"The prohibition to the partners *en commandite* to take a share in its management would be practically good for nothing." "*Commandite*" is a French commercial term signifying *Partnership, in which the acting partners are responsible without limitation and the sleeping ones to the extent of their share of capital only.* "*Société en commandite*" means "*Company in a partnership of the above description.*"

En connaisseur. Fr.—"As a good judge, as one competent to form an opinion, as one conversant with certain matters."

En dernier ressort. Fr.—"As a last resource, expedient, shift." N.B. "*Ressort*" is one of those French words which we nearly always see spelled incorrectly in English works, thus: *resort* instead of *ressort.*

En déshabille. Fr.—"In undress." "The excellence of DRYDEN's prose is an ease and apparent negligence of phrase, which shows, as it were, a powerful mind *en déshabille,* and free from the fetters of study."

Εν ελπισι χρη τους σοφους εχειν βιον.
Ανθρωπος ατυχων σωζεται ὑπο της ελπιδος. Gr. MENANDER.—
"It behooves the wise to live in hope. The man who is in adversity is sustained, buoyed up, supported, by hope."

En émoi. Fr.—"In a flutter; in commotion; in a thorough ferment."

En famille. Fr.—"Alone, by themselves." "The imperial party dined *en famille.*"

En flûte. Fr.—A large vessel is said to be *en flûte* when she carries only her upper tier of guns; her hold being filled with stores. She is then only a transport of greater force.

En grand seigneur. Fr.—"As a nobleman of the highest rank, distinction: in a lordly style." "MONSIEUR DE TALLEYRAND lived *en grand seigneur,* and saw a great deal of company."

En grande tenue. Fr.—"In full dress."

En grande toilette. Fr.—"Full-dressed," or, as the Anglo-Indians say, "in full fig."

En habiles gens. Fr.—"Like able men, clever fellows."

En mangeant l'appétit se perd. Fr. prov.—"The appetite goes away by eating." Eating and drinking take away one's stomach.

En masse. Fr.—"In a body."

En mauvaise odeur. Fr.—"In bad odor, repute."

Ην νεος, αλλα πενης· νυν γηρων, πλουσιος ειμι.
Ω μονος εκ παντων οικτρος εν αμφοτεροις
Ὁς τοτε μεν χρησθαι δυναμην, ὁποτ' ουδε ἑν ειχον.
Νυν δ' ὁποτε χρησθαι μη δυναμαι, τοτ' εχω. Gr. ANTIPHILUS.—

"Young was I once and poor, now rich and old:
A harder case than mine was never told:
Blest with the power to use them, I had none;
Loaded with riches now, the power is gone."

Εν οἱς αν ατυχηση ανθρωπος τοποις, τουτοις ἡκιστα πλησιαζων ἡδεται. Gr. STOBAEUS.—"Very little pleasure does a man take in visiting places in which he has been unfortunate, has met with misfortunes."

En papillote. Fr.—"In curl-papers." "Her hair was *en papillote.*"

En passant. Fr.—"By the way, by-the-bye;" often applied to a remark *casually* made. "It may be remarked, *en passant*, that his opinion is against the measure."

En pension. Fr.—An old lady, not understanding the convenient system of boarding *en pension* abroad, read a letter from her son, who was then traveling on the continent, and exclaimed, with a look of great delight, "I can't tell what Tom has done to deserve it, but he is now living on a pension at Naples; probably the King has taken a fancy to him: he is, certainly, a very fine lad!" N.B. Boarding *en pension* means *boarding and lodging at a boarding house, or school.*

En plein jour. Fr.—"In open day."

En présence. Fr.—"The *initiative* of operations between two armies *en présence* is a great advantage," that is, "*in sight of each other.*"

En prince. Fr.—"As a prince, like a prince, in the character of a prince."

En rapport. Fr.—"In communication." "He placed himself *en rapport* with the Baron."

En reconnaissance. Fr.—"To verify the correctness of the information, I sent there, *en reconnaissance*, a captain with some volunteers," that is, "*to make personal examination.*"

En règle. Fr.—"In order, as it should be."

En résumé. Fr.—"On the whole."

En revanche. Fr.—"In return, to make up for it." To make amends or requital.

En route. Fr.—"On one's way." "*En route* to Constantinople."

En spectacle. Fr.—"As a show, a gazing-stock." "The author seems to disdain giving himself *en spectacle* to his readers."

En titre. Fr.—"Titular, in name only, having only the name." "The bishop *en titre* of London."

Εν τῳ φρονειν μηδεν ἡδιστος βιος. Gr. Sophocles.—"Sweetest, most pleasant, agreeable, is the life, that is never troubled with thought, with thinking, with indulging in thought." See "*Quibus vivere est cogitare.*"

En tutelle. Fr.—"Under guardianship, wardship." "*Tutelle*" means the "custody by a guardian of a child under age."

En vieillissant on devient plus fou et plus sage. Fr. La Rochefoucault.—"When men grow old, they become more foolish and more wise." At that period of life, some obstinate follies are found to have struck deeper root, whilst others have been stunted, blunted, by the lapse of time and by experience.

Enceinte. Fr.—"An inclosure, inclosed space" [in a cathedral, public building]. "A portion of the *enceinte* was reserved for the members of the Congress."

Encore. Fr.—"Again." The exclamation of the spectators when they wish to hear a public performance repeated.

Endurer la soif auprès d'une fontaine. Fr. prov.—"To put up with thirst near a fountain." What! starve in a cook's shop!

Energie. Fr.—"Energy, activity in-working; inward, or mental, working."

Ενεστι παντων πρωτον ειδεναι ταυτα
Φερειν τα συμπιπτοντα μη παλιγκοτως. Gr. EURIPIDES.—
"It behooves us, as one of our first duties, to know how to bear adversity, a reverse of fortune, with an unruffled mind."

Enfant gâté. Fr.—"A spoiled child." "Is there a cultivated man in Europe, who cannot read with pleasure, long after the occasion has gone by, this reckless, thoughtless, wild, wandering, discursive, gay, good-humored, fertile, fanciful, and sensible writer, this *enfant gâté d'un monde qu'il gâte?*" that is, this spoiled child of a world that he himself spoils [MONSIEUR JULES JANIN].

Enfant terrible. Fr.—"The 'Oxford Union Debating Society' [that nursery of *enfants terribles*] goes on convulsing the nation every week by the most ridiculous debates:" that is to say [according to the idea of the writer of the above sentence], that nursery of *formidable youngsters, in their* OWN *estimation*, of *important personages, &c.* N.B. An "*enfant terrible*" does not mean a *wild young rascal*, or a *pickle*, as many suppose, nor does it mean an *ungovernable, unmanageable, or terrible child*, but *a child that, by ill-timed remarks, innocently made, causes* OTHERS *to have terrible, or terribly annoying, feelings:* for instance, A child may observe, on seeing a smell-feast unexpectedly enter his papa's dining-room, "Oh, Mr. Jones! I didn't think you'd come here to-day; Mamma said she hoped you wouldn't, as you came here *so very often.*" We can readily understand Mamma's feelings on hearing such a remark.

Enfant trouvé. Fr.—"A found child, foundling."

Enfants et fols sont devins. Fr. prov.—"Children and fools speak the truth."

Enfants perdus. Fr.—"Lost children." Those troops which are stationed at the advanced or dangerous posts: in English termed *the forlorn hope* of the army.

Enfermer le loup dans la bergerie. Fr. prov.—"To shut up the wolf in the sheepfold." Metaphorically, to patch up a disease.

Enfilade. Fr. military term.—"A row." Where a battery is placed so that it can fire along a pass, it is said to *enfilade* that pass. The troops within its range are *enfiladed.*

Enfin les renards se trouvent chez le pelletier. Fr. prov.—"The foxes find themselves at length at the fellmonger's, skindealer's." Every fox must pay his own skin to the flayer.

Engouement. Fr.—"Infatuation." "A scene of vulgar *engouement.*" N.B. "*Engouement*" is nearly always spelled wrong in English works, thus, "*engoument.*"

Enjouement. Fr.—"Cheerfulness, gayety, mirth, sprightliness, good humor."

Ennui. Fr.—"Weariness, the not knowing what to do with one's self."

Ennuyant. Fr.—"Annoying, tiresome, irksome."

Ennuyé. Fr.—"Wearied, tired, thoroughly done up." "The diary of an *ennuyé.*"

Ense petit placidam, non libertate, quietem. Lat.—"He seeks to attain, aims at attaining, gentle peace, calm repose, by the sword, and not by giving liberty, freedom, to those under his sway." "There can be no doubt that, *for the moment*, the sword of a dictator is the best, if not the only, safeguard for persons and property; even a patriot might be forgiven for a various reading of ALGERNON SIDNEY's adage:—'*Ense petit,' &c.*" [Written in reference to a notorious character of the present day.]

Enseignement mutuel. Fr.—[The system of] "mutual, or reciprocal, teaching, instruction."

Entente cordiale. Fr.—"A true, good, cordial understanding."

Entourage. Fr.—"Considering the *entourage*, in contact with which the King of Prussia lives daily, it is surprising that he has maintained even a neutral position," that is, "Considering the *persons*, in contact with whom," &c.

Entre deux vins. Fr.—"Between two wines." Neither absolutely drunk nor sober.

Entre le marteau et l'enclume. Fr.—"Between the hammer and the anvil." N.B. "*Être entre le marteau et l'enclume*" is a proverbial expression, signifying, "*to be pressed on all sides with difficulties, to be in a sad mess, fix, position.*"

Entre nous. Fr.—"Between ourselves."

Entrée. Fr.—"Admission, means of admission, entrance, privilege of entrance."

Entremetteuse. Fr.—"An intermediate agent, go-between." N.B. "*Entremetteur*" is the *masculine* form.

Entrepôt. Fr.—"A mart."

Eo magis praefulgebat, quod non videbatur. Lat. TACITUS.—"He shone with the greater splendor, because he was not seen." This expression is used by the historian when speaking of the statue of a great man, which was invidiously removed from the view of a popular procession. It is not improperly employed in speaking of a retired statesman, who may live in the endeared recollection of the people, though withdrawn from their immediate notice.

Eo nomine. Lat. CICERO.—"On this, or that, account; for this, or that, reason."

Eodem collyrio omnibus mederi. Lat.—"To cure all diseases with the same salve." To play the quack, and vend a *panacea* [which see] for the cure of all disorders.

Epanchement. Fr.—"The natural overflow [of familiar confidence]."

Επεα πτεροεντα. Gr. HOMER.—"Winged words." "Read by itself, the translation is good; but along with the original, somewhat tame. We desiderate the *επεα πτεροεντα* of the rushing original."

Επει όστις, αλογησας την ύπερ των πεπραγμενων αισχυνην, ουκ απαξιοι τοις ευτυγχανουσι βδελυρος φαινεσθαι, τουτῳ δη ουδεμια παρανομιας αταρπος αβατος· αλλα την αναιδειαν αει του μετωπου προβεβλημενος ῥαστα τε και ουδενι πονῳ ς των πραξεων τας μιαρωτατας χωρει. Gr. PROCOPIUS.—"When a man stands in no awe of the disgrace which attends bad actions, and has no concern for his character, there is no way of transgression in which that man may not walk. With a countenance clothed in shamelessness and audacity, he easily and naturally proceeds from one bad action to the most profligate attempts."

Επι δυοιν ὁρμειν. Gr. prov.—"To ride at two anchors, to be at harbor, in security:"—

"Good riding at two anchors men have told;
For if one break, the other may hold."

Επι ξυρου, or, επι ξυρου ακμης. Gr. prov.—"In great peril, in most critical circumstances," literally, "on the edge of a razor."

Epicuri de grege porcus. Lat. HORACE.—"Lavish, profligate idle, a mere sensualist, Jerome would have been well selected for the monarch of Westphalia, had Westphalia consisted of nothing but its hogs: '*Epicuri de grege porcus:*'" that is to say, *a hog from the sty of Epicurus, a glutton, a high feeder:*—

"A hog by Epicurus fed."

N.B. The Epicureans [the disciples of Epicurus, the Athenian philosopher], in consequence of the corrupt and degenerate maxims of some of their number, relative to pleasure, were stigmatized, in the popular language of the day, as mere sensualists, though many of them were most undeserving of this obloquy.

Epimuthion. Gr. in Roman characters.—"That which is subjoined to a fable, the moral." "Our conclusion, therefore, the *epimuthion* of our review, is this: that, considered as a man of the world, keenly engaged in the chase after rank and riches, DR. PARR must be pronounced to have failed."

Episcopatus non est artificium transigendae vitae. Lat. ST. AUGUSTINE.—"The office of a Bishop was not devised merely to pass away life [but it is an office of duty, labor, and attention]."

Epithalamium. From the Gr.—"A hymn in honor of a marriage."

Epitome. Gr. in Roman characters.—"A summary, abstract, abridgment, a short cut to, or the nearest way to [any art, science, language, &c.]." "An *epitome* of chemistry."

Equitare in arundine longa. Lat. HORACE.—"There is one mode of exercise, which we venture to recommend to our sedentary friends, which is a sort of compromise between riding and walking, a mode of exercise sanctioned by the philosophic Socrates, the regal Agesilaus, and that versatile genius, Alcibiades—a man who was 'all things to all men,'—we allude to the salutary exercise, immortalized by Horace, that of *equitare in arundine longa:*" that is to say, of *riding on a long stick*, of *riding the reedy cane.*

**————Equitis quoque jam migravit ab aure voluptas
Omnis ad incertos oculos et gaudia vana.** Lat. HORACE.—"Our gentry no longer receive any pleasure through the ear, and relish only delusive shows and barren pomp:"

"But now our knights from wit and genius fly
To pageant shows, that charm the wandering eye."

Corruption of taste now spreads even to the more educated classes.

Equity. [In Law.]—The rules of decision observed by the Court of Chancery. "In the Court of Chancery there are two distinct tribunals; the one ordinary, being a court of common law; the other extraordinary, being a court of equity."—BLACKSTONE.

Era già l'ora, che volge 'l disio
A'naviganti, e'ntenerisce il cuore
Lo dì ch'han detto a dolci amici a Dio;
E che lo nuovo peregrin d'amore
Punge, se ode squilla di lontano,
Che paia 'l giorno pianger, che si muore. Ital. DANTE.—
"It was the hour that wakes regret anew
In men at sea, and melts the heart to tears,
The day whereon they bade sweet friends adieu:—
And thrills the youthful pilgrim on his way
With thoughts of love, if from afar he hears
The vesper bell, that mourns the dying day."—WRIGHT.

Or:—

"'Twas now the hour when fond desire renews
To him who wanders o'er the pathless main,
Raising unbidden tears, the last adieus
Of tender friends, whom fancy shapes again;
When the late-parted pilgrim thrills with thought
Of his loved home, if o'er the distant plain
Perchance his ears the village chimes have caught,
Seeming to mourn the close of dying day."—MERIVALE.

N.B. To the above beautiful lines of DANTE, GRAY was indebted for the opening of his famous "Elegy."

Erat homo ingeniosus, acutus, acer, et qui plurimum et salis habebat et fellis, nec candoris minus. Lat. PLINY.—"He was an ingenious, sharp, and pleasant fellow, and one who had a great deal of wit and satire, with an equal share of good humor." This has been applied to SHERIDAN.

Erectos ad sidera tollere vultus. Lat. OVID.—"To bear themselves proudly as men." "Relieve the lower orders of Ireland from the pressure of want and desperation, teach them to think and to reason, raise them to stand upon their feet, and once more as liberated slaves *erectos ad sidera tollere vultus*, and the tyranny of their priesthood will soon pass away."

Ergo. Lat.—"Therefore."

Eripe turpi colla jugo. Liber, liber sum, dic age. Lat. HORACE.—"For shame, slip your neck out of the collar, and boldly say, I am, and will be, free." An incitement to obtain freedom, and also a stimulus to self-reliance.

Eripuit coelo fulmen, sceptrumque tyrannis. Lat.—"He snatched lightning from heaven, and the scepter from tyrants." This was the exergue of a medal struck in honor of BENJAMIN FRANKLIN, when Ambassador from the United States of America to France. The allusion is to his discovery that the electrical fire and that of lightning are absolutely the same, and to the eminent share which he had in establishing the independence of America, his native country.

——————————**Errat, et illinc**
Huc venit, hinc illuc, et quoslibet occupat artus
Spiritus; eque feris humana in corpora transit,
Inque feras noster. Lat. OVID.—

"Now all things are but altered, nothing dies—
And here and there th' unbodied spirit flies,
By time, or force, or sickness dispossessed,
And lodges, where it lights, in man or beast."

The system of PYTHAGORAS, the celebrated Greek philosopher of Samos [one of the principal islands of that part of the Mediterranean Sea which is now called the *Archipelago*], who believed in the transmigration of souls, and is said to have pretended that he had been EUPHORBUS, the son of PANTHOS, in the Trojan war, as well as various other characters.

———Errat longe, mea quidem sententia,
Qui imperium credat gravius esse aut stabilius,
Vi quod fit, quam illud, quod amicitia adjungitur.

Lat. TERENCE.—"In my judgment, he deceives himself greatly, who imagines that an authority established by force can be more lasting, or of greater weight, than that which is founded on friendship."

Errata. Lat.—"Errors, or misprints. Table of errors, or misprints."

Error personae. Law Latin.—"A mistake in the person." "Such contracts are plainly voidable from *error personae*."

Eruditi. Lat.—"Learned men, men of learning."

Escapade. Fr.—"Prank; frolic; lark; spree."

Escheat. From the old Fr. verb "*escheoir*," to fall out, to expire.—Hence "*escheat*,"—that which becomes forfeited to the king, or other over-lord.

Espion. Fr.—"A spy."

Espionnage. Fr.—"Spying, the spy system."

Esprit de ceux qui n'en ont pas. Fr.—"APPARENT intelligence of those who have no REAL intelligence." "Frank-collecting [among collecting manias [*hobbies*], that *esprit de ceux qui n'en ont pas*] became to persons of large correspondence the nuisance of the day."

Esprit de corps. Fr.—"Brotherhood, brotherly feeling:" literally, the "spirit of the body." That zeal for their mutual honor, which pervades every collective body, such as the gentleman of the army, the bar, &c.

Esprit délicat. Fr.—"A person of refined, of correct, taste."

Esprit épicier. Fr.—"There are coarse and narrow understandings in France, which have neither the creed and feelings of the past, nor those of the future, and which maintain a fixed middle point amid the movement of ideas. This is called *l'esprit épicier*. Applied to literature, to the arts, to the mode of living, and manifesting itself in manner, style, and taste, by something obsolete, vulgar, and awkward, tinged with the ridiculous, this spirit has created what is called *le genre épicier*:" that is to say, This is called *the huckstering mind, intellect, understanding*;—the mind, that bears a close relationship to that which savors of naught but "pounds, shillings, and pence," an "L. S. D. intellect." "*Le genre épicier*" means, *the huckstering, groveling, sordid, grasping, close-fisted, hunks-like tone of mind, style, way, manner, or fashion.*

Esprit fort. Fr.—"A freethinker, rationalist; one who places himself above, or who makes a stand against, generally-received opinions."

Esprit moutonnier. Fr.—"A sheeplike, sheepish, disposition."

"This *esprit moutonnier*, this submission of man to the world's laugh, pervades all ranks."

Esse quam videri malim. Lat.—"I should wish to *be* rather than to *seem*." I should prefer being really estimable to merely being regarded as such by the world.

Est ardelionum quaedam [Romae] natio,
Trepide concursans, occupata in otio,
Gratis anhelans, multa agendo nihil agens,
Sibi molesta, et aliis odiosissima. Lat. PHAEDRUS.—
"There is in every town a certain set of busybodies who are always trotting about in a hurry, hurriedly: very active, though having in reality naught to do: always in a bustle, though they are really idle: panting without a cause, and, in affecting to do much, doing in fact nothing whatever: troublesome to themselves, and a perfect nuisance to others."

Est brevitate opus, ut currat sententia, neu se
Impediat verbis lassas onerantibus aures. Lat. HORACE.—
"There must be a certain brevity in the style [of literary composition], that the sentences may run smoothly, and not overcharge the ear with a useless load of words:"—

"Close be your language: let your sense be clear,
Nor with a weight of words fatigue the ear."

Est demum vera felicitas, felicitate dignum videri. Lat.—PLINY.—"Real happiness consists in appearing to be really deserving of happiness." Splendor which is obtained by dark and tortuous means gains no respect. On worldly greatness it is character alone that stamps the value:—

"Worth makes the *man*, the want of it the *fellow*."

Est furor haud dubius, est manifesta phrenesis,
Ut locuples moriaris, egenti vivere fato. Lat. JUVENAL.—
"It is undoubted, unmistakable, madness, palpable insanity, to live a beggar's life, simply that you may die rich:—

"Now 'tis the veriest madness, to live poor,
And die with bags and coffers running o'er."

Est genus hominum, qui esse primos se omnium rerum volunt,
Nec sunt: hos consector: hisce ego non paro me ut rideant,
Sed eis ultro arrideo, et eorum ingenia admiror simul.
Quidquid dicunt, laudo: id rursum si negant, laudo id quoque:
Negat quis? nego: ait? aio: postremo, imperavi egomet mihi
Omnia assentari: is quaestus nunc est multo uberrimus.
Lat. TERENCE.—
"There is a race of men, who would needs be accounted the first in every thing, but they are not so. These are the men for my purpose. I make court to them not to be laughed at, but to be the first to laugh at them; and at the same time I seem, pretend, to admire their abilities. Whatever they say, I praise it: if they say just the contrary again, I praise that too: does any one deny? I deny: does he affirm? I affirm. In short, I

have made it a law with myself to humor them in every thing. This method of gain is now by far the most profitable."

Compare SHAKSPEARE:—

"*Ham.* Your bonnet to its right use: 'tis for the head.
Osr. I thank your lordship, 'tis very hot.
Ham. No, believe me, 'tis very cold; the wind is northerly.
Osr. It is indifferent cold, my lord, indeed.
Ham. But yet, methinks, it is very sultry and hot for my complexion.
Osr. Exceedingly, my lord; it is very sultry, as it were; I can't tell how."

Compare also JUVENAL:—

"Natio comoeda est. Rides? Majore cachinno
Concutitur: flet, si lacrimas adspexit amici:
Nec dolet. Igniculum brumae si tempore poscas,
Accipit endromidem: si dixeris, aestuo! sudat."

"There [in Greece] every man's an actor, every man acts a part. Do you smile? He is convulsed with a laugh far more hearty: if he spies a tear in his friend's eye, he bursts into a flood of weeping, though in reality he feels no grief. If at the winter solstice you ask for a little fire, he calls for his thick coat. If you say, I am hot! he breaks into a sweat:"—

"GREECE IS A THEATER, WHERE ALL ARE PLAYERS.
For, lo, their patron smiles,—they burst with mirth;
He weeps,—they droop, the saddest souls on earth;
He calls for fire,—they court the mantle's heat;
'Tis warm, he cries,—and they dissolve in sweat."

Est modus in rebus. Lat. HORACE.—"There is a medium in all things." There's reason in roasting eggs.

Est modus in rebus; sunt certi denique fines,
Quos ultra citraque nequit consistere rectum.

Lat. HORACE.—

"There is a medium in all things; there are, in short, certain fixed limits, on either side of which what is right, or rectitude, cannot be found, cannot exist."

"Some certain mean in all things may be found,
To mark our virtues, and our vices bound."

This is a very popular quotation: it is used to illustrate the position that every virtue consists in a due medium. Thus, generosity is the middle virtue, of which avarice and prodigality constitute the two extremes.

Est natura hominum novitatis avida. Lat. PLINY.—"Human nature is fond of novelty."

Est proprium stultitiae aliorum cernere vitia, oblivisci suorum. Lat. CICERO.—"It is the peculiar faculty of fools to discern the faults of others, while they forget their own."

————Est quaedam flere voluptas.
Expletur lacrimis, egeriturque dolor. Lat. OVID.—

"There is a certain pleasure in weeping: grief finds in tears both a satisfaction and a cure." There is, as SHAKSPEARE tells us, "a luxury in grief:" and those know not the workings of the human heart, who attempt the task of consolation before the first bursts of anguish have found free vent.

Est quodam prodire tenus, si non datur ultra.
Lat. HORACE.—
"It is always in our power to advance to a certain point, to arrive at a certain point of wisdom, even if we are not permitted to go further:"—

"Though of exact perfection you despair,
Yet every step to virtue's worth your care."

N.B. In Bentley's Horace the reading of the above line is, "*Est* QUADAM *prodire*," *&c.*

Est quoque cunctarum novitas carissima rerum. Lat. OVID.—"Novelty is the most delightful of all things." It is the constant pursuit of the "idly busy," who constitute so large a portion of mankind. See "*Est natura,*" *&c.* and "*Est ardelionum,*" *&c.*

Est sapientis, quidquid homini accidere possit, id praemeditari ferendum modice esse, si evenerit. Majoris omnino est consilii providere ne quid tale accidat: sed animi non minoris fortiter ferre, si evenerit. Lat. CICERO.—"It is the mark of a wise man ever to consider, reflect, that whatever may happen to him should be borne with patience. It is, however, a mark of greater wisdom to take every precaution against the occurrence of any thing unpleasant, of a reverse of fortune; but it is an indication of a mind in no wise inferior bravely and manfully to submit to any change of fortune, however unpleasant, untoward, unfavorable, unpropitious."

Εσθλον αλεξικακον παση ανιη. Gr.—ATHENAEUS [a learned Greek grammarian, of Naucratis in Egypt, the author of the "*Deipnosophistae,*" that is, the "*Banquet of the Learned,*" a work consisting of an immense mass of anecdotes, of extracts from the ancient writers, and of discussions on almost every conceivable subject, especially on Gastronomy, that is, "the whole mystery of good eating and drinking, of good living"]. —[Wine is] "a potent remedy for sadness."

Estne Dei sedes nisi terra et pontus et aër
Et coelum et virtus? Superos quid quaerimus ultra?
Jupiter est quodcunque vides, quocunque moveris.
Lat. LUCAN.—
"Is there any other seat of the Divinity than the earth, the sea, the air, the heavens, and virtue? Why, then, do we seek a GOD beyond? HE is whatever you see, HE is wherever you move." This passage is often quoted as containing a sublime idea of the Deity, though falling from the pen of a heathen.

Esto perpetua. Lat. FATHER PAUL.—"Be thou perpetual, enduring, lasting." This has often been applied to THE CHURCH, the "*entente cordiale*" [which see], any "*benevolent institution,*" *&c.*

Esto quod esse videris. Lat.—"Be what you seem to be."

Esto (ut nunc multi) dives tibi, pauper amicis.
Lat. JUVENAL.—
"Be (as many in the world now-a-days are) rich to yourself, and poor to your friends: luxurious when alone, parsimonious to your guests:"—

"Be worldly wise; and be, like numbers more,
Rich to yourself, to your dependents poor!"

Esurienti ne occurras. Lat.—"Do not encounter a hungry man." Risk not a contest with desperate necessity.

Et adhuc sub judice lis est. Lat. HORACE.—"And the matter, dispute, is still before the judge, is still pending, is as yet undecided." "He puts in claims to perform the same kind of office, *et adhuc*," *&c.*

Et cetera. Lat.—"And the rest."

Et genus et formam Regina Pecunia donat. Lat. HORACE.—"All-powerful wealth, Sovereign Money, gives both birth and beauty:"—

"Gold, Gold, the Sovereign Queen of all below,
Friends, Honor, Birth, and Beauty can bestow."

Et genus, et virtus, nisi cum re, vilior alga est. Lat. HORACE.—"Both birth and merit, unless accompanied by riches, are held in lower estimation than sea-weed:"—

"But high descent and meritorious deeds,
Unblest with wealth, are viler than sea-weeds."

A maxim that has been consecrated by time and truth.

Et hoc genus omne. Lat.—"And every thing of this kind." When applied to any particular class of individuals, it means, "And all of that kidney [disposition]."

Et male tornatos incudi reddere versus. Lat. HORACE.—"And to return thy badly-polished verses to the *anvil*, to fashion anew every harsh, ill-running verse:"—

"Haste to an anvil with thine ill-formed strain."

Such is the wise recommendation of this great poet. Modern writers, however, are generally too indolent to have recourse to this species of *forgery*.

Et nati natorum, et qui nascentur ab illis. Lat. VIRGIL.—"And the children of our children, and those who shall be born of them."

"From a long line of grandams draws his blood,
And counts his great-great-grandsires from the Flood."

"These things we shall feel and remember, and our *nati natorum*," *&c.* Our posterity to the latest period.

Et quiescenti agendum est, et agenti quiescendum est. Lat. SENECA.—"The active should occasionally rest, and the inactive should apply to labor." The mind as well as the body requires alternate action and repose. Compare OVID:—

"Quod caret alterna requie durabile non est."

"Whatever is without alternate rest, repose [or, as the Scotch say, 'rest turn about'], is not, cannot be durable, lasting, of long continuance."

Et qui nolunt occidere quenquam, posse volunt. Lat. JUVENAL.—"Even those, who do not wish to kill a man, are willing to have that power, would gladly have the *power*."

"'Tis nature, this; e'en those who want the will,
Pant for the dreadful privilege to kill."

Such is the spirit of ambition in the human mind, that even those, who are least likely to abuse their power, wish for a control over their equals.

Et sic de similibus. Lat.—"And so of the like." What is said of this will apply to every thing similar.

Et spes, et ratio studiorum in CAESARE tantum. Lat. JUVENAL.—"All our hope and inducement to study rest on CAESAR [the Sovereign] alone:"

"Yes, all the hopes of learning, 'tis confest,
And all the patronage, on CAESAR rest."

Compare TACITUS:—*Sublatis studiorum pretiis, etiam studia peritura.* "Take away the rewards for study, and study would soon be altogether neglected."

Étalage. Fr.—"Display; show; parade; ostentation."

État-major. Fr.—"A military staff."

Ethel. Sax.—"Noble."

Ethel-bald. "Noble and bold."

Ethel-bert. "Noble advised."

Ethel-bild. "Noble image."

Ethel-burg. "Noble fortress."

Ethel-frid. "Noble peace."

Ethel-gund. "Noble favor bearing."

Ethel-stan. "Noblest."

Ethel-ulph. "Noble help."

Ethel-wald. "Upholder of honor."

Ethel-ward. "Conserver of nobility."

Ethel-win. "Winner of nobility."

Ethics. From the Gr.—The science of morals.

Etiam fortes viri subitis terrentur. Lat. TACITUS.—"Even bold men are shaken by sudden events." Events that are unforeseen will sometimes ruffle the most even temper and disturb the firmest mind. The strongest mind is not proof against the influx of surprise.

Etiam in falso verax. Lat.—"*Intentionally* true, true of speech, truthful even in false, *unintentionally* erroneous, assertions."

Etiam oblivisci quod scis interdum expedit. Lat. PUBLIUS SYRUS.—"It is sometimes expedient to forget [to seem to forget] what you know." It is sometimes expedient, a measure of policy, to dissemble, and to withhold even the positive knowledge of facts, when one has to deal with an artful adversary.

Étourderie. Fr.—"A thoughtless or giddy act, action." "A piece of thoughtlessness, heedlessness."

Être au bout de son rôlet, ou rouleau. Fr.—"To be at one's wits' end."

Être pauvre sans être libre, c'est le pire état où l'homme puisse tomber. Fr. ROUSSEAU.—"To be poor without being free, is the worst state into which man can fall." Poverty and slavery united undoubtedly form the worst condition of human existence.

Être sur un grand pied dans le monde. Fr. prov.—"To be on a great foot, footing, in the world." This proverb originated at the time when a man's rank was known by the size of his shoes. Those of a prince measured two feet and a half, a plain cit. was allowed only twelve inches.

Εν μεταφορειν εστιν εν θεωρειν. Gr. ARISTOTLE.—"To manage metaphors with discretion is the mark of a just and comprehensive mind." See "*Et male tornatos*," *&c.*

Ευδαιμονιας χαριν τα λοιπα παντες παντα πραττομεν. Gr. ARISTOTLE.—"'Tis for the sake of happiness that we all of us do all other things whatsoever."

Ευδαιμων ὁ μηδεν οφειλων. Gr.—"Happy is the man who owes nothing." Out of debt out of danger.

Ευδαιμονια χρασις αρετας εν ευτυχια. Gr. ARCHYTAS.—"Happiness is the use or exercise of virtue, attended with external good fortune." N.B. ARCHYTAS was one of the Pythagoric preceptors of Plato [the Athenian philosopher, the most learned and eloquent of all the Greeks], and a native of Tarentum [an important Greek city in Italy]. He excelled not only in speculative philosophy, but also in geometry and mechanics, and is said to have invented a kind of winged *automaton* [*any piece of art that seems to move of itself, as a clock, jack, &c.*], and several curious hydraulic machines [machines moved by water]. He was also a distinguished general and statesman.

Euge! Gr. in Roman letters.—An expression of encouragement or praise. "Well done! very well, bravo!"

Euphemism. From the Gr.—A mode of expression by which one avoids making direct mention of indecent, melancholy, or disagreeable things: thus, the Furies [the avenging deities of the heathen Mythology, TISIPHONE, ALECTO, and MEGAERA] are denominated EUMENIDES, "the benign, well-meaning, soothed, goddesses."

Euthanasia. Gr. in Roman letters.—"A mild, happy, easy, honorable, death." "He can tolerate the Church of England, when it has acquired a capacity of witnessing to the great and final truth, that the *euthanasia* of the Church is absorption in the State." N.B. "*Euthanasia*" among divines [writers or speakers on divinity, theology, that is, "the science which treats of the origin of religious worship," "the act of giving instruction in religious matters"] means "*death in a state of grace.*"

Evènement. Fr.—"An event." A grand affair.

Everso [missus] succurrere seculo. Lat. VIRGIL.—"Sent to succor the troubled ages, or times:"

"A Prince now sent to save a sinking age."

Applied to THE YOUNG PRETENDER.

Evitata Charybdi in Scyllam incidere. Lat. prov.—"To fall into [the clutches of] SCYLLA, after escaping CHARYBDIS." Out of the frying-pan into the fire. N.B. "SCYLLA and CHARYBDIS were the names of two rocks between Italy and Sicily. In the one nearest to Italy was a cave, in which dwelt SCYLLA, a daughter of CRATAEIS, a fearful monster, barking like a dog, with twelve feet, and six long necks and heads, each of which contained three rows of sharp teeth. The opposite rock, which was much lower, contained an immense fig-tree, under which dwelt CHARYBDIS, who thrice every day swallowed down the waters of the sea, and thrice threw them up again. This is the Homeric account."—DR. WILLIAM SMITH.

Ex abundantia. Lat.—"From one's inexhaustible stock, resources." "We like his outpourings, *ex abundantia*, of various and copious reading."

Ex abusu non arguitur in usum. Lat. Law maxim.—"No argument can be drawn from the abuse of a thing against its use." If a principle or practice be perverted from its right meaning or end, no solid argument against either can be drawn from such perversion. We have heard of debtors having been made the victims of personal spleen by their creditors; but it would not be fair to argue, on this ground alone, against the practice of imprisonment for debt.

Ex acervo. Lat.—"Out of, or from, a heap." "Unfortunately they [certain ruffian expressions] are selected *ex acervo* [of similar expressions], and, still more unfortunately, they need no comment."

Ex adverso. Lat.—"On an opposite principle, in opposition [to some thing or other]."

Ex animo. Lat.—"Conscientiously, in perfect sincerity, heartily, from the heart."

Ex aperto. Lat.—"Openly."

Ex cathedra. Lat.—"From the professional chair, with an air of authority." "To the readers of this review the cardinal speaks *ex cathedra.*"

Ex commodo. Lat.—"Leisurely."

Ex concesso. Lat.—"From what has been granted." "Arguments *ex concesso*, that is, Arguments from admissions made by an adversary, an opponent."

Ex confesso. Lat.—"By one's own confession, confessedly." N.B. "*In confesso*" may be used to express the same idea.

Ex continenti. Lat.—"Immediately."

Ex curia. Lat.—"Out of court."

Ex debito justitiae. Lat.—"From what is due to justice."

Ex delicto. Lat.—"From the crime."

Ex dono Dei. Lat.—"By the gift of GOD."

Ex facie. Lat.—"Manifestly, evidently." "The languages of this country and of France are, *ex facie* [on the very face of them], those of the two *active* nations of modern Christendom."

Ex facili. Lat.—"Easily."

Ex facto jus oritur. Lat. Law maxim.—"The law arises out of the fact." Until the fact be settled, the law cannot apply.

Ex fide. Lat.—"Faithfully."

Ex fumo dare lucem. Lat. HORACE.—"Out of smoke to bring glorious light:"—

"Thus from a cloud of smoke to break to light."

"After an hour's toilsome pruning and interlining, I succeeded in reducing the metaphysical *chaos* to something like 'pure reason,' so as *ex fumo dare lucem.*" See "CHAOS," and "*Non fumum ex fulgore,*" *&c.*

Ex. gra. Lat.—"For instance, example." "*Ex. gra.*" is an abridgment of "*Exempli gratia,*" which *literally* means "*for the sake of an instance*, or *example* [a thing brought in, forward, a thing adduced, for the proof and declaration of a matter]."

Ex hoc malo proveniat aliquod bonum. Lat.—"From this evil some real good may spring." "If stage-plays," said he, "must be tolerated, let every stage in London pay a weekly pension to the poor, that *ex hoc malo proveniat aliquod bonum.*"

——————**Ex humili magna ad fastigia rerum**
Extollit, quoties voluit Fortuna jocari. Lat. JUVENAL.—"Fortune, whenever she is in a sportive mood, raises fools, low-minded, vulgar fellows, from the dust to the highest pinnacle of greatness:"—

"Fortune, I loud proclaim, Dame Fortune throws
Her more peculiar smiles on such as those,
Whene'er, to wanton merriment inclined,
She lifts to thrones the dregs of human kind!"

Ex hypothesi. Lat.—"On a supposition, suppositionally, hypothetically." An "*hypothesis*" is a supposition, founded on a principle assumed, and sometimes also an imaginary principle, or subject, maintained for the sake of argument in schools of rhetoric [the art of oratory].

Ex illo fluere ac retro sublapsa referri. Lat. VIRGIL.—"From that time their prospects vanished and rapidly took an unfavorable turn." "From this very period [the Revolution of July] must the decline of journalism in France be dated—*ex illo fluere ac retro sublapsa referri*—prosperity paved the way for corruption; another such victory, and they are undone."

Ex improviso. Lat.—"Suddenly, unawares."

Ex industria. Lat.—"On purpose, purposely."

Ex insidiis. Lat.—"Privily."

Ex insperato. Lat.—"Unexpectedly."

Ex integro. Lat.—"Afresh, anew."

Ex intervallo. Lat.—"At some distance."

Ex longinquo. Lat.—"From a great distance, a great way off."

Ex materna. Lat.—"By the mother's side." See "*Ex paterna.*"

Ex mero motu. Lat.—"From a mere motion." From a man's own free will, without suggestion or constraint. This formula [set form of words] is sometimes inserted in charters and letters-patent, as a bar to exceptions, signifying that the king acted from his own free will, and was not influenced by false suggestions.

Ex necessitate. Lat.—"Necessarily."

Ex necessitate rei. Lat.—"From the necessity of the case." Arising from the urgency of circumstances.

Ex nihilo nihil fit. Lat.—"Nothing can come of nothing: out of nothing nothing is made, created." No beneficial result can be expected where the basis is unsolid.

Ex obliquo. Lat.—"Athwart, across, overthwart."

Ex occulto. Lat.—"Secretly."

Ex officio. Lat.—"By virtue of his office, officially." "He is a trustee *ex officio.*"

Ex ordine. Lat.—"Orderly, in order."

Ex parte. Lat.—"Partly, on one side." "*Ex parte* evidence," that testimony which, as before a grand jury, is delivered in only on the side of the prosecution. "An *ex parte* statement," that is, a *one-sided* statement.

Ex parte regis. Lat.—"On the king's side."

Ex paterna. Lat.—"By the father's side." "She claimed as nearest of kin *ex paterna.*"

Ex pede Herculem. Lat.—"You may judge of the size of the statue of HERCULES from that of the foot." You may decide upon the whole from the specimen which is furnished. N.B. HERCULES, called HERACLES by the Greeks, was the most celebrated of all the heroes of antiquity.

Ex professo. Lat.—"Professedly, avowedly."

Ex proposito. Lat.—"Purposely, designedly."

Ex quovis ligno non fit Mercurius. Lat. prov.—"A Mercury is not made, not carved, out of every, any, piece of wood." You cannot make a silk purse out of a sow's ear: you can't make a horn of a pig's tail. N.B. MERCURY was a Roman divinity of commerce and gain.

Ex schedis. Lat.—"The book is one of those which are only allowed to be read *ex schedis;* in other words, prohibited."

Ex supervacuo. Lat.—"Superfluously."

Ex tempore. Lat.—"Without premeditation, without previous study, off-hand." "He prays *ex tempore,* he preaches *ex tempore.*" N.B. "*Extemporary*" is preferable as an adjective to *ex tempore,* which is used as an adverb, and ought, for the sake of precision, to be confined to that use. Thus we say with propriety, an *extemporary prayer,* an *extemporary sermon,* but, He speaks *ex tempore.*

Ex transverso. Lat.—"Across."

Ex tuto. Lat.—"Safely."

Ex ungue leonem. Lat. prov.—"To judge of the whole by a part," *literally,* to judge of the size of the lion by his claw.

Ex vano. Lat.—"Foolishly, without cause, falsely."

Ex vero. Lat.—"Truly."

Ex voto. Lat.—"From a vow, in consequence of a vow." "This group of three figures is what the learned call an *ex voto,*" that is, a *votive offering.*

Ex viribus vivimus. Lat. GALEN [A very celebrated physician born at Pergamum, a city of Asia Minor].—"We live on our forces, by our strength."

Exaltado progresista. Span.—"A radical."

Excelsior. Lat.—"Higher." "EXCELSIOR" should be inscribed on one of the walls of every counting-house. One's hold of present good can only be insured by his struggling after greater; that is, "HIGHER AND HIGHER STILL" should be, &c.

"It boots not," says ARNOLD, "to look backwards. Forwards! forwards! forwards! should be one's motto."

Compare SHAKSPEARE:—

"'Tis but a base, ignoble mind
That mounts no higher than a bird can soar."

"EXCELSIOR" has been adopted by the United States as a motto, to intimate the soaring character of that republic.

Exceptio probat regulam. Lat. Law maxim.—"The exception proves the rule, the existence of the rule; proves that the rule exists, or is in existence."

Excerpta. Lat.—"Extracts." Abridged notices taken from books, newspapers, &c. Passages selected, culled, from various authors.

Excessus in jure reprobatur. Lat. Law maxim.—"All excess is condemned by the law." Whatever the law ordains must be within the rules of reason. Thus, the law awards liberal, but by no means allows excessive, damages.

Excursions dans l'infini. Fr.—"Excursions into the deep, boundless, and unfathomable: excursions in the region of theories." See "*In nubibus.*"

Excursus. Lat.—"A digression, running-off, from the main subject:" an "*episode,*" which see. "Still more uncalled for is an *excursus* concerning BUCHANAN."

Exeat. Lat.—A term in use at the University of CAMBRIDGE, signifying, "He may go out [of college to his home, may go home], may take his departure, may withdraw for a time." A written permission for a student to go home, signed by the College Tutor.

Exeat aula, qui vult esse pius. Lat. LUCRETIUS.—"Let him, who wishes to be good, upright, uncorrupted, unpolluted, uncontaminated, withdraw from Court." The early satirists looked upon Courts as hotbeds of immorality.

Exegi monumentum. Lat. HORACE.—"I have reared, erected, completed, a monument, or memorial." "The nation which erected Greenwich Hospital may reply to the Utilitarians, 'If I prefer this mode, what is that to you? *exegi monumentum.*'" N.B. The *full* expression is, "*Exegi monumentum aere perennius,*" "I have reared a memorial of myself more enduring than brass:"

"More durable than brass the frame
Which here I consecrate to Fame."

This line was penned in allusion to the poems that HORACE had written, which he was conscious would endure to the end of time. The expression is now generally used in an ironical sense.

Exemplar vitiis imitabile. Lat. HORACE.—"An example easy to be imitated in its faults." The *full* expression is, "*Decipit exemplar vitiis imitabile,*" "An example easy to be imitated in its faults is sure to deceive the ignorant:"—

"By such examples many a coxcomb's caught,
Whose utmost art can imitate a fault."

**———————Exemplaria Graeca
Nocturna versate manu, versate diurna.** Lat. HORACE.—"Consider well, pore over, ruminate or reflect on, the Greek originals [the writings of the Greeks], and study them both day and night:"—

"Make the Greek authors your supreme delight;
Read them by day, and study them by night."

A precept not to be lost sight of, even by a modern.

Exemplo plus quam ratione vivimus. Lat.—"We live more by example than by reason." Most men act rather on the precedents set by others, in like cases, than on their own individual judgment.

**Exemplo quodcunque malo committitur, ipsi
Displicet auctori.** Lat. JUVENAL.—"Every act that is perpetrated, that will furnish a precedent for crime, is loathsome even to the author himself:"—

"Man, wretched man, whene'er he stoops to sin,
Feels, with the act, a strong remorse within."

Exeunt omnes. Lat.—"All go, take their departure."

Exigence. Fr.—"Exaction, expected observance, requirement." "*Exigence* of certain customary forms." N.B. "*Exigence*" is very often *incorrectly* written *exigeance.*

Exigite ut mores teneros ceu pollice ducat,
Ut si quis cera vultum facit. Lat. JUVENAL.—
"Require, ye parents, of him that is to teach your boys, that he mold their youthful morals as one models a face in wax:"

"Bid him, besides, his daily pains employ
To form the tender manners of the boy,
And work him, like a waxen babe, with art,
To perfect symmetry in every part."

The effect of a liberal education on the character.

Exigui numero, sed bello vivida virtus. Lat. VIRGIL.—"Small in number, but of tried and war-proof valor." A quotation frequently resorted to for the purpose of encouraging the smaller to resist the greater force.

Exit. Lat.—"A walking off, away, a departure." The *literal* meaning of "*exit*" is, "he or she goes out." "He effected his *exit* with the cash."

Exit, et obducto late tenet omnia limo. Lat. VIRGIL.—"He goes forth, and slashes at everybody and every thing right and left with the outpourings of his filth."

Exitus acta probat. Lat. OVID.—"The issue, end, of a business proves the nature of the acts, deeds." "All's well that ends well. The evening crowns the day."

Exodus. From the Gr.—"Departure, going out, forth." The book which describes the departure of the Israelites from Egypt.

Exordium. Lat.—"A beginning, preface, preamble, proem, commencement, introduction to a discourse." "His *exordium* was admirable." "A pithy *exordium.*"

Exoteric. From the Gr.—"External." "Εξωτερικοι" [*exoterikoi*], *applied to the disciples of philosophers*, means, those who were *not* as yet admitted to the study of the more abstruse branches of science, or to whom the more secret parts of the doctrine of their master were not revealed; *the others were denominated* "εσωτερικοι" [*esoterikoi*]. **Esoteric,** from the Gr.—"Internal."

———————**Experiar quid concedatur in illos,**
Quorum Flaminia tegitur cinis, atque Latina.
Lat. JUVENAL.—
"I will try what I may be allowed to vent on those, whose ashes are covered by the Flaminian or Latin road:"

"Yet I MUST write: and since these iron times
From living knaves preclude my angry rhymes,
I point my pen against the guilty dead,
And pour its gall on each obnoxious head."

Experientia docet. Lat.—"Experience teaches us, is our instructor." Compare SHAKSPEARE:—"Experience is a jewel. And it had need be so: for it is often purchased at an infinite rate."—*Merry Wives of Windsor.* Again:—"Many gain experience at a price that makes them sad "—*As You like it.* "To wish that others should learn by our experience is sometimes as idle as to think that we can eat and they be filled. But, when we find that we have eaten poison, it is, doubtless, mercy to warn them against the dish."

Experientia stultorum magistra. Lat. prov.—"Experience is the mistress of fools."

Experimenta in corpore vili. Lat.—"Experiments on the insignificant human frame, experiments on the human frame, that cost one nothing."

Experimentum crucis. Lat.—"The experiment of the cross." A bold and decisive experiment. The original use of this phrase is unknown. It is variously said to be a *cross* or direction-post for the guidance of others; or a sort of torture, by which truth has been elicited by force.

Experto crede. Lat. VIRGIL.—"Believe one, who has experience to justify his opinion." N.B. In the *original* passage the words are, "*Experto credite.*"

Expertus metuit. Lat. HORACE.—"The man who has had experience of it, dreads it." The original application was to the friendship of the great. The phrase, however, is often and variously applied.

Explebo numerum, reddarque tenebris. Lat. VIRGIL.—"I will fill up the number [*of the ghosts, departed spirits*], and be rendered back to darkness; I will quit the scene, mingle with the 'madding crowd,' and then sink into oblivion [the fate of all mankind]."

"The number I'll complete,
Then to obscurity well pleased retreat."

Explorant adversa viros. Perque aspera dura
Nititur ad laudem virtus interrita clivo.

Lat. SILIUS ITALICUS.—

"Adversity tries men; but virtue struggles after, strives to attain, fame regardless of the adverse heights." The former portion of this quotation refers to an axiom which is universally admitted.

Exposé. Fr.—"An exposure, showing-up." N.B. "*Exposition,*" and not "*exposé,*" is the *right* French term.

Exposé de motifs. Fr.—"A statement of reasons, motives, grounds, causes."

Expressio unius est exclusio alterius. Lat. Law maxim.—"The naming of one man is the exclusion of the other."

Expressum facit cessare tacitum. Lat. Law maxim.—"A matter expressed causes that to cease which otherwise, by intendment of law, would have been implied." An express covenant qualifies the generality of the law, and restrains it from going further than is warranted by the agreement of the parties.

Exsilium non supplicium est, sed perfugium portusque supplicii. Lat. CICERO.—"Banishment from one's country is not [in all cases] punishment, but a place of refuge and shelter from punishment." The Roman senator, however, thought very differently of the matter when banishment fell to his own lot. N.B. DR. LANG took the above celebrated expression for the *motto* to his "History of New South Wales."

Extra Ecclesiam Anglicanam. Lat.—"Out of the pale of the

Church of England," in opposition to "*Intra Ecclesiam Anglicanum,*" Within the pale of the Church of England.

Extra muros. Lat.—"Beyond the walls [of a city]."

Extravagants. From the Lat.—One portion of the Canon Law. "Gratian's decree, Gregory's decretals, the sixth decretal, the Clementine Constitutions, and the *extravagants* of JOHN and his successors, form the *corpus juris canonici,*" that is, "the body of the canon law."—BLACKSTONE.

Extravaganza. Ital.—"A thoroughly outrageous performance, any thing outrageous, preposterous."

Extrema gaudii luctus occupat. Lat.—"Often does sorrow succeed, take the place of, intense joy." No joy without annoy.

F.

Fa buono a te e tuoi, e poi agli altri se tu puoi. Ital. prov.—"Do good to, for, thyself and thine, and afterwards to, for, others if thou canst." Charity begins at home.

Faber compedes, quas fecit ipse, gestet. Lat. prov.—"Let the smith wear the fetters which he himself made." Every bird must hatch her own egg.

Faber fortunae suae. Lat.—"The architect, founder, of his own fortune." N.B. The *original* expression, which occurs in SALLUST [the distinguished Roman historian], is, "*Suae quisque fortunae faber,*" "Every one is [more or less] the maker of his own fortune."

Fac simile. Lat.—"Do the like thing." A close imitation: An engraved or lithographed resemblance of a person's handwriting.

Façade. Fr.—"The front of a building."

Facetiae. Lat.—"Jests, jokes, repartees, facetiousness, drollery, raillery, witty and pleasant sayings."

Facetiarum apud praepotentes in longum memoria est. Lat. TACITUS.—"The powerful hold in deep remembrance an ill-timed pleasantry." It is dangerous to sport with the feelings of the great. An unlucky jest has often been construed into a crime by a despotic sovereign, or an arbitrary government.

Facienda. Lat.—"Things to be done."

————————Facies non omnibus una,
Nec diversa tamen, qualem debet esse sororum.

Lat. OVID.—

"The face was not the same with all: it was not, however, materially different: the resemblance was such as should appear between sisters." These lines, which were originally used to express a family likeness, are now employed to mark those political circumstances which, from their similitude, bespeak the same political parent.

Facies tua computat annos. Lat. JUVENAL.—"Your face shows, proclaims, is the tell-tale of, your years." A man need not look in your mouth to know how old you are.

Facile est inventis addere. Lat.—"It is easy to add to things already invented, easy to improve an invention." A maxim frequently quoted abroad, in order to vilify the English genius. But, leaving our original inventions out of the question, every unprejudiced man will allow that the improvements which this country has made have incalculably outvalued the hints which, in some particular cases, we have borrowed.

Facile invenies et pejorem, et pejus moratam:
Meliorem neque tu reperies, neque sol videt.

Lat. PLAUTUS.—

"You will easily find a worse woman: a better the sun ne'er shone upon."

Facile omnes, cum valemus, recta consilia aegrotis damus.
Tu si hic sis, aliter sentias. Lat. TERENCE.—

"We can all, when we are well, give good counsel to the sick. Were you in my place, you would feel otherwise, you'd think very differently." We think and feel for others differently from what we should do for ourselves were we in a similar situation.

——————**Facile omnes perferre ac pati,**
Cum quibus erat cunque una: his sese dedere,
Eorum obsequi studiis, advorsus nemini,
Nunquam praeponens se aliis: ita facillime
Sine invidia invenias laudem, et amicos pares.

Lat. TERENCE.—

"To bear with everybody's humors, to comply with the inclinations and pursuits of those with whom one converses, to contradict no one, and never to assume a superiority over others. This is the ready way to gain applause and to make friends, without exciting envy." The way to obtain general approbation.

Facile princeps. Lat. CICERO.—"The admitted, acknowledged, chief." The first man, without dispute. "ERATOSTHENES was one of the most distinguished of Greek men of learning, ranking, probably, next to the *facile princeps* of them all,—ARISTOTLE."

——————**Facilis descensus Averni:**
Sed revocare gradum superasque evadere ad auras,
Hoc opus, hic labor est. Lat. VIRGIL.—

"Easy is the descent from Avernus to the lower world: but, to retrace one's steps, and escape to the upper regions, this is, indeed, a work of difficulty, this is, indeed, a task:"—

"Avernus' gates are open night and day,
Smooth the descent, and easy is the way:
But to return to heaven's pure light again,
This is a work of labor and of pain."

The poet speaks of the descent of AENEAS [the Trojan hero] into the infernal regions, in order to have an interview with his father ANCHISES. In its general application, it means that it is much easier for a man to get into difficulty or danger than to extricate himself from it.

Facilis rigidi cuivis censura cachinni. Lat. JUVENAL.—"Easy enough to any one is the stern censure of a sneering laugh."

Facilius crescit quam inchoatur dignitas. Lat. LABERIUS.—"It is more easy to obtain an accession of dignity than to acquire it in the first instance." It is with respect as with opulence: the first beginnings of both are difficult, but each is afterwards easily increased.

Facillime princeps. Lat.—"The undoubted chief, the leading man, by far the most distinguished character."

Facinus, quos inquinat, aequat. Lat. LUCAN.—"Those whom guilt stains, it equals." This expression is nervous and happy. Nothing can be so great a leveler as the mutual consciousness of criminality.

Facit indignatio versus. Lat. JUVENAL.—"Indignation, anger, gives birth to verses, prompts one to write verses, poetry; verses often flow from indignation." Strong feelings impel one to write.

Faciunt nae intelligendo ut nihil intelligant. Lat. TERENCE. —"Truly, by affectation of knowledge men often make it plain that they know nothing at all; while some individuals pretend to know more than others, they in reality know nothing." Pretenders to superior knowledge are often mere impostors.

Façon de parler. Fr.—"A form of speech, mode, manner of speaking."

Factotum.—A word compounded of the two Latin words "*Fac*," do thou, and "*totum*," the whole. One who does all sorts of work, a do-all, drudge, jack of all trades.

"He had one male attendant, thin and lean
As Romeo's Mantuan apothecary,
Who daily swept his dusty office clean,
And copied his accounts with caution wary;
In short, was his *factotum* every way,
Burdened with labor, and but little pay."

Faex populi. Lat.—"The dregs of the people." Contemptuously applied to the lower classes.

Fainéantise. Fr.—"Idleness, sluggishness, laziness." N.B. "*Fainéantise*" is often incorrectly written by English persons "*fainéantisme*," a word which does not exist.

Faire bonne mine à mauvais jeu. Fr.—"To set the best face on the matter."

Faire de l'esprit. Fr.—"To be witty, show off one's wit."

Faire planche. Fr.—"To pave the way, be a stepping-stone to any thing."

Faire sans dire. Fr.—"To act without ostentation, parade, display."

Faire une chose à bis et à blanc, or **à bâtons rompus.** Fr.—"To do a thing by hook or by crook, by fits and starts."

Faire valoir. Fr.—"To bring [things] to bear."

Faire voile à tout vent. Fr. prov.—"To set up one's sail to every wind."

Fait accompli. Fr.—"A deed that has been brought to bear, brought to completion."

Fakeer.—A wandering Indian beggar.

Fallacia alia aliam trudit. Lat. TERENCE.—"One imposture or fallacy produces another." Any one falsehood or deceit is naturally the parent of many others.

Fallentis semita vitae. Lat. HORACE.—"The path of a life that passes unnoticed by the world, path of an humble life."

Fallit [enim] vitium, specie virtutis et umbra,
Cum sit triste habitu, vultuque et veste severum.
Lat. JUVENAL.—"Vice deceives men under the guise and semblance of virtue, since it is frequently grave in bearing, and austere in look and in dress:"—

"Vice oft is hid in virtue's fair disguise,
And in her borrowed form escapes inquiring eyes."

Such is the garb and appearance which is generally worn by profound hypocrisy.

Fallitur egregio quisquis sub principe credet
Servitium. Nunquam libertas gratior exstat
Quam sub rege pio. Lat. CLAUDIAN.—"He who thinks it slavery to live under an excellent prince, is deceived. Never does liberty appear in a more gracious form than under a pious king." This was at one time poetic incense offered to an Emperor. It is now quoted as an axiom by the advocates for absolute monarchy.

Falsum in uno, falsum in omni. Lat.—"False, or erroneous, in one point, false in every point, or respect." "There is no juster maxim of general law than *falsum in uno, falsum in omni*."

Falsus honor juvat, et mendax infamia terret
Quem, nisi mendosum et medicandum? Lat. HORACE.—"Whom does undeserved honor delight, and lying calumny terrify, but the vicious man, and him that stands in need of a cure?"—

"False praise can charm, unreal shame control,
Whom, but a vicious or a sickly soul?"

If the judgment of an unreasonable multitude can make an impression on you, if you rejoice in being falsely thought virtuous, or if you are afflicted in being unjustly believed a dishonest man, your weakness proceeds from the same vicious principle, and you must apply to reason and philosophy for a cure.

Fama. Lat.—"A rumor, report." "A committee was appointed for the purpose of instituting the necessary inquiries in regard to the *fama*."

Famae damna majora quam quae aestimari possint. Lat. LIVY.—"The injury done to character is greater than can possibly be estimated." Compare SHAKSPEARE:—

"Good name in man or woman, dear my lord,
Is the immediate jewel of their soul.
Who steals my purse, steals trash;
'Tis something, nothing: 'twas mine, 'tis his,
And has been slave to thousands:
But he, who filches from me my good name,
Robs me of that which not enriches him,
And makes me poor indeed!"

Familiare est hominibus omnia sibi ignoscere nihil aliis remittere. Lat. VELLEIUS PATERCULUS.—"It is a common practice to overlook every fault in ourselves, but none in others." "It is our own vanity," says ROCHEFOUCAULT, "that makes the vanity of others intolerable."

Famosi libelli. Lat. SUETONIUS.—"Libels on the state, scurrilous pamphlets."

Fanaticus verius quam impostor, qui sibi aeque ac aliis imposuit. Lat.—"A fanatic, a frantic, mad enthusiast, rather than an impostor, who imposed on himself as much as on others." Applied by VENEMA to MANI, the founder of the sect of the Manicheans.

Fanfaron. Fr.—"A bully, boaster, braggadocio."

Fanfaronnade. Fr.—"Swaggering, boasting, bragging."

Far niente. Ital.—"A do-nothing, frivolous kind of fellow."

Fari quae sentiat. Lat. HORACE.—"To say what one thinks." To speak openly and honestly.

Farrago. Lat.—"A mixture, jumble, hodgepodge."

Farrago libelli. Lat. JUVENAL.—"A hotch-potch of a book, the motley subject of one's page." "The remainder of the *farrago libelli* is hashed up chiefly from exaggerated statements, collected from hearsay only."

Fas est et ab hoste doceri. Lat. OVID.—"It is allowable to derive instruction even from an enemy; we may learn something even from an enemy." He who notices the mistakes of a foe gains thereby a lesson of advantage. "It is," says COLTON, "always safe to learn, even from our enemies: seldom safe to venture to instruct, even our friends."

Fasciculus. Lat.—"A packet, parcel [of letters, books], mass of [literary] information, details, particulars." "This agreeable *Fasciculus* has been most judiciously arranged."

Fastens-e'en.—Shrove-Tuesday, the day following which is Ash-Wednesday, the first day of Lent; the *eve*, or *evening* [contracted to *e'en*], of the fasting days.

Fastidientis stomachi est multa degustare. Lat. SENECA.—"It shows a squeamish stomach to taste of many things." A weak appetite, taken in any sense, is only to be allured by variety.

Fata obstant. Lat. VIRGIL.—"The fates oppose it." It is in the destiny of things that the matters should be otherwise settled.

Fata volentem ducunt, nolentem trahunt. Lat.—"The fates lead the willing, and drag the unwilling." A sentiment in accordance with the Pagan and Mohammedan doctrine of Predestination.

Fatetur facinus, qui judicium fugit. Lat. Law maxim.—"He who flies from judgment confesses his crime." His flight is a tacit admission of his guilt.

———————Fatis accede Deisque
Et cole felices: miseros fuge. Sidera coelo
Ut distant, ut flamma mari, sic utile recto. Lat. LUCAN.—

"Still follow where auspicious Fates invite,
Caress the happy, and the wretched slight.
Sooner shall jarring elements unite,
Than truth with gain, than interest with right."

Faubourg. Fr.—"A suburb." "Suburbs," houses or villages near a city, a little way out of town.

Favete linguis. Lat. HORACE.—"Favor by tongues." Preserve a religious silence, give attention whilst the business proceeds. A solemn admonition repeatedly given whilst the superstitious rites of the Romans were in the act of being performed.

Fecundi calices quem non fecere disertum? Lat. HORACE.—"Whom have not the soul-inspiring cups, has not the inspiring bowl, made eloquent?"

"Whom hath not an inspiring bumper taught
A flow of words, and loftiness of thought?"

Again:—

"The fool sucks wisdom, as he porter sups,
And cobblers grow fine speakers in their cups."

Every man can converse with fluency when his spirits have been raised by wine.

N.B. The epithet "*fecundi*," as employed in the above quotation, is made by some to signify "full," or "overflowing," but with much less propriety. It is precisely equivalent to *animum fecundum reddentes*, that is, "that increase, enlarge, the natural stores of the mind, the native ability."

Felices ter et amplius,
Quos irrupta tenet copula, nec malis
Divulsus querimoniis
Suprema citius solvet amor die. Lat. HORACE.—"Happy and thrice happy are those who enjoy an uninterrupted union, and whose love, unbroken by any sour complaints, shall not dissolve until the last day of their existence:"—

"Thrice happy they, whose hearts are tied
In love's mysterious knot so close,
No strife, no quarrels, can divide,
And only death, fell death, can loose."

Felicitas multos habet amicos. Lat.—"Prosperity, a man in prosperous circumstances, has many friends."—See "*Donec eris felix.*"

Felicitas nutrix est iracundiae. Lat. prov.—"Prosperity is the nurse of anger." It leads men to indulge their passions and forget themselves.

Feliciter is sapit, qui periculo alieno sapit. Lat. PLAUTUS.—"To some purpose is that man wise, who gains his wisdom at another's expense."

Felicium multi cognati. Lat. prov.—"The wealthy have many who claim kindred with them."

"I wot well how the world wags:
He is most loved that hath most bags."

Felix quem faciunt aliena pericula cautum. Lat.—"Happy is he who learns prudence from the danger of others, from others' dangers." As he does not purchase it by personal suffering.

Felix qui nihil debet. Lat.—"Happy is he who owes nothing."

Felix qui potuit rerum cognoscere causas. Lat. VIRGIL.—"Happy is he who is skilled in tracing effects up to their causes."

Felo de se. Lat. Law term.—"A felon of himself." One who is supposed to have killed himself when in a sound state of mind.

Femme couverte. Fr.—"A married woman."

Femme rit quand elle peut, et pleure quand elle veut. Fr. prov.—"Women laugh when they can, and weep when they will."

Femme sole. Old Fr.—"A spinster, unmarried woman."

Femme sotte se cognoit à la cotte. Old Fr. prov.—"You may know a foolish woman by her finery."

Ferae naturae. Lat.—"Of a wild, or savage, nature." This phrase is generally used to describe those animals which, being of a wild and savage nature, roaming at large, undomesticated, are the common property of all. Tame animals, on the other hand, which are the absolute property of man, are called *Mansueta*, from *manui assueta*, "accustomed to the hand;" or *domitae naturae*, "of a tamed and subdued nature."

Fere libenter homines id, quod volunt, credunt.
Lat. JULIUS CÆSAR.—"Men generally believe with willingness, are quite ready to believe, what they wish to be true."

Feringee.—Frank, or European: more commonly applied by the natives of India to the descendants of the Portuguese, or the half-castes.

Feriunt summos fulmina montes. Lat. HORACE.—"Thunderbolts strike the tops of the highest mountains." Huge winds blow on high hills.

Ferme modèle. Fr.—"A model farm."

Ferme ornée. Fr.—"A decorated farm." A farm in which, though ornament is introduced, its useful purposes are not overlooked.

Fertilior seges est alienis semper in agris,
Vicinumque pecus grandius uber habet. Lat. OVID.—
"The crop is always greater on the lands of another, and our neighbors' cattle are thought more productive than our own." Such is the nature of man; most persons are of opinion that they have not their proper share of the goods of Fortune.

Fervet opus. Lat. VIRGIL.—"The work is warmly plied, the work thrives." "Pastor and people are embarked in a common cause; *fervet opus*."

Festina lente. Lat. AUGUSTUS CÆSAR.—"Hasten slowly." Most haste, worse speed. Let not impetuosity betray you into imprudence. "Hurry and Cunning," says Colton, "are the two apprentices of Dispatch and of Skill, but neither of them ever learns their master's trade."

Festinare nocet, nocet et cunctatio saepe:
Tempore quaeque suo qui facit, ille sapit. Lat. OVID.—
"It is injurious to hasten, and delay is also frequently injurious. That man is wise, who does every thing at its proper time." The prudent man will equally avoid the extremes of tardiness and of precipitation.

——————————**Festinat decurrere velox**
Flosculus, angustae miseraeque brevissima vitae
Portio: dum bibimus, dum serta, unguenta, puellas
Poscimus, obrepit non intellecta senectus. Lat. JUVENAL.—
"The short-lived bloom and contracted span of a brief and wretched life is fast fleeting away! While we are drinking and calling for garlands, and perfumes, and the society of the female sex, old age steals on us unperceived!"

"Ah! youth, too transient flower! of life's short day
The shortest part, but blossoms to decay.

Lo! while we give the unregarded hour
To revelry and joy, in pleasure's bower,
While now for rosy wreaths our brows to twine,
And now for nymphs, we call, and now for wine,
The noiseless foot of Time steals swiftly by,
And ere we dream of manhood, age is nigh!"

Festinatio tarda est. Lat.—"Haste is slow." Precipitancy seldom attains its object.

Festinatione nil tutius in discordiis civilibus. Lat. TACITUS.—"In civil discords, dissensions, commotions, nothing is safer than bringing matters to a speedy issue, than resorting to a *coup d'état*" [which see].

Fête. Fr.—"An entertainment."

Fête champêtre. Fr.—"An entertainment given in the open air."

Fetiche.—A corruption of the Portuguese word *fetiço*, a charm or witchcraft. Many of the negroes wear about them, and keep also in their dwellings, a charm against evil: this charm is called a *fetiche.*

Feu sacré. Fr.—"Inward inspiration."

Feuilleton. Fr.—The bottom of the pages of French newspapers, which is generally devoted to light literature or criticism.

Feuilletoniste. Fr.—"A writer of *feuilletons.*"

Fiacre. Fr.—"A hackney-coach."

Fiançailles. Fr.—"A betrothal, betrothing, an affiancing."

Fiat. Lat.—"Let it be made, done, enacted." A decree. A word used to signify a peremptory and decisive order.

Fiat confirmatio. Lat.—"Let the confirmation [of the person appointed] be made, or take place." "The archbishop indorsed the letters-patent directed to him with these words, *Fiat confirmatio.*"

Fiat justitia, ruat coelum. Lat.—"Let justice be done, though the heavens should fall." Though ruin should ensue, let justice take its course.

Fiat lux. Lat.—"Let there be light."

Fiat observatio. Lat.—"Let an observation be made."

Ficta voluptatis causa sint proxima veris. Lat. HORACE.—"Let your fictions have as near a resemblance as possible to truth:"—

"Fictions, to please, should wear the face of truth."

Fidei defensor. Lat.—"Defender of the faith." One of the titles of the monarchs of the British Empire. N.B. As a *queen* is now the reigning monarch, the *correct* designation is *Fidei* DEFENSATRIX, DEFENDRESS of the faith.

Fides ante intellectum. Lat.—"Faith before intellect." Believe first, and then try to understand, if you can. One of the old scholastic doctrines.

Fides sit penes auctorem. Lat.—"Let the faith be with the author." A phrase often used when a writer, citing a supposed fact, chooses to cast the responsibility on the person who had previously given it to the public.

Fidus interpres. Lat. HORACE.—"One who translates from one language into another, word for word: a literal translator."

Fieri facias. Law Lat.—"Cause it to be done." A judicial writ addressed to the sheriff, empowering him to levy the amount of a debt, or damages recovered.

Figure d'occasion. Fr.—"A countenance adapted to the occasion."

Filius nullius. Lat.—"The son of nobody." A bastard; so called, because by common law he cannot have an inheritance.

Fille de chambre. Fr.—"A lady's maid."

Finale. Lat. and Ital.—"The conclusion."

Finesse. Fr.—"Artifice, craftiness, slyness, cunning."

Finis. Lat.—"The end." "To this, as to all other human works, is appended that incomprehensible word, 'FINIS.'"

Finis chartaeque viaeque. Lat. HORACE.—"The end both of one's journey and of one's paper [traveling journal, note-book]."

Finis coronat opus. Lat.—"The end crowns the work, puts the finishing-stroke to the work." It is impossible to decide on the merits of an affair until it is completely terminated.

Fiord. Norwegian.—"An arm of the sea," the same as the Scottish term "*firth*." N.B. In the island of Cape Breton is a large arm of the sea, called by the French *le bras d'or*, whence probably the name LABRADOR.

Firmaun,—commonly written "*Firman*."—A decree, order, warrant, or passport, issued by the Shah of Persia, or the Sultan of Turkey. No subject dares to disobey the *firmaun* of the sovereign; it supersedes all laws and regulations, and renders those who pass it independent of their immediate local governors.—STOCQUELER.

Fiscal.—"Belonging to the treasury." From the Lat. *fiscus*, "the exchequer, public treasury." In Scotland, the expression "*Procurator fiscal*" is applied to one who looks after other interests of the public besides pecuniary ones, and, in particular, prosecutes crimes. This may have arisen from his levying fines.

————Fit, ut raro, qui se vixisse beatum
Dicat, et exacto contentus tempore vitae
Cedat, uti conviva satur, reperire queamus.

Lat. HORACE.—

"It unfortunately happens, comes to pass, that we seldom meet with a man who can say he has lived happily, and, when the term of his life is expired, can contentedly quit this world like a well-satisfied guest:"—

"From hence, how few, like sated guests, depart
From life's full banquet with a cheerful heart."

Flagrante bello. Lat.—"While the war is raging, going on." During hostilities.

Flagranti delicto. Lat.—"In the commission of the crime." A person apprehended *flagranti delicto*, with full evidence of his guilt.

Flamma per incensas citius sedetur aristas. Lat. PROPERTIUS.—"Sooner may the flames be extinguished when once spread amongst the standing corn." This is figuratively applied to the rapid propagation of any destructive opinion, whether political or religious.

Flaneur. Fr.—"A lounger."

Flebile ludibrium. Lat.—"A deplorable, sad mockery." A lamentable derision, or turning into derision, of any thing venerable or respectable.

Flebile remedium. Lat.—"A doleful, bewailable, lamentable, remedy."

Flèche. Fr. military term.—"An arrow." A small fort open to your army, but with a ditch and breast-work towards the enemy. It is so called from its resemblance to the point of that weapon.

Flectere si nequeo Superos, Acheronta movebo. Lat. VIRGIL. —"If I cannot influence the gods, bend the gods to my purpose, I will move all hell, will leave no stone unturned to accomplish my design." This language is frequently put into the mouth of a political opponent, of whom it is supposed that, if he cannot effect his purposes by laudable means, he will still endeavor to effect them by resorting to the worst and lowest agency. N.B. ACHERON, in the Pagan mythology, was a river of the lower world, round which the shades, departed spirits, hovered, and into which the Pyriphlegethon and Cocytus [other rivers] flowed. In late writers the name of ACHERON is used to designate the whole of the lower world.

Fleurs-de-lis. Fr.—"Flowers-de-luce, lilies."

Flocci, nauci, nihili, pili. Lat.—The initial words of a syntactical rule in the ETON LATIN GRAMMAR, which many of the users of this volume have not yet forgotten. "Government," says SOUTHEY, "must reform the populace, the people must reform themselves. This is the true reform; and, compared with this, all else is *flocci, nauci, nihili, pili,*" that is, "mere moonshine, all stuff, humbug, not worth talking about, not worth a straw, a mere waste of words."

Floriferis ut apes in saltibus omnia libant. Lat. LUCRETIUS.—"As bees, taste of every thing in flowery lawns." They collect the most precious juices of every flower. The motto is generally chosen by selectors, who either cull, or affect to cull, the beauties of many authors.

Flumina libant summa leves. Lat. VIRGIL.—

"They lightly skim,
And gently sip the dimply river's brim."

This may be applied to superficial scholars or readers.

Foenum habet in cornu, longe fuge; dummodo risum
Excutiat sibi, non hic cuiquam parcet amico.

Lat. HORACE.—

"He has hay on his horn [he is a dangerous creature], keep at a respectful distance from him; inasmuch as if he can but excite a little laughter, he will not spare even his best friend:"—

"Yonder he drives, avoid that furious beast:
Let him but have his jest, he never cares
At whose expense; nor friend nor patron spares."

A jester, or professed wit, is bound by no principle of honor or feeling.

N.B. The expression "*Foenum habet in cornu*" is a figurative one, and is taken from the Roman custom of tying hay on the horns of such of their cattle as were mischievous and given to pushing, in order to warn passengers to be on their guard.

Fogir do fumo, e cair no fogo. Port. prov.—"To escape from the smoke, and fall into the fire." Out of the frying-pan into the fire.

Foi est tout. Fr.—"Faith is every thing." "Similar examples of remarkable cures every medical man of experience could contribute in partial confirmation of the old adage '*Foi est tout:*' and of all moral engines, I conceive that faith, which is inspired by a religious creed, to be the most powerful."

Fol est qui plus depend que sa rente ne vaut. Old Fr. prov.—"Foolish is he who spends more than his income." You must cut your coat according to your cloth. Compare PLAUTUS: *Sumtus censum ne superet,* "Let not your expenditure, expenses, exceed your income."

Fonda. Span.—"A hotel."

Fons et origo. Lat.—"The source, chief cause, and origin." "He accuses the House of Orange of being the *fons et origo* of the whole evil."

Fons malorum. Lat.—"The source, or origin, of evils, of vice, sin, wickedness, misfortunes." "He pores over philosophy and history to find the *fons malorum.*"

Fool.—Probably from *fouler*, Fr., "to trample on, crush, pound." An abridgment of "Gooseberry-fool." A fluid mess made of gooseberries scalded and pounded, and of cream:—

"Thou full dish of fool."—SHAKSPEARE.

"Fall to your cheese-cakes, curds, and clouted cream,
Your fool, your flaunes."—BEN JONSON.

Formam quidem ipsam, et tanquam faciem honesti vides: quae, si oculis cerneretur, mirabiles amores [ut ait PLATO] excitaret sapientiae. Lat. CICERO.—"You see the very shape and countenance, as it were, of virtue: now, if this could be made the object of sight, it would [as PLATO says] excite in us a wonderful love of wisdom." Virtue cannot be depicted.

**Format enim natura prius nos intus ad omnem
Fortunarum habitum; juvat aut impellit ad iram,
Aut ad humum moerore gravi deducit et angit;
Post effert animi motus, interprete lingua.** Lat. HORACE.—"Nature begins from our very birth to form the mind to be differently affected according to the vicissitudes of Fortune; it enchants us with pleasure, or stimulates us to anger and resentment, or sinks us under a load of woe, and then, in process of time, teaches the tongue to utter the feelings of the heart." Speech is the best delineator of the passions.

Formidabilior cervorum exercitus, duce leone, quam leonum, cervo. Lat. prov.—"An army of stags is more to be feared, more formidable, under the command of a lion, than an army of lions led by a stag." A proverb which intimates that less depends on the discipline or valor of an army than on the skill and ability of its general.

Formosa facies muta commendatio est. Lat. LABERIUS.—"A pleasing countenance is a silent recommendation."

————**Forsan et haec olim meminisse juvabit:
Durate et vosmet rebus servate secundis.** Lat. VIRGIL.—"Perhaps the remembrance of these events may prove a source of future pleasure. Endure them, therefore, like men, and reserve yourselves for more prosperous circumstances." A most powerful appeal to companions in adversity.

Forsan miseros meliora sequentur. Lat. VIRGIL.—"Perhaps a better fate awaits, is in store for, the afflicted." A topic of consolation similar to the preceding.

Forte. Lat.—"The author's *forte* does not lie in that direction," that is, "The ability in which he shines most, or in which his powers come out the strongest."

Forte è l'aceto di vin dolce. Ital. prov.—"Strong is the vinegar from sweet wine." The sweetest wine makes the sharpest vinegar. Compare "*Corruptio optimi pessima,*" which see.

Forte scutum salus ducum. Lat.—"A strong shield is the safety, safeguard, of military or naval commanders." The first three syllables of "forte scutum" form a pun on the name FORTESCUE.

Fortem posce animum. Lat. JUVENAL.—"Pray for a bold spirit, a strong mind:"—

"Ask thou of GOD content and strength of mind."

Fortes fortuna adjuvat. Lat. TERENCE.—"Fortune helps, assists, the brave." Vigorous enterprise is commonly successful.

Forti et fideli nil difficile. Lat.—"To the brave and faithful nothing is difficult."

Fortior est, qui se quam qui fortissima moenia vincit. Lat. OVID.—"Braver, stronger, more valiant, is he who conquers, gains the victory over himself, than he who succeeds in taking the strongest, the most strongly fortified, cities." Compare the Hebrew maxim:—"He that ruleth his spirit is better than he that taketh a city," Prov. xvi. 32, and see "*Latius regnes,*" *&c.*

Fortior et potentior est dispositio legis quam hominis. Lat. Law maxim.—"The disposition of the law is of greater force and potency than the disposition of man." Thus, a man having granted a lease for years cannot overthrow this grant by any surrender of his interests.

Fortis cadere, cedere non potest. Lat.—"The brave man may fall, but cannot yield."

Fortiter in re. Lat.—"Vigorously, firmly, in action, deed, or execution."

Fortuna favet fatuis. Lat. prov.—"Fortune favors fools: fools have the best luck."

Fortuna multis dat nimis, satis nulli. Lat. MARTIAL [the epigrammatic poet].—"Fortune gives too much to many, enough to none." No man, be his possessions ever so great, is content with that which he actually possesses.

Fortuna, nimium quem fovet, stultum facit. Lat. prov.—"When Fortune caresses a man too much, she makes him a fool." Even the wisest may be intoxicated by a long succession of prosperity.

Fortuna non mutat genus. Lat. HORACE.—"Fortune changes not the nature of the individual."

Fortuna opes auferre, non animum, potest. Lat. SENECA.—"Fortune can take away riches, but cannot deprive of courage." A man of strong mind rises superior to all the changes of fortune.

Fortuna saevo laeta negotio, et
Ludum insolentem ludere pertinax,

Transmutat incertos honores,
Nunc mihi, nunc alii, benigna. Lat. HORACE.—"Fortune, exulting in her cruel employment, and persisting in playing her haughty game, constantly transfers her unstable gifts, sometimes favorable to one, and sometimes to another:"—

"Fortune, that ever-changing dame,
Indulges her malicious joy,
And constant plays her haughty game,
Proud of her office to destroy;
To-day to me her bounty flows,
And now on others she the bliss bestows."

Fortuna, viris invida fortibus,
Quam non aequa bonis praemia dividis! Lat. SENECA.—

"Capricious Fortune ever joys
With partial hand to deal the prize,
To crush the brave and cheat the wise."

See preceding quotation.

Fortuna vitrea est, quae, cum maxime splendet, frangitur. Lat. PUBLIUS SYRUS.—"Fortune is brittle as glass, and when she shines the most, when she is most refulgent, she is often most unexpectedly broken, smashed."

Fortunae cetera mando. Lat.—"I commit the rest to Fortune." I have made the wisest arrangements in my power, but I still know that I am not beyond the reach of accident.

Fortunae filius. Lat.—"A son of Fortune." A favorite of Fortune. A person highly favored by that blind deity.

Fortunae majoris honos, erectus et acer. Lat. CLAUDIAN.—"A man, who reflects honor on his distinguished position, and of an erect and bold spirit."

Fortunatos nimium, sua si bona norint! Lat. VIRGIL.—"Happy, too happy, indeed, would be numbers of individuals, did they but know, were they but sensible of, the inestimable blessings, privileges, they enjoy!"

Fortune de la guerre. Fr.—

"When the soldier's coin is spent,
He has but to fight for more;
He pays neither tax nor rent,
He's but where he was before.
If he conquer, if he fall—
Fortune de la guerre, that's all!"

that is, *The fortune of war*, or *'Tis but the fortune of war*, &c. N.B. The *full* expression is "*La fortune de la guerre.*"

Fortune du pot. Fr.—"Pot-luck."

Fosseway.—From the old Fr. "*fosse*," a ditch. One of the Roman roads through England, with a ditch on each side.

Fragili quaerens illidere dentem offendet solido. Lat. HORACE.—"Envy, while seeking to fix its tooth in something brittle, shall strike against the solid," that is, while endeavoring to find some weak point of attack in me, shall discover that I am on all sides proof against its envenomed assaults." The idea is borrowed from the apologue [narrative, tale] of the viper and the file. "My adversary, envious of my fame, in seeking to fasten on a weak part, shall find a firm resistance." If his malice be directed towards me, he shall meet with an unlooked-for and plenary punishment.

Fraises. Fr.—Pointed stakes used in fortification.

Frange, miser, calamos, vigilataque proelia dele,
Qui facis in parva sublimia carmina cella,
Ut dignus venias hederis, et imagine macra.
Spes nulla ulterior. Lat. JUVENAL.—

"Destroy your pens, poor wretch! blot out your battles, that have lost you your night's rest—you that write sublime poetry in your narrow garret, that you may come forth worthy of an ivy crown and meager image. You have nothing further to hope for." Compare BEN JONSON:—

"I, that spend half my nights and half my days
Here in a cell, to get a dark, pale face,
To come forth worth the ivy or the bays,
And in this age can hope no other grace."

The reward of Authorship is generally empty praise.

Frankpledge.—Surety for freemen.

Fraus est celare fraudem. Lat. Law maxim.—"It is a fraud to conceal a fraud." On such a concealment devolves a share in the guilt.

Fræna mordere. Lat. STATIUS.—"To receive the bridle, to submit, yield submission."

Frères d'armes. Fr.—"Brothers, companions in arms, in warfare."

Frondeur. Fr.—"An exclaimer, declaimer, against the existing administration."

Fronti nulla fides. Lat. JUVENAL.—"There is no trusting to the mere outside, the appearance, the countenance." Trust not to outward show. All is not gold that glitters. N.B. The quotation is sometimes met with in this form, "FRONTIS NULLA FIDES."

Fruges consumere nati. Lat. HORACE.—"Born merely to consume the fruits of the earth, to eat and drink, to devour provisions:"—

"Born but to eat and drink the fruits of earth."

The worthless, who live and die without having rendered any service to society. Drones in the social hive, whose only business is to devour the fruits of other men's labor.

Frustra fit per plura, quod fieri potest per pauciora. Lat.—"That is idly done by many, which may be done by a few." This maxim, though variously applied, is generally used to enforce the position, that it is better to proceed by negotiation than by warfare.

Frustra laborat, qui omnibus placere studet. Lat. prov.—"He who studies to please every one labors in vain."

Fugam fecit. Lat. Law phrase.—"He has taken to flight." Used when it is found by inquisition that a person has fled for felony, &c.

——————**Fuge magna: licet sub paupere tecto**
Reges et regum vita praecurrere amicos. Lat. HORACE.—

"Avoid, eschew, shun, greatness: beneath an humble roof one may live more happily than the powerful and the friends of the powerful:"—

"Leave then the gaudy blessings of the great:
The cottage offers a secure retreat,
Where you may make a solid bliss your own,
To kings, and favorites of kings, unknown."

Fugiendo in media saepe ruitur fata. Lat. LIVY.—"By flying, men often meet the very fate which they wish to avoid." Prudence is sometimes defeated by chance, and produces the same consequences as rashness.

Fugit irreparabile tempus. Lat. VIRGIL.—"Time, that cannot be recalled, flies, passes away. Irretrievable, irrecoverable, time wends its rapid way."

Fugitation. From the Lat. verb "*fugio*," to flee.—A Scots law term for "*outlawry*."

Fuit Ilium. Lat. VIRGIL.—"Troy *has* been." That which was the object of contention exists no more.

Fulgente trahit constrictos Gloria curru
Non minus ignotos generosis. Lat. HORACE.—
"Glory holds equally attached to her splendid chariot the ignoble and the lofty. Glory leads all men captive at the wheels of her glittering car." An allusion, beautifully figurative, to the triumphal chariot of a conqueror.

"Chained to her beamy car Fame drags along
The mean, the great: an undistinguished throng."

Functus officio. Lat. CICERO.—"Exempt from duty:" one whose official power or duties have ceased, no longer exist.

Fungar inani munere. Lat. VIRGIL.—"I will discharge a fruitless and unavailing duty." A common prefix to an elegy on a deceased friend.

——————Fungar vice cotis, acutum
Reddere quae ferrum valet, exsors ipsa secandi.
Lat. HORACE.—
"I will perform the office of a whet-stone, which, though itself incapable of cutting, yet serves to sharpen the razor, can make other things sharp." A didactic writer may instruct others to do that well, which he himself is wholly incapable of performing.

"Then let me sharpen others, as the hone
Gives edge to razors, though itself has none."

Or: –

"I'll play the whet-stone: useless and unfit
Myself to cut, I'll sharpen others' wit."

Furiosus furore suo punitur. Lat. Law maxim.—"A madman or lunatic is punished by his own madness." If a madman kill any one, he shall not suffer for the act, because, being deprived of memory and understanding by the hand of GOD, he is regarded as having broken the mere words of the law, but not the law itself.

Furor arma ministrat. Lat. VIRGIL.—"Fury, rage, supplies them [the rabble] with arms, weapons."

Furor fit laesa saepius patientia. Lat. prov.—"Patience, when too often outraged, is converted into madness." There is a certain degree of irritation, which is beyond all endurance.

Furor iraque mentem praecipitant. Lat. VIRGIL.—"Anger and rage h rry on, impel, the mind." Angry men seldom want woe.

Furore. Ital.—"Excitement."

Fusillade. Fr.—"A discharge of musketry."

Fuyez les procès sur toutes choses: la conscience s'y interesse, la santé y altère, les biens s'y dissipent. Fr. LA BRUYÈRE.—"Avoid law-suits above all things: they affect your conscience, impair your health, and dissipate your property."

G.

Gabelle. Fr.—"The salt tax." "The odious *gabelle* was said to have been the principal grievance which irritated the people to rise in the First Revolution. It is still a royal monopoly [the sole sale of any class of commodities, exclusive privilege of selling any particular article]."

Gage d'amour. Fr.—"Pledge, token of love, keepsake."

Gageure est la preuve des sots. Fr. prov.—"A wager is a fool's argument."

Gaiété de coeur. Fr.—"Gayety of heart." Sportiveness, high animal spirits.

Galantuomo. Ital.—"An honest man."

Gallus in suo sterquilinio plurimum potest. Lat. SENECA.—"Every cock is proud, feels himself an important personage, on his own dunghill."

Gamin. Fr.—"A young blackguard."

Γαμος ανϑρωποισιν ευκταιον κακον. Gr.—"Marriage is with men a wished-for evil, an evil they desire, a desirable evil:"—

"Wedlock's an ill men eagerly embrace."

Garçon. Fr.—"A boy," but in common use in France to signify "a waiter at an inn, hotel, dining-rooms," &c.

Garçon de bureau. Fr.—"An office-boy." A boy employed in an office to make himself generally useful.

Garçon d'esprit. Fr.—"A clever fellow."

Garde à vous! Fr.—"Our bugles sounded the *garde à vous!*" that is, "the military order of ATTENTION!"

Garde-chasse. Fr.—"A gamekeeper." N.B. "*Garde-chasse*" is very often incorrectly written *garde de chasse.* The plural of *garde-chasse* is either *gardes-chasse*, or *gardes-chasses.*

Garde du corps. Fr.—"A body-guard." N.B. "*Garde du corps*" is very often incorrectly written *garde de corps.*

Gardez la foy [foi]. Fr.—"Keep faith. Guard the faith."

Gardez la langue, ouvrez les yeux, si vous désirez être heureux. Fr. prov.—"Keep your mouth shut, and your eyes open, if you will lead a peaceful life."

Garrit aniles ex re fabellas. Lat. HORACE.—"He prates away old wives' tales, traditionary stories, adapted to the subject in hand He tells old wives' tales rather pertinently:"—

"The cheerful sage, when solemn dictates fail,
Conceals the moral counsel in a tale."

This quotation is sometimes addressed to an opponent who is possessed of more anecdote than argument.

Gasconnade. Fr.—"Boasting, bragging."

Gato miolador no es buen cazador. Span. prov.—"A mewing cat is not a good hunter, is not a good mouser."

Gatta guantata non piglia mai sorice. Ital. prov.—"A gloved cat, cat with gloves on, never catches mice." A muffled cat is no good mouser.

Gatto, che lecca cenere, non fidar farina. Ital. prov.—"Trust not with meal the cat that licks ashes." The *English* proverb is, The dog that licks ashes, trust not with meal.

Gauche. Fr.—"Clumsy, awkward, ungainly."

Gaucherie. Fr.—"Awkwardness, untowardness, clumsiness."

Gaudent scribentes, et se venerantur, et ultro,
Si taceas, laudant, quidquid scripsere, beati.

Lat. HORACE.—"They [bad poets] are charmed with their own performances, compositions: they admire them, and, happy in the extreme, liberally bestow upon them those praises which you refuse." Every poet, at the moment of writing, fancies he performs wonders; but, when the ardor of imagination has gone by, a good poet will examine his work in cool blood, and will find it sink greatly in his own esteem. On the other hand, the more a bad poet reads his productions over, the more he is charmed with them.

Gaudet viam fecisse ruina. Lat. LUCAN.—"He rejoices to have made his way by ruin." This is the character given by the poet to CAESAR. It will equally suit any other ambitious despot who, in the pursuit of his object, is regardless of the havoc which he may occasion among the human race.

Gaulois. Fr.—"Old French, the French people of old."

Gaunt.—"Ghent," in Belgium. JOHN OF GAUNT, Duke of Lancaster, was the fourth son of EDWARD III., and was born at Ghent in 1340.

Gavelkind.—A Saxon law, signifying "Give all kind, or, give all the kin alike:" kind, or kin, signifying "child." "This law," says MINSHEW, "continues in Kent; and, in the 18th of HENRY VI., there were not above thirty or forty persons in Kent that held by any other tenure; though now both the name and nature of the law are altered: for the modern term," continues he, "is *gavelet*, by which the tenant forfeits his lands and tenements to the lord of whom they are holden, if he withdraws from his lord his due rents and services."

Γελως ακαιρος εν βροτοις δεινον κακον. Gr.—"Mirth out of season is a grievous ill."

Gendarme. Fr.—"An armed policeman."

Gendarmerie. Fr.—"The armed police force."

Gêne. Fr.—"Constraint."

Genera. Lat.—The plural of "*genus*," which see. "Kinds." "The European *genera* of grasses."

Generalissimo. Ital.—"A commander-in-chief."

Genius loci. Lat. VIRGIL.—"The tutelary [guardian] deity of a place."

Gens de bureau. Fr.—"The officials of a public, a government office."

Gens de condition. Fr.—"Persons of rank, distinction."

Gens de guerre. Fr.—"Military men."

Gens de l'église. Fr.—"Churchmen."

Gens de peu. Fr.—"The lower sort of persons, lower classes."

Gens desouevrés. Fr.—"Persons without employment."

Gens du monde. Fr.—"Persons in active life."

Gens inimica sibi. Lat. VIRGIL.—"A nation that is hostile to them, that is so decidedly their enemy." "Italy, in the mean time, has not been safe from the *gens inimica sibi* [AUSTRIA]."

Gens togata. Lat. VIRGIL.—"The gowned nation," that is, the Roman nation. See "*Jus togae.*"

Gent libérale. Fr.—"Persons of liberal sentiments."

Gentilhombre. Span.—"A gentleman."

Gentilhommerie. Fr.—"Around him might have grouped themselves the whole *gentilhommerie* of the kingdom:" that is, the whole "gentility" of the kingdom, all that was "genteel" in, &c. N.B. "*Gentilhommerie*" is only used in derision, ironically, jocosely.

Genus. Lat.—"The Circassian *genus*," that is, the Circassian "race," or "stock." "A fair specimen of the *genus*," that is, of the "kind."

Genus dicendi. Lat. QUINTILIAN.—"A style of speaking." "The '*genus dicendi*,' of which Messrs. FINLAY and PHILLIPS are the chief patrons [and indeed models] in the present day [1817], does not appear to have been known to the ancient masters. We look in vain for any description of it in CICERO or QUINTILIAN. In the Middle Ages, however, it was abundantly practiced. The rule, in which its whole mystery may be summed up, is to give utterance to all the ideas, and in all the words, that present themselves [and as near as possible all at once] upon any matter, without regard to order or selection, and how remote soever their reference may be to the subject."

————**Genus, et proavos, et quae non fecimus ipsi,**
Vix ea nostra voco. Lat. OVID.—

"Birth [HIGH BIRTH, as it is called] and ancestry, and all other things which we ourselves have not acquired, can scarcely be called our own:"—

"Naught from my birth or ancestors I claim;
All is my own, my honor and my shame."

Genus homo. Lat.—"The human species."

Genus humanum ingenio superavit. Lat. LUCRETIUS.—"He surpassed the human race in ability, left them at an immeasurable distance." The above quotation is inscribed on the pedestal of the statue of SIR ISAAC NEWTON. N.B. In the original the *full* passage stands thus:—

"Qui genus humanum ingenio superavit, et omnes
Restinxit stellas, exortus uti aërius sol."

"His genius quite obscured the brightest ray
Of human thought, as Sol's effulgent beams,
At morn's approach, extinguish all the stars."

———**Genus humanum multo fuit illud in arvis Durius.** Lat. LUCRETIUS.—
"A hardy race of mortals, trained to sports:
The field their joy, unpolished yet by courts."

———**Genus immortale manet, multosque per annos Stat fortuna domus et avi numerantur avorum.** Lat. VIRGIL.—
"The immortal line in sure succession reigns,
The fortune of the family remains,
And grandsires' grandsons the long list contains."

This quotation has been applied to a long dynasty [sway, rule, sovereign power].

Genus irritabile. Lat. HORACE.—"An irritable race, a race quickly made angry, a fretful tribe." "Artists are a *genus irritabile.*"

Genus irritabile vatum. Lat. HORACE.—"The irritable tribe of poets." Proverbially used, in consequence of the acrimony which generally enters into any contest between writers of this class. An English poet has described, in terms still more forcible,
"The jealous, waspish, wrong-head, rhyming race."

Γηρασκω αιει πολλα διδασκομενος. Gr.—"I grow old as I make constant accessions to my knowledge; ever learning something, I advance in years and in wisdom." Older and wiser. One may "LIVE AND LEARN." A saying of Solon, one of the seven wise men of Greece, and the lawgiver of the Athenians.

Ghaut. Hindostanee.—"A mountain." It also implies a landing-place or wharf on the Ganges [a river in India].

Ghee. Hindostanee.—"The butter produced from the milk of the Indian buffalo."

Gibier de potence. Fr.—"Game for the gallows." Newgate-birds, jail-birds, scapegraces.

Giovane ozioso, vecchio bisognoso. Ital. prov.—"A young man idle, an old man needy."

Gîte. Fr.—"Gist." "The real *gîte* of the whole case."

Glacier. Fr.—"Permanent ice." "A *glacier*, in the customary meaning of the term, is a mass of ice, which, descending below the usual snow-line, prolongs its course down the cavity of one of those vast gorges which furrow the sides of most mountain-ranges. It is better represented by a frozen torrent than by a frozen ocean. Any one placed so as to see a *glacier* in connection with the range from which it has its origin at once infers that it is, in some sense or other, the outlet of the vast snow-fields which occupy the higher regions. It is impossible to doubt that it results from, and is renewed by, the eternal ice-springs of those riverless wilds."

Gladiator in arena consilium capit. Lat.—"The gladiator, sword-player, takes counsel on the stage where he is to fight." The man asks for that advice in the very hour of danger, which he should previously and in a cooler moment have solicited.

Gli ornamenti nei vestimenti delle figure vogliono esser messi con sobrietà, e fa bisogno ricordarsi di colui che altre volte diceva a quello artifice, "Tristo a te! non sapesti far Ellena

bella, la facesti ricca." Ital. ALGAROTTI.—"Richness in the drapery, dress, costume, of the human figure should be sparingly introduced, introduced with discretion, by the artist, and we should ever bear in mind the remark of APELLES [the distinguished painter of old] to one of his pupils:—'Unhappy, unfortunate, boy, youth! thou couldst not make HELEN [the most beautiful woman of her time] beautiful, lovely, and so thou hast made her gorgeous.'" The classic scholar will be pleased to see the original Greek:—"*Απελλης ὁ ζωγραφος θεασαμενος τινα των μαθητων Ἑλενην ονοματι πολυχρυσον γραψαντα, Ω μειρακιον, ειπεν, μη δυναμενος γραψαι καλην, πλουσιαν πεποιηκας.*"

Gloria in excelsis. Lat.—"Glory to GOD in the highest [a hymn of the churches of Rome and of England]." "The feathered songster and the poet are friends and fellow-worshipers, and, though dwelling in a lowly vale, their hymn is *Gloria in excelsis.*"

Gloria virtutis umbra. Lat.—"Glory is the shadow, the companion, of virtue."

Gnostics. From the Gr. word *γνωστικος* [gnostikos], "pertaining to knowledge, intelligent, possessing profound knowledge, intelligence, discernment, or penetration." The *Gnostics* were a sect who boasted of their superior *knowledge* in the mysteries of religion, and might sarcastically have been called *the knowing ones.*

Γνωθι καιρον [Gnothi kairon]. Gr.—"Know the time, opportunity," the fit, proper, convenient, or suitable time, *in reference to circumstances of persons, or things, for speaking, or acting.* Compare SHAKSPEARE:—"When our fates seem to open their hand to us, let our spirit embrace them in all that is wise and honorable." Again:—

"Who seeks and will not take when once 'tis offered,
Shall never find it more."

Gobe-mouches. Fr.—"Persons who have no opinions of their own, gulls, triflers." "The world contains a large number of *gobe-mouches.*"

Gorge. Fr. military term.—"A strait or narrow pass."

Goths. An ancient people in the northern parts of Europe: Danes, Swedes, and Norwegians. The term is often used to signify, "Any nation deficient in general knowledge." "What do you think of the late extraordinary event in Spain? Could you have ever imagined that those ignorant *Goths* would have dared to banish the Jesuits?"—LORD CHESTERFIELD.

1. *Gothic* is often used to signify, "Uncivilized." "Ah! rustic ruder than *Gothic.*"—CONGREVE.

2. *Gothicism.* "The state of barbarians." "Night, *Gothicism,* confusion, and absolute chaos [which see] are come again."—SHENSTONE.

Gourmand. Fr.—"He was a thorough *gourmand:*" that is to say, a thorough *glutton,* or, to use a milder term, *gastronomist,* or *gastrophilist.* N.B. "*Gourmet*" is often erroneously used in England for "*gourmand:*" the meaning, however, is very different, as *gourmet* signifies *a judge of wine, a wine-taster.* A "*gastronomist*" is *one who understands the whole mystery of good eating and drinking, of good living, one who has made the laws of* sensual *taste, of* palatial *taste in particular, his peculiar study.* A "*gastrophilist*" is *one who loves his belly. who makes a god of his belly.*

Goût. Fr.—"Taste, peculiar fancy, inclination."

Goute à goute. Fr.—"Drop by drop."

Gracieux accueil vaut la chère la plus delicate. Fr. prov.—"Welcome is the best cheer."

Gradatim. Lat.—"By degrees, by little and little, gradually."

GRADUS AD PARNASSUM. Lat.—"A step, way, to Parnassus." "GRADUS AD PARNASSUM" is a well-known and very useful school-book, in great requisition with those who try their hands at Latin versification, verse-making. N.B. Parnassus is the highest mountain in Central Greece, and is covered with snow during the greater portion of the year. The Castalian spring [a fountain sacred to the Muses] is fed by these perpetual snows, and pours down the chasm between the two summits. These are two lofty rocks rising perpendicularly from Delphi [a city seated on the hill of Parnassus, where the oracle of Apollo was]. These heights were sacred to BACCHUS and the MUSES, and those who slept in their neighborhood were supposed to receive inspiration from them.

Graeculus esuriens, in coelum jusseris, ibit. Lat. JUVENAL.—"A poor hungry Greek, if you order him, will e'en go to heaven! Bid the hungry Greekling go to Heaven—He'll go." That is, will attempt the thing most difficult. This was the reproach of Imperial Rome to the Greek provincials who resorted to that metropolis. It has often been applied to those supple Frenchmen who swarm in every capital, as in the following lines:—

"All trades his own your hungry Frenchman counts,
And bid him mount the sky, the sky he mounts!"

Gram. loquitur, Dia. vera docet, Rhe. verba colorat,
Mu. canit, Ar. numerat, Geo. ponderat, As. docet astra.
Lat.—

This is a memorial, definition, given by the schoolmen in verse, of what are called the seven liberal sciences: "*Grammar* speaks, *Dialectics* teach the truth, *Rhetoric* gives coloring to our speech, *Music* sings, *Arithmetic* numbers, *Geometry* weighs, and *Astronomy* teaches the knowledge of the stars."

Gramercies and Gramercy.—Both from the Fr., and signifying, "Great thanks to you:"—

"*Gramercies*, Tranio, well dost thou advise."
SHAKSPEARE—*Taming of the Shrew.*

"*Gramercy*, Mammon, said the gentle knight,
For so great grace and offered high estate."
SPENSER.

Grammatici certant, et adhuc sub judice lis est.
Lat. HORACE.—

"Grammarians, teachers of Grammar, dispute the point, and the matter in question is still, even yet, before the judge, is as yet undecided:" *in other words*, "Good judges of the matter in question are at issue on the subject, and the point is still undecided."

"By whom invented critics yet contend,
And of their vain disputings find no end."

Gran victoria es la que sin sangre se alcanza. Span. prov.—"Great is the victory that costs no blood, no bloodshed."

Grand bien vous fasse! Fr.—"Much good may it do you!"

Grand cordon. Fr.—"The great [*broad*] ribbon [of the Legion of honor, an order of knighthood]." "He was decorated with the *grand cordon* by LOUIS PHILIPPE."

Grand diseur n'est pas grand faiseur. Fr. prov.—"Great talkers are but little doers, indifferent doers, performers."

Grand gourmand. Fr.—"A great glutton, gastronomist, gastrophilist." "Eating much, eating long, and eating of the best which is to be had, are the distinguishing characteristics of a *grand gourmand*." See "*Gourmand*."

Grand homme. Fr.—"A great man." N.B. *Un homme grand* means *a tall man;* un grand homme, *a great man, a distinguished man.*

Grand homme de province. Fr.—"A distinguished provincial, provincial celebrity."

Grand siècle. Fr.—"A great, distinguished, age." "He was among the most brilliant and respectable illustrations of the *grand siècle* [the age of LOUIS XIV. of France]."

Grande arma es la necesidad. Span. prov.—"Necessity is a powerful, vigorous, strong, stout, arm." Necessity is the mother of invention, stimulates to exertion.

Grande déraison de prétendre toujours avoir raison. Fr. prov. —"It shows a remarkable want of reason to be always fancying one's self in the right."

Grandee. Span.—"Ostentation in the *parvenu millionnaire* is quite a distinct thing from ostentation in the hereditary *grandee* [nobleman]:" that is to say, Ostentation in the *upstart man who is worth a million*, or *millions, man of millions*, is quite, &c. N.B. "*Millionnaire*" is nearly always *incorrectly* spelled with *one* n instead of with *two*. The *true* meaning of the word "*grandee*" is, a Spanish nobleman who has the privilege of wearing his hat in the presence of his sovereign, like *Lord Kinsale* in this country.

Grandes promesses et peu d'effets. Fr. prov.—"Great promises and but little deeds." Great cry and little wool.

Grandeur. Fr.—"Greatness." "Intellectual *grandeur*."

Grands vanteurs, petits faiseurs. Fr. prov.—"Great boasters, little doers." Great boast, small roast.

Grata superveniet, quae non sperabitur, hora. Lat. HORACE.—"The hour that comes unexpectedly, the time that you could never venture to say you would be sure to live to see, will come on you with infinitely greater pleasure:"—

"So, if to-morrow's sun be thine,
With double luster shall it shine."

Blessings anticipated are not by any means so well relished as those which come upon us by surprise.

Gratia ab officio, quod mora tardat, abest. Lat. OVID.—"Thanks are lost in a kindness which delay keeps back." He loseth his thanks, who promiseth and delayeth.

Gratia gratiam parit. Lat. SENECA.—"Kindness begets kindness" One good turn deserves another.

Grassa cucina, magro testamento. Ital. prov.—"A fat kitchen, a lean will."

Grasse panse, maigre cervelle. Fr. prov.—"A fat belly, a lean brain."

Gratior et pulcro veniens in corpore virtus. Lat. VIRGIL.—"Even virtue is more fair when it appears in a beautiful person:"—

"More lovely virtue in a lovely form."

Beauty lends a grace even to intrinsic worth. This corresponds in some degree with the aphorism [a short sentence, in which the principal matter of a subject is comprised in a very few words, or in which the properties of a thing are expressed] of QUEEN ELIZABETH, "that a good face is the best letter of recommendation."

"Becoming graces, and a virtuous mind,
More lovely in a beauteous form enshrined."

Gratis. Lat.—"For nothing, without pay, gratuitously, free of cost."

Gratis anhelans, multa agendo nihil agens. Lat. PHAEDRUS.—"Panting without a cause, to no purpose, for naught; putting one's self to a great deal of trouble, and, in affecting to do much, really doing nothing—and, though busily engaged in many things, yet in reality doing nothing." The description of a busy, pompous blockhead. The quotation was applied to the late LORD DURHAM, when Governor of the Canadas; and it is a droll coincidence that among the strange personages whom PANTAGRUEL met in his voyages, RABELAIS should have hit upon "THE DICTATOR of MUSTARDLAND," of whom he says that "*when he scratched himself there came new proclamations, when he talked it was of last year's snow, when he dreamed it was of a cock and a bull, if he thought to himself it was whimsies and maggots;*" and, in short, "*he* was one *who used to work doing nothing, and do nothing though he worked.*" PANTAGRUEL seems to have had a *second sight* of Lower Canada in 1838. See "*Est ardelionum,*" *&c.*

Gratus dictum. Lat.—"Said for nothing, a gratuitous assertion." Spoken of a transitory observation, which says nothing for the argument.

Gratulor quod eum, quem necesse erat diligere, qualiscunque esset, talem habemus ut libenter quoque diligamus. Lat. TREBONIUS.—"I rejoice, am glad, that the person whom it was my duty to love, good or bad, is such a one as I can love from inclination, with a willing mind." This is a well-turned compliment, either from a subject to his sovereign, or from a parent to his son, as it intimates the presence of qualities which conciliate esteem and regard, independently of all relative considerations.

Gratum est quod patriae civem populoque dedisti,
Si facis ut patriae sit idoneus, utilis agris,
Utilis et bellorum et pacis rebus agendis.
Plurimum enim intererit quibus artibus, et quibus hunc tu
Moribus instituas. Lat. JUVENAL.—

"It deserves our gratitude that you have presented a citizen to your country and people, if you take care that he prove useful to the state, of service to her lands; useful in transacting the affairs both of war and peace. For it will be a matter of the highest moment in what pursuits and moral discipline you train him." The advantage of a son to society depends on his training.

Gravamen. Lat.—"A grievance." "The *gravamen* of the offense."

Grave delictum. Lat.—"A serious offense."

Graviora quaedam sunt remedia periculus. Lat. prov.—"Some remedies are worse than the disease."

Gravis ira regum semper. Lat. SENECA.—"The anger of kings is always severe." Those who possess unlimited power are vindictive from habit.

GRECIAN.—A name given to the boys who are in the first form at Christ's Hospital [The Blue-Coat School].

Grenadiers. Fr.—The tallest soldiers in a regiment, because they used to be selected to throw *grenades* [hollow balls filled with powder, which in bursting were very destructive].

——————Grex totus in agris
Unius scabie cadit, et porrigine porci. Lat. JUVENAL.—"A whole flock perishes in the fields from the scab of one sheep, and pigs from mange." One scabbed sheep will mar a whole flock.

Gribouille, qui se cacha dans l'eau crainte de la pluie. Fr. prov.—"His pretext is no better than the proverbial absurdity of *Gribouille, qui se cacha dans l'eau crainte de la pluie:* he has plunged the country into the abyss of December for fear of a shower in May:" that is to say, of *Gribouille, who hid himself in the water for fear of the rain* [for fear of getting wet through]. N.B. The proverb is generally used in reference to those silly persons who, to avoid an inconvenience of one kind, rush into another infinitely worse, jump out of the frying-pan into the fire; and also to those who have the misfortune to be ill advised, and who, in consequence, are easily imposed on. The *entire* proverb is, "*Fin comme Gribouille, qui se cache dans l'eau, crainte de la pluie:*" that is, *Cunning, or clever, as G., who hides himself in the water for fear of the rain.* The proverb is nearly always quoted *incorrectly;* thus, *Fin comme G., qui se* jette *dans l'eau,* de peur *de la pluie.*

Grist. Saxon.—"Crushed, ground." Hence *grist,* corn to be ground; *grist for the mill* is a figurative expression implying profit or gain.

Gros maigre. Fr.—"A tall, gaunt, brown, hard-featured, lantern-jawed fellow."

Grosse tête, peu de sens. Fr. prov.—"A great head and little brains." A proverb that does not invariably hold good.

Grossièreté. Fr.—"Grossness, coarseness, uncouthness of ideas:" a plain, unvarnished mode of expression.

Guardati da chi non ha che perdere. Ital. prov.—"Beware of him, keep aloof from him, who has naught to lose."

Guerilla. Span.—"Little war, petty warfare." A term applied to an irregular mode of carrying on war against an enemy by the constant attacks of independent bands. It was adopted in the north of Spain during the Peninsular War. The term is, for the most part, used adjectively: as, *guerilla* bands, *guerilla* chief, *guerilla* soldier, *guerilla* command [military command of an irregular character].

Guerra, y caça, y amores, por un plazer mil dolores. Span.

prov.—"War, hunting, and love bring a thousand pains for one pleasure, are as full of trouble as of pleasure." Wars bring scars.

Guerre à mort. Fr.—"War till death."

Guerre à outrance. Fr.—"War to the uttermost, utmost." Two phrases which, it is to be hoped, posterity will remember only as having disgraced the commencement of the 19th century. See "*À outrance.*"

Gueux comme un peintre. Fr. prov.—"As poor as a church mouse."

Guillotine. Fr.—This instrument of death was not, as is generally supposed, invented by DR. GUILLOTIN, nor was he one of its victims, as has been frequently asserted. DR. GUILLOTIN had nothing whatever to do with it, though by a combination of circumstances it came to be eventually called by *his* name. It was first called *La Louison*, from LOUIS, an eminent surgeon and secretary to the College of Surgeons in Paris, who, in March, 1792, improved the mechanism and recommended the adoption of an old instrument of the same kind. DR. GUILLOTIN was very much annoyed at finding his name attached to this instrument of death; but he lived to the Restoration in extensive professional practice, and is still much respected, in spite of the afflicting associations of his name.

Guillotinade. Fr.—"Execution by the *guillotine* on a large, gigantic, scale."

Γυναικι κοσμος ὁ τροπος, κ' ου χρυσια. Gr.—"Cultivation of mind, mental cultivation, is the [real] ornament of a woman, is a woman's best recommendation, and not gold."

Γυναικος ουδε χρημ' ανηρ ληϊζεται
Εσθλης αμεινον, ουδε ῥιγιον κακης. Gr. SIMONIDES.—
"Man gains, acquires, no possession better than a good wife, nor worse than a bad one:"

"Of earthly goods the best is a good wife:
A bad, the bitterest curse of human life."

Γυνη πολυτελης εστ' οχληρον, ουκ εᾳ
Ζην τον λαβονθ' ὡς βουλεται· αλλ ενεστι τι
Αγαθον απ' αυτης, παιδες· ελθοντ' εις νοσον
Τον εχοντα ταυτην εθεραπευσεν επιμελως.
Ατυχουντι συμπαρεμεινεν· αποθανοντα σε
Εθαψε, περιεστειλεν οικειως· ὁρα
Εις ταυθ', ὁταν λυπῃ τι των κατ' ἡμεραν.
Οὑτω γαρ οισεις παν το πραγμα. Gr. MENANDER.—

"A spendthrift wife's a troublesome appendage,
Nor lets man live as likes him: yet the jade
Yields goodly fruit too, children; fall you sick,
She tends your bed with ministering cares;
In sorrow clings she to your side; in death
Swathes with fond hand your limbs and smooths your grave:
Look then to this, when daily frets annoy,
For thus you'll lightliest bear th' appointed burden!"

Compare the beautifully delicate, but still kindred, lines of SIR WALTER SCOTT:—

"O woman! in our hours of ease,
Uncertain, coy, and hard to please,
And variable as the shade
By the light quivering aspen made;
When pain and anguish wring the brow,
A ministering angel thou!"

Or the more passionate breathings of Zuleika's tenderness, in the verses of LORD BYRON:—

"To soothe thy sickness, watch thy health,
Partake, but never waste, thy wealth,
Or stand with smiles unmurmuring by,
And lighten half thy poverty;
Do all but close thy dying eye,
For that I could not live to try;
To these alone my thoughts aspire:
More can I do? or thou require?"

Gusto. Ital.—"Taste." "They paint their personages with *gusto*."

**————Gustus elementa per omnia quaerunt,
Nunquam animo pretiis obstantibus.** Lat. JUVENAL.—"They [epicures] ransack all the elements for dainties; the price never standing in the way of their gratification:"

"They ransack every element for choice
Of every fish and fowl, at any price."

Compare SENECA:—

Quidquid avium volitat, quidquid piscium natat, quidquid ferarum discurrit, nostris sepelitur ventribus. "Every kind of bird, fish, and quadruped finds its way into our insides," *literally*, "is buried, entombed, in our bellies."

Gutta cavat lapidem non vi sed saepe cadendo. Lat. OVID.—"A drop [of water] hollows a stone not by its force, power, mere weight, but by its frequently falling, by the frequency of its falling." That may be done by gradual effort which is not to be accomplished by sudden violence.

Gutta fortunae prae dolio sapientiae. Lat. prov.—"The slightest portion of good fortune before, in preference to, a hogshead of wisdom." An ounce of discretion is worth a pound of wit. 'Tis better to be happy than wise.

Gutta percha. A substance extracted from the tuban-tree of the Straits of Malacca: it is of a dirty white color, greasy in texture, and of a leathery smell.

H.

Habeas corpus. Law Lat.—"You may have the body." This is the great writ of English liberty. It lies where a person, being indicted and imprisoned, has offered sufficient bail, which has been refused, though the case was bailable; in this case he may have a *habeas corpus* out of the King's Bench, in order to remove himself thither, and to answer the cause at the bar of that court.

The "HABEAS CORPUS ACT" is the famous statute 31 Charles II. cap. 2.

"The oppression of an obscure individual," says JUDGE BLACKSTONE, "gave rise to the famous *Habeas Corpus* Act."

"The individual here alluded to was one Francis Jenks, who," says De Lolme, "having made a motion at Guildhall, in the year 1676, to petition the king for a new parliament, was examined before the Privy Council, and afterwards committed to the Gate-House, where he was kept about two months through the delays made by the several judges, to whom he applied, in granting him a *Habeas Corpus*." See *State Trials*, vol. vii. anno 1676.

Mr. Fox, in his *Life of James the Second*, p. 35, has characterized this Act as "the most important barrier against tyranny, and best-framed protection for the liberty of individuals, that has ever existed in any ancient or modern commonwealth."

Habeas corpus ad prosequendum. Law Lat.—"You may have the body, in order to prosecute." A writ for the removal of a person for the purpose of prosecution and trial in the proper county.

Habeas corpus ad respondendum. Law Lat.—"You may have the body to answer." A writ to remove a person confined in any other prison, to answer to an action in the King's Bench.

Habeas corpus ad satisfaciendum. Law Lat.—"You may have the body to satisfy." A writ which lies against a person in prison, to charge him in execution.

Habemus confitentem reum. Lat. CICERO.—"We have before us a person accused, who confesses his guilt."

Habemus luxuriam atque avaritiam, publice egestatem, privatim opulentiam. Lat. SALLUST.—"We have luxury and avarice, public debt and private opulence, wealth." This is the description of Rome put by the historian in the mouth of Cato.

Habent et sua fata libelli. Lat.—"Books have their peculiar destiny, their phases, run their peculiar course."

Habent insidias hominis blanditiae mali. Lat. PHAEDRUS.—"The fair speeches of a bad man are designed for treachery, have a treacherous object in view, are replete with treachery."

Habeo senectuti magnam gratiam, quae mihi sermonis aviditatem auxit, potionis et cibi sustulit. Lat. CICERO.—"I am greatly indebted, much beholden, to old age, which has increased my eagerness for conversation in proportion as it has lessened my appetites of hunger and thirst, my appetite for eating and drinking, my love of the pleasures of the table."

Habere facias possessionem. Lat. Law phrase.—"You shall cause to take possession." This is a writ which lies where a man has recovered a term for years in an action of ejectment, and it is directed to the sheriff in order to put the plaintiff into possession.

Habere facias visum. Lat. Law phrase.—"You shall cause a view to be taken." This is a writ which lies in several cases, as in Dower, Formedon, &c., where a view is to be taken of the lands or tenements in question.

Habet aliquid ex iniquo omne magnum exemplum, quod contra singulos utilitate publica rependitur. Lat. TACITUS.—

"Every great example of punishment has in it some tincture of injustice: the sufferings of individuals, however, are compensated by the promotion of the public good."

Habet in adversis auxilia, qui in secundis commodat. Lat. Publius Syrus.—"He who lends in the day of prosperity finds, meets with, help, assistance, in the day of adversity."

Habet Natura ut aliarum omnium rerum sic vivendi modum: senectus autem peractio aetatis est tanquam fabulae: cujus defatigationem fugere debemus praesertim adjuncta satietate. Lat. Cicero.—"Life, as well as all other things, has its bounds assigned by Nature; and its conclusion, like the last act of a play, is old age; the fatigue of which we ought to shun, especially when our appetites are fully satisfied."

Habitat. Lat.—Literally, "He dwells, inhabits, lives" [at such a place]: but used, in the burlesque style, to signify "a dwelling-place, abode, habitation," or, to use a Londonism, "one's whereabouts."

Habitué. Fr.—"A frequenter," particularly of places of public amusement.

Hablar sin pensar es tirar sin encarar. Span. prov.—"To speak without thinking is like shooting without taking aim."

Hac mercede placet. Lat.—"I am pleased, satisfied, with such conditions." "If knowledge and a respectable situation are to be purchased only on these terms, I, for my part, can readily say, *hac mercede placet.*"

Hacienda. Span.—"An estate."

Hactenus. Lat.—"Thus far." "*Hactenus* of plants," that is, Thus far [have I spoken] of plants.

Hadjee.—A pilgrim of the East, an Eastern pilgrim.

Hae nugae seria ducent in mala. Lat. Horace.—"These trifles, trifles such as these, will lead into serious mischief, evils: will involve one in serious mischief, trouble." That which is considered as mere sport may have a ruinous tendency.

Hae tibi erunt artes, pacisque imponere morem,
Parcere subjectis, et debellare superbos. Lat. Virgil.—
"Be these thy peculiar employments, the especial objects of thy attention, to impose the conditions of peace, to spare the lowly and humble the proud:"—

"Be these thine arts, to bid contention cease,
Chain up stern war, and give the nations peace;
O'er subject lands extend thy gentle sway,
And teach with iron rod the haughty to obey."

This is the character of a beneficent conqueror.

Haec olim meminisse juvabit. Lat. Virgil.—"It will be pleasing to call to mind these things hereafter, at a future period. The remembrance of these things will hereafter be a source of pleasure." There is a melancholy pleasure in the recollection of past misfortunes.

Haec perinde sunt, ut illius animus, qui ea possidet:
Qui uti scit, ei bona; illi, qui non utitur recte, malo.
Lat. Terence.—

"These [all earthly blessings], indeed, are all to be estimated by the temper of mind of him who possesses them: to him who knows the right use of them they are blessings; but to the man who does not make a right use of them they are naught but plagues, torments." Compare these admirable lines of HORACE:—

"Non domus et fundus, non aeris acervus et auri
Aegroto domini deduxit corpore febres,
Non animo curas. Valeat possessor oportet,
Si comportatis rebus bene cogitat uti."

"Neither houses, nor lands, nor heaps of gold and silver, can fence the body against the attacks of fever, or free the mind from anxiety and cares. Without health both of body and of mind we can have no relish for the provisions and enjoyments of life:"—

"[Who hath sufficient, should not covet more:]
Nor house, nor lands, nor heaps of labored ore
Can give the feverish lord one moment's rest,
Or drive one sorrow from his anxious breast;
The fond possessor must be blessed with health,
To reap the comforts of his hoarded wealth."

Haec sunt solatia, haec fomenta dolorum. Lat. CICERO.—"These things, such things as these, afford one some degree of consolation, and tend to soften down, allay, one's annoyances, vexations, grievances, griefs, sorrows."

Haeret lateri letalis arundo. Lat. VIRGIL.—"The Reviewer affects to have forgotten my name; but he has not forgotten 'The Beauties of the Edinburgh Review, *alias* the Stinkpot of Literature,' as it is called by Dr. Thompson:

'Haeret lateri letalis arundo.'

I will not say, It is an arrow in the hand of a giant; but this I will say, it was felt by those who are not accustomed to feel. They may exclaim with the Psalmist, 'The iron entered into our soul:'" that is to say, *The fatal shaft sticks in her side, The deadly arrow,* &c. [spoken of Dido, one of Virgil's characters]:—

"Fixed in her side she feels the painful dart,
The deadly weapon rankles in her heart."

N.B. This passage may be applied to any one who is wounded by calumny, censure, or remorse.

Haereticis non est servanda fides. Lat.—"No faith should be kept with heretics." [A tenet, dogma, of the Church of Rome.] N.B. The *true* meaning of the word "*heretic*" is, as every Greek scholar knows, or at any rate *ought* to know, *one who chooses to think for himself, or to form his own opinions on any subject.*

Hagiographa.—From the Gr. words *αγιος* [hagios], holy, and *γραφω* [grapho], I write. "The writings of holy men, the Holy Scriptures."

Αἱ δ' ελπιδες βοσκουσι φυγαδας, ὡς λογος,
Καλως βλεπουσιν ομμασι, μελλουσι δε. Gr. EURIPIDES.—

"Exiles, the proverb says, subsist on hope:
Delusive hope still points to distant good,
To good that mocks approach."

Halcyonei dies. Lat. COLUMELLA.—"Halcyon days." "The days he spent at that lovely spot he always spoke of as his *Halcyonei dies.*" N.B. The *Alcedo* [or kingfisher] was supposed by ARISTOTLE and PLINY to have only sat for seven days, in the depth of winter, and that, during that period, the mariner might sail in full security; hence the expression "*Halcyon days,*" a term used to express any season of happiness, prosperity, or peace, as, the Halcyon days of the poets; the brief tranquillity, the *septem placidi dies* [the seven calm, or smoothly-flowing, days], of human life, existence.

Halo. Lat.—From the Gr. word ἁλως [halos], a thrashing-floor. The luminous circle which appears sometimes round the moon, the apparent circumference of the sun or moon. N.B. The ancient Greek thrashing-floors were of a circular form.

Hanc veniam petimusque damusque vicissim. Lat. HORACE.—"We frankly give and take this liberty; we give, concede, this privilege, and receive it in turn." This line is applied and is particularly applicable to authors, who, as none of their works can attain perfection, should be mutually indulgent. It is scarcely necessary to remark how much the reverse of this precept prevails in practice.

'Απλουν το δικαιον· ῥᾳδιον το αληθες. Gr. LYCURGUS.—"Right, justice, equity, is a simple matter: truth an easy one [an easy thing]."

Hardi gagneur, hardi mangeur. Fr. prov.—"Quick at meat, quick at work."

Harem. Turkish.—The ladies' apartment, the abode of the females in an Eastern household. "The Turkish is the only European language," says Mr. URQUHART, in his *Spirit of the East,* "which possesses, in the word *harem,* a synonym [a word of the same meaning] for home; but it implies a great deal more. To picture a Turkish woman, I would beg the reader, if possible, to fancy to himself a woman without vanity or affectation, perfectly simple and natural, and preserving the manners and the type of her childhood in the full blossom and fructification of her passions and her charms." N.B. The *correct* spelling of the Turkish word is *haréem,* or *hharéem.*

Hatta Scherif. Turkish.—A warrant, proclamation, or decree, issued by the Sultan of Turkey.

Haud facile emergunt, quorum virtutibus obstat
Res angusta domi. Lat. JUVENAL.—
"Difficult indeed is it for those to emerge from obscurity, whose noble qualities are cramped by narrow means, straitened circumstances, at home:"—

"Rarely they rise by virtue's aid, who lie
Plunged in the depth of helpless poverty."

Haud facilem esse viam voluit. Lat. VIRGIL.—"The Almighty hath willed it that the way [to accomplish any thing great or valuable] should not be easy, should not be without difficulty, should not be unattended with difficulty." "*Haud facilem esse viam voluit* is the condition under which it has pleased Divine Providence that all the valuable objects of human aspiration should be attained." See "*Nil sine magno,*" *&c.*, and compare Shakspeare:—

"Too light winning makes the prize light."

Haud ulli veterum virtute secundus. Lat. VIRGIL.—"A man not inferior to any of the ancients in valor."

Haut goût. Fr.—A "high flavor," as in venison, &c. long kept: a "zest, relish, seasoning." By many the expression is used to denote a near approach to putrescence. N.B. *Haut goût* properly means *high-seasoned*, as, *viande de haut goût*, high-seasoned meat.

Hauteur. Fr.—"Height." Metaphorically used to signify "haughtiness, pride."

'Η *αιδως ανθος επισπειρει.* Gr. LYCOPHRONIDES.—"Modesty engenders, originates, gives rise to, grace, gracefulness." Every seed of beauty is sown by modesty.

'Η *ευδαιμονια ενεργεια τις εστι.* Gr. ARISTOTLE.—"Happiness is a certain energizing, activity both mental and bodily,—consists in putting forth, in calling into play, one's energies."

'Η *ζωη ενεργεια τις εστι, και ἑκαστος περι ταυτα και τουτοις ενεργει ἁ και μαλιστα αγαπᾳ· οἱον ὁ μεν μουσικος, τῃ ακοῃ περι τα μελη, ὁ δε φιλομαθης, τῃ διανοιᾳ περι τα θεωρηματα· οὑτω δε και των λοιπων ἑκαστος.* Gr. ARISTOTLE.—"Life is a certain energy, and each man energizes about those subjects, and with those faculties, for which he has the greatest affection; the musician, with his hearing, about sounds harmonious; the studious man, with his intellect, about matters of speculation; and in like manner each man else of the various sorts beside."

'Η *πρωτη φιλοσοφια.* Gr.—"THE FIRST PHILOSOPHY." The science of *Causes*, and, above all others, of causes *efficient* and *final*.

'Η *των θεων επιμελεια πασας μεν τας ανθρωπινας πραξεις επισκοπει, μαλιστα δε την περι τους γονεας, και τους τετελευτηκοτας, και την προς αὑτους ευσεβειαν. Εικοτως. Παρ' ὡν γαρ την αρχην του ζην ειληφαμεν, και πλειστα αγαθα πεπονθαμεν, εις τουτους μη ὁτι ἁμαρτειν, αλλ' ὁτι μη ενεργουντας τον αὑτων βιον καταναλωσαι, μεγιστον ασεβημα εστι.* Gr. LYCURGUS.—"The providence of GOD o'erlooks, o'ersees, all human actions, and, in particular, the dutiful and affectionate bearing, conduct, of children towards their parents, towards those who have died, and towards themselves and each other. And this justly, with reason; inasmuch as it not only betokens the utmost impiety to be wanting in our duty towards those from whom we have received our existence, and who have been constantly loading us with kindness, but also to be reluctant to lay down our lives for them, if necessary, in return for what they have again and again done for us."

'Η *φιλια εν μονοις τοις σπουδαιοις εστι.* Gr. DIOGENES LAERTIUS.—"Friendship exists among the virtuous alone."

Headborough. According to DR. JOHNSON, a "constable:" what *kind* of constable may be best seen by what follows:

"KING ALFRED instituted tithings, so called from the Saxon, because ten freeholders and their families composed one. These all dwelt together, and were sureties or free pledges to the king for the good behavior of each other. One of the tithing is annually appointed to preside over the rest, being called the tithing-man or *headborough*."—BLACKSTONE.

Hecatomb. From the Gr.—"A sacrifice of a hundred oxen or victims."

Hectare. Fr.—A "*hectare*" of land is 2,473,614 acres.

Ἡδονη μαλλον εν ηρεμιᾳ εστιν η εν κινησει· μεταβολη δε παντων γλυκυ, κατα τον ποιητην, δια πονηριαν τινα· ὡσπερ γαρ ανθρωπος ευμεταβολος ὁ πονηρος, και ἡ φυσις ἡ δεομενη μεταβολης· ου γαρ ἁπλη, ουδ' επιεικης. Gr. ARISTOTLE.—"Pleasure exists rather in rest than in motion, change of all things being sweet [according to the poet] only from a principle of pravity in those who believe so. For in the same manner as the bad man is fickle and changeable, so is that nature bad that requireth variety, inasmuch as such nature is neither simple nor even."

Hegira.—The Mohammedan era, which dates from the flight of MOHAMMED to Medina, on the 15th of July, A.D. 622.

Heimweh. Germ.—A hankering after home, literally "home-grief:" an inordinate and morbid desire of returning to one's home; the Swiss malady, the disease called by medical men "*nostalgia.*"

Helluo librorum. Lat. CICERO.—"A great reader;" literally, "a glutton with respect to books, a devourer of books."

Ἡπερ μεγιστη γιγνεται σωτηρια,
Ὁταν γυνη προς ανδρα μη διχοστατῃ. Gr. EURIPIDES.—
"This is the chief felicity of life,
When woman wars not on her lawful lord,
[does not quarrel with her husband]."

Heredis fletus sub persona risus est. Lat. prov.—"The weeping of an heir is laughter under a mask." He affects to mourn, in order to conceal his secret joy.

Heres jure repraesentationis. Lat.—"An heir by the right of representation." This is spoken of a grandson, who shall inherit from his grandfather, because in such case he represents and stands in place of his father.

Heres legitimus est quem nuptiae demonstrant. Lat. Law maxim.—"He is the lawful heir whom marriage points out to be such." A child born in wedlock, be it ever so soon after, is, in law, legitimate, and heir to the husband of his mother.

Hermes. Gr. in Roman letters.—The god MERCURY of the heathen mythology, supposed to have been the inventor of chemistry. Hence *hermetical*, chemical. To seal *hermetically* is to heat the neck of a glass till it is about to melt, and in this state with a pair of hot pincers to twist its parts together.

Herr. Germ.—"Master, lord, mister [Mr.], Sir [in addressing, *mein Herr*, Sir!], gentleman."

Heu! quam difficile est crimen non prodere vultu!
Lat. OVID.—
"How in the looks does conscious guilt appear!"

Heu! quam difficilis gloriae custodia est!
Lat. PUBLIUS SYRUS.—
"How difficult, alas! is the custody of glory!" How much more easy it is, in many cases, to attain, than to preserve, a high reputation!

Ἑυρηκα. Gr. [Heureka.]—"I have found it out." This was the exclamation of ARCHIMEDES, the famous geometrician and astronomer of Syracuse, when, on immersing his body in the bath, he discovered the means of ascertaining the purity of the golden crown made for HIERO, king of Sicily, from the space which it would occupy in water. It is now used mostly in ridicule, to mark an affected importance annexed to an insignificant discovery.

Heureux commencement est la moitié de l'oeuvre. Fr. prov. —"A good beginning is half the battle."

Heureux hasard. Fr.—"A fortunate chance."

'Εξομεν δι' οὺ τοὺ ανθρωπον τουτον διακριναι τε απο των αλλων ζωων, και ειλικρινως νοησαι δυνησομεθα. Gr. SEXTUS EMPIRICUS.—"We shall now have a criterion [test, by which one may judge] to distinguish this man from all other living beings, and be enabled thoroughly and distinctly to understand the whole of him." N.B. This was applied last century to WILLIAM GODWIN by the author of "THE PURSUITS OF LITERATURE."

Hi motus animorum atque haec certamina tanta
Pulveris exigui jactu compressa quiescent. Lat. VIRGIL.—
"These movements of their minds, and these violent contests, will cease and be repressed only by throwing a little dust." This is used by the poet, when speaking of a conflict between two swarms of bees. It is applied in a different sense to the contests of the ambitious.

"Yet all those dreadful deeds, this doubtful fray,
A cast of scattered dust will soon allay."

Hiatus maxime, *or*, **valde, deflendus.** Lat.—"A chasm, deficiency, gap, break, very much to be lamented, greatly to be deplored, bewailed." This is a phrase of frequent occurrence in the editions of the Grecian and Roman classics, to mark some loss sustained through the ravages of time. It is now sometimes used in ridicule, or to mark some passage omitted through design.

Hibernis ipsis Hiberniores. Lat.—"More Irish than the Irish themselves." "Liking the tyranny they were enabled to inflict under the Irish law, they found it at once profitable and pleasant to become *Hibernis ipsis Hiberniores.*"

Hic dies, vere mihi festus, atras
Eximet curas. Lat. HORACE.—
"This day [any day of rejoicing], truly a day of feasting to me, shall deliver me from all anxious cares."

IMITATED.

"Of all the days are in the week,
I dearly love but one day;
And that's the day that comes between
A Saturday and Monday." OLD BALLAD.

Hic est, aut nusquam, quod quaerimus. Lat. HORACE.—"What we seek after, want, is either here or nowhere." In our search after happiness we miss the good which is immediately before us, and direct our inquiries to that which either does not exist or is unattainable.

Hic et ubique. Lat.—"Here and there and everywhere." Used to mark a perpetual change of place.

Hic jacet. Lat.—"Here he, or she, lies."

"Where some surviving friend supplies
Hic jacet, and a hundred lies."

Hic manus, ob patriam pugnando vulnera passi,
Quique pii vates, et Phoebo digna locuti,
Inventas aut qui vitam excoluere per artes,
Quique sui memores alios fecere merendo. Lat. VIRGIL.—
"Here patriots live, who, for their country's good,
In fighting fields were prodigal of blood:—
Here poets, worthy their inspiring god,
And of unblemished life, make their abode:
And searching wits, of more mechanic parts,
Who graced their age with new-invented arts:
Those who to worth their bounty did extend;
And those who knew that bounty to commend."—DRYDEN.

May be applied to any country, that is a seat for talents and patronage.

—————Hic murus aëneus esto,
Nil conscire sibi, nulla pallescere culpa. Lat. HORACE.—
"Be this thy brazen wall of defense, to be conscious of no guilt, and not to turn pale on any charge [being brought against thee]." These oft-quoted lines import in substance that the consciousness of innocence forms our best security.

IMITATED.

"True, conscious honor is to feel no sin:
He's armed without who's innocent within:
Be this thy screen, and this thy wall of brass."—POPE.

Hic niger est: hunc tu, Romane, caveto. Lat. HORACE.—"This man, fellow, is of a black character: do you, Roman, beware of him, be on your guard against him. This fellow is black of heart; shun him, thou that hast the spirit of a Roman." The word "*niger*" [black] was used by the Latins to mark every thing which they deemed either wicked or unfortunate. The quotation is frequently used as a conclusion after summing up a man's bad qualities.

Hic patet ingeniis campus: certusque merenti
Stat favor: ornatur propriis Industria donis.
Lat. CLAUDIAN.—
"Here is a field open to talent: here merit will have certain, sure, favor: and industry will have its due reward." Such a field, however, but rarely offers. The quotation often presents itself to projectors, whose hopes are bolder than their expectations.

Hic vivimus ambitiosa paupertate omnes. Lat. JUVENAL.—"Here we all live in a state of ostentatious poverty:" here we all live with a poverty that apes our betters. With most men it is the business of their lives to conceal their wants:—

"The face of wealth in poverty we wear."

Poverty is often accompanied by pride of the most preposterous and outrageous description.

Hidalgo. Span.—A person of noble birth, a man of consequence, consideration: it is a compound of the words *hijo di alguno*, a son of SOMEBODY, as opposed to those who are *terrae filii*, obscure persons [literally, *sons of the earth*], sons of NOBODY.

Hidalguia. Span.—"Nobility." "He obtained for himself and descendants a patent of *Hidalguia.*"

Hinc illae lacrimae! Lat. TERENCE.—"Hence these tears, lamentations; hence proceed those tears." This is the secret or remote cause of the discontents which have been expressed. N.B. HORACE uses the expression with a different meaning: "Hence all this spite and malice!" See HORACE, Ep. i. 19, v. 41.

Hinc subitae mortes, atque intestata senectus. Lat. JUVENAL.—"Hence proceeds the number of sudden deaths, and of old men dying without making their wills, dying intestate." The poet is speaking of luxurious living [the pleasures of the table], which shortens the life of man, and most frequently takes off the hoary epicure by surprise.

Hinc vos, vos hinc mutatis discedite partibus. Lat. HORACE.—"Exit [begone], and change characters:"—you are at liberty to choose another station of life. The phraseology of the poet seems borrowed from the stage.

Hippodrome. From the Gr. word ἱπποδρομος [hippodromos].—"A place where horse-races are held, a race-course."

Hippomania. Gr. in Roman letters.—"Horse-madness, a rage for possessing horses, an extravagant fondness for horses and horse-racing."

His nunc praemium est, qui recta prava faciunt. Lat. TERENCE.—"There is a recompense, reward, in these days for those who can make a right conduct appear in a wrong point of view, for those who confound right and wrong." There are to be found in all ages unprincipled men, whose bills of misrepresentation, to borrow a mercantile phrase, are accepted and paid by persons as unprincipled as themselves.

His saltem accumulem donis, et fungar inani
Munere. Lat. VIRGIL.—
"I may at least bestow upon him these last offerings, and discharge a vain and unavailing duty." This quotation often serves to introduce a eulogy on some celebrated man, or some friend deceased.

"These gifts, at least, these honors I'll bestow,
And do what's right, though e'en a task of woe."

'Ιστορια φιλοσοφια εστιν εκ παραδειγματων. Gr.—"History is philosophy teaching by example."

"Sundry critics," says EDWARD KENEALY, in his *Brallaghan,* "have made a great fuss about LORD BOLINGBROKE'S celebrated definition—'History is philosophy teaching by example.' BOLINGBROKE himself admits that he took it from DIONYSIUS HALICARNASSENSIS; but the learned Thebans, who prate so much about their knowledge of Greek, have never been able to find the passage. Certainly, I have never seen it pointed out by any. All this is very funny in literary *Hidalgos,* who, like the man in RABELAIS, 'monochordize with their fingers, and barytonize with their tails;' and has often made me laugh heartily. The original of the definition is as follows—*Περι Λογων Εξετασεως—Τουτο και Θουκυδιδης εοικε λεγειν περι ιστοριας, λεγων, 'ότι και ιστορια φιλοσοφια εστιν εκ παραδειγματων.'* So that, after all, THUCYDIDES was the original author of this famous and certainly beautiful aphorism."

Historia quoquo modo scripta delectat. Lat. PLINY.—"History is always pleasing, write it as you will."

'Ο αγαθος φιλαυτος εστι· και γαρ αυτος ονησεται τα καλα πραττων, και τους αλλους ωφελησει. Gr. ARISTOTLE.—"The good man is a friend to self: for by doing what is laudable, he will always himself be profited as well as at the same time be beneficial to others."

'Ο ανθρωπος ευεργετος πεφυκως. Gr. MARCUS ANTONINUS.—"Man is naturally a beneficent creature."

'Ο ελαχιστων δεομενος εγγιστα θεων. Gr. SOCRATES.—"He who wants the least, whose wants are but few, bears the closest resemblance to the gods."

'Ο κοσμος οὗτος μια πολις εστι. Gr. EPICTETUS.—"This whole universe is one city, commonwealth." A doctrine of the Stoics [an ancient sect of philosophers, of which ZENO was the founder; so called from the Greek word *στοα* [stoa], a porch, a walking-place with pillars, in Athens, spacious, and finely embellished, where they used to meet and dispute].

'Ο μεν αγαθος ανηρ ουκ ευθεως ευδαιμων εξ αναγκας εστιν· ὁ δε ευδαιμων και αγαθος ανηρ εστι. Gr. ARCHYTAS.—"The good man is not of necessity happy: but the happy man is of necessity good."

'Ο πανυ. Gr.—"A man of supreme eminence."

Hoc age. Lat.—"Do, or mind, this." Attend without distraction to the object immediately before you.

Hoc erat in votis. Lat. HORACE.—"This was in my wishes." This was the chief or immediate object of my desire.

——————————Hoc est
Vivere bis, vita posse priore frui. Lat. MARTIAL.—
"It is living twice, when you can enjoy the recollection of your former life:"—

"The present joys of life we doubly taste
By looking back with pleasure on the past."

Hoc fonte derivata clades
In patriam populumque fluxit. Lat. HORACE.—
"From this source have been derived those calamities which have overwhelmed our country and our people." Used to mark the person who has originated, or the circumstance which has occasioned, any great political mischief. N.B. The term "*patriam*" contains an allusion to public calamities, while "*populum*," on the other hand, refers to such as are of a private nature, the loss of property, of rank, of character, &c.

Hoc indictum volo. Lat.—"I wish, could wish, such language to be unsaid." I recall, so far as I can, such language, the language to which I once gave utterance.

Hoc juvat, et melli est. Lat. HORACE.—"This is a source of delight, and is extremely pleasing to me:"—

"This pleases, and, to tell the truth,
It is as honey to the tooth."

Hoc maxime officii est, ut quisque maxime opis indigeat, ita ei potissimum opitulari. Lat. CICERO.—"It is a principal point of duty to assist another most, when he stands most in need of assistance."

Hoc non solum ingenii ac literarum, verum etiam naturae atque virtutis fuit. Lat. CICERO.—"This [literary work of his] was a monument not more of his talents as an author, than of his pure and upright character as a man."

Hoc opus, hic labor est. Lat. VIRGIL.—"This is, indeed, a task, this is a work [of no little difficulty]."

"This is a work of labor and of pain."

Hoc patrium est, potius consuefacere filium
Sua sponte recte facere, quam alieno metu. Lat. TERENCE.—"This, indeed, is the duty of a father, to accustom his son to what is right, more from his own choice than from any outward fear."

Hoc sustinete, majus ne veniat malum. Lat. PHAEDRUS.—"Bear with, submit to, put up with, this misfortune, lest a greater should befall you." Compare SHAKSPEARE:—"Better to bear the ills we have, than fly to others that we know not of."

Hoc volo—sic jubeo—sit pro ratione voluntas. Lat. JUVENAL.—"I WILL it—I INSIST on it!—let my will stand instead of reason!"

"You scruple, silly lout!—'tis my command—
My will—let that, Sir, for a reason stand."

The language of the tyrannical *virago* [manlike woman] when lording it over her husband: a character so admirably delineated and immortalized by JUVENAL. Compare SHAKSPEARE:—

"Passion the obstinate, not reason, rules,
For what they will they will; and there's an end."

Again—

"Lawless are they that make their wills their law."

Hoccine credibile est, aut memorabile,
Tanta vecordia innata cuiquam ut siet,
Ut malis gaudeat alienis, atque ex incommodis
Alterius sua ut comparet commoda? Ah!
Idne est verum? Lat. TERENCE.—"Is this a thing to be believed or related, that any one should be possessed of so untoward a soul as to rejoice at the misfortunes of others and build all his hopes of success upon their ruin? Ah! Can such a thing really be?"

Hochelaga.—The ancient, but little known, name of CANADA.

Hodie mihi, cras tibi. Lat.—"To-day to me, to-morrow it belongs to you." A phrase very happily descriptive of the vicissitude of human affairs.

Hodie vivendum, omissa praeteritorum cura. Lat.—"To-day we must live, enjoy the pleasures of the table, forgetting the cares that are past." This is an Epicurean maxim, used in the moments of conviviality.

Οἱ ποιηται, μιμουμενοι τον ανθρωπινον βιον, τα καλλιστα των εργων εκλεξαμενοι, μετα λογου και αποδειξεως τους ανθρωπους συμπειθουσι. Gr. LYCURGUS.—"Poets, by their delineations of human life, and by selecting for their subjects the most renowned actions of men, of the human race, persuade their fellow-men, by means of reason and powerful representation, to emulate such distinguished examples, models, of excellence."

Hoi polloi. Gr. in Roman letters.—"The many, the multitude." "Hoi polloi" is a term applied at Cambridge to those students who do not graduate in honors; *in other words*, who, with a few honorable exceptions, do just as much as is required for their degree, *and* NO MORE.

Οἱ θεοι ουδεν προτερον ποιουσιν η των πονηρων ανθρωπων την διανοιαν παραγουσι. Και μοι δοκουσι των αρχαιων τινες ποιητων, ὡσπερ χρησμους γραψαντες τοις επιγενομενοις, ταδε τα ιαμβεια καταλιπειν—

'Οταν γαρ οργη δαιμονων βλαπτῃ τινα,
Τουτ' αυτο πρωτον εξαφαιρειται φρενων,
Τον νουν τον εσθλον, εις δε την χειρω τρεπει
Γνωμην· ἱν' ειδῃ μηδεν ὡν ἁμαρτανει. Gr. LYCURGUS.—

"In their punishment of the wicked the gods first deprive them of their senses; and some of the ancient poets, writing, as it were, oracularly for posterity, seem to have expressed themselves to this effect:—'When the anger of the gods inflicts punishment on any one, they first deprive him of every right feeling, and divert his mind into a wrong channel, so that he has no longer any idea of the crimes that he has committed.'"

Holocaust. From the Gr. words *ὁλος* [holos], "whole," and *καυστος* [kaustos], "burnt." A sacrifice, in which the whole victim was burnt. "*Holocaust*" is, *literally*, "whole burnt."

Holograph. From the Gr. words *ὁλος* [holos], "whole," and *γραφη* [graphe], "a writing." Applied to a document written entirely by the granter, and said by DR. JOHNSON to be merely a technical word of Scots law.

Homily. From the Gr. word *ὁμιλια* [homilia], "familiar intercourse, a familiar discourse, conversation, persuasion." Used in the present day to signify one of a series of printed discourses, occasionally read by the clergy of the Church of England to their congregations.

Homine imperito nunquam quidquam injustius,
Qui, nisi quod ipse facit, nil rectum putat. Lat. TERENCE.—"There is nothing more unreasonable than a man without experience of the world, who will allow nothing to be right but what he does himself."

Hominem pagina nostra sapit. Lat. MARTIAL.—"Our page, book, relates to man." Our themes are drawn from observation, and are intended for the practical use of mankind.

Homines ad deos nulla re propius accedunt quam salutem hominibus dando. Lat. CICERO.—A contributor to the "Lancet" lately made the following communication to the Editor, in reference to this *oft-misapplied* quotation:—

SIR,—Once more, in an Introductory Lecture delivered at the commencement of the present session, and subsequently printed and circulated, the familiar sentence from Cicero's Oration "Pro Q. Ligario" has been misinterpreted and misapplied:—

"*Homines ad deos nulla re propius accedunt quam* salutem *hominibus dando.*" Now, every schoolboy knows that the word *salutem* does not here mean *bodily health* or *life*, but *personal security* or *safety*. The sense is clear from the context.

This fine expression of the great orator's would, perhaps, be still nobler had the original idea been that which we now so graciously accord to it, but it would not have been apposite to the purpose of his appeal. However, it is certainly time for us to leave off the quotation; for we have thoroughly worn it out, and it never belonged to us.

I am, Sir, yours, &c.

November, 1855. AZYGOS.

N.B. In the following extract from the pen of a distinguished writer the quotation is *correctly* applied:—

"Monsieur Guizot," says he [1837], "is just the sort of man to make a *great Protestant leader*—and just the sort of Minister to save France from anarchy and revolution on the one hand, and from Papal intrigue and *ultra*-Romanist reaction on the other: '*Homines ad deos nulla re propius accedunt quam* salutem *hominibus dando*';" that is to say, *In nothing do men approach so nearly to the gods as in*, or *by*, *giving* personal security, or safety, *to men, mortals, human beings.*

Homines amplius oculis quam auribus credunt. Longum iter est per praecepta, breve et efficax per exempla. Lat. SENECA.—"Men trust rather to their eyes than to their ears: the effect of precepts is therefore slow and tedious, whilst that of examples is summary and effectual." See "*Segnius irritant*," &c.

Homines nihil agendo discunt male agere. Lat. CATO.—"By doing nothing, men learn to do ill." Idleness is the parent of almost every vice.

Homini homo quid praestat! stulto intelligens quid interest! Lat. TERENCE.—"How much does one man excel another! What a difference there is betwixt a wise man and a fool!"

Homme d'état. Fr.—"A statesman."

Homme d'honneur n'a qu'une parole. Fr. prov.—"The man of honor has but one word, but one way of expressing himself [says what he means]."

Homme instruit. Fr.—"A literary man, learned man, man of learning."

Homme médiocre. Fr.—"A man who has but mediocrity of talent."

Homme propose, mais Dieu dispose. Fr. prov.—"Man proposes, but GOD disposes."

Homo doctus in se semper divitias habet. Lat. PHAEDRUS.—"A learned man has always riches in himself."

Homo extra est corpus suum cum irascitur.

Lat. PUBLIUS SYRUS.—"A man, when angry, is beside himself." See "*Ira furor*," &c.

Homo homini aut deus aut lupus. Lat. ERASMUS.—"Man is to man either a god or a wolf." Nothing can be more contrasted than the human character. The benevolence of some consoles and relieves, whilst the persecution of others destroys, their fellow-men.

Homo homini lupus. Lat. ERASMUS.—"Man is a wolf to man." The human race have been preying on each other ever since the Creation.

Homo, in periculum simul ac venit, callidus
Reperire effugium alterius quaerit malo.

Lat. PHAEDRUS.—"Whenever a cunning man, a man who is wide awake, falls into danger, he endeavors to find the means of escape by taking advantage of the weak side of another, by getting another in the same danger." Whenever a clever fellow gets into a mess, he tries to get out of it by making a cat's-paw of some one who is not quite so clever as himself.

Homo multarum literarum. Lat.—"A man of great, distinguished, learning."

Homo, naturae minister et interpres, de naturae ordine tantum scit et potest, quantum observaverit, nec amplius scit aut potest. Lat. LORD BACON.—"Man, the servant, attendant on, and interpreter of, nature, knows naught of the order of nature but what he has actually observed, what has fallen within the scope of his observation, nor knows he, nor can he know, aught beyond."

Homo nullorum hominum. Lat. TERENCE.—"A man fit for nobody's acquaintance, a man who has no fool like himself."

Homo perpaucorum hominum. Lat. TERENCE.—"A man of very few men." One of a thousand, one who admits but few into familiarity with him; one so delicate, so choice in his associates, that few seem to have merit enough to deserve his friendship.

Homo solus aut deus aut daemon. Lat.—"Man alone is either a god or a devil." No other being in existence is capable of such violent extremes.

Homo sum: humani nihil a me alienum puto. Lat. TERENCE.—"I am a man, and deem nothing that relates to mankind foreign to my feelings, beneath my notice, unworthy of my consideration." This is the strong phrase of a philanthropist, which it is to be feared is less frequently felt than quoted.

Homunculi quanti sunt! Lat. PLAUTUS.—"How great in number, how numerous, are the little-minded men!"

'Ον οἱ ϑεοι φιλουσιν, αποϑνησκει νεος. Gr. prov.—"He whom the gods love dies young." "GIBBON," says SOUTHEY, "has said of himself that, as a mere philosopher, he could not agree with the Greeks in thinking that those who die in their youth are favored by the gods: *'Ον οἱ ϑεοι φιλουσιν, αποϑνησκει νεος.*' It was because he was 'a mere philosopher' that he failed to perceive a truth which the religious heathen acknowledged, and which is so trivial, and of such practical value, that it may now be seen inscribed upon village tombstones. The Christian knows that 'blessed are the dead that die in the Lord; even so, saith the Spirit.' And the heart of the Christian mourner, in its deepest distress, hath the witness of the Spirit to that consolatory assurance."

Honesta mors turpi vita potior. Lat. TACITUS.—"An honorable death is preferable to a base, degraded, life." Our revealed religion forbids the act of suicide; but among the ancients it was a prevalent maxim, that a self-inflicted death was preferable to a life of disgrace.

Honesta quaedam scelera successus facit. Lat. SENECA.—"Success makes some species of wickedness appear honorable." This cannot be better illustrated than by the English epigram:—

"Treason does never prosper: what's the reason?
That if it prospers, none dare call it treason."

Honestas aliquando cum utilitate pugnat. Lat. CICERO.—"Honesty is sometimes opposed to interest, principle." Honesty says one thing, a crooked policy another.

Hong, *or* **Cohong.** Chinese.—"Security." The Chinese government continues wedded to certain maxims of commercial policy. They have not, indeed, attempted to suppress foreign trade, but they have subjected it to certain regulations. Among others, they have established, not in Canton only, but in every port of the empire, a limited number of persons denominated *Hong* or *security* merchants; and every foreign ship must, on her arrival, get one of these merchants to become security for the import and export duties payable on the inward and outward cargoes, and for the conduct of the crew.

Honi soit qui mal y pense. Old Fr.—"Evil be to him that evil thinks." "The Garter, like the Rose, was an old emblem of confidence, and the knighthood established under such an emblem was to be considered as pledged to the most intimate and unchangeable fidelity. 'As close to you as your garter' is an old phrase expressive of this sentiment. And the '*Honi soit qui mal y pense*' was a motto not unsuitably corrective of the suspicions that in such times might have been produced by such intercourse." "*Honi soit qui mal y pense*" is the motto of the Sovereigns of the British Empire, and also that of the Order of the Garter. A Duke of Orleans, perhaps in ridicule of the British monarch's motto, had "honi soit qui mal y *panse*" [*Evil be to him, or Woe betide him, who in these stables looks badly after the horses:* Shame on bad grooms] inscribed over the entrance of his princely stables at Chantilly. N.B. There is no such word as "*honi:*" it ought to be spelled "*honni.*"

Honnêtes gens. Fr.—"Honest people, upright persons."

Honor est a Nilo. Lat.—"Honor is from the Nile." "There seems to be a secret meaning in the very letters of a name, which only require to be decompounded and newly arranged, to reveal the life and character of the wearer. Let those, who may be disposed to laugh at this theory as fanciful, remember that they might in this manner have read the history of the battle of the Nile at the christening of HORATIO NELSON: *Honor est a Nilo* [a sentence composed of the letters of Lord Nelson's Christian name and surname, a *metagram*]." The metagram is attributed to the celebrated DOCTOR BURNEY.

———**Honor et nomen divinis vatibus atque**
Carminibus venit. Lat. HORACE.—

"Honor and renown have daily increased to Poetry and the divine race of Poets:"—

"Thus Verse became divine, and Poets gained applause."

Honorarium. Lat.—Used in the present day to signify "a fee." The *true* meaning, however, is, "A free gift, that was given to the Roman consul when he came into his province," and also, "A present, which officers paid on their first entry upon their office."

Honores mutant mores. Lat.—"Honors change manners."

Honos alit artes. Lat.—"Honor supports the arts." The liberal arts have never thriven in any state where the professors did not receive, in addition to the mere reward of their labor, the honorary marks of attention and distinction.

Honos est praemium virtutis. Lat. CICERO.—"Honor is the reward of virtue." An adage not always verified.

Horae momento aut cita mors venit, aut victoria laeta. Lat.

HORACE.—"In the short space of an hour comes either a speedy death or joyful victory:"—

"[The battle joins,] and in a moment's flight,
Death, or a joyful conquest, ends the fight."

Spoken of a military life, in which the suspense, however painful, is seldom protracted.

Horrea formicae tendunt ad inania nunquam:
Nullus ad amissas ibit amicus opes. Lat. OVID.—
"As the ant does not bend its way to empty barns, so no friend will be found to haunt the place of departed wealth." See "*Donec eris felix,*" *&c.*, and "*Ubi mel, ibi apes.*"

Horresco referens. Lat. VIRGIL.—"I shudder, while I pen these words, while I chronicle my tale."

Horribile dictu. Lat.—"Horrible to tell."

Hors de combat. Fr. military phrase.—"Out of condition for fighting." Applied to an army, or division of an army, so far discomfited and shattered as not to be able to resume offensive operations.

Hors de propos. Fr.—"Out of place, not to the purpose."

Hors la loi. Fr.—"Out of the pale of the law, outlawed." "He was declared *hors la loi.*"

Hortus siccus. Lat.—Literally, "A dry garden." A collection of plants preserved in a dried state.

Hos ego versiculos feci, tulit alter honores:
Sic vos non vobis nidificatis, aves.
Sic vos non vobis vellera fertis, oves.
Sic vos non vobis mellificatis, apes.
Sic vos non vobis fertis aratra, boves. Lat. VIRGIL.—
"I wrote these little verses, these versicles; but another had the credit of them: Thus do ye birds build nests not for yourselves. Thus do ye sheep wear fleeces not for yourselves. Thus do ye bees make honey not for yourselves. Thus do ye oxen bear the yoke not for yourselves." The application of these lines is to those who have suffered by the profit and honor of their labors being usurped by others. The history of these lines is curious. VIRGIL, the Latin poet, having written and posted up, in a conspicuous place, a distich [a couple of lines] highly flattering to the emperor AUGUSTUS, but without discovering himself, a poet of the name of BATHYLLUS pretended to be the author, and was consequently much noticed and rewarded by the prince. VIRGIL, not brooking the injustice patiently, wrote under the distich the words "*Sic vos non vobis,*" four times. No one having been able to complete the lines of which these are the beginning, except VIRGIL himself, the imposture of BATHYLLUS was detected, and VIRGIL recognized as the author of the applauded distich.

Hospice. Fr.—"A hospital," that affords a provision for helpless infancy, and poor persons afflicted with incurable diseases.

Hospice d'accouchement. Fr.—"A Lying-in Hospital."

Hospice d'allaitement. Fr.—"A Foundling Hospital."

'Οστις δ' απ' αλλης πολεως οικιζει πολιν,
Αρμος πονηρος ὡσπερ εν ξυλῳ παγεις,
Λογῳ πολιτης εστι, τοις δ' εργοισιν ου. Gr. EURIPIDES.—

"He who leaves his own country to take up his permanent abode in another, like a piece of wood that is badly joined to another piece, is a citizen of such country in name, but not in deed, in reality."

Hôtel de Ville. Fr.—"The Town Hall."

Hôtel des Invalides, or, **Les Invalides** [for *both* expressions are equally in use], is an hospital in Paris for old, infirm, and disabled soldiers: it was founded in 1669 by LEWIS THE FOURTEENTH.

Hôtel-Dieu. Fr.—"The house of GOD." The name of the principal hospital of a city or town in France.

Hottentot. A corruption of *Hollontontes*, an African tribe, known by the general name of Gallas, or perhaps Hollontontes from it. N.B. The Hottentots are also called Kaffers, or Zoolos.

——————————————**Huc propius me,**
Dum doceo insanire omnes vos, ordine adite.
Lat. HORACE.—

"Attend my lecture, whilst I plainly show
That all mankind are mad, from high to low."

Huic maxime putamus malo fuisse nimiam opinionem ingenii atque virtutis. Lat. CORNELIUS NEPOS, in reference to THEMISTOCLES.—"What led in our opinion to his greatest misfortunes, was, that he entertained too high an opinion of his own valor and talents." It has occurred in every age, and in every department of life, that men of the greatest ability have sunk and failed, merely from the overrated opinion which they entertained of their own qualifications.

Huic versatile ingenium sic pariter ad omnia fuit, ut natum ad id unum diceres, quodcunque ageret. Lat. LIVY.—"This man's talents were so convertible to all uses, that you would have declared him to have been born for that particular object on which he was at any time engaged." This is the character of the elder CATO.

Humano capiti cervicem pictor equinam
Jungere si velit, et varias inducere plumas
Undique collatis membris, ut turpiter atrum
Desinat in piscem mulier formosa superne,
Spectatum admissi risum teneatis, amici?
Credite, Pisones, isti tabulae fore librum
Persimilem, cujus, velut aegri somnia, vanae
Fingentur species, ut nec pes, nec caput uni
Reddatur formae. Lat. HORACE.—

"Should a painter take it into his head to join a mare's neck to a human head, and, borrowing limbs from every kind of animal, cover all with the feathers of various birds, in such manner that, being in the upper part of the figure a beautiful woman, it should terminate in a hideous fish; if admitted to see this fantastic piece, would you be able to refrain from laughter? Believe me, PISOS, that nothing more resembles this picture than a book in which the ideas are vague and confusedly jumbled together; in which the ideas are formed without any regard to sober reality, like the dreams of a disordered brain, and where the head and the feet have no relation to the other parts." An admirable satire on books that are pompously written.

Humanitati qui se non accommodat,
Plerumque poenas oppetit superbiae. Lat. PHAEDRUS.—"He who in his intercourse with others shows a want of good breeding, who is deficient in complaisance to others, is, generally speaking, in the long run, punished for his haughty demeanor."

Humanum est errare. Lat.—"It is natural to man, is the lot of humanity, to err." This phrase was happily seized by the poet, when he, at the same time, availed himself of the contrast:

"To err is *human:* to forgive, *divine.*"

Humiles laborant, ubi potentes dissident. Lat. PHAEDRUS.—"Those who are inferior in power or strength are oppressed whenever the powerful are at variance."

Hung-maow. Chinese.—"Redpates." The Chinese designation of the English.

Hurler avec les loups. Fr.—"To howl with the wolves, howl when others yell, do like the rest, accommodate one's self to the whims and fancies of others, follow the fashion."

Hurrah!—This word is pure Slavonian, and is commonly heard from the coast of Dalmatia to Behring's Straits, when any of the population within these limits are called on to give proof of courage and valor. The origin of the word belongs to the primitive idea that every man that dies heroically for his country goes straight to heaven, *Hu-raj* ["to paradise"]; and so it is that in the shock and ardor of battle the combatants utter that cry, as the Turks do that of "*Allah!*" each animating himself, by the certainty of immediate reward, to forget earth and to despise death.

Hurtar el puerco, y dar los pies por Dios. Span. prov.—"To steal a hog, and give away the feet in alms." A reflection upon those who are charitable with the wealth, property, of others.

———————*'Υφηγητηρος ουδενος φιλων,*
Αλλ' αυτος ἡμιν πασιν εξηγουμενος. Gr. SOPHOCLES.—"Loving no leader, indifferent to any leader or instructor, he was himself the leader, guide, instructor, of us all."

Hygiène. Fr.—"The art of estimating the bodily powers, of exciting and sustaining them so as to preserve life as much as possible, as well as possible, and as long as possible." This is the definition of *Monsieur Reveillé-Parise*, a distinguished physician, whose loss was universally regretted.

Hypotheses non fingo. Lat. SIR ISAAC NEWTON.—"I make no suppositions, I deal not with suppositions [but with facts]."

Hysterica passio. Lat.—"Hysteric passion [suffering, ailing, disorder], passion of the mind, *Hysterics.*"

"Oh! how this mother swells up towards my heart!
Hysterica passio—Down, thou climbing sorrow!
Thy element's below." SHAKSPEARE.

'Υστερον προτερον. Gr. [Hysteron proteron].—"The last put first." The positions or arguments inverted from their natural order; or, as we familiarly say, "Putting the cart before the horse." A way of speaking when we place that after which should come before, as, "*Let us die, and rush into the midst of the fight.*"

I.

———**I, demens, et saevas curre per Alpes,**
Ut pueris placeas, et declamatio fias. Lat. JUVENAL.—"Go then, madman, and hurry over the rugged Alps, that you may be the delight of boys, and furnish subjects for declamation!" Go, desperate man, and encounter the severest hazards, to be rewarded only by the most trivial consolations. A sarcasm [*literally*, "tearing off the flesh," cutting raillery, a bitter taunt] on HANNIBAL [the distinguished Carthaginian commander] and those who are ambitious of military fame:—

"Go, madman, go! at toil and danger mock,
Pierce the deep snow, and scale the eternal rock,
To please the rhetoricians, and become
A DECLAMATION for the boys of Rome!"

I fatti sono maschii, le parole femine. Ital. prov.—"Deeds are males, and words are females."

I matti fanno le feste, ed i savj se le godono. Ital. prov.—"Fools make feasts, and wise men enjoy them."

I sciocchi e gli ostinati
Arrichiscon gli avvocati. Ital. prov.—"Fools and obstinate persons enrich the lawyers."

I secundo omine. Lat. HORACE.—"Go with a favorable anticipation of good luck. Go, and may good luck attend thee!"

Ibant obscuri sola sub nocte per umbram. Lat. VIRGIL.—"They went alone, by themselves, in the gloom and stillness of night." "Whatever guides we chanced to follow, '*ibant obscuri sola sub nocte per umbram:*' they led us into the regions of darkness, and left us there."

Ibidem. Lat.—"In the same place." A note of reference. **N.B.** Often written in an abridged form: thus, *Ibid.*

Ibit eo, quo vis, qui zonam perdidit. Lat. HORACE.—"He who has lost his purse will go whither you will." Poverty incites men to the most desperate actions.

Ιβυκου εκδικοι. Gr.—"The avengers of IBYCUS." IBYCUS, an amatory poet of Rhegium in Italy, is more known by the circumstances related of his death than by any thing now remaining of him. The story is, that he was waylaid by thieves, who murdered him; and that, in dying, he remarked some cranes flying overhead, and said that perhaps those birds would be the avengers of his death! Afterwards, two of the murderers being seated in the theater, one of them saw some cranes, and said jocularly to his fellow, "Behold the avengers of IBYCUS!" This was overheard, supicion was excited, and ultimately the truth was discovered. Hence *Ιβυκου εκδικοι* became proverbial of a culprit punished, or felony brought to light.

Ich dien. German.—"I serve." The motto of the Prince of Wales. This motto was first assumed by EDWARD, THE BLACK PRINCE, who took it from the King of Bohemia, who was killed at the battle of Cressy, in which he served as a volunteer.

Içi on parle Français. Fr.—"Here French is spoken." A very common notification in shop-windows.

————————————Id arbitror
Adprime in vita esse utile, ut NE QUID NIMIS.

Lat. TERENCE.—"I take it to be a very useful maxim in life, a maxim of the greatest utility in life, not to do any thing too much, to follow nothing too eagerly, not to be too much addicted to any one thing." N.B. "NE QUID NIMIS" was a common proverb. General sentences, such as these, are, for the most part, observations drawn from life itself, the very dictates of wisdom, and confirmed to be just by long experience. Their simplicity and brevity make us often overlook the deep sense contained in them. The present may serve as an instance of it, being in no respect different from these two celebrated and oft-quoted lines of HORACE:—

"Est modus in rebus, sunt certi denique fines,
Quos ultra citraque nequit consistere rectum."

[Which see.] PLATO observes that the ancients included their whole system of morality in these short proverbial sentences.

Id est. Lat.—"That is." Hence our contraction *i.e.*, as when we say, "momentum, *i.e.* moving force."

Id facere laus est quod decet, non quod licet. Lat. SENECA.—"It is a glory [*praiseworthy*] to do what is fit, proper, becoming, right, and not merely that which the law allows or does not actually disallow."

————Id genus est hominum pessumum,
In denegando modo queis pudor est paululum;
Post ubi jam tempus est promissa perfici,
Tum coacti necessario se aperiunt, et timent:
Et tamen res cogit eos denegare. Lat. TERENCE.—

"These are undoubtedly the worst and most dangerous of all men, who are ashamed of giving a downright refusal, but when the time for performance comes, finding themselves hard pressed, are necessarily obliged to take off the mask; they are afraid, and yet the thing itself obliges them to deny."

Id maxime quemque decet, quod est cujusque suum maxime. Lat. CICERO.—"That best becomes every man, which is more particularly his own," or, in other and coarser words, "which he is *best at*."

Idem inficeto est inficetior rure,
Simul poëmata attigit; neque idem unquam
Aeque est beatus, ac poëma cum scribit:
Tam gaudet in se, tamque se ipse miratur.
Nimirum idem omnes fallimur: neque est quisquam
Quem non in aliqua re videre Suffenum
Possis. Lat. CATULLUS.—

"Suffenus has no more wit than a mere clown when he attempts to write verses; and yet he is never happier than when he is scribbling: so much does he admire himself and his compositions. And, indeed, this is the foible [weakness] of every one of us; for there is no man living, who is not a Suffenus in one thing or other."

Idem sonans. Lat.—"The verb was unluckily *idem sonans* with another word," that is, "sounding alike, or of the same sound," with," &c.

Idem velle, et idem nolle, ea demum firma amicitia est. Lat. SALLUST.—"To live in friendship is to have the same desires and the same aversions. To wish for and reject things with similar feelings is the only foundation of friendship." True friendship can only spring from perfect sympathy [feeling with one].

Idoneus homo. Lat. CICERO.—"A fit man." A man of known ability.

Idoneus quidem mea sententia, praesertim quum et ipse eum audiverit, et scribat de mortuo; ex quo nulla suspicio est amicitiae causa eum esse mentitum. Lat. CICERO.—"A competent person, in my opinion [to write of the deceased], as he was accustomed often to hear him, and as he published his sentiments after the subject of them was no more: there is no reason, therefore, to suppose that his partiality has misled him from the truth."

Ignavissimus quisque, et, ut res docuit, in periculo non ausurus, nimio verbis et lingua ferox. Lat. TACITUS.—"Every recreant who proved his timidity in the hour of danger was afterwards the most talkative and bold in his discourse." The greatest coward in the field is generally found to be the loudest boaster after the battle.

Ignis fatuus. Lat.—*Literally*, "A foolish fire." An igneous meteor, seen in moist places. The meteor, or ignited vapor, commonly known by the name of "WILL o' the wisp, WILL with a wisp." It is applied metaphorically to a discourse or treatise which, whilst it affects to enlighten, tends only to confound and mislead.

"*Ignis fatuus*" is also sometimes used to signify "mere moonshine:"—

"Sorrow is my perpetual guest,
The constant inmate of my mournful breast;
Joy but an *ignis fatuus* light at best,
Just seen and gone!"

LADY E. STUART WORTLEY.

Ignobile vulgus. Lat. VIRGIL.—"The ignoble vulgar, the rude multitude, the mob, the rabble, the rascality."

Ignoramus. Lat.—"We are ignorant." This is the term used when the grand jury, impanneled on the inquisition of criminal causes, reject the evidence as too weak to make good the presentment or indictment brought against a person so as to bring him on his trial by a petty jury. This word, in that case, is indorsed on the back of the indictment, and all further proceedings against the individual are stopped. "*Ignoramus*" is also used to signify "a blockhead, an uninformed person, an ignorant fellow."

Ignorantia facti excusat. Lat. Law maxim.—"Ignorance of the fact excuses." If an illiterate man seals a deed which is read to him falsely, the same shall be void.

Ignorantia non excusat legem. Lat. Law maxim.—"The ignorance of the individual does not prevent the operation of the law." Every one in the kingdom is subject to the penalty of laws which have, perhaps, never been duly promulgated.

Ignorare mala, bonum est. Lat. SENECA.– "To be ignorant of evil, a stranger to wickedness, is a positive good, a blessing."

Ignorent populi, si non in morte probaris
An scieris adversa pati. Lat. LUCAN.—
"Future ages might be ignorant of your greatness of mind, if you had not proved in death that you knew how to bear up against adverse circumstances." This praise, applied to Pompey [a valiant and successful Roman warrior], has successively been given to others who, deeming themselves engaged in a good cause, have known how to suffer death itself with magnanimity.

Ignoscas aliis multa, nil tibi. Lat. AUSONIUS.—"Forgive many things in others, but naught in thyself."

Ignoscito saepe aliis, nunquam tibi. Lat. PUBLIUS SYRUS.—"Often forgive others, but never thyself."

Ignoti nulla cupido. Lat.—"No desire is felt for that which is unknown." The African or American savage does not feel the want of European luxuries; or, coming nearer home, the villagers, the peasantry, feel not the want of things which, among their superiors, are considered as necessaries.

Ignotum per ignotius. Lat.—"That which is unknown by something more unknown." He has explained the matter *ignotum per ignotius:* he has offered as an illustration that which tends to involve the matter in deeper obscurity.

Ihr sagt es sey nichts als das Glück
Zu siegen ohne die Tactick;
Doch besser ohne Tactick siegen
Als mit derselben unterliegen. TYROLESE EPIGRAM.—
"You say 'tis luck alone when those
Unskilled in tactics beat their foes;
But better 'tis without to win,
Than with these tactics to give in."

Ικμας φροντιδος. Gr.—"The mental sap;" literally, "The moisture of thought, reflection." "Ten or twelve hours of active intellectual exertion, in the course of the twenty-four, are enough for any man who wishes to keep the *ικμας φροντιδος* circulating briskly through his brains. Deprived of that wholesome circulation, the brains turn moldy; and moldy brains breed maggots."

Il a semé des fleurs sur un terrain aride. Fr.—"He has planted flowers on a barren soil." He has bestowed literary decoration on a work where the nature of the subject rendered it almost impossible.

Il arrive beaucoup de choses entre la bouche et le ventre; de la main à la bouche se perd souvent la soupe. Fr. prov.—"There's many a slip 'twixt the cup and the lip."

Il conduit bien sa barque. Fr. prov.—"He steers his boat well." He knows how to make his way through the world.

Il coûte peu à amasser beaucoup de richesses, et beaucoup à en amasser peu. Fr.—"It requires but little effort to amass considerable riches, but much effort to collect but little." The man of property can easily enlarge his wealth; but the man who has nothing has to maintain a hard struggle in his weak beginnings. "The first thousand," it has been elsewhere said, "is more difficult of acquisition than the last million."

Il diavolo tenta tutti, ma l'ozioso tenta il diavolo. Ital. prov. —"The devil tempts every one, but the lazy man tempts the devil."

Il en est d'un homme qui aime comme d'un moineau pris à la glu; plus il se débat, plus il s'embarrasse. Fr.—"It is with a man in love as with a sparrow caught with bird-lime: the more he strives, the more he is entangled."

Il en fait ses choux gras. Fr. prov.—"He thereby makes his cabbages fat." He feathers his nest by it.

Il est bas, or, **bas percé.** Fr.—"He is at a low ebb, it goes hard with him." In reference to want of money.

Il est bon d'être habile, mais non pas de le paraître. Fr. prov. —"'Tis a good thing to be clever, but not to appear so."

Il est bon de parler, et meilleur de se taire. Fr. prov.—"'Tis a good thing to speak, but 'tis better to be silent."

Il est comme l'oiseau sur la branche. Fr. prov.—"He is like the bird on the branch." His disposition is too wavering.

Il est du bois dont on fait les flûtes, il est de tous bons accords. Fr.—"He is anybody's man; he will chime in with any thing."

Il est plus aisé d'être sage pour les autres que pour soi-même. Fr. Rochefoucault.—"It is easier to be wise for other persons than for ourselves." We can judge with more coolness where our own feelings are not immediately concerned.

Il est plus honteux de se défier de ses amis que d'en être trompé. Fr. Rochefoucault.—"It is more disgraceful to suspect our friends than to be deceived by them."

Il fait déjà le barbon. Fr. prov.—"He already plays the graybeard, he is a young Solomon."

Il faut attendre le boiteux. Fr. prov.—"We must wait for the lame man." This news is doubtful: we must wait for the truth, which comes haltingly behind.

Il faut battre le fer pendant qu'il est chaud. Fr.—"We must strike the iron while it is hot: we must make hay while the sun shines."

Il faut de plus grandes vertus pour soutenir la bonne fortune que la mauvaise. Fr.—"It requires a greater share of virtue to sustain a situation of prosperity than to support one of adversity." Good fortune is apt to intoxicate the mind, which, on the contrary, is subdued and ameliorated in an adverse situation.

Il faut être reservé même avec son meilleur ami, lorsque cet ami témoigne trop de curiosité pour pénétrer votre secret. Fr. La Bruyère.—"It is prudent to be on the reserve even with your best friend, when he shows himself over-anxious to develop your secret."

Il faut gouverner la fortune comme la santé; en jouir quand elle est bonne, prendre patience quand elle est mauvaise, et ne faire jamais de grands remèdes sans un extrême besoin. Fr. Rochefoucault.—"We must regulate our fortune like our health; enjoy it when it is good, have patience when it is bad, and never resort to powerful remedies except in extreme cases."

Il faut ôter tout afin de donner quelque chose. Fr.—"We must take every thing, all, so that we may have something to give." A favorite maxim of despotic powers.

Il gran maestro di color chi sanno. Ital.—"The great master of those who know any thing; the Coryphaeus [which see] of the knowing ones." Has been applied, and very justly, to LORD BACON.

Il monde è fatto a scale;
Chi le scende, e chi le sale. Ital. prov.—"The world is like a staircase, up which one goes, and down which another comes."

Il n'a ni bouche ni éperon. Fr. prov.—"He has neither mouth nor spur." He has neither wit nor courage.

Il n'a pas inventé la poudre. Fr. prov.—"He was not the inventor of gunpowder." He is no conjurer.

Il n'appartient qu'aux grands hommes d'avoir de grands défauts. Fr. ROCHEFOUCAULT.—"It belongs only to great men to have great defects." Such defects are palliated, at least, where great qualities can be pleaded as a set-off.

Il n'est d'heureux que qui croit l'être. Fr. prov.—"The only happy man is he who thinks himself so."

Il n'est de pire sourd que celui qui ne veut ouïr. Fr. prov.—"Who so deaf as they that will not hear?"

Il n'est meilleur ami, ni parent, que soi-même. Fr. prov.—"There is no better friend or relation than one's self."

Il n'est orgueil que de pauvre enrichi. Fr. prov.—"No pride is like that of a poor man who has once become rich."

Il n'est rien d'inutile aux personnes de sens. Fr. prov.—"Nothing, no kind of knowledge, is useless to persons of sense, to sensible persons."

Il n'est sauce que d'appétit. Fr. prov.—"Hunger is the best sauce."

Il n'est si homme de bien qu'il mette à l'examen des loix toutes ses actions et pensées, qui ne soit pendable dix fois en sa vie. Fr. MONTAIGNE.—"The most virtuous man would, ten times at least, in the course of his life, be considered a fit subject for the gallows, were he to submit all his thoughts and actions to the rigid scrutiny of the laws of his country."

Il ne faut pas éveiller le chat qui dort. Fr. prov.—"We must not awaken the sleeping cat." One should not bring into question a dormant secret, nor stir a sleeping mischief; one should not rake up old grievances.

Il ne faut pas manger tout son bien en un jour. Fr. prov.—"We should not make away with all we have in one day, in a single day: he who spends more than he should will not have to spend when he would."

Il ne faut pas mettre le doigt entre le bois et l'écorce. Fr. prov.—"Put not your finger between the bark and the wood:" one must not part man and wife.

Il ne faut pas nous fâcher des choses passées. Fr. NAPOLEON

BONAPARTE.—"We should not put ourselves out, not annoy ourselves, about things that are passed."

Il ne faut qu'une brebis galeuse pour gâter tout un troupeau. Fr. prov.—"One scabbed sheep will taint a whole flock."

Il ne sait plus de quel bois faire flèche. Fr. prov.—"He is at his last shift:" *literally*, "He knows not of what wood to make his arrow."

Il ne sait sur quel pied danser. Fr. prov.—"He knows not on which leg to dance." He is at his wits' end.

Il n'y a pas de bien sans mélange de mal. Fr. prov.—"There is no good without alloy." See "*Nihil est ab omni*," *&c.*

Il n'y a point au monde un si pénible métier que celui de se faire un grand nom; la vie s'achève avant que l'on a à peine ébauché son ouvrage. Fr. LA BRUYÈRE.—"No undertaking is so difficult as that of getting a great name; life is closed when the task has scarcely been begun."

Il n'y a point de gens qui sont plus méprisés que les petits beaux esprits, et les grands sans probité. Fr. MONTESQUIEU.—"There is no description of men so much despised as your *minor* wits, and men of rank without probity."

Il n'y a point d'homme vertueux qui n'ait quelque vice, et de méchant qui n'ait quelque vertu. Fr.—"There is no virtuous man without some vice or weakness, nor any wicked man without some virtue, some redeeming point in his character."

Il n'y a qu'un pas du sublime au ridicule. Fr. SIEYES.—"From the sublime to the absurd there is but one step, a step."

Il n'y a que la vérité qui blesse. Fr.—"Truth is the only thing that is offensive, unpalatable, that wounds our feelings, our self-esteem."

Il n'y a que le premier pas qui coûte. Fr. prov.—"The only difficulty is the first step: it is only the first step that gives trouble." N.B. The French proverb is often quoted *erroneously*, thus: "*c'est le premier pas qui coûte.*"

Il piccol prestito fa un amico; e il grande, un nemico. Ital. prov.—"A small loan makes a friend, a great one an enemy."

Il poco mangiar e poco parlare non fece mai male. Ital. prov. —"Eating little and speaking little have never injured any one."

Il sabio muda conscio, il nescio no. Port. prov.—"A wise man changes his mind, a fool never." The former will reflect and recall his opinions; the obstinacy of the latter is proportioned to his ignorance.

Il satollo non crede al digiuno. Ital. prov.—"A full belly knows not the meaning of hunger."

Il savio udendo più savio diventa. Ital. prov.—"The wise man by listening becomes still wiser."

Il va du blanc au noir. Fr. prov.—"He runs into extremes:" *literally*, "He goes from white to black."

Il vaut mieux employer notre esprit à supporter les infortunes, qui nous arrivent, qu'à prévoir celles qui nous peuvent arriver. Fr. ROCHEFOUCAULT.—"It is better to turn our attention to supporting the misfortunes which happen to us, than in anticipating those which may, *perhaps*, happen."

Il vaut mieux être oiseau de campagne qu'oiseau de cage. Fr. prov.—"It is better to be a bird at liberty than a bird in a cage. Poverty at large is better than wealth in a prison."

Il vaut mieux tâcher d'oublier ses malheurs que d'en parler. Fr.—"It is better for a man to forget his misfortunes than to talk of them." He who is too querulous not only feeds his own regret, but excites disgust in others.

Il veut être ou César, ou rien, Fr. prov.—"He will be either every thing or nothing."

Il volto sciolto ed i pensieri stretti. Ital.—"The countenance open, but the thoughts strictly reserved." This is the difficult maxim so strongly recommended by Lord Chesterfield. The man who can assume an apparent frankness, and at the same time keep his opinions impenetrably concealed, is fit for a politician, *or any thing else.*

Il y a anguille sous roche. Fr. prov.—"There is an eel under the rock." There is a mystery in the affair.

Il y a bien des gens qu'on estime parce qu'on ne les connoît point. Fr.—"There are many persons who are esteemed only because they are not known." There are many who mask their real dispositions so successfully as to be esteemed for qualities which they never possessed.

Il y a des gens à qui la vertu sied presque aussi mal que la vice. Fr. Bouhours.—"There are some persons on whom virtue sits almost as ungraciously as vice." There are those who detract from the intrinsic dignity of virtue by their arrogance or austerity.

Il y a des gens dégoûtants avec du mérite, et d'autres qui plaisent avec des défauts. Fr.—"There are persons of merit who are disgusting, and there are others who please with all their defects." So much depends upon manner, suavity, and conciliation.

Il y a des gens qui ressemblent aux vaudevilles, qu'on ne chante qu'un certain temps. Fr. Rochefoucault.—"There are certain persons whose fame is like that of a popular ballad, which is sung for a certain time and is then forgotten."

Il y a des reproches qui louent, et des louanges qui médisent. Fr. Rochefoucault.—"There are some reproaches which form a commendation, and some praises which are, in fact, a slander." There are some persons whose censure is praise, and whose praise is infamy.

Il y a du haut et du bas dans la vie. Fr. prov.—"There are ups and downs in life, in the world."

Il y a encore de quoi glaner. Fr. prov.—"There is something yet to be gleaned." The subject is not wholly exhausted.

Il y a plus de fous acheteurs que de fous vendeurs. Fr. prov.—"There are more foolish buyers than sellers."

Iliacos intra muros peccatur, et extra. Lat. Horace.—"They sin both within and without the walls of Troy." There are faults to be found on both sides.

Illa dolet vere, quae sine teste dolet. Lat. Martial.—"She who grieves unseen grieves sincerely." Before company her grief might possibly be suspected of affectation.

**Illam, quicquid agit, quoquo vestigia flectit,
Componit furtim, subsequiturque decor.** Lat. TIBULLUS.—
"Whate'er she does, where'er her steps she bends,
Grace on each action silently attends:"—
Compare MILTON:—
"Grace was in all her steps, heaven in her eye,
In every gesture dignity and love."

Ille crucem pretium sceleris tulit, hic diadema! Lat. JUVENAL. —"One man receives crucifixion as the reward of his villainy; another a regal crown!" One murderer, for instance, ascends a throne, whilst another mounts a scaffold. See "*Multi committunt,*" *&c.*

**Ille igitur nunquam direxit brachia contra
Torrentem, nec civis erat, qui libera posset
Verba animi proferre, et vitam impendere vero.**
Lat. JUVENAL.—
"He, therefore, never attempted to swim against the stream, nor was he a citizen who dared give vent to the free sentiments of his soul, and devote his life to the cause of truth." This is an admirable description, though in negative terms, of the qualities of a good patriot.

**——————Ille potens sui
Laetusque deget, cui licet in diem
Dixisse, Vixi.** Lat. HORACE.—
"That man will live happy and master of himself, and in command of himself, who from day to day can say, *I have lived:*" that is, I have enjoyed, as they should be enjoyed, the blessings of existence:—
"Happy the man, and happy he alone,
He who can call to-day his own;
He who, secure within, can say,
To-morrow do thy worst, for I have lived to-day."
DRYDEN.
The man who has lived for beneficent purposes, and has laid up a store of good actions, has little to fear from any change while "*all is peace within.*"

**Ille sinistrorsum, hic dextrorsum abit; unus utrique
Error, sed variis illudit partibus.** Lat. HORACE.—
"One deviates, takes, to the right, another to the left; the error is the same with all, but it deceives them in different ways; each errs, but in a different way from the other:"—
"One reels to this, another to that wall:
'Tis the same error that deludes them all."

**Ille terrarum mihi praeter omnes
Angulus ridet.** Lat. HORACE.—
"So congenial has the Cape of Good Hope [1837] been found with the feelings and pursuits of that amiable and accomplished scholar and philosopher, Sir John Herschel, that, hardly able to tear himself away, he is ready to say with Horace [as indeed he *has* said in other and stronger words],
'*Ille terrarum mihi praeter omnes
Angulus ridet:*'
that is, 'That corner of the earth possesses charms for me more than,

over and above, all other places,' possesses more charms for me than any other spot on earth, on the face of the globe:—

'No spot so joyous smiles to me
Of this wide globe's extended shores.'"

Illi mors gravis incubat,
Qui, notus nimis omnibus,
Ignotus moritur sibi. Lat. Seneca.—
"Death presses heavily on that man who, being but too well known to others, dies at last in ignorance of himself:"—

"He who is taken unprepared,
Finds death an evil to be feared,
Who dies to others too much known,
A stranger to himself alone."

Again:—

"To him, alas! to him, I fear,
The face of death will terrible appear,
Who, in his life, flattering his senseless pride,
By being known to all the world beside,
Does not himself, when he is dying, know,
Nor what he is, nor whither he's to go."—Cowley.

Illic enim debet toto animo a poëta in dissolutionem nodi agi; eaque praecipua fabulae pars est, quae requirit plurimum diligentiae. Lat. Cicero.—"The poet ought to exert his whole strength and spirit in the solution of his plot, which is the principal part of the fable, and requires the utmost diligence and care."

Illud amicitiae sanctum ac venerabile nomen
Nunc tibi pro vili, sub pedibusque jacet. Lat. Ovid.—
"The sacred and venerable name of friendship is now trampled on and despised by you." You have perfidiously burst those bonds of friendship by which we were so closely united.

Illud maxime rarum genus est eorum, qui aut excellente ingenii magnitudine, aut praeclara eruditione atque doctrina, aut utraque re ornati, spatium deliberandi habuerunt, quem potissimum vitae cursum sequi vellent. Lat. Cicero.—"There are very few persons of extraordinary genius, or eminent for learning and other noble endowments, who have had sufficient time to consider what particular course of life they ought to pursue."

Ils se sont mangé le blanc des yeux. Fr.—"They have been at daggers-drawing, have fallen out seriously," *literally*, "They have eaten the white of each other's eyes."

Imbécile. Fr.—"A fool," an idiot.

Imitatores, servum pecus! Lat. Horace.—"Ye imitators, a vile, servile herd!" Addressed to servile copyists, who show at once their meanness and their weakness by living on the borrowed spoils of others.

Immer wird, nie ist. German, Schiller.—[Truth] "never is, always is a-being."

Immortale odium, et nunquam sanabile vulnus:
Inde furor vulgo, quod numina vicinorum
Odit uterque locus; cum solos credat habendos
Esse deos, quos ipse colit. Lat. Juvenal.—

"There is a deathless hatred and a rankling wound, that knows no cure [between these two sections of the community]. On both sides, the principal rancor arises from the fact that each of these hates its neighbor's gods, and believes those only ought to be held as deities which itself worships:"

"Between two neighboring towns a deadly hate,
Sprung from a sacred grudge of ancient date,
Yet burns; a hate no lenients can assuage,
No time subdue, a rooted, rancorous rage!
Blind bigotry, at first, the evil wrought:
For each despised the other's gods, and thought
Its own the true, the genuine,—in a word,
The only deities to be adored!"

Imperat aut servit collecta pecunia cuique. Lat. HORACE.—"Money is always either our master or our slave."

Imperium facile iis artibus retinetur, quibus initio partum est. Lat. SALLUST.—"Power is easily retained by those means by which it was first acquired." It is generally gained by conciliation, and kept whilst that is continued. It is lost by oppression and intolerance.

Imperium flagitio acquisitum nemo unquam bonis artibus exercuit. Lat. TACITUS.—"The power which was acquired by guilt has never been directed to any good end, or any useful purpose." When command is obtained by crime, the power which is thus usurped is most generally abused.

Imperium in imperio. Lat.—"A government existing in, within, another government." An establishment existing under, but wholly independent of, a superior establishment. An arrangement, where the clashing interests must inevitably lead to confusion. "The East India Company has been described as an anomalous body exercising a sort of *imperium in imperio.*"

Impetus. Lat.—"An impulse, an inducement."

Impossible! c'est le mot d'un fou! Fr.—"Impossible! that is the word of a fool, a madman!" There is nothing in the world impracticable; and NAPOLEON never spoke a truer sentiment than when he said —*Impossible! c'est le mot d'un fou!* Compare SHAKSPEARE:—

"With caution judge of possibility,
Things *thought* unlikely, e'en impossible,
Experience often shows us to be true."

Impotentia excusat legem. Lat. Law maxim.—"Impotency does away the law." This maxim relates to the infirmity of certain persons, whom the law excuses from doing certain acts: as, men in prison, idiots and lunatics, persons blind and dumb, &c.

Impransus. Lat.—"A man who has not dined." Frequently applied to one who is without the means of obtaining a dinner. The plural is *impransi.*

Imprimatur. Lat.—"Let it be printed." The phrase of permission to print in countries where the press is under a vexatious control. The word is figuratively used to denote that sort of authority.

Imprimis. Lat.—"In the first place, first of all."

—— ——————Improbae
Crescunt divitiae: tamen
Curtae nescio quid semper abest rei. Lat. HORACE.—
"Riches, dishonestly acquired, increase; yet something or other is ever wanting to what seems an imperfect fortune in the eyes of its possessor."

Improbe amor, quid non mortalia pectora cogis? Lat. VIRGIL.—"O wretched love! to what dost thou not impel the human breast?" to what excesses dost thou not drive that heart of which thou hast once taken possession?

Improbe Neptunum accusat, qui naufragium iterum facit. Lat. prov.—"The man improperly blames the sea, who is a second time shipwrecked." He should have learned prudence from his first misfortune. N.B. NEPTUNE, the god of the sea, is here figuratively used for the sea itself.

Improbis aliena virtus semper formidolosa est. Lat. SALLUST.—"To the wicked the virtue of other men is ever formidable." They dread that which lowers them by comparison, and hate the excellence to which they cannot aspire.

Impromptu. Lat.—"Without study, off-hand." *Literally*, "In readiness, at hand." A short extemporaneous composition. N.B. The word *ought* to be written "*In promptu.*"

Improvisatore. Ital.—"An extemporaneous composer, an off-hand composer, a composer without previous study." N.B. *Improvisatore* is sometimes very incorrectly written *improvisator*.

Impune potius laedi, quam dedi alteri. Lat. PHAEDRUS.—"It is better to submit to an injury without seeking redress, than to be given up to the rule of another, to be brought under subjection to another."

In absolutissima forma. Lat.—"In the most absolute form [of words]."

In ambiguo. Lat.—"A matter of doubt." The case is not *in ambiguo.*

In amore haec omnia insunt vitia: injuriae,
Suspiciones, inimicitiae, induciae,
Bellum, pax rursum. Lat. TERENCE.—
"All these inconveniences are incident to love; love is necessarily subjected to a long train of evils: reproaches, suspicions, jealousies, quarrels, parleys, truces, war, and then peace."

In articulo mortis. Lat.—"At the point of death." "The deceased was *in articulo mortis* at the time of the execution of the will."

In caldo, e'n gielo. Ital. DANTE.—"The wretch that would wish the Poetry of life and feeling to be extinct, let him forever dwell *in caldo, e'n gielo:*" that is,
"In flame, in frost, in ever-during night."

In capita. Lat.—"To the polls, heads." "Challenges to the polls, *in capita*, are exceptions to particular persons, and must be made, in each instance, as the person comes to the box to be sworn, and before he is sworn; for, when the oath is once taken, the challenge is too late."

In capite. Lat.—"In chief." "We have not had the means of ascertaining whether there were any of these persons, who had no holding at all *in capite.*"

In causa facili cuivis licet esse diserto. Lat. OVID.—"In an easy cause any man may be eloquent." The most indifferent orator may assume a triumphant air when he occupies "the vantage-ground."

In coelo quies. Lat.—"There is rest in heaven." A motto often found on funeral achievements, commonly called "hatchments."

In commendam. Lat.—"In trust, or holding an office in trust for another." This phrase of modern Latin is used to denote a person "*commended*," or recommended to the care of a living whilst the church is vacant. It is used by a fiction to permit a bishop to retain the emoluments of a living within or without his own diocese. N.B. "*Commenda*" means "the advowson [patronage] of a living, benefice, rectory, or vicarage, ecclesiastical charge."

In culpa est animus, qui se non effugit unquam. Lat. HORACE. "The mind alone is in fault, which can never fly from itself:"—

"'Tis in the mind alone our follies lie,
The mind, that never from itself can fly."

See "*Quid terras*," *&c.*, and "*Coelum non animum*," *&c.*

In cumulo. Lat.—"In a heap, in a lump, all at once." "With all his defects, he is fully entitled to claim his degrees *in cumulo*."

In curia. Lat.—"In the court."

In deliciis habuit. Lat. CICERO.—"It [the work] was a great favorite with him, he was very fond of it."

In diem, or, **In horam, vivere.** Lat. CICERO.—"To live from hand to mouth." N.B. PERSIUS, the distinguished satirist and philosopher, uses the expression "*Ex tempore vivere*" in nearly the same sense.

In disciplinis mathematicis et physicis. Lat.—"Honors are awarded, not only *in literis humanioribus*, but also *in disciplinis mathematicis et physicis*:" that is, not only "in classics, in classical learning or literature, in Greek and Latin," but also "in mathematical and physical science, in mathematics and natural philosophy." "He took a first-class degree *in literis humanioribus*."

In disgrazia della giustizia. Ital.—"In fear of the law, under a cloud."

In dubiis. Lat.—"In matters of doubt." In cases of uncertainty.

In eadem conditione. Lat.—"In the same condition, predicament." "All these vessels stood *in eadem conditione*."

In eadem re utilitas et turpitudo esse non potest. Lat. CICERO. —"Usefulness and baseness cannot exist in the same thing." It is in vain to plead the advantages of a proceeding when those advantages are to be purchased by the loss of honesty or of honor.

In embryo.—"*Embryo*" is from the Greek, and means "the infant in the womb, the young of animals in the womb." "The business is now *in embryo*," that is, "is progressing, is in an unfinished state, is, as it were, in its infancy."

In eo facetiae erant, quae nulla arte tradi possunt. Lat. CICERO, in reference to MARC ANTONY.—"He had a witty mirth, which could be acquired by no art."

In esse. Lat.—"In being." "Members *in esse* and members *in posse* are here and there over the country, addressing their constituents:" that is, *Actual* members, and *persons who may possibly become* members, &c.

In extenso. Lat.—"In full, at length." "We now give their opinion *in extenso.*" This is a diplomatic phrase. "The paper was submitted *in extenso,*" that is, in its full extent, and not by way of abstract.

In extremis. Lat.—"The Free Library is, if not *in extremis,* dragging on a miserable existence," that is, "on its last legs," or, to use a Londonism, "in a shaky condition."

In flagranti crimine. Lat.—"In the very commission of the crime. "In order to prove the fact, the perpetrator must be taken *in flagranti crimine.*"

In flagranti, or **flagrante, delicto.** Lat.—The same meaning as the preceding expression, but *much more frequently used.* "The working man goes to the park, and catches the governing class *in flagrante delicto,*" that is, "committing the very faults that they themselves so loudly condemn in the lower grades of society."

In fore. Lat.—"In prospective." "He, the editor *in fore,* did not hesitate to undertake for three-fourths of the letter-press."

In forma pauperis. Lat. Law phrase.—"In the form, shape, of a poor man. As a pauper, as a person without pecuniary means or resources." According to the statute 11 HENRY VII., any man who is too poor to meet the expenses of suing at law or in equity, making oath that he is not worth more than £5 after his debts are paid, and producing a certificate from a lawyer that he has just cause of suit, the judge in this case is to admit him to sue *in forma pauperis;* that is, without paying any fees to the counsel, attorney, or clerks.

In foro conscientiae. Lat.—"Before the tribunal of conscience." In a man's own conviction of what is equitable.

In foro contentiosissimo. Lat.—"In a very contentious, or disputatious, court; in a court in which the opinions broached were of a very conflicting character."

In foro divino. Lat.—"Before the divine tribunal, the tribunal of GOD, GOD'S tribunal. In the sight of GOD."

In foro humano. Lat.—"Before a human tribunal." "PALEY reprehensibly asserted that so long as we keep within the design and intention of a law, that law will justify us *in foro conscientiae* as well as *in foro humano,* whatever be the equity or expediency of the law itself." See "*In foro conscientiae.*"

In foro poëtico. Lat.—"Before a tribunal of poets, a poetic tribunal."

In furore. Lat.—"In a rage, a towering passion."

In futuro. Lat.—"At a future period."

In futurum. Lat.—"At a future period, hereafter."

In generalibus latet dolus. Lat.—"In general assertions, some fallacy, wile, trick, or other, lies hid, or concealed."

In gremio legis. Lat. Law phrase.—"In the lap or bosom of the law." "Is an estate without any visible owner?—the law, with an Oriental boldness of imagery, declareth that it is *in nubibus!* or, adopting a more tender and beautiful phrase, saith it reposeth *in gremio legis.*"

In hoc signo vinces. Lat.—"In this sign thou shalt conquer." This was the motto assumed by the EMPEROR CONSTANTINE after seeing a *cross* in the air, which he considered as the presage of victory.

In horas. Lat. HORACE.—"Every hour."

In illo viro tantum robur et corporis et animi fuit ut, quocunque loco natus esset, fortunam sibi facturus videretur. Lat. LIVY.—"In that man was displayed so much strength both of body and mind that, in whatever place or position he might have been born, it was evident that he would be the architect of his own fortune." "Of NAPOLEON BONAPARTE it may be said, in the words of LIVY, as applied to CATO MAJOR, *In illo viro*," *&c.*

In initio. Lat.—"In the beginning, at the outset."

In limine. Lat.—"From the very first." "We may, however, *in limine*, object to this."

In literis humanioribus. Lat.—See "*In disciplinis*," *&c.*

In loco. Lat.—"In the place; in the proper place; on, or upon, the spot; in season."

In loco parentis. Lat.—"In the place, position, of a parent."

In medias res. Lat. HORACE.—"Into the midst of things, into the midst of his subject." Sometimes spoken of an author who rushes abruptly and without preparation into his subject. "He thus plunges at once *in medias res.*"

In mercatura facienda multae fallaciae et quasi praestigiae exercentur. Lat. CICERO.—"In commerce, commercial transactions, many deceptions are practiced, and various tricks are played off." "At no time, perhaps, could it with greater truth be observed than at the present that *in mercatura*," *&c.*

In nomine Domini. Lat.—"In the name of the LORD."

In nova fert animus mutatus dicere formas. Lat. OVID.—"My mind, disposition, leads, or prompts, me to speak of bodies changed into new forms, bodies transformed in a new manner." I am now to dwell on transformations or changes of a most singular nature. N.B. "*In nova fert animus*" is a phrase often used by itself. "My mind, or disposition, leads me to new matters, or to discuss new topics."

In nubibus. Lat.—"In the clouds, in the region of theories." "Parliamentary discussions have often the unintended effect of taking a subject from the order of facts and the sphere of experience, and leaving it *in nubibus*." See "*In gremio legis*."

In nullum avarus bonus est, in se pessimus. Lat. prov.—"The avaricious man is kind to no person, but he is most unkind to himself."

In nullum reipublicae usum ambitiosa loquela inclaruit. Lat. TACITUS.—"He became celebrated for an affected and ambitious verbosity, attended with no advantage whatever to the state."

In nullo est erratum. Lat. Law phrase.—"There is no error in the record."

In obscuro. Lat.—"In obscurity, a matter of obscurity." "Why no appointment was offered him remains *in obscuro*."

In oculis civium. Lat. CICERO.—"In public, before the public."

In omnem sensus actum influit imaginatio. Lat.—A maxim of the old Schoolmen. "The imagination exercises a powerful influence over every act of sense, thought, reason,—over every idea."

In omnibus fere minori aetati succurritur. Lat. Law maxim.—"In all cases relief is afforded to persons under age." The law is so careful of persons of this description that it will not suffer them to alienate, sell, or bind themselves by deed, unless it be for eating, drinking, schooling, physic, or such other matters as are absolutely necessary.

In omnibus quidem, maxime tamen in jure, aequitas est. Lat. Law maxim.—"In all things, but particularly in the law, there is equity." Equity is said to be a corrective of the law, where the latter is deficient on account of its generality.

In otio et negotio probus. Lat.—"Upright in business and out of business, upright in every relation of life."

In pace leones, in proelio cervi. Lat.—"In peace they are lions, in the battle deer." They are blusterers and cowards. "Lion-talkers, lamb-like fighters."

In pari materia. Lat.—"Of a similar nature, on a like matter, subject." "Several cases *in pari materia* have fallen under our notice."

In partibus infidelium. Lat.—"In countries inhabited by those who are strangers to Christianity." "He was appointed a bishop *in partibus infidelium.*" An ecclesiastical phrase.

In partibus transmarinis. Lat.—"In countries beyond sea."

In perpetuam rei memoriam. Lat.—"As a perpetual memorial of the thing, matter,—of any particular thing, or matter. To perpetuate the memory of the thing." An inscription generally found upon pillars, &c. raised to commemorate any particular incident.

In perpetuum. Lat.—"Forever, for ever and ever, in perpetuity." "*In aeternum*" and "*In omne aevum*" have the same meaning.

In pertusum ingerimus dicta dolium. Lat. PLAUTUS.—"We fling our sayings into a cask that is bored through, that has holes in it." Our advice is wholly thrown away in that quarter; we spend our breath in vain; we talk to no purpose.

In petto. Ital.—Literally, "In, or within, the breast." In reserve, held in reserve, kept back. N.B. The Pope often creates cardinals *in petto,* that is, keeping the matter to himself, until he may think fit to proclaim it to the world.

In pontificalibus. Lat.—"In his pontificals, episcopal robes." "In the chapel of Our Lady [in the Church of St. Savior, Southwark] is a gravestone of a bishop *in pontificalibus.*"

In posse. Lat.—See "*In esse.*"

In praesenti. Lat.—"For the present [time]: at the present [time]." N.B. We may also say *In praesens, praesens in tempus,* or *in praesentia,* to express the same idea as "*In praesenti.*" See "*In futuro.*"

In primis hominis est propria veri inquisitio atque investigatio. Lat. CICERO.—"The searching out and thorough investigation of truth is [or *ought to be*] the first, the primary study of man." "*In primis*" has the same meaning as "*Imprimis,*" which see.

In procinctu. Lat.—"In readiness."

In propria persona. Lat.—"In his own person." In personal attendance.

In prospectu. Lat.—"In prospect, in view."

In puris naturalibus. Lat.—"In a purely natural state." "Every vegetable," observes a German traveler in England, "appears at table *in puris naturalibus;*" that is, in its natural state [without the addition of sauce or any thing else].

In re. Lat.—"In the matter of." "*In re* JOHN ROBINSON, deceased." "SIR HUMPHRY DAVY got some credit for his directions *in re* Salmon: 'Carry him to the pot, and before you put in a slice let the water and salt boil furiously, and give time to the water to recover its heat before you throw in another; and so proceed with the whole fish.'" Salmonia, or Days of Fly-Fishing, p. 188.

In rebus jucundis vive beatus. Lat. HORACE.—"Live merrily, joyously."

In rerum natura. Lat. CICERO.—"In the nature, the very nature, of things." "An English garrison without a horse-race is scarcely a thing *in rerum natura.*"

In sacris. Lat.—"In sacred things, matters."

In se ipso totus, teres, atque rotundus. Lat. HORACE.—"A man who relies solely on himself, regular and even in his disposition and desires." According to the Stoics [an ancient sect of Grecian philosophers], since those things only are truly good which are becoming and virtuous, and since virtue, which is seated in the mind, is alone sufficient for happiness, external things contribute nothing towards happiness. The wise man, in every condition, is happy in the possession of a mind accommodated to nature, and all external things are consequently indifferent. In reference to the words "*teres atque rotundus,*" the metaphor is taken from a globe. Our defects are so many inequalities and roughnesses, which wisdom polishes and rubs off. The image, too, suits extremely well with the other part of the description, "*in se ipso totus.*"

In se magna ruunt. Lat. LUCAN.—"Great things are apt to rush against each other." Two great powers are naturally inclined to jealousy, and thence to hostility.

In secula seculorum. Lat.—"For ever and ever, to the end of time."

In situ. Lat.—"In its position."

In spiritualibus. Lat.—"In spiritual matters."

In statu esse. Lat. PLAUTUS.—"To be upon, on, one's guard."

In statu pupillari. Lat.—"In the position of a student [at college], during the under-graduateship of a student [at college]."

In statu quo. Lat.—"In the position in which it was, he was, they were."

In suo proprio loco. Lat.—"In its own peculiar, proper, place."

In temporalibus. Lat.—"In temporal matters."

In tempore veni. Lat. TERENCE.—"I came in time, in good time:"—

"To tithe-pig, when roasted,
He still has a keen eye,
And oft has he boasted,
In tempore veni."

In tempore veni; quod rerum omnium est primum. Lat. TERENCE.—"I came at the critical moment, in the nick of time; which is the main business of all, the chief thing of all, the grand article in every thing, in all the affairs of life."

In tenui labor. Lat. VIRGIL.—"Labor on a small object:"—

"Though low the subject, it deserves our pains."

Nothing is so mean as to be unworthy of our attention.

In tenui labor, at tenuis non gloria. Lat. VIRGIL.—"The labor is bestowed on a small object, but the fame of the achievement is not the less." To do little things well is in some cases highly honorable.

In terrorem. Lat.—"They held him up *in terrorem* over the latter;" that is, "as a bugbear" over the latter, "an intimidation" to the latter, or "to intimidate" the latter. "*In terrorem,*" "as a warning."

In toto. Lat.—"Wholly, altogether, utterly." "We object *in toto* to this new system."

In transitu. Lat.—"The matter was then *in transitu,*" that is, was then "progressing, going on, on its passage." N.B. Goods *in transitu* ["on the passage"] are goods consigned by one person to another, and which have not yet reached the consignee. QUINTILIAN uses "*In transitu*" to signify "by-the-bye, by the way."

In turbas et discordias pessimo cuique plurima vis; pax et quies bonis artibus indigent. Lat. TACITUS.—"In seasons of tumult and discord bad men have most power; genius and goodness are only fostered by repose." In times of revolution and disorder the dregs are forced upward, and talent and virtue are depressed. This, however, is only for a season, and that which is the scum will soon become the sediment.

In ultimato. Lat.—"At last." "He was told, *in ultimato,* that the decision of the ministers would not be overruled." N.B. "*Ultimo*" is preferable to "*in ultimato,*" which is unclassical.

In usum vulgi. Lat.—"For the use of the people at large, of the masses, of the million." N.B. We may also say "*ad usum vulgi.*"

In verbo principis. Lat.—"On the word of a prince."

In vino veritas. Lat.—"There is truth in wine." It extracts secrets from the reserved, from those who are ordinarily on their guard, and puts the habitual liar off his guard.

Inca.—The title of the native sovereigns of Peru. "Thus, according to the Indian tradition, was founded the empire of the *Incas,* or lords of Peru."—ROBERTSON.

Incedis per ignes suppositos cineri doloso. Lat. HORACE.—"You walk over, are walking over, fire that lies hidden under deceitful ashes." You are occupied in describing times in which the most calamitous events burst forth as suddenly as flames from under ashes. The reference is to C. ASINIUS POLLIO, who was engaged in writing a history of the civil war, "an undertaking," according to the poet, "full of danger and of hazard."

Inclusio unius est exclusio alterius. Lat. Law maxim.—"The name of one being included supposes an exclusion of the other." This is a maxim frequently used in arguments on testamentary devises. If, of two persons of equal affinity, one is especially mentioned, it is supposed that the other is out of the intention of the testator.

Incognita. Ital.—"She came to reside *incognita* amidst the scenes of her youth;" that is, "as a person unknown to the inhabitants; as a stranger, concealing her true name and position;" to reside "in privacy," &c.

Incognito. Ital.—"They drove out in a small private carriage, and quite *incognito;*" that is, and quite "undistinguishable as to their rank and position." N.B. "*Incognito*" is frequently used in an abridged form: thus, *incog.*

Inconnu. Fr.—"A stranger." "The door opens, and an *inconnu* appears."

Incredibile dictu. Lat. CICERO.—"Strange, marvelous to say: unbelievable to tell." "Greek affairs were mentioned, upon which [*incredibile dictu!*] MR. HUME could not keep silent."

Incredulus odi. Lat. HORACE.—"I view with feelings of incredulity and disgust." "To all extravagant and monstrous inventions the *incredulus odi* opposes itself in every bosom of sound taste and sound understanding."

Incubus. Lat.—A disease, or disagreeable sensation, called *the nightmare*, lying like a load upon one, so that one can neither move nor speak. "Let not classical learning sit thus like an *incubus* upon the expanding intellects of our youth, and as a counterpoise to the mighty efforts which science is making to elevate the physical condition of our species." There is in VIRGIL a very fine description of the nightmare, which it may gratify the reader to see:—

"Ac velut in somnis, oculos ubi languida pressit
Nocte quies, nequidquam avidos extendere cursus
Velle videmur, et in mediis conatibus aegri
Succidimus: non lingua valet, non corpore notae
Sufficiunt vires, nec vox aut verba sequuntur."

"And as in dreams, when languid sleep has closed our eyes in the night, we seem in vain to make efforts to prolong a race on which we are intent, and in the midst of our efforts sink down quite faint; nor is there power in the tongue, nor in the body a competency of the usual strength, and neither voice nor words obey the dictates of our will [just so from Turnus does the accursed fiend withhold success, by whatever efforts of valor he sought the way to insure it]."

Inde irae. Lat.—"Hence [proceed] those resentments."

Index Expurgatorius. Lat.—The "*Index Expurgatorius*" means at Rome, where the expression originated, "A catalogue of the books whose publication is only prohibited until they have been purged or corrected." The "*Index Purgatorius,*" or simply the "*Index,*" means "A catalogue of the books actually and strictly forbidden or prohibited to be read."

Indict.—"On this verb," says JOHNSON, "see *Indite* and its derivatives." Now, this short sentence is a string of blunders throughout. *Indite* [as an article] is not in the original edition of JOHNSON, but *Endict;* and of its *derivatives* he has but *one* in any orthography. The verb [in its legal sense] is always *indict:*

"Hold up your head; hold up your hand:
Would it were not my lot to show ye
This cruel writ, wherein you stand
Indicted by the name of Chloe!"—PRIOR.

**Indignor quidquam reprehendi, non quia crasse
Compositum illepideve putetur, sed quia nuper;
Nec veniam antiquis, sed honorem et praemia posci.**
Lat. HORACE.—
"It raises my indignation to see a work undervalued, not because gross and ungenteel, but because of modern date; and that we demand for the ancients, not barely indulgence, but honors and rewards:"—

"I feel my honest indignation rise
When, with affected air, a coxcomb cries,
'The work, I own, has elegance and ease,
But sure no modern should presume to please:'
Then for his favorite ancients dares to claim
Not pardon only, but rewards and fame."

Indocti discant, et ament meminisse periti. Lat.—
"Content, if here th' unlearn'd their wants may view,
The learn'd reflect on what before they knew."—POPE.
A motto frequently prefixed to works of a general and useful tendency.

Inerat Vitellio simplicitas ac liberalitas, quae, nisi adsit modus, in exitium vertuntur. Lat. TACITUS.—"There was in VITELLIUS [the ninth Roman emperor] a simplicity and a liberality, qualities which, unless taken in the degree, are generally ruinous to the possessor." There are virtues the most amiable in private life, which, exercised by a public man beyond their due bounds, will ever be found dangerous in the extreme.

Inest sua gratia parvis. Lat. LUCAN.—"Little things have their value." Trifles are not to be despised.

Infant [in law].—A young person, to the age of one-and-twenty. "Male or female till twenty-one years is an *infant*, and so styled in law." BLACKSTONE. "*Infant*" is also the title of a prince of Spain:—
"The *Infant* hearkened wisely to her tale."—SPENSER.

Infanta.—A princess of Spain.

Infantry.—In some early poets used for an *Infant*:—
"No careful nurse should wet her watchful eye,
When any pangs should gripe her *infantry*."—W. BROWNE.

Infelix ager. Lat.—"An unprolific, barren, unproductive, or unfruitful ground." "The great *arena* of the imagination should not be allowed to lie fallow as an *infelix ager*." See "*Arena*."

Infelix operis summa. Lat. HORACE.—"Unfortunate, or unsuccessful, in the close of his work; unsuccessful in bringing his work to a good, perfect, accurate, well-finished, conclusion." "Neither poet nor painter must be *infelix operis summa*." Of neither poet nor painter ought it to be said that
"He fails of just perfection in his art."

Infinita est velocitas temporis, quae magis apparet respicientibus. Lat. SENECA.—"The swiftness of time is infinite, as is most evident to those who look back." It is only by a retrospect of the years that have passed and have been misspent, that we can discern and regret the velocity with which they have escaped us.

Infra dignitatem. Lat.—"Beneath one's dignity: derogatory to one's dignity." N.B. Often used in an abridged form: thus, *infra dig.*

Ingenia gravia ac sollemnia, et mutare nescia, plus plerumque habent dignitatis quam felicitatis. Lat. LORD BACON.—"Men of a grave and serious deportment, and who have no disposition to change their principles according to circumstances [to rat: to jump Jim Crow], have generally more dignity about them than good fortune, good luck, worldly prosperity attending them." "I could not," says BISHOP WATSON, "adopt the versatility of sentiment which LORD BACON, with more of worldly wisdom than of honor, recommends as necessary to a man occupied in the fabrication of his own fortune: '*Ingenia,*' he says, '*gravia,*' " &c.

Ingenii largitor venter. Lat. PERSIUS.—"The belly is the giver, the bestower, of genius." Ironically spoken of those whose only *stimulus* to authorship is their poverty, but who, thus impelled,

"Still, in despite
Of nature and their stars, will write."

See "*Magister artis,*" &c.

Ingenio stat sine morte decus. Lat. PROPERTIUS.—"The honors of genius are eternal." This is the boast of many a poet. We know when it has been realized, as in the "*Exegi monumentum,*" &c. of HORACE [which see]; but most probably in a myriad of instances it has been made in vain.

**Ingenium cui sit, cui mens divinior, atque os
Magna sonaturum, des nominis hujus honorem.**
Lat. HORACE.—

"Honor with the illustrious name of 'poet' the man who has a genius, who has a heaven-born soul, and eloquence that can give utterance to great things:"—

"Is there a man whom real genius fires,
Whom the diviner soul of verse inspires,
Who talks true greatness? let him boldly claim
The sacred honors of a poet's name."

Ingenium illustre altioribus studiis juvenis admodum dedit; non, ut plerique, ut nomine magnifico seque otium velaret, sed quo firmior adversus fortuita rempublicam capesseret. Lat. TACITUS.—"In early youth he devoted all the powers of his illustrious mind to the higher philosophy; not, as the manner of some is, to shelter sloth under the covert of a splendid name, but, by a steady and deliberate firmness against the accidents of life, to prepare himself for the administration of the affairs of the state." Has been applied to WILLIAM PITT.

Ingenium ingens inculto latet hoc sub corpore. Lat. HORACE.—"A mighty intellect is encased, enshrined, in this unpolished, rough carcass: in this unlicked cub's bodily tenement, unprepossessing exterior, outer man:"—

"But underneath this rough, uncouth disguise
A genius of extensive knowledge lies."

"The person of BEETHOVEN is, in this volume, described as filthy, and his manners as bearish; but *Ingenium ingens*," &c.

Ingenium res adversae nudare solent, celare secundae. Lat. HORACE.—"In adversity those talents are called forth which are concealed by prosperity;" or, "Success in the affairs of life often serves to hide one's abilities, whereas adversity frequently gives one an opportunity to discover them."

Ingens telum necessitas. Lat. SENECA.—"Necessity is a powerful weapon:" "Need, want, indigence, is a powerful *stimulus* to exertion."

Ingentes dominos, et clarae nomina famae,
Illustrique graves nobilitate domos
Devita, et longe cautus fuge; contrahe vela,
Et te litoribus cymba propinqua vehat. Lat. SENECA.—
"Each mighty lord, big with a pompous name,
And each high house of fortune and of fame,
With caution fly; contract thy ample sails,
And near the shore improve the gentle gales."—ELPHINSTON.

———Ingenuas didicisse fideliter artes
Emollit mores, nec sinit esse feros. Lat. OVID.—
"Learning the liberal arts and sciences thoroughly softens men's manners, and prevents their being a pack of brutes or unlicked cubs."
"Learning, if deep, if useful, and refined,
Communicates its polish to the mind."

Again:—
"Ingenuous arts, where they an entrance find,
Soften the manners, and subdue the mind."

N.B. The rule, however, admits of exceptions innumerable, as we may daily and hourly see.

Ingrata patria. Lat.—"Ungrateful native country! O native country, that hast been so unjust and ungrateful to me!" "He is not the first great man over whose tomb has been written, *Ingrata patria!*"

Ingrato homine terra pejus nil creat. Lat. AUSONIUS.—"The earth produces nothing worse than an ungrateful man."

Ingratus unus miseris omnibus nocet. Lat. PUBLIUS SYRUS.—"One ungrateful man does an injury to all who are wretched." By his baseness he has, perhaps, steeled the heart which might otherwise have relieved their distresses.

Iniqua nunquam regna perpetua manent. Lat. SENECA.—"Authority founded on, or maintained by, injustice, is never of long duration."

Iniquissimam pacem justissimo bello antefero. Lat.—"I should prefer the *hardest* terms of peace to the most just war." [The favorite maxim of CHARLES JAMES FOX.] The horrors of war are so numerous and so afflicting, that peace should, at all times, be purchased at any price short of national dishonor. Compare CICERO:—*Pax vel injusta utilior est quam justissimum bellum,* "Even an unjust peace is more advantageous than the justest war."

Initia magistratuum nostrorum meliora ferme, et finis inclinat. Lat. TACITUS.—"The discharge of our public offices is generally more exemplary at the commencement; its vigor declines towards the conclusion." When men first enter upon office they are alert and punctual, but towards the close of their functions they become relaxed and indifferent. Our proverb of "New brooms" gives of this an apt, though homely, illustration.

Injuria absque damno. Lat.—"Injury without loss."

Injuriarum remedium est oblivio. Lat.—"The best remedy for injuries is to forget them." This maxim is not of universal application; but there are certain injuries which cannot too soon be consigned to oblivion.

Innubilus aether. Lat. LUCRETIUS.—"A cloudless sky, firmament, atmosphere." "There is an *innubilus aether* over both those countries."

Innuendo. Lat. Law term.—"By signifying." Thereby intimating. A word much used in declarations of slander and libel, to ascertain the application to a person or thing which was previously named. An oblique hint.

Innumerabiles morbos non miraberis, coquos numera. Lat. —"Reckon up the number of dishes prepared for our tables, and you will then no longer marvel at the innumerable diseases to which mortals are subject."

Inopem copia fecit. Lat.—"His plenty made him poor." His copiousness of ideas retarded and embarrassed his language.

Inopes rerum, nugaeque canorae. Lat. HORACE.—"Words destitute of sense combined with harmonious trifles." "It is a part of excellent policy in a minister of the crown to be never unprovided with a certain number of voices *inopes rerum, nugaeque canorae*, which, when the subject lags, may fill a pause, and run an extempore *cantabile* of any required length without breaking down:" that is, of voices "that can only give utterance to the most unmeaning jargon and silly trifling," &c. N.B. "*Cantabile*" means "something to be sung:" it is a term applied to movements intended to be performed in a graceful, elegant, and melodious style.

Inops, potentem dum vult imitari, perit. Lat. PHAEDRUS.—"A poor man, who aspires to imitate the rich, to ape the manners and habits of the rich, is sure to be undone, sure to be ruined."

Inquinat egregios adjuncta superbia mores. Lat. CLAUDIAN.—"The best manners are stained by the addition of pride." Even virtue itself is disgusting in a severe and haughty garb.

Insanire certa ratione modoque. Lat. HORACE.– "To play the madman in accordance with fixed reason and measure, by right reason and rule." "There is in such a state of things a sort of realization of HORACE's impossibility, of the *insanire certa ratione modoque:*" that is, of the "possibility of acting the madman with a certain appearance or show of reason and method."

Insanus omnis furere credit ceteros. Lat. prov.—"Every madman thinks that all the rest of the world is mad."

————Insanus paucis videatur, eo quod
Maxima pars hominum morbo jactatur eodem. Lat. HORACE. —"The covetous man, the miser, may, perhaps, seem mad only to a few, because the greater part of mankind labor under the same disease, are tossed to and fro by the same disease."

"By few, forsooth, a madman he is thought,
For half mankind the same disease have caught."

Insignia. Lat.—"The distinguishing emblems." "The *insignia* of *Britain*."

Insita hominibus libido alendi de industria rumores. Lat.—"Men have in them a natural desire to propagate rumors, reports." All are eager to circulate the reports which have reached them, and, it may be stated also, to add by way of embellishment something of their own.

Insita hominibus natura violentiae resistere. Lat. TACITUS.—"To resist violence is implanted in the nature of man." The most degraded people will be roused to action when oppression has reached a certain degree.

Insolation.—"[In medicine] The influence of a scorching sun on the brain." "One case of consequential madness is an effect of *insolation*, or what the French call *coup de soleil*."—BATTIE *on Madness*.

Insouciance. Fr.—"Carelessness, heedlessness, thoughtlessness, unconcern."

Insouciant. Fr.—"Careless, heedless, thoughtless, listless, reckless, unconcerned."

Inspicere tanquam in speculum in vitas omnium
Jubeo, atque ex aliis sumere exemplum sibi. Lat. TERENCE.—"The lives of men should be regarded as a mirror, from which we may take an example and a rule of conduct for ourselves." In observing the follies of others, the accurate observer of human life will thereby gain so many lessons of caution and correctness.

Instanter. Lat.—"Instantly, at once."

Instantiae ostensivae. Lat. LORD BACON.—"Glaring instances."

Instruction préalable. Fr. Law phrase.—"Preliminary measures."

Integer vitae scelerisque purus. Lat. HORACE.—"A man of upright life, and free from wickedness." "He is liberal, like most men of science, and *integer vitae*," *&c.*

Integra mens augustissima possessio. Lat.—"A mind imbued with integrity is the most august possession."

Intellectus communis. Lat. QUINTILIAN.—"Common sense."

Intellectus humanus, mens hominis. Lat. LORD BACON.—"The human intellect exhibits the mind of the man." The human understanding, in all its conscious presentations and reflexes, is itself only a phenomenon of the inner sense, and requires the same corrections as the appearances transmitted by the outward senses.

Intelligibilia, non intellectum, fero. Lat.—"If Pindar [a Greek poet of sublime genius, accounted the chief of the nine Lyric poets] seems obscure or rambling to us, we must surely in all modesty suppose that a part of the fault is in ourselves. We ought to give this learned Theban the benefit of the old retort, *intelligibilia, non intellectum, fero*:" that is, "I bring before you intelligible things, things that may be understood, understandable things; but I do not profess or undertake to find you an understanding, or brains to comprehend what I have written."

Intemperans adolescentia effetum corpus tradet senectuti. Lat. CICERO.—"An intemperate, disorderly, youthhood will bring to old age, old agehood, a feeble and worn-out bodily frame."

Intemperantia bibendi. Lat. SENECA.—"Intemperance, excess, want of moderation, in drinking." "The austere CATO and the voluptuous CÆSAR were each given to what SENECA calls *intemperantia bibendi.*"

Intemperantia est a tota mente ac a recta ratione defectio. Lat. CICERO.—"Intemperance [unableness or inability to rule and moderate one's appetites and passions] betrays a total aberration of mind and right reason."

Inter alia. Lat.—"Among other things or matters."

Inter arma silent leges. Lat. CICERO.—"The laws are not regarded in the midst of arms, while war is going on, is raging." During the violence of hostilities but little attention is paid to the precepts of justice.

Inter causas malorum nostrorum est quod vivimus ad exempla. Lat. SENECA.—"Among the causes of our misfortunes, of the evils into which we fall, may be reckoned the circumstance of our living by the example of others." Example in mere human morality is omnipotent, and certainly the contagion of bad example is deplorable; but, on the other hand, there is more than a compensating attractiveness in the exhibition of moral beauty.

Inter folia fructus. Lat.—"We will be wise, and ever bear in mind our motto, *inter folia fructus;*" that is, "Fruit among our leaves [the leaves of our book]."

Inter ignes luna minores. Lat. HORACE.—"As the moon [shines] among the feebler fires [of the night], the stars." "However high may be our comparative rank, however we may shine by the force of contrast, *inter ignes luna minores,* there is still too fatal a scope for the benevolent exertions of the philosopher and the philanthropist to authorize the inactivity of either."

Inter nos. Lat.—"Between ourselves."

Inter se. Lat.—"Among themselves."

Inter spem curamque, timores inter et iras,
Omnem crede diem tibi diluxisse supremum:
Grata superveniet, quae non sperabitur, hora. Lat. HORACE.—"Imagine every day to be the last of a life surrounded with hopes, cares, anger, and fear. The hours that come unexpectedly will be so much the more grateful:"—

"By hope inspired, depressed with fear,
By passion warmed, perplexed with care,
Believe that every morning's ray
Hath lighted up thy latest day:
Then if to-morrow's sun be thine,
With double luster shall it shine."

Compare SENECA:—

"*In somnum ituri laeti hilaresque dicamus, 'Vixi,' et quem dederat cursum fortuna peregi. Crastinum si adjecerit Deus, laeti recipiamus. Ille beatissimus et securus est sui possessor, qui crastinum sine solicitudine exspectat. Quisquis dixit 'Vixi,' quotidie ad lucrum surgit.*" "When we go to sleep, let us calmly say, 'I have lived, and have finished the course allotted me by fate.' If Heaven adds another day to our life, let us receive it with joy. He alone is truly happy, and calmly possesses himself, who expects the morrow without anxiety. Whoever can say, when he goes to sleep, 'I have lived,' enjoys the following day as so much pure gain."

Inter utrumque tene. Lat. prov.—"Keep between both." Steer through life a safe and middle course, avoiding equally all extremes.

Inter vivos. Lat.—"Among the living." "He is still, we believe, *inter vivos.*"

Interdum et insanire jucundum est. Lat. SENECA.—"It is sometimes, at times, pleasant, delightful, gratifying, to play the fool." See "*Dulce est desipere,*" *&c.*

Interdum lacrymae pondera vocis habent. Lat. OVID.—"Tears are sometimes equal in weight to words." The poet might have said that they are in general of more effect.

Interdum stultus bene loquitur. Lat.—"A fool sometimes speaks well." Every man is entitled to attention, as a wise remark may occasionally drop from a person whose previous discourse had offered no ground of expectation.

Interdum vulgus rectum videt; est ubi peccat. Lat. HORACE. —"The people sometimes see what is right, judge well; and sometimes they form erroneous conclusions:"—

"Sometimes the crowd a proper judgment makes,
But oft they labor under gross mistakes."

Interea dulces pendent circum oscula nati:
Casta pudicitiam servat domus. Lat. VIRGIL.—

"His cares are eased with intervals of bliss:
His little children, climbing for a kiss,
Welcome their father's late return at night;
His faithful bed is crowned with chaste delight."—DRYDEN.

Intererit multum, Davusne loquatur, an heros. Lat. HORACE. -"There will be a great difference when *Davus* is speaking, and when a hero." The former is a servant: the rule is addressed to dramatic writers, who should always make their characters speak an appropriate language.

Intérêt bien entendu. Fr.—"One's own interest well or thoroughly understood: a sharp, keen eye to one's own interest." "We put at once out of court the recent, we hope we may say the late, French system of *l'intérêt bien entendu,* which we take to be this: that its followers think it to be quite right to be generous and honest, and so forth, but that it would be most absurd to be either honest or generous, except on a long-sighted view of advantage to be derived from such faithfulness or magnanimity to their own particular selves."

Interim. Lat.—"In the mean time, in the mean while." "An *interim*-sheriff-substitute," that is, a "*temporary* sheriff-substitute." "An *interim*-viceroy."

Interiora rerum. Lat.—"The inmost recesses of creation."

Interlocutor. Lat.—In Scots law, "an order of court."

Internuncio.—"The Pope's *Internuncio* left Paris on 'urgent private affairs,' thus conveniently relieving himself of the awkward *dilemma* of meeting a sovereign under the ban of excommunication:" that is, The

Pope's *Vice-ambassador* left . . . . the awkward *difficulty*, *fix*, of meeting, &c. N.B. An "*Internuncio*" supplies the place of a Papal ambassador [an ambassador, or *nuncio*, from the Pope] during his absence from court, or when the office of *Nuncio* [ambassador] is vacant. The *right* meaning of "*dilemma*" is, an argument containing two contradictory propositions, the choice of one of which is left to the opponent [opposing person], in order to bring thorough conviction to his mind, whichever side he may take up or espouse.

Interregnum. Lat.—"The space between two reigns or governments."

Intima praecordia. Lat. OVID.—"The innermost thoughts and affections." "The bells of Bow Church are supposed to thrill the *intima praecordia* of every Londoner's memory in every part of the globe."

Intra Ecclesiam Anglicanam. Lat.—"Within the pale of the Church of England." See "*Pale.*"

Intra fortunam debet quisque manere suam. Lat. OVID.—"Every man should confine himself within the bounds, limits, of his own fortune."

Intra, and **extra, muros.** Lat.—"The commissioners have succeeded in attaining an amount of unpopularity, both *intra* and *extra muros*, completely unparalleled:" that is, both "in the city *and* out of it."

Intuta quae indecora. Lat. TACITUS.—"Those things that are unseemly are unsafe." In certain situations men should remember that as much danger frequently arises from forfeiting the respect as from incurring the resentment of those who are beneath them.

Inveniam viam aut faciam. Lat.—"I will either find a way or I will make one: I will either find the means of accomplishing my object, of bringing the matter to bear, or will compass it in some way or other." "On he would go right to his end, through flood and fell, with the obstinacy of a Roman road. *Inveniam viam aut faciam.*"

Invidus alterius macrescit rebus opimis. Lat. HORACE.—"The envious man pines at the success, prosperity, of another, of his neighbor:"—

"The man who envies must behold with pain
Another's joys, and sicken at his gain."

Nothing can exceed the pining of the envious man under the supposition that a rival has outstripped him and may possibly succeed.

**Invidus, iracundus, iners, vinosus, amator;
Nemo adeo ferus est, ut non mitescere possit,
Si modo culturae patientem commodet aurem.**

Lat. HORACE.—

"The slave to envy, anger, wine, or love,
The slothful, wisdom's excellence shall prove:
Fierceness itself shall bear its rage away,
When listening calmly to the instructive lay."

Invisa potentia, atque miseranda vita eorum qui se metui quam amari malunt. Lat. CORNELIUS NEPOS.—"Hateful is the power, and pitiable is the life, of those who wish to be feared rather than be loved." Every government must be odious, which takes for its basis the terrors instead of the good wishes of the people.

Invita MINERVA. Lat. CICERO and HORACE.—"Against one's

inclination: MINERVA being unwilling." HAYDN never began a symphony "*invita* MINERVA:" that is, "when he felt himself unequal to the task; when he was not in the humor for composing." N.B. "*Invita* MINERVA" was a proverbial form of expression among the Romans. The mind could accomplish nothing unless MINERVA, the Goddess of Wisdom, lent her favoring aid.

Invitat culpam, qui peccatum praeterit. Lat. PUBLIUS SYRUS. —"He who overlooks one crime invites the commission of another."

Iota. Gr. in Roman letters.—The ninth letter of the Greek alphabet. "A jot, the least thing that is." "They never contribute one *iota* to the revenue:" that is, one "jot," one "single fraction," &c.

Ipse dixit. Lat.—"He himself said it." "On his *ipse dixit:*" on his sole assertion. "The connection between a nation's morals and its literature rests far too deeply below the surface to be filliped off with a few sentences of *ipse dixit*, be the authority ever so trustworthy:" that is, with a continued repetition of "*Oh, sir, but HE said so, I do assure you,*" &c. [in allusion to some great name, or to some one of high standing in the literary world, some big-wig].

Ipse viam tantum potui docuisse repertam
Aonas ad montes, longeque ostendere Musas
Plaudentes celsae choreas in vertice rupis. Lat. VIDA.—
"I only pointed out the paths that lead
The panting youth to steep Parnassus' head,
And showed the tuneful Muses from afar,
Mixed in a solemn choir, and dancing there."

Youth may be excited to emulation by example.

Ipsissima verba. Lat. PLAUTUS.—"The very identical, very same, words."

Ipso facto. Lat.—"In the fact itself." By the fact when it shall appear. "They thereby *ipso facto* deliver themselves up to the protection of another prince:" that is, "by the very fact, act, or deed."

Ipso jure. Lat.—"By the law itself." By the law when it shall be pronounced.

Ira furor brevis est. Lat. HORACE.—"Anger is a short madness; rage is a brief insanity." All the mischiefs of madness may be produced by a momentary passion. "Look at a man shaken by wrath as a tree is shaken by the wind. Here the passion rages paramount, and every thing else is forgotten. Consciousness is extinguished; and hence the expression of the poet, *Ira furor brevis est*, is strictly and pathologically true; because consciousness, the condition upon which all sanity depends, is for the time absent from the man. Hence also the ordinary phrase, that rage transports a man *out of himself*, is closely and philosophically correct. Properly interpreted, it means that the man is taken completely out of the pole where consciousness abides, and is rested entirely in the opposite pole where passion dwells; or rather we should say that *as a man* he is extinct, and lives only *as a machine*. In both of these cases the men lose their personality. They are played upon by a foreign agency."

———————**Ira quae tegitur nocet;**
Professa perdunt odia vindictae locum. Lat. SENECA.—

"It is only concealed resentment that is dangerous." Hatred, when openly avowed, loses its opportunity of revenge.

Iracundior est paulo, minus aptus acutis
Naribus horum hominum; rideri possit eo, quod
Rusticius tonso toga defluit, et male laxus
In pede calceus haeret; at est bonus, ut melior vir
Non alius quisquam, at tibi amicus, at ingenium ingens
Inculto latet hoc sub corpore. Lat. HORACE.—

"Your friend is passionate, perhaps unfit
For the brisk petulance of modern wit;
His hair ill cut, his robe, that awkward flows,
Or his large shoes, to raillery expose
The man you love; yet is he not possessed
Of virtues with which very few are blest?
And underneath this rough, uncouth disguise
A genius of extensive knowledge lies."

Genius and distinguished virtues are often hidden under an uncouth appearance.

Iram qui vincit, hostem superat maximum. Lat.—"He who subdues, gets the mastery of, his anger, conquers his greatest enemy." See "*Fortior est*," *&c.*, and "*Latius regnes*," *&c.*

Iras et verba locant. Lat. MARTIAL.—"They let out for hire their passions and their words." This is the severest sarcasm ever uttered against the gentlemen of the long robe, who, it intimates, not only hire out their eloquence, but can also feign a degree of passion proportioned to the magnitude of the fee.

Irony. From the Gr. word *Ειρωνεια* [eironeia].—A mode of speech in which the meaning is directly contrary to the words: as when, in speaking of a coward, we say, "This brave man."

Irrevocabile verbum. Lat. HORACE.—"A word that cannot be recalled, an un-call-back-able word."

Is maxime divitiis utitur, qui minime divitiis indiget. Lat. SENECA.—"He who has the smallest share of personal wants makes the best use of riches." By his self-denial, he has a larger disposable share to relieve the distresses of others.

Is mihi demum vivere et frui anima videtur, qui, aliquo negotio intentus, praeclari facinoris aut artis bonae famam quaerit. Lat. SALLUST.—"In my opinion, he only may be truly said to live, and enjoy his being, who is engaged in some praiseworthy pursuit, and acquires a name by some illustrious action or useful art."

Is ordo vitio careto, ceteris specimen esto. Lat.—"Let that order be free from vice, and afford an example to all others." This was an ordinance contained in the Roman laws of the Twelve Tables, and addressed to the senatorial or patrician order. The best example should come from the highest place.

Is suarum rerum satagit. Lat. TERENCE.—"He has enough upon his hands; he has more upon his hands than he can well manage."

Is unus bibliotheca magna. Lat.—"He alone, in himself, is a great library." FATHER FINARDI, with great felicity, said of MAGLIABECHI, the celebrated librarian of the Grand Duke of Tuscany, *Is unus bibliotheca magna*, that being the metagram [transposition of letters] of his Latinized name, ANTONIUS MAGLIABBECHIUS. See "*Honor est a Nilo*," and "*Anagram*."

Iskander.—The name by which ALEXANDER THE GREAT is known and celebrated all over the East.

Ist dir wohl, so bleibe. German prov.—"Are you in good circumstances, well off, well to do in the world, in a good position? be satisfied with it, without endeavoring to be better off."

Ista colluvies vitiorum. Lat.—"That sink, kennel of vices [of every kind and degree]." "There is in the work in question a knowledge of the component parts of society in 'high life:' of that society which is commonly called GOOD society, *ista colluvies vitiorum!*"

Istaec commemoratio quasi exprobratio est immemoris beneficii. Lat. TERENCE.—"Your reminding me in this manner of what you have done for me seems to reproach me with a forgetfulness of your favors." It was a saying among the Greeks, "When you receive a kindness, remember it; when you do a kindness, forget it." To reproach persons with the favors we do them, is canceling the obligation at once. The only excuse we can plead in this case is where the person obliged proves ungrateful.

Istamboul.—The Turkish title for Constantinople.

Istuc est sapere non quod ante pedes modo est
Videre, sed etiam illa quae futura sunt,
Prospicere. Lat. TERENCE.—

"True wisdom consists not in seeing that which is immediately before our eyes, but in the foresight of that which is to arrive." The ordinary politician judges of events only as they pass before him in review; but the exalted statesman, by combining the present with probable circumstances, will form something like an insight into futurity.

Istuc est sapere, qui, ubicunque opus sit, animum possis flectere. Lat. TERENCE.—"It is an evidence, a proof, of wisdom, to bring one's self to comply with the occasion, to bring one's self to bend to circumstances."

Ita finitima sunt falsa veris ut in praecipitem locum non debeat se sapiens committere. Lat. CICERO.—"Falsehood frequently borders so nearly on the truth, that a wise man should not trust himself to the precipice." He should be cautious of being deceived by appearances.

Ita fugias, ne praeter casam, quod aiunt. Lat. TERENCE.—"Run so as not to pass your own gate, as the saying is." Fly so as not to go beyond the proper bounds, and lose sight of relief: so avoid one danger, as not to run into a greater.

Ita lex scripta est. Lat.—"Thus the law is written." A phrase used in polemics, to refer the adversary to the letter of the text in question

Ita plerique ingenio sumus omnes: nostri nosmet poenitet. Lat. TERENCE.—"Such in troth we are almost all of us by nature, never to be contented with our own condition, our lot in life."

Ita servus homo est! Lat. JUVENAL.—"So [you dolt, addressing her husband] a slave is a MAN, then!" "Slavery under the Romans gave the master the power of life and death over his bondsman; this is undeniable, known to everybody: *Ita servus homo est!* are the words put by the greatest of satirists into the mouth of the fine lady, the lady in HIGH LIFE! who calls upon her husband to crucify his slave."

Ita vita est hominum, quasi cum ludas tesseris;
Si illud, quod maxume opus est jactu, non cadit,
Illud, quod cecidit forte, id arte ut corrigas. Lat. TERENCE.

"The life of man is as when we play at dice; if the throw that was most wanted comes not up, we must correct that by skill which chance has sent us." The poet had probably in his eye a passage of the tenth book of PLATO's Commonwealth, where that philosopher says "that we should make it our endeavor to reap the fruits of wisdom from the operations of chance, and, as in a game at dice, employ all our skill in turning that to our profit which fortune has thrown up to us; that by thus using the lights which reason gives us, we may turn even seeming misfortunes into benefits."

Itan' comparatam esse hominum naturam omnium,
Aliena ut melius videant et dijudicent
Quam sua! Lat. TERENCE.—

"Strange that men should be all so constituted by nature as to be better judges of what regards others than themselves!" In the latter instance we are blinded by our feelings and prejudices: in the former there is nothing to impede our natural perspicacity.

Iterum. Lat.—"Again."

J.

J'ai eu toujours pour principe de ne faire jamais par autrui ce que je pouvais faire par moi-même. Fr. MONTESQUIEU.—"I have ever held it as a maxim, never to do that through another which it was possible for me to execute myself."

Jacquerie, or **Jaquerie.** Fr.—"It is indeed no light matter to stir up a rude, uncivilized peasantry, and array them in battle upon pretenses of which they are entirely incapable of judging, against men who, as men, cannot even be said to have done them any harm; neither is it a light matter to create a *Jacquerie.*" N.B. A "*Jacquerie,*" or "*Jaquerie,*" was the name of an association of rebellious peasants, which was formed in Picardy [a province of France] in 1358, during the captivity of King John. The object of these men was to exterminate the nobles. "*Jacquerie*" took its name from the nobles of that day calling the peasant in derision *un Jacques bon homme,* that is, *a James goodman,* Jemmy Goodman. *Un bon homme* is often used in France to signify *a peasant.* "*Jacquerie*" is used at the present day for *a rebellion* or *revolt of the lower orders.*

Jacta est alea. Lat.—"The die is cast." "Nothing venture, nothing have!" "I have put every thing to venture, and must now stand the hazard, run the risk."

Jactitatio. Lat.—"A boasting." Jactitation of marriage is cognizable in the Ecclesiastical Court.

Jam omnibus in ore est, qui semotus sit ab oculis eundem quoque ab animo semotum esse. Lat. ERASMUS.—"It is now in everybody's mouth, that he who is out of your sight is also out of your mind, thoughts." Out of sight, out of mind.

Jamais arrière. Fr.—"Never behind."

Jamais, quoiqu'il fasse, un mortel ici-bas
Ne peut aux yeux du monde être ce qu'il n'est pas.
Fr. BOILEAU.—"Never can a mortal with all his exertions, or, exert himself as he will, appear in the estimation of the world what he is not, in any character but his own true one."

Jambe. Fr.—"A leg." Hence *jambs,* supports of any thing on each side; as, *the jambs of a door.*

Jamne igitur laudas quod de sapientibus alter
Ridebat, quoties a limine moverat unum
Protuleratque pedem flebat contrarius alter? Lat. JUVENAL.

"Will ye not now the pair of sages praise,
Who the same end pursued by several ways?
One pitied, one contemned the woeful times,
One laughed at follies, one lamented crimes."

Jamque opus exegi, quod nec Jovis ira, nec ignes,
Nec poterit ferrum, nec edax abolere vetustas. Lat. OVID.—"I have now completed a work, which neither the wrath of Jove, nor fire, nor sword, nor the corroding tooth of time, will be able to destroy." This triumphant boast of the poet with respect to his own productions has certainly been realized. But at present this passage, as well as the *exegi monumentum,* &c. of Horace, are chiefly used in an ironical sense, and for the purpose of holding up some proud boaster to ridicule.

Janissary.—A European corruption of "*Yeni-tchiri,*" a member of a body of Turkish infantry soldiery, now no longer in existence. STOCQUELER. N.B. The janissaries were destroyed by the Sultan MAHMOUD in 1826.

Janitor. Lat.—"A porter, door-keeper, keeper of a gate, gatekeeper." A word much used in SCOTLAND. "*Janitor*" comes from the Latin word "*janua,*" a gate, so called from JANUS [an ancient Latin divinity, who was worshiped as the sun], because this god was the guardian deity of gates.

Janotisme. Fr.—An improper inversion of the members of a sentence, thus:—"*Je viens chercher une médecine pour mon père, qui est malade dans une bouteille.* I am come for some medicine for my father, who is ill in a little bottle."

Januae mentis. Lat.—"Gates of the mind." Sources of knowledge. "LOCKE admits two *januae mentis* [sensation and reflection]."

Januis clausis. Lat.—"The doors being shut, or closed; with closed doors." "The matter was debated *januis clausis.*"

Jardin des plantes. Fr.—"A botanical garden, garden of plants."

Jargon. Fr.—This word is often used to signify "*unintelligible talk,* *gibberish, lingo:*" but the *true* meaning of the word is "SLANG," such as is used by bull-fighters in Spain, and the "gentlemen of the fancy" [*les messieurs de l'imagination*, as the Frenchman translated this very queer phrase], the pugilists and prize-fighters of England. This peculiar dialect, or language, has long been reduced to a system in Spain, where it is termed "*germania*," "*xerge:*" [the "*argot*" of France, the "*gauner sprache*" of Germany, the "*gerga*" of Italy:] a regular vocabulary was published at Barcelona in 1609. The "*fancy*" Spaniards honor the author as their DR. JOHNSON, and his dictionary has gone through many editions. It is very useful to the reader of QUEVEDO. A similar vocabulary of Venetian slang was published in 1549 at Venice, by Zindone Mapheo, "Nuevo Modo de intendere la Lengua Zerga; cioè parlare forbesco." It was from Italy that Mendoza and others imported their picaresque novels. The circus has long been the school of that particular language which prevails in the ring and seems peculiar to roguery and low company in all ages and countries. See "*Mots d'argot.*"

Je ne sais quoi. Fr.—"I know not what." "You might find ten artists more capable of playing *drame* without having the *je ne sais quoi* which places her so high in public admiration:" that is to say, of playing *dramatic parts* without having the *indescribable charm, that inexplicable manner, &c.*

Je suis oiseau—voyez mes ailes:
Je suis souris—vivent les rats! Fr.—
"I am a bird, look at my wings: I am a mouse, long live the rats!" N.B. Said in allusion to the bat. "Louis Philippe endeavors [1834] to steer between the two antagonist principles of monarchy and revolution, and is therefore obliged to appeal alternately to one and the other, and to be in turns a citizen king and a legitimate sovereign:—

"*Je suis oiseau—voyez mes ailes:*
Je suis souris—vivent les rats!"

Jee. Hindostanee.—"Sir, mister." The word is found terminating the names of Parsees and Hindoos, as Cursetjee, or Ragojee; familiarly "Curset" or "Rago." See "*Parsees*" and "*Hindoos.*"

Jejunus raro stomachus vulgaria temnit. Lat. HORACE.—"The hungry stomach seldom despises vulgar fare." Or, as it may be differently translated, "The stomach which is seldom hungry holds vulgar fare in contempt." In construction [if the line be genuine] *raro* must be joined with *jejunus*, and the allusion is to the stomach of the rich, which is described by the satirist as "rarely hungry."

Jeu d'esprit. Fr.—"A witticism, piece of wit."

Jeu de main, jeu de vilain. Fr.—"None but fools show their wit by their finger, or by pawing." Practical tricks belong only to the lowest classes. No gentleman should deal in horse-play or vulgar roughness.

Jeu de mots. Fr.—"A quibble, pun, play upon words, quirk."

Jeu de théâtre. Fr.—"Dumb show, attitude, gesture."

Jeune chair et vieux poisson. Fr.—"Young flesh and old fish." To intimate that the flesh of young eatable quadrupeds is the most delicious, but that the largest fish is the best.

Jeune on conserve pour la vieillesse: vieux on épargne pour

la mort. Fr. La Bruyère.—"When young, men lay up for old age; when aged, they hoard for death." It is in the nature of parsimony to confirm itself, and to increase.

Jour de fête. Fr.—"A saint's day, festival, holiday."

Jour de l'an. Fr.—"New-year's day."

Jour gras. Fr.—"A flesh-day." A day on which Papists are allowed to eat the flesh of oxen, sheep, swine, fowls, &c.

Jour maigre. Fr.—"A fish-day, meager day." A day of abstinence from beef, mutton, lamb, pork, fowls, &c.

Journal des débats. Fr.—"The Journal of the Parliamentary debates." A French newspaper, published in Paris.

Journal pour rire. Fr.—"The laughter-exciting Journal." A French comic periodical like our unrivaled "Punch."

Jucunda est memoria praeteritorum malorum. Lat. Cicero.—"Pleasing, pleasure-exciting, is the remembrance of ills that are past."

Jucunda et idonea dicere vitae. Lat. Horace.—"To describe whatever is pleasant and proper, for regulating the conduct of life, our conduct through life." This line well describes the duty of the didactic poet.

Jucundi acti labores. Lat. Cicero.—"The labors and difficulties through which we have passed are pleasing to the recollection."

Jucunditas quaedam. Lat. Quintilian.—"A certain pleasingness [in literary composition]." An indescribable fascination in literary productions, poems, odes, &c. "It is certain that a great deal of poetry was admitted into the lyric class without having any of its peculiar spirit; such poetry, however, appears rather a forced addition than a natural accession to the family: and it is impossible to think the *jucunditas quaedam* of Simonides so proper an attribute of the species as the fire of Alcaeus."

Jucundum nihil est nisi quod reficit varietas. Lat. Publius Syrus.—"Nothing is pleasant but what variety renews."

Judex curiae. Lat.—"The judge of the court."

Judex damnatur cum nocens absolvitur. Lat. Publius Syrus.—"The judge is found guilty, is censured, when a criminal is acquitted." This is to be understood as applying only where prejudice or corruption has dictated the sentence. "The motto of the Edinburgh Review truly says, *Judex damnatur cum nocens absolvitur*, but not the *judge* alone, for, what is worse, the plaintiff and the witness suffer the punishment, which the offender escapes."

Judicandum est legibus, non exemplis. Lat. Law maxim.—"The judgment must be pronounced, or we must judge, from law, not from precedent." As no two precedents, in the legal phrase, run together "on four legs," the strict letter of the law must be consulted.

Judicium Dei. Lat.—"The judgment of God." This was the name given by our ancestors to the "ordeal," *i.e.* walking blindfold over red-hot plowshares, &c., which has been long since disused.

Judicium parium, aut leges terrae. Lat.—"The judgment of our peers, the verdict of a jury, or the law of the land."—It is only by these, according to Magna Charta, that an Englishman can be condemned. This quotation from the Great Charter was adopted as his motto by the first Lord Camden.

Juge de paix. Fr.—"A justice of the peace, legal arbiter in petty disputes."

Jugulare mortuos. Lat.—"To stab the dead." To exercise superfluous cruelty.

Juncta juvant. Lat.—"These things, when conjoined, mutually aid each other." Individually considered, they are of little avail; but, taken conjunctively, they form a strong body of evidence.

Jungle. Forest, wilderness. The term *jungle* is very ill understood by European readers, who generally associate it with uninhabited forests and almost impenetrable thickets, whereas all the desert and uncultivated parts of India, whether covered with wood or merely suffered to run to waste, are styled jungles; and *jungle-wallah* is a term indiscriminately applied to a wild-cat, or to a gentleman who has been quartered for a considerable period in some desolate part of the country. Persons who are attached to very small stations in remote places, or who reside in solitary houses, surrounded only by the habitations of the natives, are said to be living in the jungles.—STOCQUELER.

Junks.—"Chinese trading-vessels."

Jupiter est quodcunque vides. Lat. LUCAN.—"Where'er you turn your eyes, 'tis GOD you see."

Jura negat sibi nata, nihil non arrogat armis. Lat. HORACE.—"He says that laws were not made for him, but that he claims for himself all he can get in war, in open warfare, in fair fight:"—

"Like Homer's hero, he does spurn all laws,
And by the sword alone asserts his cause."

This applies to the arrogant tyrant or usurper,

"Who scorns all judges and all law but arms."

Jura singulorum. Lat.—"The rights of individuals."

Juramentum contra utilitatem ecclesiasticam praestitum non tenet. Lat.—"No oath, contrary to ecclesiastical utility [meaning *the interests of the Church*], is binding." N.B. One of the canons of the CHURCH OF ROME.

Jurare et fallere numen. Lat. VIRGIL.—"To swear and forswear, violate one's oath." The motto prefixed to one of the cleverest of Mr. Canning's Essays in the "*Microcosm*," an essay on the vice of swearing.

Jure devoluto. Lat.—"The right [of doing any thing] having come to, devolved on, some other person, or body of persons." "By the existing statute law of Scotland, if the patron [of a church-living] failed to present within six months, the right of presentation fell *jure devolutc* [that is, *by lapse*], as it is called, to the presbytery."

Jure divino. Lat.—"By divine law." This is the tenure by which, according to certain high-fliers, kings hold their crowns, without any reference to the will of the people.

Jure humano. Lat.—"By human law." By that law which is founded on the assent of men. It is generally used in opposition to the foregoing.

Jure matrimonii. Lat.—"By reason, or in right, of his or her marriage."

Jure metropolitico. Lat.—"In his right as Metropolitan, or Head

.f the Episcopal College." Said of the ARCHBISHOP OF CANTERBURY, as head of the Church of England.

Jure naturae aequum est neminem cum alterius detrimento et injuria fieri locupletiorem. Lat.—"It is certainly not agreeable to natural justice that a *stranger* should reap the *beneficial pecuniary produce of another man's work.*" Said by LORD MANSFIELD in speaking on the "Law of Copyright."

Jus civile. Lat.—"The civil law." The law of many European nations, and of some of our courts, particularly the ecclesiastical, founded on the code of JUSTINIAN.

Jus dare and **Jus dicere.** Lat.—"To give a judicial decision, *and* To give a decision according to law, in conformity with the law of the land." *Jus dederunt, non jus dixerunt.* "They [the House of Lords] have given a judicial decision, but they have not given a decision according to the law of the land."

Jus et consuetudines gentium. Lat.—"The law and the customs, usages, of nations."

Jus gentium. Lat.—"The law of nations."

Jus in casu necessitatis. Lat.—"A right of desperate extremity."

Jus parliamentarium. Lat.—"The law, usage, or custom of Parliament." See "*Parliament.*"

Jus primogeniturae. Lat.—"The right of eldership."

Jus sanguinis, quod in legitimis successionibus spectatur, ipso nativitatis tempore quaesitum est. Lat. Law maxim.—"The right of blood, which is regarded in all lawful inheritances, is found in the very time of nativity." It is the *jus primogeniturae,* or right of eldership, that is principally respected, the maxim being that the next of worthiest blood should always inherit.

Jus summum saepe summa est malitia. Lat. TERENCE.—"Law enforced to strictness sometimes becomes the severest injustice." The more law, the less justice.

Jus togae. Lat.—"The right to the gown, right to wear the gown." "Dress is a greater ingredient in the formation of character than is generally supposed, and we may be strictly called in more senses than one the creatures of *habit.* The Romans were aware of this when they gave their citizens the exclusive *jus togae,* as a garment which might distinguish them in every quarter of the world, and stimulate them to uphold the national reputation." N.B. The "*toga*" was the principal outer garment worn by the Romans. It was the peculiar distinction of the Romans, who were thence called *togati,* or *gens togata* [the *gowned* nation]. It was originally worn only in Rome itself, and the use of it was forbidden alike to exiles and to foreigners.

Jusq'au revoir. Fr.—"Good-by."

Juste milieu. Fr.—"The golden mean, a medium, a just medium, an intermediate course." "The count stood between the Pope's Nuncio and the Turk. '*Voilà le juste milieu!*' said some one, and '*juste milieu*' was echoed around."

Justement, vous avez rencontré. Fr.—"Right, you have hit the nail on the head."

Justesse de l'esprit. Fr.—"Correctness of mind, a truly philosophical discrimination." "I had been far from doing adequate justice to the variety of his knowledge, and, above all, to that *justesse de l'esprit,* which judges the past as it would judge the present." N.B. Often used *incorrectly,* thus: "*justesse d'esprit,*" instead of the above.

Justitia regnorum fundamentum. Lat.—"Justice is the foundation, or main-stay, of kingdoms, the rock on which kingdoms are founded." "The prevailing features in the character of FRANCIS THE FIRST of Austria were his extreme craft and narrow-mindedness; he trusted no one. He was not a cruel man; but no contemporary prince inflicted a greater mass of moral and physical sufferings upon his subjects; none ever understood better how to give a gloss unto his violence. He had adopted for his motto, '*Justitia regnorum fundamentum,*' but he was a relentless persecutor, and the men whom he believed to entertain liberal sentiments in politics, or to harbor a feeling of nationality, were his personal foes. He never desisted from a pursuit, and the keys of his state prisons were in no hands but his own."

Justitiae fundamentum est fides. Lat. CICERO.—"Faith, fidelity, truth, honesty, is the groundwork of justice."

Justitiae partes sunt non violare homines: verecundiae non offendere. Lat. CICERO.—"Justice consists in doing no injury to men: decency, in giving them no offense."

Justitiae soror fides. Lat. HORACE.—"Faith, fidelity, is the sister of justice:"—

"Unsullied faith, of soul sincere,
Of justice pure the sister fair."

Justum ac tenacem propositi virum
Non civium ardor prava jubentium,
Non vultus instantis tyranni,
Mente quatit solida. Lat. HORACE.—

"The man who is just and firm to his purpose will not be shaken from his fixed resolution, either by the misdirecting ardor of his fellow-citizens, or by the threats of any imperious tyrant." *Or,* "Neither the wild fury of his fellow-citizens ordering evil measures to be pursued, nor the look of the threatening tyrant, shakes from his settled purpose the man who is just and firm in his resolve." This passage is often and properly quoted. It offers the finest picture of a statesman whose calmness and perseverance can equally resist the excesses of popular tumult, or the menaces of an arbitrary sovereign.

"The man in conscious virtue bold,
Who dares his secret purpose hold,
Unshaken hears the crowd's tumultuous cries,
And the impetuous tyrant's angry brow defies."

Juvenile vitium regere non posse impetum. Lat. SENECA.—"It is the fault of youth that it cannot govern its own violence." It either knows not, or will not consider, where the danger lies.

Juvenis. Lat.—"A young man, or woman." "Till a man is called to the degree of Serjeant at Law, or appointed King's Counsel, he is always called 'young gentleman,' let him be as old as he will; just as at our universities, the man who graduates *bachelor of arts* is called *juvenis*, whether he be twenty or forty years of age."

JUWAUB.—Literally, "an answer," but familiarly used in Anglo-Indian colloquy to imply a *negatur* [a denial, refusal] to the matrimonial proposal. "He has got his *juwaub*," or "He has been *juwaubbed*," denotes the failure of an *aspirant* to obtain the hand of the object of his devotion.—STOCQUELER.

K.

Kaffir.—In the Persian language this word is used to indicate an infidel, or unbeliever in MOHAMMED. At the Cape of Good Hope it implies the Hottentot race. N.B. The silly appellation of "*Caffres*" was given to the natives of a district of Africa by the early Portuguese voyagers, from the word "*Kaffir*."

Καιρον γνωθι. Gr.—"Know your opportunity." This was the advice of PITTACUS, one of the seven wise men of Greece. To let slip a favorable opportunity is the greatest proof of imbecility.

Kalends. From the Lat.—The first day of the Roman month, on which the people used anciently to be called together for particular purposes. On the first day of every month debtors were called upon by their creditors to pay their interest-money.

Κατ' αναλογιαν. Gr.—"According to analogy [reasoning by comparison]."

Κατ' εμφασιν. Gr.—"Emphatically."

Κατ' εξοχην. Gr.—"By excellence, pre-eminently."

Κατα σταγονα. Gr.—"By drops, drop by drop." "The cup of horror must be poured out before the reader only *κατα σταγονα*."

Kesar. [The same as CAESAR.]—"An emperor."

"Whilest kings and *kesars* at her feet did them prostrate."

SPENSER.

"Fayre fell good ORPHEUS, that would rather be
King of a mole-hill, than a *keysar's* slave."

RETURN FROM PARNASSUS.

Khan. Persian.—A title equivalent to the word "*Lord*."

Kirk. [Preferably, *Kyrk.*]—Derived from Κυριου οικος, "the house of the LORD," or, according to CLELAND, from the Celtic *kir* or *cir*, signifying "*a church, shire, or community*." An old word for a church. "The *Kirk* of Scotland."

Kitcat.—A technical term with painters of portraits, for that size of canvas which is between one serving for a mere head, and what is appropriated to a half-length.

Κοινος νους. Gr.—"COMMON SENSE." "There are truths or universals of so *obvious* a kind that *every mind* or *intellect* not absolutely depraved can, without the least help of art, hardly fail to recognize them. The *recognition* of these, or at least the *ability* to recognize them, is called *κοινος νους*, COMMON SENSE, as being *a sense common to all*, except lunatics and idiots."—JAMES HARRIS.

Κοινωνικον ζωον ὁ ανθρωπος. Gr. AMMONIUS.—"Man is by nature, naturally, a social animal."

Koran. Arabic.—The book which contains the doctrines and the precepts of MOHAMMED. N.B. The word "*Koran*" is spelled by some authors "*Kur'an:*" by others "*Chooran.*"

Κρονος. Gr.—The heathen deity SATURN: but often used by the ancients in the same sense as our English expression "*old fool.*"

Ksar.—MILTON's word for "*Czar.*"

——————————"The Russian *Ksar*
In Mosco."

Κτημα ες αει. Gr. THUCYDIDES.—"An imperishable, undying, possession." "The tooth of time will not injure the pages of ANASTASIUS: they bear the stamp of immortality, *κτημα ες αει.*"

Kuzzilbash. Turkish.—"Red Head." The word is employed in the present day to designate a Persian soldier, though in former times it was exclusively applied to seven tribes, who in the reign of SHAH ISMAEL the First formed a sort of body-guard to their monarch, and were bound by covenant to defend the Sheah [heretic or unorthodox] faith against the followers of OMAR.

Kyapootee oil, or **Cajeput oil.**—The volatile oil obtained from the leaves of the cajeput-tree, a tree growing in abundance on the mountains of Amboyna and the other Molucca Islands. It is much used as an embrocation in rheumatism, lumbago, &c.

L.

L'adversité fait l'homme, et le bonheur les monstres. Fr.——"Adversity makes men, but prosperity makes monsters." The former braces and strengthens, whilst the latter relaxes and debases, the powers of the mind. To this general rule, however, there are great and numerous exceptions.

L'affaire s'achèmine. Fr.—"The business is going forward, is progressing, progresses."

L'aimable siècle où l'homme dit à l'homme,
"Soyons frères, ou je t'assomme!" Fr. LE BRUN.—
"The amiable or glorious days, in which man said to his fellow-man, 'Let us be brothers, or I will knock your brains out.'" Fraternity or death. Applied to the FRENCH REVOLUTION of the last century.

L'allegorie habite un palais diaphane. Fr. LE MIERRE.—"Allegory dwells in a transparent palace." Its only use being to offer truth from the mirror of reflection, it should not be dimmed by obscurity.

L'amour de la justice n'est, en la plupart des hommes, que la crainte de souffrir l'injustice. Fr. ROCHEFOUCAULT.—"The love of justice is, in most men, nothing more than the fear of suffering injustice." Our anxiety on this subject may be traced to a motive of selfishness.

L'amour est une passion qui vient souvent sans savoir comment, et qui s'en va aussi de même. Fr.—"Love is a passion which frequently comes we know not how, and which quits us exactly in the same manner."

L'amour et la fumée ne peuvent se cacher. Fr. prov.—"Love and smoke are two things which cannot be concealed." Of the passion of love the faintest glimmerings give a strong light, as the smallest crevice will suffer a volume of smoke to escape.

L'amour propre est le plus grand de tous les flatteurs. Fr. ROCHEFOUCAULT.—"Self-love is the greatest of all flatterers." It is the lot of almost every man to flatter himself into a higher self-opinion than can possibly be effected by the adulation of others.

L'argent est un bon serviteur et un méchant maître. Fr. BOUHOURS.—"Money is a good servant, but a bad master." It is useful when well employed, but mischievous when men devote themselves wholly to its acquisition.

L'art de vaincre est celui de mépriser la mort. Fr. DE SIVRY.—"The art of conquering is that of despising death."

L'Empire! c'est la paix! Fr.—"The Empire! Peace is the Empire!" "The Napoleon dynasty imports something the very reverse of the policy of its founder—*L'Empire, c'est la paix.* Public opinion has effected this change:" that is to say, *The Empire! Peace is the Empire:* in other words, *Peace is the only sure foundation on which the Empire rests, or the only sure guarantee for the continuance of the Imperial Government.*

L'empire des lettres. Fr.—"The republic of letters, the learned [as a body], the commonwealth of the learned."

L'ennui du beau amène le goût du singulier. Fr. prov.—"A disgust of that which is proper leads to a taste for singularity."—Men who are tired of conforming to established modes and habits take up new ones of their own, and, since they cannot otherwise distinguish themselves, claim a notice from their affected peculiarities.

L'esclavage moins la honte. Fr.—"Slavery, serfdom, only without the shame, baseness, disgrace, degradation, or infamy attending it." N.B. A noted hit in one of CHATEAUBRIAND's harangues, in which he speaks of the condition of the French under NAPOLEON, as contrasted with their position under the CITIZEN-KING.

L'espérance est le songe d'un homme éveillé. Fr. prov.—"Hope is the dream of a man awake." It is properly called a dream, because it is allied, not with the judgment, but with the imagination.

L'esprit a son ordre, qui est par principes et démonstrations; le cœur en a un autre. Fr. PASCAL.—"The mind has its arrangement; it proceeds from principles to demonstrations. The heart has a different mode of proceeding." Lovers conclude first, and reason afterwards.

L'esprit est toujours la dupe du cœur. Fr. ROCHEFOUCAULT. "The understanding is ever the dupe of the heart." Our feelings are in general sure to get the better of our reason.

L'esprit qu'on veut avoir, gâte celui qu'on a. Fr. GRESSET.—"Extravagant pretensions to wit or wisdom depreciate the value of either, in the hands of their actual possessor."

L'esprit ressemble aux coquettes; ceux, qui courent après

lui sont ceux qu'il favorise le moins. Fr.—"Wit is like a coquette; those who run after it are the least favored." Those who laboriously hunt after wit generally find themselves deluded in the pursuit; it is an electric flash, which comes unbidden by any previous solicitation.

L'état!—c'est moi! Fr.—"The state! *I* am the state!" The phrase of LEWIS THE FOURTEENTH of France.

L'Europe est pourrie. Fr.—"Europe is rotten, rotten at the core." A favorite saying of late among the advocates of organic changes.

L'homme nécessaire. Fr.—"THE RIGHT MAN."

L'hypocrisie est un hommage que le vice rend à la vertu. Fr. ROCHEFOUCAULT.—"Hypocrisy is a homage which vice renders or pays to virtue." Vicious persons put on a mask, as being ashamed of appearing to the world in the features of their own consciousness.

L'imagination galope, le jugement ne va que le pas. Fr.—"The imagination gallops, the judgment only goes a foot-pace." The former anticipates the conclusion, which the latter awaits in sober leisure.

L'industrie des hommes s'épuise à briguer les charges; il ne leur en reste plus pour en remplir les devoirs. Fr. D'ALEMBERT.—"The industry of men is now so far exhausted in canvassing for places, that none is left for fulfilling the duties of them." A self-evident maxim with respect to the majority of courtiers.

L'injustice à la fin produit l'indépendance. Fr. VOLTAIRE.—"Injustice is in the end productive of independence, freedom."

L'une des marques de la médiocrité de l'esprit est de toujours conter. Fr. LA BRUYÈRE.—"One of the marks of mediocrity of understanding is to be fond of telling long stories."

L'usage fréquent des finesses est toujours l'effet d'une grande incapacité, et la marque d'un petit esprit. Fr.—"The frequent use of artifices and cunning is ever the effect of incapacity, and the mark of a narrow mind." A man of talent takes in the whole of a business at a single view, and proceeds directly to his end; those in general advance circuitously who are not certain either of their end or of their means.

La beauté sans vertu est une fleur sans parfum. Fr. prov.—"Beauty without virtue is like a flower without perfume." It may retain its color, but is without its essence.

a carrière des armes. Fr.—"The career of arms.

a carrière ouverte aux talents. Fr.—"The course, or race, open to talent, to the best man, to the *right man for the right place.*" "*La carrière ouverte aux talents* carried Napoleon in triumph over Europe."

La clémence des princes n'est souvent qu'une politique pour gagner l'affection des peuples. Fr. ROCHEFOUCAULT.—"The clemency of princes appears frequently to be nothing more than a measure of policy, calculated to gain the affections of the people."

La confiance fournit plus à la conversation que l'esprit. Fr. ROCHEFOUCAULT.—"Confidence is generally found to supply more materials for conversation than either wit or talent."

La cour ne rend pas content; mais elle empêche qu'on ne le soit ailleurs. Fr. LA BRUYÈRE.—"The court does not make a man-happy, but its habits prevent a man from enjoying happiness elsewhere." He who has long been busied in ambitious pursuits can find little pleasure in quiet and retirement.

La criaillerie ordinaire fait qu'on s'y accoutume, et que chacun la méprise. Fr.—"Clamorous abuse, too often repeated, becomes so familiar to the ear as to lose its effect." If you scold your servant inordinately for not rinsing a glass, he will scarcely feel your rebuke when you charge him with robbery.

La décence est le teint naturel de la vertu, et le fard du vice. Fr. prov.—"Decency is the genuine tint of virtue, and the false coloring of vice."

La docte antiquité fut toujours vénérable :
Je ne la trouve pas cependant adorable. Fr. BOILEAU.—"To the learning of antiquity I pay all due respect and veneration, but I do not therefore hold it as sacred." Some deference is due to that which the lapse of time has rendered venerable, but a gem dug from a *modern* is equally valuable with one that is taken from an *ancient* mine.

La faiblesse de l'ennemi fait notre propre force. Fr.—"The weakness of the enemy constitutes our own strength." This is a maxim in war, where all advantages may fairly be taken. There is a similar sentiment in another language:—*Dolus, an virtus, quis in hoste requirat?* (Lat.)—"What matters it, whether the enemy has been defeated by stratagem or by valor?" or rather, "Who questions in an enemy, or asks of an enemy, whether he has carried on his operations by stratagem or by valor?"

La faim chasse le loup hors du bois. Fr. prov.—"Hunger will break through stone walls."

La faim épouse la soif. Fr. prov.—"It is hunger marrying thirst." Said of men and women marrying without having any thing to live on.

La faim rend un homme excusable. Fr.—"Hunger, starvation, excuses a man in some degree for the commission of crime."

La fleur des pois. Fr.—"The very pink of the fashion." "But look! here comes *la fleur des pois!*" Applied to bipeds, in the shape of men, who can find nothing better to do with themselves than decorating their pretty persons.

La fleur des troupes. Fr.—"Choice men, picked men." A military expression.

La fortune du pot. Fr.—"Pot-luck."

La France est un soldat. Fr.—"France is [essentially] a military nation." A saying of CHATEAUBRIAND'S.

La grande nation. Fr.—"The great nation." The designation given by *Frenchmen* to France.

La grande pensée. Fr.—"The grand idea, The all-absorbing thought." The term familiarly employed by the Parisians before the overthrow of NAPOLEON, to express their national scheme of universal subjugation.

La grande sagesse de l'homme consiste à connaître ses folies. Fr.—"The great wisdom of man consists in the knowledge of his follies." To be convinced of our false steps is in some degree an advance towards wisdom.

La journée sera dure, mais elle se passera. Fr.—"The day, the season of trial, will be severe, hard to bear, but it will pass away, will have an end." The words of DAMIENS, who derived fortitude and consolation from reflecting that the day would run its inevitable course.

La langue des femmes est leur épée, et elles ne la laissent pas rouiller. Fr. prov.—"The tongue of a woman is her sword, which she seldom suffers to rust." A sarcasm sufficiently severe on the proverbial loquacity of the sex in general.

La libéralité consiste moins à donner beaucoup qu'à donner à propos. Fr. LA BRUYÈRE.—"Liberality does not consist so much in giving a great deal as in giving seasonably."

La liberté est ancienne; c'est le despotisme qui est nouveau. Fr.—"Liberty is a thing of the olden time, an institution of ancient standing, whereas despotism is something comparatively new, modern."

La maladie sans maladie. Fr.—"The disease without a disease." The hypochondriac distemper.

La marque d'un mérite extraordinaire, c'est de voir que ceux qui l'envient le plus sont contraints de le louer. Fr.—"The proof of extraordinary merit is to see that it extorts praise even from those with whom it is an object of envy."

La moitié du monde prend plaisir à médire, et l'autre moitié à croire les médisances. Fr. prov.—"One half of the world takes pleasure in detraction, and the other half in believing all that detraction utters."

La moquerie est souvent une indigence d'esprit. Fr. LA BRUYÈRE.—"Jesting, in some cases, only proves a want of understanding."

La mort est plus aisée à supporter sans y penser, que la pensée de la mort sans péril. Fr. PASCAL.—"Death is itself more easy when it comes without previous reflection, than the thought of death even without the danger."

La nuit donne, or, **porte conseil.** Fr. prov.—"Night gives counsel; advise, or take counsel, with your pillow."

La parfaite valeur est de faire sans témoins ce qu'on serait capable de faire devant tout le monde. Fr. ROCHEFOUCAULT.—"True courage is shown in doing, without witnesses, that which a man is capable of doing in the face of the whole world." In the former case it is certain that ostentation has no share in the effort.

La passion fait souvent un fou du plus habile homme, et rend souvent habiles les plus sots. Fr. ROCHEFOUCAULT.—"Love often makes a fool of the cleverest man, and as often gives cleverness to the most foolish."

La patience est amère, mais son fruit est doux. Fr. J. J. ROUSSEAU.—"Patience is bitter, but its fruit is sweet." Men are generally the better for suffering.

La patience est le remède le plus sûr contre les calomnies: le temps tôt ou tard découvre la vérité. Fr. prov.—"Patience is the surest antidote against calumny. Time, sooner or later, will discover the truth."

La philosophie qui nous promet de nous rendre heureux

nous trompe. Fr.—"Philosophy, which promises to render us happy, deceives us."

La philosophie triomphe aisément des maux passés et des maux à venir; mais les maux présents triomphent d'elle. Fr. ROCHEFOUCAULT.—"Philosophy holds an easy triumph over misfortunes which are past and those that are to come; but those which are present triumph over her." By philosophy we are taught to dismiss our regrets for past and our apprehensions of future evils; but the immediate sense of suffering she cannot teach us to subdue.

La plupart des hommes n'ont pas le courage de corriger les autres, parcequ'ils n'ont pas le courage de souffrir qu'on les corrige. Fr.—"The generality of mankind have not sufficient courage to correct others, because they themselves are wanting in fortitude to submit to correction." An adviser should not only have wisdom to admonish, but be also fortified, in conscious innocence, to bear the retort which his advice may possibly provoke.

La politesse est l'art de rendre à chacun sans effort ce qui lui est socialement dû. Fr.—"Politeness is the art of giving to every one in an easy and unconstrained manner those particular marks of attention which are his due, which he has a right to expect as a member of the universal brotherhood of the human family."

La propriété est un vol. Fr.—"Property is robbery!" One of the vile watchwords of the French Communists and Socialists.

La réputation d'un homme est comme son ombre, qui tantôt le suit et tantôt le précède; quelquefois elle est plus longue et quelquefois plus courte que lui. Fr. prov.—"The reputation of a man is like his shadow: it sometimes follows and sometimes precedes him; it is sometimes longer, and sometimes shorter, than his natural size." As our shadows vary in their length and direction according to our relative position to the sun, so is the reputation of many men either magnified or diminished from relative situations and circumstances.

La sauce vaut mieux que le poisson. Fr. prov.—"The sauce is better, or more relishing, than the fish." The accompaniments are better than the thing [dish] itself. N.B. The remark made by SCALIGER concerning the "PERSIUS" of CASAUBON.

La science du gouvernement n'est qu'une science de combinaisons, d'applications, et d'exceptions, selon les temps, les lieux, et les circonstances. Fr. ROUSSEAU.—"The science of government is only a science of combinations, of applications, and of exceptions, according to times, places, and circumstances."

La verità è figlia del tempo. Ital. prov.—"Truth is the daughter of time."

La vérité appartient à l'histoire. Fr.—"Truth belongs to history, Truth ought to be the distinguishing characteristic of history." "Whosoever," says Sir Walter Raleigh, "in writing a modern history, shall follow truth too near the heels, it may haply strike out his teeth. There is no mistress or guide that hath led her followers and servants into greater miseries. He that goes after her too far off loseth her sight, and loseth himself; and he that walks after her at a middle distance, I know not whether I should call that kind of course *temper or baseness.*" The above motto was prefixed to the *second* edition of a celebrated French work, which appeared ten years after the publication of the *first* edition. The *second* edition contained information which would have put in jeopardy the life of the author had such information appeared in the *first* edition: the motto has, therefore, been pointedly translated,—"*The teeth are no longer in danger.*"

La vérité est cachée au fond du puits. Fr. prov.—"Truth is, or lies, hidden at the bottom of a well."

La vérité ne fait pas autant de bien dans le monde, que ses apparences y font de mal. Fr.—"Truth does not so much good in the world, as the appearances of it do mischief." The deceit and hypocrisy of men are the prime sources of evil in the moral world.

La vertu dans l'indigence est comme un voyageur que le vent et la pluie contraignent de s'envelopper de son manteau. Fr. prov.—"Virtue in indigence is like a traveler, who is compelled by the wind and the rain to wrap himself up in his cloak." In this situation the virtuous man is overlooked, and the passing world is heedless of his merits and his qualifications. Compare "*Laudo manentem.*" &c.

La vertu n'irait pas si loin si la vanité ne lui tenait compagnie. Fr. ROCHEFOUCAULT.—"Virtue would not go so far, if vanity did not bear her company." We are forwarded in our best actions by a secret wish to gain the good opinion of others.

La volonté générale. Fr.—"The voluntary system." A system which is highly praised by some of the French religionists.

Labitur, et labetur in omne volubilis aevum. Lat. HORACE.—"The stream or river flows, and will continue to flow through all ages to the end of time." "What is a country life but a mere repetition of the same things, a very roundabout, the *labitur, et labetur in omne volubilis aevum?*" that is to say, the *onward flowing and never-varying stream of time*, the *same undying monotony.*

Labor ipse voluptas. Lat.—"Labor, or toil, itself is a pleasure." "*Labor ipse voluptas* is indeed the principle upon which most men who devote themselves to labor for the public can alone regard themselves as fully compensated."

Labor omnia vincit. Lat. VIRGIL.—"Labor conquers every thing." There are few difficulties which will not yield to perseverance. The *full* expression is—

——————Labor omnia vincit
Improbus, et duris urgens in rebus egestas:

that is to say, *Severe and continuous toil, combined with the pressure of want in the day of trouble, in hard times, surmounts every difficulty:*—

"Thus labor conquers, and compelling need."

Laborum dulce lenimen. Lat. HORACE.—"Sweet solace of my labors or toils:"—

"Hear thou thy poet's solemn prayer,
Thou softener of each anxious care!"

The appellation is given by the poet to his lyre [one of the most ancient musical instruments of the stringed kind]. N.B. "*Laborum dulce lenimen*" is also applied by sundry gents to *tobacco-smoking*, *snuff-taking*, *&c.*

LAC.—One hundred thousand. A lac of rupees (£10,000) was once the desiderated maximum of an Anglo-Indian fortune. The "nabobs" of the last century, and a few of the present, often returned to England with several lacs. At the present day, the accumulation of a single lac is a matter of difficulty.—STOCQUELER.

Lâches. Law French.—An abridgment of the old Norman-French word "*lâchesse*," meaning "*laxity, laxness, looseness in the administration of justice, negligence, slackness.*" "It would have the effect of preventing a failure of justice, should any *lâches* occur on the part of the local authorities."

Laconic. From the Greek.—"Brief," the Laconians or Lacedaemonians [the inhabitants of Laconica or Laconia, a country of ancient Greece] being in the habit of using but few words, of expressing themselves briefly. "*Verborum multitudine supersedendum est*" [We must forbear using, or abstain from using, a great number of words. We must avoid being verbose, or wordy; otherwise we run the risk of becoming prosy] is an adage that will recur to the memory of many of the users of this volume, such "*wise saw*" having been well drilled into them during "*the happiest days of their lives*," that is, their school-boy days! N.B. "LACON: or, Many things in few words; addressed to those who think," by the Rev. C. C. Colton; and a somewhat similar work, entitled "The Pocket LACON," may be safely recommended to those who crave for something better than the trash that is continually teeming from the press.

Lacunae. Lat.—"Gaps or empty places, when any thing is wanting in an author; gaps in a manuscript."

Laesio majestatis. Lat.—"High treason." See "*Crimen Majestatis.*"

Laetus in praesens animus, quod ultra est
Oderit curare, et amara lento
Temperet risu. NIHIL EST AB OMNI PARTE
BEATUM. Lat. HORACE.—

"Let the mind that is contented with its present lot dislike disquieting itself about the events of the future, and temper the troubles of life, the bitters of existence, with a placid smile [*a calm, philosophic smile*]."

"He, who can taste without allay
The present pleasures of the day,
Should with an easy, cheerful smile
The bitterness of life beguile,—
Should all of future care detest,
FOR NOTHING IS COMPLETELY BLEST."

Laisser-aller. Fr.—"To let matters go on as they list, as listeth them." The phrase is said of "ease, freeness, freedom, easiness, or yieldingness of disposition, too great a readiness to adopt the opinions of others, or to allow one's self to be led by the nose, a kind of negligence in the demeanor and manner of acting and speaking."

1. "An invincible tendency to '*laissez-aller*' was the basis of the character of HORACE WALPOLE. But he did not lie by and observe

events, like Metternich and Talleyrand, to become imbued with their tendency, and ultimately gain the mastery of them; he let them take their course, and in reality cared very little for the result."

2. "Excellent!" said he, "only not so much *laisser-aller;* a little more stiff, more drawn up! That will do: oh, it's perfect!"

Laisser dire le monde, et toujours bien faire, c'est une maxime qui, étant bien observée, assure notre repos, et établit enfin notre réputation. Fr.—"To let the world talk, and always to act well, is a principle of action which, well observed, will secure our repose, and in the end establish our reputation."

Laissez-faire. Fr.—"Let or leave doing alone." Let things take their course, go on without interruption, go on without meddling with them. This oft-used phrase will be best explained by a few quotations:—

1. "With the '*absolute shall*' of Mr. Dunlop and the abolitionists on one side, and the *laissez-faire* of Dr. Chalmers and the concessionists on the other, what is even the Procurator for the Church [*of Scotland*] among so many?"

2. "That the *laissez-faire* [let-alone] system is incompetent to the moral management of the new economical conditions under which society exists, is the inference generally drawn from the frightful mass of Practical Heathenism existing in the heart of Christian countries."

3. "*Laissez-faire* has long been a favorite maxim of our statesmen and lawyers: to seek for no remedy till some partial evil has grown to such a height as absolutely to force itself on the notice of the physician, and even then to admit it only to the extent of the actual exigency."

4. "Reforming abuses gives trouble, creates ill blood, and puts coldness between friends; while *laissez-faire* conciliates amity, strews roses instead of thorns, and makes the world run smoothly."

LA-MAH-E-IL-ALLAH! Persian.—"There is no God but God!" The first part of the Mohammedan confession of faith. It is in constant colloquial use, as an exclamation of astonishment, grief, or pleasure, or even as an occasional ejaculation without any meaning at all.

Lang festjen is nin brae sperjen. Frisian prov.—"Long fasting spares no bread."

Lapsus linguae. Lat.—"A slip of the tongue."

Lasciate ogni speranza, voi ch'entrate. Ital. Dante.—"Leave hope behind, all ye who enter here," or "Discard all hope, ye who do enter here." Applied as a motto to the Revolutionary tribunal of France. "In France there are none of those hateful institutions styled workhouses, over whose gates are written, at least in imagination, the words devised by Dante for the infernal portals—*Lasciate ogni speranza, voi ch'entrate.*"

Lateat scintillula forsan. Lat.—"A small spark may lurk unseen." This hemistich, alluding to the vital spark, is very happily adoped as the motto of the Royal Humane Society for the recovery of persons apparently drowned.

Latet anguis in herba. Lat. Virgil.—"There is a snake concealed in the grass." There is a lurking danger before you which you do not immediately perceive.

Latitat. Law Lat.—"He lurks, lies hid, does not appear, when summoned by law, skulks and keeps out of the way." A writ of summons issuing from the King's Bench, which by a fiction states the defendant to be in a state of concealment. See "*Mandamus*."

Latius regnes avidum domando
Spiritum, quam si Libyam remotis
Gadibus jungas, et uterque Poenus
Serviat uni. Lat. HORACE.—
"You may have an infinitely more extensive sway by subduing, gaining the mastery over, a greedy disposition, than if you were to join Africa to distant, remote Gades [*Cadiz*], and both Carthages [*one in Spain and the other in Africa*] were to be in subjection to you alone, were to be under your own absolute control:"—

"By virtue's precepts to control
The thirsty cravings of the soul,
Is over wider realms to reign
Unenvied monarch, than if Spain
Thou could'st to distant Libya join,
And both the Carthages were thine."

Laudant quod non intelligunt. Lat.—"They praise what they do not understand." A very common practice; much more so, indeed, than is generally imagined. The author of "Adventures in the North of Europe, illustrative of the Poetry and Philosophy of Travel," a man, by-the-by, who confesses himself utterly ignorant of the Danish language, says, "The clergyman [of the Lutheran Church at Elsinore] had a quiet earnestness of manner, and a persuasive eloquence, that pleased and attracted. I admired his discourse, though I did not understand a word of it."

A DUTCHMAN'S TESTIMONY.

"I vill tell you, such is de powers of de Shakspeer, that I vunce saw de plays arcted in Anglish languish, in Holland, where der vas not vun persons in all de house but myself could onderstond it; yet dare vas not a persons in all dat house but vat vas in tears, dat is, all crying, blowing de nose, and veep very mouch, couldn't onderstond vun vurd of de play, yet all veeping. Such vas de powers of de Shakspeer."

Laudari a viro laudato. Lat. CICERO.—"To be praised by a man who has himself been oft the subject of praise." This is certainly the most valuable species of commendation.

Laudato ingentia rura, exiguum colito. Lat. VIRGIL.—"Bestow your praise upon large domains, but your preference on a small estate." The latter to a contented mind is likely to produce the greater share of happiness.

Laus Deo. Lat.—"Praise be to GOD."

Laus est facere quod decet, non quod licet. Lat.—"It is a praiseworthy action to do what is fit, proper, becoming, right, and not merely that which is lawful, which the law allows, or does not actually disallow." "When pressed by the legal opinion upon a certain question, Cardinal Wolsey took the distinction between law and conscience, and said, 'It is proper to have a respect to conscience before the rigor of the common law, for *laus est facere quod decet, non qvod licet.*'"

Layman.—From the Greek word λαος, the people: a *layman*, then, is a *people-man, one of the people.* The word is now used to signify "*one who is not a clergyman.*"

Lazzaroni. Ital.—The *Lazzaroni* are a very peculiar class of society, the *very dregs of the people* at Naples, and their misery, idleness, and utter want of thought or consideration are proverbial. At the end of the last century they numbered 40,000. "*Lazzaroni*" is the *plural* of *Lazzarone*, one of their number.

Le beau monde. Fr.—"The gay world, people of fashion."

Le bien cherche le bien. Fr. prov.—"Every one bastes the fat hog, while the lean one burneth; money bets money." Property, wealth, money, goes to those who have already enough of it.

Le bien ne se fait jamais mieux que lorsqu'il s'opère lentement. Fr. De Moy.—"Good is never effected more happily than when it is produced slowly." Sudden changes, either in the affairs of empires or of individuals, are seldom productive of beneficial consequences.

Le bon estomac et le mauvais cœur. Fr.—"A good stomach and a bad heart; a good digestion and a heart impervious to the whisperings of conscience." "Shame never visits her, for ''tis conscience that makes cowards of us all,' and she has none. She realizes that *ne plus ultra* of sublunary comfort, which it was reserved for a Frenchman to define,—the blessed combination of *le bon estomac et le mauvais cœur.*"

Le bon temps viendra. Fr.—"The good time will come, there's a good time coming." "The common bias of the mind undoubtedly is (such is the benevolent appointment of Providence) to think favorably of the future; to overvalue the chances of possible good, and to underrate the risks of possible evil; and in the case of some fortunate individuals, this disposition remains after a thousand disappointments. To what this bias of our nature is owing, it is not material for us to inquire: the fact is certain, and it is an important one to our happiness. It supports us under the real distresses of life, and cheers and animates all our labors."

"There's a good time coming yet,
  A good time coming;
The pen shall supersede the sword,
And *right*, not *might*, shall be the lord,
  In the good time coming.
Worth, not *birth*, shall rule mankind,
  And be acknowledged stronger;
The proper impulse has been given,
  Wait a little longer.

"There's a good time coming yet,
  A good time coming:
War in all men's eyes shall be
A monster of iniquity
  In the good time coming;
Nations shall not quarrel then,
  To prove which is the stronger,
Nor slaughter men for glory's sake,—
  Wait a little longer."

Le bonheur de l'homme en cette vie ne consiste pas à être sans passions: il consiste à en être le maître. Fr.—"The happiness of man in this life does not consist in the absence, but in the mastery, of his passions."

Le bonheur des peuples dépend et de la félicité dont ils jouissent au dedans, et du respect qu'ils inspirent au dehors. Fr. HELVETIUS.—"The welfare of nations depends on the happiness they enjoy within themselves, and the respect with which they inspire other countries."

Le bonheur ou le malheur des hommes ne dépend pas moins de leur humeur que de la fortune. Fr. ROCHEFOUCAULT.—"The good or bad fortune of men depends as much on their own disposition as on chance."

Le bonheur ou le malheur vont d'ordinaire à ceux qui ont le plus de l'un ou de l'autre. Fr. ROCHEFOUCAULT.—"Good and bad fortune are found severally to visit those who have the most of the one or the other." The prosperous man has in general nothing but lucky additions; whilst those in adversity find only new visitations of misfortune.

Le Bourgeois Gentilhomme. Fr.—"The citizen who would needs be a fine gentleman, an apish imitator of the higher classes of society." "*Le Bourgeois Gentilhomme* is in London daily enacted with even more farcical pretension than Molière would have ventured to delineate." N.B. "*Le Bourgeois Gentilhomme*" is one of Molière's comedies.

Le coût fait perdre le goût. Fr. prov.—"The cost puts one out of conceit with it." I should like the thing, but I dislike the expense.

Le crime fait la honte, et non pas l'échafaud. Fr. CORNEILLE.—"It is crime that causes shame, and not the scaffold."

Le Grand Monarque. Fr.—"The Great Monarch." LEWIS THE FOURTEENTH of France.

Le grand œuvre. Fr.—"The great work," namely, the philosopher's stone.

Le Jesuitisme est une épée, dont la poignée est à Rome, et la pointe partout. Fr. DUPIN.—"Jesuitism is a sword, the handle or hilt of which is at Rome, and the point everywhere." One of DUPIN's lucky hits.

Le jeu est le fils de l'avarice, et le père du désespoir. Fr. prov.—"Gaming is the son of avarice, and the father of despair."

Le jeu ne vaut pas la chandelle. Fr.—"The game is not worth the candle, or candles." The business will not quit cost, is not worth one's while.

Le mérite est souvent un obstacle à la fortune, et la raison de cela c'est qu'il produit toujours deux mauvais effets, l'envie et la crainte. Fr.—"Merit is often an obstacle to success, and the reason is, that it ever produces two bad effects, envy and fear;"—envy from those who cannot reach the same effort, and fear from those whom it may possibly supplant.

Le mieux est l'ennemi du bien. Fr.—"The best is the enemy of well." In endeavoring to make a thing better, beware lest you make it worse. We lose our present advantages in seeking after those that are unattainable. We often spoil a good thing in wishing to make it better.

Le moineau en la main vaut mieux que l'oie qui vole. Fr. prov.—"A sparrow in the hand is better than a goose on the wing." A bird in the hand is worth two in the bush.

Le monde est le livre des femmes. Fr. ROUSSEAU.—"The world is the women's book." They are generally supposed to profit more from observation than from reading.

Le monde poli. Fr.—"The gay or fashionable world, people of fashion." N.B. The same as "*Le beau monde.*"

Le monde savant. Fr.—"The learned world, the learned."

Le mot de l'énigme. Fr.—"The meaning of the riddle, the secret." The key to the mystery.

• **Le moyen le plus sûr de se consoler de tout ce qui peut arriver, c'est d'attendre toujours au pire.** Fr.—"The most certain consolation against all that can happen, is always to expect the worst." Those whose hopes are too much buoyed up have always to meet the severest mortification.

Le nœud de l'affaire. Fr.—"The difficulty of the business, the main or chief point."

Le patriotisme le plus pur. Fr.—"The purest patriotism, patriotism of the most disinterested character." "In France—as, we suspect, all over the reformed world—*le patriotisme le plus pur* is evinced by a very hungry attention to one's own personal interests."

• **Le pays du mariage a cela de particulier, que les étrangers ont envie de l'habiter, et les habitants naturels voudroient en être exilés.** Fr. MONTAIGNE.—"The land of marriage has this peculiarity, that strangers are desiring of inhabiting it, while its natural inhabitants would willingly be banished from thence." This is a sarcasm upon matrimony, which unfortunately, in many cases, is not more biting than just.

Le petit caporal. Fr.—"The little corporal." A familiar name given to NAPOLEON by the French soldiers after the battle of Lodi.

Le petit monde. Fr.—"The lower classes."

Le petit peuple. Fr.—"The mob, the meaner or lower sort of people, mobility, populace."

Le plus lent à promettre est toujours le plus fidèle à tenir. Fr.—"The man who is most slow, or the slowest, in promising is most sure to keep his word."

Le plus sage est celui qui ne pense point l'être. Fr. BOILEAU.—"The wisest man is generally he who does not think that he is so." The truly wise bear with them a consciousness of their own failings.

Le présent est pour ceux qui jouissent; l'avenir pour ceux qui souffrent. Fr.—"The present is for those who enjoy; the future for those who suffer."

Le refus des louanges est souvent un désir d'être loué deux fois. Fr.—"The refusal of praise often intimates nothing less than that the praise is regarded as insufficient;" and of course that a double portion would be more acceptable. An honest mind will fairly take the eulogy which is due: a vain one will inhale the incense of flattery almost to suffocation.

Le roi le veut. Fr.—"The king wills it, or will have it so."

Le roi s'en avisera. Fr.—"The king will consider or think of it." These are phrases derived from the Normans, by which the king either gives his sanction to an act of Parliament or postpones his assent. The latter is disused in practice. N.B. "*Le roi le veut*" was the imperious term used by the kings of France previous to the REVOLUTION, in sending their ordinances to the parliament to be enregistered. "*Le roi s'en avisera*" is another French phrase, that was used by the same monarchs to express their dissent from any act submitted for their approval, and was considered as an absolute *veto* [prohibition].

Le sage entend à demi mot. Fr.—"The sensible man understands half a word." He can take a brief intimation.

Le sage songe avant que de parler à ce qu'il doit dire; le fou parle, et ensuite songe à ce qu'il a dit. Fr. prov.—"A wise man thinks before he speaks; but a fool speaks, and then thinks of what he has been saying."

Le savoir faire. Fr.—"The knowledge how to act." Address. "Could we not gain some Indian officers, men of *savoir-faire?*" that is to say, *men who have their wits about them, men who have heads to contrive and hands to execute.*

Le savoir vivre. Fr.—"The knowledge how to live." An acquaintance with life and manners.

Le secret d'ennuyer est celui de tout dire. Fr. VOLTAIRE.—"The secret of tiring and disgusting is to say all that can be said." Applied to those dull, plodding writers who think it necessary to exhaust their subject, without leaving any thing to be supplied by the judgment or imagination of their readers.

Le silence du peuple est la leçon des rois. Fr.—"The silence of the people is a lesson for kings, or reads a lesson to kings."

Le silence est le parti le plus sûr de celui qui se défie de soi-même. Fr. ROCHEFOUCAULT.—"To be silent is the safest choice for the man who distrusts his own powers." He will in that case be insured against incurring disgrace.

Le style c'est l'homme. Fr.—"The style is the man; the style shows or betrays the man." "As nothing is more difficult, we might say impossible, than to disguise, through a long series of compositions, those features of the mind which we term STYLE, *le style c'est l'homme*, it seems certain that the daring satirist would have been readily detected had any writings of consequence previously proceeded from his pen, or had he figured in any department of public life."

Le temps présent est gros de l'avenir. Fr. LEIBNITZ.—"The present time is big with the future." Great events are in the womb of time.

Le travail du corps délivre des peines de l'esprit; et c'est ce qui rend les pauvres heureux. Fr. ROCHEFOUCAULT.—"The labor of the body relieves us from the fatigues of the mind; and this it is which forms the happiness of the poor."

Le travail éloigne de nous trois grands maux, l'ennui, le

vice, et le besoin. Fr. VOLTAIRE.—"Labor rids us of three great evils—irksomeness, vice, and poverty."

Le vent du bureau est bon. Fr.—"The official wind is good, things take a good turn, he is [you, we are] likely to carry our measure, our object." Appearances are favorable for the success of an affair.

Le vent du bureau n'est pas pour vous. Fr.—"The cause is likely to go against you."

Le vrai mérite ne dépend point du temps ni de la mode. Fr. prov.—"True merit depends not on the time or on the fashion." It avails itself not of modes or opinions, but rests securely on its intrinsic strength.

Le vrai moyen d'être trompé, c'est de se croire plus fin que les autres. Fr. ROCHEFOUCAULT.—"The sure mode of being deceived is to believe ourselves to be more cunning than the rest of the world."

Le vrai n'est pas toujours vraisemblable. Fr.—"The true, or That which is true, is not always probable or likely, is not always a matter of probability or likelihood."

Lector benevole. Lat.—"Kind or gentle reader."

Legant prius et postea despiciant, ne videantur non ex judicio sed ex odii praesumptione ignorata damnare. Lat. LOPE DE VEGA.—"Let them read my book before they give an opinion respecting it, and then despise it if they choose: read it first of all, I say, that they may not subject themselves to the charge of ignorantly condemning a work merely from a hateful spirit of prejudice, and not from the actual exercise of their judgment." The motto prefixed by LOPE to his "JERUSALEM," a work against which an unfavorable prepossession had gone forth. The practice, so common with a number of would-be critics, of condemning books without reading them, or at any rate with only a superficial knowledge of their contents, has now become proverbial—*Damnant quod nesciunt!*

Legimus, ne legantur. Lat. LACTANTIUS—"We [reviewers] read such works [objectionable though they are] to prevent [if possible] their being read by others." Our notice, we trust, will be sufficient to deter others from wasting their time on such garbage.

Legis constructio non facit injuriam. Lat. Law maxim.—"The interpretative construction of the law shall wrong no person." If a person, for instance, grants away all his goods and chattels, those of which he is possessed as an executor shall not pass, for that would be a wrong to the estate of the testator.

Lene tormentum. Lat. HORACE.—"Gentle violence." "These learned thieves first laid down the rule that in cases of 'slow coaches' operations were to be quickened, and a loyal zeal excited, by the *lene tormentum* of a fine upon delays."

Lenior et melior fis, accedente senecta? Lat. HORACE.—"Do you grow, become, milder and better on the approach of old age, as old age approaches?"

"My worthy friend, say, dost thou grow
More mild and virtuous as thy seasons flow?"

The experience and reflections of past years contribute, or ought to ontribute, *to make us better*.

Leniter ex merito quidquid patiare ferendum est,
Quae venit indigne poena dolenda venit. Lat. Ovid.—"That which is deservedly suffered must be borne with calmness, but when the pain is unmerited, the grief is resistless." The poet is justifying his own strong feelings on having been banished, as he states, without having deserved that punishment.

Leonina societas. Lat.—"A lion's company." That dangerous association where the whole of the prey is monopolized by the strongest and most powerful.

Les amertumes sont en morale ce que sont les amers en médecine. Fr.—"Misfortunes, the bitternesses of existence, are in morals what bitters are in medicine." They are equally disagreeable in the first instance, but they act in the same manner as corroborants, strengtheners.

Les bras croisés. Fr.—"With folded arms, idle." "He could not, as he expressed it, rest '*les bras croisés*.'"

Les cartes sont brouillées. Fr.—"The cards are mixed." "Matters are embroiled." There is a violent misunderstanding.

Les consolations indiscrètes ne font qu'aigrir les violentes afflictions. Fr. Rousseau.—"Consolation, when improperly administered, does but irritate the affliction."

Les eaux sont basses chez lui. Fr.—"The waters are low with him, he is at low water, hard up." His resources are exhausted.

Les esprits médiocres condamnent d'ordinaire tout ce qui passe leur portée. Fr. Rochefoucault.—"Men of confined understandings generally find fault with every thing that is beyond their comprehension."

Les extrêmes se touchent. Fr.—"Extremes meet."

Les femmes peuvent tout, parcequ'elles gouvernent les personnes qui gouvernent tous. Fr. prov.—"Women can do every thing, because they rule those who command every thing."

Les femmes sont extrêmes: elles sont meilleures ou pires que les hommes. Fr. La Bruyère.—"The character of women is in extremes. They are always better or worse than men."

Les fous font les festins, et les sages les mangent. Fr. prov. —"Fools make feasts, and wise men eat them."

Les fous inventent les modes, et les sages les suivent. Fr. prov.—"Fools invent fashions, and wise men follow them."

Les Français inventent, mais les Anglais perfectionnent. Fr. —"The French invent things, but the English make them perfect, bring them to perfection."

Les gens qui ont peu d'affaires sont de très grands parleurs. Moins on pense, plus on parle. Fr. Montesquieu.—"Men who have little business are great talkers. The more one thinks, the less one speaks."

Les grands noms abaissent, au lieu d'élever, ceux qui ne les savent pas soutenir. Fr. Rochefoucault.—"Great names debase, instead of raising, those who know not how to sustain them." A title stained by vice, or degraded by ignorance, is but a higher claim to contempt.

Les grandes pensées viennent du cœur! Fr.—"Great or sublime thoughts come, or spring, from the heart!"

Les hommes sont égaux: ce n'est point la naissance,
C'est la seûle vertu, qui fait la différence. Fr. VOLTAIRE.—"All men are equal: it is not birth, but virtue alone, that makes the difference." This is the only proper ground on which the much-contested doctrine of *equality* can be founded: including, however, the principle of *equal* rights.

Les hommes sont la cause que les femmes ne s'aiment point. Fr. LA BRUYÈRE.—"It is the men that cause the women to dislike each other."

Les jeunes gens disent ce qu'ils font, les vieillards ce qu'ils ont fait, et les sots ce qu'ils ont envie de faire. Fr.—"Young folks tell what they are doing, old ones what they have done, and fools what they wish to do."

Les malheureux, qui ont de l'esprit, trouvent des ressources en eux-mêmes. Fr. BOUHOURS.—"Unfortunate men of genius find or have resources in themselves." They have that within which tends to console them for the neglect of the world.

Les mœurs. Fr.—"Manners or morals." Neither of these English words, however, conveys the idea of the original, "Manners" comprehending too little, and "Morals" too much. The ingenious author of "The World" defines it thus—"A general exterior, decency, fitness, and propriety of conduct, in the common intercourse of life."

Les murs ont des oreilles, les murailles parlent. Fr. prov.—"Walls have ears." Be cautious how you speak.

Les passions sont les vents, qui font aller notre vaisseau, et la raison est le pilote, qui le conduit; le vaisseau n'irait point sans les vents, et se perdrait sans le pilote. Fr.—"The passions are the winds, which urge our vessel forward, and reason is the pilot, which steers it; the vessel could not advance without the winds, and without the pilot it would be lost."

Les plaisirs sont amers sitôt qu'on en abuse. Fr. prov.—"Pleasures become bitter as soon as they are abused." Amusement which exceeds the measure of reason ceases to be pleasure.

Les querelles ne dureraient pas longtemps, si le tort n'était que d'un côté. Fr. ROCHEFOUCAULT.—"Disputes would not continue so long, if the wrong lay but on one side." As both parties, generally speaking, are in fault, the dispute is prolonged by their mutual recriminations.

Les roués de la Révolution. Fr.—"The scamps, scampish fellows, rascals of the Revolution; the scamps, rogues, and rascals who had been engaged in, or had taken part in, the Revolution." N.B. "*Roué*" properly signifies, "a criminal, that has been broken on the wheel," and figuratively as above, "an unprincipled fellow, a rake, profligate, man about town." The origin of the term is as follows: Philip, Duke of Orleans, Regent of France, a prince gifted with an amiable countenance, with a mild and affable character, much wit, agreeable and varied talents, knowledge tolerably extensive for a man of his rank, worthy of praise on many accounts, merits none on that of his morals. Corrupted in his youth by the Abbé Dubois, his sub-preceptor, he surrounded himself, as soon as he came to the regency, with men and women who partook of his inclination for debauchery. It was then that all the courtiers who directed or imitated this prince received the appellation of *roués*, or persons who deserved to be broken on the wheel. The greater number were men of abandoned characters, who were proud of their depravity, and sold to the enemies of the state their influence over the mind of the regent. This prince gave to the above appellation another sense; his *roués* were, in his estimation, persons who would suffer themselves to be broken on the wheel for him; but the public, more just, gave to this word the meaning which it now bears. The dukes, the counts, the valets, whom he named his *roués*, the actresses, the duchesses, the dancers, the princesses, the ladies of honor, &c., all eagerly participated in his profligacy.

Les talents sont distribués par la nature, sans égard aux généalogies. Fr. FREDERIC THE GREAT.—"Talents are distributed by nature without the slightest regard, or respect, to genealogies, pedigrees, ancestry, and all that kind of thing."

Les vertus se perdent dans l'intérêt, comme les fleuves se perdent dans la mer. Fr. ROCHEFOUCAULT.—"Our virtues lose themselves in our interest, as the rivers lose themselves in the ocean."

Lettre de cachet. Fr. — A "*lettre de cachet*" was "an arbitrary order of the kings of France in the form of a letter, addressed to a person in order to banish him, or even to imprison him." An arbitrary warrant of imprisonment without accusation or trial.

Leve fit, quod bene fertur onus. Lat. OVID.—"The load or burden becomes light, feels light, which is cheerfully borne." If the spirits are buoyant, they greatly diminish the weight of suffering.

Levia perpessi sumus, si flenda patimur. Lat. SENECA.—"We have suffered but lightly, if we have suffered that which we should only weep for." We have been so deeply injured that not our tears but our acts must speak for us.

Levis est dolor qui capere consilium potest. Lat. SENECA.—"That grief is light which can take counsel." On excessive grief all advice is thrown away.

Levius fit patientia quidquid corrigere est nefas. Lat. HORACE.—"Whatever cannot possibly, or by any possibility, be amended is made more easy by bearing patiently." *What can't be cured must be endured:*

"Bear up! for patience must endure,
And soothe the woes it cannot cure."

Levius solet timere, qui propius timet. Lat. SENECA.—"Less does he usually fear, who fears when nearer danger than at some distance from it. The man, who fears when close on danger, usually fears less than he did when he was further off it." The man, whom danger stares in the face, fears less than if he were far away from it. Our apprehensions generally diminish with the approach of the object. "Examinations" [when contemplated at a distance], says Colton in his "LACON," "are formidable even to the best prepared, for the greatest fool may ask more than the wisest man can answer."

Lex et consuetudo Parliamenti. Lat.—"The law and custom of Parliament."

Lex loci. Lat.—"The law of the place."

Lex loquens. Lat.—"The speaking law." A living arbitrator In this country, the king has been justly termed "*lex loquens.*"

Lex neminem cogit ad impossibilia. Lat. Law maxim.—"The law compels no man to do impossibilities." Thus, the condition of a bond to go to Vienna or Constantinople in a few hours would be void from its impossibility.

Lex non scripta. Lat.—"The unwritten law." The common law of England.

Lex scripta. Lat.—"The written law." The statute law of this country. The former, though not originally set down in writing, is paramount to all modern enactments, in clearness, brevity, and authority. "Shakspeare doubtless intended by using the phrase '*though it be not written down*, remember,' and so on, to allude to the laws of England, the *lex non scripta* being there of equal force with the *lex scripta.*"

Lex talionis. Lat.—"The law of retaliation." The law of requital in kind, as alluded to in the Scriptures, of "an eye for an eye, a tooth for a tooth," &c.

Lex terrae. Lat.—"The law of the land." Taken generally in contradistinction to the civil law, or code of JUSTINIAN.

Lex universa est quae jubet nasci et mori. Lat. PUBLIUS SYRUS.—"Universal is the law which summons us into existence and calls us hence."

Libertas est potestas faciendi id quod jure liceat. Lat. CICERO. —"Liberty consists in the power of doing that which is permitted by the law." This is certainly a just definition. There cannot be rational freedom where there are arbitrary restraints.

Libertas ultima mundi
Quo steterit ferienda loco. Lat. LUCAN.—
"The remaining liberty of the world was in that precise place to be smitten and destroyed." This is the sentiment attributed by the poet to Caesar. It has been used in many a subsequent struggle for freedom, which, it has been said, "if there subdued, could ne'er revive." Factions, however, are temporary, but principles are everlasting.

Liberum arbitrium. Lat. LIVY.—"Free choice." The power of judgment. N.B. For "free choice," CICERO uses "*libera voluntas.*"

Liberum veto. Lat.—"Free forbiddance, free prohibition, freedom of forbidding or prohibiting." "The monstrous privilege of the *liberum veto* [in Poland, when independent], by which any one representative could break up the diet [legislative assembly], and nullify its acts." N.B. "*Veto*" signifies "*I forbid, prohibit.*"

Licet superbus ambules pecunia,
Fortuna non mutat genus. Lat. HORACE.—
"Though you strut proud of your money, yet fortune has not changed your birth." Addressed to a wealthy upstart.

"Fortune cannot change your blood,
Though you strut as if it could:"—

Or,— "Though wealth thy native insolence inflame,
An upstart ever is the same."

——————**Licuit, semperque licebit**
Parcere personis, dicere de vitiis. Lat.—
"It has ever been, and ever will be, lawful to attack vice, sparing at the same time the individual." Or, as thus translated,

"The best and surest method of advice
Should spare the person, though it brands the vice."
Burton's Anat. of Melancholy.

Liegepoustie.—A Scots law term, signifying, "The time of health, during which a man has full power to settle his affairs." Corrupted from "*in legitima potestate.*" Lat.—"In legitimate, lawful, complete, full power."

Limae labor ac mora. Lat. HORACE.—"The labor and delay of the file of correction." The slow process of polishing a literary production. This is a process now nearly forgotten. "Most men write now," says Lord Orford, "as if they expected that their works should live no more than a month."

Lingua mali pars pessima servi. Lat. JUVENAL.—"The tongue is the worst part of a bad servant:"—

"A servant's tongue! Oh! lay this truth to heart,
The tongue is the vile servant's vilest part."

Lingua Professoria. Lat. TACITUS.—"Professional Language." "On a memorable occasion, one, who deserves to be called the most eminent person at the English bar, said publicly, 'I shall attend to the interests of my client alone. I cast my country to the winds!' Other considerations, which, to a righteous man, should be dearer than life, must have been cast to them, before such an avowal could have been made! *Sans doute*, says Bayle, *Tacitus a compris bien des défauts sous les termes de* LINGUA PROFESSORIA:" that is to say, *Tacitus has undoubtedly included, comprised, comprehended, many defects, faults, blemishes, imperfections, in the term* PROFESSIONAL LANGUAGE.

Lingua volgare. Ital.—"The vulgar tongue." Applied to *the common Italian*, as opposed to the numerous *dialects* of Italy. N.B. Some would-be witty, but very ignorant, fellows often make merry with the concluding words of the clergyman in "The Ministration of Publick Baptism of Infants"—"Ye are to take care that this child be brought to the Bishop to be confirmed by him, so soon as he can say the Creed, the Lord's Prayer, and the Ten Commandments, in the *vulgar* tongue," &c., not considering that the *true* and *primary* meaning of "*vulgar*" is, "belonging or relating to the common people, the people at large, the masses," or, to use a Londonism, "THE MILLION." On the *secondary* meaning of "*vulgar*," the following remark will be found interesting:—"Cervantes, the Shakspeare of Spain, puts this sentiment into the mouth of Don Quixote, who, albeit deprived of the sovereignty of reason on one subject, was in others the model of a high-bred man of the world, and, in fact, the mouthpiece of the opinions of Cervantes, himself a soldier and a gentleman:—'Do not imagine that I consider as *vulgar* those only of the poor and humble classes: but all who are *ignorant*, even be they lords or princes, they must be classed under this denomination—vulgar.'"

Lis sub judice. Lat. HORACE.—"A disputed point submitted to the decision of an umpire and not yet settled, and as yet unsettled."

Litera scripta manet. Lat.—"The written letter remains as evidence in black and white." Words may pass away and be forgotten, but that which is committed to writing will remain as evidence.

Literae humaniores. Lat.—A phrase in use at the University of Oxford, signifying "learning of a rather polite cast, or learning of a description more polite than usual," namely, "Greek and Latin, the Classics:" a queer expression, forsooth! and one, in good sober truth, the correctness of which may very properly be called in question.

Literae inhumaniores. Lat.—"Learning of rather an inhuman or barbarous tendency."

Literae vocales. Lat.—"Vocal letters." The designation given by BACON to the popular lawyers of the House of Commons, in the reign of JAMES THE FIRST, meaning those lawyers who were bold enough to speak their minds and to stand up for the rights of their constituents.

Literati. Lat.—"Learned men, literary men, literary characters."

Literatim. Lat.—"Word for word." "He always repeated the suggestion *literatim*."

Littérateur. Fr.—"A literary man, man of letters."

Litus ama, altum alii teneant! Lat. VIRGIL.—"Do you keep close to the shore, let others venture on the deep, stand out to sea." Consult your own safety, and let others indulge in the spirit of adventure. An honorable baronet having remarked that "those only wished to displace the ministers who looked for power, or emoluments, or honors from their removal," Mr. Canning, in a happy vein of irony, retorted the imputation on the baronet; but gravely admonished him in the above words of VIRGIL. The effect was astounding.

Livres défendus. Fr.—"Prohibited books, books not allowed by the Pope to be read."

Loafer. American.—The word *loafer* is so very common in America, that, although closely approximating to a slang term, it cannot be overlooked here. The expression only found its way into writing about the year 1830, but had been in use long before, especially in the vicinity of the markets. It is equivalent to "vagabond" *intensified*, and its personal application is one of the greatest insults that can be offered to an American, something like calling a Frenchman *canaille*. It is singular that the verb (of later formation) has not necessarily a bad meaning; a man will say of himself, "I have been loafing about:" that is, I have been lounging, or idling. As to the derivation, it clearly has nothing to do with *loaf*. We must seek the root in Dutch. It *may* be from *loof*, primarily *weary*, *tired*, thence *faint-hearted*, *lazy*, *cowardly;* but it more probably comes from *loopen* (=German *laufen;* compare in English inter-*loper*). The term *loper*, applied to deserters from South-Sea whalers, and Jack Tar's familiar land-*lubber*, are probably connected. *Looper* in old Dutch, such Dutch as honest old Peter Stuyvesant may have used, meant a running footman, so that perhaps the idea of "lackey" or "flunkey" was mixed up with the term of contempt.

Loc. cit. Lat.—An abridgment of *Loco citato.* "In the place or passage [of an author's work] quoted."

Loca nocte silentia, or **tacentia late.** Lat. VIRGIL.—"Places where the silence of night prevails, a night-like silence prevails." Applied, *though not quite correctly*, to the Reading Room of the British Museum.

Loca parallela. Lat.—"Parallel passages in the works of authors, passages that are alike, or nearly so."

Locofocos.—The term by which the ultra-Radicals of the United States are designated. When the constitution of the United States was discussed, the parties were so equally divided, that the decision often hung upon a vote. But after the death of Washington the popular party rapidly gained ground, and the election of Jefferson to the Presidency in 1801 was the crowning triumph of democracy. His friends then took the name of *Democrats* or *Republicans*. The name of Federalist continued till a much later period; but in 1824, when John Quincy Adams was elected President, it was changed for that of *National Republicans*, and about the same period the democrats who opposed him began to be called *Jackson-men*. In 1834 both parties were baptized anew. The old federalists, or aristocrats, were christened *Whigs;* and the democrats (who supported Van Buren) *Tories*, which had been regarded as a term of opprobrium ever since the Revolution, when the adherents of the mother-country were so called. Some of these new Tories had a meeting at Tammany Hall, New York: the lamps being accidentally extinguished, the hall was re-lighted by Locofoco (Lucifer) matches, and thus arose the term *Locofocos*.

Locum tenens. Lat.—"One who holds or fills [often only for a time] the place of another." A deputy, a substitute.

Locus in quo. Lat.—"The spot or place in question."

Locus poenitentiae. Lat.—"A place, an institution, for repentance and reformation."

Locus sigilli. Lat.—"The place for the seal." Denoted by L. S. on all diplomatic papers.

Locus standi. Lat.—"A place for standing." "The vendor could have no claim, no *locus standi*, in a prize court:" that is to say, not *a leg to stand on*, &c.

Lollard. From Lothard, a German.—A name given to the first reformers of the Roman Catholic religion in England. "The Lollards."

Londinensium more. Lat.—"After the fashion of the Londoners, the London fashion."

Longa est injuria, longae ambages. Lat. Virgil.—"Tedious is the relation, the recital, of my wrongs, and intricate are the circumstances." Used as an apology in recounting one's wrongs.

Longe fugit, qui suos fugit. Lat. Varro.—"Far doth he flee who self and clan doth shun:"—

"Closer, closer let us knit
Hearts and hands together,
Where our fireside-comforts sit
In the wildest weather:—
Oh! they wander wide who roam
For the joys of life from home!"

Longo intervallo. Lat.—"At a great, an immense, distance." We believe Foote to be, after Molière [and not *longo intervallo*], the greatest master of comic humor that ever lived."

Longum iter est per praecepta, breve et efficax per exempla. Lat. SENECA.—"Long or tedious is the way [to instil instruction] by precepts, dogmas, adages, or 'old saws,' but short and effectual, effect-producing, by examples [of what is right and proper in your own person]."

Loquendum ut vulgus, sentiendum ut sapientes. Lat.—"We must speak, give utterance to opinions, as THE PEOPLE AT LARGE do [*that is*, without reflection], but we must, or should in reality, think as the WISE." See "*Lingua volgare.*"

Los dias de la esclavitud son contados! Span.—"The days of slavery are numbered."

Los muertos no tienen amigos. Span.—"The dead have no friends, have [very often] none to say a good word for them."

Louis or **louis d'or.** Fr.—A French gold coin, worth 16*s.* 8*d.*

Louis le Bien-aimé. Fr.—"Lewis the Beloved, or well-loved." The designation *at one time* of LEWIS THE FIFTEENTH of France.

Louis le Grand. Fr.—"Lewis the Great." [LEWIS THE FOURTEENTH of France]. See "*Le Grand Monarque.*"

Lubricum linguae non facile in poenam est trahendum. Lat. Law maxim.—"A light expression (or, as it is familiarly called, 'a slip of the tongue') is not easily punishable, ought not to be rashly or inconsiderately punished." Words of heat, such as to call a man rogue, knave, &c., will bear no action, at law, unless they are specifically applied, as, in such an affair, to a certain person, &c.

Lucerna Dei, spiraculum hominis. Lat.—"The lamp of GOD is the breath, the life of man." "The powers of BACON were varied, and in great perfection; his senses were exquisitely acute, and he used them to dissipate illusions, by holding firm to the works of GOD and to the sense, which is GOD'S lamp,—*Lucerna Dei, spiraculum hominis.*"

Lucidus ordo. Lat. HORACE.—"The lucid, clear, method or judicious arrangement [of a literary work]."

Lucri bonus est odor ex re qualibet. Lat. JUVENAL.—"The smell of gain is good from any thing whatever, from any source, no matter what:"

"All gain smells sweet, from whatsoe'er it springs."

Again:—

"No! though compell'd beyond the Tiber's flood
To move your tan-yard, swear the smell is good,
Myrrh, cassia, frankincense; and wisely think
That what is lucrative can never stink."

Lucus a non lucendo. Lat.—"If there was one official more incapable than his brethren, it was Dr. Andrew Smith, its 'director- [*quasi lucus a non lucendo*] general:'" that is to say, its "director" from not directing at all, from taking no part in the direction [*even as a grove is in Latin called "lucus,"* a place resplendent with light, *from not shining, from not being illumined by the rays of the sun, from having any thing but a brilliant or shining appearance*]. N.B. The word "*lucus,*" a grove, is derived from "*lucere,*" to shine, because the rays of the sun are supposed rarely to penetrate through its foliage. The phrase is generally used to mark an absurd or discordant etymology.

Ludibria ficta et composita. Lat.—"Cunningly-devised tricks." Often applied to the Romish miracles.

Lugete, Veneres Cupidinesque. Lat. CATULLUS.—"Weep, all ye Venuses and Cupids." Mourn, all ye loves and graces. This quotation is generally used in an ironical sense.

Lumina civitatis. Lat. CICERO.—"Luminaries of the state, ornaments to the state." Brave, gallant persons. Persons distinguished or remarkable for excellence of any kind.

Lunatic.—From "*Luna*," the Latin word for "*the moon.*" "The terms '*luna*-tic' and 'lucid intervals' are commonly supposed to be based on the *hypothesis* that the moon exercises a decided influence on the insane, as well as upon various morbid *phases* of the intellect not amounting to derangement:" that is to say, on the *supposition* that . . . morbid *appearances* of the intellect, &c. N.B. A "*lunatic*" is one who is affected with "*lunacy*," that is, madness, supposed to be influenced by the "*luna*," that is, the *moon*. A "*lucid*" interval is a "*shining*" interval, a time when the reason, which has been absent, or in abeyance, again *shines forth*. "*Lucid*" comes from the Latin word "*lucidus*," which means *shining*, *sparkling*, *glittering*. See "*Lucidus ordo.*"

Lunette d'approche, *or*, **Lunette de longue vue.** Fr.—"A perspective-glass, telescope, spying-glass." "*Distance* [from the object of his affection] had proved to him but a *lunette d'approche*, bringing him acquainted with those rare qualities in his fair mistress which had been imperceptible during their personal intercourse."

Lupus pilum mutat, non mentem. Lat. prov.—"The wolf changes his coat, but not his disposition." No change of appearance can alter that which is radically bad or perverse.

Lusisti satis, edisti satis, atque bibisti:
Tempus abire tibi est. Lat. HORACE.—
"Thou hast sported, or trifled, enough, and hast eaten and drunk enough: it is time for thee to depart, to quit the scene." May be addressed to any worn-out rake, man about town, who still clings to existence:—

"Already glutted with a farce of age,
'Tis time for thee to quit the wanton stage."

Lusus naturae. Lat.—"A sport of nature." A deformed or unnaturally-formed animal: a cow, for instance, with two heads. "The man who has no love for children is a species of *lusus naturae*," that is, is a species of *one of nature's freaks, a social monster*.

Lux Intellectus, lumen siccum. Lat. BACON.—"The Pure and Impersonal Reason," as beautifully interpreted by COLERIDGE.

Lymphatici nummi aurei. Lat. PLAUTUS.—"The golden coins of a madman." A fool's money, which he fancies will never come to an end. Money, that burns in one's pocket.

Lynch law. An American term.—Lynch law originated in what is now known as the Piedmont country of Virginia, which was at the time the western frontier. The nearest court of criminal jurisdiction held its sessions at Williamsburg, which is but seven miles from Jamestown, where the first settlement was made. When the condition of the country at that time is duly considered, it will be seen that practically the inhabitants of the Piedmont country had no law, and were actually forced to be a law unto themselves. Misdemeanors and crimes of every sort were of frequent occurrence; and yet the apprehension and delivery of a criminal involved an arduous journey of hundreds of miles, mostly through a wilderness, which not only occupied weeks, but months. Now, in every district there were men of sound judgment and high character, to whom controversies were constantly referred, and whose decisions were regarded as final. Prominent among these was a man named Lynch, whose awards exhibited so much justice, judgment, and impartiality, that he was known throughout the country as Judge Lynch. In the course of time, criminals were brought before him, and he awarded such punishments as he considered just and proper. There were other persons, in different districts, who acted as arbitrators, and who awarded punishments; but Judge Lynch was the most conspicuous, and consequently the system took his name, and was called Lynch Law. This was a compliment to his integrity and high character. But of late years the term has been regarded as a reproach, because violent and unprincipled men, such as Lynch was accustomed to punish, have set the law at defiance, and while inflamed with passion, or maddened by a thirst for revenge, have usurped the prerogative of the courts of justice.

Lyts to let, folle to let. Frisian.—"Little too late, all too late."

M.

Macte virtute. Lat. VIRGIL.—"Proceed in virtue." "Go on as you have begun." Often used ironically, as we sneeringly say, "*Go on and prosper.*"

Maculae, quas incuria fudit. Lat. HORACE.—"Errors, or blemishes, which carelessness, want of care, has produced, or occasioned."

Madonna. Ital.—1. A name generally given to pictures of the VIRGIN MARY: 2. Used by SHAKSPEARE for "*Madam:*"—"Two faults, *Madonna*, that drink and good counsel will amend."—*Twelfth Night.*

Magasins de nouveautés. Fr.—"Repositories for the sale of fancy articles, or goods."

Magister artis, ingenîque largitor venter. Lat. PERSIUS.—"The belly is the master of all art, and the bounteous giver, the bestower, of genius:"—

"The BELLY: Master he of Arts,
Bestower of ingenious parts."

N.B. Thus translated by a school-boy, who for some misconduct was ordered to give a metrical version of it:—

"Hunger a master is of arts,
Who brightens much the mental parts."

MAGNA CHARTA. Lat.—"The Great Charter." [THE BASIS OF OUR LAWS AND LIBERTIES.] The charter of our liberties, obtained from King JOHN by the Barons of England, in the year 1215.

Magna civitas, magna solitudo. Lat. prov.—"A great city is a great desert wilderness, a dreary solitude." N.B. Cato used to say that he was never less alone than when alone, nor less at leisure than when at leisure.

Magna est veritas et praevalebit. Lat.—"Great, or powerful, is truth, and it will *ultimately* prevail, will throw down every obstacle."

Magna minaris, extricas nihil. Lat. PHAEDRUS.—"You promise great things, you raise high expectations, and in reality accomplish nothing, bring nothing worth mentioning to bear." See "*Parturiunt montes," &c.*

Magna servitus est magna fortuna. Lat. SENECA.—"A great fortune is a great slavery." It brings with it many peculiar burdens and inconveniences.

Magnae periclo sunt opes obnoxiae. Lat. PHAEDRUS.—"Great riches are exposed to danger, the chance of danger, often render the possessor of them liable to danger, to the risk of losing them."

Magnas inter opes inops. Lat. HORACE.—"Poor in the midst of wealth, riches." A just description of a rich miser.

Magnates. Lat.—"Great men, peers, nobles, grandees, dons."

Magni Dei datum. Lat.—"The gift of the great GOD, of the Great Supreme."

Magni nominis umbra. Lat. LUCAN.—"The shadow of a mighty name." Applied to a man who inherits the name or title of a great ancestor, but without any indication of greatness in himself.

Magni refert quibuscum vixeris. Lat. prov.—"It is of great importance with whom you live [on terms of intimacy]." It is a point of great importance to consider well with whom you associate.

Magnificabo apostolatum meum. Lat.—"I will magnify my office, my peculiar mission, or vocation, the dignity of my art."

Magnificat. Lat.—"He, or she, magnifies." The name given in the service of the Romish Church, and also in that of the Church of England, to the Song of the Virgin Mary, drawn from Luke i. 46, in the Vulgate [The Latin version of the Scriptures, made by JEROME about the year 385. The Vulgate was the first book ever printed].

Magnis excidit ausis. Lat. OVID.—"He failed in his bold attempts."

Magno conatu magnas nugas [dicere]. Lat. TERENCE.—"With great efforts to be delivered of, to deliver one's self of, some mighty trifle." To waste much labor on inadequate objects, on trifling matters.

Magnos homines virtute metimur, non fortuna. Lat. CORNELIUS NEPOS.—"We estimate great men by their virtue (or valor), and not by their success." This is unhappily the philosophic, but not the worldly, admeasurement. Men now look less to the means than to the end, and it is the absolute result which, generally speaking, stamps the character.

Magnum est argumentum in utroque fuisse moderatum. Lat. —"It is a great argument in favor of a man, that when placed in different situations he displayed in each the same spirit of moderation."

Magnum est vectigal parcimonia. Lat. CICERO.—"Economy is of itself a great revenue." Many men get rich by their savings, rather than by their gains. "In a debate on some economical question, BURKE was guilty of a false quantity [pronouncing a Latin or Greek word incorrectly]. *Magnum vectĭgal parcimonia.* '*Vectīgal*,' said Lord North in an audible under-tone. 'I thank the noble lord for his correction,' resumed the orator, 'since it gives me an opportunity of repeating the inestimable adage, *Magnum vectigal parcimonia.*'"

Magnum opus. Lat.—"The great work, grand business."

**Magnum pauperies opprobrium jubet
Quidvis et facere et pati.** Lat. HORACE.—
"Poverty, which is considered a great reproach, forces us to attempt or submit to any thing, in order that we may avoid it."

Magnus Apollo. Lat.—"The great Apollo." N.B. Often used for "the most distinguished professor of any art or science." Apollo was one of the great divinities of the Greeks, the god of prophecy, the god of song and music, the god of the Sun; the god who punished; the god who afforded help and warded off evil; the god who protected the flocks and cattle; and the god who delighted in the foundation of towns and the establishment of civil constitutions.

Maison d'arrêt. Fr.—"House of custody, prison-house, prison."

Maison de détention. Fr.—"House of detention."

Maison de force. Fr.—"House of correction, bridewell."

Maison de santé. Fr.—"Private hospital."

Maison de ville. Fr.—"Town-house, guildhall."

Maître d'hôtel. Fr.—"House-steward."

Maître des hautes-œuvres. Fr.—"The master of the high works." The hangman, the executioner.

Maître des requêtes. Fr.—"Master of Requests, Referendary [a kind of magistrate]."

Major e longinquo reverentia. Lat.—"Respect is greater when coming from a distance." The persons and objects, with which we are familiar, seldom excite a high degree of reverence. "No man," it has been well observed, "was ever a hero to his valet."

**———————Major famae sitis est quam
Virtutis; quis enim virtutem amplectitur ipsam
Praemia si tollas?** Lat. JUVENAL.—
"The thirst after fame is greater than that after virtue; for who embraces virtue if you take away its rewards?"

"So much the raging thirst of fame exceeds
The generous warmth which prompts to worthy deeds,
That none confess fair virtue's genuine power
Or woo her to their breast without a dower."

Major hereditas venit unicuique nostrum a jure et legibus, quam a parentibus. Lat. CICERO.—"A greater inheritance comes to each of us from our rights and laws than from our parents." The security which we enjoy from the protection of the laws, when well administered, is the most valuable possession we derive from our ancestors.

Major privato visus, dum privatus fuit, et omnium consensu capax imperii, nisi imperasset. Lat. TACITUS.—"He was regarded as greater than a private man whilst he remained in privacy, and would have been deemed worthy of governing if he had never governed." A political maxim of very general application. Said in reference to the Roman Emperor GALBA.

Major rerum nascitur ordo. Lat. VIRGIL.—"A greater series of incidents arises." A more extended order of things presents itself.

Major videri. Lat. VIRGIL.—"To appear greater than usual, than before." "Reality has outgrown fiction, and has become the '*major videri,*'" that is, *the more important object, the main point.*

Majora canere. Lat. VIRGIL.—"To sing higher strains." To enter into matters of greater moment, to take a higher range.

Majore fama quam emolumento docuit. Lat.—"He taught with greater reputation than gain, got more reputation than lucre by his teaching."

Majorem turbam punitorum reperies.
Paucis temeritas est bono, multis malo. Lat. PHAEDRUS.—"[Of those who have become possessed of property by unjust means] you will find that the majority have met with punishment in one form or other. Rashness and foolhardiness in the acquisition of property are advantageous to but few, while they are a positive misfortune to the many."

Majus et minus non variant speciem. Lat.—"Greater and less do not change the nature of a thing." A maxim of morality no less than of law: the *first step* in the career of iniquity is the one which must be resisted; when it is once taken, the difficulty of ulterior resistance is increased with every deviation from rectitude. See "*Principiis obsta,*" *&c.*

Mal à propos. Fr.—"Unseasonably, impertinently, improperly, ill timed, out of place, preposterously."

Mal-entendu. Fr.—"Mistake, misunderstanding, misapprehension."

Mala fide. Lat.—"Fraudulently, falsely." A *mala fide* witness, that is, a witness who is unworthy of belief, on whose testimony no reliance can be placed.

Mala fides. Lat.—"Want of good faith, want of integrity."

Mala grammatica non vitiat chartam. Lat. Law maxim.—"Bad grammar does not vitiate the deed." An error in the language is not to be regarded, if it do not involve some ambiguity.

Mala mens, malus animus. Lat. TERENCE.—"An evil head, an evil heart." In other words, "A wicked heart always suggests wicked projects." *Animus*, the *heart*, conceives wicked designs—*Mens*, the *mind*, devises the means of reducing them to practice.

Malades imaginaires. Fr.—"Persons who fancy themselves ill, sick; hypochondriacs, hippish individuals."

Maladie du pays. Fr.—"An itching or longing to return to one's native country. A hankering after home, home-sickness."

Maladresse. Fr.—"Unskillfulness, want of management or tact, awkwardness, clumsiness."

Malaria. Ital.—Sometimes written, *Mal Aria.* An unhealthy constitution of the atmosphere, or of the soil. The disease communicated by "*Malaria*" is no other than an intermittent, or an ague of the worst kind; such as will be long remembered in England by the name of the *Walcheren* fever.

Male cuncta ministrat
Impetus. Lat. STATIUS.—
"Anger manages every thing badly." We seldom act rightly when under the dominion of passion.

Male imperando summum imperium amittitur. Lat. PUBLIUS SYRUS.—"The greatest empire may be lost by the misrule of its governors." A political maxim, the truth of which has been proved in every age and country.

Male parta male dilabuntur. Lat. CICERO.—"Things ill acquired are as badly expended."

Male sarta amicitia. Lat.—"A badly or ill patched-up friendship, a bungling kind of friendship." N.B. The *correct* expression occurs in HORACE:—

"[Debes hoc etiam rescribere] an male sarta
Gratia nequicquam coit ac rescinditur:"—
"Say, was the reconciliation made in vain,
And, like an ill-cured wound, breaks forth again?"

Male verum examinat omnis corruptus judex. Lat. HORACE.—"A corrupt judge decides ill in matters of right and property:"—

"A judge, when bribed, but ill to truth attends."

Maledicus a malefico non distat nisi occasione. Lat. QUINTILIAN.—"An evil-sayer differs only from an evil-doer in the want of opportunity." The difference is but slight between a calumniator and an assassin.

Malefacere qui vult nusquam non causam invenit. Lat. PUBLIUS SYRUS.—"He who has a mind to do mischief will always find a pretense."

Malheureux celui qui est en avance de son siècle. Fr. prov.—"Unfortunate, or unlucky, is he who is in advance of his age, who knows more than his contemporaries."

Malim inquietam libertatem quam quietum servitium. Lat.—"I would rather have disturbed liberty than a quiet slavery." The ferment of a free government is preferable to the torpor of a despotic one.

Malle-poste. Fr.—"The mail-coach, mail."

Malo indisertam prudentiam, quam loquacem stultitiam. Lat. CICERO.—"I prefer silent prudence to loquacious folly." That sober sense, which neither wants nor cultivates the flowers of speech, is infinitely preferable to all the coarse fluency of ignorance.

Malo mihi male quam molliter esse. Lat. SENECA.—"I would rather be sick than idle." The evil of a slight indisposition is transient: the mischiefs of idleness, when once rooted, are incurable.

Malo mori quam foedari. Lat.—"I had rather die than be debased."

Malorum facinorum ministri quasi exprobantes aspiciuntur. Lat. TACITUS.—"The agents in evil actions are regarded as reproaching the deed." There is a jealousy between the principals and the agents on such occasions, which is productive, and that in a very early stage, of mutual contempt and distrust.

Malum in se. Lat.—"A thing evil in itself." *Malum prohibitum:* "A thing evil because forbidden." To illustrate the legal distinction between these two species of evil, it is only necessary to observe that murder is "an evil in itself." The exportation of wool, commonly called "owling," was not punishable as an evil, until it was prohibited by the law.

Malum nascens facile opprimitur, inveteratum fit robustius. Lat. CICERO.—"An evil at its birth is easily crushed, but it grows and strengthens by endurance." See "*Majus et minus,*" *&c.*, and "*Principiis obsta,*" *&c.*

Malum vas non frangitur. Lat. prov.—"A bad vessel is seldom broken." Things which are held most cheaply are in general the most secure from danger.

Malus usus abolendus est. Lat. Law maxim.—"A bad custom is to be, or ought to be, abolished, or done away with." A custom in local jurisdictions, existing from time immemorial, has the force of a law; but if that custom be proved to be a bad one, such proof will set it aside.

Mandamus. Lat.—A writ granted by the Sovereign [King, or Queen, as the case may be]. More properly, however, "by the Court of King's Bench." "A *mandamus,*" says Blackstone, "is in general a writ issuing in the King's name from the Court of King's Bench." N.B. The meaning of "*mandamus*" is, *we* [that is, the Lord Chief Justice of the Court of King's Bench, acting in the name and on the behalf of the Queen] *command.* A "*mandamus*" often means a *writ* from the King's Bench, commanding any corporate body [the city of London, for instance] to admit a person to any privilege or office. Many persons are great sticklers for the use of "QUEEN'S Bench" instead of "KING'S Bench," for *the very wise reason* that the reigning sovereign is a QUEEN. Such persons, however, would do well to bear in mind that "KING'S Bench" means MONARCH'S or REIGNING SOVEREIGN'S Bench, without the slightest reference to the mere sex of the Potentate. If we substitute "*Queen's Bench*" for "*King's Bench,*" we should, to be consistent, substitute QUEENdom for KINGdom.

Manes. Lat.—The name which the Romans gave to the souls of the departed, who were worshiped as gods. Hence on sepulchres we find D. M. S., that is, *Dîs Manibus Sacrum*—"Sacred to the departed spirits, whom we now look on as gods."

Manet alta mente repostum. Lat. VIRGIL.—"It [*the remembrance of the quarrel, the grievance*] continues, or remains deeply fixed in the mind." It has taken deep root in the mind, and lurks there still:—

"*Fixed it remains, and rankles in the breast.*"

N.B. This phrase, by which the poet describes the inveterate resentment of JUNO [the queen of heaven, or the female JUPITER, according to the heathen mythology], is now frequently used to denote a long embosomed sense of injury.

Mange-tout. Fr.—"A spendthrift, squanderer." Literally, "an eat-all."

Mania. Gr.—"Madness." Frequently used to signify a *modified* form of insanity, a rage for, or craving after, particular objects.

Manibus pedibusque. Lat. TERENCE.—"With hands and feet, with all one's power." It was a struggle *manibus pedibusque*, or, as we should express it in English, "with tooth and nail."

Manière d'être. Fr.—"Manner, peculiar manner, deportment, bearing." An indescribable *manière d'être,* which is inseparable from high birth and breeding.

Manœuvre. Fr.—"A move, movement, dodge, artful dodge, way of going to work."

Μαντις αριστος, ὁστις εικαζει καλως. Gr.—"He's the best prophet who conjectures well."

Μαντις κακων. Gr. HOMER.—"A prophet of evils, misfortunes, disasters, a prognosticator of unpleasant events."

Manus justa nardus. Lat.—"The just hand is as precious ointment."

Manus manum fricat. Lat. prov.—"One hand rubs the other." Applied to two persons, who gratify the vanity, or forward the views, of each other by mutual adulation. The sense is much the same as that of the homely English proverb, "Do you tickle me, and I'll tickle you."

Marchandise, qui plaît, est à demi vendue. Fr. prov.—"The goods which please are already half sold." We have a corresponding proverb in English, "Please the eye and pick the purse."

Mare clausum. Lat.—"A closed or shut-up sea, a sea not open to commerce." N.B. "*Mare clausum*" meant in the days of CICERO [the illustrious Latin orator] "*The winter-time:*" namely, from the 10th of November to the 10th of March, during which period navigation ceased among the Romans.

Mare, ignis, et mulier sunt tria mala. Lat. prov.—"The sea, fire, and woman are three evils."

Mare liberum. Lat.—"A sea open, or free to all the world."

Mare magnum. Lat.—"The great sea, the ocean, the vast ocean." "The *mare magnum* of philosophical interpretation."

Marie ton fils quand tu voudras, mais ta fille quand tu pourras. Fr. prov.—"Marry your son when you will, and your daughter when you can." Get rid of the latter precarious charge as soon as possible.

Marqué au bon coin. Fr.—"Marked with a good stamp, a man of the right stamp." A man possessed of superior qualities. N.B. This phrase is nearly always quoted *incorrectly:* thus, "Marqué DU bon coin."

Marquess.—The *right* word for what is now usually written and called *Marquis.*

Mars gravior sub pace latet. Lat. CLAUDIAN.—"A severer war lurks under the show of peace."

Martinet.—"A strict military disciplinarian, one particularly *fussy* about trifles." N.B. "*Martinet*" [French] was the name of an individual who, at one time, had the regulation of the French infantry. "*Martinet*" has various meanings, among others, a *cat-o'-nine-tails,* one of the emblems of our *civilization.*

Mashallah! Persian.—"Praised be the LORD!"

Materfamilias. Lat.—"The lady, mistress, or good wife of the house, the mother of a family."

Materiam superabat opus. Lat. OVID.—"The workmanship surpassed the materials." This applies either to great genius employed on a slight subject, or to that mechanical ingenuity which, when employed upon, can heighten the value even of the most precious materials.

Matres omnes filiis in peccato adjutrices, auxilio in paterna

injuria solent esse. Lat. TERENCE.—"Mothers are always advocates for their sons' faults, and take part with them against the father."

Mature fias senex. Lat. CICERO.—"May you early prove an old man." May you learn the wisdom of age long before you are depressed with its infirmities.

Maundy Thursday.—This day, which is always the Thursday before Easter, is called in Latin *Dies Mandati*, that is, *The day of the command*, being the day on which our LORD washed the feet of his disciples and commanded them to wash one another's feet. This practice was long kept up in the monasteries. After the ceremony, liberal donations were made to the poor in clothing and in silver money; and refreshment was given them to mitigate the severity of the fast. A relic of this custom is still preserved in the donations dispensed at St. James's on this day.

Mausoleum. Gr.—A pompous funeral monument. The word signified originally *the sepulcher of* MAUSOLUS [king of Caria, a district of Asia Minor, that is, of *Anatolia*], which was a magnificent monument erected at Halicarnassus [now *Budrum*] B.C. 353, by ARTEMISIA, the widow of MAUSOLUS. It was adorned with beautiful works of art, and was regarded as one of the seven wonders of the world. The word "*Mausoleum*" was used by the Romans as a generic name for any magnificent sepulchral edifice.

Mauvais pas. Fr.—"A dilemma, scrape, awkward fix, mess."

Mauvais sujet. Fr.—"A bad subject, bad fellow, worthless fellow."

Mauvais ton. Fr.—"Ill manners, vulgarity, *unmannerliness, want of good breeding*."

Mauvaise honte. Fr.—"Bashfulness, sheepishness, shyness." COUNT EDOUARD DE MELFORT, in his "Impressions of England" [London: 1836], says "*Mauvaise honte* renders but a very imperfect meaning of the word SHYNESS: one may say of a man, 'he is shy;' but to say, 'he is *honteux*,' which is the only word that I know of, to translate it, may give you the idea of something ignoble or base, whilst the character that I wish to paint is one which inspires me with great interest, and is just the contrary." *Mauvaise honte* betrays itself in different ways in England. In a room full of company there are many women who dare not move from a sofa, upon which they condemn themselves to pass whole hours; and if at last one of them ventures to cross the room, it is with an embarrassment and awkwardness which shows itself at every step, and which she would not perhaps exhibit if a fewer number of eyes or none at all were on her. The greater number of the men too, from the same reason, remain nailed to the wall, half hidden by a curtain, or else they never venture much beyond the door of the drawing-room.

Mauvaise langue. Fr.—"An ill tongue, a malicious, slanderous person."

Mauvaise plaisanterie. Fr.—"A scurvy jest, a mere joke, sorry pleasantry."

Maxima debetur puero reverentia. Lat. JUVENAL.—"The greatest reverence, or respect, is due to a child:"—

"His child's unsullied purity demands
The deepest reverence at a parent's hands."

N.B. Nearly always quoted *incorrectly:* thus, *pueris* instead of *puero*.

Maxima illecebra est peccandi impunitatis spes. Lat. CICERO.—"The greatest excitement to guilt is the hope of sinning with impunity." In order to deter men from crimes, it is not so necessary that the punishment should be *severe* as that it should be *certain*.

Maxima pars eorum quae scimus, est minima pars eorum quae nescimus. Lat.—"What we know bears, in magnitude at least, no proportion to that of which we are ignorant."

Maxima quaeque domus servis est plena superbis. Lat. JUVENAL.—"Every great house is proportionably full of saucy menials."

Maximus virtutes jacere omnes necesse est, voluptate dominante. Lat. CICERO.—"Where pleasure is the all-engrossing consideration, the fairest virtues will, as a matter of course, be lost sight of, be in abeyance."

Maximum. Lat.—Literally, "The greatest thing, or a very great thing." "A *maximum* of labor," *that is, a very large amount* of labor.

Maximum est vitium carere virtutibus. Lat.—"It is a very great fault or misfortune to be without virtues, to have no virtuous endowments."

Maximus in minimis. Lat.—"Very great in very little things." A studious attention to petty objects is the sure sign of a narrow mind. When Cardinal Chigi told another member of the *corps diplomatique* that the same pen had served him for three years, he was instantly and properly set down as a man whose mind was not framed for any enlarged or liberal discussion.

Maximus novator tempus. Lat.—"Time is a very great innovator, repairer, or redresser of faults, or defects." "The whole British constitution underwent a mighty change in the last century: it *settled*, to use the builder's phrase; it shifted its center of gravity; and the political theorems [speculative propositions, imaginings, conjectures] of past times are no longer applicable to it. The hand of the great reformer [OLD FATHER TIME] has passed over the fabric. It is in vain that an English jurist proves from his GLANVIL and his FLETA that our government subsisted under HENRY THE SECOND; the philosophic eye perceives nothing but contrast, even in ages less remote. The REVOLUTION is the great epoch, so far as gradual alterations can relate to one epoch, from which our new constitution is dated."

————Me Parnassi deserta per ardua dulcis
Raptat amor: juvat ire jugis, qua nulla priorum
Castaliam molli devertitur orbita clivo. Lat. VIRGIL.—

"But the commanding Muse my chariot guides,
Which o'er the dubious cliff securely rides:
And pleased I am no beaten road to take,
But first the way to new discoveries make."

Mea maxima culpa. Lat.—"Through my very great fault; *that is*, I am the most to blame in the matter." N.B. The quotation is part of a sentence that occurs in the Romish Breviary [Prayer-Book, or Liturgy]: "Mea culpa, mea culpa, *mea maxima culpa*."

Mea virtute me involvo. Lat. HORACE.—"And virtue, though in rags, will keep me warm." The wise man wraps himself up in the mantle of his own integrity, and bids defiance to the storms and changes of fortune.

Méchant écrivain. Fr.—"A poor writer, author; a mere scribbler, a mere paper-stainer; a sorry or paltry scribe."

Μεγα βιβλιον, μεγα κακον. Gr.—"A great book is a great evil." This is a charge which voluminous authors are perpetually shifting to the shoulders of their neighbors.

Μηδεν αγαν. Gr.—"Too much of one thing is good for nothing." Follow nothing too eagerly. N.B. This adage is precisely similar to the "*Ne quid nimis*" of TERENCE.

Medica manus. Lat. VIRGIL.—"The healing hand." "We gave up his minor faults as beyond our *medica manus:*" that is, our *corrective skill, or treatment.*

————————Medio de fonte leporum
Surgit amari aliquid, quod in ipsis floribus angat.

Lat. LUCRETIUS.—

Even in the midst of our pleasures [*when we are surrounded by every earthly blessing*] something bitter arises, or is sure to arise, to vex, annoy, and harass us, when our happiness is at the very highest, at its height, when every thing is "*couleur de rose*" [which see].

"Days '*all serene,*' and pleasures ever pure,
Are not for man; dark clouds at times obscure
The sky most favored with the sun's blest rays:
The blithest heart will have its sorrowing days."

"Full from the fount of joy's delicious springs
Some bitter o'er the flowers its bubbling venom flings."—BYRON.

Medio tutissimus ibis. Lat. OVID.—"You will advance most safely in the middle." To consult your safety, you should through life avoid all extremes.

Mediocria firma. Lat.—"The middle station is the safest." See "*Auream quisquis,*" &c.

Mediocribus esse poëtis
Non homines, non Di, non concessere columnae.

Lat. HORACE.—

"Mediocrity is not allowed to poets, either by the gods, or men, or the pillars which sustain the booksellers' shops." By this whimsical periphrase the poet means simply to say that mediocrity, which in other pursuits is respectable, in that of poetry is generally disregarded. N.B. Books, at Rome, were exposed for sale, either in regular establishments [*tabernae librariae*], or on shelves around the pillars of porticos and public buildings.

Medium. Lat.—"The great *medium* of entertainment:" *that is,* The great *means, instrument, method, way,* of, &c. N.B. The *literal* meaning of "*medium*" is *the midst or middle* of a thing, *any thing intervening or that comes between.*

Meilleure pâte d'homme. Fr.—"A good-natured man, fellow, soul: the best-natured soul that ever lived."

Mel in ore, verba lactis,
Fel in corde, fraus in factis. Lat.—

"Honey in his mouth, words of milk, gall in his heart, and fraud in his acts." These are monkish rhymes, in which a mischievous hypocrite is not ill described.

Μελετη το παν. Gr.—"Care and industry do every thing." This was the saying of PERIANDER, one of the seven sages of Greece. To unceasing industry nothing is impracticable that is not physically impossible.

Meliores priores. Lat.—"The better men, the better or prior claim."

Melius est cavere semper quam pati semel. Lat. prov.—"It is better to be always on our guard, than to suffer once." A life of caution is overpaid by the avoidance of one serious misfortune.

Melius non tangere, clamo. Lat. HORACE.—"I cry out, it is better not to touch me." This is the language of the satirist, who has his quiver full of defense.

Mellitum venenum, blanda oratio. Lat. prov.—"A smooth speech is honeyed poison." We should distrust the intention of that speaker who mingles too many eloquent blandishments in his discourse. Truth wants neither disguise nor ornament.

Memento mori. Lat.—"Remember death, that you must one day die." "A *memento mori* style:" *that is,* A style *that is enough to bore you to death.*

Meminerunt omnia amantes. Lat. OVID.—"Lovers remember every thing." Nothing escapes their notice or recollection.

Mémoires pour servir à l'histoire. Fr.—"Materials, papers, notes, memorandums, for composing history." N.B. Often used in an abridged form: thus, "*Mémoires pour servir.*"

Memorabile nomen. Lat.—"A memorable, notable, or remarkable name, character, individual."

Memorabilia. Lat.—"Things to be remembered, memorable acts or deeds." Matters deserving of record. "*Memorabilia*" is often used in reference to a work that was written by XENOPHON, the Athenian.

Memoria in aeterna. Lat.—"In eternal remembrance."

Memoria technica. Lat.—"An artificial system of memory."

Mens divinior. Lat. HORACE.—"A mind that soars, or towers, above the average intellectual *caliber;* a mind imbued with that enthusiasm, or poetic inspiration, which can alone give success to the votaries of the epic, tragic, or lyric muse."

Mens immota manet: lacrimae volvuntur inanes. Lat. VIRGIL.—

"Sighs, groans, and tears proclaim his inward pains,
But the firm purpose of his heart remains."

Mens invicta manet. Lat.—"The mind remains unconquered." The body may sink under its sufferings, but the mind of a brave man will hold itself aloof, and despise the afflictions of adversity, and even the aggravations of torture.

Mens pati durum sustinet aegra nihil. Lat. OVID.—"The sick mind cannot bear any thing which is harsh." The mind of affliction is so sensitive as to shrink from the slightest touch of offense.

Mens sana in corpore sano. Lat. JUVENAL.—"A sound mind in a sound body." Moral and mental rectitude combined in the same individual. N.B. The above quotation has, by a judicious writer, been styled "*the golden rule of education.*"

Mens sibi conscia recti. Lat. VIRGIL.—"A mind conscious to itself of rectitude or undeviating integrity."

Mensura juris vis erat. Lat. LUCAN.—"Power was the measure of right." A good description of a state of anarchy, where every man feels that what he *can* do he *may* do.

Mentis gratissimus error. Lat. HORACE.—"A most gratifying mental delusion."

Meo periculo. Lat.—"At my own risk."

Meo sum pauper in aere. Lat. HORACE.—"I am poor, 'tis true: but I owe nothing." If I have abridged my own comforts, my consolation is that I owe nothing to others.

Mercatura non derogat nobilitati. Lat.—"Trade is no abatement of honor."

Mero motu suo. Lat.—"Of his own accord."

Metempsychosis. Gr.—"The transmigration of souls, the passage of a soul from one body into another."

Metiri se quemque suo modulo ac pede verum est. Lat. HORACE.—"It is just, a good rule, that every man should measure himself by his own model and standard," *literally*, "by his own last and foot," *that is*, by the measure of his own foot, by his own proper standard. It is not fitting that any man should put forth his pretensions beyond his strength, or that men of slender abilities should aim at high and weighty situations:—

"The human race should rightly be confined
Within the bounds which Nature has assigned."

Meum et tuum. Lat.—"Mine and thine." It is a question of *meum et tuum;* the dispute is respecting the distinct rights of property.

Meus mihi, suus cuique carus. Lat. PLAUTUS.—"My own is dear to me, and dear is his own to every man." Every one has his own prepossessions and predilections.

Mey lege hannen ist quae haucken faen. Frisian prov.—"With emptie hands men may no hawkës lure."—CHAUCER.

Mezzo cammin della nostra vita. Ital. DANTE.—"The mid-way, mid-journey, of our life, or existence."

Mezzo termino. Ital.—"Something in the shape of a compromise, a stop-gap, a sort of half concession."

Mihi cura futuri. Lat.—"My care is for the future life, the life to come."

Mihi tarda fluunt ingrataque tempora. Lat. HORACE.—

"How heavily my time revolves along!"

Miles perpetuus. Lat.—"A standing army, or standing armies."

Militavi non sine gloria. Lat. HORACE.—"I served with some degree of repute." "LORD CAMPBELL said that he himself could say, '*Militavi non sine gloria,*' for he had served as a volunteer during the war with France."

Mille hominum species, et rerum discolor usus;
Velle suum cuique est, nec voto vivitur uno. Lat. PERSIUS.—"There are a thousand kinds of men, and equally diversified is their

pursuit of objects; each has his own peculiar desire [his hobby], nor do men live with one single wish:"

"Countless the various species of mankind,
Countless the shades which separate mind from mind;
No general object of desire is known;
Each has his will, and each pursues his own."

Millionnaire. Fr.—"A man worth a million, or millions, a man of millions." N.B. "*Millionnaire*" is nearly always *incorrectly* spelled with one *n* instead of with *two*.

Minimum. Lat.—"The smallest thing, or a very small thing." "A *minimum* of wages," *that is*, *A very small amount* of, &c. "The *minimum* quantity, that can be sold wholesale," *that is*, the *smallest* quantity, &c.

Minor est quam servus dominus qui servos timet. Lat. prov. —"That master, who is in fear of his servants, is lower than a servant."

Minus. Lat.—"Less."

Minus caute locuti sunt. Lat.—"They have spoken somewhat incautiously, with less caution than usual."

Minus in parvos fortuna furit,
Leviusque ferit leviora Deus. Lat. SENECA.—
"The rage of fortune is less directed against the humble, and Providence strikes more lightly on the low." Those of humble condition are exempt from the violent reverses which frequently afflict their superiors.

Minus sufficiens in literatura. Lat.—"By no means sufficiently learned, up to the mark, as a scholar."

Minuti semper et infirmi est animi exiguique voluptas ultio. Lat. JUVENAL.—"Revenge is ever the pleasure of a paltry spirit, a weak and abject mind." No man of an enlarged understanding indulges in so dark a passion:—

"Revenge we ever find
The weakest frailty of a feeble mind."

Minutiae. Lat.—"Trifles." "To enter into *minutiae*," to discuss the most minute and trifling parts of the business.

Mirabile dictu. Lat. VIRGIL.—"Wonderful to tell."

Miramur ex intervallo fallentia. Lat.—"We admire at a distance the things that deceive us." Our sight is apt to misrepresent remote objects, but the deception vanishes on a nearer approach.

Mirantur taciti, et dubio pro fulmine pendent. Lat. STATIUS. —"They stand in silent astonishment, and wait for the fall of the yet doubtful thunderbolt." Used to describe a general apprehension and consternation.

Mirum. Lat.—"Wonderful."

Misce stultitiam consiliis brevem. Lat. HORACE.—"Mix short follies with wise counsels. Blend a little folly with thy worldly plans." Let your moments of dissipation bear no proportion to those of sober reflection.

Misera est magni custodia census. Lat. JUVENAL.—"The care of a large estate is an unpleasant thing." Even wealth itself brings with it its cares and inconveniences.

Misera est servitus, ubi jus est aut vagum aut incognitum

Lat. Law maxim.—"The servitude is miserable in that country in which the law is either vague or unknown." In every good government the laws should be precisely defined and generally promulgated.

Miseriarum portus est patientia. Lat. PUBLIUS SYRUS.—"Patience is the asylum [*place of refuge*] of affliction."

Miseris succurrere disco. Lat. VIRGIL.—"I learn to relieve the wretched," having personally, in person, borne the scourge of affliction.

Miserrima est fortuna quae inimico caret. Lat. PUBLIUS SYRUS. —"That is a most wretched fortune which is without an enemy." His condition must be low indeed, who possesses not any thing for which he can be envied.

Miserum est aliorum incumbere famae. Lat. JUVENAL.—"It is a wretched thing to live on the fame of others." Nothing can be more pitiable than authors who, without proper resources, assume a borrowed splendor from the talents of others.

Μισω μνημονα συμποτην. Gr. prov.—

"Far from my table be the tell-tale guest!"

Mitte superba pati fastidia, spemque caducam
Despice; vive tibi, nam moriere tibi. Lat. SENECA.—

"Bow to no patron's insolence: rely
On no frail hopes: in freedom live and die."

A stimulus to mental independence, self-reliance.

Mittimus. Lat.—"We send." The writ by which a magistrate commits an offender to prison.

Mobilitate viget, viresque acquirit eundo. Lat. VIRGIL.—"It flourishes in its quickness of motion, and gains new strength in its progress." The poet speaks of fame or common report, which gathers strength as it proceeds, and swells, like the snowball, as it rolls along.

Moderado. Spanish.—"A conservative."

Moderato durant. Lat. SENECA.—"Things enjoyed in moderation are of long continuance." Power, health, and faculties are exhausted by excess.

Modicum. Lat.—"A little." "The smallest *modicum*:" that is, the smallest *possible quantity*.

Modus in rebus. Lat. HORACE.—"A mean, or medium, in all things."

Modus operandi. Lat.—"The way of proceeding, of setting to work."

Moestae urbes et publica vota vicerunt. Lat. JUVENAL.—"Sorrowing, grieving, or mourning cities and their public prayers prevailed [with Heaven to spare his life]:"—

"But lo! a thousand suppliant altars rise,
And public prayers obtain him from the skies."

N.B. Applied to LEWIS THE FIFTEENTH of France in 1744, at a time when he was lying dangerously ill.

Mœurs politiques. Fr.—"The political character."

Molle meum levibus cor est violabile telis. Lat. OVID.—

"Cupid's light darts my tender bosom move."

Mollia tempora fandi. Lat.—"The favorable occasions for speaking." These are to be sought for with great men. That request may succeed at one time, which at another may be considered as an importunity. N.B. *Not* in HORACE, nor in any other poet, as is generally imagined. An analogous expression occurs in VIRGIL, "*Mollissima fandi tempora,*" the most favorable time for speaking to an individual, to a rich man, for instance, *after* he has had his dinner. "*L'homme riche,*" says a French writer, "*quand il a bien diné, voit tout le monde heureux:*" that is, *When a rich man has dined well, he not only feels happy himself, but also fancies every biped in the universe happy.*

——————————Mollissima corda
Humano generi dare se natura fatetur
Quae lacrimas dedit. Lat. JUVENAL.—
"Nature confesses that she has bestowed on the human race hearts of softest mold, in that she has given us tears:"—

"NATURE, who gave us tears, by that alone,
Proclaims she made the feeling heart our own."

Or:—

"Compassion proper to mankind appears,
Which Nature witnessed when she gave us tears."

Molliter manus imposuit. Lat. Law term.—"He but gently laid hands." This phrase is used in a defense set up against an action or indictment for an assault. "He but gently laid hands" on the prosecutor, for the purpose of expelling him, as he had a right to do, from the premises.

Momentum. Lat.—"Force." "The stone had not sufficient *momentum* to hurt any one."

Moniti, meliora sequamur. Lat. VIRGIL.—"Being admonished, let us pursue a better course, let us act more judiciously." Having had the lessons of experience, let our future prudence attest their effects.

Monomania. Gr.—"Madness, or insanity, on one particular point."

Μονον αργυρον βλεπουσι. Gr. ANACREON.—"Men look only at, care for naught but, money."

Monsoon.—A regular or periodical wind in the East Indian and other Asiatic seas, which blows constantly in the same direction during six months of the year, and contrariwise the remaining six months. In the Indian Ocean the winds are partly general, and blow the whole year round from the same points, as in the Ethiopic Ocean; and partly periodical, namely, half the year from one way, and the other half year nearly on the opposite points: these points and times of alteration differ in different parts of the Indian Seas, and these latter winds are termed *monsoons*. The change of the monsoon does not occur at one precise period of time; in some places the time of the change is accompanied by calm weather, at others, by variable winds; those of China in particular, on ceasing to blow westerly, are very liable to be tempestuous; such is their violence (appearing to be similar to the West Indian hurricanes) that the navigation of those seas is very hazardous in those seasons. These tempests the seamen call the *breaking up of the monsoons*. —STOCQUELER.

Monstra evenerunt mihi:
Introiit in aedes ater alienus canis!
Anguis per impluvium decidit de tegulis!
Gallina cecinit! Lat. TERENCE.—

"What unlucky prodigies have befallen me! a strange black dog came into the house! a snake fell from the tiles into the courtyard! a hen crowed!"

Monstrum eruditionis. Lat.—"A prodigy of learning, erudition; a literary prodigy." Applied by BOERHAAVE to CONRAD GESNER, the German PLINY [the naturalist].

Monstrum horrendum, informe, ingens, cui lumen ademtum. Lat. VIRGIL.—"A frightful, horrid, horrible, terrible, or terrific monster, a misshapen mass of flesh and blood, huge in size, and deprived of his visual organ, deprived of sight." This is the description given by VIRGIL of the giant POLYPHEMUS when his one eye had been bored out by ULYSSES. It is sometimes applied to an absurd proposition, conceived in ignorance, and brought forth by presumption.

Monstrum, nulla virtute redemtum a vitiis. Lat. JUVENAL.—

"Without one sneaking virtue in thy train,
O precious villain! scoundrel! rogue in grain!"

Monumentum aere perennius. Lat. HORACE.—"A monument more durable than brass, a memorial more enduring than brass." Applied by HORACE to the unrivaled effusions of his genius, which will be read till time shall be no more. Respecting the *Odes* of this distinguished poet, it has been justly observed that "as works of refined art, of the most skillful felicities of language and of measure, of translucent expression, and of agreeable images embodied in words which imprint themselves indelibly on the memory, they are altogether unsurpassed."

Moonshee, or linguist. Ordinarily a teacher of some language, particularly the Persian, Hindostanee, and Hindee, though numbers are employed only as interpreters, or as scribes. Learning is their sole pursuit: and so far as that can reach in a country where but little is understood of philosophy and mathematics, some of them advance themselves considerably. Generally speaking, however, a few volumes of tales, the lives of those great men who have either invaded or ruled the empire, some moral tracts, and the Koran (for *moonshees* are Mussulmans), constitute the acquirements of this class of servants.—STOCQUELER.

Morceaux d'ensemble. Fr.—"Concerted parts in music, pieces of music sung by different voices."

More majorum. Lat.—"After the manner, or according to the fashion, of his ancestors, or forefathers."

More philosophico. Lat.—"In a philosophic manner." "He spent a few days with him *more philosophico*."

More probato. Lat.—"After, or according to, the approved fashion, or practice."

More suo. Lat.—"In his own way, his own peculiar manner, or fashion."

Mores hominum multorum vidit. Lat. HORACE.—"He many men and many manners saw."

Morgue. Fr.—"The Dead-house," a place in which persons found dead are laid to be owned by their friends or relatives.

Mors janua vitae. Lat.—"Death is the gate of life eternal. the entrance to immortal life."

Mors sola fatetur quantula sint hominum corpuscula! Lat. JUVENAL.—"Death alone confesses, or discloses, how very small, or insignificant, are the puny bodies of mortals!" Death shows us the weakness of ambition, and the emptiness of a proud and haughty spirit:—

"Death, the great teacher, Death alone proclaims
The true dimensions of our puny frames."

Mors ultima linea rerum est. Lat. HORACE.—"Death is the end of all human miseries:"

"Death is that course where human sorrow ends."

Mortuo leoni et lepores insultant. Lat. prov.—"Even hares [the most timid of animals] can insult a dead lion." The mightiest of the dead may be insulted by the weakest of the living.

Mos majorum. Lat.—"The custom, or practice, of one's ancestors, or forefathers." "Every thing among the Hindoos or Hindus [the *aborigines or first inhabitants of India*] is regulated by the *mos majorum* and the book of precedents."

Mos pro lege. Lat. Law maxim.—"Custom for law." Long-established usage, as in the case of a fixed *modus* for tithes, will stand in the place of law.

Moslems. Hindostanee [The common language of India].—*Moslems* has the same meaning as *Moosulmans or Mussulmans*, namely, "true believers, persons resigned in every respect to the will of GOD." The Mohammedans arrogate this title to themselves as the only elect of GOD. N.B. The Moslems, and other natives of India descended from foreign races, are properly called *Hindustanis*, while the first inhabitants [the *aborigines*] are the *Hindus*,—a distinction not well understood in Europe. The former take their name from the country, as *natives of Hindustan*, which has derived its own name from the latter, as being the *country of the Hindus*.

Mot d'ordre or **mot de l'ordre.** Fr.—"The word that is given daily to soldiers on duty to enable them to distinguish friends from enemies: the pass-word."

Mot du guet, or simply **Mot.** Fr.—"A watch-word." A war-term, or term used during war. The *mot du guet* enables the soldiers to distinguish each other from the enemy.

Mot pour rire. Fr.—"A jest or joke."

Mots à double entente. Fr.—"Ambiguous or doubtful words, words with a double meaning." N.B. "*Double entendres*," which is in almost everybody's mouth, is bad French: the *right* and *full* expression is *mots à double entente*, words that have a twofold meaning: the singular is *mot à double entente*, a word that has a twofold meaning.

Mots d'argot. Fr.—"Slang, slang phrases, professional slang, words intelligible only to thieves, beggars, pickpockets, sharpers, &c., thieves' language." N.B. Two especial new *mots d'argot* came in vogue in Paris between twenty and thirty years ago. On these two words Mrs. Trollope, in her "Paris and the Parisians in 1835," observes: "The first appears to me to be applied by the young and innovating to every thing which bears the stamp of the taste, principles, or feelings of time past. That part of the French population to which the epithet '*rococo*' is thus applied may be understood to combine all varieties of old-fashionism, from the gentle advocate for laced coats and diamond sword-knots, up to the high-minded, venerable loyalist, who only loves his rightful king the better because he has no means left to requite his love. Such is the interpretation of *rococo* in the mouth of a *doctrinaire.* But if a republican speaks it, he means that it should include also every gradation of orderly obedience, even to the powers that be, and, in fact, whatever else may be considered as essentially connected either with law or gospel. There is another adjective, which appears also to recur so frequently as fully to merit, in the same manner, the distinction of being considered as fashionable. It is, however, a good old legitimate word, admirably expressive too, and at present of more than ordinary utility. This is '*décousu;*' and it seems to be the epithet given by the sober-minded to all that smacks of the rambling nonsense of the new school of literature, and of all those fragments of opinions which hang so loosely about the minds of the young men who discourse fashionably of philosophy in Paris."

She goes on to remark:

"Were the whole population to be classed under two great divisions, I doubt if they would be more expressively designated than by these two appellations, the *décousu* and the *rococo.* I have already stated who it is form the *rococo* class; the *décousu* division, as embracing the whole of the ultra-romantic school of authors, be they novelists, dramatists, or poets, all shades of republicans, from the avowed eulogists of the 'spirited Robespierre,' to the gentler disciples of Lamennais, most of the schoolboys, and all the *poissardes* of Paris."

Mots d'usages. Fr.—"Words in common use, of daily occurrence."

Movet cornicula risum furtivis nudata coloribus. Lat. HORACE. —"The jackdaw, divested of her borrowed plumes, becomes the jest of the whole world, provokes our laughter." No object is more ridiculous than the plagiarist when deprived of his stolen ornaments:—

"Stripped of his stolen pride, the crow forlorn
Now stands the laughter of the public scorn."

N.B. An application of the well-known fable of Æsop, except that for the more common term "*graculus*" we have here "*cornicula.*"

Mugitus labyrinthi. Lat. JUVENAL.—"The bellowing of the labyrinth." This was a favorite topic with the Roman poetasters. It is therefore put for any commonplace topic of ordinary poets or writers.

Mulier est hominis confusio. Lat.—"Woman is man's confusion." But malevolent would be the man who should thus *mistranslate* it; for—

"Madam, the meaning of this Latin is,
That womankind to man is sovereign bliss."—DRYDEN.

Multa. Lat.—"Many things."

Multa cadunt inter calicem supremaque labra. Lat. LABERIUS. —"Many things fall between the cup and the lip." Disappointment will interfere between us and our nearest expectations. "There's many a slip 'twixt the cup and the lip."

Multa docet fames. Lat. prov.—"Hunger teaches many things." Necessity is the mother of invention.

**Multa ferunt anni venientes commoda secum,
Multa recedentes adimunt.** Lat. HORACE.—

"The coming years bring many advantages with them; when retreating, they take away as many." There is a tide in the affairs of men. What we gain by the influx, we miserably lose by the reflux, of that tide.

"The blessings flowing in with life's full tide,
Down with our ebb of life decreasing glide."

Multa gemens. Lat. VIRGIL.—"Groaning much, with many a groan bitterly lamenting." "He complied *multa gemens*, with every expression of grief."

Multa litura. Lat. HORACE.—"The many a blotting out, the repeated correction," or what Pope calls the noblest art, "the art to blot."

Multa petentibus desunt multa. Lat. HORACE.—"Much is wanting to those that seek or covet much:"—

"In troth, the state of man is such,
They greatly want who covet much."

Compare SHAKSPEARE:—

"Poor, and content, is rich, and rich enough:
But riches, fineless, is as poor as winter
To him that ever fears he shall be poor."

Multa renascentur, quae jam cecidere; cadentque
Quae nunc sunt in honore vocabula, si volet usus,
Quem penes arbitrium est et jus et norma loquendi.

Lat. HORACE.—

"Many terms now out of use will revive; and many now in vogue will sink into oblivion, if custom will have it so,—custom, the sovereign arbitrator of language."

Multa viri nequidquam inter se vulnera jactant,
Multa cavo lateri ingeminant, et pectore vastos
Dant sonitus: erratque aures et tempora circum,
Crebra manus: duro crepitant sub vulnere malae.

Lat. VIRGIL.—

"Thumps following thumps, and blows succeeding blows,
Swell the black eye, and crush the bleeding nose:
Beneath the ponderous fist the jaw-bone cracks:
And the cheeks ring with their redoubled thwacks."

————————————————**Multi**
Committunt eadem diverso crimina fato.
Ille crucem pretium sceleris tulit, hic diadema.

Lat. JUVENAL.—

"Many commit the same crimes with results widely different. One man receives crucifixion as the reward of his villainy; another, a regal crown!"

"Some made by villainy, and some undone,
And THIS ascends a scaffold, THAT a throne!"

Multi te oderint, si teipsum ames. Lat.—"Many will hate you if you love yourself." Self-love, when strongly manifested, is of all things the most disgusting.

Multis ille bonis flebilis occidit. Lat. HORACE.—"He died lamented by many good men."

Multis parasse divitias non finis miseriarum fuit, sed mutatio. Non est in rebus vitium, sed in animo. Lat. SENECA.—"To have acquired riches is with many not to put an end to, but to change the nature of, their misery. The fault, however, is not in the riches, but in the mind." Wealth is very properly compared to manure: both are useless when in the heap, and both are thrown away upon an unkindly soil.

Multis terribilis, caveto multos. Lat. AUSONIUS.—"If thou art terrible to many, then beware of many."

Multos ingratos invenimus, plures facimus. Lat.—"We find many ungrateful men, and we make more." Ingratitude is but too frequent, yet it is sometimes provoked by the arrogance of the benefactor.

Multos in summa pericula misit,
Venturi timor ipse mali. Lat. LUCAN.—
"The mere apprehension of a coming evil has put many into a situation of the utmost danger." Our alarms frequently lead us into perils more fearful even than those which we first apprehended.

Multum. Lat.—"Much." "This sect has a great deal to say for itself, especially if by a great deal is meant *multa* and not *multum:*" that is to say, *many things* and not *much* [in those things after all]: *much* [worth notice]. See "*Multa.*"

Multum in parvo. Lat.—"Much in little." A great deal in a few words, a great deal in a small compass. A compendium of knowledge.

Mundae parvo sub lare pauperum
Coenae, sine aulaeis et ostro,
Sollicitam explicuere frontem. Lat. HORACE.—
"To frugal treats and humble cells
With grateful change the wealthy fly,
Where health-preserving plainness dwells,
Far from the carpet's gaudy dye.
Such scenes have charm'd the pangs of care,
And smoothed the clouded forehead of despair."

Retirement is often courted by the wealthy.

Mundus edibilis. Lat.—"The eatable world." The world of things good to eat.

Mundus universus exercet histrioniam. Lat. PETRONIUS ARBITER.—"All the world practices the art of acting." Compare SHAKSPEARE:—

"All the world's a stage,
And all the men and women merely players."

Munitions de guerre et de bouche. Fr.—"Ammunition and provisions."

Mus in pice. Lat. prov.—"A mouse in a pitch-barrel." Applied to a man who is always perplexing himself in useless disquisitions and inquiries.

Mussulman.—See "*Moslems.*"

Mutata forma, interimitur prope substantia rei. Lat. Law maxim.—"The form being changed, the substance of the thing is destroyed." Thus, if trees are improperly cut down, and laid as beams in a house, their nature is so far altered, that they cannot be seized in that shape: but the owner is to bring his action for the damage.

Mutatio elenchi. Lat.—"A change, or shifting, of the argument:" commonly *a sophistical one.* "The sophistry of the whole pamphlet is not an *ignoratio* [an ignorance of], but a *mutatio, elenchi;* of which the lofty aim is to impose on the simplicity of those readers who may rely on the author's veracity."

Mutatis mutandis. Law Lat.—"After making the necessary changes." Thus, what was law for A. and B. shall apply to C. and D., only altering terms according to circumstances.

Mutato nomine de te fabula narratur. Lat. HORACE.—"Change but the name, the tale is told of you." You smile at the satire whilst you supposed it leveled at another; yet, if the name were altered, you would find it reach to "*your own business and bosom.*"

N.

N'importe. Fr.—"No matter; it does not signify; never mind."

Nadir. Arab.—"The point under foot." Hence "*nadir,*" opposed to "*zenith,*" which see.

Nagree.—The character used in Sanscrit [the ancient language of Hindostan] works, and sometimes called "*Deva Nagree.*"

Naïveté. Fr.—"Artlessness, unaffected simplicity, ingenuousness."

Nam genus et proavos, et quae non fecimus ipsi,
Vix ea nostra voco. Lat. OVID.—
"For birth and ancestry, and that which we have not ourselves achieved, we can scarcely call our own." The man who prides himself, not on his personal conduct, but on a long line of ancestry, has been ludicrously, but justly, compared to the potato-plant, the best part of which is under ground.

Natio comoeda est. Lat. JUVENAL.—"The whole nation appears like a set of stage-players.—There every one's an actor:"—

"GREECE IS A THEATER, WHERE ALL ARE PLAYERS."

N.B. Applied by the satirist to Greece, but of late years by modern writers to France. Compare SHAKSPEARE:—

"All the world's a stage,
And all the men and women merely players."

————————————**Natura beatis**
Omnibus esse dedit, si quis cognoverit uti. Lat. CLAUDIAN.—
"Nature has granted to all to be happy, if they did but know how to use her benefits."

Natura ipsa valere, et mentis viribus excitari, et quasi quodam divino spiritu afflari. Lat. CICERO.—"To be strong from nature; to be excited by the powers of the mind; and to be inspired, as it were, by a divine spirit." Such is the definition of genius, given by this great orator.

Natura lo fece, et poi ruppa la stampa. Ital. ARIOSTO.—

"Nature, after making him, broke the mold." This eulogy has all the extravagance of the Italian school. It imports of the subject, what no man can predict, that future time shall never see his equal.

Natura! quam te colimus inviti quoque! Lat. SENECA.—"O Nature! how we worship thee, however unwilling!" How potent are thy dictates, and how resistless are thy laws!

Natura tenacissimi sumus eorum, quae pueri percipimus, ut sapor, quo nova vasa imbuuntur, durat. Lat. SENECA.—"We are naturally very tenacious of, we very naturally cling to, those ideas which we receive when boys, in our boyhood, just the same as the flavor continues in those vessels [casks, &c., of a porous nature] with which they were imbued, saturated, impregnated, when new, fresh from the hands of the mechanic." See "*Quo semel est,*" *&c.*

Naturam expelles furca, tamen usque recurret,
Et mala perrumpet furtim fastidia victrix. Lat. HORACE.—"You may endeavor [vain though the task] to crush all that is natural; but nature will be nature still, and by slow, but sure, degrees will eventually and victoriously break through all conventional absurdities."

"Though nature's driven out with proud disdain,
The powerful goddess will return again:
Return in silent triumph to deride
The weak attempts of luxury and pride."

NAWAB.—A species of Mohammedan sovereign; a very great deputy, vicegerent, or viceroy. A governor of a province under the Mogul government, and popularly called by the English a *nabob.* The title of Nawab is also by courtesy often given to persons of high rank or station. It was formerly used (under the corruption *nabob*) to designate wealthy Englishmen who returned from India laden with wealth.

Ne cui de te plus quam tibi credas. Lat.—"Do not believe any man more than yourself, when he speaks of you." When a man flatters you, you should correct his assertions by your own consciousness.

Ne mente quidem recte uti possumus, multo cibo et potione completi. Lat. CICERO.—"We cannot make a right use of our intellectual faculties, understanding, of the powers of the mind, when gorged with an excess of meat and drink, when we have been making beasts of ourselves by eating and drinking too much."

Ne plus supra. Lat.—"Nothing above [one], superior to [one]." "A great worldling himself, he stood the *ne plus supra* to worldlings," the *very summit of human ambition* to worldlings.

Ne plus ultra. Lat.—"Nothing more beyond." He was arrived at his *ne plus ultra.* His utmost efforts could not carry him any further. "The *ne plus ultra* of political perfection," that is, the *very extreme* of, &c. "The *ne plus ultra* of art," that is, the *utmost point* of art, the *very perfection* of art.

Né pour la digestion. Fr. LA BRUYÈRE.—"Born merely for the purpose of digestion." A man who comes into life merely to enjoy what are called its good things, without rendering any service to the community. See "*Fruges consumere nati.*"

Ne puero gladium. Lat. prov.—"Do not trust a boy with a sword." Do not commit a strong measure to inconsiderate hands.

Ne quid abjecte, ne quid timide, facias. Lat. CICERO.—"Do naught meanly, abjectly, contemptibly, dispiritedly, despondingly, naught timidly, fearfully, timorously, faintly, with a faint heart."

Ne quid detrimenti Respublica capiat. Lat.—"[To take care] that the Republic, commonwealth, common weal, receive no injury, detriment." "Until that event, no permanent appointment will take place: no more will be done than is necessary to secure *ne quid detrimenti Respublica capiat.*" N.B. The above Latin words were the injunction given by the Roman Republic on investing a Dictator with supreme power, authority. This attention to domestic security, in contra-distinction to foreign conquest, is often intimated to the statesman at the helm of affairs as forming his first and most important duty.

Ne quid falsi dicere audeat, ne quid veri non audeat. Lat. CICERO.—"Let him not presume to utter any falsehood, but be bold in promulgating every truth." In this brief direction are comprised the principal duties of the historian.

Ne quid nimis. Lat. TERENCE.—"Do not pursue an object too far, too eagerly." "I shall now close my observations on the work, lest *Ne quid nimis* should be thrown in my teeth:" that is, lest [the observation of] *Too much of one thing is good for nothing* should, &c. A golden proverb, repeatedly employed by the best classic writers. ALCAEUS: *το μηδεν αγαν αγαν με τερπει.* MENANDER: *ἡ μεσοτης εν πασιν ασφαλεστερον.* HORACE alludes to it by "*aurea mediocritas,*" and OVID by "*medio tutissimus ibis.*" The origin of the proverb is generally ascribed to PITTACUS of Mytilene, one of "the seven wise men" of Greece. N.B. See the above quotations in their proper places.

Ne remettez pas à demain ce que vous pouvez faire aujourd'hui. Fr. prov.—"Do not defer until to-morrow that which you have it in your power to do to-day."

Ne scutica dignum horribili sectere flagello. Lat. HORACE.—"Do not pursue him, who merely deserves a slight whipping, with the weightier scourge." The advice is to the satirist, whose severities should ever be proportioned to the offense. N.B. The "*scutica*" was a simple *strap*, or thong of leather, used for slight offenses, particularly by schoolmasters, in correcting their pupils. The "*flagellum,*" on the other hand, was a *lash*, or whip, made of leathern thongs or twisted cords, tied to the end of a stick, sometimes sharpened with small bits of iron or lead at the end. This was used in correcting great offenders.

Ne sus Minervam. Lat.—"Let not a pig presume to teach Minerva, [one of the great divinities of the Greeks, a goddess in whom power and wisdom were harmoniously blended]." The proverb is applied to a stupid person, who presumes to set right an intelligent one. "Teach not thy granny to suck eggs."

Ne sutor ultra crepidam. Lat.—"Let not the shoemaker go beyond his last." N.B. This censure was very properly addressed by Apelles [a distinguished painter, who flourished in the time of Alexander the Great] to a certain shoemaker [*cobbler*], who found fault with an ill-painted slipper in one of his pictures; but when he presumed to extend his criticism to other parts of the painting, he betrayed so much ignorance as to elicit from the painter this rebuke. No one should presume to give his opinion in a province of art in which he is only a dabbler. It is worthy of remark that throughout his life Apelles labored to improve himself, especially in drawing, which he never spent a day without practicing. Hence the proverb, "*Nulla dies sine linea.*"

Ne tentes aut perfice. Lat.—"Attempt not, or accomplish what you have in view,—or bring the matter to bear."

Ne vile velis. Lat.—"Incline to nothing base, mean, disgraceful."

Nebulae. Lat.—"Mists, fogs, clouds." "We lament that such *nebulae* should be found upon the broad and luminous disk of these 'Imaginary Conversations.'"

Nec aliud quidquam per fabellas quaeritur,
Quam corrigatur error ut mortalium,
Acuatque sese diligens industria. Lat. PHAEDRUS.—
"Naught else is aimed at in fables, fables have in view no other end, object, than that the mistakes of mankind be corrected, amended, and that diligent industry, assiduity, may sharpen itself, may rouse itself to more vigorous exertion, may receive an additional stimulus to exertion."

Nec bella, nec puella. Lat.—"Neither beautiful nor young [not a girl]." The description of Sir Thomas More's second wife [a perfect shrew], as given by himself.

Nec deus intersit, nisi dignus vindice nodus inciderit. Lat. HORACE.—"Nor let a god interfere, unless a difficulty present itself worthy a god's unraveling." The poet is advising play-writers. Do not introduce an extraordinary or supernatural appearance, unless on an occasion of the highest importance.

"Nor let a god in person stand display'd,
Unless the laboring plot deserve his aid."

N.B. Horace intends this precept as a censure upon a common fault among the ancient tragic poets, that of having recourse to some deity for the unraveling of the plot, whenever they were at a loss in relation to it. He was made to descend in a species of machine; whence the expression, *Deus ex machina* [a god out of a machine]. The passage is often quoted in an abridged form: thus, "*Nec deus intersit.*"

Nec fas est propius mortali attingere Divum. Lat.—"Nor is any mortal permitted to make a nearer approximation to the Deity." "While we agree with Halley that no mortal can ever approach more nearly to the divine intelligence than NEWTON, *Nec fas est propius mortali attingere Divum,*—we must at the same time admit that no one has approached more nearly to NEWTON than LAPLACE."

——————**Nec lex est aequior ulla**
Quam necis artifices arte perire sua. Lat. OVID.—
"Nor is any law more just, or impartial, than that the plotters or contrivers of death [and destruction] should perish or fall by their own machinations, should themselves fall into the trap that they had prepared for others."

Nec liber indicium est animi, sed honesta voluntas
Plurima mulcendis auribus apta refert.

Accius esset atrox; conviva Terentius esset:
Essent pugnaces, qui fera bella canunt. Lat. Ovid.—
"Nor is the book the index of the mind,
But just we feel an honest wish, to find
Some way of pleasing, be it grave or witty.
Accius were else the greatest brute in Rome,
Terence a rake, that never dined at home;
All epic poets, cut-throats and banditti!"

"The influence which our knowledge, or, in the absence of knowledge, our idea, of the personal character of a poet has on our reception of his works is not used to be sufficiently considered; nor the natural propriety of this dependence enough perceived. For although the abstract moral quality of a work of art is not of that vast importance which is often made of it, the *animus* of the author is greatly to be considered. This will appear the more, when we reflect that the tenor and character of an author's works are not always a faithful copy of his mind; and that the total amount of his meaning, as well as that which is of still more consequence, the amount of moral influence which his life and writings ought to have in the world, are only to be collected from investigation by parallel. Ovid has noticed this contradiction between man and book, where he says, prettily, *Nec liber*," &c. [as above].

Nec lusisse pudet, sed non incidere ludum. Lat. Horace.—"Nor is it a shame to have been a little wild, but it is a shame not to put an end to such follies:" that is, by calling maturer judgment to our aid. The levities of youth are pardonable, but if not discontinued in time, they form the strongest reproach to maturity and age.

"Once to be wild is not a foul disgrace.
The blame is to pursue the frantic race."

Or:— "Nor do I blush to own my follies past,
But own those follies should no longer last."

Nec me pudet, ut istos, fateri nescire quod nesciam. Lat. Cicero.—"I am not ashamed, as some men are, to confess my ignorance of that which I do not know." "Whoever would be cured of ignorance," says Montaigne, "must confess it. Great abuse in the world is begot, or, to speak more boldly, all the abuses in the world are begot, by our being taught to be afraid of professing our ignorance." "All that I know," said Socrates, the celebrated Athenian philosopher, "is that I know nothing."

Nec mirum. Lat.—"And no wonder, nor is it marvelous, wonderful, surprising."

Nec mora, nec requies. Lat. Virgil.—"No stop, no stay, neither rest nor cessation [from the business in hand]."

Nec placidam membris dat cura quietem. Lat. Virgil.—"Care allows no calm repose to limbs [that are wearied with excess of toil, with care], to the care-worn mind."

Nec pluribus impar. Lat.—"Not an unequal match for numbers, for many." This was the vain-glorious motto adopted by Louis XIV. when he formed his dreamy project of universal empire.

Nec prosunt domino quae prosunt omnibus artes. Lat.—"The arts [of literary composition, production], peculiar features of knowledge, which are profitable, beneficial, to all, are [too frequently] of but little benefit to their possessor." Applied at one time, in an especial manner, to authors, who were *compelled* to give eleven copies of their works to various institutions. See "*Sic vos non vobis.*"

Nec Sarmata, nec Thrax, mediis sed natus Athenis. Lat. JUVENAL.—"Neither a Sarmatian, nor a Thracian [neither a Pole, nor a Turk], but one born in the heart of Athens." "Without attempting to show, as they [Junius and Casaubon], under the influence of fancy, have endeavored to do, that unlettered rustics unwittingly speak Greek, and that many a word with a barbarous and discordant sound is *nec Sarmata, nec Thrax, mediis sed natus Athenis*, we cannot but avow the conviction that the uneducated classes of an agricultural district have mainly contributed to sustain the national idiom in a state of incorruptness and stability."

Nec satis apparet cur versus factitet. Lat. HORACE.—"It is by no means easy to discover why he has been seized with this vein of rhyming, why he bothers himself about writing, or making verses:"

"Nor is it plain for what atrocious crime
The gods have plagued him with this curse of rhyme."

"When a man can write such excellent prose, it may well be said with the poet, '*Nec satis apparet cur versus factitet.*'"

Nec scire fas est omnia. Lat. HORACE.—"We cannot know, or be expected to know, every thing." "We are surrounded with mysteries on every side, which baffle our inquiries, and the result of all our boasted knowledge

'Is but to know how little can be known.'"

"One science only can one genius fit,
So vast is art, so narrow human wit."

Nec semper feriet quodcunque minabitur arcus. Lat. HORACE.—"The arrow will not always hit the object which it threatens." The most skillful archer cannot always hit the object at which he aims. The best aims are often fruitless.

"Nor always will the bow, though famed for art,
With speed unerring wing the threatening dart."

Nec si non obstatur propterea etiam permittitur. Lat. CICERO.—"On the supposition that an act is not expressly forbidden, we must not therefore imagine that it is permitted, allowed" [to any one who has a correct idea of "right and wrong"].

Nec sibi, sed toti genitum se credere mundo. Lat. LUCAN.—"To think that he was born not for himself alone, but for the whole human race." This is the rare character of an enlarged and philosophic mind. "None of us," says the Apostle Paul, "liveth to himself."

——————Nec studium sine divite vena,
Nec rude, quid prosit, video ingenium. Lat. HORACE.—"I neither see what art can do without a rich vein [of fancy, imagination], nor a fine genius without the help of art:"

"Now, art, if not enriched by nature's vein,
And a rude genius of uncultured strain,
Are useless both."

Nec tibi quid liceat, sed quid fecisse decebit
Occurrat: mentemque domet respectus honesti.
Lat. CLAUDIAN.—
"Do not consider what you may do, but what it will become you to do, and let the sense of honor govern, regulate, your mind." This is a most admirable epitome of ethics. Were men to look, not to the extent of their power, but to that mode of conduct which would bear reflection, the great would be more respected, and the powerless more happy.

Nec vera virtus, quum semel excidit, curat reponi deterioribus. Lat. HORACE.—"True valor, when it has once fallen from its dignity, cares not to be restored by minds that have become degraded by cowardice:"—

"True valor, failing in the soldier's breast,
Scorns to resume what cowardice possessed."

Nec verbum verbo curabis reddere fidus
Interpres. Lat. HORACE.—
"Do not, faithful translator though you are, aim at rendering the original word for word." In this servility of translation the spirit of the original will certainly evaporate.

Nec vixit male, qui natus moriensque fefellit. Lat. HORACE. —"Nor has he spent his life badly who has passed it from his birth to his burial in privacy." The man is fortunate who escapes completely from the cares of public life.

"Nor ill he lives, who lives and dies unknown."

N.B. This beautiful adage of the poet will remind many of a parallel passage in Gray's "Elegy written in a Country Churchyard:"—

"Far from the madding crowd's ignoble strife,
Their sober wishes never learned to stray;
Along the cool sequestered vale of life
They kept the noiseless tenor of their way."

Necesse est cum insanientibus furere, nisi solus relinquereris. Lat. PETRONIUS.—"It is necessary to be mad with the insane, unless you would be left quite alone." Even the wise man will bend and accommodate himself in some degree to the follies and prejudices of those around him, in order to avoid the reproach of singularity.

Necesse est facere sumtum, qui quaerit lucrum. Lat. PLAUTUS.—"It is necessary that he who looks for gain should incur expense." No profit in common life can be made without previous risk and expenditure.

Necesse est in immensum exeat cupiditas, quae naturalem modum transiliit. Lat. SENECA.—"When once ambition has passed its natural bounds, its progress is sure to be immense." It is so with avarice, which the word *cupiditas* may imply, and indeed with the whole train of evil passions. When the first restraints are got over, their further progress mocks all calculation.

Necesse est, qui mare tenet, eum rerum potiri. Lat.—"He who is in possession of the sea, master of the sea, is, as a matter of course, master of a monarchy." "To be master of the sea," says BACON, "is an abridgment of a monarchy."

Necesse est ut multos timeat, quem multi timent. Lat. PUBLIUS SYRUS.—"He that is feared by many must be in fear of many." The tyrant, who governs others by terror, has cause to be himself the most terrified.

Necessitas non habet legem. Lat. Law maxim.—"Necessity has no law." Any man may justify, for instance, the pulling down the house of another, if it be done to prevent the spreading of a dangerous fire.

Nefas nocere vel malo fratri puta. Lat. SENECA.—"You should deem it a crime to hurt even a bad brother." You should enlighten, admonish, and if possible reform, him, but abstain from injury or violence. This maxim should in a great degree govern our conduct towards all our fellow-men.

Negatas artifex sequi voces. Lat. PERSIUS.—"He attempts to express himself in a language which nature has denied him."

Nem. con.—Abbreviation for *nemine contradicente.*

Nem. dis.—Abbreviation for *nemine dissentiente.* "No person opposing or disagreeing." These two phrases are in fact synonymous. The latter, however, is exclusively used in the House of Peers.

Neminem id agere ut ex alterius praedetur inscitia. Lat. CICERO.—"[It is only right and proper that] no man should so act as to take advantage of another's folly." This is a precept which those must admire in theory who outrage in practice.

Nemo allegans suam turpitudinem audiendus est. Lat. Law maxim.—"No man alleging his own baseness is to be heard." The evidence of spies, informers, and of every man who does not come into court with clean hands, is to be listened to with distrust.

Nemo bis punitur pro eodem delicto. Lat. Law maxim.—"No man can be twice punished for the same crime."

Nemo malus felix. Lat. JUVENAL.—"No bad man is ever happy." "There is no peace, saith the LORD, unto the wicked."

Nemo me impune lacesset. Lat.—"No man shall provoke me with impunity." The motto of the Order of the *Thistle,* to the rough nature of which plant it has reference.

Nemo mortalium omnibus horis sapit. Lat. PLINY.—"No man is wise at all times." This phrase, so frequently employed, enforces a serious truth,—that the wisest of mankind have their lapses of indiscretion.

Nemo punitur pro alieno delicto. Lat. Law maxim.—"No man is to be punished for the crime of another." It is to be observed, that this is a *law,* and not a *state,* maxim. The people in every state are punished for the sins of those who administer the government.

Nemo repente fuit stultissimus. Lat.—"No one ever became, or has ever become, exceedingly foolish, or a very great fool, all on a sudden, or all at once."

Nemo repente fuit turpissimus. Lat. JUVENAL.—"No one ever became thoroughly base, vicious, profligate, debased, or lost to all sense of decency, all at once, all on a sudden,—no one ever reached the climax [which see] of vice at one step:"—

"MARK! NONE BECOME, AT ONCE, COMPLETELY VILE.
Or,— None ever reached the height of vice at first."

Nemo solus sapit. Lat. PLAUTUS.—"No man is wise alone, of himself." No man should be so confident in his own opinion as to reject all advice. "In the multitude of counselors," says Solomon, "there is safety."

Nemo tenebitur prodere seipsum. Lat.—"No one shall be held bound, or liable, to betray himself."

Nemo tenetur ad impossibile. Lat.—"No one is bound to an impossibility, no one is expected to do what is impossible." There is an old saying to this effect, that "though Solomon was wise, and Samson was strong, neither of them could pay money if they hadn't it."

Nemo vir magnus sine afflatu aliquo divino unquam fuit. Lat. CICERO.—"No man was ever great, no one ever became a great man, without some degree or measure of divine inspiration." Education can form men after its own image, or, rather, after the image of the school-master; but not all the education in the world will, of itself, make a man a Newton, a Locke, a Porson, a Richard Owen, or a Faraday. In all such cases there must be in-born talent of the very highest order, the gift of Omnipotence alone, for, as Cicero tells us, *Nemo vir magnus sine afflatu aliquo divino unquam fuit.*

Νηφε, και μεμνησ' απιστειν· αρϑρα ταυτα των φρενων. Gr. EPICHARMUS.—"Be discreet, and bethink thee to be mistrustful, to disbelieve rather than otherwise: for this, in troth, is the very essence of wisdom." "In no study more than in that of historical antiquities is it expedient to keep in view the maxim of EPICHARMUS, '*Νηφε, και μεμνησ' απιστειν· αρϑρα ταυτα των φρενων.*'"

Nepotism.—The *true* meaning of this oft-used, but not well-understood, word is *the too great influence of the nephews*, or *possessed by the nephews, of a reigning Pope*, in consequence of the important positions which they usually fill. The word is *generally* used to signify *undue partiality to one's own relations*, in putting them if possible into good berths, or situations, irrespective of their merits.

Neque caecum ducem neque amentem consultorem. Lat. from ARISTOPHANES.—"Do not take either a blind guide, or a weak adviser." The former is not more dangerous than the latter.

Neque culpa neque lauda teipsum. Lat.—"Neither blame nor applaud thyself." The latter, in conversation, is a silly egotism, and the former is most frequently to be traced to an affectation as absurd.

Neque extra necessitates belli praecipuum odium gero. Lat. —"I bear no particular hatred beyond the necessity of war." I feel no resentment beyond that which is justified by the occasion.

Neque mala vel bona quae vulgus putet. Lat. TACITUS.—"Things are neither good nor bad, as they appear to the judgment of the multitude."

Neque semper arcum tendit Apollo. Lat. HORACE.—"Nor does Apollo always bend his bow." This phrase is generally used as an apology for those who, being engaged in grave pursuits, indulge themselves in occasional relaxation; but sometimes in a different sense,—that men of talent [who at one time were supposed to be under the special protection of Apollo] do not at all times reach by their exertion the level of their usual merits.

Nequeo monstrare, et sentio tantum. Lat. JUVENAL.—"I cannot embody it in words, but can feel it in my soul;"—what I can fancy, but cannot express. Used in speaking of an indefinable sensation. "This do I feel, but want the power to paint." N.B. "*Nequeo monstrare*," &c. has been appositely used in reference to SHAKSPEARE, him of whom TUPPER thus sings in his beautiful lines to Brother Jonathan:—

"There lived a man, a man of men,
A king on fancy's throne;
We ne'er shall see his like again:
The globe is all his own;
And if we claim him of our clan,
He half belongs to you,
For Shakspeare, happy Jonathan,
Is yours and Britain's too!"

Nequicquam sapit, qui sibi non sapit. Lat.—"To no purpose is he wise who is not wise for himself, wise for his own interest or benefit."

Nervis alienis mobile lignum. Lat. HORACE.—"A puppet moved by wires in the hands of others." Applied to politicians of a certain class, whose motions are dictated, and whose proceedings are regulated, by persons unseen, or by what is called "*an interior cabinet*."

Nescia mens hominum fati sortisque futurae,
Et servare modum, rebus sublata secundis. Lat. VIRGIL.—
"The mind of man is ignorant of fate and future destiny, or of keeping within due bounds when elated by prosperity." How blind is the mind of man to fate and future events! how unwilling, reluctant, to practice moderation! how puffed up, inflated with prosperity! The rich and the great in their proudest career should bear in mind the vicissitudes of fortune, and be humble.

Nescio qua natale solum dulcedine cunctos
Ducit, et immemores non sinit esse sui. Lat. OVID.—
"I know not by what sweetness, attractions, our native soil attaches all men to it, and permits them not to be unmindful of it." Neither time nor distance can eradicate the attachment which MOST men feel for the spot that gave them birth:—

"A nameless fondness for our native clime
Triumphs o'er change and all-devouring time;
Our next regards our friends and kindred claim,
And every bosom feels the sympathetic flame."

"That we should love the land of our birth, of our happiness, of that social system under which our happiness has been produced and protected, the land of our ancestors, of all the great names and great deeds which we have been taught most early to venerate, is surely as little wonderful as that we should feel, what we all feel, a sort of affection for the most trifling object which we have merely borne about with us for any length of time. Loving the very land of our birth, we love those who inhabit it, who are to us a part, as it were, of the land itself, and the part which brings it most immediately home to our affections and services. It is a greater recommendation to our good will, indeed, to be a relative, or a friend, or a benefactor; but it is no slight recommendation, even without any of these powerful titles, to be a fellow-countryman, to have breathed the same air, and trod the same soil, and lent vigor to the same political institutions, to which our own aid has actively or passively contributed."—*Brown's Lectures.*

"Breathes there the man, with soul so dead,
Who never to himself hath said,
'This is my own, my native land!'
Whose heart has ne'er within him burned,
As home his footsteps he hath turned,
From wandering on a foreign strand!
If such there breathe, go, mark him well:
For him no minstrel raptures swell:
High though his titles, proud his name,
Boundless his wealth as wish can claim,
Despite those titles, power, and pelf,
The wretch, concentered all in self,
Living, shall forfeit fair renown,
And, doubly dying, shall go down
To the vile dust from whence he sprung,
Unwept, unhonored, and unsung."—SCOTT.

"I traveled among unknown men
In lands beyond the sea:
Nor, England! did I know till then
What love I bore to thee.

"'Tis past, that melancholy dream!
Nor will I quit thy shore
A second time: for still I seem
To love thee more and more."—WORDSWORTH.

Nescio quid profecto mi animus praesagit mali. Lat. TERENCE. —"I know not, in troth, what misfortune my mind presages, or forebodes; my mind anticipates something indescribably unpleasant."

Nescire quid antea quam natus sis acciderit, id est semper esse puerum. Lat. CICERO.—"To be ignorant of what happened before you were born, of by-gone times, of the days that are past, is ever to be like a child [in knowledge]."

Nescis, mi fili, quantula sapientia gubernatur mundus! Lat. OXENSTIERN.—"Thou knowest not, my son [thou hast yet to learn], with how little wisdom the world is governed!" "Civilization has never been granted an opportunity of suddenly making such an immense step, or rather such an incalculable stride, as is now offered [1838]; but it is humiliating to reflect how little apprehension we have shown for the heavenly gift which has been imparted to us,—how strongly our conduct respecting it exemplifies the observation, '*Nescis, mi fili, quantula sapientia gubernatur mundus!*'"

Nescit vox missa reverti. Lat. HORACE.—"The word which has once escaped can never be recalled." We should be careful of what we say. The impression made by an indiscreet word is scarcely ever erased

——————**Nessun maggior dolore**
Che ricordarsi del tempo felice
Nella miseria. Ital. DANTE.—

"There is no greater woe
Than to remember days of happiness
Amid affliction."

**Neutiquam officium liberi esse hominus puto,
Cum is nil promereat, postulare id gratiae apponi sibi.** Lat. TERENCE.—"I think it below a man of honor to lay claim to an obligation, where he has done nothing to merit any." A man of liberal sentiments will not stoop to ask that as a favor, which he cannot claim as a reward.

Ni plus ni moins. Fr.—"Neither more nor less."

——————————————————**Ni
Posces ante diem librum cum lumine, si non
Intendes animum studiis et rebus honestis—
Invidia vel amore vigil torquebere.** Lat. HORACE.—"Unless before daybreak you call for a book and a light, and if you do not apply your mind to study and honorable pursuits, love or envy will torture you and keep you awake:"

"Unless you light your early lamp to find
A moral book,—unless you form your mind
To nobler studies,—you will forfeit rest,
And love or envy will distract your breast."

Niaiseries. Fr.—"Follies, fooleries, absurdities, sillinesses, nonsense." "The *niaiseries* of fashionable West-End life can scarcely be understood in other localities."

Niger est—hunc tu, Romane, caveto. Lat. HORACE.—"He is black in heart; shun him, then, thou that hast the spirit of a Roman; do thou, O Roman, beware of him, be on thy guard against him." The delineation of a hypocrite. N.B. The *entire* passage, of which the above words are an extract, is so remarkably beautiful as to render any apology for its introduction, by way of appendage, unnecessary:—

——————Absentem qui rodit amicum
Qui non defendit, alio culpante; solutos
Qui captat risus hominum, famamque dicacis;
Fingere qui non visa potest, commissa tacere
Qui nequit; hic niger est—hunc tu, Romane, caveto.

"He who malignant tears an absent friend,
Or, when attacked by others, don't defend;
Who trivial bursts of laughter strives to raise,
And courts of prating petulance the praise;
Of things he never saw who tells his tale,
And friendship's secrets knows not to conceal,
This man is vile; here, Roman, fix your mark;
His soul is black, as is his nature dark."

ROGERS, the distinguished poet and lover of punning, and Father Mahony once walking down the Strand, a *Black* approached, when Rogers, in affected alarm, exclaimed,—

"Hic *niger* est—hunc tu, *Romane*, caveto."

Nihil ad rem. Lat.—"Nothing to the purpose." "We have in these Lectures a display of learning to little purpose, quotations from Latin and Greek, really *nihil ad rem;* the φαντασιαι [vain shows, or displays, pompous exhibitions, or parade of learning] of the Greek, and *visiones* of the Romans."

Nihil agas quod non prosit. Lat. PHAEDRUS.—"Do nothing but what may be profitable, may turn to some account, to good account."

Nihil agit qui diffidentem verbis solatur suis:
Is est amicus, qui in re dubia re juvat, ubi re est opus.
Lat. PLAUTUS.—
"He who comforts, administers consolation to, a man who is down in the world, who is on his beam-ends, who has no shot in the locker, who has nothing to fall back upon, with mere words, does nothing worth mentioning; but a true friend is he who in circumstances of difficulty comes to the rescue, *purse in hand*, with open hand and open heart."

Nihil credo auguribus qui aures verbis divitant
Alienas, suas et auro locupletent domos. Lat. ATTIUS.—
"I put no faith in augurs, I give no credit to augurs, conjurers, fortune-tellers, who enrich the ears of others with [lying] words, that they may replenish their own houses with gold:"—

"I trust not augurs, who enrich our ears with fables old,
In order to replenish their own abodes with gold."

Nihil erat quod non tetigit: nihil quod tetigit non ornavit. Lat. Dr. JOHNSON on GOLDSMITH.—"In his writings he touched on every subject, so versatile was his genius: and naught did he touch upon without adorning it." "The star of the race-course of modern times was Colonel Mellish. *Nihil erat quod non tetigit: nihil quod tetigit non ornavit* He was a clever painter, a fine horseman, a brave soldier, a scientific farmer, and an exquisite coachman."

Nihil eripit fortuna nisi quod et dedit. Lat. PUBLIUS SYRUS.—"Fortune takes naught from us but what she first gave us."

Nihil est ab omni parte beatum. Lat. HORACE.—"There is nothing that is in every respect, in every instance, in every point of view, blessed, happy, or perfect:"—

"Naught is there that's completely blest."

There is no perfect happiness in the world; no state, condition of life is without its disadvantages. Nothing human is or can be perfect. See "*Laetus in praesens animus*," &c.

Nihil est aliud magnum quam multa minuta. Lat. prov.—"Every thing great is composed of many things which are small." This ancient adage is admirably illustrated by YOUNG, when he says,—

"Sands form the mountain, moments make the year."

Nihil est aptius ad delectationem lectoris, quam temporum varietates, fortunaeque vicissitudines. Lat. CICERO.—"Nothing is more calculated to entertain a reader, than the variety of times, and the vicissitudes of fortune." In the perusal either of history or romance, the pleasure of the reader arises chiefly from variety and contrast.

Nihil est in intellectu quod non prius fuit in sensu. Lat.—"There is nothing in intelligence, which did not previously exist in sense."

"In Nature as well as in Art, there are intelligible forms, which to the sensible are subsequent. Hence then we see the meaning of that noted School axiom, *Nihil est in Intellectu quod non prius fuit in Sensu;* an axiom which we must own to be so far allowable, as it respects the Ideas *of a mere contemplator.*"

Nihil est quin male narrando possit depravari. Lat. TERENCE. —"There is nothing but by ill telling, by suppressing the good and bringing forward the evil, may be made to appear the worse."

Nihil est quod non expugnet pertinax opera, et intenta ac diligens cura. Lat. SENECA.—"There is nothing which persevering industry, and unwearied and unremitted exertion, may not completely and thoroughly surmount, overcome." "KING ROBERT BRUCE, being out on an expedition to reconnoiter the enemy, had occasion to sleep at night in a barn. In the morning, still reclining his head on a pillow of straw, he beheld a spider climbing up a beam of the roof. The insect fell to the ground, but immediately made a second essay to ascend. This attracted the notice of the hero, who, with regret, saw the spider fall a second time from the same eminence. It made a third unsuccessful attempt. Not without a mixture of concern and curiosity, the monarch twelve times beheld the insect baffled in its aim; but the thirteenth essay was crowned with success. It gained the summit of the barn, and the king, starting from his couch, exclaimed, 'This poor insect has taught me perseverance! I will follow its example. Have I not been twelve times defeated by the enemy's superior force? On one fight more hangs the independence of my country!' In a few days his anticipations were fully realized by the glorious result to Scotland of the Battle of Bannockburn."—*Goodrich's Fireside Education.*

Nihil est tam utile quod in transitu prosit. Lat. SENECA.— "No book can be so good as to be profitable when carelessly read."

Nihil est tam volucre quam maledictum: nihil facilius emittitur, nihil citius excipitur, nihil latius dissipatur. Lat. CICERO. —"Nothing is so swift in its progress as calumny; nothing is more easily circulated, nothing more readily received, and nothing can be more widely spread abroad." Or, as our poet has it,—

"On eagles' wings immortal scandals fly."

Nihil magis consentaneum est quam ut iisdem modis res dissolvatur, quibus constituitur. Lat. Law maxim.—"Nothing is more equitable than that every thing should be dissolved by the same means by which it was constituted." A deed under hand and seal can only be released by a similar deed. An obligation in writing cannot be discharged by a verbal agreement.

Nihil omni ex parte perfectum atque beatum. Lat. CICERO.— "There is nothing that is in every point of view blessed or happy and perfect." See "*Nihil est ab omni,*" *&c.*

Nihil potest rex nisi quod de jure potest. Lat. Law maxim.— "The king can do nothing but what he can do by law." He cannot, for instance, order a man to prison without the writs and processes of law.

Nihil quod tetigit non ornavit. Lat.—"Naught did he touch [write about] that he did not adorn, embellish." See "*Nihil erat quod non* *tetigit,*" *&c.* "We are obliged to pass by a variety of minor matters which, in its thousand abortive motions, and in its multifarious and fruitless debates, the Reformed house has *touched.* In the opinion of the pamphleteers, *nihil quod tetigit non ornavit:* we, on the contrary, think that it has touched nothing which it has not disturbed; and, what with committees within doors and commissioners without, we really know not what spot of the old *terra firma* of British institutions has not been turned into a quicksand."

Nihil scriptum miraculi causa. Lat. TACITUS.—"Nothing composed for the sake of exhibiting prodigies, or exciting wonder." Applied to a history which narrates simple facts in plain terms.

Nihil semper floret; aetas succedit aetati. Lat. CICERO.—"Nothing is at all times in a flourishing condition, in its prime, nothing perpetually flourishes: age succeeds age, the several stages of existence succeed each other."

Nihil sub sole novi. Lat.—"There is nothing new under the sun." "There is no new thing," says Solomon, "under the sun. Is there any thing, whereof it may be said, See, this is new? it hath been already of old time which was before us." Compare CHAUCER:—

"For out of the olde feldis, as men saieth,
Comith all this new corne, fro yere to yere;
And out of olde bokis, in good faith,
Comith all this newe science, that men lere."

Horace Walpole, remarking to Selwyn one day, at a time of considerable popular discontent, that the measures of government were as feeble and confused as in the reign of the first Georges, and saying, "There is nothing new under the sun:" "No," replied Selwyn, "nor under the grand*son* [GEORGE THE THIRD]."

Nihil tam firmum est, cui periculum non sit etiam ab invalido. Lat. QUINTUS CURTIUS.—"Nothing is so firm, secure, as to be impregnable to the attacks even of the very weakest." See "*Quamvis sublimes,*" *&c.*

Nihil tam firmum est, quod non expugnari pecunia possit. Lat. CICERO.—"Nothing is so secure, firm, stable as not to be overcome, gotten the weather-gage of, by means of money." See "*Aurum per medios,*" &c. "We are not," says Colton, "more ingenious in searching out bad motives for good actions, when performed by others, than good motives for bad actions, when performed by ourselves. I have observed elsewhere, that no swindler has assumed so many names as self-love, nor is so much ashamed of his own; self-love can gild the most nauseous pill, and can make the grossest venality, when tinseled over with the semblance of gratitude, sit easy on the weakest stomach."

"There is," says a writer in the *Spectator*, "a way of reasoning which seldom fails. I mean, convincing a man by ready money, or, as it is ordinarily called, bribing a man to an opinion. This method has often proved successful when all others have been made use of to no purpose. A man who is furnished with arguments from the Mint, will convince his antagonist much sooner than one who draws them from reason and philosophy. Gold is a wonderful clearer of the understanding; it dissipates every doubt and scruple in an instant; accommodates itself to the meanest capacities; silences the loud and clamorous, and brings over the most obstinate and inflexible. *Philip of Macedon* was a man of most invincible reason this way. He refuted by it all the wisdom of Athens, confounded their statesmen, struck their orators dumb, and at length argued them out of all their liberties."

Nihil tam incredibile est, quod non dicendo fiat probabile: nihil tam horridum, tam incultum, quod non splendescat oratione, et tanquam excolatur. Lat. Cicero.—"Nothing is so incredible, unbelievable, as not to appear probable by the way in which it is told: nothing so horrid or revolting, nothing so ugly or devoid of ornament, as not to appear fair or bright by being arrayed in gorgeousness of language, and decked out, as it were, in the garb of loveliness."

Nihil turpius est quam gravis aetate senex, qui nullum aliud habet argumentum, quo se probet diu vixisse, praeter aetatem. Lat. Seneca.—"Nothing is more base, contemptible, than an old man who can exhibit no other proof of having lived a long time but his mere age." We should all try to show by some generous act, some brave exertions, or some scientific efforts, that we have not lived in vain, been mere cumberers of the soil.

Nil actum reputans, dum quid superesset agendum. Lat. Lucan.—"Thinking that nothing was done whilst any thing remained to be done." This is the character of a man of talent and enterprise. He never sits down indolently contented with half measures:—

"He reckoned not the past, whilst aught remained
Great to be done, or mighty to be gained."

"Adopting the noble maxim of considering nothing done *dum quid superesset agendum*, they would feel the very spires of our cathedrals an eyesore, and would never rest until they were overthrown."

Nil admirari prope res est una, Numici,
Solaque, quae possit facere et servare beatum.

Lat. Horace.—

"To wonder at nothing, *that is*, to be astonished at nothing that we see around us, or that occurs to us in the path of our existence, to look on every thing with a cool and undisturbed eye, to judge of every thing dispassionately, to value or estimate nothing above itself, and consequently to covet nothing immoderately, and to think nothing more alarming or adverse than it really is, is almost the only way, Numicius, to make us happy and to continue to keep us so."

"Not to admire is of all means the best,
The only means to make and keep us blest."

Happiness does not arise from those things which men are apt to admire, but from virtue, and a mind not subject to idle wonder and admiration. "Very large sums are wasted every year on the Continent by our countrymen in pursuit of the 'antique,' though it might be difficult to determine to what extent public credulity is thus annually imposed upon; difficult, because self-love is here at variance with self-interest (*silencing* many a victim, who fears lest, if his mistakes were blabbed abroad, the world might append some more unflattering name to his own than that of *dupe*); and difficult again, because there are gulls that *will not* be so called; and *gud-*

geons who *won't* believe in a pike till he swallows them up alive! Thus while the fraud practiced is great, the stir it makes, in consequence of these things, is small; and it becomes, therefore, the more necessary to apprize amateurs, that the money laid out to *learn* experience may come to more than would purchase them a commission in the Guards!"

"Not to admire's the simplest art we know
To keep your fortune in its *statu quo;*
Who holds loose cash, nor *cheques* his changeling gold,
Buy what he will, is certain to be *sold.*"

Nil agit exemplum, litem quod lite resolvit. Lat. HORACE.—"That example does nothing, which in removing one difficulty introduces another. An instance, which solves one difficulty by raising another, concludes nothing." That arbitration is of no avail, which leaves behind it as great a difficulty as it found in the first instance.

Nil conscire sibi, nulla pallescere culpa. Lat. HORACE.—"To be conscious of no guilt, and to turn pale at no charge." The latter is the strongest proof of a pure mind and unsullied conscience.

THE PULTENEY GUINEA.

William Pulteney, afterwards Earl of Bath, was remarkable alike for his oratorical talents and his long and consistent opposition to the measures of Sir Robert Walpole, the great Whig Minister. On the 11th of February, 1741, a time when party feeling was at its height, Walpole received an intimation in the House of Commons that it was the intention of the Opposition to impeach him. To this menace he replied with his usual composure and self-complacence, merely requesting a fair and candid hearing, and winding up his speech with the quotation,—

"Nil conscire sibi, null*i* pallescere culp*ae*."

With his usual tact, Pulteney immediately rose, and observed, "that the right honorable gentleman's logic and Latin were alike inaccurate, and that Horace, whom he had just misquoted, had written '*nulla pallescere culpa.*'" Walpole maintained that his quotation was correct, and a bet was offered. The matter was thereupon referred to Nicholas Hardinge, Clerk of the House, an excellent classical scholar, who decided against Walpole. The Minister accordingly took a guinea from his pocket, and flung it across the house to Pulteney. The latter caught it, and, holding it up, exclaimed, "It's the only money I have received from the Treasury for many years, and it shall be the last." This guinea, having been carefully preserved, finally came into the hands of Sir John Murray, by whom it was presented, in 1828, to the British Museum. The following memorandum, in the handwriting of Pulteney, is attached to it: "This guinea I desire may be kept as an heir-loom. It was won of Sir Robert Walpole in the House of Commons; he asserting the verse in Horace to be 'nulli pallescere culpae,' whereas I laid the wager of a guinea that it was 'nulla pallescere culpa.' He sent for the book, and, being convinced that he had lost, gave me this guinea. I told him I could take the money without any blush on my side, but believed it was the only money he ever gave in the House where the giver and the receiver ought not equally to blush. This guinea, I hope, will prove to my posterity the use of knowing Latin, and encourage them in their learning."

Nil debet. Lat. Law term.—"He owes nothing." The usual plea in an action for debt.

Nil desperandum. Lat. HORACE.—"Let us despair of nothing, let us never despair, be cast down." "MAN, amidst the fluctuations of his own feelings and of passing events, ought to resemble the ship, which currents may carry and winds may impel from her course, but which, amidst every deviation, still presses onward to her port with unremitted perseverance. In the coolness of reflection, he ought to survey his affairs with a dispassionate and comprehensive eye, and, having fixed on his plan, take the necessary steps to accomplish it, regardless of the temporary mutations of his mind, the monotony of the same track, the apathy of exhausted attention, or the blandishments of new projects."—*Essays on the Formation and Publication of Opinions.*

"Never give up! it is wiser and better
Always to hope, than once to despair!
Fling off the load of Doubt's heavy fetter,
And break the dark spell of tyrannical care;
Never give up! or the burden may sink you:
Providence kindly has mingled the cup,
And in all trials or troubles, bethink you,
The watchword of life must be, Never give up!

"Never give up! there are chances and changes
Helping the hopeful a hundred to one,
And through the chaos High Wisdom arranges
Ever success,—if you'll only hope on:
Never give up! for the wisest is boldest,
Knowing that Providence mingles the cup,
And of all maxims the best, as the oldest,
Is the true watchword of, Never give up.

"Never give up! though the grape-shot may rattle,
Or the full thunder-cloud over you burst:
Stand like a rock,—and the storm or the battle
Little shall harm you, though doing the worst:
Never give up! if adversity presses,
Providence wisely has mingled the cup,
And the best counsel in all your distresses,
Is the stout watchword of, Never give up!"

TUPPER'S *Ballads and Poems.*

Nil dicit. Lat. Law term.—"He says nothing." This plea intimates a failure in the defendant, in not putting in his answer to the plaintiff's declaration.

Nil dictu foedum visuque haec limina tangat,
Intra quae puer est. Lat. JUVENAL.—"Let nothing shocking to eyes or ears approach those doors that close upon your child." Nothing indecent or criminal should be mentioned within the early and eager hearing of children. "Little pitchers have large ears." See "*Maxima debetur*," &c.

Nil ego contulerim jucundo sanus amico. Lat. HORACE.—

"Ne'er shall I, while in my senses, ever think any blessing equal to that of an agreeable true friend:"—

"Surely no blessing in the power of fate
Can be compared, in sanity of mind,
To friends of a companionable kind."

Nil erit ulterius, quod nostris moribus addat
Posteritas: eadem cupient facientque minores,
Omne in praecipiti vitium stetit. Lat. JUVENAL.—
"There is nothing further, that future times can add to our immorality. Our posterity must have the same desires, and perpetrate the same acts. Every vice has reached its climax:"—

"NOTHING is left, NOTHING, for future times
To add to the full catalogue of crimes;
The baffled sons must feel the same desires,
And act the same mad follies, as their sires.
VICE HAS ATTAINED ITS ZENITH."

This is the complaint of every century, since a picture of national manners was first drawn. The inventive genius of each succeeding age has continued, however, to mock the prediction.

Nil falsi audeat, nil veri non audeat dicere. Lat. CICERO.—"That he should not dare to tell a falsehood, or to leave a truth untold." This is the brief but just character of an honest historian.

Nil fuit unquam sic impar sibi. Lat. HORACE.—"Nothing was ever so unlike itself." "No man's conclusions are more discordant with one another than those of Milton, *Nil fuit unquam sic impar sibi:" Nothing was ever so unlike itself:* that is, *No man ever exhibited in his own person such a mass of inconsistencies and contradictions:*—

"Sure such a various creature ne'er was known."

N.B. This quotation has often been applied to BYRON.

Nil habet infelix paupertas durius in se
Quam quod ridiculos homines facit. Lat. JUVENAL.—
"The greatest hardship of poverty is, that it tends to make men ridiculous."

"Want is the scorn of every wealthy fool,
And wit in rags is turned to ridicule."

Nil intra est olea, nil extra in nuce duri. Lat. HORACE.—"There is nothing hard within the olive, there is nothing hard without in the nut." There is no trusting even to physical evidence, admitting the above assertion to be true. The idea intended to be conveyed in the original passage, of which the above words are a portion, is this: To assert that, because the oldest Greek writers are the best, the oldest Roman ones are also to be considered superior to those who have come after, is just as absurd as to say that the olive has no stone, and the nut no shell, or to maintain that our countrymen [the Romans] excel the Greeks in music, painting, and wrestling.

Nil mortalibus arduum est. Lat. HORACE.—"Nothing is difficult to mortals." Nothing is too difficult for mortals to attempt:—

"No work too high for man's audacious force."

Nil oriturum alias, nil ortum tale fatentes. Lat. HORACE.—

"Acknowledging that never yet hath appeared, nor ever will appear, your equal:"—

"We all confess no prince so great, so wise,
Hath ever risen, or shall ever rise."

Admitting the existence of a *unique*, an object not to be equaled.

Nil proprium ducas, quod mutarier potest. Lat. PUBLIUS SYRUS.—"Never deem that your own which can be transferred." All worldly possessions are precarious, but philosophy and virtue we may call our own.

Nil similius insano quam ebrius. Lat. prov.—"Nothing is more like a madman than a man who is drunk." Insanity and ebriety produce effects so similar, that the principal distinction between them lies in the continuance of the former.

Nil sine magno vita labore dedit mortalibus. Lat. HORACE.—"In this life nothing is given to man without great labor."

"There is nothing gotten in this life
Without a world of toil and strife!"

No man can achieve the possession of fame, wealth, or influence, without incessant pains and application to his object.

Nil tam difficile est, quin quaerendo investigari possit. Lat. TERENCE.—"Nothing is so difficult but by industry it may be accomplished." Compare MENANDER [a very distinguished Athenian poet]:—*'Αλωτα γιγνετ' επιμελεια και πονῳ ἁπαντα.*—"All things are capturable, seizable, may be done, managed, accomplished, by application and toil, labor, exertion, trouble." Compare also PHILEMON [another celebrated Athenian poet]:—*Παντ' εστιν εξευρειν, εαν μη τον πονον φευγῃ τις, ὁς προσεστι τοις ζητουμενοις.*—"Every thing may be discovered, if we do not shun the necessary labor, which, however, is generally the attendant of those who are engaged in difficult researches, investigations."

"See first that the design is wise and just:
That ascertained, pursue it resolutely.
Do not for one repulse forego the purpose
That you resolved to effect."—SHAKSPEARE.

"Make not impossible that which but seems unlike."—SHAKSPEARE.

Nil tam difficile est, quod non solertia vincat. Lat. prov.—"Nothing is so difficult but that by diligence and practice it may be overcome."

Ni l'un ni l'autre. Fr.—"Neither the one nor the other."

Nimia est miseria pulcrum esse hominem nimis. Lat. PLAUTUS.—"It is a very great misfortune for a man to be too handsome." The words of a coxcomb.

**Nimia illaec licentia
Profecto evadet in aliquod magnum malum.** Lat. TERENCE.—"This excessive licentiousness will most certainly terminate in some great mischief." This is a maxim often resorted to in political discussions. That licentiousness is mischievous no man will dispute; but in contending parties, there are few who can draw the line exactly between the improper license and the fair freedom of discussion.

Nimia subtilitas in jure reprobatur; et talis certitudo cer-

titudinem confundit. Lat. Law maxim.—"Too much subtilty, shrewdness, acuteness, *close shaving*, in legal matters is very properly con demned; and 'certainty to a certain intent in every particular' throws into utter confusion every thing in the shape of certainty."

Nimirum insanus paucis videatur, eo quod
Maxima pars hominum morbo jactatur eodem. Lat. HORACE.—"This man may, perhaps, seem mad only to a few, because the greater part of mankind labor under the same disease:"—

"By few, forsooth, a madman he is thought,
For half mankind the same disease have caught."

Nimis poeta. Lat.—"Too much of a poet." "There is a great difference in being *poeta* and *nimis poeta*, if we may believe Catullus, as much as betwixt a modest behavior and affectation:" that is to say, in being *a poet* and *too much of a poet*, if we may, &c.

Nimium altercando veritas amittitur. Lat. prov.—"In excessive altercation truth is lost." In protracted disputes, men forget both themselves and the subject.

Nimium premendo litus. Lat. HORACE.—"By keeping too near the shore." By keeping out of danger. "His policy, like Walpole's, was characterized by an extreme solicitude for peace: on this point also he was perhaps inclined to err, *nimium premendo litus*."

Nimium risus pretium est, si probitatis impendio constat. Lat. QUINTILIAN.—"That laughter costs too much, which is purchased by the sacrifice of decency or propriety."

Nimius in veritate, et similitudinis quam pulcritudinis amantior. Lat. QUINTILIAN.—"Too exact, so far as truth is concerned, and rather studious of similitude than of beauty." In the fine arts, even nature may be too closely copied. None seem to be more aware of this maxim than the *portrait-painters* who are fashionable and successful.

Nimm die Zögernde zum Rath,
Nicht zum Werkseug deiner That. Germ.—"Take plenty of time to consider your plan [in any thing you project], but not in carrying it out, not in carrying out, in putting into execution, your operations." Compare SALLUST: *Priusquam incipias consulto, et, ubi consulueris, mature facto opus est.* "Deliberate well before you begin: but, when you have so deliberated, then act with promptitude, decision." "We may wait, it is true, and consign to centuries to come, the toils, the glories, and the hopes of science, or we may rely on an easy effort distributed over length of years for the accomplishment of much that vigorous exertion might now effect; but we should recollect the admonition of the poet,—

'Nimm die Zögernde zum Rath,
Nicht zum *Werkzeug* deiner That.'

"The feeling of the astronomer, laboring under the weight of his vast cycles, patiently watching the slow evolutions of cosmical events, and breathing forth his aspirations after a perfection which he perceives to be attainable in that tone of protracted hope which borders on resignation, has somewhat too much pervaded other sciences. There are secrets of nature we would fain see revealed while we yet live in the flesh, resources hidden in her fertile bosom for the well-being of man upon earth we would fain see opened up for the use of the generation to which we belong. But if we would be enlightened by the one or benefited by the other, we must *lay on power*, both moral and physical, without grudging and without stint."

Nin ting mey'er haest as flien to faen. FRISIAN.—"Nothing in haste except to catch fleas."

Nisi Dominus, frustra. Lat.—"Unless the Lord be with you, all your efforts are in vain." This, which is the motto of the city of Edinburgh, has been thus whimsically translated: "You can do nothing here unless you are a lord!"

Nisi prius. Law Lat.—"Unless before." A judicial writ, by which the sheriff is to bring a jury to Westminster-hall on a certain day, "unless before" that day the lords justices of the sovereign go into his county to take assizes. They there dispose of the cause, and thus save expense and trouble to the parties, jury, and witnesses.

Nisi utile est quod facimus, stulta est gloria. Lat. PHAEDRUS.—"Unless what we do be useful, foolish is the pride we assume in consequence of our achievements."

Nitimur in vetitum semper, cupimusque negata. Lat. OVID.—"We always struggle for the things which are forbidden, and covet those denied to us."

NIZAMUT ADAWLUT.—The Court of criminal justice in India, the principal offices in which are filled by some of the oldest of the Company's servants.

No saber firmar. Span.—"Not to know how to sign one's name." "*No saber firmar* is jokingly held in Spain to be one of the attributes of grandeeship [nobility]."

Nobiles fontes. Lat. HORACE.—"The noble fountains, the noble founts of classic song." N.B. By the noble or famous fountains are meant *Hippocrene*, *Dirce*, *Arethusa*, &c., fountains often alluded to by the Grecian and Roman writers.

Nobilitas sola est atque unica virtus. Lat. JUVENAL.—"Virtue is the only and true nobility." The pride of birth, and the sound of titles, disappear before the intrinsic dignity of virtue.

"Conceited souls! pray take this truth from me,
VIRTUE ALONE IS TRUE NOBILITY."

Nobilitatis virtus, non stemma, character. Lat.—"Virtue, not pedigree, should characterize nobility."

Nobis judicibus. Lat.—"We being judges of the matter, in our opinion, in our humble opinion."

Nobis non licet esse tam disertis,
Qui musas colimus severiores. Lat. MARTIAL.
—"We, who cultivate the muses of a graver spirit, cannot indulge in such license or extravagance." The nature of our pursuit is such as to exclude those licentious freedoms.

Noblesse oblige. Fr. prov.—"Nobility binds to noble conduct; nobility imposes the obligation of nobleness of feeling and conduct" A maxim not the less true because it is old.

Noblesse vient de vertu. Fr. prov.—"True nobility consists in virtue."

Nocet differre paratis. Lat.—"Those who are prepared should never delay." When your preparations are complete, it is injudicious to grant a further time to your adversary. See "*Nimm die Zögernde*," *&c.*

Nocet emta dolore voluptas. Lat. HORACE.—"That pleasure is injurious, which is bought at the price of pain." We should carefully look to the perils which wait upon certain enjoyments.

Noctes coenaeque Deum. Lat. HORACE.—"Nights and refections of the gods, worthy of the gods, fit for the gods to partake of:"—

"O nights, that furnish such a feast
As even gods themselves might taste."

N.B. "*Coena*" was the principal meal of the Greeks and Romans, THE DINNER.

Nocturna versate manu, versate diurna. Lat. HORACE.—"Be these your studies by day and by night." Let these objects be never out of your contemplation. The reference in Horace is to the Greek authors, the careful and diligent study of which he strongly recommends:—

"Make the Greek authors your supreme delight:
Read them by day, and study them by night."

Nolens volens. Lat.—"Whether he or she will or not." The plural is *nolentes volentes*, "whether they will or not."

Noli adfectare, quod tibi non est datum,
Delusa ne spes ad querelam recidat. Lat. PHAEDRUS.—"Do not aspire to, aim at, that which has not been given or granted you by the Great Supreme, lest your deluded hopes, disappointed expectations, should end in complaint, complainings." Aspire not to become a second NEWTON, when you find that, even with the closest application, you can scarcely understand the very first proposition of Euclid's Elements.

Noli me tangere. Lat.—"Do not touch me." A name given to a very tender complaint in the nose; or, ironically, to a person who is over-sensitive.

Nolle prosequi. Law Lat.—"To be unwilling to proceed." This is used in law when a plaintiff, having commenced an action, declines to proceed therein. It is also entered by the Queen's Attorney-General, to stay any further proceedings in certain cases.

Nolo episcopari. Lat.—"I do not wish to be made a bishop." This is a phrase of form, put into the mouth of the person appointed to this high office. It is now applied ironically to those who affectedly disclaim that which is the secret and sole object of their ambition.

Nolumus leges Angliae mutari. Lat.—"We are unwilling that the laws of England should be changed." "We really think that those who feel with the noble Baron on this subject, and on such fundamental and constitutional questions are ready to say, with the Barons of old, *Nolumus leges Angliae mutari*, must consider him as entitled to great praise for the manly and able manner in which he has conducted this appeal, both in his private and his legislative capacity, undeterred by the clamors of ignorance and folly."

Nom de guerre. Fr.—"A war-name." An assumed or traveling title. "Captain" is excellent as a *nom de guerre.*

Nominatim. Lat.—"By name."

Nominis umbra. Lat. LUCAN.—"The shadow of a name." He is a mere *nominis umbra.*

Non amo te, Sabidi, nec possum dicere quare;
Hoc tantum possum dicere, non amo te. Lat. MARTIAL.—"I do not love you, Sabidius, I cannot assign a reason for it; but this alone can I say, I do not love you." Such an unaccountable prejudice finds its way, at times, into every human breast. The epigram has been thus pleasantly translated:—

"I do not love you, Dr. Fell,
The reason why, I cannot tell;
But this indeed I know full well,
I do not love you, Dr. Fell."

Non ampliter sed munditer convivium; plus salis quam sumtus. Lat. CORNELIUS NEPOS.—"The entertainment was more neat than ample; there was more relish in it than cost."

Non assumpsit. Law Lat.—"He did not assume," or, take to himself. A plea in personal actions, when the defendant denies that any promise was made.

Non bene conveniunt, nec in una sede morantur,
Majestas et amor. Lat. OVID.—"Dignity and love do not blend well, nor do they continue long together." Where one of the married individuals is greatly superior to the other, there cannot be found that energy of passion which is reciprocally felt when the situations are more on an equality. "The vigor of mind which can explore the abstrusest depths of philosophy must meet with the fine sensibility to the beauties of eloquence and poetry:—

'*Non bene conveniunt, nec in una sede morantur,*
Majestas et amor—'

—laborious diligence in collecting materials, with dexterous skill in harmonizing and arranging them; the vast range of knowledge requisite for compiling a useful and instructive book, with the more delicate art of writing an agreeable one."

Non compos mentis. Lat.—"Not of sound mind, not in his right senses." In a delirium or state of lunacy.

Non constat. Law Lat.—"It does not appear." It is not before the court in evidence.

Non cuivis homini contingit adire Corinthum. Lat. HORACE.—"It does not happen to every man to go to Corinth; it is not every man who is lucky enough to pay a visit to Corinth." It is not to be supposed that all men can possess the same opportunities, or recur to the same sources of information. "On leaving home, he had made up his mind that the highest satisfaction would consist in returning to England, and being able to say, in reference to having actually been within the walls of Pekin, *Non cuivis homini contingit adire Corinthum:*" [a very populous and wealthy city of ancient Greece]. N.B. "*Non cuivis,*" *&c.*, is a proverbial form of expression, and is said of things that are arduous and perilous, and which it is not the fortune of every one to surmount.

——Non domus accipiet te laeta, neque uxor
Optima, nec dulces occurrent oscula nati
Praeripere, et tacita pectus dulcedine tangent.

Lat. LUCRETIUS.—"No joyous home shall receive thee, nor admirable wife, nor will any dear children of thine run out to meet thee and vie with each other in snatching kisses from thee, and raise a tumult of sweet but unutterable affection in thy breast." GRAY must have had this passage in his mind's eye, when he penned the following sweet stanza:—

"For them no more the blazing hearth shall burn,
Or busy housewife ply her evening care:
No children run to lisp their sire's return,
Or climb his knees the envied kiss to share."

"See the married man in that best position, in the old monuments of James's time, kneeling with his spouse opposite at the same table, with their seven sons and seven daughters, sons behind the father, and daughters behind the mother. It is worth looking a day or two beyond the turmoil or even joys of our life, and to contemplate in the mind's eye one's own *post mortem* and monumental honor. Such a sight, with all the loving thoughts of loving life, ere this maturity of family repose, is it not enough to make old bachelors gaze with envy, and go and advertise for wives? each one sighing as he goes, that he has no happy home to receive him, no best of womankind his spouse, no children to run and meet him and devour him with kisses, while secret sweetness is overflowing at his heart; and so he beats it like a poor player, and says, that is, if he be a Latinist,—

"Non domus accipiet te laeta, neque uxor
Optima, nec dulces occurrent oscula nati
Praeripere, et tacita pectus dulcedine tangent."

Non domus et fundus, non aeris acervus et auri
Aegroto domini deduxit corpore febres,
Non animo curas.

Lat. HORACE.—"Neither houses, nor lands, nor heaps of gold and silver, can fence the body against the attacks of fever, nor can they free the mind from anxiety and corroding cares:"—

"Nor house, nor lands, nor heaps of labored ore,
Can give the feverish lord one moment's rest,
Or drive one sorrow from his anxious breast."

Non eadem est aetas, non mens. Lat. HORACE.—"I am not now of the same age or disposition as I was formerly. My age is not the same, my habits of thinking are changed." I am not inclined to engage actively in the contest for which I feel myself disqualified.

Non ego illam mihi dotem esse puto, quae dos dicitur,
Sed pudicitiam, et pudorem, et sedatam cupidinem.

Lat. PLAUTUS.—"A woman's true dowry, in my opinion, is not that which is commonly so called; but virtue, modesty, and desires kept in due subjection."

Non ego mordaci distrinxi carmine quenquam,
Nulla venenato est litera mista joco. Lat. OVID.—
"I have not attacked any one with biting verse, nor does any envenomed jest lurk in what I have written." I always meant to be playful rather than satirical.

————————————**Non ego paucis**
Offendar maculis, quas aut incuria fudit,
Aut humana parum cavit natura. Lat. HORACE.—
"[In a literary composition] I shall not be offended with a few slight faults which may be owing to a pardonable neglect, to mere inadvertence, and to that frailty which is natural to man, which is inseparable from human nature:"—

"[But where the beauties more in number shine],
I am not angry when a casual line,
That with some trivial faults unequal flows,
A careless hand or human frailty shows."

Non ego ventosae plebis suffragia venor. Lat. HORACE.—"I do not hunt for, or court, the votes of the light and veering rabble, of the mob, that are changeable as the wind."

Non enim gazae neque consularis
Submovet lictor miseros tumultus
Mentis, et curas laqueata circum
Tecta volantes. Lat. HORACE.—
"It is not in the power of wealth, or of the consul's lictor (*i.e.* of any of the appendages of greatness), to subdue the conflicts of a wretched mind, or to remove the cares which hover around the splendid ceilings of the great." The last image has been thus beautifully rendered by WARREN HASTINGS:—

"Where care, like smoke, in turbid wreaths
Round the gay ceiling flies."

Non enim tam auctoritatis in disputando, quam rationis momenta quaerenda sunt. Lat. CICERO.—"In every disputation, we should hope more from the influence of reason than from the weight of authorities."

Non equidem invideo, miror magis. Lat. VIRGIL.—"I do not indeed envy your position, but am rather surprised at it."

Non est ad astra mollis a terris via. Lat. SENECA.—"There is no easy way from the earth to the stars." It is not by common efforts that men can attain immortality.

Non est inventus. Lat. Law term.—"He has not been found." The return made by the sheriff when the defendant is not to be found in his bailiwick. It is sometimes used, in the way of pleasantry, to mark a sudden disappearance.

Non est loquax deprecatio, quamdiu respondit affectui;—non est BATTOLOGIA, quibus ardor animi, veluti flamma, subinde major emicans, exprimit easdem voces. Lat. ERASMUS.—"Prayer must not be considered or looked upon as verbose or wordy, so long as it is in unison with the feelings of the heart; nor must the frequent repetition of the same words be considered as TAUTOLOGY, when the ardor of the feelings, bursting forth like a flame ever and anon gaining strength, gives utterance again and again to the very same ideas." N.B. "*Tautology*" means "the repetition of a word, or of an idea, that has been fully expressed or implied before." "The human mind in distress instinctively indulges in repetition; the earliest cries of a child for pardon are repetition; the urgency of manhood for any desired object vents itself in repetition; in the extremities of punishment, and on the bed of death, the soul exhales itself in petitions and repetitions, for cure, for mercy, or for pardon. It is the common language of human nature, of all ages, of all countries. It was the practice of our Lord himself in his agony; and if a Christian be awakened to a true sense of his transgressions, and if he pours out his soul in a *sincere* prayer for mercy, he will naturally indulge in the *universal form of repetition*, he will ask for the bread of life with '*importunity*,' and he will '*knock*' till the door of mercy be opened to him!"

Non est tanti. Lat. CICERO.—"It is not worth while, worth the while." "The cold iron and *non est tanti* feelings or no feelings of fashionable folks," that is, the *contemptuously indifferent and scornful* feelings, &c., the feelings that in their magnificent estimate of themselves tell them that it is not worth their while to make themselves agreeable to those in a lower walk of life.

Non est vivere, sed valere, vita. Lat. MARTIAL.—"Life is not life but with the enjoyment of health." The invalid can scarcely be said to live, when the faculties, either of the mind or of the body, are seriously impaired.

Non exercitus, neque thesauri, praesidia regni sunt, verum amici. Lat. SALLUST.—"The safety of a kingdom does not depend so much upon its armies, or its treasures, as upon its alliances." The tranquillity of a nation, like that of an individual, is best secured by cultivating the good will of its neighbors.

Non facile solus serves, quod multis placet. Lat. PUBLIUS SYRUS.—"Not easily canst thou retain or keep for thyself that which many have a particular fancy for, longing for, craving after."

Non fidatevi al alchemista povero, o al medico ammalato. Ital. prov.—"Do not trust to a poor alchemist, or a sick physician." Do not take the advice of those who have not been able to act properly for themselves.

Non fumum ex fulgore sed ex fumo dare lucem. Lat. HORACE. —"Not to bring smoke from light, but out of darkness to produce splendor." This is the difference, as stated by the satirist, between a bad poet and a good one. The former exhausts himself in the glare of his opening, and loses himself in smoke. The latter proceeds from a more modest opening to disclose all the radiance of poetry.

"He strikes out light from smoke, not smoke from light,
New scenes of wonder opening to the sight."

N.B. A good motto for the Gas Companies.

Non gemmis, neque purpura venale, neque auro. Lat. HORACE. —"Not to be purchased, not purchasable, by gems, nor by purple, nor by gold." "That must be an unpurchasable commodity: *non gemmis*," &c.

Non hiemes illam, non flabra, neque imbres
Convellunt; immota manet, multosque nepotes,
Multa virum volvens durando saecula vincit. Lat. VIRGIL.
—"Nor wintry storms, nor blasts of winds, nor showers, can uproot it; unmoved it remains, and while countless races of mortals pass from this earthly scene, it outlasts them in surviving:"—

"Unshaken, therefore, by the wintry blast,
Unmoved by storms, it shall for ages last.
It, while the race of man consumes away,
Shall vanquish time, unconscious of decay."

"In attempting to vilify Mr. Fox, he has only shown us that there was no labor from which that great man shrunk, and that no object connected with his history was too minute for his investigation. He has thoroughly convinced us that Mr. Fox was as industrious, and as accurate, as if these were the only qualities upon which he had ever rested his hope of fortune or of fame. Such, indeed, are the customary results when little people sit down to debase the characters of great men, and to exalt themselves upon the ruins of what they have pulled down. They only provoke a spirit of inquiry, which places every thing in its true light and magnitude, shows those who appear little to be still less, and displays new and unexpected excellence in others who were before known to excel. These are the usual consequences of such attacks. The fame of Mr. Fox has stood this, and will stand much ruder shocks.

"*Non hiemes illam, non flabra, neque imbres*
Convellunt; immota manet, multosque nepotes,
Multa virum volvens durando saecula vincit."

Non homines, non di, non concessere columnae. Lat. HORACE. —"Neither men, nor gods, nor booksellers have ever tolerated or will tolerate [mediocrity in poetry]." "If this be the kind of Latin now taught and written in the University of OXFORD, we have only to observe that it is an original indigenous speech of their own. The proper and discriminate use, indeed, of the indicative and subjunctive moods is, in many cases, a point of such extreme nicety as may excuse error; but such a phrase as the one to which we have alluded, *Non homines, non di, non concessere columnae:* at least in places where ignorance is not privileged by titular degrees of science."

Non ignara mali miseris succurrere disco. Lat. VIRGIL.— "Not being myself a stranger to suffering, I have learned to relieve the calamities of others." The words of DIDO, the reputed foundress of Carthage, to AENEAS, the Trojan hero. The school of misfortune is (with a few exceptions) the only one which can endue the mind with sympathy.

Non ille pro caris amicis
Aut patria timidus perire. Lat. HORACE.—
"He dares for his country or his friends to die." This is a flower frequently strewed over the tomb of a hero.

Non licet hominem esse saepe ita ut vult, si res non sinit. Lat. TERENCE.—"Often does it happen that a man, a human being, can neither be, nor do, as he would: especially if circumstances prevent it."

It seldom happens that we can be situated as we please, while circumstances oppose our wishes.

Non licet in bello bis peccare. Lat.—"It is not permitted in war to err twice." At other games a blot may be got over, but at this most dangerous game a mistake is generally to be considered as irretrievable.

Non magni pendis, quia contigit. Lat. HORACE.—"You do not value it highly, because it came unexpectedly." The *windfalls* of fortune are less valued than the *usufruct* of our own industry.

Non maximas, quae maximae sunt interdum irae, injurias
Faciunt: nam saepe est, quibus in rebus alius ne iratus quidem est.
Quum de eadem causa est iracundus factus inimicissimus.
Lat. TERENCE.—

"Quarrels, even the fiercest, do not always argue the greatest offenses. For it often happens that what would not in the least provoke another will make a wrathful man your mortal enemy."

Non misere vivit, qui parce vivit. Lat.—"Not wretchedly, miserably, does he live who lives sparingly [CORNARO, for instance]." "*Non misere vivit, qui parce vivit*, is an acknowledged truism; but during the racing season, a jockey in high practice, who—as was the case with Chifney, Robinson, Dockeray, and Scott—is naturally above our light racing weights, is subject to no trifling mortification. Like the good Catholic, however, when Lent expires, he feels himself at liberty when the racing season is at an end; and on the last day of the Houghton meeting, Frank Buckle had always a *goose for supper!* his labors for the season being then concluded."

Non missura cutem, nisi plena cruoris, hirudo. Lat. HORACE. —"Like a leech, which does not quit the skin until it is full of blood." Used to mark a pertinacious claimant or applicant, who cannot be induced to retire until he has obtained his purpose.

"He, like a leech, voracious of his food,
Quits not his cruel hold, till gorged with blood."

Non multa, sed multum. Lat.—"Not many things, but much." "His system of reading smacks of the old school; little, but good, '*non multa, sed multum.*'"

Non nobis. Lat.—"Not unto us." The commencement of the Latin version of the 115th Psalm, part of which Psalm is frequently sung as a grace after public dinners. "*Non nobis, Domine, sed tibi sit gloria:*" "Not unto us, O LORD, but unto THEE be the glory!"

Non nobis solum, sed toti mundo nati. Lat.—"Not born for ourselves alone, but for the whole world." Altered from LUCAN. See "*Nec sibi, sed toti,*" &c.

Non nostrum inter vos tantas componere lites. Lat. VIRGIL. —"It is not for us to adjust such grave disputes, such serious matters, to determine so great a controversy between you." Ironically quoted, in general, and when the contest is of a trivial nature. It is also often quoted in an *abridged* form: thus, "*Non nostrum.*"

Non numero haec judicantur, sed pondere. Lat. CICERO.— "These things are not judged of by their number, but by their weight."

He is speaking of actions useful to the state, one of which may, f om intrinsic circumstances, outvalue and outweigh a host of others.

Non nunc agitur de vectigalibus, non de sociorum injuriis: libertas et anima nostra in dubio est. Lat. CICERO.—"The question is not now respecting our revenues, or the injuries done to our allies: our liberties and lives are all at stake."

Non obstante. Lat.—"Notwithstanding." "Some of the fleet are to winter in Cork harbor, *non obstante* Sir Charles Wood;" that is to say, *notwithstanding* Sir C. Wood.

Non omnia possumus omnes. Lat. VIRGIL.—"We cannot all of us do every thing." The human faculties are generally confined to a narrow line of operation.

Non omnis error stultitia est dicenda. Lat.—"Every error is not to be called folly." Fatuity is not to be inferred from a single circumstance of mistake.

Non omnis moriar. Lat. HORACE.—"I shall not altogether, or entirely, die." My works, writings, will survive me. Horace's anticipation of immortality.

Non posse bene geri rempublicam multorum imperiis. Lat. CORNELIUS NEPOS.—"[He said that] a commonwealth could not be well conducted under the command of many."

Non possidentem multa vocaveris
Recte beatum: rectius occupat
Nomen beati, qui Deorum
Muneribus sapienter uti,
Duramque callet pauperiem pati,
Pejusque leto flagitium timet. Lat. HORACE.—

"It is not always with justice, consistently with true wisdom, that we call him happy who has large possessions: better does he deserve that name, with far more propriety does that man lay claim to the title of happy, who well knows how to make a wise improvement of the bounty of the gods: who can bear, with patience and courage, the hardships of poverty, and fears crime, the commission of crime, more than death:—

"Not he of wealth immense possessed,
Tasteless who piles his massy gold,
Among the number of the blest
Should have his glorious name enrolled:
He better claims the glorious name, who knows
With wisdom to enjoy what Heaven bestows:"

"Who knows the wrongs of want to bear,
E'en in its lowest, last extreme;
Yet can with conscious virtue fear,
Far worse than death, a deed of shame."

Non propter vitam faciunt patrimonia quidam,
Sed vitio caeci propter patrimonia vivunt. Lat. JUVENAL.—

"Some men do not make fortunes for the purpose of enjoying life, but, blinded by avarice, live only for money-getting." They are so besotted, as to mistake the means for the end:—

"Few GAIN TO LIVE [pray listen], few or none,
But, blind with avarice, LIVE TO GAIN alone."

Non quo, sed quomodo. Lat.—"Not by whom, but in what manner [the business is done]."

Non res, sed spes erat. Lat.—"No great matters did he accomplish, but there was a well-grounded expectation that he would have done much [had his life been spared]." "He has sunk in the prime of life, exhausted by his labors ere their fruits had been given to the public. *Non res, sed spes erat;* but how well-grounded and sure a hope, all who know Cambridge can say."

————Non rete accipitri tenditur, neque milvo,
Qui male faciunt nobis: illis, qui nil faciunt, tenditur:
Quia enim in illis fructus est: in illis opera luditur.
Aliis aliunde est periclum, unde aliquid abradi potest.
Lat. TERENCE.—

"The net is never spread either for the hawk or for the kite, that do mischief, but for such birds as are quite harmless; because in these last there is some profit, the others were lost labor. And just in the same manner, they only are in danger from others, who have any thing to lose."

Non satis est pulcra esse poemata; dulcia sunto. Lat. HORACE.—"It is not enough that poems be beautiful; let them also be affecting." "*Poemata*" refers principally to dramatic compositions.

Non scribit ille, cujus carmina nemo legit. Lat. MARTIAL.—"That man does not write, whose verses no one reads." They are as much unknown as if they had never existed.

Non semper ea sunt, quae videntur; decipit
Frons prima multos. Lat. PHAEDRUS.—

"Things are not always what they seem, or appear to be: the first appearance, glance, view, deceives, or imposes on, many."

Non sequitur. Lat.—"It does not follow as a matter of course, it is not a necessary deduction." "Was there ever a more outrageous *non sequitur* than is contained in this line?" that is to say, a more outrageous *non-sequence, inconsequence, non-conclusion, non-inference, non-deduction,* than is contained, &c.

Non si male nunc et elim sic erit. Lat. HORACE.—"If matters go on badly at present, they may take a better turn hereafter." One of the usual phrases of encouragement under misfortune. Compare SHAKSPEARE:—

"Things at the worst will cease; or e'en climb upward
To what they were before."

Non sibi sed patriae. Lat.—"Not for himself, but for his country."

Non sibi, sed toti genitum se credere mundo. Lat. LUCAN, in reference to CATO.—"Believing himself to be born not for himself, but for the whole world." Or thus, more freely translated:—

"Born not to serve himself, his generous plan
Takes in the universe, nor ends in man."

Non simul cuiquam conceditur amare et sapere. Lat.—"To no one is it granted, permitted, allowed, at the same time both to be in love and to be [really and truly] wise." "Love is an overwhelming passion; and no man, who gives way to it, can ever say into what excesses he may not be hurried: *Non simul cuiquam conceditur amare et sapere.*" Compare SHAKSPEARE:—

"Love's mind of judgment rarely hath a taste:
Wings, and no eyes, figure unheedy haste."

Again:— "Reason and Love oft keep not company."

Non sine dis animosus infans. Lat. HORACE.—"A bold, courageous, spirited, fearless child, deriving courage from the manifest protection of the gods." Horace alludes to the Muses, of whom there were nine [the inspiring goddesses of song, divinities presiding over the different kinds of poetry, and over the arts and sciences]. "Three months ago he [WILLIAM PITT, at the age of seven] told me [his tutor, Mr. Wilson] in a very serious conversation that he was glad he was not the eldest son, but that he *could serve his country in the House of Commons like his papa.* '*Non sine dis animosus infans!*'"

Non sum qualis eram. Lat. HORACE.—"I am not now what I once was." I feel the natural decay of my vigor and of my faculties.

Non tali auxilio, nec defensoribus istis tempus eget. Lat. VIRGIL.—"These times stand in need of different help and of defenders of a very different description. The present conjuncture has need of no such aid, nor of such defense:"—

"No aid like this this dreadful hour demands,
But asks far other strength, far other hands."

These times want other aids. Those who are at the helm of affairs are inadequate to their duty. N.B. The quotation is often used in an *abridged* form: thus, "*Non tali auxilio.*"

Non tam portas intrare patentes
Quam fregisse juvat: nec tam patiente colono
Arva premi, quam si ferro populetur et igni.
Concessa pudet ire via. Lat. LUCAN.—

"The conqueror is not so much pleased by entering through open gates as by forcing his way. He desires not the fields to be cultivated by the patient husbandman; he would have them depopulated by fire and sword. It would be his shame to go by a way already granted to his passage." This is the angry language of the poet, animadverting on the conduct of CAESAR. In modern history this conduct has been too often realized.

Non tangenda, non movenda. Lat.—"Things that are neither to be touched, nor to be moved." "These important privileges have formed the deep foundations, *non tangenda, non movenda*, of the Scottish criminal jurisprudence:" that is to say, that are *neither to be touched, meddled with, interfered with*, nor *to be moved, rescinded, altered, made void.*

Non temerarium est, ubi dives blande appellat pauperem. Lat. PLAUTUS.—"It is not without cause, without some substantial reason, whenever a rich man addresses a poor man, speaks to a poor man, in a familiar tone, familiarly." Witness the conduct of certain candidates for seats in the HOUSE OF COMMONS.

Non tutti van per la medesma strada,
Ne la cosa medesma a tutti piace:
A chi lo mare, a chi la terra aggrada. Ital.—

"Not by the same road do all go, proceed, nor does the same thing please every one: some have a fancy for the sea, and some for the land." The difference of men's pursuits and the various roads they take are here aptly pointed out. See "*De gustibus non est,*" *&c.*

Non ut diu vivamus curandum est, sed ut satis. Lat. SENECA.—"Our care should be not so much to live long, as to live to some purpose." The proper estimate of human life should be taken, not from the years through which it has been protracted, but from the good actions by which it has been distinguished.

Non vi, sed saepe cadendo. Lat. OVID.—"Not by strength, but by frequently falling." Every thing is to be effected by incessant efforts. The idea is taken from drops of water, which unremittingly falling will hollow out a stone. "They are laboring to effect their mischievous purposes *non vi, sed saepe cadendo:*" that is to say, *not by downright force, but by frequently falling to in an underhand manner.*

Non vultus, non color. Lat. VIRGIL.—"There is neither the same countenance, nor the same color in the complexion." This quotation is differently used. It is employed to repel a testimony where there is no semblance of truth, or to rebut the imputation of writings to an author which bear not the features of his style, or the complexion of his sentiments.

Nonchalance. Fr.—"Coolness, indifference."

Nonchalant. Fr.—"Cool, sluggish, inactive." "*Nonchalant* manners were the tone of the time:" that is to say, Manners *implying coolness, listless indifference: cool, sluggish, inactive* manners were, &c.

Nonumque prematur in annum. Lat. HORACE.—"Let your literary compositions be kept from the public eye for nine years at least." It was a saying of ZEUXIS, the celebrated Greek painter, that "he was long in giving the finishing-strokes to his paintings, because he was painting for immortality, painting to gain an imperishable name." "Scripta," says QUINTILIAN, "reponantur ad aliquod tempus, ut ad ea post intervallum velut nova atque aliena redeamus," that is, "Let our literary compositions be laid aside for some time, that we may after a reasonable period return to their perusal, and find them, as it were, altogether new to us." N.B. The practice of locking up, or stowing away for a season, old coats, waistcoats, "*et hoc genus omne,*" is somewhat analogous to the Horatian precept, and has been sedulously carried out by many distinguished individuals,—among others, by the late Dr. NORBURY, of Eton. The reverend gentleman's celebrated black wardrobe, and the suits which reappeared, in the order of the Pythagoric *rotation*, from the chest or ark, were matters of notoriety:—

Supera ut convexa REVISANT,
Rursus et incipiant IN CORPORA VELLE REVERTI.—VIRGIL.

"That they may *revisit* the superior regions [come again into the light of day], and again manifest an inclination to return to their *bodily, visible forms.*" It is hardly possible to translate the spirit, peculiar point, of this quotation in English.

Nos besoins sont nos forces. Fr.—"Our wants are our strength." Our wants compel us to put forth our energies, make us stir our stumps. See "*Magister artis,*" *&c.*

Nos omnes, quibus est alicunde aliquis objectus labos,
Omne quod est interea tempus, prius quam id rescitum est, lucro est. Lat. TERENCE.—"It is an undoubted maxim with all men, that, when any disaster happens to us, all the time that passes before we come to the knowledge of it is so much clear gain."

Nos patriam fugimus, nos dulcia linquimus arva. Lat. VIRGIL. —"We flee from our country, we quit our delightful plains, our pleasant fields."

"Whence does this love of our country, this universal passion, proceed? Why does the eye ever dwell with fondness upon the scenes of infant life? Why do we breathe with greater joy the breath of our youth? Why are not other soils as grateful, and other heavens as gay? Why does the soul of man ever cling to that earth where it first knew pleasure and pain, and under the rough discipline of the passions was roused to the dignity of moral life? Is it only that our country contains our kindred and our friends? And is it nothing but a name for our social affections? It cannot be this; the most friendless of human beings has a country which he admires and extols, and which he would, in the same circumstances, prefer to all others under heaven. Tempt him with the fairest face of nature, place him by living waters under shadowy trees of Lebanon, open to his view all the gorgeous allurements of the climates of the sun, he will love the rocks and deserts of his childhood better than all these, and thou canst not bribe his soul to forget the land of his nativity; he will sit down and weep by the waters of Babylon when he remembers thee, O Sion!"—*Rev. Sydney Smith.*

Noscitur ex sociis. Lat. prov.—"He is known by his companions." "Tell me," says the Spanish proverb, "what company you keep, and I'll tell you what you are."

Nosology.—"A description of diseases."

Nosse omnia haec salus est adolescentulis. Lat. TERENCE.—"To know all these things is the sure preservation of young men; it is salutary, good, for young men to be informed of these things, these important matters."

Nostrapte culpa facimus, ut malos expediat esse,
Dum nimium dici nos bonos studemus et benignos.
Lat. TERENCE.—"'Tis our own fault that some men find their account in being knaves; while we too much affect to be thought good and generous."

Nostri farrago libelli. Lat. JUVENAL.—"The hotch-potch of my book, the motley subject of my page." Applied by the satirist to the multifarious subjects on which he descants.

Nostri fundi calamitas. Lat. TERENCE.—"The flood that ravages our fields, the curse of our land."

Nostro periculo. Lat.—"At our own risk."

Nostrum. Lat.—"Ours, our own thing or property." A medicine, the composition of which is supposed to be known only to the inventor; JAMES'S FEVER POWDERS, for instance. "Physicians have no *nostrums* that will agree with every constitution:" that is to say, have no *medicines* *of their own invention of universal and indiscriminate use*, that will, &c. N.B. "*Nostrum*" is used *absolutely*, as scholars say, that is, *alone*, or *by itself*, to signify *our own*, that is, *my own peculiar medicine*, *remedy*, or *means of cure*. The *full* expression is *nostrum remedium:* that is to say, *our own peculiar*, &c., as above. A *quack* medicine is often called a *nostrum*.

Nota bene. Lat.—"Mark well, pay particular attention; pray, bear in mind." Used in referring to some remarkable object or circumstance, and generally in an *abridged* form: thus, N.B.

Notanda. Lat.—"Remarks, matters, things, points, deserving of notice."

Notre-Dame. Fr.—"Our Lady." This term "*Notre-Dame*" is used in France in reference to churches dedicated to the Virgin Mary. The Church of "*Notre-Dame*" is the Cathedral of Paris, just as St. Paul's is the Cathedral [chief church, metropolitan, or mother-church] of the city of London.

Notre défiance justifie la tromperie d'autrui. Fr. ROCHEFOUCAULT.—"Our mistrust justifies the deceit of others." Men are neither happy nor safe but in mutual confidence.

Notre mal s'empoisonne
Du secours qu'on lui donne. Fr. prov.—
"Our disease is aggravated by the remedies which are administered."

ΝΟΥΝ *ουδεν* ΣΩΜΑ *γεννα· πως γαρ αν τα* ΑΝΟΗΤΑ ΝΟΥΝ *γεννησοι.* Gr. SALLUST de Diis et Mundo.—"No BODY produces MIND: for how should THINGS DEVOID OF MIND produce MIND?" See "Νους."

Nourriture passe nature. Fr. prov.—"Nurture goes beyond nature; birth is much, but good breeding is more."

Νους. Gr.—"Mind." The inductive faculty, the faculty which, *by induction of similar individuals*, forms out of the *particular* and the *many* what is *general* and *one*. N.B. This species of *apprehension* is evidently our *first* and *earliest* knowledge, because all knowledge by *reasoning* dates its origin from it, and because, except *these two*, no other knowledge is possible.——The word "*νους*," NOUS, is often used as synonymous with a very funny but expressive word, "GUMPTION:" "He is not devoid of *nous*," that is, "He knows what's what; he has a spice of *gumption* about him."

Nous aurions souvent honte de nos plus belles actions, si le monde voyait tous les motifs qui les produisent. Fr. ROCHEFOUCAULT.—"We should often be ashamed of our brightest actions, were the world but to see the motives by which they are produced." That this is frequently true must be conceded to those who trace every spring of action up to the source of self-love. It is more benign, however, though it may be less in the spirit of this philosophy, to accept of the best motives that can be assigned for a good action.

Nous avons changé tout cela. Fr. MOLIÈRE.—"We have changed all that, all that kind of thing:"—

"GERONTE. It is impossible to reason better, Doctor. But, dear Sir, there is one thing that staggers me in your lucid explanation. I always thought till now that the heart was on the left side, and the liver on the right.

MOCK DOCTOR. Ay, Sir, so they were formerly; but *we have changed all that.* The College at present, Sir, proceeds upon an entire new method.
GERONTE. I ask your pardon, Sir.
MOCK DOCTOR. Oh, Sir! there is no harm,—you're not obliged to know so much as we do.
GERONTE. Very true, Doctor, very true."

Nous avons donné à penser. Fr.—"We have given [*our readers*] materials for thought, ample subject for serious reflection."

Nous avons tous assez de force pour supporter les maux d'autrui. Fr. ROCHEFOUCAULT.—"We have all of us sufficient strength to bear the misfortunes of others." A sneer is of course meant at the selfish and unfeeling part of mankind.

Nous désirerions peu de choses avec ardeur, si nous connaissions parfaitement ce que nous désirons. Fr. ROCHEFOUCAULT.—"We should wish for few things with eagerness, if we perfectly knew the nature of that which was the object of our desire."

Nous ne savons ce que c'est que bonheur ou malheur absolu. Fr. ROUSSEAU.—"We do not know what is absolutely good or bad fortune." The condition of life is mixed. The highest have their sufferings, and the lowest their consolations.

Nous ne trouvons guère de gens de bon sens que ceux qui sont de notre avis. Fr. ROCHEFOUCAULT.—"We seldom find any persons of good sense but such as are of our opinion." Our self-love on such occasions induces us to pass a favorable judgment.

Novissima verba. Lat.—"The last words [of a person on earth]." N.B. "*Novissima*" is used by itself in the Latin authors to signify DEATH.

Novos amicos dum paras, veteres cole. Lat.—"Whilst you are seeking new friendships, take care to cultivate the old." Do not lose sight of old attachments for the sake of making new connections.

Novus homo. Lat.—"A new man." A man who has only recently become *somebody*, an upstart. N.B. CICERO uses "*novi homines*," the plural of the above, to signify "the first noblemen of their respective families, those who had been first ennobled."

Nuces relinquere. Lat. PERSIUS.—"To abandon our childhood's nuts, our playthings, to cease to be children."

Nucleus. Lat.—"The germ of any thing." "The *nucleus* of a good standard library." N.B. *Nucleus* is properly *the kernel of a nut;* but, in usage, any body or thing about which matter is collected. An almond-kernel, for instance, may be the *nucleus* of a *sugared* almond, sugar being the *matter* or *stuff* collected around it.

Nudum pactum. Lat.—"A naked agreement." A promise unconfirmed by any written obligation.

Nugae canorae. Lat. HORACE.—"Melodious trifles." Mere sing-song without meaning.

Nugis addere pondus. Lat. HORACE.—"To give weight to trifles, to give an air of importance to trifles." To give consequence to matters of slight moment.

Nul n'aura de l'esprit,
Hors nous et nos amis. Fr. MOLIÈRE.—

"No person shall be allowed to have wit out of our circle and that of our friends." This alludes to the little *juntos* of witlings to be found in almost every town, who associate to be-praise and be-puff each other, with a view of excluding the pretensions of those who are not of the party of these monopolists.

Nul n'est content de sa fortune,
Ni mécontent de son esprit. Fr. DESHOULIÈRES.—
"No one is either satisfied with his fortune, or dissatisfied with the tone of his mind, intellect, or understanding." "Madame Deshoulières ought to be held in grateful recollection, if for nothing else, at least for having written these incisive lines,—

'Nul n'est content de sa fortune,
Ni mécontent de son esprit,'—

an epigram to which Rochefoucault has given a new dress in his Maxims."

Nulla aconita bibuntur fictilibus. Lat. JUVENAL.—"No wolf's-bane is drunk out of earthenware." The danger of poison is reserved for those who drink out of vessels of plate.

Nulla bona. Lat.—"No goods, effects, assets."

Nulla dies sine linea. Lat. prov.—"No day without a line." (without having done something). Throughout his life APELLES, the most celebrated of Grecian painters, labored to improve himself, especially in drawing, which he never spent a day without practicing. Hence the above proverb.

Nulla est sincera voluptas,
Sollicitique aliquid laetis intervenit. Lat. OVID.—
"No joy comes unmixed, and some anxiety invariably interferes with every pleasure." See "*Medio de fonte*," *&c.*

Nulla est tam facilis res, quin difficilis siet,
Quam invitus facias. Lat. TERENCE.—
"There is nothing so easy but it becomes difficult when we set about it unwillingly."

Nulla falsa doctrina est, quae non permisceat aliquid veritatis. Lat.—"There is no doctrine so false, but that it may be intermixed with some degree of truth."

Nulla fere causa est, in qua non femina litem
Moverit. Lat. JUVENAL.—
"There are few disputes in life which may not, on investigation, be found to originate with a woman. There is scarcely a single cause in a court of law in which a woman is not engaged in some way or other in fomenting the suit." We pretend to command, but in fact are often mere instruments in the hands of the weaker sex.

Nulla fides regni sociis, omnisque potestas
Impatiens consortis erit. Lat. LUCAN.—
"There will be no common faith between those who share in power, and each man will be jealous of his associate." This is a strong description of the jealous and distracted councils of a nation on the eve of ruin.

Nulla pallescere culpa. Lat. HORACE.—"Not to turn pale on any imputation of guilt, through consciousness of guilt; ne'er to turn pale with guilt, or through guilt." This is frequently used as a motto to a declaration of conscious innocence. See "*Nil conscire sibi*," &c.

Nulla unquam de morte hominis cunctatio longa est. Lat. JUVENAL.—"Where man's life is at stake, is in question, no deliberation can be too long:"—

"Mark! when the life of MAN is in debate,
No time can be too long, no care too great."

Nulla venenato litera mixta joco est. Lat. OVID.—"Not a line in my writings is polluted with any envenomed jest, jeer, gibe:"—

"My writings flow from no satiric vein,
Contain no poison, and convey no pain."

Nulla virtute redemtum. Lat. JUVENAL.—"A monster with no redeeming points in his character." A complete incarnation of SATAN.

Nulli jactantius moerent, quam qui maxime laetantur. Lat. TACITUS.—"None mourn with more affectation of sorrow than those who are inwardly rejoiced." Those who assume sorrow, or affect grief, in general overact their part.

Nulli negabimus, nulli differemus justitiam. Lat.—"We will neither refuse nor postpone the administration of justice which is due to any man." This emphatic phrase is in MAGNA CHARTA, the "Great Charter" of our rights. "That grand principle of the English MAGNA CHARTA, '*Nulli differemus justitiam*,' is in Sicily wholly unknown." Mr. Hughes, the author of "Travels in Sicily," witnessed two executions at Palermo, in 1813, "for crimes committed and condemned, the one eleven, the other fifteen, years before."

Nulli nocendum: si quis vero laeserit,
Multandum simili jure. Lat. PHAEDRUS.—

"We must injure, hurt, no one, do harm to no one: and if any one has injured his fellow-creature, it is only right and proper that he should be punished with like justice, should be repaid in kind."

Nullius addictus jurare in verba magistri. Lat. HORACE.—"Not being bound to swear or speak according to the dictates of any master." This quotation is fairly used by a writer professing to give, and using only, his own free, honest, and independent opinions. "His pre-eminence [as a scholar] cannot be disputed: pity only it is that he wishes to reign like the Turk, with no brother near the throne; and declares war against all and sundry who will not join his party, *addicti jurare in verba magistri*:" that is to say, *blindly addicted to the tenets* [opinions] *of their master, teacher*; literally, *bound*, or *compelled, to swear to the opinions of their teacher*:—

"Sworn to no master, of no sect am I:
As drives the storm, at any door I knock,
And house with MONTAIGNE now, and now with LOCKE."

N.B. "*Addicti*" were properly those debtors whom the Praetor [a legal officer of ancient Rome] adjudged to their creditors, to be committed to prison, or otherwise secured, until satisfaction was made. Soldiers, however, were also called "*addicti*," in allusion to the military oath, which they took when enrolled. We have a pleasant use of the word in Shakspeare: *Leave off all thin potations*, says Falstaff, *and* addict *thyself unto Sack*.

Nullius in bonis. Lat.—"In the goods of no one, among the possessions of no one." The property of no one.

Nullum beneficium esse duco id quod, cui facias, non placet. Lat PLAUTUS.—"I consider, look upon, those attentions as not worth a straw, which are distasteful to the individual to whom they are offered shown."

Nullum elementum in suo proprio loco est grave. Lat.—"No element in its own peculiar place is heavy, in its own proper place is heavy." "Our student shall observe that the knowledge of the law is like a deep well, out of which each man draweth according to the strength of his understanding. He that reacheth deepest, he seeth the amiable and admirable secrets of the law, wherein I assure you the sages of the law in former times have had the deepest reach. And as the bucket in the depth is easily drawn to the uppermost part of the water [for *nullum elementum in suo proprio loco est grave*], but take it from the water it cannot be drawn up without great difficulty; so albeit beginnings of this study seem difficult, yet, when the professor of the law can dive into the depth, it is delightful, easy, and without any heavy burthen, so long as he keep himself in his own proper element."

Nullum est jam dictum, quod non dictum sit prius. Lat. TERENCE.—"Nothing can be said now that may not have been said before." This line, which is often quoted, is not to be taken in a sense absolutely literal. The meaning is that, in these latter days, it is difficult to arrive at novelty.

Nullum imperium tutum, nisi benevolentia munitum. Lat. CORNELIUS NEPOS.—"No government is safe, unless it be fortified by the good will of the community at large." The strongest powers, when they branch into tyranny and oppression, are certain to perish from their very roots. "Peace and good will towards men" are the buttresses to support an empire which looks for an indeterminate duration.

Nullum iniquum in jure praesumendum est. Lat. Law maxim. —"Nothing unjust is to be presumed in the law." All things are taken to be lawfully done until proof is adduced to the contrary. Fraud shall never be intended or presumed by the law, unless it be expressly averred.

Nullum magnum ingenium sine mixtura dementiae. Lat. SENECA.—"Never is there, never does there appear, a great genius without some tinge of insanity, madness." This assertion is, perhaps, too broad and general: it is thus properly qualified by DRYDEN:—

"Great wit to madness sure is near allied,
And thin partitions do their bounds divide."

Nullum magnum malum quod extremum est. Lat. CORNELIUS NEPOS.—"That evil can never be great which is the last." A man can undergo almost any suffering under the persuasion that it is the last that he shall endure. This quotation is, however, generally employed against the fear of death, which terminates all our sufferings.

Nullum medicamentum est idem omnibus. Lat. prov.—"No medicine is the same for, is equally adapted to, all persons." *Freely* translated, "What's one man's meat is another man's poison."

Nullum numen abest, si sit prudentia. Lat. JUVENAL.—"No protecting power is wanting, if prudence be but employed; no other protection is wanting, provided you are under the guidance of prudence." If men generally acted with prudence, they would be under no necessity of invoking any other *human* aid.

"No god is absent, where calm prudence dwells."

Nullum tempus occurrit regi. Lat. Law maxim.—"No time impedes the king, reigning monarch, sovereign: no lapse of time bars the rights of the crown." The rights of the crown are indefeasible by any lapse of time.

Nullus argento color est, nisi temperato splendeat usu. Lat. HORACE.—"There is neither beauty nor value in money unless it derive its luster from temperate and judicious application."

"Gold hath no luster of its own,
It shines by temperate use alone."

Nullus commodum capere potest de injuria sua propria. Lat. Law maxim.—"No man can take advantage of his own wrong." If a lessor and a lessee of lands for years join in the cutting down of timber, the lessor shall not afterwards punish the lessee for waste, as this would be to take advantage of his own wrong.

Nullus esse potest ambigendi locus. Lat.—"There can be no reason for doubt [in the matter in question]."

Nullus tantus quaestus quam quod habes parcere. Lat. prov. —"There is no gain so certain as that which arises from sparing what you have." There is no road to wealth more certain than that of economy.

Numeri innumeri. Lat. VARRO.—"The innumerable, numberless, countless, number [of books]."

Numerisque fertur lege solutis. Lat. HORACE.—"He is borne along in numbers free from law, in unshackled numbers." His verses are licentious, or unrestrained by any of the existing rules. The poet alludes to the privilege, enjoyed by dithyrambic poets, of passing rapidly and at pleasure from one measure to another.

Numerus certus pro incerto ponitur. Lat.—"A certain is put for an uncertain number." As we say a thousand, or a million, to express a large number, but without meaning to ascertain the precise amount.

Nunc adbibe puro pectore verba. Lat. HORACE.—"Now, in the days of thy youth, drink deep into thy pure breast the language of instruction."

Nunc aut nunquam. Lat.—"Now or never."

Nunc omnis ager, nunc omnis parturit arbos;
Nunc frondent silvae, nunc formosissimus annus.
Lat. VIRGIL.—"Now every field and every tree are in bloom; the woods are in full leaf, and the year in its highest beauty." Used generally to introduce a poetical description of summer.

"The fields with grass, the trees with leaves, abound,
The groves are now with freshest verdure crowned;
Unnumbered flowers adorn the rising year,
And all the beauties of the spring appear."

Nunc patimur longae pacis mala; saevior armis
Luxuria incubuit, victumque ulciscitur orbem.

Lat. JUVENAL.—"Now we suffer the mischiefs of a long peace. Luxury, more destructive than war, has engrossed us, and avenges the vanquished world." This is a fine description of Rome in its decline; it exhibits what SHAKSPEARE calls

"The cankers of a calm world, and a long peace."

Nunquam ad liquidum fama perducitur. Lat.—"Fame never reports things in their true light." The strongest impressions are often produced from beginnings the most idle and rumors the most frivolous.

Nunquam aliud natura, aliud sapientia dicit. Lat. JUVENAL.—"Nature never says one thing, and wisdom another." Their dictates are always in complete accordance.

Nunquam animum quaesti gratia ad malas adducam partes. Lat. TERENCE.—"Never shall gain be an inducement to me to do a base thing."

Nunquam est fidelis cum potente societas. Lat. PHAEDRUS.—"An alliance with a powerful individual is never to be relied or depended on, is never rely-upon-able."

Nunquam ita quisquam bene subducta ratione ad vitam fuit
Quin res, aetas, usus semper aliquid apportet novi,
Aliquid moneat, ut illa, quae te scire credas, nescias:
Et quae tibi putaris prima, in experiundo repudies.

Lat. TERENCE.—"No man has so well computed the measures of life but that experience, years, and custom will be still bringing something new, still furnishing some lesson,—insomuch that you must own your ignorance of many things you fancied you knew, and often reject upon trial what before you believed unexceptionable."

Nunquam libertas gratior extat quam sub rege pio. Lat. CLAUDIAN.—"Liberty never existed in a more gracious form than under a pious king." Monarchy is not unfavorable to liberty, if the monarch adheres to the obligations which exist between him and the people.

Nunquam minus solus, quam cum solus. Lat.—"Never less alone than when alone." This was the saying of the ancient philosopher, who found his greatest luxury in solitude.

O.

——————————**O caeca nocentum**
Consilia! O semper timidum scelus! Lat. STATIUS.—"Oh! the blind counsels of the guilty! Oh! how ever cowardly is wickedness!" It has often been remarked that Providence seems to darken the understandings, and to depress the spirits, of great criminals.

O curas hominum! O quantum est in rebus inane! Lat. PERSIUS.—"Oh! the cares, anxieties, of men! how much emptiness, frivolity, in their affairs!"

O curvae in terris animae, et coelestium inanes! Lat. PERSIUS.
"O souls, in whom no heavenly fire is found,
Fat minds, and ever groveling on the ground!"—DRYDEN.

O faciles dare summa deos, eademque tueri
Difficiles! Lat. LUCAN.—
"Oh! how gracious are the gods in bestowing high situations, positions, and how reluctant are they to insure them when given!" This is an apostrophe [a figure in rhetoric, *when the speaker abruptly leaves his subject to direct his speech to a person*] strictly in unison with the ancient mythology. In its more recent application, it can serve only to denote the precarious tenure by which high places are held.

O fortuna, ut nunquam perpetuo es bona! Lat. TERENCE.—"O fortune! strange that thou art never constant, never to be depended on, in thy favors!"

O fortunatos nimium, sua si bona norint,
Agricolas, quibus ipsa, procul discordibus armis,
Fundit humo facilem victum justissima tellus! Lat. VIRGIL.
"O only too happy husbandmen, if they knew but their own advantages!—for whom, in the absence of clashing arms, the grateful earth pours forth an easy sustenance, support." A eulogy often quoted on the condition of agriculturists. The first line is sometimes taken apart, and applied to those who either rightly or without reason urge any motives of political discontent.

O imitatores, servum pecus! Lat. HORACE.—"Away, ye imitators, servile herd!" Generally applied to plagiarists.

O lepidum caput! Lat. TERENCE.—"O you clever fellow!" Often applied ironically to quacks, state quacks, literary quacks, &c.

O major, tandem parcas, insane, minori. Lat. HORACE.—
"O sovereign madman! abstain from taxing the faults of one who comes so far short of thee in madness:"—
"Thou mightier fool, inferior idiots spare!"
An expression often used ironically in a paper war.

O miseras hominum mentes! o pectora caeca!
Lat. LUCRETIUS.—
"How wretched are the minds of men, how blind their understandings!" A quotation frequently and well applied in a moment of popular delusion.

O munera nondum intellecta deum! Lat. LUCAN.—
"Thou chiefest good!
Bestowed by Heaven, but seldom understood."
In allusion to health, which is seldom appreciated.

Ω πατρις, ειθε παντες οἱ ναιουσι σε,
Οὑτω φιλοιεν ὡς εγω· και γε ῥᾳδιως
Οικοιμεν αν σε, κουδεν αν πασχοις κακον. Gr. EURIPIDES.—
"Dear native land! would that all who inhabit thee loved thee as I do! then indeed should we be better denizens of thy soil, and naught wouldst thou sustain of evil!" Compare the following quotation:—

Ω φιλτατη γη μητερ, ὡς σεμνον σφοδρ' ει
Τοις νουν εχουσι κτημα. Gr. MENANDER.—

"Dear native land! how do the good and wise
Thy happy clime and countless blessings prize!"

Compare "*Nescio qua natale,*" *&c.*

O quanta species! cerebrum non habet. Lat. PHAEDRUS.—

"In outward show so splendid and so vain,
'Tis but a gilded block without a brain."

Applied to fops, coxcombs, *et hoc genus omne* [which see].

**O qui perpetua mundum ratione gubernas,
Terrarum coelique sator!—
Disjice terrenae nebulas et pondera molis,
Atque tuo splendore mica! Tu namque serenum,
Tu requies tranquilla piis. Te cernere, finis,
Principium, vector, dux, semita, terminus, idem.**
Lat. BOETHIUS.—

"O Thou, whose power o'er moving worlds presides,
Whose voice created, and whose wisdom guides,
On darkling man in pure effulgence shine,
And cheer the clouded mind with light divine.
'Tis thine alone to calm the pious breast
With silent confidence and holy rest:
From Thee, great GOD, we spring; to Thee we tend;
Path, motive, guide, original, and end."

A beautiful invocation to Heaven, to enlighten the human mind. Compare POPE's "Universal Prayer."

**O rus, quando ego te adspiciam? quandoque licebit,
Nunc veterum libris, nunc somno et inertibus horis
Ducere sollicitae jucunda oblivia vitae?** Lat. HORACE.—

"Oh! when again
Shall I behold the rural plain?
And when, with books of sages deep,
Sequestered ease, and gentle sleep,
In sweet oblivion, blissful balm!
The busy cares of life becalm?"

O si sic omnia! Lat.—"Oh! had he thus conducted himself in every respect, had all his actions been equally consistent!" Applied to an inconsistent character, who is as meritorious in one great instance as he is censurable in other points of his conduct.

O tempora! O mores!—Senatus haec intelligit; consul vidit, hic tamen vivit; vivit?—immo vero etiam in senatum venit, fit publici concilii particeps! Lat. CICERO, in reference to CATILINE, the noted Roman conspirator.—"Oh! the strangeness of the times! Oh! the laxity of men's manners, principles! The senate clearly understands, sees through these things; the consul is also a witness of such atrocities, and yet this miscreant still lives. Lives, did I say? in troth, he e'en comes into the senate-house, and takes part in the deliberations of this august assembly!" "Might we not ask in reference to some of the men returned to Parliament, as we happen to know an elector in one of the metropolitan boroughs did, in speaking with a brother tradesmen, 'How can any men of common sense confide the care of their lives and properties to persons whom in their individual capacities they would not trust with ten pounds' worth of their goods?' One or two names might justify the indignant exclamation of CICERO—'*O tempora,*'" *&c.*

O vita misero longa! felici brevis! Lat. PUBLIUS SYRUS.—

"O Life! to Misery how drear,
To Bliss how short, dost thou appear!"

Again:—

"O Life! how long to him thy course appears,
Who counts its progress by his sighs and tears!
To him how short, whose happy lot beguiles
The gliding moments with perpetual smiles!"—NEAVES.

O vitae Philosophia dux, virtutis indagatrix! Lat. CICERO.—"O Philosophy, thou guide of life and discoverer of virtue!"

Obiter. Lat.—"By-the-by, by the way." "My remark is only *obiter:*" that is, *a passing* or *casual observation.* N.B. The *full* Latin expression is "*obiter dictum,*" which is sometimes used in the plural: thus, "*obiter dicta.*"

Oblitusque suorum, obliviscendus et illis. Lat. HORACE.—"His friends forgetting, by his friends forgot." "SHAKSPEARE produced his OTHELLO in 1611, at the age of *forty-seven,* and immediately afterwards withdrew from the stage, from literature, from London, contented to linger on the remaining five years of his life in his native village, *oblitusque suorum,*" *&c.* N.B. In the *original* passage we have *meorum.*

Obreros á no ver, dineros á perder. Span. prov.—"Neglect watching over your workmen, and you will throw your money away."

Obruat illud male partum, male retentum, male gestum imperium. Lat. CICERO.—"Perish that power which has been obtained by evil means, retained by similar practices, and which is administered as badly as it was acquired." Such a power in any state can never be of long duration.

Obscuris vera involvens. Lat. VIRGIL.—"Involving the truth in obscure terms." Often applied to a political adversary who, not being able to deny the main fact, envelops himself in dark or cloudy circumlocution.

Obscurum per obscurius. Lat.—"To explain what was obscure by something more obscure." This phrase occurs, and frequently with justice, in polemic [contentious, vehement, wrangling] argument, when the opponent, professing to explain, involves himself in a cloud of words, and thus renders more dark what was sufficiently dark before.

Obsequium amicos, veritas odium parit. Lat. TERENCE.—"Obsequiousness gains friends, but truth begets hatred." Deference and adulation will excite kindness, where the honest bluntness of truth must have provoked enmity.

Obstupui, steteruntque comae, et vox faucibus haesit. Lat. VIRGIL.—"I was astounded, my hair stood on end, and my voice stuck in my throat." A description of an extreme degree of consternation.

Occasions manquées. Fr.—"Favorable opportunities missed, let slip."

Occupet extremum scabies. Lat. HORACE.—"Shame come upon

all that lag behind, that do not push onwards, that do not '*go ahead.*' Plague take the hindmost." A proverbial form of expression, borrowed from the sports of the young.

Octroi. Fr.—A municipal tax, which articles pay on entering the barriers of a town.

Oculi sunt in amore duces. Lat. PROPERTIUS.—"The eyes are the leaders, pioneers, organs that first whisper 'the soft tale' in love, in love-affairs." Compare GARTH:—

"Sighs with success their own soft passion tell,
And eyes shall utter what the lips conceal."

"A lady's tears," says CRASHAW, "are silent orators." It seems that lovers' eyes are equally eloquent.

Oderint dum metuant. Lat. CALIGULA.—"Let them hate me, provided they do but fear me." The sentiment of a tyrant towards his subjects, briefly and characteristically expressed.

Oderunt hilarem tristes, tristemque jocosi. Lat. HORACE.—

"The grave a gay companion shun,
Far from the sad the jovial run."

Oderunt peccare boni virtutis amore. Lat. HORACE.—"Good men forbear to sin from their love of virtue." Those who love virtue for her own sake will act solely from her impulses, and without any regard to extrinsic circumstances.

Odi, vedi, e taci, se vuoi vivere in pace. Ital. prov.—"Listen, see, and hold your tongue, if you wish to live in peace."

Odia in longum cocta. Lat.—"Long-cherished, well-digested, hatred, resentment."

Odia in longum jaciens, quae reconderet, auctaque promeret. Lat. TACITUS.—"A man who lays aside his resentment, but stores it up to bring it forward with additional acrimony." This, as JUNIUS observes, is a description of the very worst of characters. The man who can dissemble his resentment until occasion serves, is the basest of all hypocrites, and the most dangerous of all enemies.

Odia qui nimium timet regnare nescit. Lat. SENECA.—"He who is too fearfully alive to hatred is ignorant of the art of reigning." The sovereign who aims at the general good of his people should learn to despise the resentments of individuals.

Odimus accipitrem quia semper vivit in armis. Lat. prov.—"We hate the hawk, because it always lives in arms." All men must detest that power which is in a state of eternal hostility.

Odimus quem laesimus. Lat.—"We hate the man whom we have injured."

Odium theologicum. Lat.—"Theological rancor, hatred; rancor or hatred that cloaks itself under the name of religion." The hatred of divines, theologians. It has been observed that divines bear with them a greater degree of rancor than any other class of disputants.

Odium vicinorum. Lat.—"The hatred of one's neighbors." "The *odium vicinorum* pervades the common language of every Italian state, which fixes the climax of vituperation in the mere mention of the country of the offender."

Officier d'ordonnance. Fr.—An "orderly officer."

Officina gentium. Lat.—"The workshop of nations." "England can never reasonably expect to become the absolute *officina gentium* to the exclusion of their own industry."

Ogni debole ha sempre il suo tiranno. Ital. prov.—"The weak man will always have some one to tyrannize over him."

Ogni medaglio ha il suo reverso. Ital. prov.—"Every medal has its reverse." There are two sides to every statement.

Ohe! jam satis est. Lat. HORACE.—"Enough and more than enough; enough of this." An expression used to denote satiety and disgust.

Ohne Hast, aber ohne Rast. Ger.—"Without haste, but without rest, repose:" in other words, "Haste not, rest not." The motto on GOETHE's ring.

Οικεια ξυνεσει, φυσεως μεν δυναμει, μελετης δε βραχυτητι, κρατιστος δη οὑτος αυτοσχεδιαζειν τα δεοντα. Gr. THUCYDIDES.—"His sagacity was peculiarly his own; gifted by nature with intuitive skill, he had, moreover, such promptitude of counsel as gave him a decided superiority in advancing all that was necessary upon any subject, and on the spur of the occasion." Was applied to WILLIAM PITT.

Olim. Lat.—"Formerly; in time past; some time since."

Olla Podrida, or simply, **Olla.** Span.—"*Olla Podrida*" [Putrid Mixture] is the name of a favorite dish with all classes in Spain. It consists of a mixture of all kinds of meat cut into small pieces, and stewed with various kinds of vegetables. When long kept, it has a disagreeable odor; hence the name. In *England* the phrase is used metaphorically for any incongruous mixture.

Omne actum ab agentis intentione est judicandum. Lat. Law maxim.—"Every act is to be judged from the intention of the agent." In contracts and obligations the law particularly looks to the intention of the parties. In wills the intent of the testator is to be religiously regarded.

Omne animi vitium tanto conspectius in se
Crimen habet, quanto major, qui peccat, habetur.
Lat. JUVENAL.—

"Every fault of the mind becomes more conspicuous and more guilty, in proportion to the rank of the offender." Persons in high stations are not only answerable for their own conduct, but also for the example which they may hold out to others. This, joined to their advantages of education, aggravates their vices, and loads them with a greater share of responsibility.

Omne capax movet urna nomen. Lat. HORACE.—"The capacious urn shakes every name alike; in the capacious urn of death every name is shaken." All are subject to the law of mortality.

Omne ignotum pro magnifico. Lat.—"Every thing of which we are ignorant is taken for something magnificent." We are apt to attach the idea of greatness, magnificence, to that which is mysterious or unknown to us.

Omne in praecipiti vitium stetit. Lat. JUVENAL.—"Every kind of vice has reached its summit." Nothing remains for posterity to add. One of the commonplace remarks on the profligacy of the present day

Omne nimium vertitur in vitium. Lat. prov.—"Every excess becomes a vice." Even our virtues are changed into vices, when pushed to extremes.

Omne scibile. Lat.—"Every thing that may be known, every thing knowable." "Crude and dull compendiums [short cuts to, nearest ways to] of the *omne scibile.*"

Omne solum forti patria est. Lat. OVID.—"Every country is the brave man's land, or the brave man makes every country his own."

Omne supervacuum pleno de pectore manat. Lat. HORACE.—"Whatever is superfluous soon flows away, and is forgotten."

"If in dull length your moral is expressed,
The tedious wisdom overflows the breast."

The writer who wishes to interest should not overload his subject with unnecessary description or improbable aggravation. N.B. HORACE's expression is a metaphor taken from a vessel, which, once full, can receive no more, as all that is afterwards poured into it flows over.

Omne tulit punctum, qui miscuit utile dulci. Lat. HORACE.—"He has accomplished every thing, has carried every point, who has well blended the useful with the agreeable, what is useful with what is agreeable." In allusion to authors.

Omne vafer vitium ridenti Flaccus amico
Tangit: et admissus circum praecordia ludit
Callidus excusso populum suspendere naso. Lat. PERSIUS.—

"Horace, with sly insinuating grace,
Laughed at his friend, and looked him in the face:
Would raise a blush where secret vice he found,
And tickle while he gently probed the wound:
With seeming innocence the crowd beguiled,
But made the desperate passes when he smiled."—DRYDEN.

The satirist may, if he will, e'en wound with pleasantry. The quotation has been applied, and very appositely, to several poets of modern times.

Omne verum utile dictu. Lat.—"Every thing that is true is fit, proper, to be said, spoken, uttered."

Omnem jecit aleam. Lat.—"It was neck or nothing with him."

Omnes amicos habere operosum est; satis est inimicos non habere. Lat. SENECA.—"It is impracticable to have all men as your friends; it is enough if you have no enemies."

——————**Omnes, cum secundae res sunt maxume, tum maxume**
Meditari secum oportet, quo pacto advorsam aerumnam ferant.
Quidquid praeter spem eveniat, omne id deputare esse in lucro. Lat. TERENCE.—

"When Fortune smiles most upon us, we ought all to consider with ourselves in what manner to bear adversity, so that if things fall out differently from what we apprehended, we may account it so much clear gain."

Omnes eodem cogimur: omnium
Versatur urna serius ocius
Sors exitura. Lat. HORACE.—"We are all driven towards the same quarter [deathwards]: the lots of all are shaken in the urn, destined sooner or later to come forth."

"Now all must tread the paths of Fate,
And ever shakes the mortal urn,
Whose lot compels us, soon or late,
To wend our course, and ne'er return."

Omnes, et habentur et dicuntur tyranni, qui potestate sunt perpetua in ea civitate quae libertate usa est. Lat. CORNELIUS NEPOS.—"All those are accounted and denominated tyrants who exercise perpetual power in that state which was before free."

Omnes quibu' res sunt minu' secundae, magi' sunt nescio quo modo
Suspiciosi: ad contumeliam omnia accipiunt magis:
Propter suam impotentiam se semper credunt negligi.
Lat. TERENCE.—"Persons in circumstances of distress are always, I know not how, more apt to be suspicious: they construe every thing into an affront, and fancy themselves slighted because of their poverty."

Omnes sibi malle melius esse quam alteri. Lat. TERENCE.—"[It is an undoubted truth that] it is in the nature of man that every individual should wish for his own advantage in preference to that of others." "Every man for himself."

Omni aetati mors est communis. Lat. CICERO.—"Death is common to every period of life, stage of existence."

Omni exceptione major. Lat.—"Superior to all exception." Applied in the first instance to the competence and credibility of a legal witness, or more generally to the character of a man, which is to be considered as unimpeachable.

Omnia Castor emit; sic fiet ut omnia vendet. Lat. MARTIAL.—"CASTOR buys every thing, and almost as a matter of course he will be compelled to sell every thing."

"Such *bargains* purchased by his dear,
Her taste at auctions showing,
Himself must turn an auctioneer—
'A-going, a-going, a-going.'"

A good lesson for the frequenters of sale-rooms.

Omnia cum amico delibera, sed de ipso prius. Lat. SENECA.—"Consult with your friend on every thing, but particularly on that which respects yourself."

Omnia fert aetas, animum quoque. Lat. VIRGIL.—"Time deprives us of every thing, even the powers of the mind." A reflection that renders comment altogether unnecessary.

————————————Omnia Graece,
Cum sit turpe magis nostris nescire Latine. Lat. JUVENAL.—"They [the fashionable Romans] give utterance to every thing in Greek,

though it is in troth more discreditable for them to be ignorant of Latin [their mother-tongue]." A sarcasm on those who devote themselves to the study of other languages without having previously mastered their own.

Omnia inconsulti impetus coepta, initiis valida, spatio languescunt. Lat. TACITUS.—"All matters commenced with hasty violence are strenuous in the beginning, but languish in the end." That fervor which seeks no aid from wisdom soon evaporates: the means are, therefore, exhausted before the end can be attained.

Omnia mea mecum porto. Lat. AUSONIUS, from the Greek of STOBAEUS.—"I carry all I have with me. All that I can properly call my own I carry with me," namely, MY LEARNING. The saying of BIAS, one of the Seven Wise Men of Greece, on leaving Priene, his native city, on the occasion of its being taken. When the inhabitants were carrying away all they could, some one asked him why he was going away empty, to which he made the above reply. N.B. The quotation has been waggishly translated, "All my property is *personal.*"

Omnia non pariter rerum sunt omnibus apta. Lat. PROPERTIUS.—"All things are not alike for all men fit."

Omnia novit Graeculus esuriens. Lat. JUVENAL.—"A hungry or starving Greekling knows, *or rather*, pretends to know, every thing." A man in a state of starvation will often profess to do things of which he is utterly incapable.

Omnia praeclara sunt rara. Lat.—"Every thing of superlative, surpassing, excellence is [comparatively speaking] rare, of unusual occurrence."

Omnia prius experiri verbis, quam armis, sapientem decet. Lat. TERENCE.—"A wise commander ought to try all means, to try all that can be done by negotiation, before coming to an open assault, before recourse is had to arms." Every practicable expedient should be tried by statesmen, before they consent to rush into the horrid, inexpiable mischief of war. See "*A cuspide corona.*"

Omnia profecto, cum se a coelestibus rebus referet ad humanas, excelsius magnificentiusque et dicet et sentiet. Lat. CICERO.—"The contemplation of celestial things will make a man both speak and think more sublimely and magnificently when he descends to human affairs."

Omnia, quae nunc vetustissima creduntur, nova fuere; et quod hodie exemplis tuemur inter exempla erit. Lat. TACITUS.—"Every thing, that we now deem of antiquity, was at one time new; and what we now defend by examples will, at a future period, stand as precedents." This just observation is frequently turned against those who wish to rest every thing on the authority of musty records and antiquated precedents.

Omnia quae sensu volvuntur vota diurno,
Pectore sopito reddit amica quies. Lat. CLAUDIAN.—
"In sleep, when fancy is let loose to play,
Our dreams repeat the wishes of the day."

Omnia tuta timens. Lat. VIRGIL.—"Fearing all things, even those which are safe." A mind long harassed with dangers cannot look with confidence to any quarter for security or repose.

Omnia tecum una perierunt gaudia nostra,
Quae tuus in vita dulcis alebat amor. Lat.—
"All our joys, pleasures, all the pleasures of our existence, have perished with thee,—pleasures to which thy sweet affection ever contributed during thy sojourn on earth." Addressed to a dear departed friend or relative.

Omnia transformat sese in miracula rerum. Lat. VIRGIL.—"He [PROTEUS, one of the gods of the sea in the heathen mythology] transforms himself into all the wondrous shapes in nature." Frequently applied to political characters, from their readiness in changing sides.

Omnia vincit Amor; nos et cedamus Amori. Lat. VIRGIL.—"Love conquers all things; let us yield then to Love." So despotic is his power that nothing is left to mortals but submission.

Omnibus. Lat.—"For all persons, for everybody." A name given to a carriage for the conveyance of passengers. Frequently contracted into "*Bus*" by those who know not the *true* meaning of the word.

Omnibus invideas; nemo tibi. Lat. MARTIAL.—"Thou enviest all men; but no man envies thee." The envier is never envied.

Omnibus nobis ut res dant sese, ita magni atque humiles sumus. Lat. TERENCE.—"We are all elated or depressed, according as Fortune smiles or frowns upon us."

Omnibus notum tonsoribus. Lat. HORACE.—"A thing well known to every barber [to every gossip, chatterbox]." The loquacity of barbers, and their love of small talk, ever have been, and still are, proverbial.

————————————Omnis [enim] res
Virtus, fama, decus, divina humanaque pulcris
Divitiis parent. Lat. HORACE.—
"All things, virtue, reputation, beauty, in short, every thing both human and divine, now give place to riches."

"Now virtue, glory, beauty, all divine
And human powers, immortal gold! are thine."

It was said in the days of this poet that "at *Rome* all things were venal." Had he lived in later days, he could have furnished even a stronger description of the omnipotence of wealth, and of the yieldings of venality.

Omnis loquendi elegantia augetur legendis oratoribus et poetis. Lat. CICERO.—"All elegance in speech, in oratory, is increased by reading [carefully and attentively] the orators and the poets." "As the poets," says DR. LAWSON, "abound most in figures, it might be fit that all who mean to excel in eloquence should, at least in their youth, be conversant with their writings."

Omnis poena corporalis, quamvis minima, major est omni poena pecuniaria quamvis maxima. Lat. Law maxim.—"The slightest corporal punishment falls on the culprit with more weight than the largest pecuniary penalty."

Omnium consensu capax imperii, nisi imperasset. Lat. TACITUS.—"In the opinion of all men he would have been regarded as capable of governing, if he had never governed." This was the language of this great historian respecting the Emperor Galba. It is now frequently applied to others, who exhibit something like a show of talent, but which, when brought to the test, proves to be nothing but mere superficialness; more talk than talent.

Omnium-gatherum.—A cant term for a miscellaneous collection of things.

Omnium prope quibus affligimur morborum origo et quasi semen. Lat. MORGAGNI.—"The origin and as it were the germ of almost all the diseases with which we are afflicted." Said by MORGAGNI in reference to "a SLIGHT COLD."

On a beau prêcher à qui n'a cure de bien faire. Fr. prov.—"It is in vain to preach to those who care not to mend."

On commence par être dupe, on finit par être fripon. Fr. Mad. DESHOUILLÈRES.—"They begin by being fools, and end in being knaves." This is a just description as it is applied to the progress of a gambler.

"Such is the equal progress of deceit,
The early dupe oft closes in the cheat."

On dit. Fr.—"It is said." "I give the story only as an *on dit*," that is, only as a *report*, a *rumor*, as *what persons say*, as a *hearsay*.

On doit être heureux sans trop penser à l'être. Fr.—"We ought to be happy, to endeavor to make ourselves happy, without thinking too much of being so."

On est mieux seul qu'avec un sot. Fr. prov.—"We are better alone than with a fool."

On fait souvent tort à la vérité par la manière dont on se sert pour la défendre. Fr.—"An injury is frequently done to the cause of truth by the manner in which some men attempt to defend it." An injudicious advocate is sometimes more hurtful than a violent adversary.

On parle peu quand la vanité ne fait pas parler. Fr. ROCHEFOUCAULT.—"Men speak but little when vanity does not induce them to speak." When a person speaks much in company, it is done, in most instances, with a view to distinguish himself.

On perd tout le temps qu'on peut mieux employer. Fr. ROUSSEAU.—"All that time is lost which might be better employed."

On peut attirer les cœurs par les qualités qu'on montre, mais on ne les fixe que par celles qu'on a. Fr. DE MOY.—"Hearts may be attracted by assumed qualities, but the affections are not to be fixed but by those which are real."

On peut mépriser le monde, mais on ne peut pas s'en passer. Fr. BARON WESSENBERG.—"We may despise the world, but we cannot do without it."

On prend le peuple par les oreilles, comme on fait un pot par les anses. Fr. prov.—"The people are to be taken by the ears, as a pot is by the handle." A reflection often cast, and frequently with justice, on the credulity of the mass of the people.

On prend souvent l'indolence pour la patience. Fr. prov.—"Indolence is often taken for patience."

On n'a jamais bon marché de mauvaise marchandise. Fr. prov.—"The best is always the cheapest."

On n'aime guère d'être empoisonné même avec esprit de rose. Fr.—"We by no means like to be poisoned even with the very essence of the rose." What is meant to be an unmixed pleasure will not long be available as a pleasure at all.

On n'aurait guère de plaisir si l'on ne se flattait point. Fr. —"A man would have but little pleasure if he did not sometimes flatter himself."

On n'est jamais bien juste à l'égard d'un rival. Fr. prov.— "We are never very just towards a rival."

On n'est jamais si heureux, ni si malheureux, qu'on se l'imagine. Fr. ROCHEFOUCAULT.—"We are never so happy, nor so unhappy, as we suppose ourselves to be." In either case the feeling is exaggerated. We are ever too much elated, or too much depressed.

On n'est jamais si ridicule par les qualités que l'on a, que par celles que l'on affecte d'avoir. Fr. ROCHEFOUCAULT.—"Men are never so ridiculous from the qualities which really belong to them, as from those which they pretend to have." Affectation is even more contemptible than weakness.

On n'est souvent mécontent des autres que parcequ'on l'est de soi-même. Fr. BARON WESSENBERG.—"We are often dissatisfied with others only because we are so with ourselves."

On ne cherche point à prouver la lumière. Fr. prov.—"There is no necessity for proving the existence of light." It is idle to adduce proofs of that which is self-evident.

On ne donne rien si libéralement que ses conseils. Fr. ROCHEFOUCAULT.—"Men give away nothing so liberally as their advice."

On ne loue d'ordinaire que pour être loué. Fr. ROCHEFOUCAULT. —"We generally praise only to be praised in return." Applied, and justly so, to the bandying of compliments between two vain persons.

On ne méprise pas tous ceux qui ont des vices, mais on méprise tous ceux qui n'ont aucune vertu. Fr. ROCHEFOUCAULT.— "We do not despise all who have vices, but we despise those who have no virtues." In the former case there may be some good qualities to make atonement, some redeeming qualities.

On ne saurait faire boire un âne s'il n'a soif. Fr. prov.—"A man may lead his horse to the water, but cannot make him drink unless he list."

On ne saurait si peu boire qu'on ne s'en sente. Fr. prov.— "When the wine is in, the wit is out."

On ne se blâme que pour être loué. Fr. ROCHEFOUCAULT.—"We only blame ourselves to be praised in return." When we impute to ourselves a fault, we generally expect to receive a compliment in return.

On ne sent bien que ses propres maux. Fr. prov.—"Our own misfortunes are the only ones that we *really* feel, that *really* affect us."

On ne trouve guère d'ingrats, tant qu'on est en état de faire du bien. Fr. ROCHEFOUCAULT.—"We find but few persons ungrateful, so long as we are in a condition to serve them." Expectation in such cases sustains the office of gratitude.

On ne vaut point dans ce monde que ce qu'on veut valoir.

Fr. La Bruyère.—"A man of the world must seem to be what he wishes to be." In other words, the interested man, or the man of the world, must, to forward his purposes, carry his pretensions far beyond his realities.

On se fait cuisinier, mais on est né rôtisseur. Fr.—"A man may make himself a cook, but he must be born a roaster, be born with ability to roast in perfection." A favorite maxim of the French cooks.

On se sent toujours de la bassesse de sa naissance, ou de son extraction. Fr.—"People can never help giving indications of the meanness of their birth, origin, or extraction."

Onor di bocca assai giova e poco costa. Ital. prov.—"Kind words are of great value, are very gratifying, and cost little."

Ontology. From the Gr.—"Metaphysics," the science which treats of the general affections of beings,—the study of the mind. See "*Quand celui, qui écoute,*" *&c.*

Onus. Lat.—"A burden, task." "The real *onus* imposed on his party [in Parliament]."

Onus probandi. Lat.—"The burden, task, of proving." The *onus probandi* should lie on the person making a charge. He is bound to prove what he asserts.

Opera omnia. Lat.—"The whole, entire, works [of an author]."

Opere in longo fas est obrepere somnum. Lat. Horace.—"In a long work it is excusable that sleep should sometimes creep on the writer, excusable if at times we are surprised by sleep." [In the composition of a long work it is excusable if the author be sometimes found tripping.]

Opes animi irritamen avari. Lat. Ovid.—"Riches are the ruling passion, the only stimulants, of an avaricious disposition."

Opes invisae merito sunt forti viro,
Quia dives arca veram laudem intercipit. Lat. Phaedrus.—"Riches are deservedly odious to a brave man, a man of generous feeling, because great wealth carries off, intercepts, the glory that is due to true merit."

Opes irritamenta malorum. Lat. Ovid.—"Riches are the incentives to every kind of wickedness."

Opinionum commenta delet dies, naturae judicia confirmat. Lat. Cicero.—"Time effaces the comments of opinion, but confirms the judgments of nature." Speculative opinions pass away, whilst inferences drawn from nature and truth remain permanently on record.

Opprobrium. Lat.—"A reproach, disgrace, taunt, scandal." "The barbarous system of legal technicalities may justly be styled the *opprobrium* of human reason."

Opprobrium medicorum. Lat.—"The reproach of the faculty, medical body." A name given to a disorder which is generally considered as incurable. "Insanity has for ages continued the *opprobrium medicorum.*"

Optat ephippia bos piger, optat arare caballus. Lat. Horace.—"The lazy ox wishes for horse-trappings, and the horse wishes to plow." A proverbial expression, leveled at such as are dissatisfied with their position, and envy that of others.

Optima est lex quae minimum relinquit arbitrio judicis. Lat. Lord Bacon.—"That law is the best, which leaves as little as possible to the mere discretion of the judge." The business of the judge is, after investigation, to say under what class of cases, provided for by the legislature, the individual case which he has to deal with is included.

Optime traducitur illud Phocionis a moribus ad intellectualia; ut statim se examinare debeant homines, quid erraverint aut peccaverint, si multitudo consentiat et complaudat. Lat. LORD BACON.—"Right well, admirably, correctly, is that maxim of PHOCION'S [a distinguished Athenian, who was most basely treated by his countrymen] as to moral matters transferred to intellectual—namely, that, if the multitude shall assent and applaud, a man should forthwith examine himself to find wherein he has erred."

Optimi quidem, sed nec satis eruditi et paulo iracundiores viri, aetate jam provectiores quam ut pravi quidquam dedoceantur vel recti quidquam addiscant. Lat. PROFESSOR PORSON.—"There are some excellent men, not troubled, however, with too much learning, and moreover of rather irritable dispositions, who are too old either to disabuse their minds of their erroneous impressions, or to ingraft any thing accurate on their very scanty stock of knowledge." Such individuals we may daily meet with. "When the abscess over ZADIG'S eye broke, in opposition to the judgment of the doctor, the doctor wrote a treatise to prove that the abscess ought not to have broken."

Optimism.—The doctrine, that every thing in nature is ordered for the best, that all things are arranged in the manner best calculated for the good of mankind, by the overruling Providence of GOD. N.B. Instead of this *omitted* word, JOHNSON has *optimity*, a word of his own coinage.

Optimum est pati quod emendare non possis. Lat. SENECA.—"It is the best thing you can do to bear patiently what you cannot amend, correct, or make better." What cannot be cured must be endured.

Opum contemtor, recti pervicax, constans adversus metus. Lat. TACITUS.—"A man superior to avarice, of a persevering rectitude of principle, and unmoved by fear." Has been applied, and justly, to WILLIAM PITT.

Opum furiata cupido. Lat. OVID.—"An ungovernable craving after wealth." An avarice which knows no bounds.

Opuscule. Fr.—"A tract, small treatise or work." "A very interesting *opuscule*."

Opusculum. Lat.—The same meaning as the above.

——————————Ora negatur
Dulcia conspicere; at flere et meminisse relictum est.
Lat. PETRARCH.—

"No longer is it permitted me to see the dear countenance of my departed friend; but I may still weep and brood over the remembrance of what I have lost."

Orandum est ut sit mens sana in corpore sano. Lat. JUVENAL.—"Our prayers should be for a sound mind in a sound body." The first great requisites to human happiness.

Ore tenus. Lat.—"From the mouth, by word of mouth." "The testimony was *ore tenus*," that is, *oral testimony* in contradistinction to *written evidence*. "He can plead *ore tenus*." N.B. CICERO uses "*Verbo tenus*" with the same meaning.

Origo mali. Lat.—"The source of the evil, misfortune, the origin of the grievance." "This appears to have been the *origo mali.*"

Origo malorum. Lat.—"The source of evils, misfortunes."

Ortus a quercu non a salice. Lat.—"Sprung from an oak, and not from a willow." A sturdy fellow, and no sycophant, lickspittle, spaniel, *muff.*

Os à ronger. Fr.—"A bone to pick, bones to pick." "Plenty of *os à ronger* he has left scattered throughout his works."

Os durum. Lat. TERENCE.—"A brazen-faced fellow, an impudent fellow."

Os homini sublime dedit coelumque tueri. Lat. OVID.—"To man the Almighty has given the sublime countenance, magnificent visage, and the power to raise his eyes to heaven, to survey the heavens." In contradistinction to other animals, who move in a horizontal posture.

Os magna sonaturum. Lat. HORACE.—"A mouth fitted to speak great things:" in other words, "eloquence that can give utterance to flashes of genius; eloquence pregnant with the celestial fire of genius."

Os sublime. Lat. OVID.—"The sublime countenance; magnificent visage; human form divine." "Many of those human bipeds, to whom nature has given the *os sublime,* have little more perception or enjoyment of her charms than a 'cow on a common, or goose on a green.'"

Otia si tollas, periere Cupidinis arcus. Lat. OVID.—"Remove but the temptations of leisure, and the bow of Cupid will lose its effect." The passions produce but little effect on the mind that is absorbed in business and industry.

Otium cum dignitate. Lat.—"Ease, the pleasures of retirement from business, the pleasures of privacy combined with the dignity of position in society." "He now enjoys the *otium cum dignitate.*"

Otium sine dignitate. Lat.—"Ease, the pleasures of retirement from business, the pleasures of privacy without any portion of dignity." A character precisely the reverse of the preceding.

Ottava rima. Ital.—"The eight-lined stanza."

Ου δικαιον την των ανθρωπων πονηριαν επι τα πραγματα μεταφερειν· αλλ' αυτοις εκεινοις ψεγειν όσοι τοις αγαθοις κακως χρωνται, και τοις ωφελειν δυναμενοις τουτοις βλαπτειν τοις συμπολιτευμενοις επιχειρουσι. Gr. ISOCRATES.—"It is not fitting that the evil produced by men should be imputed to things: let those bear the blame, who make an ill use of things in themselves good and hesitate not to injure their fellow-citizens by any means which will conduce to their own profit."

Ου γαρ εν μεσοισι κειται
Δωρα δυσμαχητα Μοισαν
Τῳ 'πιτυχοντι φερειν. Gr.—

"The gifts of the Muses are not offered to every one who passes by, as common favors; they must be sought after, and obtained with difficulty."

Ου λογῳ, αλλ' εργῳ. Gr. LYCURGUS.—"Not theoretically, but practically." See "*Res, non verba.*"

Ου το ζην περι πλειστον ποιητεον, αλλα τε ευ ζην. Gr. PLATO.—"We should not set the highest value on mere existence, but on living well, or living to some useful purpose."

Ουϑεν ματην ή φυσις ποιει. Gr. ARISTOTLE.—"Nature makes nothing in vain." Every thing is created for some wise purpose.

Oui et Non sont bien courts à dire, mais avant que de les dire il y faut penser long-temps. Fr. GRACIAN.—"Yes and No are very easily said, but before they are said one should think a long time." In matters of consequence, it is most necessary to deliberate before we give a precipitate assent, or a hasty negative.

Ουκ εστιν ήδεως ζην ανευ του φρονιμως, και καλως, και δικαιως· ουδε φρονιμως, και καλως, και δικαιως ανευ του ήδεως. Gr. EPICURUS.—"'Tis impossible to live pleasurably without living prudently, and honorably, and justly; or to live prudently, and honorably, and justly without living pleasurably."

Ουτ' ευτυχων περιχαρης, ουτε δυστυχων περιλυπος εση. Gr. ISOCRATES.—"Be not too much elated in prosperity, nor too much downcast, dispirited, in adversity."

Outré. Fr.—"Outrageous, unreasonable." "A most *outré* costume."

Ouvrage de longue haleine. Fr.—"A long-winded business." "A work too tediously spun out."

——————————*Ουχ εὑδει Διος*
Οφθαλμος· εγγυς δ'εστι και παρων πονῳ. Gr.—
"No slumber seals the eye of Providence,
Present to every action we commence."

Ovem lupo commisisti. Lat. prov.—"You have set the fox to keep the geese:" *literally,* "You have intrusted the sheep to the care of the wolf."

Oyer. Old Norman-French.—"To hear." Hence, a court of *Oyer and Terminer,* "to hear and determine:" *Oyes,* a corruption of *oyez,* "hear,"—a word three times repeated by public criers before making a proclamation.

P.

Pabulum. Lat.—"Food, aliment." "*Pabulum* for the news-writers," that is, *matters, topics, for consideration or discussion.*

Pabulum Acherontis. Lat. PLAUTUS.—"Food for the Acheron," a fabled river in the infernal regions, according to the heathen mythology [fabulous history]. Used to signify "an old fellow just ready to drop into the grave."

Pace tanti nominis. Lat.—"With due submission or deference to so great, illustrious, or distinguished a name;" *literally,* "by leave or permission of so great a man." N.B. "*Pace tanti viri*" has the same meaning.

Pace tua. Lat. TERENCE.—"With thy leave, permission." "Let me venture, *pace tua* [lector benevole, *which see*], to present thee with a short report of the case."

Pacha.—A Turkish title, signifying "a governor, prince, or viceroy."

Pacta conventa. Lat.—"Conditions agreed upon." A diplomatic phrase used to describe certain articles which are to be observed by the contracting parties.

Pacte de famille. Fr.—"A family compact." "He had concluded a *pacte de famille* with LOUIS PHILIPPE."

Pactum illicitum. Lat.—"An unlawful, illegal, illicit, compact, contract, or agreement." "An illegal consideration, or *pactum illicitum*, affects the validity of the whole transaction."

Paean. Lat. from the Gr. *παιαν* [paian].—A name given to APOLLO; a song of triumph, as such songs generally commenced with the invocation *Io Paean*. Hence *Paean*, a song of triumph.

Pagan.—"Pagan Archaeology," that is, "A discourse on heathen antiquities, or on the antiquities of the heathen." "*Pagan*," which comes from the Latin word *paganus*, and that from *pagus*, a village, originally meant a *villager*, a *peasant*, *any one that was not a soldier:* it afterwards meant a *heathen*, because, according to some, the villages continued heathen after the cities became Christian; according to others, because the heathen refused to serve as soldiers under the Christian banner.

Palam mutire plebeio piaculum est. Lat. PHAEDRUS.—"It is a dangerous thing, matter, for a plebeian, for one of the common people, one of the lower orders, publicly or openly to grumble and growl against the government, the existing state of things."

Pale.—From the Lat. word *palus*, "a pale or stake," and metaphorically, "a place of protection." "Within the *pale* of the church."

Palimpsest.—A manuscript so called from the Greek adjective *παλιμψαιστος*, or *παλιμψηστος*, signifying "twice rubbed;" not, as the glossary [dictionary to show the signification of words] of DU CANGE [*membrana iterum abrasa, charta deletilis*] would seem to denote, because the parchment had twice undergone erasure, or the writing been twice obliterated, but because it had been twice prepared for writing, which was principally effected by rubbing it with pumice, first in the course of manufacture, after the skin had been cured, and again by the same process, after the original writing had been taken away by washing or in any other manner. The strict and precise sense of *Palimpsest* is, therefore, "twice prepared for writing;" the repetition of such preparation being the prevailing idea in the etymology, and not erasure, as some have erroneously supposed.

Palinodiam canere. Lat. CICERO.—"To make one's recantation; to retract what one has written or spoken; to eat one's words." "*Palinode*," from the Gr.—"A recantation." "Subsequent and humiliating *palinodes* have sufficiently attested the calumnious nature of their statements."

Palladium. Lat. from PALLAS, another name for MINERVA, the goddess of wisdom, in the heathen mythology.—A statue of PALLAS, pretended to be the guardian of Troy. Hence *palladium*, "a protection." "That great *palladium*, the liberty of the press."

Pallida Mors aequo pulsat pede pauperum tabernas,
Regumque turres. Lat. HORACE.—

"Pale Death knocks with impartial foot at the cottages of the poor and the palaces of kings."

"With equal foot stern and impartial Fate
Knocks at the cottage and the palace gate."

Compare the beautiful lines of MALHERBE, the first who personified Death, and *saw* the livid specter knocking at the doors of her destined victims:

"Le pauvre en sa cabane, où le chaume le couvre,
Est sujet à ses lois,
Et la garde, qui veille aux barrières du Louvre,
N'en défend pas nos rois."

Palmam qui meruit, ferat. Lat.—"Be his the palm [the mark or token of victory, or of excelling others] who hath the conquest gained." The motto of the illustrious NELSON. N.B. Besides the crown, a palm-branch was presented to the conqueror at the Grecian games, as a general token of victory: this he carried in his hand.

Panacea. Lat. from the Gr.—"A general or universal remedy or medicine for all diseases." "A *panacea* for every disease."

Pandite, atque aperite propere januam hanc Orci, obsecro:
Nam equidem haud aliter esse duco: quippe quo nemo advenit,
Nisi quem spes reliquere omnes. Lat. PLAUTUS.—

N.B. The passage from which DANTE adopted his inscription for the portal of Hell. See "*Lasciate ogni speranza,*" &c.

————————*Παντα τα ζητουμενα*
Δεισθαι μεριμνης φασιν οἱ σοφωτατοι. Gr. MENANDER.—

"The wisest men tell us that all subjects of inquiry, investigation, require the deepest thought and reflection."

Παντα ὑποληψις. Gr.—"All things are matter of opinion." The motto on the title-page of LORD SHAFTESBURY'S "Characteristics."

Pape des fous. Fr.—"The fools' pope." A functionary who appears to answer pretty closely to the "*lord of misrule*" of our early English history.

Papier mâché. Fr.—"Chewed paper." That mashed substance of which snuff-boxes and other articles are made.

Par-ci par-là. Fr.—"Here and there." "A few words really bearing on the subject may be found scattered up and down these volumes, *par-ci par-là.*"

Par excellence. Fr.—"By way of eminence, or pre-eminently." "He defended Lord Palmerston as the British Minister *par excellence,*" that is, as "THE minister."

Par exemple. Fr.—"For instance."

Par hasard. Fr.—"By chance."

Par le droit du plus fort. Fr. prov.—"By the right of the strongest." A right more frequently acted upon than pleaded.

Par les mêmes voies on ne va pas toujours aux mêmes fins. Fr. ST. REAL.—"By the same means we do not always arrive at the same ends." Though acting from the best experience, our plans may be deranged by unforeseen circumstances.

Par manière d'acquit. Fr.—"By way of discharge." Carelessly.

Par negotiis neque supra. Lat. TACITUS.—"Neither above nor below his business. Equal to his business, but not fitted for a position requiring greater ability." Used to describe a man whose abilities are exactly fitted to his station.

Par nobile fratrum. Lat. HORACE.—"A noble pair of brothers."

Used ironically to denote two associates exactly suited to each other. N.B. Often used in an abridged form, thus: "*Par nobile.*"

Par parenthèse. Fr.—"By the way." "He tells it you quite *par parenthèse*, as it were."

Par principe. Fr.—"On principle." "He was an aristocrat *par principe.*"

Par privilège. Fr.—"By way of privilege."

Par profession. Fr.—"By profession." "He felt the whole discomfort of democrat *par profession.*"

Par signe de mépris. Fr.—"As a token of contempt."

Parce gaudere oportet, et sensim queri;
Totam quia vitam miscet dolor et gaudium. Lat. PHAEDRUS.—"We ought to rejoice sparingly, and to complain moderately, in moderation, inasmuch as joy and grief checker the whole of human existence."

Parcendum est animo miserabile vulnus habenti. Lat. OVID.—"We must be slow in reproving, blaming, censuring, one who is suffering from the pangs of sorrow, grief, distress."

Parcere personis, dicere de vitiis. Lat.—"To be sparing of persons, but to speak of, denounce, their crimes or vices." A precept of which the honest satirist should never lose sight. Lash vices in general terms, but descend not to personalities.

Parcere subjectis, et debellare superbos. Lat. VIRGIL.—[Be it thy care, O warrior,] "to spare the humbled, but to crush the proud."

Parcite paucorum diffundere crimen in omnes. Lat. OVID.—"Ever abstain from laying the fault of a few on the many, on the masses, on the people at large." Indulge not in generalizing from individual instances.

Parens patriae. Lat. PLINY, in reference to CICERO.—"The father of his, one's, country." "To the House [of Commons], then, as the *parens patriae*, as the people's House, bound to maintain the people's rights, I now appeal."

Pares cum paribus facillime congregantur. Lat. PLAUTUS.—"Birds of a feather flock together."

Pari passu. Lat.—"With an equal pace; by a similar gradation; in the same degree or proportion."

Pari ratione. Lat.—"By like reasoning; by parity of reasoning."

Paria copulantur paribus. Lat. prov. or Law maxim.—"Birds of a feather flock together."

Paribus sententiis reus absolvitur. Lat. Law maxim.—"When the opinions of those who sit in judgment are equally divided, the accused is [or ought to be] acquitted."

Paritur pax bello. Lat. CORNELIUS NEPOS.—"Peace is gotten or procured by war." The party desirous of peace is often compelled to make a greater show of hostile preparation, in order to bring about the return of that inestimable blessing.

Parla bene, ma parla poco, se vuoi esser stimato. Ital. prov.—"Speak well, to the purpose, but speak little, if you wish to be esteemed, thought well of."

Parlez du loup, et vous verrez sa queue. Fr. prov.—"Speak of the wolf, and you will see his tail." Mention but a person's name, and he instantly makes his appearance.

Parlez peu et bien, si vous voulez qu'on vous regarde comme un homme de mérite. Fr.—"Speak but little and well, if you would be esteemed, looked on, as a man of merit."

Parliament.—"When the institutions of the Anglo-Saxons were superseded by, or incorporated with, those of the Normans, even the right or the power of conquest did not overthrow the acknowledged principle on which this assembly was summoned, and the Norman term *Parle-a-ment,* by which it was now denominated, and which remains in use to this day, continued to inform the subjects of the Anglo-Norman kings and their posterity, that it met to *speak* the *mind:* at first, as is well known, of the clergy and military barons, but afterwards, of the commons, or people, also." N.B. The French word "*parler*" means *to speak,* and "*ment*" is only a slight change from the Latin word "*mens,*" which signifies *the mind* [thought, judgment, opinion].

Parole. Fr.—"Word." "His *parole* bound him," that is, "His *word, mere word, promise,* bound him." His *word was his bond.*

Pars beneficii est, quod petitur, si cito neges. Lat. Publius Syrus.—"It is something like kindness at once to refuse what you have no intention of granting." It is charity not to excite hopes that must end in disappointment.

Pars hominum vitiis gaudet constanter, et urget
Propositum: pars multa natat, modo recta capessens,
Interdum pravis obnoxia. Lat. Horace.—

"Some men constantly exult in their vices, and pursue their vicious objects: the greater part, however, fluctuate, sometimes undertaking what is right and sometimes exposed to the contamination of evil:"—

"Among mankind, while some with steady view
One constant course of darling vice pursue,
Most others float along the changing tide,
And now to virtue, now to vice, they glide."

Pars magna. Lat. Virgil.—"The main-spring; the main-stay; the chief support." "Of this ministry Farini himself was *pars magna.*" N.B. In Virgil, however, "*pars magna*" signifies "a great share: a conspicuous part."

Pars minima est ipse poeta sui. Lat. Ovid.—"The poet himself is [often] the smallest part of himself." "How much has been written upon Shakespeare and Shakspere—what long pedigrees of the Halls, Harts, and Hathaways—while the reader, amidst the profusion of learning, searches in vain for a vestige of the manners and opinions of him in whom alone he is interested. *Pars minima est ipse poeta sui!*"

Pars minima sui. Lat. Ovid.—"The smallest part of the man, individual, thing." The poor shadowy remains of the man, or the frittered remnant of the subject.

Pars pro toto. Lat.—"A part for the whole." "An extension of the rule of *pars pro toto.*"

Pars sanitatis velle sanari est. Lat. SENECA.—"The wish to be cured is of itself an advance to health." Metaphorically: To be conscious of one's folly is a negative advance to amendment.

"To yield to remedies is half the cure."

Partage du lion. Fr.—"The lion's portion, share."

Parte tamen meliore mei super alta perennis
Astra ferar, nomenque erit indelebile nostrum. Lat. OVID.—"[Though I must needs 'shuffle off this mortal coil'], yet in the most memorable portion of my soul's frail tenement shall I still survive, and go down the stream of time with a name 'familiar in the mouth as household words;' with a name ne'er to be forgotten, ne'er to be buried in oblivion."

Particeps criminis. Lat.—"A partaker of, sharer or accomplice in, the crime or guilt." The plural is *participes criminis.* N.B. "*Particeps criminis*" is applied to an accessory either before or after the fact; and also to one who instigates another to commit a foul or dishonest action.

Partie carrée. Fr.—Often used *incorrectly* by English writers and speakers to signify "a small and select party:" the *true* meaning, however, is, "a party composed of TWO gentlemen and TWO ladies." N.B. The expression is sometimes erroneously written thus: "*partie quarrée.*"

Parturiunt montes, nascetur ridiculus mus. Lat. HORACE.—"The mountains are in labor, and only bring forth a mouse:"—

"The mountains labor with prodigious throes,
And lo! a mouse ridiculous outgoes."

An allusion to the well-known fable of The Mountain and the Mouse, and applied, as a proverbial expression, to all pompous and imposing beginnings, which result in nothing, end in smoke.

Parva leves capiunt animos. Lat. OVID.—"Little minds are pleased with trifles; trifles captivate weak minds." Frivolous minds are captivated by silly or trifling pursuits. See "*Maximus in minimis.*"

Parva metu primo, mox sese attollit in auras. Lat. VIRGIL.—"Cautious, wary, guarded, at first, through fear, it [slander] by-and-by throws off all restraint, and assumes a bold and shameless front." In reference to outrageous demands on the Government by furious and unprincipled demagogues, the passage may be thus translated: "Moderate at first in their demands through [apparent] diffidence, they at length assume a haughty and arrogant tone." "Their arguments have gradually grown up from the humbler suggestion of *expediency* into the imperative assertion of *right: 'Parva metu primo, mox sese attollit in auras.'* "

Parvenu. Fr.—An "upstart." "He is ready to take offense with all the susceptibility of a *parvenu.*" The *correct* definition of a *parvenu* is, "*one who from an humble origin rises to an elevated position, forgets what he once was, and consequently makes a fool of himself.*" The feminine of *parvenu* is *parvenue.*

Parvenu millionnaire. Fr.—"An upstart who is worth a million, or millions; a man of millions." "Ostentation in the *parvenu millionnaire* is quite a distinct thing from ostentation in the hereditary *grandee* [nobleman]." N.B. "*Millionnaire*" is nearly always *incorrectly* spelled with *one n* instead of with *two.* The *true* meaning of the word "*grandee*" is, a Spanish nobleman, who has the privilege of wearing his hat in the presence of his sovereign, like *Lord Kinsale* in this country.

Parvis componere magna. Lat. VIRGIL.—"To compare great things with small."

Parvum parva decent. Lat. HORACE.—"Little things become the humble man; ordinary things best become ordinary men." The man in a low station never makes himself ridiculous but when his efforts exceed his means.

Pas. Fr.—"A step, precedence." "To him I gave the *pas*."

Pas à pas on va bien loin. Fr. prov.—"Step by step one goes very far." To advance by degrees is in general the most secure as well as the most successful mode of proceeding. N.B. This proverb is a counterpart to the ancient Cornish, "*Cusal ha teg, sirra wheage, moaz pell:*" a literal translation of which, "Soft and fair, sweet Sir, goes far," is as common in Britain and North America as it is appropriate in Australia or at the Cape.

Pascitur in vivos livor, post fata quiescit:
Tunc suus, ex merito, quemque tuetur honor. Lat. OVID.—"Envy is nourished against the living, but ceases when the object is dead: his deserved honors will then defend him against calumny." The sentiment that the world seldom does justice to living merit, will be found, varied only in the expression, in different passages of this Dictionary.

Πασιν ευφρονουσι συμμαχει τυχη. Gr. fragment of an ancient poet.—"Fortune affords aid or succor to the prudent, assists the prudent."

Πασων τουτων των αρετων το τελος ειναι, το ακολουθως τῃ φυσει ζῃν· ἑκαστην δε τουτων δια των ιδιων παρεχεσθαι τυγχανοντα τον ανθρωπον. Gr. STOBAEUS.—"[It is clearly manifest that] the end of all these virtues [the primary virtues, PRUDENCE, TEMPERANCE, FORTITUDE, and JUSTICE] is, to live agreeably to nature; and each of them, by those means which are peculiar to itself, is found to put a man in possession of this end."

Passato il pericolo, gabbato il santo. Ital. prov.—"When the danger is passed, the saint is mocked." In Catholic countries, in every case of danger and difficulty prayers are eagerly offered to some peculiar saint. If the peril be avoided, the patron saint relapses into cold neglect, until he is elevated into respect by the approach of new danger. It applies to cases of friendship exerted, or protection extended, which are too often forgotten with the occasion.

Passe-partout. Fr.—"A pass-key, master-key, universal passport." N.B. "*Passe-partout*" is often incorrectly written *Passe par-tout.*

Passe-port de mer. Fr.—"A sea passport." Permission, leave, authority, to travel by sea, to traverse or cross the sea. "The consul refused the vessel a *passe-port de mer*."

Passibus ambiguis Fortuna volubilis errat,
Et manet in nullo certa tenaxque loco. Lat. OVID.—"With dubious steps does inconstant, fleeting, Fortune wander about, and remains not in any one place for a constancy and so as to be relied upon, depended upon."

Passim. Lat.—"Everywhere, all through, in many or innumerable places or passages." "See 'Roscoe's two Essays' *passim*."

Passim spargere lucem. Lat.—"Everywhere to throw light" on a subject, on the subject in hand, on the subject under consideration.

Pater est quem nuptiae demonstrant. Lat. Law maxim.—"The father is he whom marriage points out as the husband: the husband of the woman is [in the eye of the law] the [reputed] father of her children."

——————————**Pater ipse colendi**
Haud facilem esse viam voluit, primusque per artem
Movit agros, curis acuens mortalia corda. Lat. VIRGIL.—"The father himself [in allusion to JUPITER, the supreme god of the heathens] willed not, was unwilling, that the art of husbandry, art of cultivating the soil, should be easy, and was the first to upturn the ground, to plow the land, by art, by calling in the assistance of art, thus rousing the mind to exertion by anxious care and solicitude." Providence has put care and labor in our way, as blessings too easily enjoyed are soon neglected, if not despised.

Pater noster. Lat.—"Our Father." The commencing words of the Latin version of the Lord's Prayer.

Pater patriae. Lat.—"The father of one's, of his, country, native land." "*Pater patriae* is, with German sovereigns, no rhetorical flourish, but a part of their royal style and dignity. In the preamble of their statutes they say, 'Having taken such or such a subject into our *fatherlandly* consideration.'" N.B. CICERO uses the expression "*Patriae pater*" to signify "*a preserver of one's country.*"

Patere quod emendare non possis. Lat. SENECA.—"Bear patiently what you cannot amend, correct, or make better." What cannot be cured must be endured. See "*Durum!*" *&c.;* and "*Miseriarum portus,*" *&c.*

Paterfamilias. Lat.—"The master, head, or father, of the family."

Pathos. Gr. in Roman letters.—"Feeling." "An inexhaustible mine of *pathos.*"

Pati nos oportet quod ille faciat cujus potestas plus potest. Lat. PLAUTUS.—"It becomes us patiently to bear, submit to, whatever he may inflict whose power is supreme."

Patientia paupertatis ornati. Lat.—"Men distinguished and adorned by their patient endurance of poverty, by honorable poverty."

Patriae fumus igne alieno luculentior. Lat. prov.—"The smoke of one's own country appears brighter than the fire of another country, of any other country."

Patriae impendere vitam. Lat. LUCAN.—"To devote one's life to the service of one's country."

Patriae pietatis imago. Lat. VIRGIL.—"An image of paternal tenderness, affection."

Patris est filius. Lat. prov.—"He is the son of his father." A chip of the old block.

Patte de velours. Fr.—"A velvet paw." Sometimes used to signify "*kindness,*" or "*the semblance of kindness.*"

Paucis carior est fides quam pecunia. Lat. SALLUST.—"There are few who do not set a higher value on their money than on their good faith." The historian wrote at a time when the finer feelings were almost universally absorbed in the prevailing passion of avarice.

Paucis verbis. Lat.—"In a few words." "The details may be given *paucis verbis.*"

Paullo majora canere. Lat. VIRGIL.—"To sing somewhat higher strains." To enter into or upon matters of greater moment; to take a higher range.

Paullum sepultae distat inertiae celata virtus. Lat. HORACE.—"Virtue or energy when concealed differs but little from buried inertness, sluggishness, sloth." If a man can serve his country or his friend, and withholds his exertions, he is as liable to blame for his indolence as another for his incapacity. N.B. The above translation may pass muster when the quotation is used without reference to the context of the original. Viewed, however, in connection with the context, the *true* meaning of the passage is—"Bravery, when concealed and unknown, or Merit, when uncelebrated [when concealed from the knowledge of posterity, for want of a bard or historian to celebrate its praises], differs but little from indolence and obscurity:"

"In earth if it forgotten lies,
What is the valor of the brave?
What difference, when the coward dies
And sinks in silence to his grave?"

Pauper Aristoteles cogitur ire pedes. Lat.—"Poor ARISTOTLE [the distinguished philosopher] is compelled to go about on foot, to trudge it, to pad the hoof." The literary history of all countries and of all ages proves but too plainly that philosophy has never yet been the high road to riches.

Pauper eris semper, si pauper es, Aemiliane;
Dantur opes nullis nunc nisi divitibus. Lat. MARTIAL.—
"Once poor, my friend, still poor you must remain;
The rich alone have all the means of gain."

Poverty is a boundary difficult to pass.

Pauper non est, cui rerum suppetit usus. Lat. HORACE.—"That man is not poor, who has a sufficiency for all his wants:"—

"He is not poor, to whom kind Fortune grants
E'en with a frugal hand what nature wants."

Pauperes necessitas, divites satias in melius mutat. Lat. TACITUS.—"Necessity reforms the poor, and satiety the rich." Compare ROCHEFOUCAULT:—"Fortune breaks us of many faults which reason cannot."

Paupertas fugitur, totoque arcessitur orbe. Lat. LUCAN.—"Poverty is shunned and persecuted, impeached, looked upon as a crime, throughout or all over the world."

Paupertas omnes artes perdocet. Lat. PLAUTUS.—"Poverty teaches us perfectly, or instructs us thoroughly in, every art and science." See "*Magister artis,*" *&c.*, and "*Omnia novit,*" *&c.*

Paupertas onus et miserum et grave. Lat. TERENCE.—"Poverty is a grievous and heavy burden."

Paupertatis pudor et fuga. Lat. HORACE.—"A shame of narrow means, and an aversion to them." A dread of narrow means, and an anxious care to avoid them.

——————"The dread of nothing more
Than to be thought necessitous and poor."

The imputation of poverty is repugnant to the feelings. See "*Nil habet infelix,*" *&c.*

Pauvres gens, je les plains; car on a pour les fous
Plus de pitié que de courroux. Fr. BOILEAU.—

"Poor fellows, I pity them: as one always has for fools more pity than anger." A sarcasm leveled at a class of disappointed authors.

Pauvreté n'est pas vice. Fr. prov.—"Poverty is not a vice, is no vice."

Pavé. Fr.—"Pavement." "The *pavé* of this huge metropolis."

Pax in bello. Lat.—"Peace in war." A war carried on without energy, spirit. "The king," says DOCTOR JOHNSON, "who makes war on his enemies tenderly, distresses his subjects most cruelly."

Pax potior bello. Lat.—"Peace is better than, preferable to, war."

Pax vel injusta utilior est quam justissimum bellum. Lat. CICERO.—"Even unjust peace is better, more advantageous, than the justest war." See "*Iniquissimam pacem,*" *&c.*

Pax vobiscum. Lat.—"Peace be with you." A sentence of the Romish Breviary [Prayer-book of the Roman Catholic Church].

Pays de Cocagne. Fr.—A country in which things are to be had for nothing. N.B. "*Cocagne*" is an imaginary country, where every thing is to be had in abundance and without labor.

Pays Latin. Fr.—*Literally*, "The Latin territory, district, region." "The students of the *Pays Latin,*" that is, of the *University.*

Peccavi. Lat.—"I have sinned." To make one cry *peccavi:* to compel him to acknowledge his transgression. To cry *peccavi* is to acknowledge one's self in the wrong.

Pectus praeceptis format amicis. Lat. HORACE.—"Poetry molds the tender minds of youth to virtue by its friendly precepts." Poetry serves to form our riper age, which it does with all the address and tenderness of friendship, by the sanctity and wisdom of the lessons which it inculcates.

Pecuniae fugienda cupiditas; nihil est tam angusti animi tamque parvi quam amare divitias. Lat. CICERO.—"The insatiable craving after money should be carefully shunned, as nothing so strongly indicates a contracted, base, and groveling mind as the idolizing of wealth."

Pecuniam in loco negligere maxumum interdum est lucrum. Lat. TERENCE.—"To seem to slight, despise, money on some occasions, is sometimes the surest gain, sometimes leads to the greatest gain." There are circumstances in which nothing is to be expected but from a liberal expenditure.

Peine forte et dure. Fr.—"Harsh and severe pain." This was applied in the old law to the punishment of laying under heavy weights, and feeding only with bread and water, the culprit who refused to plead on his arraignment. This severity has been done away with by an Act of Parliament, which enacts that the culprit so refusing to plead shall be held to have pleaded guilty.

Pékin. Fr.—"*Pékin* employment." "*Pékin* is used in France to signify *civil* as opposed to *military*. The soldiers of that country call *pékin* [a word of contempt] all those who are not soldiers. A distinguished officer had been invited to a dinner-party at TALLEYRAND's. He kept the party waiting for almost half an hour; at last he came and excused himself by saying that he had been detained so long by a "*pékin*." TALLEYRAND asked the meaning of the word. "Nous appelons pékin," said the other, "tout ce qui n'est pas militaire [We call every one who is not a soldier, a pékin]." "Ah!" answered the diplomatist, "c'est comme nous, qui appelons militaire tout ce qui n'est pas civil [Ah! that's something like *our* fashion, as *we* call every one who is not civil, a soldier]." N.B. "*Pékin*" is nearly always incorrectly spelled by English writers, thus—*Péquin*, a word that does not exist.

Πελαγος κακων. Gr.—"A sea of troubles."

Pells. From the Latin word *pellis*, "the skin or hide of a beast."—"Skins, parchment rolls." "The clerk of the *pells*."

Penates. Lat.—"The household gods" of the Romans. Small images of the heathen gods, worshiped at home. N.B. "*Penates*" is often used to signify "one's home, fixed habitation or abode." "He could not bear to think of a permanent separation from the humble *Penates*."

Penchant. Fr.—"A peculiar propensity." The plural is *penchants*.

Pendente lite. Lat.—"While the suit or contest is pending, depending; during the continuance of the suit."

Penitus toto divisi orbe Britanni. Lat. VIRGIL.—"The Britons, a race of beings almost separated from the rest of the world, from the rest of mankind." When the poet wrote thus, he did not combine the prophetic office with the poetic. Little did he think that this remote island would arrive at a height of greatness, that would leave proud Rome herself in comparative insignificance, and only as a speck upon the globe!

Pennas incidere alicui. Lat. prov.—"To clip one's wings, lessen one's authority." To bring one from one's high horse; to take him down a peg.

Per acclamationem. Lat.—"By acclamation, with shouts of applause." "He is invested, *per acclamationem*,
——————with robes and ring,
Crozier and miter, seals and every thing."

Per adoptionem. Lat.—"By, on account of, adoption."

Per aetatem. Lat.—"By reason of, because of, on account of, one's age, time of life."

Per aevum. Lat.—"Eternally, forever."

Per annum. Lat.—"By the year, yearly, annually; a year." "A thousand a year."

Per capita. Lat. Law phrase.—"By the head [individually]." "How may they vote? in a lump, or *per capita?*"

Per centum. Lat. commercial term.—"By the hundred." Generally used in an abridged form: thus, *Per cent.* "The property pays him ten *per cent.*"

Per contra. Lat. commercial term.—"On the other side." "There is a *per contra*," that is, "There is a *something to counterbalance this*."

Per damna, pei caedes, ab ipso
Ducit opes animumque ferro. Lat. HORACE.—
"Through seeming losses and wounds it derives strength from the iron itself."

"Through wounds, through losses, no decay can feel,
Collecting strength and spirit from the steel."

"The increase in our mercantile shipping has proceeded with so regular a pace, that the war seems to have had no other effect on it, than to give consistency and firmness to its growth; like the oak of which it is built, '*Per damna,' &c.*"

Per devia loca vagamur. Lat.—"We wander through trackless wilds." "Some title-pages hang out false lights, and so bewilder our expectations; *per devia loca vagamur*, and at last get nothing but weariness and fatigue for our pains."

Per diem. Lat.—"Daily, every day, or a day." "Those omnibuses make scores of journeys *per diem.*"

Per far effetto. Ital.—"To do the thing [any thing] in style; to come out strong."

Per fas et nefas. Lat.—"Through right and wrong; justly or unjustly; through thick and thin; by every means, good, bad, or indifferent." "They strive to gain their ends *per fas et nefas.*"

Per incuriam. Lat.—"Through carelessness, negligence, heedlessness." "The whole passed *per incuriam* on the part of the officer."

Per legem terrae. Lat.—"By the law of the land."

Per multa disspergitur cor, et hic illucque quaerit ubi requiescere possit, et nihil invenit quod ei sufficiat, donec ad Deum redeat. Lat. ST. BERNARD.—"Tossed to and fro in every direction is the heart of man, and on all sides does it seek a resting-place, but seek in vain, until it returns to the bosom of its GOD."

Per multum risum poteris cognoscere stultum. Lat.—"By his incessant laughter, you will always be able to discover, distinguish, a fool." Habitual indulgence in laughter betrays a weak mind.

Per plures. Lat.—"By a majority, the majority." "It was agreed *per plures* that he should be fined and imprisoned."

Per quod servitium amisit. Lat. Law phrase.—"By which he lost her services." Words used to describe the injury sustained by the plaintiff when the defendant has seduced his daughter.

Per saltum. Lat.—"By a leap." Passing over the intermediate steps or degrees. "The Lord Chancellor Hatton was much celebrated for his saltatory abilities; and, indeed, may be said to have stepped to the wool-sack *per saltum.* He was first taken notice of by the Queen, for the comeliness of his person, and for his graceful dancing in a mask at court; but more afterwards, for his great abilities." N.B. At the University of Cambridge, a clergyman who takes the degree of Doctor in Divinity without first taking that of Bachelor in Divinity is said to take such degree "*per saltum.*"

Per scelera semper sceleribus certum est iter. Lat. SENECA.—"The sure, certain, way to wickedness is always through wickedness." The perpetration of one crime generally leads to the commission of another.

Per se. Lat.—"By itself, or of itself." "The act was not a contract *per se.*"

Per se aut per alium. Lat.—"By himself or by another." "He must often, *per se aut per alium*, have enslaved his fellow-whites."

Per se sibi quisque carus est. Lat. CICERO.—"Every one is naturally dear to himself."

Per tot discrimina rerum. Lat. VIRGIL.—"Through so many dangers, hazards, perils, ups and downs." "After so many storms, which have been weathered by the directors *per tot discrimina rerum*, they have at length safely gained a port;" that is, *after struggling with so many dangers and difficulties, after being plunged in a sea of troubles*, they have, &c.

Per varios casus. Lat. VIRGIL.—"Through various chances, hazards, risks, stirring adventures." N.B. This and the preceding quotation form a single line in the original: thus,

"*Per varios casus, per tot discrimina rerum.*"

———————Peragit tranquilla potestas
Quod violenta nequit: mandataque fortius urget
Imperiosa quies. Lat. CLAUDIAN.—

"The calm exercise of power, power calmly exercised, accomplishes what violence fails in, cannot do: and cool and deliberate measures enforce more vigorously the mandates of those who bear imperial or regal sway, the behests of monarchs." Things lawfully and mildly commanded exact performance; but if harshly and illegally required, produce dislike, and sometimes occasion refusal and resistance.

Peras imposuit Jupiter nobis duas:
Propriis repletam vitiis post tergum dedit,
Alienis ante pectus suspendit gravem. Lat. PHAEDRUS.—

"JUPITER [the supreme god of the heathens] has bestowed on us two wallets, bags: the one, filled with our own vices, faults, defects, he has placed behind us, on our backs; the other, heavy with those of others, he has hung, suspended, in front of us, before us." We are all remarkably quick in discovering the faults of others, though but slow either in seeing or acknowledging our own.

Percontare a peritis. Lat. CICERO.—"Ask, make inquiries of, seek information from, those who are well skilled, are adepts, in any branch of knowledge [if you wish to improve yourself, to become a proficient in any thing]."

Percontatorem fugito, nam garrulus idem est. Lat. HORACE.—"Shun an inquisitive person, as he is always a tattler, a babbler."

"Shun the inquisitive, they'll talk again."

Or:— "Th' impertinent be sure to hate:
Who loves to ask will love to prate."

Again:— "Shun the inquisitive and curious man:
For what he hears he will relate again."

Those who inquire much into the affairs of others are seldom capable of retaining the secrets that they learn.

Perdidit arma, locum virtutis deseruit, qui
Semper in augenda festinat et obruitur re. Lat. HORACE.—

"The man, who is perpetually busy and wrapped up, altogether engrossed, in amassing wealth, has thrown down his arms, and has basely abandoned the post of virtue."

"The man, who thirsts for gold, hath left the post
Where virtue placed him, and his arms hath lost:
To purchase hasty wealth his force applies,
And overwhelmed beneath his burden lies."

N.B. By *arma* the poet means the precepts of virtue and wisdom. The Deity has sent us into this world to combat our passions. The man, who gives ground, is like the coward that has thrown away his arms, and abandoned the post it was his duty to preserve.

Père La Chaise. Fr.—The name of the eastern cemetery of Paris, so called from the circumstance of its site having belonged to a Jesuit named "*La Chaise.*" N.B. Cemeteries in France are not allowed to be *within* the towns or cities.

Pereant amici, dum una inimici intercidant. Lat. CICERO.—"Let our friends perish, provided our enemies fall at the same time." This, which was a proverb both with the Greeks and the Romans, is quoted by the orator only to be marked by his reprobation. It is a sentiment which bears the stamp of a cold, or rather of a most detestable, selfishness.

Pereant, qui ante nos nostra dixerunt! Lat. DONATUS [a learned grammarian: the instructor of Saint Jerome, and a commentator on Terence.]—"Would that those persons had never existed, who gave utterance to the very same thoughts that occur to ourselves!" By this exclamation DONATUS acknowledged the truth of the adage, "*Nihil dictum, quod non dictum prius*" [*which see*]: an adage in some measure resembling our English one, "There is nothing new under the sun!"

Pereunt, et imputantur. Lat. MARTIAL.—"They [the hours] disappear, vanish, pass away, and are charged to us, are placed to our account."

Perfer et obdura. Lat. OVID.—"Bear with, bear patiently, submit with resignation to, any trouble that presses on you, that oppresses or overwhelms you, and show yourself unmoved by it, steel yourself against it."

Perfervidum ingenium. Lat.—"A very hot, hasty, fierce, fiery, disposition."

Perfide Albion. Fr.—"Perfidious, false, or treacherous, Albion [England]." "No longer do the French look on England as the *perfide Albion:* the day has gone by."

Perfulgent eo ipso quod non videantur. Lat.—"They beam forth, shine more refulgently, are infinitely more conspicuous, inasmuch as they are not seen, are not patent to the sight." "Nor is it the *works of man* only that testify by their ruin, *perfulgent eo ipso quod non videantur*, the divine truth; the very *features of Nature* herself have accommodated themselves to the most improbable predictions [of Scripture]; the prophetic curses of barrenness, desolation, affliction, and slavery, pronounced against the rich, flourishing, and powerful countries and inhabitants of Egypt, Judea, Assyria, and Arabia, have been, to our own ocular knowledge, rigorously fulfilled, and are still in unmitigated force. In short, it may be asserted that what we venture, for conciseness, to call the *geographical denunciations* of the prophecies have been all executed with the most surprising, but most indisputable, accuracy."

Periculosae plenum opus aleae. Lat. HORACE.—"A work full of dangerous hazard, an undertaking full of danger and of hazard."

"Doubtful the die, and dire the cast!"

N.B. The metaphor of the poet is borrowed from the Roman games of chance: hence the quotation has been applied to the gamester.

"Curst is the wretch, enslaved to such a vice,
Who ventures life and soul upon the dice."

Periculosum est credere et non credere:
Ergo exploranda est veritas multum, prius
Quam stulta prave judicet sententia. Lat. PHAEDRUS.—"It is equally dangerous [hastily] to believe and not to believe: the truth should, therefore, be most rigidly investigated before we suffer ourselves, lest we suffer ourselves, to be led away by an erroneous conclusion, opinion."

Periculum ex aliis facito, tibi quod ex usu siet. Lat. TERENCE.—"Take example from others of, learn from the example of others, what may be to your own advantage." See "*Felix quem faciunt,*" *&c.*, and "*Aliena optimum,*" *&c.*

Periere mores, jus, decus, pietas, fides,
Et, qui redire nescit, cum perit, pudor. Lat. SENECA.—"We have lost our morals, justice, honor, piety, and integrity, and with these that modest sense of shame which, when once extinguished, can never be restored." This is one of the complaints that are frequently, and at all times, repeated of the dissoluteness of the existing age.

Periturae parcite chartae. Lat. JUVENAL.—"Spare the paper, which is fated to perish." A phrase of supplication, phrase intended to bespeak the tender mercies of the reader, which is sometimes prefixed to a work of a light and fugitive character.

"In pity spare us when we do our best
To make as much waste paper as the rest."

Perjurii poena divina exitium, humana dedecus. Lat.—"The crime of perjury is punished by Heaven with perdition, and by man with disgrace." This, which was one of the laws of the Romans, called the laws of the "*Twelve Tables,*" is sometimes quoted as a maxim by modern judges and lawyers. N.B. In the year of the city 300, the Romans, who had hitherto been governed by very imperfect laws, sent three deputies to Greece to make an exact collection of the laws of SOLON [one of the wise men of Greece, and the lawgiver of the Athenians]. On the return of the deputies, the *Decemviri* were created; that is, ten of the most distinguished citizens were appointed with sovereign authority to dispose these laws under proper heads and propose them to the people. They were at first summed up in ten tables, but in the following year two more were added. Hence they were called "THE LAWS OF THE TWELVE TABLES [the foundation of the Roman jurisprudence]."

Permissu superiorum. Lat.—"By or with the leave, permission, of the [*ecclesiastical*] superiors [the Romish Prelates, Archbishops and Bishops]." "Such meetings had been recommended *permissu superiorum.*"

Permitte Divis cetera. Lat. HORACE.—"Leave the rest to the gods." Discharge your duty, and leave the rest to Providence.

Permittes ipsis expendere numinibus quid
Conveniat nobis, rebusque sit utile nostris.
Carior est illis homo quam sibi. Lat. JUVENAL.—"Leave the gods to consider, judge, what is proper for us, and suitable to our peculiar sphere in life, inasmuch as man is dearer to them than he is to himself."

"Intrust thy fortune to the powers above:
Leave them to manage for thee, and to grant
What their unerring wisdom sees thee want.
In goodness as in greatness they excel:
Ah! that we loved ourselves but half so well!"

Pernicibus alis. Lat. VIRGIL.—"With swift wings." With rapid flight. "Scandal passes *pernicibus alis* from house to house."

Perpetuum mobile. Lat.—"Perpetual motion." "They are not hurried on by those admirers of change for change's sake, who so felicitously jumble physics and ethics, looking for the *summum bonum* [which see], and finding the *perpetuum mobile.*"

——————**Perpetuus nulli datur usus, et heres**
Heredem alterius, velut unda supervenit undam.
Lat. HORACE.—"The perpetual enjoyment of things is given to no one, and one heir gives place to another, as wave succeeds wave."

Perruques. Fr.—*Literally*, "Wigs, perukes," but often used to signify "Prejudiced old men." "The gallant old soldier speaks a different language from what our ancient *perruques* here drivel."

Persiflage. Fr.—"Quizzing." The external faculty of polite contempt, and also—The art of general inward contempt. The two are frequently combined in the same individual.

Persifleur. Fr.—"A quizzer." One who indulges in *persiflage.*

Persona ingrata. Lat.—"They assume that he is a *persona ingrata* to his Majesty," that is, a "person unacceptable, offensive, or objectionable," to, &c.

Personnel. Fr.—"Body or staff." "The entire *personnel* of the Embassy."

Persta atque obdura. Lat. HORACE.—"Persevere and hold out." Constantly bear in mind the adage of "NEVER GIVE UP."

Pessimae reipublicae plurimae leges. Lat. TACITUS.—"A very bad republic has generally a vast number of laws." "He adds that the weakness and fragility of a constitution are in exact proportion to the multiplicity of written laws to which it has given rise; thus commenting the well-known sentence of TACITUS: *Pessimae,*" *&c.*

Pessimum genus inimicorum laudantes. Lat. TACITUS.—"Flatterers are the worst kind of enemies." You cannot guard against their attacks. A secret mine is more to be dreaded than an open assault.

Petit bourgeois. Fr.—"A second-rate citizen, cit."

Petit littérateur. Fr.—"A petty man of letters, literary man: mere dabbler in literature, mere cipher in the republic of letters."

Petit maître. Fr.—"A fop, coxcomb, spark, conceited puppy."

——————**Petite hinc, juvenesque senesque,**
Finem animo certum, miserisque viatica canis.

Lat. PERSIUS.—

"Now hence, both old and young, with profit learn
The bounds of good and evil to discern."

Or:— "Seek here, ye young, the anchor of your mind;
Here, suffering age, a blest provision find."

N.B. The poet alludes to the study of philosophy: the quotation has, however, been applied to the best of all philosophy, to the cultivation of true religion, as a solace to high and low, old and young, rich and poor.

Petites affiches. Fr.—"Advertisements."

Petitio ad misericordiam. Lat.—"An appeal to mercy, compassion."

Petitio principii. Lat.—"A begging of the question." N.B. "A *petitio principii*," which is a logical term, is the supposition of what is not granted, or a supposed proof, by stating the question in other words.

Petits soins. Fr.—"Little attentions." "All his *petits soins* were addressed to her ladyship."

Petulanti splene cachinno. Lat. PERSIUS.—"A great laugher, scorner, or scoffer, of a waggish, sportive, sarcastic, turn of mind." "The professor had sometimes an auditor or two of another stamp, some *petulanti splene cachinno*, who came to spy out the barrenness of the land and bring back to the evening party a few precious fragments of sounding inanity or dexterous sophistry."

Peu de bien, peu de soin. Fr. prov.—"He, who has not much wealth, has not much care, is not overburdened with cares."

Peu de gens savent être vieux. Fr. ROCHEFOUCAULT.—"Few persons know how to be old." When the manners of youth are suffered to accompany old age, they only tend to make it ridiculous.

Peu de gens sont assez sages pour préférer le blâme, qui leur est utile, à la louange, qui les trahit. Fr. ROCHEFOUCAULT.—"Few are so wise as to prefer the censure which may be useful to them, to the flattery which betrays them."

Phase. From the Gr. word *φασις* [phasis]—"an appearance."—The appearance exhibited by any body, such as a change of the moon. "There are various morbid *phases* of the intellect, that do not amount to derangement." "The man has three *phases* [aspects]: diurnal, general, and metaphorical."

Φημι πολυχρονιην μελετην εμμεναι, φιλε· και δη
Ταυτην ανθρωποισι τελευτωσαν φυσιν ειναι. Gr.—

"Long exercise, my friend, inures the mind;
And what we once disliked, we pleasing find."

Custom is second nature.

Philippic.—An invective, severe castigation, animadversion, reproof, reprimand; "calling over the coals." "*Philippics*" was the name given to the orations of DEMOSTHENES [the most distinguished orator of Greece] against PHILIP, King of Macedon, to rouse the Athenians against PHILIP, and guard against his crafty policy. They are esteemed the master-pieces of that great orator. CICERO's *Philippics* [written in imitation of those of DEMOSTHENES] cost him his life, MARC ANTONY having been so exasperated by them that, when he became one of the triumvirate [the government of three individuals, each possessing like authority], he procured CICERO's murder, cut off his head, and stuck it up in the very place where the orator had delivered his *philippics*.

Philosophia nec aliud quicquam est, si interpretari velis, quam amor sapientiae. Lat. CICERO.—"Philosophy, if rightly defined, is naught but the [true] love of wisdom."

Philosophia simulari potest; eloquentia non potest. Lat. QUINTILIAN.—"Philosophy may be feigned, counterfeited, pretended; eloquence cannot." On some subjects our knowledge cannot be instinctive, but must be acquired. A neglect of this distinction necessarily leads to erroneous inferences. Compare *Poeta nascitur, non fit*, which see.

Philosophia stemma non inspicit. Platonem non accepit nobilem philosophia, sed fecit. Lat. SENECA.—"Philosophy does not look into pedigrees. She did not find PLATO noble [by nature], but she made him so." In the eye of true philosophy, all men are equal; distinction is only to be acquired by superior worth and talents.

Phoenix literarum. Lat.—"The phoenix of literature: the reviver of learning, the restorer of classical literature [and classical literature involved literature in general]." Applied by the learned throughout Europe to REUCHLIN, the most distinguished luminary of the fifteenth century. He was also looked up to as the "*eruditorum αλφα*," "the first of the learned." CARDINAL FISHER, who made a pilgrimage from England for the sole purpose of visiting this brilliant scholar, candidly confesses to ERASMUS that he regarded REUCHLIN as "bearing off from all men the palm of knowledge, especially in what pertained to the hidden matters of religion and philosophy." N.B. "The phoenix," says PLINY, "is a bird of Arabia, of the size of an eagle, and of which there is never but one. It lives five hundred years, according to most writers, though some say three hundred and forty, but others four hundred and sixty; and, when come to its end, makes its nest of hot spices, which being set on fire by the heat of the sun, it burns, and from the ashes arises a worm, which afterwards grows to be a phoenix." TERTULLIAN, ST. AMBROSE, and others cite this [fabulous] bird as a rational argument for the resurrection of the human body.

Φωναντα συνετοισι. Gr.—"Observations addressed to the wise, intelligent, to those who can understand, who are *wide awake*."

Phrenology.—From the Gr. words *φρην* [phren], and *λογος* [logos], a word. A new science, or pretended science, which professes to teach the knowledge of the mind from the form of the head. This modern system of Cranioscopy [Skull-Examination] is misnamed. It is not entitled to the appellation of Phrenology. *Φρην* properly signifies "the membranes of the heart," but especially "the diaphragm." The term has no relation whatever to the substance of the brain, or the skull, which incloses it. The diaphragm was originally thought to be the seat of the mind, and the term, analogically, and not properly, came to be used to signify "mind." With what propriety, therefore, is it adopted to distinguish a science of mind which expressly removes its seat from the heart to the brain?

Φυγη μονον προς μονον. Gr. PLOTINUS.—"The ascent or flight of the soul, which is one, simple, and uncompounded, to that Being, who is ONE and ALONE in an eminent and incommunicable sense; GOD HIMSELF!" N.B. The language of PLOTINUS in this passage is so sublime and full of meaning, that, without a paraphrase, it is absolutely *impossible* to express the ideas contained in it. Every Greek scholar will readily coincide in this opinion.

Φυσει εισι φιλοτεκνοι πασαι αἱ γυναικες. Gr. LYCURGUS.—"All women are naturally fond of their children, naturally love their children."

Physique du globe. Fr.—"Terrestrial physics, the natural philosophy of the earth."

Pia fraus. Lat.—"A pious fraud, a charitable fraud, fraud originating in motives of benevolence." "He finds it impossible to ascribe the rarity of convictions to any *pia fraus* of grand jurors in defeating the law."

————————————Pia mater
Plus quam se sapere, et virtutibus esse priorem
Vult. Lat. HORACE.—

"An affectionate mother wishes that her offspring may be wiser and better than herself."

"With sage advice, and many a sober truth,
The pious mother molds to shape the youth."

Willingly does she give her children the benefit of her experience.

————————Pictoribus atque poetis
Quidlibet audendi semper fuit aequa potestas.
Lat. HORACE.—

"Painters and poets have always had the privilege to attempt whatever they pleased."

"Painters and poets our indulgence claim,
Their daring equal, and their art the same."

The sister arts are entitled to avail themselves of equal boldness of invention.

Pie poudre. Law Fr.—"The court of *pie poudre* is the lowest court recognized by the law of England." N.B. "*Pie poudre*" means *dusty feet.* The etymology [account of the true origin of words] of the name is somewhat doubtful. Sir EDWARD COKE says that it has its name, because justice is done "as speedily as dust can fall from the foot," while others derive it from the "dusty feet" of the suitors. Mr. Barrington derives it more satisfactorily from *pieds puldreaux*, a peddler in old French—a court of petty chapmen, such as resort to fairs and markets.

Pièce de position. Fr.—"Heavy guns." "They lined the heights of the right bank with *pièces de position.*"

Pièce de résistance. Fr.—"A solid joint of meat."

Pièces de théâtre. Fr.—"Plays of every description: theatrical pieces or compositions."

Pied-à-terre. Fr.—"She strains her strength to hold a *pied-à-terre* on that side of the Black Sea:" that is, to hold a *position*, &c.

Piensa el ladron que todos son de su condicion. Span. prov.—"The thief thinks that all persons are like himself, are of his profession."

Pietate adversum Deum sublata, fides etiam et societas

humani generis tollitur. Lat. CICERO.—"Piety, religious feeling, being once lost sight of, there is an end to all integrity and social intercourse"

—————Piger scribendi ferre laborem,
Scribendi recte; nam ut multum, nil moror. Lat. HORACE.—"He was too indolent to undergo the toil of writing, I mean of writing correctly; for, as to how much he wrote, I do not at all concern myself about that." The poet alludes to LUCILIUS, a Roman knight, who was a very voluminous writer. The quotation may be applied with propriety to the numerous tribe of careless writers, who cannot endure the labor of revising or correcting their works.

Pindarum quisquis studet aemulari,
Iule, ceratis ope Daedalea
Nititur pennis, vitreo daturus
Nomina ponto. Lat. HORACE.—"Whoever attempts to rival PINDAR trusts to waxen wings, first contrived by the art of DAEDALUS, and will give his name to the sparkling deep, to the glassy ocean, the sea, that sparkles like glass:" in other words, Whoever shall attempt to imitate PINDAR will experience as terrible a downfall as ICARUS.

"He, who to PINDAR's height attempts to rise,
Like ICARUS, with waxen pinions tries
His pathless way, and from the venturous theme
Shall leave to azure seas his falling name."

The allusion is to ICARUS, the son of DAEDALUS, who is fabled to have fled from Crete on artificial wings, when, the sun melting his waxen pinions, he fell into the Icarian Sea. The lesson has reference to the difficulty of what is called Pindaric poetry; the ancient and modern imitators of that bard having generally given naught but flights of extravagance instead of flights of genius.

Piquant. Fr.—"Pungent." "The smallest trait of *piquant* truth excites their anger."

Pis-aller. Fr.—"A last shift, make-shift."

Place aux dames. Fr.—"Room, make room, for the ladies." "*Place aux dames* is a maxim of gallantry."

Place de Grève. Fr.—A public square in Paris, where executions formerly took place. N.B. Very generally *incorrectly* written; thus, *Place de la Grève,* instead of as above.

Placeat homini quidquid Deo placet. Lat. SENECA.—"Whatever is pleasing to GOD should be pleasing, satisfactory, to man."

Plausibus ex ipsis populi, laetoque furore,
Ingenium quodvis incaluisse potest. Lat. OVID.—"Any one, however clever, may be excused for being warmed, growing warm, with the applauses of the people, and their ebullitions of joy, their transports or raptures of delight."

Plebs. Lat.—"The common people:" hence "plebeian," one of the common people.

Pleins pouvoirs. Fr.—"Full power, authority." A diplomatic phrase.

Plenus rimarum sum; hac atque illac perfluo. Lat. TERENCE.—

"I am full of holes, am a blab of my tongue; I cannot keep a secret, as whatever is told me is sure to escape me." "The writer's brains have doubtless been molded after the fashion of the servant in TERENCE:—'*Plenus rimarum,*' *&c.* All his reading has run out immediately on its entrance, and his brains have been left as dry as they were previously to that process of percolation."

Pleonasm.—From the Gr. word *πλεοναςμος* [pleonasmos], "redundancy, superfluity."—A redundancy in speech or in writing, as when we say, "I saw it with my eyes." The three last words are unnecessary.

Plerumque gratae divitibus vices. Lat. HORACE.—"Changes are generally agreeable to the wealthy: variety is, for the most part, pleasing to the great." The poet alludes to the love of variety, so generally prevalent in those who can afford to indulge in it.

——————————Plerumque modestus
Occupat obscuri speciem, taciturnus acerbi. Lat. HORACE.—"A modest man has often the appearance of one that is reserved and close, a silent man of one that is morose."

"The modest oft too dark appear,
The silent thoughtfully severe."

See "*Fronti nulla fides.*"

Plerumque stulti, risum dum captant levem,
Gravi destringunt alios contumelia,
Et sibi nocivum concitant periculum. Lat. PHAEDRUS.—"In their endeavors to have a laugh at others, fools often indulge in the most insulting conduct, and by such proceedings generally do themselves serious injury."

Plethora. Gr., in Roman letters.—An undue fullness of the vessels of the body: a fullness of body, of bodily humors.

Ploratur lacrymis amissa pecunia veris. Lat. JUVENAL.—"The loss of money is deplored with real tears." Whatever may be affected on other subjects, nothing wounds the feelings of most men so much as their pecuniary losses.

Ploravere suis non respondere favorem
Speratum meritis. Lat. HORACE.—"They found, with grief, or to their sorrow, that they were far from meeting with the acknowledgment due to their merit: they lamented that the encouragement for which they had hoped did not await upon their merits." By no means an unusual complaint of men of talent in every walk of life.

Πλουτου δ' ουδεν τερμα· χρηματα τοις θνητοις γιγνεται αφροσυνη. Gr. THEOGNIS.—"With men there is no bound, limit, to riches [they are never satisfied]: riches are the madness, insanity, of mortals." The incessant craving after wealth clearly shows that the mass of mankind are devoid of reason, labor under the loss of reason, though apparently in full possession of their senses. See "*Quid non mortalia,*" *&c.*

Plura faciunt homines e consuetudine quam e ratione. Lat.—"Men do more things from custom than from reason." In our general conduct we are found to act rather from habit than from reflection.

Plura sunt quae nos terrent quam quae premunt; et saepius opinione quam re laboramus. Lat. SENECA.—"Our alarms are much more numerous than our dangers, and we suffer much oftener in imagination than in reality." The experience of human life has proved that imaginary terrors occur more frequently than real dangers.

Plures crapula quam gladius. Lat. prov.—"Gluttony, gormandizing, over-feeding, kills more than the sword."

Pluries. Lat. Law term.—"At several times." A name given to a writ, which issues after two former writs have gone out without effect. The original writ is the *capias* [which see]; then follows an *alias* [which see]; which failing, the *pluries* issues.

——————————**Plurima sunt, quae**
Non audent homines pertusa dicere laena. Lat. JUVENAL.—"There are very many things, which men dare not give utterance to when in rags and tatters."

Plurimum facere, et minimum ipso de se loqui. Lat. TACITUS.—"To do the most and say the least of himself: to do a great deal, and say as little as possible both of himself and his deeds." The portrait given by the Roman historian of a great but unostentatious character. See "*Res, non verba.*"

Pluris est oculatus testis unus quam auriti decem. Lat. PLAUTUS.—"One eye-witness is of more weight than ten who give evidence merely from hearsay."

Plus. Lat.—"More."

Plus aloës quam mellis habet. Lat. JUVENAL.—"He has more gall than honey in him." Applied to a writer whose *forte* [which see] lies chiefly in sarcasm. The phrase may also be translated—"There is more trouble than pleasure in it: the bitter overbalances the sweet."

Plus apud nos vera ratio valeat quam vulgi opinio. Lat. CICERO.—"Right, sound, reason should have, ought to have, more influence with us than popular opinion, than the mere opinion of the people, of the masses."

Plus dolet quam necesse est, qui ante dolet quam necesse est. Lat. SENECA.—"He who grieves before it is necessary, grieves more than is necessary."

——————————**Plus est quam vita salusque**
Quod perit: in totum mundi prosternimur aevum.
Lat. LUCAN.—
"More than life and safety is lost in the present conflict: we are laid prostrate even to the last epoch of the world." Said by the poet in lamenting the consequences of the battle fought between CAESAR and POMPEY at Pharsalia. It is now often used to describe conflicts of a different kind in the way of exaggeration, and when not national but personal interest is concerned.

Plus impetus, majorem constantiam, penes miseras. Lat. TACITUS.—"There is more violence as well as greater perseverance among the lowly and the wretched." A wise government will, therefore, always be cautious of provoking this description of men to opposition or resistance.

Plus in amicitia valet similitudo morum quam affinitas. Lat. CORNELIUS NEPOS.—"Similarity of manners and congeniality of taste are stronger motives for, inducements to, friendship than mere relationship."

Plus in posse quam in actu. Lat.—"More in power than in act." "Science offers us great store of life *plus in posse,*" *&c.*

Plus negabit in una hora unus asinus quam centum doctores in centum annis probaverint. Lat.—"An ass, blockhead, will deny more in a single hour than a hundred doctors have proved in a hundred years." The remark of DR. JOHNSON to a pert dogmatician.

Plus ratio quam vis caeca valere solet. Lat. CORNELIUS GALLUS.—"Reason can generally do more than blind force." That which cannot be done by mere strength is sometimes to be accomplished by address.

Plus salis quam sumtus. Lat. CORNELIUS NEPOS.—"More sense, sound sense, refinement, than expense [displayed]." A proper definition of a philosophical entertainment.

Plutôt mourir que changer. Fr.—"Sooner die than change."

Pobres vergonzantes. Span.—"The blushing poor," the poor who would rather smother their griefs, sorrows, toils, and troubles, than proclaim them to an unfeeling world. The French have a similar expression, though not quite so expressive, "*pauvres honteux.*" See "*Curae leves loquuntur,*" *&c.*

Poco curante. Ital.—"The *poco curante* inhabitants of Naples enjoy their refreshments *al fresco*" [which see]: that is, The *listless, free-from-care, or give-themselves-no-trouble* inhabitants, &c.

Poco di matto. Ital.—"Slight tinge of madness." "Feeding constantly on lofty hopes, COLUMBUS acquired an exaltation of character, which fools thought madness; but there was a method in that enthusiasm, that '*poco di matto,*' which BACON thought essential to those who aspired to great things."

Podestà. Ital.—"Chief magistrate."

Poëmatis personae. Lat.—"Poetic personages or characters: persons who figure in a poem."

Poena ad paucos, metus ad omnes. Lat.—"Punishment for the few, fear for all."

Poëta nascitur, non fit. Lat. prov.—"The poet is born a poet, and not made so by artificial means." Education can form men after its own image, or rather, after the image of the schoolmaster, but not all the education in the world will of itself make a man a SHAKSPEARE, a NEWTON, a LOCKE, a PORSON, or a FARADAY; in all such cases there must be inborn talent of the very highest order, the gift of Omnipotence alone; for, as CICERO tells us, *Nemo vir magnus sine afflatu aliquo divino unquam fuit;* that is, No one has ever become a great man without some degree or measure of divine inspiration.

Point d'argent, point de Suisse. Fr. prov.—"No money, no Swiss [to fight for you]." An allusion to the mercenary services of that people. "No longer pipe, no longer dance."

———————————**Pol, me occidistis, amici,**
Non servastis, ait, cui sic extorta voluptas,
Et demtus per vim mentis gratissimus error. Lat. HORACE.—"Verily, my friends," says he, "far from curing, you have undone me, in thus depriving me of so great a pleasure, and forcibly tearing from me the grateful illusion." Your misplaced zeal has inflicted on me an irreparable

injury. The poet alludes to a monomaniac [one who is mad on a *single* point] who would infinitely rather have remained uncured.

Πολλοι μαθηται κρειττονες διδασκαλων. Gr. prov.—

"Full many a pupil has become
More famous than his master."

Πολυ το μεσον. Gr. EURIPIDES.—"There is a great difference." The passage that WORDSWORTH had in view when he said of his Lucy, "*Oh! the difference to me.*"

Πολυτελες βρωμα. Gr. ATHENAEUS.—"Very expensive eating." In reference to pheasants, that had been reared for a royal table.

Pompa mortis magis terret quam mors ipsa. Lat.—"The solemnity of death is more terrible than death itself."

Ponamus nimios gemitus; flagrantior aequo
Non debet dolor esse viri, nec vulnere major. Lat. JUVENAL. "Let us dismiss all excessive sorrow; a man's grief should not pass the bounds of propriety, or show itself greater than the infliction." A man is degraded by that womanish sorrow which knows no bounds and passes far beyond the occasion.

Ponderanda sunt testimonia, non numeranda. Lat. ULPIAN. —"Testimonies [on every point] should be well considered, weighed, and not merely counted, reckoned up."

Pons asinorum. Lat.—"The asses' bridge." The name given by the students at Cambridge to the Fifth Proposition of the first book of EUCLID.

Pontifex maximus. Lat.—"The highest pontiff, or chief priest." One of the designations of the Pope.

Ponton. Fr. military term.—"A temporary bridge for an army." *Pontonniers*, men who are employed in the construction of such bridges.

Popularis aura. Lat. HORACE.—"The breath of popular favor or applause: the humor of the mob."

Populum falsis dedocet uti vocibus. Lat. HORACE.—[Philosophy, true wisdom] "teaches the populace to disuse false names for things: rectifies the judgment of the vulgar, who are accustomed to use names for things."

"From cheats of words the crowd he brings
To real estimates of men and things:"

Or:— "True virtue can the crowd unteach
Their false, mistaken forms of speech."

The masses, in a false use of words, disguise the real nature of things by mistaken names. "*Auferre, trucidare, rapere,*" says TACITUS, "FALSIS NOMINIBUS, *imperium; atque, ubi solitudinem faciunt, pacem appellant.*" See the quotation.

————**Populus me sibilat, at mihi plaudo**
Ipse domi, simul ac nummos contemplor in arca.
Lat. HORACE.—

"The people hiss me, but I applaud or congratulate myself at home, as often as I gloat over the money in my chest, cash-box."

————"Let them hiss on [he cries],
While, in my own opinion fully blest,
I count my money, and enjoy my chest."

The consolation of misers, SECRETARIES, AND DIRECTORS! OF SWINDLING COMPANIES.

Populus vult decipi et decipiatur. Lat.—"The people like to be imposed on; so let them be imposed on."

Port de relâche. Fr.—"A place, or port, at which ships may touch, call, or put into."

Porte.—In the metaphorical language of the East, the state is represented as a palace, or rather as a tent; its foundations are the law [the Koran], the customs, and the decrees of the ruling Sultan. The gate [the *Porte*] is, as it were, an image of the whole edifice; it signifies the whole government, in allusion to the patriarchal times, when the head of the tribe sat as judge and ruler "in the gate." The term Gate, or *Porte*, is likewise used in a subordinate sense for the whole military array; and, thirdly, it is applied to the inner palace or harem. In this sense it is the gate of "bliss;" in the former the sublime *Porte* of the empire, or the gate of "good fortune." Within this inner gate "of bliss" is not only the harem, but the treasury, and the divan.

Porte-monnaie. Fr.—"A flat purse:" literally, a "coin-holder, coin-case."

Posse comitatus. Lat.—"The power of the county: the armed force of a county," whence *posse*, any armed force. A levy, which the sheriff is authorized to call forth whenever opposition is made to the King's writ or to the execution of justice.

Possunt, quia posse videntur. Lat. VIRGIL.—"They are able to accomplish any thing they take in hand, because they seem to themselves to have the power necessary for so doing."

"For they can conquer, who believe they can."

The advantage of self-confidence, self-reliance.

"To what," says KENEALY in his "Brallaghan, or the Deipnosophists," "is not this little sentence applicable? In company we please, because we try to please. In politics, in law, in every science or pursuit in the world, we succeed, because we *think* we shall succeed, and therefore exert our best efforts to do so. If EPICTETUS, in his epitome of all worldly philosophy, 'BEAR AND FORBEAR,' teaches the true rule for the government of man, VIRGIL teaches the surest path to success. I do not know a nobler motto for a young man."

Post amicitiam credendum est, ante amicitiam judicandum. Lat. SENECA.—"After forming a friendship you should place the utmost confidence; before that period you should exercise your judgment." In a state of perfect friendship, there should be nothing like hesitation or distrust on either side.

Post bellum auxilium. Lat.—"Help after the war." Vain and superfluous assistance, offered when the difficulty or danger is passed.

Post-captain.—"The origin of this strange term '*post*-captain,'" says a writer in the Quarterly Review, "now abolished in the navy, we conceive to be this: masters and commanders, or even lieutenants, commanding a vessel, though popularly called *captains*, have no claim to that title nor to regular advancement by seniority, but may be promoted to the superior ranks over the heads of their seniors; while the *captain*, properly so called, when once placed on the list, *took his post*, and proceeded to the rank of admiral by mere seniority, from which there could be no deviation: so that, when an officer obtained that rank, he was said to be *posted;* that is, placed beyond the reach of favor or other contingencies."

Post cineres gloria sera venit. Lat. MARTIAL.—"Glory comes too late when we are naught but dust and ashes."

"Fame to our ashes comes, alas! too late:
And praise smells rank upon the coffin-plate."

Post equitem sedet atra cura. Lat. HORACE.—"Behind the horseman sits carking care."

"And when he mounts the flying steed,
Sits gloomy Care behind."

Said of a man whose conscience is ill at ease, and who vainly endeavors to fly from his own reflections.

Post factum nullum consilium. Lat.—"After the deed is done, consultation is useless, to no purpose." When an affair is irretrievable, nothing is more absurd than the discussion of what might have been done.

Post hoc. Lat.—"After this, this thing, matter, or circumstance."

Post homines natos. Lat. CICERO.—"Since the world began: since the creation of the world."

Post hominum memoriam. Lat. CICERO.—The same meaning as the preceding example.

Post malam segetem serendum est. Lat. SENECA.—"After a bad crop, you should instantly sow again." Instead of sinking under misfortune, we should immediately think of renewing our industry, of calling all our energies into play. See "*Tu ne cede malis,*" *&c.*

Post meridiem. Lat.—"After noon, noontide, mid-day." Usually written P.M.

Post mortem. Lat.—"After death." "A *post mortem* examination."

Post nubila Phoebus. Lat.—"After cloudy weather comes, shines forth, the sun." After adversity sometimes comes prosperity.

Post prandium. Lat.—"After dinner." "A very respectable *post prandium* speech."

Post tenebras lux. Lat.—"After darkness comes light." After so much concealment, we at length arrive at the truth.

Post tot naufragia portum. Lat.—"After so many shipwrecks, we get into port." After so many dangers, an asylum at length presents itself.

Postea. Lat. Law term.—"Afterwards." The name given to the writ by which the proceedings by *nisi prius* [which see] are returned after the verdict into the Court of Common Pleas.

Postulata. Lat.—"Postulates, things required." The admissions demanded from an adversary or opponent, before the main argument is entered upon. N.B. A "*postulate*" is that which in argument is demanded to be conceded or granted without proof.

Potentia cautis quam acribus consiliis tutius habetur. Lat. TACITUS.—"Power is more safely retained by cautious than by severe counsels." Mildness combined with vigilance, as a prop of power, is more to be relied upon than a system of irritating severity.

Potentissimus est qui se habet in potestate. Lat. SENECA.—

"Most powerful is he who has himself in his power:" who is able to command himself. See "*Latius regnes,*" *&c.*, and "*Fortior est qui se,*" *&c.*

Pour avoir du goût, il faut avoir de l'âme. Fr. VAUVENARGUES.—"In order to have [*critical*] taste, we must have a soul [*that can feel, feelingly alive*], we must have a heart and an imagination."

Pour bien instruire, il ne faut pas dire tout ce qu'on sait, mais seulement ce qui convient à ceux qu'on instruit. Fr. LA HARPE.—"To instruct well, we must not tell all that we know, but simply what is suitable to those whom we are teaching." The master should carefully avoid any ostentatious display of his own learning.

Pour comble de bonheur. Fr.—"As the height, the completion, of happiness."

Pour connaître le prix de l'argent, il faut être obligé d'en emprunter. Fr.—"In order to know the value of money, a man must be obliged to borrow some." To know the value of money, try to borrow some from your *friends*.

Pour connaitre un homme, il faut avoir mangé un muid de sel avec lui. Fr. prov.—"To know a man thoroughly, you must have eaten a bushel of salt with him." You must be long acquainted with a man, ere you can know him thoroughly.

Pour encourager les autres. Fr.—"To encourage, or by way of encouragement to, others." Often used ironically. N.B. The above phrase is often used in an *abridged* form: thus, "*Pour encourager.*"

Pour faire de l'esprit. Fr.—"To be witty: to show off one's wit, one's witty disposition."

Pour faire rire. Fr.—"To excite laughter." "It was expressly written *pour faire rire.*"

Pour la populace ce n'est jamais par envie d'attaquer qu'elle se soulève, mais par impatience de souffrir. Fr. SULLY.—"It is never from a wish to attack that the mob rise, but simply because they are tired of suffering." A similar sentiment is expressed by BURKE in his pamphlet entitled "Thoughts on the Causes of the Present Discontents," published in 1770. "When," says he, "popular discontents have been prevalent, it may be well affirmed and supported, that there has been generally something found amiss with the constitution, or in the conduct of government: the people have no interest in disorder; when they do wrong it is their error, not their crime; but with the governing part of the state it is far otherwise."

Pour la représentation. Fr.—"To do the honors."

Pour passer le temps. Fr.—"To while away the time, to get over the time."

Pour s'établir dans le monde, on fait tout ce que l'on peut pour y paraître établi. Fr. ROCHEFOUCAULT.—"When a man has to establish himself in the world, he makes every effort in his power to exhibit himself as being already established."

Pour se faire valoir. Fr.—"To make one's self of value." "He spoke largely *pour se faire valoir,*" that is, to intimate that he should be looked upon as a man of consequence.

Pour toujours. Fr.—"Forever."

Pour un point, Martin perdit son âne. Fr. prov.—The explanation given by BLACKER of this is, that Martin, the Abbot of the Abbey Asello, ordered the line,

Porta patens esto, nulli claudaris honesto:
"[Gate, be thou open, be thou shut against no honest man],"

to be placed as an inscription over the gate; but, by the workman's blunder, the comma was misplaced, making the line,

Porta patens esto nulli, claudaris honesto:
"[Gate, be thou open to no one, be thou shut against the honest man]."

The Pope, passing by, was so outraged at this apparently scandalous motto of Martin, that he deprived him, and gave the abbacy to another, who erased the offensive inscription, and substituted

Pro solo puncto, caruit Martinus Asello:
"[For a single stop, Martin lost the Abbey of Asello]."

"*Asello*" in Italian meaning an ass, the French translated it as well as the rest of the sentence.

Pour vivre longtemps, il faut être vieux de bonne heure. Fr. prov.—"In order to live long, we must be old [in knowledge] in early life."

Pourparler. Fr.—"A parley, oral treaty, private consultation."

Praecepto monitus, saepe te considera. Lat. PHAEDRUS.—"Having been warned, advised, by a precept or lesson [worth listening to], examine thyself often carefully and steadily." Compare Γνωθι σεαυτον [Gnothi seauton], "Know thyself," the saying either of THALES the Milesian, one of the seven wise men of Greece, or of CHILO the Lacedaemonian philosopher, another of the seven wise men of Greece. "This saying," says JUVENAL, the distinguished Roman satirist, "came down to us from heaven."

Praecipuum munus annalium reor, ne virtutes sileantur, utque pravis dictis, factisque, ex posteritate et infamia metus sit. Lat. TACITUS.—"The principal office of history I consider to be this: to prevent virtuous actions from being passed over in silence, and that fear of an opprobrious verdict from posterity should attach itself to foul expressions and vicious conduct." This maxim, from the pen of the great historian, shows the use and benefit of history.

Praeferre patriam liberis regem decet. Lat. SENECA.—"A king should prefer his country to his children." His duty to his subjects should be of greater consideration with him than his family affections.

Praelectiones academicae. Lat.—"Lectures given or delivered by professors of the learned languages to students at the Universities."

Praemia virtutis. Lat.—"The rewards of virtue." "Then only will virtue be at the highest when the *praemia virtutis* are at the highest."

Praemissis praemittendis. Lat.—"Passing over those things that may reasonably be omitted."

Praemoniti praemuniti. Lat. Law maxim.—"Forewarned, forearmed." "Law maxims," says a distinguished writer, "may be adduced as examples of proverbs. Lord Coke's definition of them is, 'propositions to be of all men confessed and granted, without proof, argument, or discourse.'"

Praemunire. Law Lat.—"The first word of a writ, by which offenders are, in certain cases, put out of the protection of the law." "The Dean escaped the penalties of *praemunire:*" that is, *imprisonment and forfeiture of his goods.*

Praenomen. Lat.—The *first* name of the three which the ancient Romans usually had: thus, PUBLIUS Virgilius Maro; QUINTUS Horatius Flaccus; MARCUS Tullius Cicero. N.B. The *plural* is "*Praenomina.*"

Praepropera consilia raro sunt prospera. Lat. LORD COKE.—"Very hasty, over-hasty, precipitate, counsels, advice, designs, resolutions, determinations, decisions, are seldom prosperous, successful, attended with success."

Praeproperum ac fervidum ingenium. Lat. LIVY.—"A hot-headed man, a hot-spur." "The hero of our story showed himself, even on the most trifling occasions, a *praeproperum ac fervidum ingenium.*"

Praesens in tempus. Lat. HORACE.—"For the present time; at the present time; for the present; at present."

Praesens vel imo tollere de gradu
Mortale corpus, vel superbos
Vertere funeribus triumphos. Lat. HORACE.—

"O thou, that in an instant canst raise mortal man from the lowest to the highest degree, or change pompous triumphs into funerals [thee does every one invoke]." Addressed by the poet to FORTUNE.

Praesertim, ut nunc sunt mores, adeo res redit,
Si quis quid reddit, magna habenda est gratia.

Lat. TERENCE.—

"In the present state or phase of society more especially, things have come to that pass, that if a man pays his debts, it must be considered by his creditors as a great favor."

Praeses. Lat.—"One who presides, either alone or with others, in the administration of affairs public or private, sacred or civil; a magistrate." N.B. The use of this word for "*chairman*" or "*president*" is confined to the Scotch, and they invariably make a point of spelling it wrong: thus, *preses* instead of *praeses.*

Praesidium et dulce decus. Lat. HORACE.—"A patron of literary men, and one in whose patronage, under whose protection, they may glory and exult."

Praestat amicitia propinquitati. Lat. CICERO.—"Friendship is infinitely better than relationship, kinship."

Praestat cautela potius quam medela. Lat. LORD COKE.—"Precaution, prevention, is infinitely better than cure, than remedial measures."

Praestat habere acerbos inimicos quam eos amicos, qui dulces videntur. Lat. CATO.—"Better is it to have open, avowed, enemies, than those friends who are only so in name, than those persons who merely wear the garb of friendship."

Praestat otiosum esse quam nihil agere. Lat. PLINY.—"Better is it to be idle, altogether unemployed, than to do nothing that can turn to account."

Praeteriti anni. Lat. VIRGIL.—"The years that are passed, passed and gone." "We, too, could moralize over the *praeteriti anni;* but let that pass."

PRAGMATIC SANCTION.—An expression frequently made use of and referred to, but, comparatively speaking, but very imperfectly understood. The following extracts, however, will give an insight into the *true* meaning of the expression.

"CHARLES THE SIXTH, Emperor of Germany, left no son, and had long before his death relinquished all hopes of male issue. During the latter part of his life, his principal object had been to secure to his descendants in the female line the many crowns of the house of HAPSBURG. With this view, he had promulgated a new law of succession, widely celebrated throughout Europe under the name of the '*Pragmatic Sanction.*' By virtue of this decree, his daughter, the Archduchess Maria Theresa, wife of Francis of Lorraine, succeeded to the dominions of her ancestors."

"FERDINAND THE SEVENTH, King of Spain, among whose many bad and unkingly qualities want of foresight could not be reckoned, published the '*Pragmatic Sanction,*' that secured the crown to his offspring, should it prove a girl; and a girl it was."

"ST. LOUIS, King of France, wrote repeatedly to POPE ALEXANDER THE FOURTH, to obtain some relaxation of ecclesiastical immunities, became sensible of the associations among his barons and lords, and himself promulgated the '*Pragmatic Sanction,*' the Charter of the Liberties of the Gallican Church." A *true* copy of this important document may be seen in SISMONDI.

Pravo favore labi mortales solent,
Et, pro judicio dum stant erroris sui,
Ad poenitendum rebus manifestis agi. Lat. PHAEDRUS.—"Mankind are accustomed to fall into mistakes through prejudice, through perverse or improper prepossessions in favor of any one, and whilst they boldly and doggedly stand up in defense of their erroneous judgment, are at length compelled to recant, acknowledge their error by the powerful, all-potent evidence of facts."

Prava diligentia. Lat.—"Ill-judged, misplaced, misapplied, wrongly applied, industry, labor, or toil; rascally and specious industry, labor, toil: attention to matters from purely selfish motives, from interested motives alone." "In what we have hitherto stated, we have not touched those evils, which are superadded by the elaborate errors, the *prava diligentia*, of lawyers, whose learned folly has encumbered their science with defects not necessary to it."

Précepte commence, exemple achève. Fr. prov.—"Precept begins, but example completes, puts or gives the finishing-stroke." Children will act not so much from what they are taught, as from what they see.

Preces armatae. Lat.—"Armed prayers." Claims made with feigned submission, but which at the same time will be enforced if not at once allowed or granted.

Précieuse. Fr.—"A prude, a coy, conceited, finical, or precise, woman." "She became a *précieuse.*"

Précis. Fr.—"An abstract, a summary, an epitome, an abridgment."

A *diplomatic* term. A "*précis* writer" is one who can make such abstracts, summaries, epitomes, or abridgments.

Préfet. Fr.—"A Prefect." A *Prefect* in France is a *chief magistrate or governor, invested with the general administration of a department;* as, "*The Prefect of the Department of La Seine.*"

Premier pas. Fr.—"The first or main difficulty, first step, first or chief consideration, the puzzle." "The *premier pas* was how the entrance into the city was to be effected."

Premit altum corde dolorem. Lat. VIRGIL.—"He subdues, stifles, or represses the agony that wellnigh annihilates him, the unutterable agony of his soul, the agony that bows him to the very dust; hushes, calms, or soothes the grief that threatens to burst from its mortal tenement."

Prendre la lune avec les dents. Fr.—"To seize the moon with one's teeth." To aim at impossibilities.

Prepense. Fr.—"Premeditated," as in the expression "*malice prepense,*" which is sometimes corrupted by the uneducated into "*malice propense.*"

Près de l'église, loin de Dieu. Fr. prov.—"The nearer the church, the farther from GOD."

Prestige. Fr.—"Even the *prestige* of rank has been a good deal broken of late [1839], probably with *malice prepense,* by the Emperor [of Austria], who has ennobled a great many merchants and bankers, not a few of them being Jews:" that is, "Even the *magic charm, spell, value, importance, illusion,* of rank," &c. See "*Prepense.*"

Pretiosa supellex. Lat.—"The costly, sumptuous furnishings of, or appendages to, every mansion; costly movables." "He cared not for pictures, statues, or the tribe of knicknacks, that *pretiosa supellex* of affluence."

Preux chevalier. Fr.—"A bold, valiant, or gallant knight."

Prima donna. Ital.—"The chief female singer of the Italian opera."

Prima facie. Lat.—"On the first face." On the first view of an affair: or, in Parliamentary phraseology, "on the first blush of the business." "A strong and imposing *prima facie* case," that is, A case *that at first sight might appear to be correct.*

Prima materia. Lat.—"The prime material, groundwork." "Gibraltar has been designated 'the hot-bed of contraband, the nursery of the smuggler, that *prima materia* of a robber and murderer.'"

Primi pensieri. Ital.—"The first thoughts, originations."

Primum mobile. Lat.—"The first motion." The main spring, or impulse, which puts all the other parts into activity.

Primus inter pares. Lat.—"The first among his equals:" as in a meeting of magistrates, where the senior is called upon, as a matter of course, to preside.

Principibus placuisse viris non ultima laus est. Lat. HORACE.—"To have pleased great, powerful, noble, and distinguished men is a circumstance which claims not the least degree of praise." This poet was also a courtier.

Princeps obsoniorum. Lat.—"The very prince of dishes, articles of food."

Principiis obsta. Lat. OVID.—"Meet the very beginnings." Look to the budding mischief, before it has time to ripen into maturity.

Principiis obsta. Sero medicina paratur
Cum mala per longas convaluere moras. Lat. OVID.—"Meet the disorder in its outset. Medicine may be too late, when the disease has gained ground through delay." This precept is universally just. It is at present more frequently applied to the political than to the animal economy.

Priusquam incipias consulto: et, ubi consulueris, mature facto opus est. Lat. SALLUST.—"Advise well before you begin; and when you have maturely deliberated, then act with promptitude."

Privatus illis census erat brevis, commune magnum. Lat. HORACE.—"Their private fortunes were but small; the wealth of the public was great, the public resources were extensive." This description was applied to the infancy of the Roman republic, and contrasted with the later and more corrupt times, when individuals were possessed of enormous wealth, while the public treasury was impoverished.

Pro aris et focis. Lat. CICERO.—"For our altars and our hearths." For our religion and our firesides: for GOD and one's country.

Pro bono publico. Lat.—"For the public good: for the good or benefit of the public."

Pro et con. Lat.—"For and against." The reasonings *pro et con* —on both sides of the question.

Pro forma. Lat.—"For form's sake." "The bills had been read merely *pro forma*."

Pro forma tantum. Lat.—"Only for form's sake."

Pro hac vice. Lat.—"For this turn; on this occasion; for this time." "A. shall present *pro hac vice*, when B. has an alternate right of presentation to a church living, a benefice."

Pro libertate patriae. Lat.—"For the liberty of one's country."

Pro Magna Charta. Lat.—"For, or in defense of, 'THE GREAT CHARTER.'"

Pro pudor. Lat.—"Shame! shame!"

Pro rata. Lat. LIVY.—"In proportion."

Pro rata portione. Lat. CICERO.—"In proportion."

Pro ratione voluntas. Lat. JUVENAL.—"The will, mere will, instead of reason."

Pro rege et patria. Lat.—"For my king and my country."

Pro rege, lege, grege. Lat.—"For the king, the law, and the people."

Pro re nata. Lat. CICERO.—"For special business." "A *pro re nata* meeting of the court was held on Monday:" that is, A meeting, &c. *for special business* was, &c. "This sovereign can imprison, scourge, shoot, or hang his dear subjects *pro re nata*, without troubling himself about ulterior considerations:" that is, "*as occasion serves, calls for*."

Pro salute animae. Lat.—"For the health or safety of the soul." A phrase in use in the Ecclesiastical Courts.

Pro tanto. Lat.—"For so much." "Every true philosopher is a religious man; and he who is not religious is *pro tanto* not a philosopher:" that is, "*so far as religion is concerned.*"

Pro tempore. Lat.—"For the time, for a time." "A measure *pro tempore*"—a temporary expedient. N.B. Often used in an *abridged* form: thus, *Pro tem.*

Pro virili. Lat. Cicero.—"To his utmost." "He urges *pro virili* the wisdom and necessity of giving a fair trial to the plan:" that is, "*by every argument he can adduce.*" N.B. The *full* expression is, "*pro virili parte.*"

Pro virtute felix temeritas. Lat. Seneca.—"Instead of valor, there was a happy rashness." The philosopher speaks of Alexander; but, if modern generals were to be tried in the same manner, we should find that the greater part of their "glories" should be set down, in the same manner, to a successful temerity.

Probam pauperiem sine dote quaero. Lat. Horace.—"I court virtuous poverty without a dowry." I throw myself into the embraces of poverty, unactuated by any ambitious wishes. See "*Laudo manentem,*" *&c.*

Probatum est. Lat.—"It has been proved [beyond a doubt]."

Probitas laudatur et alget. Lat. Juvenal.—"Honesty, integrity, undeviating rectitude, is praised and freezes, is slighted or disregarded." Acts of probity have too frequently no other reward than cold commendation.

Procès-verbal. Fr.—"An official report."

Procul a Jove, procul a fulmine. Lat.—"Being far from Jupiter, you are also far from this thunder." They who feel not the sunshine of court favor are in return exempt from the dangers of courtly intrigue.

Procul este, profani! Lat. Virgil.—"Avaunt, ye profane! keep off, ye vulgar!"

Procureur du roi. Fr.—"The king's attorney, the Attorney-General." N.B. "*Procureur général*" has the same meaning.

Prodesse civibus. Lat.—"To be of advantage to one's fellow-citizens." To be employed on a work, the aim of which is to be of service to the community to which one belongs.

Prodesse quam conspici. Lat.—"To do good rather than to be conspicuous."

Profanum vulgus. Lat. Horace.—"The profane or ignoble common people, rude multitude, mob, rabble, rascality, rascaldom."

Profession de foi. Fr.—"A profession of one's religious faith, creed."

Proh superi! quantum mortalia pectora caecae
Noctis habent. Lat. Ovid.—

"Heavens! what thick darkness pervades the minds of men!" How clouded is the understanding of the many!

Prohibetur ne quis faciat in suo, quod nocere possit in alieno. Lat. Law maxim.—"It is forbidden that any man should do that on his own property which may injure the property of another." If a man does any thing on his own ground which offends his neighbor, it is held to be a nuisance, and as such may be abated: such an offense is a build ing which darkens the windows of another, erecting a dye-house, forming a tan-pit, &c., the smells of which are offensive, and sometimes infectious.

Projicit ampullas et sesquipedalia verba. Lat. HORACE.—"He [the judicious writer, the writer of taste] casts or throws aside, rejects, repudiates, high-sounding expressions and words a-foot-and-a-half long [jaw-breakers]." "The style, though still carefully rounded, has relaxed from the stately march, and the sometimes tumid pomp, which it assumes in his great historical work: *Projicit ampullas et sesquipedalia verba.*" BEN JONSON terms them "*Foot and half-foot* words." The term "*ampulla*" properly denotes a species of phial or flask, for holding oil or vinegar, having a narrow neck, but swelling out below. Hence the word is figuratively taken to signify *inflated diction, tumid language, bombast, rant, swelling lines, high-flown stuff.*

Prolegomena. Gr.—"Preliminary observations, prefaces, preambles, prefatory notices or reviews." N.B. "*Prolegomena*" means *things* or *matters to be read,* or *that ought to be read, before reading the work itself to which they are prefixed.* The *singular* is "*Prolegomenon,*" —a word but little used.

Prolétaires. Fr.—"The laboring classes."

Proletarii. Lat.—"The poor and beggarly portion of the community, of the people."

Prolétariat. Fr.—"General beggary." "Agricultural reform can alone, in France, put an end to the *Prolétariat.*"

Promenades militaires. Fr.—"Military marches." "It is probably for this reason that the French are making so many *promenades militaires.*" N.B. A "*promenade militaire*" is a regimental march of several hours' duration for the purpose of exercising the soldiers, when they have little, if any thing, else to do.

Promettre monts et merveilles. Fr. prov.—"To make very great, magnificent, promises, professions, of what one is going to do [which very often end in smoke, in nothing at all]."

Propaganda. Lat.—A congregation or society at Rome, established for the propagation of Christianity.

Propagande. Fr.—An association for the spread of certain political principles. "The *propagande* of LAMARTINE and the Republic."

Propriété littéraire. Fr.—"Literary property, copyright."

Proprio Marte. Lat.—"Instead of paying others for inventing and propagating falsehood, he performed that meritorious work *proprio Marte:*" that is, "by his own peculiar skill, ability, ingenuity; by his own unrivaled powers of imagination; by his own unassisted exertions."

Proprio motu. Lat.—"Of his or her own accord, own free will· spontaneously."

Proprium humani ingenii est odisse quem laeseris. Lat. TACITUS.—"It is in the nature of man to hate those whom he has injured." It is the disposition of many never to be reconciled to those whom they have offended, supposing perhaps that the forgiveness of the opposite party cannot be sincere.

Propter hoc. Lat.—"On account of, or by reason of, this thing, matter, or circumstance."

Propter quod. Lat.—"On account of which thing, matter, or circumstance."

Pros and cons.—"The theme of this comedy involves the *pros* and *cons* of the marriage life;" that is, involves the *fors* and *againsts*, involves [the arguments] *in favor of* and *against*, the marriage life. In CICERO we meet with the expression, "*Hoc non* PRO *me, sed* CONTRA *me est potius;*" that is, This matter, thing, or circumstance, is not *in favor of* me, but rather *against* me. N.B. "*Con.*" is an abridgment of *contra.*

Prosperum et felix scelus virtus vocatur. Lat. SENECA.—"Wickedness, when successful and prosperous, is called virtue." This will be best explained by the English epigram—

"Treason does never prosper; what's the reason?
That when it prospers, none dare call it treason!"

Protectio trahit subjectionem, et subjectio protectionem. Lat. Law maxim.—"Protection implies allegiance, and allegiance should insure protection." As the subject owes the sovereign obedience, so the sovereign is bound to defend the laws, the persons, and the property of his subjects.

Protégé. Fr.—A person patronized by some one of distinction, of rank, of an elevated position in society. The *feminine* is "*Protégée.*"

Protocol. Gr.—"The king consents unreservedly to sign the *Protocol.*" "Protocol" means, the *original* copy of any writing. In *diplomacy* [forms of negotiation on political matters] it means, The *original* copy of any dispatch, treaty, or other document.

Prout occasio postulet. Lat.—"According as, even as, occasion, circumstances, may require."

Proviso. Ital.—"A condition, stipulation, agreement, understanding." "The sole *proviso.*"

Proximus ardet Ucalegon. Lat. VIRGIL.—"Your next neighbor's house is on fire." The danger is so near that it becomes you to consider your own safety.

Proximus sum egomet mihi. Lat. Law maxim.—"I am always nearest to myself." This maxim bears on certain cases, in which a man may, without injustice, give himself the preference: for instance, an executor may first pay a legacy to himself, or take his own debt before other debts of an equal degree.

Prudens futuri temporis exitum
Caliginosa nocte premit Deus:
Ridetque, si mortalis ultra
Fas trepidat. Lat. HORACE.—

"God, in his wisdom, has shrouded the future in gloomy night: and he smiles, if mortals are unduly anxious to know what is to happen."

"Our GOD, in goodness ever wise,
Hath hid, in clouds of depthless night,
All that in future prospect lies
Beyond the ken of mortal sight,
And laughs to see vain man opprest
With idle fears, and more than man distrest."

This is a sublime lesson to those who neglect their present opportunities and are continually employing their thoughts about the future.

Publiciste. Fr.—"One who writes, or makes lectures, upon public law."

Publicum bonum privato est praeferendum. Lat. Law maxim. —"The public good is to be preferred to private advantage."

Pudor rusticus. Lat.—"Rustic sheepishness, bashfulness;" in other words, "sheepishness or bashfulness," the result of living too exclusively in the country.

Pudore et liberalitate liberos
Retinere satius esse credo, quam metu. Lat. TERENCE.—"It is better to keep children to their duty by a sense of honor, and by kindness, than by fear and punishment." Severity towards children often produces an effect directly the reverse of that which was intended.

"Better far
To bind your children to you by the ties
Of gentleness and modesty, than fear."

Pulcrum est accusari ab accusandis. Lat.—"It is honorable to be accused by those who are themselves deserving of accusation."

Pulcrum est benefacere reipublicae, etiam bene dicere haud absurdum est. Lat. SALLUST.—"It is commendable to act well for the republic; even to speak well of it is not undeserving of praise."

Pulcrum est digito monstrari et dicier, Hic est. Lat. PERSIUS. —"It is pleasant to be pointed at with the finger, and to have it said of you, 'There goes the man.'" Applied to those who are fond of obtruding themselves upon public notice. See "*Digito monstrari,*" *&c.*

Pulvisires, et in pulverem reverteris! Lat.—"Dust thou art, and unto dust shalt thou return!"

Punica fides. Lat.—"Punic faith." This phrase was used in an ironical sense by the Romans, to denote the treachery of the Carthaginians, a charge from which they themselves were not exempt. It is now used generally to mark the absence of good faith, or the breach of a political engagement.

Punitis ingeniis, gliscit auctoritas. Lat. TACITUS.—"When men of talents are punished, their authority is strengthened." When the infliction of the law falls upon the witty or ingenious author of what is termed a libel, it generally serves to give weight and notoriety to that which might have been overlooked with impunity.

Puras Deus, non plenas, adspicit manus. Lat. PUBLIUS SYRUS. —"God looks only to pure, and not to full, hands." The Supreme Judge looks to the innocence, and not to the wealth, of the individual. It is often otherwise in the courts below.

Q.

Quae caret ora cruore nostro? Lat. HORACE.—"What coast is not stained with our gore?" The poet speaks exultingly of the valor and successes of the Romans. A paraphrase applied to the present century, and confining itself to the naval exploits of England, might run thus:—

"What coast, encircled by the briny flood,
Boasts not the glorious tribute of our blood?"

Quae cum ita sint. Lat.—"As or since these things are so, as such is the state of matters." An expression frequently used by logicians and discussers of mathematical subjects or points.

Quae fuerant vitia mores sunt. Lat. Seneca.—"What once were vices are now the manners of the day." Such is the general depravity, that what was at one time imputed as a crime is now exhibited as a boast.

Quae laedunt oculum festinas demere: si quid
Est animum, differs curandi tempus in annum.

Lat. Horace.—"If any thing affects your eye, you hasten to have it removed: but if your mind is disordered, you postpone the term of cure for a year:"—

"For the hurt eye an instant cure you find:
Then why neglect for years the sickening mind?"

Men are infinitely less solicitous about their moral than about their physical state.

Quae male sunt inchoata in principio, vix bono peraguntur exitu. Lat. Law maxim.—"Things badly begun seldom end well, have but rarely a good ending." Like beginning, like end.

Quae supra nos nihil ad nos. Lat. prov.—"The things which are above us are nothing to us." A maxim frequently used against astrologers, and sometimes, but falsely, applied to politicians. Every man who can understand the first principles of government has a right to examine into the conduct of his rulers.

Quae volumus et credimus libenter, et quae sentimus ipsi reliquos sentire putamus. Lat. Julius Caesar.—"What we wish to be true we readily believe to be true, and whatever opinions we form we fancy that every one else must, as a matter of course, form the same [and we are angry with him, in high dudgeon, if he presume to differ from us, especially on religious matters]."

Quaelibet concessio fortissime contra donatorem interpretanda est. Lat. Law maxim.—"Every man's grant shall be taken most strongly against himself." Whenever the words of a deed are ambiguous or uncertain, they shall be construed against the grantor. If a man grants an annuity out of land, and has no land at the time of making the grant, it shall charge his person.

Quaerenda pecunia primum, virtus post nummos! Lat. Horace.—"Money must first be scraped together, and *afterwards, forsooth!* virtue and all that is amiable MAY then receive some little portion of our attention."

"[Ye groveling louts], let money first be sought,
Virtue is only worth a second thought."

Quaerit, et inventis miser abstinet, ac timet uti. Lat. Horace.—"The miser is ever on the search, yet fears to use what he has acquired."

Quaestio fit de legibus, non de personis. Lat. Law maxim.—"The question must refer to the laws, and not to persons." In a court of judicature regard must be had to the letter and the meaning of the law, and not to the rank or situation of either of the contending parties.

**Qualem commendes, etiam atque etiam adspice, ne mox
Incutiant aliena tibi peccata pudorem.** Lat. HORACE.—"Consider again and again the character of any one whom you recom mend, commend, to the notice of others, lest the failings of the person recommended bring disgrace on you."

"With cautious judgment o'er and o'er
The man you recommend explore,
Lest when the scoundrel's better known,
You blush for errors not your own."

Qualis ab incepto processerit, et sibi constet. Lat. HORACE.—"Let the characters he delineates be consistent and uniform throughout." This was written as an instruction to the tragic poet.

Qualis rex, talis grex. Lat.—"As is the king, so will be the people."

Quam maxima possunt celeritate. Lat.—"With the greatest possible haste, the greatest quickness imaginable: in double quick time."

Quam multa injusta ac prava fiunt moribus! Lat. TERENCE.—"How many unjust and wicked things are sanctioned by custom, has custom introduced!"

**Quam saepe forte temere
Eveniunt, quae non audeas optare!** Lat. TERENCE.—"How often do things occur by mere chance, which we dared not even to hope for!" The chances of life are very often such as to transcend every prudent expectation. These, however, are rare indeed. They may be regarded as similar to the success of the Grecian painter, who, despairing of hitting off the foam at a horse's mouth, dashed his sponge against the picture, and thereby produced the desired effect.

Quam seipsum amans sine rivali. Lat. CICERO *de Hirtio.*—"How much in love with himself, and that without a rival." Describing a man absorbed in self-love, and despised by the rest of the world.

Quam temere in nosmet legem sancimus iniquam. Lat.—"How rashly do we make severe and unjust laws against ourselves!" How blindly do the unthinking part of mankind lend their aid and approbation to measures, of which, if better informed, they would perceive that they must ultimately be the victims!

Quamdiu se bene gesserit. Lat.—"As long as he shall conduct himself properly."—A phrase first used in the letters patent granted to the Chief Baron of the Exchequer. All the judges now hold their places by this tenure: they were formerly held "*Durante bene placito,*" that is, "*During the Sovereign's pleasure.*"

Quand celui, qui écoute, n'entend rien, et celui, qui parle, n'entend plus, c'est métaphysique. Fr. VOLTAIRE.—"Leeds is probably the sole place in the empire, which would have afforded a temporary refuge to the editor of Hobbes [Sir William Molesworth],—the only Metaphysician in the House [of Commons], unless, indeed, we adopt the definition of Voltaire, which would make as good a one of Mr. Joseph Hume: *Quand celui, qui écoute, n'entend rien, et celui, qui parle, n'entend plus, c'est* MÉTAPHYSIQUE:" that is to say, *When he, who listens,* or, *gives ear, does not understand a word of what is said, and the speaker himself is* *in the same fix* [is talking without either rhyme or reason], *you may then consider that you have got into* METAPHYSICS—*into the region of* METAPHYSICS." N.B. Written in 1839.

Quand les vices nous quittent, nous nous flattons que c'est nous qui les quittons. Fr.—"When our vices leave us, we flatter ourselves that we leave them."

Quand on ne trouve pas son repos en soi-même, il est inutile de le chercher ailleurs. Fr.—"When a man finds not repose in himself, it is in vain for him to seek it elsewhere." He cannot escape by change of place from the anxiety which is lodged within his bosom.

Quando aliquid prohibetur, prohibetur et omne per quod devenitur ad illud. Lat. Law maxim.—"When any thing is forbidden to be done, whatever tends or leads to it, as the means of compassing it, is at the same time forbidden."

——Quando uberior vitiorum copia? quando
Major avaritiae patuit sinus? alea quando
Hos animos? Lat. JUVENAL.—

"What age so large a crop of vices bore,
Or when was avarice extended more?
When were the dice with more profusion thrown?"

Most peculiarly and strikingly applicable to the state of society in the present day. See "*Aude aliquid,*" &c.

Quando ullum invenient parem? Lat. HORACE.—"When shall they look upon his like again, find his equal?"

Quanto mayor e la fortuna, tanto e menor secura. Sp. prov. —"The more exalted the fortune, the less secure." This requires but little comment. The oak is demolished while the willow has only bent itself before the storm.

Quanto plura recentium seu veterum revolvo, tanto ludibria rerum mortalium cunctis in negotiis observantur. Lat. TACITUS.— "The more I turn over in my mind the transactions of the ancients or the moderns, the more frivolity and absurdity does there appear to me in all human affairs." The matters which appear grave to the present spectator, will assume a lighter aspect in the estimation of the future observer, when acquainted with all their more minute circumstances.

Quanto perditior quisque est, tanto acrius urget. Lat. HORACE. —"The more profligate and abandoned, the more of a spendthrift, he perceives one to be, the more he rises in his demands." The character of the usurer.

Quanto quisque sibi plura negaverit,
Ab Dis plura feret. Nil cupientium
Nudus castra peto, et transfuga divitum
Partes linquere gestio. Lat. HORACE.—

"The more a man denies himself, the more a man restrains and moderates his desires, the more will he receive from Heaven. Divested of every desire for more than fortune has bestowed, I seek the camp of those who covet nothing, I associate with those that desire nothing, and, as a fugitive, abandon, take delight in abandoning, the party of the rich." Or, as thus quaintly translated by FANSHAWE :—

"The more a man himself denies,
The more indulgent Heaven bestows;
Let them who will side with the *I's*,
I'm with the party of the *Noes*.'

Again:—

"The more we to ourselves deny,
The more the bounteous gods supply.
Far from the quarters of the great,
Happy, though poor, I do retreat,
And to th' unwishing few with joy
A bless'd and bold deserter fly."

Quantum. Lat.—"How much." The *quantum*, "the due proportion." "His *quantum* of common sense," that is, "His *amount*," &c.

Quantum a rerum turpitudine abes, tantum te a verborum libertate sejungas. Lat. CICERO.—"We should be as careful of our words as of our actions, and as far from speaking ill as from doing ill." Defamation, calumny, and slander should be most especially guarded against.

Quantum est in rebus inane! Lat. PERSIUS.—"How much folly is there in the affairs of men! what a vast amount of emptiness in human affairs or matters!" How senseless and frivolous are the pursuits of men in general!

Quantum meruit. Lat.—"As much as he has deserved." This phrase occurs in an action for work done without a previous agreement. The law will in this case give the plaintiff "as much as he has fairly earned."

Quantum mutatus ab illo! Lat. VIRGIL.—"How changed from what he once was!" How much altered from that figure which we regarded with so much interest! "No report, which has appeared, does any thing like justice to the scene, a scene in which 'Richard was himself' again, and yet, alas! *quantum mutatus ab illo!*"

Quantum quisque sua nummorum servat in arca,
Tantum habet et fidei. Lat. JUVENAL.—
"Every man's credit and consequence are proportioned to the money that he possesses." The word "*credit*" is not here taken in the modern sense. The meaning is simply, It is wealth alone that can command respect.

Quantum Religio potuit suadere malorum! Lat. LUCRETIUS.—"To how many crimes does not what is *called* Religion persuade mankind!" The poet is speaking of the sacrifice of Iphigenia, enjoined by the priests on her father Agamemnon. The line is sometimes invidiously used, and in a broader sense.

Quantum sufficit. Lat.—"As much as may be necessary, sufficient." N.B. Often written in an *abridged* form: thus, "*Quant. suff.*" "What follows is *quant. suff.*," that is, is "*amply sufficient.*"

Quantum valeat. Lat.—"For what it is worth." "Our notice must go *quantum valeat.*"

Quare facit opium dormire? Quia in eo est virtus dormitiva. Lat.—"Why does opium induce sleep? Because it has in it a sleepy quality." This question and answer are given by MOLIÈRE, in ridicule of that pompous ignorance which affects to solve every difficulty, whilst it merely dwells in lofty no-meaning; or, as in this instance, simply retorts the terms of the original question.

Quare impedit? Lat.—"Why does he disturb?" The name of a writ, which lies for the patron of a living against the person who has disturbed his right of advowson.

Quare si fieri potest, et verba omnia et vox hujus alumnum urbis oleant: ut oratio Romana plane videatur, non civitate donata. Lat. QUINTILIAN.—"Wherefore, if it can be done, both your words and your voice should savor of a pupil of this city, in order that your speech may appear to be truly that of ROME, and not that of a foreigner, on whom it had bestowed its freedom." This, when modernized, is a good lesson against all provincial and vulgar dialects, which in a great metropolis preclude even the idea that the person so expressing himself can have made any thing like elegant acquirements.

Quare vitia sua nemo confitetur?
Quia etiam nunc in illis est. Somnum
Narrare vigilantis est. Lat. SENECA.—
"Why does no one confess his vices? It is because he is yet in them, yet their slave. It is for a *waking* man to tell his *dreams*."

————**Quas aut incuria fudit,**
Aut humana parum cavit natura. Lat. HORACE.—
"Faults originating from carelessness, from that frailty which is natural to man, or that may be owing to a pardonable neglect." Errors in a literary work either springing from haste or partaking of the infirmity of our nature.

Quas dederis solus semper habebis opes. Lat. MARTIAL.—"The wealth which you give away will ever be your own." As the poet was ignorant of the Christian precept of "laying up treasures in heaven," he seems to have placed too much reliance on human gratitude. When a gentleman, who had been accustomed to give away some thousands, was supposed to be at the point of death, his presumptive heir inquired where his fortune was to be found; to whom he answered, "that it was in the pockets of the indigent."

Quasi. Lat.—"As it were, in a manner." "A *quasi* independent member," that is, "An *apparently* independent member."

Quasi in loco parentis. Lat.—"As it were in the place or position of a parent." "It was obvious that he stood *quasi in loco parentis*."

Quem poenitet peccasse, pene est innocens. Lat. SENECA.—"He who is sorry for having sinned, is almost innocent." His penitence has nearly obliterated his fault.

Quem res plus nimio delectavere secundae,
Mutatae quatient. Lat. HORACE.—
"The man who is too much elated with prosperity, will most acutely feel the shock of adversity." He who is intoxicated by his height, will most severely feel his fall.

Quem semper acerbum
Semper honoratum (sic di voluistis) habebo. Lat. VIRGIL.—"That day I shall always recollect with grief, but, as the gods have willed it, with reverence:" referring to the day on which the speaker had lost a most valued friend.

Quemcunque miserum videris, hominem scias. Lat. SENECA.—"When you see a man in distress, acknowledge him at once your fellow-man." Recollect that he is formed of the same materials, with the same feelings, as yourself, and then relieve him as you yourself would wish to be relieved.

Qui alterum incusat probri eum ipsum se intueri oportet. Lat. PLAUTUS.—"He, who accuses another of dishonesty, of any heinous or detestable action, should look closely into himself, should rigidly scrutinize his own conduct." A man who goes into court as a witness against another should go thither with *clean hands;* and the same with the COURT OF CONSCIENCE.

Qui amicus est amat, qui amat non utique amicus est. Itaque amicitia semper prodest; amor etiam aliquando nocet. Lat. SENECA.—"He who is a friend must love, but he who loves is not therefore a friend. Thus friendship is always advantageous, whilst love is sometimes injurious."

Qui, aut tempus quid postulet non videt, aut plura loquitur, aut se ostentat, aut eorum quibuscum est rationem non habet, is ineptus esse dicitur. Lat. CICERO.—"That man is guilty of impertinence, who considers not the circumstances of time, or engrosses the conversation, or makes himself the subject of his discourse, or pays no regard to the company he is in." A good definition of impertinence.

Qui Bavium non odit, amet tua carmina Maevi! Lat. VIRGIL.—"He who does not hate BAVIUS, let him, O MAEVIUS, love thy verses." These were two of the worst poets of antiquity. He, who has so little taste as to relish one bad performance, cannot be disgusted with another equally indifferent.

Qui bellus homo est, pusillus homo est. Lat. MARTIAL.—"A pretty fellow [coxcomb] is but half a man."

Qui capit ille facit. Lat. prov.—"He, who takes it to himself, makes the allusion." If the cap fits, put it on.

Qui Curios simulant et Bacchanalia vivunt. Lat. JUVENAL.—"Who affect to be CURII, and live like Bacchanals."—Applied to men whose feigned austerity is nothing more than a mask for their debauchery.

Qui de contemnenda gloria libros scribunt, nomen suum inscribunt. Lat.—"They who write books about despising glory, inscribe their own names." They show a wish for that fame which they affect to despise.

Qui dedit beneficium, taceat: narret, qui accepit. Lat. SENECA.—"Let him who has done another a kindness, say naught about it: let the receiver, however, proclaim it to the world [if such be his pleasure]."

Qui e nuce nucleum esse vult, frangit nucem. Lat. PLAUTUS.—"He that will eat the kernel must crack the nut; he that would have the gain must take the pain."

Qui est plus esclave qu'un courtisan assidu, si ce n'est un courtisan plus assidu? Fr. LA BRUYÈRE.—"Who is a greater slave than the assiduous courtier, unless it be the one who is still more assiduous, more of a toad-eater?"

Qui facit per alium facit per se. Lat. Law maxim.—"What a man does by another, he does by or through himself." Every man must be responsible for that which he empowers or commands another to do. If he orders another to commit a trespass, he is himself a trespasser.

Qui fert malis auxilium, post tempus dolet. Lat. PHAEDRUS. —"He who renders assistance to the wicked repents of it, regrets it, ere long."

Qui fit, Maecenas, ut nemo, quam sibi sortem
Seu ratio dederit, seu fors objecerit, illa
Contentus vivat, laudet diversa sequentes. Lat. HORACE.— "How comes it, Maecenas, that no one is contented with that lot which either reflection may have given him, or chance may have thrown in his way, but rather deems the condition of those persons enviable, who follow pursuits in life that are different from his own?" The merchant envies the lawyer, and is envied in his turn. Every man, with few exceptions, seems to think that he would have thriven better in any other pursuit, than in that which he has adopted.

Qui genus humanum ingenio superavit, et omnes
Praestinxit, stellas exortus uti aetherius Sol.
Lat. LUCRETIUS.— "A man who utterly surpassed the whole human race in ability, in inborn talent, and threw all into the shade, outshone all, even as the rising sun outshines or obscures the stars." These brilliant lines were applied by the Poet to EPICURUS, the distinguished Athenian philosopher. The first clause, "*Qui genus humanum ingenio superavit,*" is inscribed on the pedestal of the statue of SIR ISAAC NEWTON in the chapel of Trinity College, Cambridge.

Qui genus jactat suum, aliena laudat. Lat. SENECA.—"He who boasts of his lineage, boasts of that which does not properly belong to him." See "*Genus et proavos,*" *&c.*, and "*Quid prodest, Pontice,*" *&c.*

Qui invidet minor est. Lat.—"He who envies admits his inferiority."

——**Qui legitimum cupiet fecisse poema,**
Cum tabulis animum censoris sumet honesti;
Andebit, quaecunque parum splendoris habebunt,
Et sine pondere erunt, et honore indigna ferentur,
Verba movere loco. Lat. HORACE.— "The author who proposes to give the public a finished poem [a genuine poem, *that is,* one composed in accordance with all the rules and precepts of art], must peruse, go over, his papers with the eye of an impartial critic. He will nicely mark what words seem to want strength and beauty, what appear low and groveling, and will resolutely retrench them, reject them, blot them out."

"The man, who studies masterly to frame
A finished piece, and build an honest fame,
Will with his papers, faithful to his trust,
Assume the spirit of a censor just;
Boldly blot out whatever seems obscure,
Or lightly mean, unworthy to procure
Immortal honor [though the words give way
With warm reluctance, and by force obey]."

N.B. The idea intended to be conveyed by the poet is this:—That such a writer as the one described will take his tablets, on which he is going to compose his strains, with the same feeling that an impartial critic will take up the tablets that are to contain his criticisms. For, as a fair and honest critic will mark whatever faults are deserving of being noted, so will a good poet correct whatever things appear in his own productions worthy of correction.

Qui male agit odit lucem. Lat. prov.—"He who commits evil actions shuns the light." The worst presumable motives will always be inferred, where the doer of an act seeks to shroud himself in darkness and in mystery.

Qui mentiri, aut fallere insuerit patrem aut
Audebit, tanto magis audebit ceteros. Lat. TERENCE.—"He who once dares to lie to, or deceive, his father, will much more readily do so by others."

Qui méprise Cotin n'estime point son roi,
Et n'a, selon Cotin, ni Dieu, ni foi, ni loi. Fr. BOILEAU.—"He who despises Cotin cannot respect his king; and, according to Cotin, knows neither a God, a faith, or a law." This is applied to the conduct of political disputants, who, when their passions are heated, do not scruple to apply to their opponents the appellations of atheists and traitors, jacobins and jacobites, or whatever may be the opprobrious terms of the day.

Qui mori didicit servire dedidicit. Supra omnem potentiam est, certe extra omnem. Lat. SENECA.—"He who has learned to die, has learned how to avoid being a slave. Such a man is most certainly beyond the reach of all human power." The writer, who afterwards suffered himself to bleed to death, when commanded by a tyrant to terminate his existence, seems, when writing this energetic passage, to have had some presentiment of his own fate. The fear of death presses heavily on the human mind: the frequent and habitual contemplation of it, however, disarms the grim and ruthless tyrant of all his terrors.

Qui n'a point de sens à trente ans, n'en aura jamais. Fr.—"He who has no sense at thirty years of age, will never have any."

Qui, ne tuberibus propriis offendat amicum,
Postulat, ignoscet verrucis illius. Lat. HORACE.—"He who expects his friend not to take offense at the bumps, swellings, that disfigure his own person, must at once o'erlook such friend's warts."

"The man who hopes his bile shall not offend
Should overlook the pimples of his friend."

We ought to overlook minor blemishes in our friends, if we expect that they should not be shocked with our greater defects.

Qui nescit dissimulare nescit regnare. Lat.—"He who knows not how to dissemble knows not how to reign." That man is little fitted for society who has not, on particular occasions, the peculiar faculty of concealing his feelings, and dissembling for the moment his resentments.

Qui nil molitur inepte. Lat. HORACE.—"Who attempts nothing injudiciously." Whose means are always suited to his end. Spoken of a wise and provident statesman.

Qui non est hodie, cras minus aptus erit. Lat. MARTIAL.—

"The man will surely fail, who dares delay,
And lose to-morrow, that has lost to-day."

Procrastination is ruinous. Aptly has it been styled by YOUNG "the thief of time."

Qui non libere veritatem pronunciat, proditor est veritatis. Lat.—"He who does not freely and boldly speak the truth is a betrayer of the truth."

Qui non proficit, deficit. Lat.—"He who does not progress, retrogades." This is a maxim for all ages; the boy at school, who is not gaining, is certainly losing ground. It will equally apply to every other position in life.

Qui non vetat peccare cum possit, jubet. Lat. SENECA.—"He who does not forbid the commission of crime, when it is in his power to do so, acts as if he actually commanded it."

Qui non vult fieri desidiosus, amet. Lat. OVID.—"Let him, who does not wish to be slothful, lazy, indolent, fall at once in love." That busy passion will call into existence, will speedily arouse, all his faculties.

Qui perd, pèche. Fr. prov.—"He who loses, sins." The man who is unsuccessful is generally held to be in the wrong.

————————————**Qui praegravat artes**
Infra se positas, extinctus amabitur idem. Lat. HORACE.—"He whose moral or intellectual excellence causes envy in his lifetime will be revered when he is dead."

"For those are hated that excel the rest,
Although, when dead, they are beloved and blest."

Qui prête à l'ami perd au double. Fr. prov.—"He who lends his money to a friend, is sure to lose both."

Qui se sent galeux se gale. Fr. prov.—"He who feels himself scabby, let him scratch." Let him who feels the allusion resent it.

Qui se sert de la lampe, au moins de l'huile y met. Fr.—"He, who makes use of the lamp, should at least supply it with oil."

Qui seipsum laudat, cito derisorem inveniet. Lat. PUBLIUS SYRUS.—"He who sounds his own praises, who is his own trumpeter, will soon meet with those who will scoff at him, will turn him into ridicule."

Qui sentit commodum, sentire debet et onus. Lat. Law maxim.—"He should endure the burden who derives the advantage."

Qui sibi amicus est, scito hunc amicum omnibus esse. Lat. SENECA.—"He who is his own friend, is a friend to all men." He who is considerate in his own concerns, will kindly extend his consideration to those of his friends.

Qui statuit aliquid, parte inaudita altera,
Aequum licet statuerit haud aequus est. Lat. SENECA.—"He who decides in any case, without hearing the other side of the question, is most certainly not just, even though he may come to a just decision."

Qui studet optatam cursu contingere metam
Multa tulit fecitque puer, sudavit et alsit. Lat. HORACE.—"He who desires to reach with speed the wished-for end (the winning-post of the race), must from his boyhood have endured and labored much, and have borne the alternate extremes of heat and cold." No man ever attained

excellence in any one art or profession, without having passed through the slow and painful process of study and preparation.

Qui sui memores alios fecere merendo. Lat. VIRGIL.—"Men, who have insured the remembrance of themselves by their merits, their deserts." Men whose good deeds live in the hearts of their survivors: HOWARD, THE PHILANTHROPIST, for instance, SIR HUMPHRY DAVY, and a few others.

Qui tam. Law Lat.—"An action in the nature of an information on a penal statute."

Qui terret, plus ipse timet. Lat. CLAUDIAN.—"He who awes others is more in fear himself." The despot keeps others in dread of his tyranny, whilst he himself is a prey to his own alarms.

Qui timide rogat, docet negare. Lat. SENECA.—"He who asks fearfully invites a denial." The claimant who has the greatest share of confidence is the most likely to succeed.

Qui trop dit, ne dit rien. Fr.—"He who says too much, says nothing [to the point or purpose]."

Qui uti scit, ei bona. Lat.—"To the man who knows how to make a proper use of them, riches are a blessing."

Qui vive? Fr.—"Who goes there?" Literally, "Who lives?" "He is on the *qui vive*," that is, "on the alert, on the tiptoe of expectation."

Qui vult decipi, decipiatur. Lat. prov.—"If a man wishes to be deceived or imposed upon, let him be imposed upon."

Quibus indiciis? quo teste probavit? Lat. JUVENAL.—"By what discoveries, by what witness, has he proved it? [the truth of his assertion]." In other words, "Where or what is his authority for his assertion?"

Quicquid agunt homines nostri est farrago libelli. Lat. JUVENAL.—"All that engrosses the attention of mankind is the heterogeneous compound of this book of mine."

"Whate'er men say, or do, or think, or dream,
Our motley paper seizes for its theme."

A motto often prefixed to periodical works.

Quidquid erit, superanda omnis fortuna ferendo est. Lat. VIRGIL.—"Whatever the event may be, whatever may turn out, we must get the better of our ill fortune by bearing it like men." The only way to overcome disaster is by fortitude and perseverance. See "*Tu ne cede malis*," &c.

Quicquid est boni moris levitate exstinguitur. Lat. SENECA.—"Levity of behavior is the bane of all that is good and virtuous."

Quicquid est illud, quod sentit, quod sapit, quod vult, quod viget, coeleste et divinum est; ob eamque rem aeternum sit necesse est. Lat. CICERO.—"Whatever that be, which thinks, which understands, which wills, which acts, it is something celestial and divine; and, upon that account, must necessarily be eternal."

Quicquid excessit modum
Pendet instabili loco. Lat. SENECA.—
"Whatever has exceeded its due bounds, is ever in a state of instability." This is a maxim equally true, whether applied to men or to governments.

In politics, as well as in physics, the power is weakened from being overstrained.

Quicquid praecipies, esto brevis. Lat. HORACE.—"Whatever precepts you give, be short: let your precepts be clear and succinct." All didactic rules should be given with brevity.

Quicunque amisit dignitatem pristinam,
Ignavis etiam jocus est in casu gravi. Lat. PHAEDRUS.—"Whoever has lost his former dignity, elevated position in the social scale, is, in his sad condition, in his misfortune, a standing jest even to the cowardly, the vilest of the vile."

Quicunque turpi fraude semel innotuit,
Etiamsi verum dicit, amittit fidem. Lat. PHAEDRUS.—"Whoever has once been notorious for an act of fraud or falsehood, can never again gain credit even when he speaks the truth."

"The wretch, who often has deceived,
Though truth he speaks, is ne'er believed."

Quid aeternis minorem consiliis animum fatigas? Lat. HORACE.—"Why dost thou disquiet thy mind, unable to take in eternal designs?" that is, to extend its vision beyond the bounds of human existence. Why torment thyself with the anticipation of future evil?

"Thus while Nature's works decay,
Busy mortal, prithee say,
Why dost thou fatigue thy mind,
Not for endless schemes designed!"

Quid brevi fortes jaculamur aevo multa? Lat. HORACE.—"Why do we, whose strength is but of short duration, aim at many things, form so many and great designs?"

"Why do we aim with eager strife
At things beyond the mark of life?
Creatures, alas! whose boasted power
Is but the blessing of an hour!"

Quid crastina volveret aetas scire nefas homini. Lat. STATIUS.—"What to-morrow may bring forth, what may happen on the morrow, 'tis not permitted man to know." See "*Prudens futuri,*" *&c.*

Quid datur a divis felici optatius hora? Lat. CATULLUS.—"What is there given by the gods more desirable than a happy hour?" The *felix hora* of the Romans implied "a lucky occasion," or what ROWE calls "a glorious, golden opportunity."

Quid de quoque viro, et cui dicas, saepe videto. Lat. HORACE.—"Take especial care what you say of any man, and to whom you say it."

"Now take my counsel, and pray have a care
Of whom you talk, to whom, and what, and where."

Nothing in human life requires more caution than the manner of making our report on the character of others.

Quid dem? quid non dem? renuis tu, quod jubet alter. Lat. HORACE.—"What shall I give? what shall I not give? What you refuse, another imperiously calls for." The poet is speaking of what authors in all ages have complained of,—the difference of taste, and the capriciousness of their readers.

Quid dignum tanto feret hic promissor hiatu? Lat. HORACE.—"What will this promiser bring forward worthy of so large a boast?" What will this boaster of what he will do bring forth, or produce, worthy of so grandiloquent an exordium, commencement, or beginning?

"How will the boaster hold this yawning rate?"

Quid dignum tanto tibi ventre gulaque precabor? Lat. MARTIAL.—

"So wide a swallow, and so vast a paunch,
Say, what shall cram?—a turbot or a haunch?"

A suitable question to city aldermen, parochial officials, and gluttons.

Quid domini facient, audent quum talia fures? Lat. VIRGIL.—"What will their masters do, when low villains thus presume?" What are we to expect from the principals, when we are thus insulted by the subalterns?

Quid est turpius quam senex vivere incipiens? Lat. SENECA.—"What is more scandalous than an old man who is only just beginning to live as he ought to do?" It is shameful to see a man in advanced life entering for the first time on the rudiments of knowledge, or the practice of virtue.

Quid ferre recusent, quid valeant humeri. Lat. HORACE.—"[Let an author well consider with himself] what his shoulders can bear, and what they cannot."

Quid leges, sine moribus vanae, proficiunt? Lat. HORACE.—"What good can laws do, unless based on the principles of morality?"

Quid mentem traxisse polo, quid profuit altum
Erexisse caput, pecudum si more pererrat? Lat. CLAUDIAN.—"What profits it a man to have had a soul infused into him, and to have had the privilege of walking with head and brow erect, if he goes astray like creatures devoid of reason?" A good lesson from a heathen.

Quid non ebrietas designat? Operta recludit;
Spes jubet esse ratas; in proelia trudit inertem. Lat. HORACE.—

"To what lengths does not wine proceed? It discloses the deepest secrets; it ratifies every hope; and urges even the coward to the battle-field." Drunkenness makes men, at the same time, confident and imprudent.

Quid non mortalia pectora cogis,
Auri sacra fames? Lat. VIRGIL.—

"Accursed thirst of gold! to what dost thou not urge the human breast?" To what atrocities cannot that mind reach, which is impelled by selfish avarice!

Quid nos dura refugimus
Aetas? quid intactum nefasti
Liquimus? Lat. HORACE.—

"What villany has this age left untried,—what wickedness unaccomplished?" By this reflection, so often employed, it is meant to intimate that the present age is worse than any of those which have preceded it.

Quid nunc? Lat.—"What now?" What is the news at present? Applied in ridicule to a person who makes the acquisition of news his principal pursuit

Quid plura. Lat.—"Why should I say any thing more,—why say any thing further?"

————————**Quid prodest, Pontice, longo**
Sanguine censeri, pictosque ostendere vultus
Majorum? Lat. JUVENAL.—

"Of what advantage is it to you, Ponticus, to quote your remote ancestors, and to exhibit their portraits?"

"Where's the advantage, where the real good,
In tracing from the source our ancient blood;
To have our ancestors, in paint or stone,
Preserved as relics, or as monsters shown?"

Quid pro quo. Lat.—"What for what." A *quid pro quo*, "a mutual consideration."

Quid quisque vitet, nunquam homini satis
Cautum est in horas. Lat. HORACE.—

"Man is never sufficiently aware of the dangers that he has every moment to avoid." That which is called misfortune contributes but little to the sufferings of human life. They are in general to be set down to our own want of caution and foresight.

Quid ratione timemus aut cupimus? Lat. JUVENAL.—"What do we dread or desire from a rational motive?"

"How void of reason are our hopes and fears!"

————**Quid rides? mutato nomine de te**
Fabula narratur. Lat. HORACE.—

"Why do you laugh? Change but the name, and the story is told of yourself." We smile, as the Satirist justly observes, at follies related under feigned names, when we should smart if they were linked with our own.

Quid Romae faciam? Mentiri nescio. Lat. JUVENAL.—"What should I do at Rome? I cannot lie." What should that man do in a great capital, who cannot adopt its manners?

Quid salvis infamia nummis? Lat. JUVENAL.—"What matters infamy, disgrace, so long as your cash is safe?" or, to use an elegant LONDONISM, "so long as you have *lots of tin*."

Quid sit futurum cras, fuge quaerere. Lat. HORACE.—"Avoid all inquiry with respect to what may happen on the morrow." Look not so anxiously into the future as to preclude all present enjoyment.

Quid sit pulcrum, quid turpe, quid utile, quid non. Lat. HORACE.—"What is praiseworthy, what is base, what is profitable, and what pernicious." These are stated by the poet as the first aims of every moral inquiry.

————————**Quid tam dextro pede concipis, ut te**
Conatus non poeniteat, votique peracti? Lat. JUVENAL.—

"What in the conduct of our life appears
So well designed, so luckily begun,
But, when we have our wish, we wish undone?"

Quid tam ridiculum quam oppetere mortem, cum vitam tibi inquietam feceris metu mortis. Lat. SENECA.—"What can be so ridiculous as to seek for death, when it is merely the fear of death that renders your existence miserable?" A similar idea which occurs in MARTIAL has been thus translated:—

"Himself he slew, when he the foe would fly.
What madness this,—for fear of death to die."

Quid te exemta juvat spinis de pluribus una? Lat. HORACE.—"What does it avail you to pull out one thorn, while so many are left behind?" How are you bettered by the removal of a single grievance, if the general pressure be suffered to continue?

**——————Quid terras alio calentes
Sole mutamus patria? Quis exsul
Se quoque fugit?** Lat. HORACE.—
"Why do we change our own country for lands warming beneath another sun? What exile, or fugitive, ever fled from himself?"

"To climates warmed by other suns
In vain the wretched exile runs."

N.B. There is another passage from the pen of the same poet, in which we are told that,

Coelum, non animum, mutant, qui trans mare currunt:

that is,

"Those wights who through the venturous ocean range,
Not their own passions, but,—the climate, change."

Again:—*In culpa est animus, qui se non effugit unquam:*—

"'Tis in the mind alone our follies lie,
The mind, that never from itself can fly."

Once more:—Varro tells us that *longe fugit, qui suos fugit:*—

"Far doth he flee, who self and clan doth shun."

Quid verum atque decens curo et rogo, et omnis in hoc sum. Lat. HORACE.—"My cares and my inquiries are directed in search of decency and truth, and in this I am wholly engrossed and occupied." This is the just motto of a satirist, whose aim should be to correct whatever is improper, and to chastise whatever is indecent.

Quid violentius aure tyranni? Lat. JUVENAL.—"What can be more violent than the ear of a tyrant?" What more dangerous than the confidence of a despot?

**Quid voveat dulci nutricula majus alumno,
Qui sapere, et fari possit quae sentiat?** Lat. HORACE.—
"What can an affectionate nurse wish more for her darling charge than for him to be wise, and to be able to express his thoughts with propriety and elegance?"

"What can the fondest mother wish for more,
E'en for her darling son, than solid sense,
Perceptions clear, and flowing eloquence?"

Quidquid delirant reges, plectuntur Achivi. Lat. HORACE.—"Whatever folly their kings may commit, the Greeks suffer for it." The unhappy people invariably suffer for the faults of their leaders.

——"When doting monarchs urge
Unsound resolves, their subjects feel the scourge."

Quidquid dicunt, laudo: id rursum si negant, laudo id quoque. Lat. TERENCE.—"Whatever they say, I praise it; if they say just the contrary again, I praise that too." The character of a toad-eater, lick-spittle.

Quidquid in altum fortuna tulit, ruitura levat. Lat. SENECA.—"Whatever fortune has raised to a height, she has raised only that it may fall." When chance, not merit, has contributed to a man's elevation, his fall may be considered as certain.

Quidquid multis peccatur inultum est. Lat. LUCAN.—"The guilt which is committed by many must pass unpunished." Where the offenders are numerous, it is sometimes prudent to overlook the crime.

Quieta non movete. Lat.—"Disturb not things or matters that are going on in the old jog-trot style." Eschew and utterly repudiate every thing in the shape of improvement, and crush, if possible, the faculties of the human mind. A maxim in high repute with a large section of what is *called* "the EDUCATED portion of the community!"

Quiete et pure atque eleganter actae aetatis placida et lenis recordatio. Lat. CICERO.—"Placid and soothing is the remembrance of a life passed in quietness, innocence, and elegance."

————————**Quis bonus, aut face dignus**
Arcana, qualem Cereris vult esse sacerdos,
Ulla aliena sibi credat mala? Lat. JUVENAL.—
"Who can all sense of others' ills escape,
Is but a brute, at best, in human shape."

See "*Homo sum: humani,*" *&c.*

Quis custodiet ipsos custodes? Lat. JUVENAL.—"Who shall guard your own guards?" What check have you upon the very spies whom you have set on this occasion?

Quis desiderio sit pudor aut modus
Tam cari capitis? Lat. HORACE.—
"What shame or bounds can be annexed to our grief, on losing an individual so intimately and justly esteemed?"—This is a common preface to an elegy or a funeral sermon.—By the poet it was originally given as a solemn tribute to the memory of an endeared friend. If Quintilian had the worth ascribed to him in the following part of the ode, HORACE must be absolved from the guilt of posthumous adulation.

Quis expedivit psittaco suum *χαιρε*? Lat. PERSIUS.—"Who taught that parrot his 'HOW D'YE DO?'"—Who instructed that pedant to quote so largely from other languages?

Quis exsul se quoque fugit? Lat. HORACE.—See "*Quid terras,*" *&c.*

Quis fallere possit amantem? Lat. VIRGIL.—"Who can deceive a lover?" What can escape a lover's jealousy and penetration?

Quis scit an adjiciant hodiernae crastina summae
Tempora Di superi? Lat. HORACE.—
"Who knows whether the Almighty will add to-morrow to the days already passed?" "Boast not thyself of to-morrow: for thou knowest not what a day may bring forth."—Prov. xxvii. 1.

Quis talia fando temperet a lacrymis? Lat. VIRGIL.—"Who in speaking of such things can abstain from tears?" Who can remain unaffected by such a narrative?

Quis tulerit Gracchos de seditione querentes? Lat. JUVENAL.—"Who could endure the Gracchi complaining of sedition?" "He complains of faction and conspiracy, forsooth! *Quis tulerit Gracchos de sedi tione querentes?*"

"[This we might bear;] but who his spleen could rein
And hear the Gracchi of the mob complain?"

Quis virtutem amplectitur ipsam, praemia si tollas? Lat. JUVENAL.—"Who embraces, cares for, e'en Virtue herself, if you take away her rewards, if you withhold every inducement to love her for her own sake?"

Quis vituperavit? Lat.—"Who has found fault with it,—who has disparaged it,—who has questioned it?"

Quisnam igitur liber? Sapiens, sibi qui imperiosus. Lat. HORACE.—"Who, then, is free? The wise man, who can command himself, who exercises dominion over himself." No man is less free than he who is a slave to his passions.

Quo animo? Lat.—"With what mind?" The *quo animo*,—the spirit and intention with which any act was performed.

Quo fata trahunt retrahuntque, sequamur. Lat. VIRGIL.—"Let us follow the fates where'er they may direct our footsteps. Let us go where Fate summons or invites us." Let us yield implicit obedience to the will of Heaven.

Quo jure. Law Lat.—"By what right." A writ that lies for him who has lands, wherein another challenges common of pasture time out of mind, whereby the party is compelled to show "by what right" he entertains this claim.

Quo me cumque rapit tempestas, deferor hospes. Lat. HORACE.—"To whatever quarter the storm may blow, it bears me as a willing guest." I endeavor to accommodate myself to every circumstance and condition of life.

Quo mihi fortuna, si non conceditur uti? Lat. HORACE.—"Of what use is fortune to me, if I am not permitted to make use of it?" Of what value is wealth, if its enjoyment be restricted?

Quo minus. Law Lat.—The appellation given to a writ issuing by fiction from the Court of Exchequer, on behalf of a person supposed to be the sovereign's farmer or debtor, against another, where there is any cause of personal action.

Quo more pyris vesci Calaber jubet hospes. Lat. HORACE.—"In the same manner as a Calabrian would insist on your eating his pears." This fruit is so plentiful in Calabria, that it is chiefly used in feeding hogs. The application is therefore to those who officiously force on you things of little value, and for which you have no liking.

Quo nihil majus meliusve terris. Lat. HORACE.—"Than whom (or which) was never any thing greater or better on earth." A convenient phrase of compliment.

Quo res cumque cadent, unum et commune periclum,
Una salus ambobus erit. Lat. VIRGIL.—"Whatever may be the issue of the affair, we (or they) will share one common danger, or rejoice in mutual safety." Whatever may be the result, our fates (or those of the parties) are united.

Quo semel est imbuta recens, servabit odorem Testa diu. Lat. HORACE.—"The jar will long retain the flavor of that with which it was first filled." The prejudices imbibed from early education will probably last through life.

"The odor of the wine that first shall stain
The virgin vessel, it will long retain!"

N.B. The vessels for holding wine, in general use among the Greeks and Romans, were of *earthenware.*

Quo teneam vultus mutantem Protea nodo? Lat. HORACE.—"By what knot, noose, or chain can I hold this Proteus, who changes his form and appearance at will?" How shall I confine to a specific point the man who so often shifts his ground of argument? N.B. According to the heathen mythology, PROTEUS was one of the gods of the sea, and could foretell future events. He could transform himself into any shape.

Quo warranto. Law Lat.—"By what warrant." A writ lying against the person who has usurped any franchise or liberty against the sovereign.

Quoad. Lat.—"So far as." "The duties of the high constables, *quoad* the collection of county rates, ceased in 1845."

Quoad hoc. Lat.—"As, or, so far as, this." "He is right *quoad hoc:*" that is, "as to this stage of the business, or point of the argument." "Each power is separately weak *quoad hoc:*" that is, "so far as this [thing or matter is concerned]."

Quoad sacra. Lat.—"A letter was read in support of an overture in favor of the extension of the parochial system to *quoad sacra* churches;" that is, "to churches *that were* [as we say in England] *chapels of ease.*" N.B. "*Quoad sacra*" means, "as to, or with respect to, sacred matters, or, so far as the offices of the church are concerned," in contradistinction to matters of a merely parochial nature.

Quocunque modo. Lat.—"By some means or other, no matter what." "His sole aim was usurpation, and as the first step to it, a breach —*quocunque modo*—of that article of the constitution which prohibited his re-election."

Quod ab initio non valet, tractu temporis convalescere non potest. Lat. Law maxim.—"That which had no force in the beginning can gain no strength from the lapse of time." A claim or title, defective in the first instance, cannot derive any additional weight from prescription.

Quod alias bonum et justum est, si per vim aut fraudem petatur, malum et injustum est. Lat. Law maxim.—"What otherwise is good and just, if it be aimed at by fraud or violence, becomes evil and unjust." Thus it is forbidden, even to those who have title of entry, to enter into lands or tenements otherwise than in a peaceable manner.

Quod caret alterna requie durabile non est. Lat. OVID.—"Alternate rest and labor long endure." "All work and no play make Jack a dull boy."

Quod certaminibus ortum ultra metam durat. Lat. VELL. PATERCULUS.—"That which arises from contest often goes beyond the mark." From all political contentions certain consequences flow, beyond what the actors in the scene had in their immediate contemplation.

Quod decet honestum est, et quod honestum est, decet. Lat CICERO.—"What is becoming is honorable, and what is honorable is becoming."

Quod Deus avertat! Lat.—"Which GOD forbid!" An exclamation frequently used when any calamity is apprehended.

Quod est inconveniens et contra rationem non est permissum in lege. Lat. Law maxim.—"Whatever is inconvenient and contrary to reason is not permitted in law." Thus, if a town has customs which can be shown to be unreasonable, they shall no longer be binding.

Quod est violentum, non est durabile. Lat. prov.—"What is violent is not durable." The most violent passions are the soonest exhausted.

Quod facit per alterum, facit per se. Lat.—"What a man does through or by another, he does of or by himself." "If sermons are worth lending, the good which one man does may extend itself to neighboring and distant parishes." "*Quod facit per alterum, facit per se.*"

Quod fuit durum pati, meminisse dulce est. Lat. SENECA.—"That which was harsh, severe, to suffer, is pleasing to remember." There is something soothing to a man, in the recollection of his past misfortunes.

Quod male fers, assuesce: feres bene. Lat. SENECA.—"Accustom yourself to that which you bear ill, and you will bear it well." Patience and resignation will lighten every difficulty.

——————**Quod medicorum est**
Promittunt medici: tractant fabrilia fabri. Lat. HORACE.—"Physicians promise that which belongs to physicians, that which comes within their skill; and artificers mind only their own peculiar calling." In these cases no man interferes with another's business.

Quod non opus est, asse carum est. Lat. CATO.—"What you do not want, of which you do not stand in need, is dear at a penny."

Quod non potest vult posse, qui nimium potest. Lat. SENECA.—"He who is too powerful still aims at that degree of power which is unattainable." It is in the nature of despotism to be insatiable.

—————— **Quod petis, hic est:**
Est Ulubris, animus si te non deficit aequus.
Lat. HORACE.—"What you are in search of is here: 'tis e'en at Ulubrae, if you do but possess a calm and unruffled mind." N.B. "*Ulubrae*" was a small town of Latium, a country of Italy. Its marshy situation is alluded to by CICERO, who calls the inhabitants *little frogs*. JUVENAL also gives us but a wretched idea of the place. And yet even here, according to HORACE, might happiness have been found, if he who sought for it possessed but a calm and unruffled mind, a mind that was not the sport of ever-varying resolves, but was contented with its lot. You look for happiness in change of place, when in fact it is everywhere within your reach, were your search but properly directed.

Quod petis, id sane est invisum acidumque duobus. Lat.

HORACE.—"What you ask is disagreeable and distasteful to two others." This is the language of an author, laboring under something worse than a *dilemma* [which see], which has but *two* horns, as not knowing how to please a *trio* of readers.

Quod praestare potes, ne bis promiseris ulli:
Ne sis verbosus, dum vis urbanus haberi. Lat. CATO.—'Promise no man twice the service or favor you are able to do him, but do it at once and without any fuss: and be not wordy about it, talk not much about it, if you wish to be looked upon as a real gentleman."

Quod ratio nequiit, saepe sanavit mora. Lat. SENECA.—"That which reason could not cure, has often been cured by delay." To forbear and wait for events is sometimes all that is left to the most consummate prudence.

Quod satis est, cui contigit, hic nihil amplius optet. Lat. HORACE.—"He who has enough should wish for nothing more." The man who has a sufficiency should learn to smile at the artificial wants of others.

Quod si deficiant vires, audacia certe
Laus erit: in magnis et voluisse sat est. Lat. PROPERTIUS.—"Even though strength should fail, still boldness shall have its praise: in great attempts 'tis enough to have made the attempt, trial." The resolution to attempt a great deed is praiseworthy, e'en though the attempt should prove unsuccessful.

Quod si in hoc erro quod animos hominum immortales esse credam, libenter erro: nec mihi hunc errorem, quo delector, dum vivo, extorqueri volo; sin mortuus, ut quidam minuti philosophi censent, nihil sentiam, non vereor ne hunc errorem meum mortui philosophi invideant. Lat. CICERO.—"If I mistake in my opinion that the human soul is immortal, I willingly err: nor would I have this pleasing error eradicated from my mind; and if, as some pretenders to philosophy, some dabblers in philosophy, suppose, death should deprive me of my being, I need not then fear the raillery of those pretended philosophers when they are no more." The belief in the soul's immortality appears to have afforded great consolation to some of the most distinguished men of ancient times.

Quod sis esse velis, nihilque malis. Lat. MARTIAL.—"Continue to wish to be simply what you are, and give the preference to naught else upon earth." Be satisfied "*to do your duty in that state of life unto which it has pleased GOD to call you.*"

Quod sors feret, feremus aequo animo. Lat. TERENCE.—"Whatever chance may lay upon us, let us bear it with courage and firmness." As we cannot control the vicissitudes of fortune, let us make sure of a relief and an asylum in our own fortitude and equanimity.

Quod vos jus cogit, id voluntate impetret. Lat. TERENCE.—"What the law insists upon, let your adversary obtain from your own free will." When the merits of a case are decidedly against a man, it is folly to persist in a vexatious course of litigation.

Quodcunque ostendis mihi sic, incredulus odi. Lat. HORACE.—"Whatever you show me in such a way as to contradict my senses, to outrage common sense, I view with feelings of incredulity and disgust."

This is applied to those poets who deal in nothing but monsters, specters, and such like extravagances.

"I hate such wild, improbable romance."

Quondam etiam victis redit in praecordia virtus. Lat.—"Valor sometimes returns even to the bosoms of the conquered." A valor of this description is sometimes found to spring e'en from the bosom of despair.

Quoniam diu vixisse denegatur, aliquid faciamus quo possimus ostendere nos vixisse. Lat. CICERO.—"As length of life is denied us, let us at least do something to show that we have lived to perpetuate the remembrance of our existence."

Quoniam id fieri quod vis non potest,
Velis id quod possit. Lat. TERENCE.—
"As you cannot effect that which you wish, you should wish for that which may possibly be effected." You should endeavor to divert your inclination from that which you cannot possibly attain.

Quorum. Lat.—"A chief judge, with only three laymen as an assistant *quorum*, decides all questions *en dernier ressort:*" that is, *without further appeal.* N.B. "*Quorum*" means "*of whom*," one of the *quorum.* This description of a justice of peace is taken from the words of his "*Dedimus.*" "*Quorum unum*"—"*One of whom,*" I have appointed N. S., Esq., to be. It is also used in another sense: "Such a number to be a *quorum*," that is, to be of sufficiency to proceed in the business. See "*Dedimus potestatem,*" and "*En dernier ressort.*"

Quorum pars. Lat. VIRGIL.—"A part of whom." "We feel that we are part of the human system, and this sort of *quorum pars* is a mighty ally to an author;" that is, and this sort of *participation in the human community, &c.*

Quorum pars magna fuit. Lat. VIRGIL.—"In which he himself acted so conspicuous a part." "To the actual correspondence of one so pre-eminently engaged in these concerns as the EARL OF CHATHAM, *quorum pars magna fuit,* we cannot but look for lights of no ordinary character."

Quos Deus vult perdere prius dementat. Lat.—"Those, whom GOD has a mind to destroy, he first deprives of their senses, reason." A phrase most frequently applied to ministers of state, whose real or imputed faults are taken as the prelude to their approaching fall.

Quot capitum vivunt, totidem studiorum millia. Lat. HORACE.—"So many men, so many minds." The number of different pursuits and passions is in proportion to the number of human beings. Each man has his own prevailing passion, which differs in some respect from that of his neighbor.

Quot homines, tot rationes docendi. Lat.—"So many men, so many ways or methods of teaching [any art or science]."

Quot homines, tot sententiae. Lat. TERENCE.—"So many men, so many different opinions." An allusion to the continued diversity of taste and opinion.

Quot servi, tot hostes. Lat. SENECA.—"So many servants, so many enemies." A servant may at any time, for aught you know, turn out your enemy.

Quota. Lat.—"Each contributed his *quota,*" that is, his "*share.*"

Quousque tandem abutere patientia nostra? Lat. CICERO.—"How long, O Catiline, wilt thou abuse our patience?" The beginning of one of Cicero's orations against Catiline, the Roman conspirator, whose plots and contrivances were found out and defeated by Cicero, who at that time was one of the consuls. The quotation is often used by political writers.

R.

Rabido ore. Lat.—"With rabid, raging, furious, or foaming mouth." "He admires, or condemns, *rabido ore.*"

Rabies canina. Lat.—"Canine madness, the madness of dogs." "The political insanity of these distinguished individuals appeared to have some relation to the *rabies canina.*"

Rabies ethnica. Lat.—"The bitter hatred of [certain] races of the earth to each other."

Raison froide. Fr.—"Indifference,"—*literally,* "cold reason or reasoning." "WALPOLE was not satisfied with the reception which 'The Castle of Otranto' met with, and he blamed for it the *raison froide* of the time."

Rampant. Fr.—"Ready for action, for fighting." A term in heraldry. "What is the creditor, quiescent and *couchant,* as heralds say, compared to the same creature *rampant,* when he sloughs his skin and passes into the *dun?*" N.B. "*Couchant*" [Fr.—"Lying down"] is also a term in heraldry, and is applied to the posture of a beast lying with his belly on the ground, his legs bent under him, and his head looking upwards.

Rara avis. Lat. JUVENAL.—"A rare or scarce bird." N.B. The expression is usually employed to denote "*a prodigy, or something very unusual.*"

Rara avis in terris, nigroque simillima cygno. Lat. JUVENAL.—"A rare bird on the earth, and very like a black swan." Something singular or wonderful. A *unique,* a prodigy.

Rara est [adeo] concordia formae atque pudicitiae! Lat. JUVENAL.—"Rare is the union of beauty and of virtue!"

Rara fides probitasque viris qui castra sequuntur. Lat. LUCAN.—"Good faith and probity are rarely found among those who are the followers of camps." A military life but too often relaxes the principles of men, and renders their feelings more callous. And yet, by a singular contradiction, it is from the midst of camps that an historian of the human heart could select the most splendid instances of nice honor and acute sensibility!

Rara mens intelligit, quod interiore condidit cura angulo. Lat. PHAEDRUS.—"Few have capacity enough to comprehend, or, it is no ordinary mind that comprehends, or, it is the well-disciplined, the penetrating mind only, that comprehends, that invaluable and priceless experience which is the result of a life of close observation, and which has been carefully laid up in the storehouse of memory."

Rara temporum felicitas, ubi sentire quae velis, et quae sentias dicere licet. Lat. TACITUS.—"Unusual was the happiness of the times, so much so that you might think as you would, and might speak as you thought." This strong description, so seldom realized, is given by the historian of the reigns of NERVA and TRAJAN.

Rarement à courir le monde on devient plus homme de bien. Fr. prov.—"Seldom do we become more virtuous by traveling o'er the world, in traversing the globe."

Rari nantes in gurgite vasto. Lat. VIRGIL.—"Swimming dispersedly in the vasty deep." This was originally used in speaking of seamen escaping from a wreck. It is now applied to a literary performance where *a few happy thoughts* are nearly lost in *an ocean of no-meanings.*

Rari quippe boni: numero vix sunt totidem, quot
Thebarum portae, vel divitis ostia Nili. Lat. JUVENAL.—"Good men are indeed scarce. Scarcely are they more in number than the (seven) gates of Thebes, or the mouths of the rich Nile." The poet alludes to the received account of the Seven Wise Men of Greece. He means the *Boeotian* Thebes, which was as remarkable for its seven gates as the *Egyptian* Thebes for its hundred gates. The mouths of the Nile were very numerous; the most celebrated of them, however, were seven in number.

"Good men are scarce, the just are thinly sown:
They thrive but ill, nor can they last when grown.
And should we count them, and our store compile,
Yet Thebes more gates could show, more mouths the Nile."

Raro antecedentem scelestum
Deseruit pede Poena claudo. Lat. HORACE.—"Justice, though moving with tardy pace, has seldom failed in overtaking the wicked in their flight." It is one of the strongest arguments for the belief of a superintending Providence, that but few men, who have been guilty of enormous crimes, have in the end escaped their well-merited punishment.

Rarus [enim] ferme sensus communis in illa
Fortuna. Lat. JUVENAL.—"We do not usually find men of humility among those of the highest fortune."

"Sure 'tis rare
If mighty fortunes humbleness can share."

Rarus sermo illis, et magna libido tacendi. Lat. JUVENAL.—"Their discourse was infrequent, and their seeming desire was to be silent." This is spoken of men who affect silence as a characteristic of gravity and wisdom. It is thus translated by Dryden:—

"Since silence seems to carry wisdom's power,
Th' affected rogues, like clocks, speak once an hour."

Ratio. Lat.—A mathematical term, signifying "Proportion." "The expansive force is always in some direct *ratio* to the resistance offered to it."

Ratio et consilium propriae duces artes. Lat. TACITUS.—"The

34

proper qualities of a general are reason and deliberation." Inconsiderate rashness may frequently do much in the first instance, but the leader who acts upon sober reflection will, in general, be found to prevail in the end.

Ratio justifica. Lat.—"The reason that does justice, or justifies."

Ratio ruentis acervi. Lat. HORACE.—"The insensibly sinking heap; the steady principle of the sinking heap," that is, the principle by which the heap keeps steadily diminishing. "We disclaim this *ratio ruentis acervi* as a meet or worthy mode of argument in the discussion of so important a subject. As profitably might we seek to calculate how many grains of corn a horse could carry, and try to ascertain the point at which the addition of a single grain must make the animal sink beneath its load."

Ratio suasoria. Lat.—"The reason which persuades." This phrase and "*Ratio justifica*" are used to distinguish when a speaker is impelled by a different motive from that by which he means to influence his audience; when he secretly *justifies* his measures on one ground, and wishes to *persuade* his hearers on another.

Ratio ultima legum. Lat.—"The last resource or expedient of the law," in reference to "MILITARY FORCE."

Rationale. Lat.—A detail with reasons: a series of reasons assigned: an account or solution of the principles of some opinion, action, hypothesis [*supposition*], phenomenon [*appearance*], &c. "The whole *rationale* of the loan."

Ratione privilegii et ratione soli. Lat. Law phrase.—"By reason of privilege, and by reason of ownership of soil." "The difference is almost imperceptible between the right *ratione privilegii et ratione soli*, and no franchise could ever be granted to any one, except on his own soil."

Ratione tenurae. Law Lat.—"By the nature of the tenure; by the condition on which property is held." "He was bound to prepare it *ratione tenurae*."

Razzia. Arabic.—"War is a *razzia* rather than an art to the impetuous and merciless PELISSIER." "*Razzia*" is an Arabic word much employed in connection with Algerine affairs, to signify—*an incursion made by military into an enemy's country, for the purpose of carrying off cattle and destroying the standing crops.* It always conveys the idea of *pillage.* Its meaning is sometimes extended to other sorts of incursions.

Re infecta. Lat. LIVY.—"The affair not having been done." "He returned *re infecta*,"—that is, "without accomplishing his purpose or object."

——————Re ipsa repperi
Facilitate nihil esse homini melius neque clementia.

Lat. TERENCE.—

"I have found by experience that nothing is more useful, beneficial, advantageous, to man than a spirit of mildness and accommodation, than an easy temper and an obliging disposition." In the various contacts of human life the man of bland and gentle manners will, generally speaking, make his way before the person who aims to gain his object by a coarse and undistinguishing austerity.

Re opitulandum, non verbis. Lat. prov.—"We should assist those who need our help, by deeds, and not by empty words."

Rebus angustis animosus atque
Fortis adpare: sapienter idem
Contrahes vento nimium secundo
Turgida vela. Lat. HORACE.—

"In adversity be spirited and firm; and with equal prudence lessen your sails, when swelled with a too fortunate gale of prosperity." The latter part of the above sentence is metaphorical. Suffer not yourself to be too far elated, or carried away, by your success.

"When Fortune, various goddess, lowers,
Collect your strength, exert your powers:
But when she breathes a kinder gale,
Wisely contract your swelling sail."

Rebus in angustis facile est contemnere mortem,
Fortiter ille facit, qui miser esse potest. Lat. MARTIAL.—

"It is easy in adversity to despise death; real fortitude has he, who can dare to be wretched."

"The coward dares to die, the brave live on."

Rebus non me trado, sed commodo. Lat. SENECA.—"I do not give, but lend, myself to business." "The inhabitants of Oenoch, a dry island near Athens, bestowed much labor to draw in a river to water it and make it fruitful: but when the sluices were opened, the water flowed so abundantly that it overflowed the island and drowned the inhabitants. The application is obvious. It was an excellent saying of SENECA, '*Rebus non me,*' *&c.*"

Rebus secundis etiam egregii duces insolescunt. Lat. TACITUS.—"In the day of prosperity even the best generals become haughty and puffed up." It is in the nature of success to intoxicate leaders of every description, and there is no season in which they are more apt to expose their weak points to a vigilant adversary.

Recalcitrat undique tutus. Lat. HORACE.—"Though bad logic may ask much dexterity to unravel, and old prescription may require much erudition to expose its rotten grounds, yet spiritual gibberish is still better intrenched, and harder to be approached, from its having no weak side of common sense; *recalcitrat undique tutus:*" that is [your ignorant opponent], *kicks back upon you, being at all quarters on his guard.*

Réchauffage. Fr.—"That chapter is an able *réchauffage* of Sextus Empiricus:" that is to say, an able *dressing-up in a new style* [literally, a *warming-up*], *giving as new what is old, plagiarism,* &c. N.B. "*Réchauffé,* which means a *warming-up* of FOOD, is often erroneously used for *réchauffage.*

Recherché. Fr.—"Refined, tasteful." "The *recherché* style of the shop has obtained a European renown."

Recipe. Lat.—"Take." The *right* word for a *physician's prescription.*

Réclame. Fr.—"A puff." "A *réclame* for his journal."

Recours en cassation. Fr.—"An appeal to the Court of Cassation, to the highest court of appeal, to the highest judicial court."

Recta fronte. Lat.—"Manifestly, evidently, at first sight of it, on the very face of it." "It is impossible for the human mind to give its assent to any doctrine which militates *recta fronte* against the testimony of sense."

Rectus in curia. Lat.—"Upright in the court." A man coming into a court of justice, as the phrase is, "with clean hands."

Reculer pour mieux sauter. Fr. prov.—"To retreat a few paces in order to leap the better." The metaphor is borrowed from the practice in what is called a running leap. To retreat with prudence for the purpose of coming forward with greater energy.

Rédacteur. Fr.—"Editor of a newspaper."

Rédacteur en chef. Fr.—"Chief editor," &c.

Reddas amicis tempora, uxori vaces,
Animum relaxes, otium des corpori,
Ut adsuetam fortius praestes vicem. Lat. PHAEDRUS.—"Return the visits of, enjoy the society of, devote your time to, your friends, have leisure to pay due attention to your wife, relax your mind, unbend from the cares of business, and allow your body some little repose, in order that you may perform or dispatch the ordinary return of business, may resume your functions with new vigor." Addressed to a man over head and ears in business.

Reddere personae scit convenientia cuique. Lat. HORACE.—"He knows how to assign what is proper and becoming to each person."

"The appropriate justice sorts each shade and hue,
And gives to each the exact proportion due."

The dramatic poet gives to every personage an apposite and characteristic expression.

Redeat miseris, abeat Fortuna superbis! Lat. HORACE.—"May Fortune, a change for the better, revisit the wretched, and keep aloof from the proud, the haughty."

"May Fortune with returning smiles now bless
Afflicted worth, and impious pride depress!"

Redire, cum perit, nescit pudor. Lat. SENECA.—"When modesty is once extinguished, it knows not how to return." The ingenuous sense of shame, when once lost, can never be restored.

——————Redit labor actus in orbem,
Atque in se sua per vestigia volvitur annus. Lat. VIRGIL.—"The man's labor, unvaried round of toil, returns in a circle, and the year rolls round, revolves, on its own steps [and witnesses the incessant fatigue and plodding of the man whose business is his god]." Has often been applied to the mere man of business.

Redit mihi res ad restim. Lat. TERENCE.—"The matter is desperate, I may go hang myself."

Redivivus. Lat.—"Mr. Harrison is but JOE MILLER, and not very *redivivus:*" that is, and not very "like his great prototype once more furbished up, modernized, or, called into existence."

Reductio ad absurdum. Lat.—"Reducing the position to an absurdity." A phrase in logic, when your adversary is, or is supposed to be, *reduced* to submission by showing him the *absurdity* of his conclusions.

Refranes que dicen las viejas tras el fuego. Span.—"Sayings of old wives, old crones, by their firesides: old wives' fables."

Refugium peccatorum. Lat.—"A refuge for sinners or delinquents." "He said that the consular system of England was a *refugium peccatorum.*"

Reges atque tetrarchas, omnia magna loquens. Lat. HORACE.—"*Monk* Lewis was fonder of great people than he ought to have been, either as a man of talent, or as a man of fashion. He had always dukes and duchesses in his mouth—*reges atque tetrarchas, omnia magna loquens,* and was pathetically fond of any one that had a title. You would have sworn he had been a *parvenu* of yesterday:" that is, *was always boasting of his intimacy with kings and tetrarchs, and all such magnificent subjects, or matters,* and was, &c. See "*Parvenu.*" N.B. A "*tetrarch*" originally denoted *one who ruled over the fourth part of a country or kingdom.* Afterwards, however, the term merely came to signify *a minor or inferior potentate, without any reference to the extent of territory governed.*

Reges dicuntur multis urgere culullis,
Et torquere mero, quem perspexisse laborant,
An sit amicitia dignus. Lat. HORACE.—
"When great men would unmask the soul, and read its deepest thoughts with a view to discover if it were worthy of trust and friendship, they are said to try it with wine, and strongly to urge the full cups."

"Wise were the kings, who never chose a friend
Till with full cups they had unmasked his soul,
And seen the bottom of his deepest thoughts."

Again:— "Monarchs, 'tis said, with many a flowing bowl
Search through the deep recesses of his soul
Whom for their future friendship they design,
And put him to the torture in his wine."

N.B. "*Torquere mero*"—"To put to the rack with wine," is a bold and beautiful expression. Wine racks the heart, and draws forth all its hidden feelings, as the torture racks the frame of the sufferer, and forces from him the secret of his breast.

Regia, crede mihi, res est succurrere lapsis. Lat. OVID.—"Believe me, 'tis a kingly, royal, regal, act, an act worthy of a king, to succor, relieve, assist, the distressed:" or, in the expressive language of "The Book of Common Prayer," "to succor, help, and comfort all that are in danger, necessity, and tribulation."

Regibus boni quam mali suspectiores sunt, semperque his aliena virtus formidolosa est. Lat. SALLUST.—"Good men are stronger objects of suspicion to kings than bad men, and the virtues of other men invariably inspire them with dread."

Régime. Fr.—"Form of government." "They have no *régime.*"

Regis ad exemplum. Lat. CLAUDIAN.—"By or according to the example of the king." "The book is translated *regis ad exemplum:*" that is, *in all the bombast of the original.*

Régisseur. Fr.—"A manager." "The *régisseur* of the theater."

Regium donum. Lat.—"A royal gift, or grant." A sum of money granted annually by the Government for distribution among certain classes of Dissenting ministers.

Regni novitas. Lat. VIRGIL.—"The novelty to one of being a ruler, of being invested with the powers of a governor." "If his lordship can find time under the *res dura* and *regni novitas* of his laborious department to give one comprehensive glance at the documents, he will infuse something of his own activity and decision into our Eastern naval stations [1846]." See "*Res dura.*"

Reipublicae formam laudare facilius quam evenire; et, si evenit, haud diuturna esse potest. Lat. TACITUS.—"It is much more easy to praise a republican form of government than to establish it; and, even if established, it cannot be of long continuance, duration." This assertion of the historian, though often made use of, it is out of our province to discuss.

Rélation historique. Fr.—"A personal narrative." "This error applies most particularly to the *rélation historique.*"

Relievo. Ital.—That part of a figure which projects beyond the ground on which it is carved. "A monumental vault adorned with *relievos,*" that is, with *figures in relievo, embossed work.*

Religentem esse oportet, religiosum nefas. Lat. AULUS GELLIUS.—"A man should be religious, but not superstitious." A maxim of the olden days, but strongly applicable, however, to modern times. N.B. "*Religentem*" is *unclassical.*

Religio est dicere. Lat. TERENCE.—"I scruple, am afraid, to say or tell."

Religio loci. Lat.—"The religion of the place: the religious or devotional feelings called forth by circumstances." "The *religio loci* cannot with impunity be disregarded, whether it be the sanctity of a spot, the mythology of a people, the tradition of a family, or the opinion of a class."

Religio temporis. Lat.—"The religion of the day, of the times."

Rem acu tetigisti. Lat. PLAUTUS.—"You have touched the matter, subject, with a needle:" *in other words,* "You have hit the right nail on the head."

——————Rem facias, rem;
Si possis, recte; si non, quocunque modo rem.

Lat. HORACE.—

"A fortune—make a fortune by honest means, if you can; but, if not, by any means make a fortune: make a fortune by hook or by crook." "Make money; money, if thou canst, by fair means; if not, money in any way." Be not too scrupulous, provided you gain your end. This language is put by the poet into the mouth of a corrupt and unscrupulous man. It has been thus well translated:—

"Get wealth and power, if possible, with grace;
If not—by any means get wealth and place."—POPE.

Again:—

"My friend, get money; get a large estate,
By honest means; but get, at any rate."

See "*Quaerenda pecunia,*" *&c.*

Rem tibi Socraticae poterunt ostendere chartae;
Verbaque provisam rem non invita sequentur.

Lat. HORACE.—

"You may rely on meeting with good sense [the source and ground of writing well] in the Philosophy of SOCRATES, in the precepts of Socratic wisdom: and when the subject on which you propose to write has been previously and carefully reflected upon [has been examined in all its various details, so that you are become thorough master of it], proper and suitable words will naturally and as a matter of course offer themselves."

"Good sense, that fountain of the muses' art,
Let the strong page of Socrates impart:
For if the mind with clear conceptions glow,
The willing words in just expressions flow."

Compare CICERO:—"Give yourself," says he, "wholly up to the study of the Academic Philosophy: for from the writings and principles of the Socratic school we may draw knowledge, history, and eloquence. There is, moreover, a great variety of arts, without the aid of which it is impossible to succeed in any considerable undertaking. These are they that have formed orators, generals, and governors of states: to descend to inferior branches, this is the school that has produced so many famous mathematicians, poets, physicians, and expert artists of all kinds."

Remeatus tessera. Lat.—"A ticket of leave." "He has returned with a *remeatus tessera*, on the strength of which he picks the pockets of his former acquaintance."

Renaissance. Fr.—"Francis the First did not contribute greatly to the *renaissance* of the Louvre:" that is, to the *regeneration*, &c. N.B. "*Renaissance*" means *the revival of any thing which has long been in decay or extinct.* The term is specially applied in France to the time of the revival of letters and arts, and still more particularly to the style of building and decoration which came into vogue in the early part of the sixteenth century.

Rencontre. Fr.—"A meeting—opportunity of seeing, or having a glimpse of, any one." "The usual *rencontre* of a country curate with his bishop is at the meetings for certain religious societies."

Rendezvous. Fr.—"The Imperial Guard of France was ordered to *rendezvous* at some distance from Paris:" that is, to *take up their quarters* at, &c., to *betake themselves*, or, *to repair* [to a spot] at some, &c. N.B. The noun "*rendezvous*" means an *appointment*, a *place appointed, meeting-place.*

Rendre l'homme infâme, et le laisser libre, est une absurdité, qui peuple nos forêts d'assassins. Fr. DIDEROT.—"To brand a man with the mark of infamy, and leave him in full possession of his liberty, is an absurdity which peoples our woods and forests with assassins." [Or, what is a worse, because a more spreading, evil, it peoples our cities with veteran delinquents, and furnishes a constant supply of professors in the arts of crime.] A good lesson for the advocates of the "TICKET-OF-LEAVE SYSTEM."

Rentes. Fr.—"The funds." "The Minister was empowered to negotiate the amount of the *rentes* necessary to produce a certain capital."

Renvoi. Fr.—"A release." "The *renvoi* of those who had been enrolled."

Repente dives nemo factus est bonus. Lat. PUBLIUS SYRUS.—'No good man ever became rich all of a sudden—all at once." Immense and rapid fortunes, generally speaking, are acquired by fraud or violence.

Répertoire. Fr.—"A collection of stock plays." "Short comedies and dramatic pieces of the French school partially dislodged the works of the old English *répertoire.*"

Réponse sans réplique. Fr.—"An answer that admits of no reply, no rejoinder."

Républicain à tout prix. Fr.—"A devoted republican."

Requiescat! Lat.—"May he, *or* she, rest!" N.B. The *full* and usual form is, "*Requiescat in pace!*"—"May he, *or* she, rest in peace!" This inscription is often found on tombstones. It is sometimes used ironically; for instance, to a minister who has resigned, or who is no longer in office. It is also frequently used in an *abridged* form: thus, R. I. P.

Rerum copia verborum copiam gignit. Lat. CICERO.—"Ample materials for literary composition naturally originate, give rise to, a command of language, an abundant supply of words." See "*Rem tibi,*" *&c.*

Rerum divinarum atque humanarum scientia. Lat.—"The knowledge of things divine and human." "Mythic tales and classical fable have been discovered to contain matters of the gravest import and meaning. Mythology is, indeed, the *rerum divinarum atque humanarum scientia* of the most remote antiquity [so HERMANN has happily called it], and, ceasing, therefore, to be an object of frivolous curiosity only, it has become an important branch of the science of antiquity, and now fully deserves the deepest attention of the divine, the philosopher and the historian."

Res adversae. Lat.—"Adversity, a reverse of fortune."

Res adversae consilium adimunt. Lat. TACITUS.—"Adversity deprives men of their reason." Compare ROCHEFOUCAULT:—"Our wisdom is no less at Fortune's mercy than our wealth."

Res angusta domi. Lat. JUVENAL.—"Very limited pecuniary means;" the severe pressure of poverty. "The *res angusta domi* caused him at first much suffering:" that is to say, The *straitened circumstances in which he found himself—the difficulty of keeping his head above water*—the *next to impossibility of knowing how to keep the pot boiling.*

Res angustae. Lat. HORACE.—"Straits, straitened circumstances, pecuniary difficulties."

Res arctae. Lat. VALERIUS FLACCUS.—"Straits, straitened circumstances, pecuniary difficulties."

Res detestabilis et caduca. Lat.—"A detestable and frail, fleeting or perishable, affair, thing, or matter." "Power without right is the most odious and detestable object that can be offered to the human imagination. It is, in fact, *Res detestabilis et caduca.*"

Res dura. Lat. VIRGIL.—"The difficulty of one's position;" particularly applicable to an *official* position, such as that of PRIME MINISTER, &c.

Res dura et regni novitas me talia cogunt
Moliri. Lat. VIRGIL.—

"The difficulty of my position and the novelty to me of being a ruler, of being invested with the powers of a governor, compel me to do these things, to adopt this course." "Up to this period, then, impolitic and even illegal as some of Lord Durham's proceedings may have been, there might still be some excuse for him—'*Res dura,*' *&c*"

Res est forma fugax. Quis sapiens bono
Confidat fragili? Lat. SENECA.—
"Beauty is sure a fleeting flower.
Then how can wisdom e'er confide
In beauty's momentary pride?"

Res est sacra miser. Lat. OVID.—"A person in affliction, distress, is a sacred object." A hallowed respect is due to the wretched, which should protect them from further insult or depression.

Res est solliciti plena timoris amor. Lat. OVID.—"Love is an affair full of anxious fear. Love is the perpetual source of fears and anxieties."

Res gestae. Lat.—"Transactions, deeds." "The parliamentary papers give but an obscure notion of the whole *res gestae*."

Res incognitae. Lat.—"Things, matters, that are unknown, of which we have no knowledge." "The secret must remain, with the authorship of Junius, the executioner of Charles the First, and the Egyptian hieroglyphics, among the *res incognitae* of the world."

Res magna. Lat. HORACE.—"An ample fortune."

Res, non verba. Lat.—"Deeds, not words."

Res secundae. Lat. TERENCE.—"Prosperity."

Res severae. Lat. CORNELIUS NEPOS.—"Business."

Res unius aetatis. Lat.—"A thing of only one age." A phrase used by civilians to denote a legal provision which by no possibility can pass beyond the first generation.

Residuum. Lat.—"A residue, remnant, arrearage." "A *residuum* of incontestable facts."

Respice, aspice, prospice. Lat. ST. BERNARD.—"Look back on the days that are passed, look at the aspect of the present day, and look also, if thou canst, into the future."

Respice finem. Lat.—"Look to the end." Before you enter on an affair, let the consequences be well considered.

Respicere exemplar vitae morumque jubebo
Doctum imitatorem, et veras hinc ducere voces.
Lat. HORACE.—
"I would direct, counsel, advise, the skillful imitator to attend to the great pattern of life and manners, which nature unfolds to the view, and to derive from this source the lineaments of truth:"—
"Keep Nature's great original in view,
And thence the truthful images pursue."
Compare the sentiments of a great poet of our own day, WORDSWORTH:—
"To the solid ground
Of NATURE trusts the mind that builds for aye:
Convinced that there, there only, she can lay
Secure foundations."

Respondeat superior. Lat. Law maxim.—"Let the principal answer." In civil cases the master is always to be considered as responsible for the acts of his servant.

Respue quod non es. Lat. PERSIUS.—"Reject, throw off, what you are not." Assume no character to which you have no legitimate claim; sail not under false colors.

Restaurateur. Fr.—"An eating-house keeper."

Restitutio in integrum. Lat.—"A restoration to one's former position, reinstatement in one's former position."

Résumé. Fr.—"A recapitulation." "The *résumé* at the end of the report."

Retraxit. Lat.—"He has recalled or revoked." A term in law, when the plaintiff or demandant says that he will proceed no further.

Réunion. Fr.—"An assembly or party."

Revenons à nos moutons. Fr. phrase.—"Let us return to our sheep:" *in other words,* Let us return to our subject, to the matter we have been discussing [from which we have digressed]. N.B. The *origin* of the apparently singular expression "*Revenons à nos moutons*" is curious:—A French lawyer pleading the cause of a client, who had lost some sheep, talked of every thing but the matter in question, when his unfortunate client recalled him [gave him a *refresher*] by the above exclamation. It is used in conversation to check any impertinent wandering from the argument.

Revocare gradum. Lat. VIRGIL.—"To retrace one's steps."

Revocate animos, moestumque timorem mittite. Lat. VIRGIL.—"Resume your courage, and dismiss your care." See "*Tu ne cede malis,*" *&c.*

Rex convivii. Lat.—"The president or chairman at a banquet or feast."

Rex datur propter regnum, non regnum propter regem. Potentia non est nisi ad bonum. Lat. Law maxim.—"A king is given to serve the kingdom, not the kingdom to serve the king. Power is conferred only for the sake of general advantage, for the general or common weal, for the public good."

Rex est, qui metuit nihil:
Rex est, qui cupit nihil. Lat. SENECA.—
"He is a king, who fears nothing: a king is he, who covets nothing." Such a man has erected in his own mind an independent sovereignty.

Rex non debet esse sub homine, sed sub Deo et lege. Lat. Law maxim. BRACTON.—"The king ought not to be under the jurisdiction of man, but under that of GOD, and the laws of the country over which he rules."

Rex regum. Lat. HORACE.—"A king of kings." The definition of the "*truly wise man,*" according to the doctrine of the Stoics [an ancient sect of philosophers, of which ZENO was the founder, so called from the Greek word στοα [*stoa*], a porch, gallery, or portico, a walking-place with pillars, in Athens, spacious and finely embellished, where they used to meet and dispute].

Rex vini. Lat. HORACE.—"The king of good fellows, master of the revels."

Ride, si sapis. Lat. MARTIAL.—"Laugh, if you are wise." Enjoy the ridicule which you will find directed against error, ignorance, and folly.

Ridentem dicere verum quid vetat? Lat. HORACE.- "What hinders or forbids one's telling the truth jocosely, facetiously?"
'But may not truth in laughing guise be dressed?"

Why may not wholesome truths be conveyed under the garb of pleasantry? See "*Ridiculum acri,*" *&c.*, and "*Risus rerum,*" *&c.*

Ridere *γελωτα Σαρδωνιον*. Lat. and Greek prov. CICERO.—"To laugh far from the heart." N.B. *Σαρδωνιος γελως* means "*a forced laugh,*" "*a bitter laugh,*" and sometimes, "*angry or scornful laughter,*" but always laughter, either involuntary, or laughter only in appearance. "A forced laughter," says AINSWORTH, "when in outward appearance one seemeth well pleased, but at his heart is discontented." *Σαρδονιον* is a species of crow's-foot, of peculiar malignancy, supposed to be a variety of *water crow's-foot—Ranunculus philonotis:* The plant is a deadly poison, producing a convulsive movement of the muscles of the face resembling laughter; hence some derive the origin of the expression, *Σαρδωνιος γελως*. The plant grows abundantly in Sardinia.

Ridetur, chorda qui semper oberrat eadem. Lat. HORACE.—"That man makes himself ridiculous who is ever harping on the same string." Nothing is more disgusting than sameness in conversation, or in writing.

——————————**Ridiculum acri**
Fortius et melius magnas plerumque secat res.

Lat. HORACE.—

"Ridicule often decides matters of importance more effectually, and in a better manner, than severity of satire: Ridicule is frequently employed with more power and success than severity."

"For ridicule shall frequently prevail,
And cut the knot, when graver reasons fail."

Again:— "A jest in scorn points out, and hits the thing
More home than the morosest satire's sting."

Playful satire may sometimes reform, where serious indignation would be of no avail. See "*Ridentem dicere,*" *&c.*, and "*Risus rerum saepe,*" *&c.*

Rien de plus éloquent que l'argent comptant. Fr. prov.—"Naught is more eloquent than ready money. Nothing can give utterance to finer language than ready money [and plenty of it], hard cash." See "*Argent comptant.*"

Rien de plus estimable que la civilité, mais rien de plus ridicule et de plus à charge que la cérémonie. Fr.—"Nothing is of more value than complaisance; nothing more ridiculous or troublesome than mere ceremony."

Rien de plus hautain qu'un homme médiocre devenu puissant. Fr. BARON WESSENBERG.—"Nothing in the world is more haughty than a man of moderate capacity when once raised to power." Nothing is more haughty, pompous, insufferably and disgustingly proud, than a man of low grade when once possessed of power, become powerful.

Rien n'empêche tant d'être naturel que l'envie de le paraître. Fr. ROCHEFOUCAULT.—"Nothing prevents a person from being natural and easy in manner so much as the desire of appearing such." The study of itself produces the opposite effect,—constraint.

Rien n'est beau que le vrai: le vrai seul est aimable. Fr. BOILEAU.—"Nothing is beautiful but truth: and truth alone is lovely."

Rien n'est si dangereux qu'un indiscret ami;
Mieux vaudrait un sage ennemi. Fr. LAFONTAINE.—

"Nothing is more dangerous than an imprudent friend; better is it to have to deal with a prudent enemy." You can more easily be on your guard against the attacks of the latter than against the indiscretions of the former.

Rien ne pèse tant qu'un secret. Fr. prov.—"Nothing so troublesome, oppressive to the mind, as a secret."

Rien ne peut arrêter sa vigilante audace.
L'été n'a point de feux, l'hiver n'a point de glace.
Fr. BOILEAU.—

"Nothing can arrest his daring vigilance. For him the summer has no heat, and the winter has no ice." This was the eulogy of the poet on LEWIS THE FOURTEENTH. It has often been quoted in reference to the great NAPOLEON.

Rien ne ressemble mieux à un honnête homme qu'un fripon. Fr. prov.—"Nothing more closely resembles an honest man than a knave."

Rien ne s'anéantit, non rien ; et la matière,
Comme un fleuve éternel, roule toujours entière.
Fr. ROUCHER.—

"Nothing whatever is annihilated. Matter, like an eternal river, still rolls on without diminution." A just philosophical maxim from the pen of but an indifferent poet. It is only necessary to look around us to be convinced that, though every thing perishes, yet—nothing is lost.

Rifacimento. Ital.—"A remodeling, a dressing-up in a somewhat different manner." "This history is a *rifacimento* of an earlier and better original."

Rira bien, qui rira le dernier. Fr. prov.—"Who laughs the last does laugh with great success." Naught is more ridiculous than when the anticipation of triumph is mocked by a defeat.

Risu inepto res ineptior nulla est. Lat. MARTIAL.—"Than silly laughter nothing is more silly. Nothing so foolish as the laughter of fools." Naught is more absurd than laughter unseasonably or causelessly indulged in.

Risum teneatis, amici? Lat. HORACE.—"Can you refrain from laughter, my friends [on hearing or witnessing any thing so truly absurd]?" "Towards the end of the seventeenth century some ignorant or knavish men sent to Paris a number of Arabic manuscripts in excellent condition and clear characters. They were rapidly purchased at a high price by the bibliomaniacs [*men who were book-mad*] ; but, lo! when they were examined by the *connaisseurs*, they were discovered to be books of accounts and registers, neatly transcribed by certain Arabian merchants. *Risum teneatis, amici?*" See "*Connaisseur.*"

Risus rerum saepe maximarum momenta vertit. Lat. QUINTILIAN.—"A lively jest is capable of disconcerting the gravest reasons and reasoners." *Literally*, "Laughter often changes or gives a turn to the force, power, or bias of the greatest things or weightiest matters." See "*Ridentum dicere,*" *&c.*, and "*Ridiculum acri,*" *&c.*

Rivalem patienter habe. Lat. OVID.—"With patience bear a rival in thy love."

Rixatur de lana caprina. Lat. HORACE.—"He wrangles about trifles, about things of no consequence whatever." *Literally*, "He disputes about goat's-wool," that is, about nothing, since a goat is covered with hair, and not with wool. A person so captious that he will dispute on every thing, however absurd or trifling. See "*Alter in obsequium*," *&c.*

Robur et corporis et animi. Lat. LIVY.—"Strength both of body and of mind: bodily and mental vigor." See "*Mens sana in corpore sano.*"

Rodomontade.—A word that is very often spelled erroneously—*rhodomontade*, instead of as above. It is derived from the Italian word "*Rodomonte*," which signifies *a blusterer, a swaggerer,—a swaggering, blustering fellow.* "*Rodomontade*" may also be written "*rodomontado*" —an empty boast.

Rôle. Fr.—"The character or part." A dramatic term. "The *rôle* of Valeria may justly be styled complex."

Rôle d'équipage. Fr.—"A list of the crew." An official list of the persons on board, which neutral vessels are compelled to produce in time of war.

Roman de longue haleine. Fr.—"A long-winded romance." N.B. Often incorrectly written, "Roman de *la* longue haleine."

Rome de Rome est le seul monument,
Et Rome Rome a veincu seulement.
Le Tybre seul, qui vers la mer s'enfuit,
Reste de Rome. O mondaine inconstance!
Ce qui est ferme est par le temps destruit,
Et ce qui fuit au temps fait résistance.

Old Fr. JOACHIM DE BELLAY [in reference to the Tiber and the ruins of Rome].

"Rome now of Rome is the only funerall,
And only Rome of Rome hath victory;
Ne ought save Tyber, hastening to his fall,
Remains of all. O world's inconstancy!
That which is firm doth flit and fall away,
And that is flitting doth abide and stay."—SPENSER.

Roture. Fr.—"Commonalty, plebeianism."

Roturier. Fr.—"A commoner," in contradistinction to a nobleman.

Roué. Fr.—"A scamp, a profligate."

Roués de la Révolution. Fr.—"The First Consul removed in succession from around him all the *roués de la Révolution*, and ere long everybody became ambitious of the honor to be received in the *salons* [drawing-rooms] of the *Tuileries*:" that is, *all the scamps, scampish fellows, rascals, of the Revolution,—all the scamps, rogues, and rascals, who had been engaged in*, or *had taken part in, the Revolution.* N.B. The "*Tuileries*," or rather *Le château*, or, *Le Palais des Tuileries*, is one of the imperial residences of the monarch of France. Instead of "*Tuileries*" we may often see the word most absurdly and incorrectly spelled *Thuilleries*.

Rouge et noir. Fr.—"Red and black." A game so called, and much in vogue at gambling-houses and in the *higher* circles of society.

Route. Fr.—"A road." "This route was agreeable to us." See "*En route.*"

Routinier. Fr.—"A man of business habits: a man whose SOLE recommendation is his regularity as a man of business."

Rubicon. Lat.—The "*Rubicon*" is a small river, which formerly parted France and Italy. "*To pass the Rubicon*" is often used to signify —*engaging in any thing in an irrevocable* [uncallbackable] *manner.* The expression has reference to the proceeding of Caesar, who passed the Rubicon to march against the Senate on his return from Gaul [*France*] in the forty-ninth year before Christ, after that body had refused him the Consulship.

Rubor efflorescens. Lat.—"The crimsoned efflorescence, crimson blush." "One of the commentators on LUCIAN [a learned and witty Greek author] mentions the delicate tinting of the *rubor efflorescens* of the cheek of beauty, as one of the many excellences of APELLES [a distinguished painter, who flourished in the time of ALEXANDER THE GREAT]." See "*Ne sutor,*" *&c.*

Rudis indigestaque moles. Lat. OVID.—"A rude and unarranged, undigested, mass." A Chaos [*which see*] of undigested matter. "He has extracted a most valuable narrative from the *rudis indigestaque moles* of the little note-books, field-books, letter-books, and imperfect journals of these travelers."

Ruhe ist die erste Burgerpflicht. German.—"Tranquillity is the foremost of civic duties." A cardinal axiom of the civic morality of Prussia and Germany.

Rumor est sermo quidam sine ullo certo auctore dispersus, cui malignitas initium dedit, incrementum credulitas. Lat. QUINTILIAN.—"Rumor is a certain kind of report widely spread, and untraceable to, unfixable on, any distinct author, originating in malignity, and constantly receiving accessions of strength from the credulity of the world of mankind."

Rura mihi et rigui placeant in vallibus amnes,
Flumina amem silvasque inglorius! Lat. VIRGIL.—
"May fields and streams meandering through the valleys be my delight, and, passing my days in obscurity, may I love the rivers and the silvan scenes!"

"My next desire is, void of care and strife,
To lead a soft, secure, inglorious life:
A country cottage near a crystal flood,
A winding valley, and a lofty wood."

Rursum si reventum in gratiam est,
Bis tanto amici sunt inter se quam prius. Lat. PLAUTUS.—
"When once they [lovers] have made it up again [after quarreling], they are twice as good friends as they were before." See "*Amantium irae,*" *&c.*

Rus in urbe. Lat.—"The country in town." A situation, residence, which partakes of the advantages of both town and country.

Rus suburbanum. Lat. CICERO.—"The country near or about a city, in the suburbs." "Not the '*rus suburbanum,*' but the veritable country, with its 'pomp of groves and garniture of fields'—nothing within thirty miles larger than a quiet market-town."

Ruse. Fr.—"An artifice, trick, stratagem."

Ruse contre ruse. Fr. phrase.—"Trick against trick." Diamond cut diamond.

Ruse de guerre. Fr. phrase.—"A trick of war, stratagem or trick in the game of war."

Ruse doublée de force. Fr. DE PRADT.—"Fraud lined with violence."

Rusticus, abnormis sapiens. Lat. HORACE.—"A rustic or peasant, a philosopher without rules." "The Charivari [the French PUNCH] represents an honest laborer inquiring who the *Communists* are; he is told that they are people who would have *l'argent commun, le terrain commun, le travail commun* [money in common, land in common, labor in common]. 'Mais,' says the *Rusticus, abnormis sapiens,—'pour commencer, n'y ont pas le* SENS COMMUN' [to begin with their project, ought they not to have sense in common, intelligence in common, COMMON SENSE]?"

Rusticus, abnormis sapiens, crassaque Minerva. Lat. HORACE.—"A rustic or peasant, a philosopher without rules, and of strong, rough, common sense." "This conception of the character is a most admirable exhibition of our old friend, *Rusticus, abnormis sapiens, crassaque Minerva.*" The expression "*abnormis sapiens*" is here used to denote one who was a follower of no sect, and who derived his doctrines and precepts from no rules of philosophizing, as laid down by others; but who drew them all from his own breast, and was guided by his own convictions respecting the fitness or unfitness of things. The phrase "*crassa Minerva*" is meant to designate one who has no acquaintance with philosophical subtleties or the precepts of art, but is swayed by the dictates and suggestions of plain native sense.

Rusticus exspectat, dum defluat amnis; at ille
Labitur, et labetur in omne volubilis aevum. Lat. HORACE.—"The peasant [in the fable] sits waiting on the bank, till the river shall have passed away; but still the stream flows on, and will continue to flow forever." Used to mark the disappointed ignorance of those who seem to be of opinion that the same causes will not continue to produce the same effects. The laws of nature are, and must ever be, unchangeable.

S.

S'abstenir pour jouir, c'est l'épicurisme de la raison. Fr. ROUSSEAU.—"One of the maxims of EPICURUS [the distinguished Athenian philosopher] was, *abstain in order to enjoy*, which meant that people should refuse to eat and drink more than their stomachs can bear, in order constantly to enjoy. The maxim was re-echoed by ROUSSEAU, who tells us that *s'abstenir pour jouir, c'est l'épicurisme de la raison:*" that is to say, *Abstaining so as* REALLY *to enjoy is the epicurism, the very perfection, of reason.* N.B. The word "*epicure*" is very generally supposed to mean the same as "*glutton.*" Now, this is a very great mistake. The *right* definition of an "*epicure*" is, one who is particularly nice in his food, and, *however humble his fare*, will have it of the best of its kind. He is not a *gormandizer*, but, generally speaking, *quite the reverse.* "You are a great

EPICURE, I believe," said a lady, addressing HUME, the historian. "No, madam," replied he, "I am only a GLUTTON."

S'embarquer sans biscuit. Fr. prov.—"To engage in an undertaking without having the things necessary to succeed."

Sa boule est demeurée. Fr. phrase.—"His bowl has stopped short of the jack." He has failed in his object.

Sacer inest in nobis spiritus bonorum malorumque custos, et observator, et quemadmodum nos illum tractamus, ita et ille nos. Lat. SENECA.—"There is a holy Spirit residing in us, who watches and observes both good and wicked men, and who will treat us after the same manner that we treat him."

Sacer vates. Lat. OVID.—"A sacred or divine poet." "Then indeed should we hear him and look upon him as the *sacer vates*, the *interpres deorum* [the interpreter of the will of the gods], whose appeal is to the hearts of all his brethren, whose language is the language of them all."

Sacra indignatio. Lat.—"Cruel indignation, furious anger: extreme, excessive, great, indignation or anger." "He, who makes it his business to watch obliquities, and see what is absurd in human manners, has not much chance of enjoyment in society. The *sacra indignatio* is a comfortless feeling."

Saepe ego audivi apud milites eum primum esse virum qui ipse consulat quid in rem sit: secundum, eum, qui bene monenti obediat: qui nec ipse consulere, nec alteri parere sciat, eum extremi ingenii esse. Lat.—"Often have I heard from military men that that man was deservedly considered the first among his fellows, who consulted with others on the point in hand, on the immediate exigency, and who made suitable provision for the occasion: that the second, the one next to him, was he, who yielded ready obedience to a good and competent adviser: but that he, who neither knew how to consult with others and to provide against emergencies, nor to yield due obedience to a superior in tact and in intellect, must, forsooth! be a man of the most astounding ability, powers of mind [the last clause, of course, *ironical*]." "The man who never changes his mind, must be about as great a fool as the man who is always changing it; and if there be an occasion when such an intellectual process ought to meet with indulgence, it is when you perhaps save a kingdom by submitting to it. *Saepe ego audivi,*" *&c.*

Saepe est sub sordido palliolo sapientia. Lat. CAECILIUS.—"Often is wisdom found, met with, discovered, under a shabby coat, in an humble garb." See "*Ingenium ingens,*" *&c.*, and "*Rusticus, abnormis,*" *&c.*

Saepe intereunt aliis meditantes necem. Lat.—"Often do they who plot the destruction of others become the victims of their own machinations." The mischiefs which men devise against others very often recoil upon themselves, and are their ruin.

Saepe piget ————————
Corrigere, et longi ferre laboris onus.
Corrigere at res est tanto magis ardua, quanto
Magnus Aristarcho major Homerus erat. Lat. OVID.—"Often is it an irksome, wearisome, toilsome, task to correct one's compositions, and to submit to the drudgery of such long-continued labor. The

work of correction, however, is infinitely greater than that of composition, just as the illustrious HOMER was greater than his severe critic ARISTARCHUS [who would not allow some verses in HOMER to be his]." See "*Limae labor ac mora.*"

Saepe rogare soles qualis sim, Prisce, futurus,
Si fiam locuples, simque repente potens.
Quemquam posse putas mores narrare futuros?
Dic mihi, si fias tu leo, qualis eris. Lat. MARTIAL.—"Often art thou accustomed, Priscus, to ask me what kind of a man I should be, were I to become rich, and all at once great and powerful. Thinkest thou, my friend, that any one can tell what his future conduct would be under such circumstances? Tell me now, if thou wert changed into a lion, what kind of a lion thou wouldst be?"

"Priscus, you've often asked me how I'd live,
Should Fate at once both wealth and honor give.
What soul his future conduct can foresee?
Tell me what sort of lion you would be."

The moral conduct of any individual cannot be foretold.

Saepe, si qua intemperantia subest, tutior est in potione quam in esca. Lat. CELSUS.—"Intemperance in eating is generally more noxious than excess in drinking." "DR. HOLLAND concurs in the maxim of CELSUS, so far as *wine* is concerned. '*Saepe, si qua,*' *&c.*"

Saepe stilum vertas, iterum, quae digna legi sint,
Scripturus. Lat. HORACE.—"Till the general introduction of the '*stilus*' and the waxen tablet, the *multa litura*, or, what Pope calls the noblest art, 'the art to blot,' as well as the other precept of the poetical critic,—

Saepe stilum vertas, iterum, quae digna legi sint,
Scripturus,—

could scarcely have been in the power of those authors whom, nevertheless, we justly admire as models of correctness:" that is to say, the *repeated correction* [literally, the *many a blotting out*] or, &c. *Turn the* stilus *often* [Be frequent in thy corrections], *if thou intendest to write what shall be worthy of a second perusal:*—

"Would you a reader's just esteem engage?
Frequent correct with care the blotted page."

N.B. In "*saepe stilum vertas,*" there is an allusion to the Roman mode of writing. The ordinary writing-materials of the Romans were tablets covered with wax, and besides these, paper and parchment. The former, however, were most commonly employed. The "*stilus,*" or instrument for writing, was a kind of iron pencil, broad at one end, and having a sharp point at the other. This was used for writing on the tablets, and when they wished to correct any thing, they turned the "*stilus*" and smoothed the wax with the broad end, that they might write on it anew. From "*stilus*" we obtain our English word *style*, the particular character of writing, speaking, painting, music, &c.; a title. The writer who wishes for permanent fame must submit to the labor of repeatedly correcting his works.

Saepe summa ingenia in occulto latent. Lat. PLAUTUS.—"Often are the most distinguished abilities, the greatest talents, buried in obscurity [frequently for want of encouragement]." Compare the beautiful stanza in GRAY'S "Elegy written in a Country Churchyard:"—

"Full many a gem of purest ray serene,
The dark unfathomed caves of ocean bear:
Full many a flower is born to blush unseen,
And waste its sweetness on the desert air."

Saepe tacens vocem verbaque vultus habet. Lat. OVID.—"Often has the countenance, though silent, unspeaking, both a voice and words, expressions, of its own." See "*Oculi sunt,*" *&c.*

Saevis compescuit ignibus ignes. Lat. OVID.—"He has quenched fires with ruthless fires." He has stilled the raging flames by adding fuel to the flame. "This stupid and irrational prejudice the author has set himself to encounter with a warmth and excitability not unlike its own. '*Saevis compescuit ignibus ignes.*'"

Saevis inter se convenit ursis. Lat. JUVENAL.—"Even bears with bears agree." Even beasts of the most savage nature do not prey upon their own kind. Man is the only animal that is perpetually at war with his fellow-men.

Saevit amor ferri, et scelerata insania belli. Lat. VIRGIL.—"The love of arms rages in their breasts, and the atrociously wicked madness for war, the ruthless thirst of war." A good description of that species of frenzy which is too frequently the sole cause of national hostilities.

**————Saevit animis ignobile vulgus:
Jamque faces et saxa volant, furor arma ministrat.**
Lat. VIRGIL.—

"The rude rabble are enraged: and now firebrands, now stones, are seen to fly about: their fury supplies them with arms."

"Now the wild rabble storms, and thirsts for blood;
Of stones and brands a mingled tempest flies,
And all those arms that sudden rage supplies."

A striking description of a popular tumult.

**Saevius ventis agitatur ingens
Pinus: et celsae graviore casu
Decidunt turres: feriuntque summos
Fulgura montes.** Lat. HORACE.—

"The lofty pine is more fiercely agitated by the winds, more exposed to the fury of the winds, than trees of lower size: and lofty towers fall to the earth with a heavier crash: and lightning strikes the tops of the highest mountains."

"When high in air the pine ascends,
To every ruder blast it bends:
The palace, from its airy height,
Falls tumbling down with heavier weight:
And when from heaven the lightning flies,
It blasts the hills which proudest rise."

N.B. The metaphors here used serve admirably well to convey to the reader's mind the ideas that the poet would impress by means of them,—namely, that the highest stations in life are most exposed to the attacks of fortune, and that the downfall of great men is often attended with heavy ruin. Daily experience confirms the justness of this observation.

Saheb. Hindostanee.—"Gentleman, Sir." It is always added in addressing or speaking of Europeans in India or Persia: as, "Colonel *Saheb*," Colonel: "Lord *Saheb*," Lord, the Bishop or Governor-General: "Elchee *Saheb*," the Ambassador. STOCQUELER.

Sain et sauf. Fr.—"Safe and sound." "I had some tremblings for the state *sain et sauf* of my friend."

Sainte-Ampoule. Fr.—"The idiotic royalism of the *Sainte-Ampoule* and the *Oriflamme* was at that time the sentiment most in vogue." N.B. The "*Sainte-Ampoule*" means "the phial, or flask of oil, which was said to have been brought from Heaven by a dove for the coronation of Clovis, King of France." The "*Oriflamme*" [Great Standard of France] means "the standard which the early kings of France caused to be borne when they went to the battle-field."

Salaam. Hindostanee.—This word is indifferently used in India to express compliments or salutations. Sending a person your "*salaam*" is equivalent to presenting your compliments. The personal "*salaam*" or salutation is an obeisance executed by bending the head slightly downwards, and placing the palm of the right hand on the forehead. This gesticulation is universal throughout India. STOCQUELER.

Salaam Aleikoom! Hindostanee.—"Peace be with you!" The ordinary Mohammedan salutation. STOCQUELER.

Salle à manger. Fr.—"A dining-room."

Salle d'asile. Fr.—"An infant school."

Salon. Fr.—"A drawing-room."

——— **Saltat Milonius, ut semel icto**
Accessit fervor capiti, numerusque lucernis. Lat. HORACE.—"As soon as his head is heated with wine, and the lamps appear double, Milonius falls to dancing." Used to describe a drunken frolic, where the actor is in other respects of a distinguished character. N.B. The Romans generally held dancing in little estimation.

Salus populi suprema est lex. Lat.—"The welfare of the people is the first great law." The main end of every government should be the well-being of the people, the establishment of order and security, and the diffusion of social happiness.

Salus populi suprema lex esto. Lat.—"Let the welfare of the people be the first great law." "'*Salus populi*,' *&c.*, was his polar star. He sealed his last vote with his blood, and died happy in the cause of Liberty." Said of LEPELETIER.

Salve, Magna Parens! Lat. VIRGIL.—"Hail, Mighty Parent!" "When we first visited Grub Street, and with bared head did reverence to the genius of the place, with a '*Salve, Magna Parens!*' we were astonished to learn on inquiry that authors did not dwell there now, but had all removed, years ago, to a sort of 'High Life below Stairs,' far in the west."

Salve, Magna Parens frugum, Saturnia tellus,
Magna virum: tibi res antiquae laudis et artis
Ingredior, sanctos ausus recludere fontes. Lat. VIRGIL.—"Hail, Saturnian land, Great Parent of fruits, Great Parent of heroes: for thee I enter on a subject of ancient renown and art, venturing to disclose the sacred springs." "An American approaches the shores of England

with all that veneration which is due to the country from which he has derived every thing that distinguishes him from the naked savage of the desert: his religion, his philosophy, his laws, his literature, and his language: '*Salve, Magna Parens,' &c.*"

"Hail, mighty Parent! blest with every store,
Much famed for fruits, for men and heroes more!
Saturnian land! for thee my voice I raise,
In lofty themes of ancient art and praise:
For thee disclosing all their sacred spring,
[Ascraean lays in Roman towns I sing]."

Salve Paeoniae largitor nobilis undae!
Salve Dardanii gloria magna soli!
Publica morborum requies, commune medentum
Auxilium, praesens numen, inemta Salus! Lat. CLAUDIAN.—"Hail, thou noble bestower of the Paeonian waters! Hail, thou distinguished glory of the Dardanian soil! thou universal relief from disease, thou common assistant to those who profess the healing art, thou benign deity, Health, unpurchasable by the wealth of worlds!"

"Hail, greatest good Dardanian fields bestow,
At whose command Paeonian waters flow;
Unpurchased Health! that dost thine aid impart
Both to the patient and the doctor's art!"

A beautiful Apostrophe [figure of speech, by which we address absent persons or inanimate objects, which we personify] to Health.

Salvo jure. Lat.—"Saving the right." A clause of exception. Such a thing shall be granted, *salvo jure Regis*, "saving the King's right," if it do not trench upon his rights or prerogative.

Salvo pudore. Lat.—"Without offense to modesty." I shall describe the matter "*salvo pudore*," that is, without offending either the eye or the ear.

Samson Agonistes.—"*Agonistes*" [a Greek word] means *one who contends for the prize in public games.* Milton has used "*Agonistes*" in this sense, and so called his tragedy from the similitude of Samson's exertions, in slaying the Philistines, to prize-fighting. "*Samson*" is a Hebrew word, and means *a little son.*

Sancta sanctorum. Lat.—"The holy of holies." "That the so-called Holy Cities, which are the *sancta sanctorum* of the Moslem faith, should excite deep and serious curiosity among Christian nations is only natural." N.B. The *singular* form is "*sanctum sanctorum*," which is often abridged to "*sanctum.*" The expression is often used in reference to a place into which persons are not usually and indiscriminately admitted,—a literary man's study, for instance; a chemist's laboratory, &c.

Sanctio justa, jubens honesta, et prohibens contraria. Lat.—"A just ordinance, commanding what is honest, and forbidding the contrary." This is the proper definition, given by BRACTON, of our municipal law.

Sanctissima res est civilis sapientia; sed quae pretio nummario non est aestimanda nec dehonestanda, quum in judicio honor petitur. Lat. JUSTINIAN.—"The wisdom of the bar, legal wisdom,

wisdom of barristers or advocates, is a very sacred and honorable thing; a thing, however, that is neither to be estimated nor dishonored, disgraced, disparaged, by mere considerations of pounds, shillings, and pence, inasmuch as honor alone is the object in view of the legal practitioner." "The Roman laws did not, any more than ours, admit in principle that an advocate should be paid for his advice: '*Sanctissima res est,' &c.* Yet advocates [we shall not speak of our barristers] professing to be in pursuit of honor, were very sharp after their fees, and, we rather think, laughed at OVID's line:—

'*Turpe reos emta miseros defendere lingua;*' " [which see].

Sanctius his animal mentisque capacius altae
Deerat adhuc, et quod dominari in cetera posset:
Natus homo est. Lat. OVID.—

"A living being more holy than the rest of the animal creation, and more capable of more exalted faculties, more fitted to receive a higher range of intellect, was still wanting; one, indeed, who could exercise dominion over all other animals: and then was man formed, summoned into existence."

"A creature of a more exalted kind
Was wanting yet, and then was man designed;
Conscious of thought, of more capacious breast,
For empire formed, and fit to rule the rest."

Man is, in most points of view, the superior of the animal creation.

Sanctum. Lat.—See "*Sancta sanctorum.*"

Sanctum est vetus omne poema. Lat. HORACE.—"Every ancient poem is sacred and venerable."

"So much can Time its awful sanction give
In sacred fame to bid a poem live."

———————————— **Sanctus haberi**
Justitiaeque tenax, factis dictisque mereris?
Agnosco procerem. Lat. JUVENAL.—

"Do you, by your words and actions, deserve to be looked upon as accounted a man of uprightness and of undeviating integrity? If so, I at once acknowledge you as a real nobleman, recognize you as a true noble."

"Convince the world that you're devout and true,
Be just in all you say, in all you do:
Whatever be your birth, you're sure to be
A peer of the first quality to me."

Lowness of birth, if accompanied by correctness of character, is no disparagement to a good man. See "*Nobilitas sola,*" *&c.*, and "*Virtus sola,*" *&c.*

Sang-froid. Fr.—Literally, "Cold blood." Indifference, apathy [which see], coolness.

Sans cérémonie. Fr.—"Without ceremony." Without any fuss or nonsense.

Sans-culotterie. Fr.—"The body of French Revolutionists of the days of LEWIS THE SIXTEENTH." "The *sans-culotterie* of Paris." See "*Sans-culottes.*"

Sans-culottes. Fr.—Literally, "Without breeches." The Revolutionists of the days of LEWIS THE SIXTEENTH: Red-hot Republicans.

"The English were then [in the reign of the great NAPOLEON] detested by her *sans-culottes* politicians and poverty-stricken beggars, whose greedy desire was to wrest the scepter of riches [in reference to our Indian Empire] from, as they supposed, the failing, enfeebling grasp of England."

Sans doute. Fr.—"Undoubtedly, indubitably, without doubt."

Sans-façon. Fr.—"Unceremonious." "His simple, quiet, and *sans-façon* manner."

Sans les femmes les deux extremités de la vie seraient sans secours, et le milieu sans plaisirs. Fr.—"Without women the two extremes of life would be without help, assistance, or succor, and the middle of it without pleasure." Were it not for the fair sex, our infancy would be without succor, our old age without relief, and our manhood without enjoyment, our manhood a complete state of monotony.

Sans oeuvre mêlée. Fr.—"Our great men have none of the *hauteur*, or of the assemblies *sans oeuvre mêlée*, of the Germans." N.B. An assembly "*sans oeuvre mêlée*" is, in the style of the German nobility, an assembly from which not only commoners are excluded, but even those whose nobility is liable to the slightest suspicion.

Sans peur. Fr.—"Without fear." "We must speak out all we think, as we are accustomed to do, *sans peur* and *sans reproche* [without reproach, blame]."

Sans tasche [the *old* French word for **tâche**].—"Without stain, without spot or blemish." The motto of LORD GORMANSTOWN.

Saper fingere qui si stima virtù. Ital. prov.—"To pretend to be wise, pretend to wisdom above one's fellows, is here [in certain circles] looked upon as virtue, as the perfection of virtue." "In one word, '*Saper fingere qui si stima virtù:*' and as 'nothing is, but thinking makes it so,' there is nothing really disgraceful in transcendentals but that evidence of the lowest imbecility and simplicity,—the being found out!"

Sapere aude. Lat. HORACE.—"Dare to be wise; be bold, and venture to be wise." Pursue the path of wisdom, without regarding the obstacles which may be thrown in your course.

————Sapere est abjectis utile nugis,
Et tempestivum pueris concedere ludum. Lat. HORACE.—"'Tis without doubt the best and wisest part for men to renounce trifles and turn to the precepts of wisdom, and to leave to youth those amusements which are more suited to, which better become, their age."

"'Tis wisdom's part to bid adieu to toys,
And yield amusements to the taste of boys."

Sapere est et principium et fons. Lat. HORACE.—"Of eloquence, whether in speaking or writing,—*SAPERE est et principium et fons:*" that is to say, *Knowledge,—sound knowledge,—a thorough knowledge of one's subject*, or *the subject in question, is both the beginning,—the very commencement,—and the true source.*

"Good sense, that fountain of the speaker's art,
Let the strong page of Pitt and Fox impart."

Sapere et fari quae sentiat. Lat. HORACE.—"To be wise and to say what he really thinks: [to speak openly and honestly]." "Through feeling the youthful heart acquires knowledge, and the wise nurse's wish is accomplished for her child,—*Sapere et fari quae sentiat.*"

Sapiens dominabitur astris. Lat.—"The wise man will govern the stars." His prudence and foresight will enable him to counteract that which, with vulgar minds, is suffered to pass for fate or destiny.

Sapiens ipse fingit fortunam sibi. Lat. PLAUTUS.—"The wise man carves out, fashions, his own destiny,—is the architect of his own fortune, own success in life." See "*Faber fortunae suae.*"

Sapiens nihil facit invitus, nihil dolens, nihil coactus. Lat. CICERO.—"The wise man does naught against his will, naught grudgingly or with a bad grace, naught by compulsion."

Sapientem pascere barbam. Lat. HORACE.—"To cherish a sage beard, to nurse a philosophic beard," that is, a long and flowing one; in the days of HORACE, *the badge of wisdom.*

Sapientia prima stultitia caruisse. Lat. HORACE.—"The first part of, step to, wisdom, the beginning of wisdom, is not to be a fool, is to be free from folly."

"When free from folly, we to wisdom rise."

Compare ROCHEFOUCAULT:—"Man's chief wisdom consists in being sensible of his follies."

Sapientissimus inter sapientes. Lat. CICERO.—"The wisest of the wise." Said in reference to THALES, the Milesian, one of the Seven Wise Men of Greece, a man remarkable for his attainments in ethics [the science of morals] and astronomy.

Sapientum octavus. Lat HORACE.—"An eighth wise man." One added to the Seven Wise Men of Greece. Used ironically in reference to an individual who plumes himself on his wisdom.

Sardonius risus. Lat.—"Forced laughter." See "*Ridere γελωτα σαρδωνιον.*"

Sassenach. The term by which the Irish, who hold extreme Catholic opinions, designate the people of England. "You would bind Ireland and England together [how can they flourish apart?], and '*Sassenach* and *Heretic*' are made convertible terms, and immediately between the two countries there opens an impassable gulf."

Sat cito, si sat bene. Lat. prov.—"Quick enough, if well enough."

Satis loquentiae, sapientiae parum. Lat. SALLUST.—"Talk, prate, enough, yet but little wisdom in it." A fluent elocution, command of language, "*gift of the gab,*" is not always a proof of intrinsic good sense. N.B. TALLEYRAND has the credit of being the first who defined speech as a "faculty given to man for concealing his thoughts;" but this sly recreant only twisted into an apophthegm what YOUNG had thrown out [nearly a hundred years before] in very scorn, when speaking of courts:—

"Where Nature's end of language is declined,
And men talk only to conceal their mind."

Satis, superque. Lat.—"Enough, and more than enough." Applied to an author who overloads his subject, and leaves his reader without ground for reflection or inference.

Satius est me meis gestis florere, quam majorum auctorita-

tibus inniti; et ita vivere ut sim posteris meis nobilitatis initium et virtutis exemplum. Lat. CICERO.—"It is infinitely better for me that I am in repute through my own achievements, rather than that I take credit to myself in consequence of the public services of my ancestors; and that I live in such a manner as to let my descendants see that I was the first man of my family, and that I exhibited in my own person a distinguished example of virtuous conduct."

Saturnalia. Lat.—"A festival among the Romans of five or seven days, though originally but of one, and afterwards of three. At this festival, which began on the 17th of December, great rejoicings and entertainments were made, and presents were given and returned. Servants also sat at table with their masters, in memory of the golden age under SATURN [a heathen deity, the father of JUPITER, the supreme god of the heathens], when all things were in common, and great hospitality was shown in memory of his coming as a stranger into Italy." N.B. The term is used by modern writers to signify "a time for festive enjoyment, mirth, jollity" such as Christmas-time, &c. "'Tis but a faint attempt to describe those delightful *saturnalia* of the heart, which once a week relieve and cheer a dull matter-of-fact existence,—

'Confined and pestered in this pin-fold here.'"

Sauces piquantes. Fr.—"Pungent sauces." Sauces that tickle the palate.

Saunterer.—A word of very singular derivation. "Our pilgrims were called '*Palmers*,' from bearing the palm-branch, and '*Saunterers*,' because returning from the Holy Land, '*La Sainte Terre*.'"

Sauter pour mieux reculer. Fr.—"They seized the reins [of government] in blind assurance by first giving head, more readily after to curb in the unruly half-jaded steed of Reform,—in reverse of the French saying, *sauter pour mieux reculer:*" that is to say, *to leap* [hastily into a responsible position] *in order to go back* [in their policy] *with a better grace.* N.B. The French proverb is,—*Il faut reculer pour mieux sauter*, that is to say, *One must go back,—draw back,—retreat a few paces, in order to take a better leap.*

Sauve qui peut. Fr.—"Save himself who can: cut, who can: run, who can." The phrase of flight, when a French army is routed.

"'Tis *sauve qui peut;*—the fruit dessert
Is fruitlessly deserted,
And homeward now you all revert,
Dull, desolate, and dirtied,—
Each gruffly grumbling, as he eyes
His soaked and sullen brother,
'If these are pic-nic pleasantries,
Preserve me from another!'"

[A storm has suddenly come on, with a perfect deluge of rain].

Savants. Fr.—"Learned men." "The *savants* of Europe." The singular is *savant.* N.B. The corresponding *Latin* term, which is in frequent use, is the *literati* [which see].

Savoir. Fr.—"Learning, scholarship, erudition." "His *savoir* was again called into requisition."

Savoir obscur de la pédanterie [le]. Fr. Molière.—"The obscure knowledge,—learning,—scholarship,—of pedantry."

Savoir-faire. Fr.—"Men of *savoir-faire*," that is, "*Men who have their wits about them,—men who have heads to contrive, and hands to execute.*"

Savoir-vivre. Fr.—"Good breeding, the manners of a lady or a gentleman."

Savoyard. Fr.—The word *Savoyard* has become quite a technical term in the French language; it is universally employed by the French to denote a chimney-sweeper, let him come from what part of the world he may. The natives of Savoy, therefore, feel that it degrades them, and they prefer taking the name of "*Savoisiens.*"

Sbirri. Ital.—"Officers of police, police agents." N.B. The singular is "*sbirro.*"

Scandalum magnatum. Law Lat.—"*Scan. mag.*" is an abridgment of *Scandalum magnatum*, that is to say, *The scandal of the Peerage,—scandalizing the Nobility*,—a reflection, or slight, thrown out against either an individual peer, or against the body of the Peerage. The name given to a statute of Richard the Second, by which punishment is to be inflicted for any scandal or wrong offered to, or uttered against, a noble personage.

Scelere velandum est scelus. Lat. Seneca.—"One crime, atrocity, has to be concealed by another." The guilt of one crime is but too frequently disguised by the perpetration of a second.

——————**Scelus est jugulare Falernum,**
Et dare campano toxica saeva mero. Lat. Martial.—
"How great the crime, how flagrant the abuse,
T' adulterate gen'rous wine with poisonous juice!"

A good lesson to our wine-merchants.

———**Scelus intra se tacitum qui cogitat ullum**
Facti crimen habet. Lat. Juvenal.—

"He who silently and secretly meditates the commission of a crime has all the guilt of the deed." The intention in certain cases is as guilty as the act itself. We have in this striking adage a tenet of Scripture purity: "that the heart is the seat of all true morality." Indeed, the universal presence of the divine mind should be as great a restraint upon our INWARD CONCEPTIONS, as the opinion of the world usually is upon our outward actions.

Scientia architectonica. Lat.—"The chief or principal knowledge; the knowledge that governs and prescribes." The art of clearing up the mysterious occurrences of Providence, by reducing them to the written word [the Word of God], and *there* lodging them as *effects* in their proper *causes.*

Scientiae, quas habemus, fere a Graecis fluxerunt. Quae enim scriptores Romani, aut Arabes, aut recentiores addiderunt, non multa, aut magni momenti sunt: et qualiacunque sint, fundata sunt super basin eorum quae inventa sunt a Graecis. Lat. Lord Bacon.—"The sciences that we possess, of which we are in possession, were for the most part derived from the Greeks. What the Roman, Arabic, or more recent writers have added, are, indeed, no great things, neither of much moment, weight, or consequence: such, however, as are their additions, they were certainly based on the inventions and discoveries of the Greeks."

Scientiarum omnium robur instar fascis illius senis; non in singulis bacillis, sed in omnibus vinculo conjunctis. Lat. LORD BACON.—"The strength of all kinds of knowledge, of every description of knowledge, may be compared to the old man's fagot in the well-known fable: not in a number of isolated facts or points, but in a well-digested arrangement of the whole, forming a compact mass, ready to be drawn upon as occasion may require."

Scindentur vestes, gemmae frangentur et aurum;
Carmina quam tribuent fama perennis erit. Lat. OVID.—"Garments, vestments, will fall to pieces, jewels and gold will lose something of their luster; but the fame that poems of a high order acquire will be ever during, will last the course of time."

Scinditur incertum studia in contraria vulgus. Lat. VIRGIL.—"The multitude, not knowing what to think, are greatly divided in their opinions." The populace, incapable of judging for themselves, and generally taking their opinions from others, are seldom to be found in a state of unanimity.

Scire facias. Law Lat.—"Cause it to be known." The name given to a judicial writ, ordering the defendant to show cause why the execution of a judgment, which has passed, should not be made out.

Scire tuum nihil est, nisi te scire hoc sciat alter. Lat. PERSIUS.—"Your own knowledge is as nothing, goes for nothing, unless others know that you possess such knowledge." "His case is precisely that in which *scire tuum nihil est, nisi te scire hoc sciat alter:* and the putting your lighted candle under a bushel is as bad as extinguishing it." Compare LUCILIUS, from whom PERSIUS took the sentiment:—

————————*Id me*
Nolo scire, mihi cujus sum consciu' solus,
Ne damnum faciam. Scire est nescire, nisi id me
Scire alius scierit.

'I should be unwilling to know any thing, were I myself to be alone conscious of it, were I myself the only one cognizant of my possessing such knowledge, lest perchance I should be a loser by it, I should sustain a loss by it [solely in consequence of not interchanging ideas with my fellow-men, an admirable means both of acquiring and increasing knowledge]. Knowledge is no knowledge at all, is not worth the name of knowledge, unless others know that I possess such knowledge." With many persons the chief value of acquired knowledge is to impress others with a sense of their acquirements.

Scire volunt omnes, mercedem solvere nemo. Lat. JUVENAL.—"All wish to possess knowledge, but few, comparatively speaking, are willing to pay the price:" to undergo the study and bear the expense, pay the fees of the schoolmaster or tutor.

Scribendi recte sapere est et principium et fons. Lat. HORACE.—"The first principle and source of all good writing is to think justly Good sense is the source and ground of writing well."

"Of writing well these are the chiefest springs,
To know the nature and the use of things."

This is the principle which Horace opposes to the ridiculous conceits of his contemporary poets: 'tis as if he had said, "You imagine that madness makes a poet; but my notion is, that good sense is the foundation of all."

Scribentem juvat ipse favor, minuitque laborem;
Cumque suo crescens pectore fervet opus. Lat. OVID.—"This very feeling of enthusiasm is a powerful auxiliary to an author, and marvelously diminishes his toil; and, as his work progresses, it glows with the feelings that animate his breast."

Scribimus indocti doctique. Lat. HORACE.—"Learned and unlearned, we all of us write, indulge in composing, indulge in literary pursuits." See "*Cacoëthes scribendi.*"

Scribimus indocti doctique poemata passim. Lat. HORACE.—"Learned and unlearned, we all of us write [what we consider deserving of the name of] poems."

"Now every desperate blockhead dares to write,
Verse is the trade of every living wight."

Other pursuits are supposed to require some previous study, but most men suppose themselves qualified to become, instinctively as it were, poets as well as politicians.

Scripta ferunt annos. Lat. OVID.—"Writings, literary compositions of adequate merit, survive the course of time, endure from age to age."

Se non è vero, è ben trovato. Ital. saying.—"If it be not true, it is at least well feigned or invented." "When we are willing to be deceived, there is but small difference between the *vero* and the *ben trovato.*"

Secret de la comédie. Fr.—"Everybody's secret." "The secret was religiously kept for three weeks; after which it became the *secret de la comédie.*"

Secrete amicos admone, lauda palam. Lat. PUBLIUS SYRUS.—"Admonish or advise your friends privately or secretly, but praise them openly."

Secrétaire des commandements. Fr.—"A private secretary."

Secundum artem. Lat.—"Scientifically, skillfully, judiciously: in an artistical manner."

Secundum formam statuti. Law Lat.—"According to the form of the statute."

Secundum usum. Lat.—"According to usage or established custom."

Sederunt. Lat.—"A session or sittings." "Wherefore is it that Parliament continues its *sederunt* through seven long months of very long days and nights?" N.B. The literal meaning of "*sederunt*" is *they have sat:* the use of the word for *session* is confined to the Scotch.

Segnius irritant animos demissa per aurem,
Quam quae sunt oculis subjecta fidelibus. Lat. HORACE.—"Things that go in at the ear [which, by-the-by, often come out at the other] impress the mind less powerfully, or forcibly, than those that actually come under our notice, or inspection, that are submitted to our in-

spection·" in other words, What we see done affects us more strongly than what we merely hear related:—

"What we hear
With weaker passion will affect the heart,
Than when the faithful eye beholds the part."

See "*Pluris est oculatus,*" *&c.*

Selectae e Profanis and **Selectae e Veteri.** Lat.—"These dancing civic dons held their solemn festivities beneath the appropriate roof of Haberdashers' Hall, deep in the labyrinth of some lane within lanes, whose name I have forgotten. It was the *Selectae e Veteri,* or rather the *Selectae e Profanis,* of Cheapside and Broad Street:" that is to say, It was a *select and choice spot, a crack locality, in the old,* or rather *the vulgar quarter of the City of the Cockneys, that takes within its range Cheapside and Broad Street.* N.B. "*Selectae e Veteri*" and "*Selectae e Profanis*" are the titles of two school-books, well known to the young gentlemen who attend the Public Schools.

Semel emissum volat irrevocabile verbum. Lat. HORACE.—"A word, when once it has escaped you, cannot be called back."

"Now you shall wish, but wish in vain,
To call the fleeting words again."

Semel in anno. Lat.—"Once in the year." "If stage plays," said he, "must be tolerated, let every stage in London pay a weekly pension to the poor, that *ex hoc malo proveniat aliquod bonum* [which see]: but it is rather to be wished that players might be used, as Apollo did his laughing,—*semel in anno.*"

Semel insanivimus omnes. Lat.—"We have all been mad [more or less] at some time or other." Every man must recollect some period in his life when his conduct was not influenced by his reason.

Semel malus semper praesumitur esse malus. Lat. Law maxim.—"A man, who has once been bad, on the wrong tack, is always presumed to be so." This is to be understood *in eodem genere mali,* "in the same kind of evil:" as persons convicted of perjury are not to be admitted as witnesses in any cause, after having once so offended.

————————————**Semita certe**
Tranquillae per virtutem patet unica vitae. Lat. JUVENAL.
—"Virtue offers the only path which, in this life, leads to tranquillity, true peace of mind."

Semper avarus eget. Lat. HORACE.—"The miser is ever in want."

"He wants forever, who would more acquire."

Semper habet lites alternaque jurgia lectus,
In quo nupta jacet: minimum dormitur in illo.
Lat. JUVENAL.—
"The bed in which a married woman lies is full of scolding and disputes: little sleep is there to be met with in such a place." One of the commonplace sarcasms on those contests which but too frequently embitter the married state.

Semper nocuit differre paratis. Lat. LUCAN.—"Delay has ever been injurious to those who are prepared." When you are ready, you should leave your adversary no further time for preparation.

Semper honos nomenque tuum laudesque manebunt. Lat. VIRGIL.—"Thy honor, thy renown, and the praises heaped on thee from every quarter, will ever continue." Thy fame will be everlasting.

Semper idem. Lat.—"Always the same [man or character]."

Semper inops quicunque cupit. Lat. CLAUDIAN.—"The man who desires more is ever poor." See "*Semper avarus*," &c.

Semper paratus. Lat.—"Always ready."

————Semper tibi pendeat hamus:
Quo minime credas gurgite, piscit erit. Lat. OVID.—
"Let thy hook be always ready, as a fish will often be in waters where thou least thinkest of it." Avail yourself of every opportunity, as good may sometimes arise from a quarter where least expected. Compare SHAKSPEARE:—

"There is a tide in the affairs of men,
Which, taken at the flood, leads on to fortune."

Sempre il mal non vien per nuocere. Ital. prov.—"Misfortune does not always come to injure." That which we take for an infliction sometimes comes as a blessing.

Senilis stultitia, quae deliratio appellari solet, senum levium est, non omnium. Lat. CICERO.—"That which is usually called dotage is not the weak point of all old men, but only of such as are distinguished by their levity."

Sentiment réligieux. Fr.—"A pious, religious, devout, sentiment or feeling: a display of religious or devout feeling."

Sequitur. Lat.—Literally, "He, she, or it follows." A consequence, sequel, or sequence.

Sequitur patrem non passibus aequis. Lat. VIRGIL.—"He follows his father, but not with equal steps or paces." He follows his predecessor, but with an inferior share of vigor, or ability.

Sera in fundo parcimonia. Lat. SENECA.—"Economy is useless when all is spent."

Sera nunquam est ad bonos mores via. Lat. SENECA.—"The way to good manners is never too late." Never too late to learn or to mend.

Sera tacitis poena venit pedibus. Lat. TIBULLUS.—"Punishment, though slow in coming, is sure to come eventually."

Seria cum possim, quod delectantia malim
Scribere, tu causa es, lector. Lat. MARTIAL.—
"That I prefer writing on lighter topics, when I could handle those of a more serious cast, thou, reader, art the sole cause." An author must strive to gratify the taste of his reader; for

"Those who live to please, must please to live."

Seriatim. Lat.—"In regular order. One after the other." "They negatived *seriatim* the different positions relied upon by the counsel."

Series implexa causarum. Lat. SENECA.—"The complicated series of causes." By this is signified what the ancients expressed by the general term FATE.

Serit arbores, quae alteri seculo prosint. Lat. CICERO.—"The country gentleman plants, and builds, and purchases for himself and for his heirs; *serit arbores, quae alteri seculo prosint:*" that is to say, *he plants* *trees, which may be profitable, a source of profit, to a future age, to posterity.* "Be aye [always] sticking in a tree, Jock," said a dying Scotch laird [a country gentleman on a small scale] to his son: "it will be growing whilst you are sleeping."

Serius aut citius sedem properamus ad unam. Lat. OVID.—"Sooner or later we all hasten to one place, to the same place." Death is the common doom of mortality.

Sero adveniat! Lat.—"She has won an honorable place in the large assembly of modern female writers, and at her death [*sero adveniat!*] deserves a monumental vault adorned with *relievos:*" that is to say, at her death [*late may it occur*, or *happen!*] deserves . . . . . with *figures in relievo, embossed work.*

Sero respicitur tellus, ubi, fune soluto,
Currit in immensum panda carina salum. Lat. OVID.—

"It is too late to look back upon the land when, the cable being loosed, the vessel is making her way into the immense deep." We should ever use all previous circumspection, when about to commit an act which in its consequences may be irretrievable.

Sero venientibus ossa. Lat.—"The bones for those who come late, for late comers." Applied to those who are always beyond their time in coming to dinner-parties.

Serum est cavendi tempus in mediis malis. Lat. SENECA.—"Too late is it to be on one's guard, to exercise caution, when plunged in misfortune." After-thought is wholly useless in many cases which, by due foresight, might have been prevented.

Serus in coelum redeas, diuque
Laetus intersis populo. Lat. HORACE.—

"Late may you return to heaven, and long may you continue to gladden your people with your presence."

"Oh! late return to heaven, and may thy reign
With lengthened blessings fill thy wide domain."

This was the flattering invocation of the poet to the Emperor AUGUSTUS. It has since become a commonplace, addressed to every potentate of every description.

Servare cives major est virtus patriae patri. Lat. SENECA.—"To preserve the lives of his fellow-citizens [and continually to watch over their interests] is the greatest virtue imaginable in the Father of his country [the reigning Monarch]."

————————————Servetur ad imum,
Qualis ab incepto processerit, et sibi constet. Lat. HORACE.

—"Let the character you delineate be preserved to the very last as it set out from the beginning, and thus be consistent with itself."

"From his first entrance to the closing scene,
Let him one equal character maintain."

Serviet aeternum, quia parvo nesciet uti. Lat. HORACE.—"He will ever be a slave, and will live in perpetual bondage, because he knows not, and will not learn, how to make a proper use of a small income." Prodigality in the first instance is the natural parent of baseness and servility in the second.

Servum pecus. Lat. HORACE.—"A slavish body [of imitators, of worshipers of rank and fashion]."

Si ad naturam vivas, nunquam eris pauper; si ad opinionem nunquam dives. Lat. SENECA.—"If you live according to the dictates of nature, you will never be poor; but if according to the opinions of the world, you will never be rich." The natural wants of man are but few, and those are easily satisfied: it is the gratification of their artificial wants that leads the proud and sensual into distress and difficulty.

Si antiquitatem spectes, est vetustissima; si dignitatem, est honoratissima; si jurisdictionem, est capacissima. Lat. COKE.—"If you look to its antiquity, it is most ancient; if to its dignity, it is most honorable; if to its jurisdiction, it is most extensive." This is the description given by one of our ablest law-writers, of the English House of Commons.

Si cadere necesse est, occurrendum discrimini. Lat. TACITUS.—"If a man must fall, he should manfully meet the hazard." When the danger is extreme, it should be met with an adequate energy.

Si celeres quatit pennas, resigno quae dedit. Lat. HORACE.—"If she [Fortune] shakes her wings [an evidence of her intending to fly off], I resign what she once bestowed."

"Now,—if she shake her rapid wings,
I can resign, with careless ease,
The richest gifts her favor brings."

N.B. *Resigno* is here used in the sense of *rescribo*, and the latter is a term borrowed from the Roman law. When an individual borrowed a sum of money, the amount received, and the borrower's name, were written in the banker's books; and when the money was repaid, another entry was made. Hence *scribere nummos*, "to borrow;" *rescribere*, "to pay back."

Si ceux, qui sont ennemis des divertissements honnêtes, avaient la direction du monde, ils voudraient ôter le printemps et la jeunesse,—l'un de l'année, et l'autre de la vie. Fr. BALZAC.—"If those who are the enemies of innocent amusements had the direction of the world, they would take away the spring and youth; the former from the year, and the latter from human life."

Si cui vis apte nubere, nube pari. Lat. OVID.—"Do you wish to marry suitably? if so, then marry your equal [in years and in position]."

Si Deus nobiscum, quis contra nos? Lat.—"If God be with us, who shall be against us?"

Si dixeris, 'Aestuo,' sudat. Lat. HORACE.—"If you say, 'I am warm,' he sweats." Spoken of such sycophants, or "water-flies," as Osric in Hamlet, who, amongst other modes of adulation, are ever of the same opinion as those to whom they address themselves.

Si foret in terris, rideret Democritus. Lat. HORACE.—"If Democritus were on earth, he would laugh at the follies of mankind."

"How these two men," says GIFFORD, speaking of DEMOCRITUS and HERACLITUS, "came to be distinguished by the names of the laughing and the crying philosophers, I know not; they certainly did not deserve such trifling appellations. DEMOCRITUS, in particular, was a man of extraordinary talents: and unless some perverted or exaggerated notions respecting the nature of his skepticism led the vulgar to form so silly an opinion of him, it will be difficult to account for this singular degradation of the first philosopher of his age: although this praise must not, as DR. IRELAND observes, go forth unqualified. He was the father of all that desolating philosophy which, placing the senses in the room of reason, tends to extinguish science, while it encourages personal gratifications. As for HERACLITUS, he was a stern and rigid moralist of what was afterwards called the Stoic school: as little likely to cry upon all occasions as the former to laugh."

Si fortuna juvat, caveto tolli;
Si fortuna tonat, caveto mergi. Lat. AUSONIUS.—

"If fortune favors you, do not be elated; if she should frown, do not despond." Preserve an unruffled mind in all situations.

Si fractus illabatur orbis,
Impavidum ferient ruinae. Lat. HORACE.—

"Should the shattered heavens descend upon him, the ruins would strike him remaining a stranger to fear."

"Let Jove's dread arm with thunders rend the spheres,
Beneath the crush of worlds undaunted he appears."

Applied to the man of undeviating integrity.

Si genus humanum, et mortalia temnitis arma,
At sperate deos memores fandi atque nefandi.
Lat. VIRGIL.—

"If you despise the human race and mortal arms, yet remember that there is a God who is mindful of right and wrong." Recollect that there is a future state of rewards and punishments.

Si in hoc erro quod animos hominum immortales esse credam, libenter erro; nec mihi hunc errorem, quo delector, dum vivo extorqueri volo. Lat. CICERO.—"If in this matter I am in error in believing the souls of men to be immortal, willingly do I err in this respect; nor, so long as I live, should I wish this error, which is altogether so pleasing to me, to be wrested from me, to be torn from my imagination."

Si incolae bene sunt morati, pulcre munitum arbitror. Lat. PLAUTUS.—"If the inhabitants, indwellers, of a town are imbued with correct principles, I consider such town fortified in the best manner imaginable."

Si judicas, cognosce; si regnas, jube. Lat. SENECA.—"If you are a judge, inquire; if you are a monarch, command." If your office be judicial, inform yourself as to the merits of the case; if regal, you may decide from your innate sense of right and wrong.

Si leonina pellis non satis est, assuenda vulpina. Lat. prov. —"If the lion's skin is not enough, sew the fox's to it." What cannot be done by might or force must be done by craft or cunning.

Si mens non laeva fuisset. Lat. VIRGIL.—"If my mind had not been perverted," *literally*, had not been on the *left* side. The Romans considered as unfortunate all omens relating to human affairs that occurred on the left side. It was the reverse of this when the heavens were to be consulted, as the right hand of the divinity was supposed to be to the left of the person looking upward, and making his appeal.

Si monumentum requiris, circumspice. Lat.—"No quotation was ever more happy or more argumentative than Mr. Baring's reply to those who complained that the House of Commons, as then constituted, was insensible to the wishes of the people, when pointing to the Reform majority he exclaimed, *Si monumentum requiris, circumspice:*" that is to say, *If you seek my monument, look around* [you]. N.B. This is a portion of the epitaph of the architect, Sir Christopher Wren, in St. Paul's Cathedral, which he designed and erected. [If you question my merit, behold my works].

Si natura negat, facit indignatio versum. Lat. JUVENAL.—"It is the adjunct of poetry, that is wanting in these letters. It makes the dullest reader feel the spark. *Si natura negat, facit indignatio versus:*" that is to say, *If nature denies* [the power], *indignation brings forth, or makes, verse.* [The verses flow from indignation,—Strong feelings impel, or prompt, one to write.] N.B. In the *original* passage "*versum*" is used: the alteration is of little, if, indeed, of any, consequence.

Si non errasset, fecerat ille minus. Lat. MARTIAL.—"Had he not committed an error, not gone wrong, he would have achieved less." Spoken of a man who has atoned for a temporary lapse by great efforts of virtue or of valor. Thus more poetically translated:—

"Had he not erred, his glory had been less."

Si nous n'avions point de défauts, nous ne prendrions pas tant de plaisir à en remarquer dans les autres. Fr. ROCHEFOUCAULT.—"If we had no defects in ourselves, we should not take so much pleasure in remarking those of others." It is the consciousness of our own weakness that forms the ground of satisfaction on seeing others brought down to the same level.

Si nous ne nous flattions pas nous-mêmes, la flatterie des autres ne pourrait nous nuire. Fr. BOUHOURS.—"Did we not flatter ourselves, the flattery of others could do us no harm." Their incense would be thrown away, were it not grateful to our self-love.

————**Si quid novisti rectius istis,**
Candidus imperti; si non, his utere mecum. Lat. HORACE.—"If you know any thing better than these maxims of mine, kindly, or candidly, impart it, communicate it, make me acquainted with it, tell it me; but if not, make use of the precepts I have laid down, and, together with me, at once reduce them to practice:"—

"Now, brother, if a better system's thine,
Impart it frankly, or make use of mine."

Or, translated in reference to *political pamphleteering:*—

"Brother! if Hume or you have writ
Aught for our common end more fit,
Send it, and earn an old man's thanks,—
[You can't be at a loss for *franks.*]
If you have *really* nothing new,
Sing these with me, and now, adieu!"

————**Si sine amore jocisque**
Nil est jucundum, vivas in amore jocisque. Lat. HORACE.—"If naught appears to you delightful, pleasant, or agreeable without the episodes of love and mirth, then live in love and sportive enjoyments."

"If life's insipid without mirth and love,
Let love and mirth insipid life improve."

A maxim of the *Epicurean* school.

**——————Si veris magna paratur
Fama bonis, et si successu nuda remoto
Inspicitur virtus, quicquid laudamus in ullo
Majorum fortuna fuit.** Lat. LUCAN.—

"If honest fame awaits upon the truly good, and if, setting aside the ultimate success, virtue and valor are alone to be considered, then was his fortune as proud as any to be found in the records of our ancestry." This is the poetic incense offered at the shrine of Pompey. It has been kindled anew, and applied to several unfortunate generals, who could not command success though they had deserved it.

**Si vis incolumem, si vis te reddere sanum,
Curas tolle graves, irasci crede profanum.** Lat.—

"If you wish to preserve yourself in health and in safety, avoid all serious cares, and never give way to vehement passion." This very useful precept has been translated into somewhat homely verse, as follows:—

"If you would safe and happy be, abstain
From anxious cares; think anger, too, profane."

**——————Si vis me flere, dolendum est
Primum ipsi tibi.** Lat. HORACE.—

"If you wish me to weep at the recital of your mournful story, of your sorrows, you must first weep yourself [and thus show that you feel what you say]."

"If you would have me weep, begin the strain
[Then I shall feel your sorrows, feel your pain]."

This was the precept of the didactic to the tragic poet. It is equally applicable to the actor in tragedy. Compare CICERO:—"*Ardeat, qui vult incendere:*" that is, "Let him, who wishes to rouse and inflame the feelings of others, show that he himself is impassioned." Compare also QUINTILIAN: "*Prius afficiamur ipsi, ut alios afficiamus:*" that is, "Let us first show by our manner that we ourselves are *really* affected by what we say, so that we may affect or influence others, may work on the feelings of others."

**——————Si volet usus,
Quem penes arbitrium est et jus et norma loquendi.** Lat. HORACE.—

"If usage, custom, so wills it, on which depend both the rule and the law of speech."

"If custom will, whose arbitrary sway
Words and the forms of language must obey."

The use and the pronunciation of particular words and expressions must, to a certain extent, be governed by the fashion of the day. Compare AULUS GELLIUS:—"*Consuetudo omnium domina rerum, tum maxime verborum est:*" that is, "Custom is the mistress of every thing, and, in a most especial manner, regulates the use of words." Compare also QUINTILIAN:—"*Ridiculum est malle sermonem, quo locuti sint, quam quo loquuntur. Sed necessarium est judicium:*" that is, "It is ridiculous and altogether preposterous to prefer the language of bygone days to the language of our own times or day. Sound judgment, however, and a power of discrimination, are, in matters of this kind, absolutely necessary." See "*Multa renascentur*," &c.

Sic delatores, genus hominum publico exitio repertum, et poenis nunquam satis coercitum, per praemia eliciebantur. Lat. TACITUS.—"Thus were informers, a race of men brought forward for the destruction of the public, and never sufficiently restrained by pains or penalties, allured and invited to action by rewards!" The historian is describing some of the worst evils of a despotic government; and he could not have chosen a stronger instance than in speaking of the race of informers,—men who have always been the bane of all social intercourse, and the curse of every civil institution.

Sic itur ad astra. Lat. VIRGIL.—"Exciting no envy or jealousy, he had every one's good word, and, accommodating himself to the humors of all, all were disposed to befriend him:—*Sic itur ad astra:*" that is to say, *Such is the way to immortality.*

——————— **Sic omnia fatis**
In pejus ruere et retro sublapsa referri. Lat. VIRGIL.—"Thus all things are changed for the worse, and at length go back, retrograde." By the greater number of the ancient poets in particular, every signal misfortune was supposed to spring from a fixed and irrevocable destiny.

Sic passim. Lat.—"So everywhere." This is used to denote that the same sentiment occurs in several passages of the same work.

Sic praesentibus utaris voluptatibus ut futuris non noceas. Lat. SENECA.—"Enjoy your present pleasures so as not to injure those which are to follow." Take care in every indulgence not to destroy your powers by excess.

———————————— **Sic quisque pavendo**
Dat vires famae, nulloque auctore malorum
Quae finxere timet. Lat. LUCAN.—"Thus each person by his fears gives wings to rumor, and, without any real source of apprehension, men fear what they themselves have imagined." Popular apprehension too often causes the mischief that it fears.

Sic sedebat. Lat.—"Thus he sat." "A colossal *sic sedebat* statue of the poet Krylow has been erected at St. Petersburg:" that is, A colossal statute of the poet *in his ordinary sitting attitude, &c.*

Sic transit gloria mundi. Lat. "Thus passes away the glory of this world." Such are the transitions and fluctuations of worldly splendor and of human happiness. "Bishops, who had ever been dull in the pulpit, now preached eloquently from their canvas on the texts, *Memento mori*, or *Sic transit gloria mundi:*" that is to say, on the texts, *Remember to die, Remember death, Remember that you must one day die*, or *Thus passes away the glory of the world.* N.B. The latter quotation is often met with in an abridged form: thus, *Sic transit*, or, *Sic transit gloria.*

Sic utere tuo ut alienum non laedas. Lat. maxim.—"Make use of your own property in such a manner as not to injure that of another." This is often applied in case of nuisances, &c.

Sic volumus. Lat.—"So we will it." "The *sic volumus* of the secretary and the commissioners superseded the directions contained in their patent:" that is, The *arbitrary decision* of the, &c.

Sic vos non vobis. Lat. VIRGIL.—"So you do not labor for yourselves." This is merely the commencement of some stanzas, in which the poet complains that as bees do not make honey, or sheep bear fleeces, for their own use, so the profit and honor of his labors had been usurped by others. The lines are these:—

"Hos ego versiculos feci, tulit alter honores:
Sic vos non vobis nidificatis aves:
Sic vos non vobis vellera fertis oves:
Sic vos non vobis mellificatis apes:
Sic vos non vobis fertis aratra boves:"

that is to say, *I write these little verses, these versicles; but another had the credit of them: Thus do ye birds build nests not for yourselves: thus do ye sheep wear fleeces not for yourselves: thus do ye bees make honey not for yourselves: thus do ye oxen bear the yoke not for yourselves.* The application of these lines is to those who have suffered by the profit and honor of their labors having been usurped by others. The history of these lines is curious. Virgil, the Latin poet, having written and posted up in a conspicuous place a distich [a couple of lines] highly flattering to the emperor Augustus, but without discovering himself, a poet of the name of Bathyllus pretended to be the author, and was consequently much noticed and rewarded by the prince. Virgil, not brooking the injustice patiently, wrote under the distich the words, "*Sic vos non vobis,*" four times. No one having been able to complete the lines, of which these are the beginning, except Virgil himself, the imposture of Bathyllus was detected, and Virgil was then recognized as the author of the applauded distich.

Siècle d'or. Fr.—"The golden age." Applied to the times of LEWIS THE FOURTEENTH of France.

Siesta. Span.—"Mid-day repose, a nap," a practice universally indulged in by the Spaniards.

Signalement. Fr.—"A written description of an individual."

Simia quam similis, turpissima bestia, nobis! Lat.—"How like to a man in shape and in action is that vile beast, the monkey!" The imitative talents of this animal give rise to the curious query:—

"Do chattering monkeys mimic men,
Or we, turned apes, out-monkey them?"

Simplex munditiis. Lat. HORACE.—"Simple in neatness, unaffectedly neat," or, as MILTON has it in his translation,—"Plain in thy neatness." Recommended by propriety of dress, but unincumbered with superfluous ornament.

Simul et jucunda et idonea dicere vitae. Lat. HORACE.—"To tell at once what is pleasant and proper in life." This is the task of the didactic poet, whose business it is to blend amusement with instruction.

Sincerum est nisi vas, quodcunque infundis acescit. Lat. HORACE.—"Unless the vessel be pure, whatever you put into it will turn sour." If the young mind be not duly prepared, all after-instructions will be thrown away.

Sine die. Lat.—"Without a day." The business was deferred *sine die:* no day was named for its reconsideration, or for a further meeting.

Sine invidia. Lat.—"Without envy." Not speaking invidiously.

Sine odio. Lat.—"Without hatred." I speak *sine odio,*—I feel divested of all animosity.

Sine qua non. Lat.—"A thing without which another cannot be." An indispensable condition. An ingredient absolutely necessary.

Sine virtute esse amicitia nullo pacto potest; quae autem inter bonos amicitia dicitur, haec inter malos factio est. Lat. SALLUST.—"There can be no friendship without virtue; for that intimacy which among good men is called friendship, becomes faction when it subsists among the unprincipled."

Singula de nobis anni praedantur euntes. Lat. HORACE.—"Each passing year robs us of a share of what we possessed."

Singula quaeque locum teneant sortita decenter. Lat. HORACE.—"Let each particular species of writing, when once it has had its proper place allotted to it, hold that place in a becoming manner."

"E'er let your style be suited to the scene,
And its peculiar character maintain."

The poet is instructing the playwright not to go into any deviation from propriety of character. The phrase is also used in a political sense to recommend that all things may preserve their due place and order.

Siste, viator! Lat.—"Stop, traveler!" "The *siste, viator!* on the tombstone at once arrested his attention."

Siste, viator! heroem calcas. Lat.—"While pointing to the grave of Lord Raglan, no Russian will refuse to say, *Siste, viator! heroem calcas:*" that is to say, "*Halt, traveler! or thou wilt trample on a hero.*" N.B. The Latin is *inaccurate;* the meaning, however, *intended* to be conveyed, is as above.

Sit meae sedes utinam senectae. Lat. HORACE.—"May such a retreat be the abode or dwelling-place of my old age." "Under the influence of such a retreat we breathe the prayer, *Sit meae,*" &c.

Sit mihi fas audita loqui. Lat. VIRGIL.—"May it be allowed me to state what I have heard."

Sit mihi quod nunc est; etiam minus: et mihi vivam,
Quod superest aevi, si quid superesse volunt Di.

Lat. HORACE.—"May what I now have continue to be mine; or even less, should Heaven deem it good for me: and may I live for my own benefit and improvement so long as the gods grant me life."

——————— "Let me possess
My present wealth, or even less:
And if the bounteous gods design
A longer life, that life be mine."

We have here a fine picture of the manner in which HORACE sought for tranquillity. So far was he from desiring more, that he could even be satisfied with less. He wanted to live for himself, cultivate his mind, and be freed from uncertainty.

Sit pro ratione voluntas. Lat. JUVENAL.—"Let my will stand instead of reason." The language of a tyrant. See "*Hoc volo,*" *&c.*

Sobriquet. Fr.—"A nickname."

Sociétés en commandite. Fr.—"*Commandite*" is a French commercial term, signifying "Partnership in which the acting partners are responsible without limitation, and the sleeping ones to the extent of their share of capital only." "*Société en commandite*" means "*A company instituted and carried on on such principles.*"

Sociétés anonymes. Fr.—"Joint-stock companies."

Soeurs de Charité. Fr.—"Tell them of the tender mercies of the *Soeurs de Charité:*" that is to say, of the *Sisters*, or *Sisterhood, of Charity* [Ladies who "go about doing good,"—who devote themselves to works of love and mercy, for the benefit of their poor fellow-creatures].

Soi-disant. Fr.—"So-called, self-styled, self-dubbed." "The *soi-disant* [*would-be*] improvers of personal appearance not only destroy health, but absolutely engender deformity."

Soirée. Fr.—"An evening party."

Sol occubuit; nox nulla secuta est. Lat.—"The sun set, but no night followed." An ingenious stroke of flattery, addressed to the successor to a throne. The meaning is, "The sun of your father's glory is set, but we feel not the loss whilst enlightened by your radiance."

Solamen curarum. Lat.—"A soother of one's cares: a comfort or consolation in one's troubles." "What an aider of thought is a pinch of snuff! what a *solamen curarum!* what a helpmate of existence!"

Solamen mali. Lat. VIRGIL.—The same meaning as the above, though not quite so expressive or full of meaning.

Solamen miseris socios habuisse doloris. Lat.—"It is a comfort to the wretched to have companions in grief, sympathizers in their woes." This maxim is true only to a certain extent. It may be admitted, however, that a man never suffers so much as when he suffers alone. The sense of sympathy, under other circumstances, tends to diminish the suffering of the individual.

Solatium. Lat.—"Comfort, consolation, solace, soothing unction." "There is nothing new in Frenchmen laying claim to the inventions and discoveries of others; and we were prepared to find Monsieur Dupin seeking his *solatium* in a recurrence to this authentic practice."

Soli Deo gloria. Lat.—"Glory to GOD alone."

Solitudinem faciunt, pacem appellant. Lat. TACITUS.—"They make a desert, and call that tranquillity." They exterminate a people, and then say that peace is restored. It will be for posterity to record that this barbarous solecism was acted upon in various places at the latter end of the eighteenth century.

Solutos qui captat risus hominum, famamque dicacis. Lat. HORACE.—"A man who seeks eagerly for the loud laughter of those around him, and who courts the reputation of a wit."

"Who trivial bursts of laughter strives to raise,
And courts of prating petulance the praise."

The allusion is to one who values not the character or the feelings of others, if he can but raise a laugh at their expense, and who will sacrifice the ties of intimacy and friendship to some paltry witticism.

Solvit ad diem. Law Lat.—"He paid to the day." This is a plea to an action of debt on a bond or penal bill, by which it is alleged that money was paid on the day assigned.

Solvuntur tabulae. Lat.—"The bills are dismissed; the indictment is quashed." The defendant is acquitted.

Somne, quies rerum, placidissime, somne, Deorum,
Pax animi, quem cura fugit, qui corda diurnis
Fessa ministeriis mulces, reparasque labori. Lat. OVID.—
"Sleep, thou repose of all things, Sleep, thou most gentle of the deities, thou peace of the mind, whom care shuns and flees from, who soothest the human frame when wearied, worn out, exhausted, with the toil and labors of the day, and infusest into it vigor and energy for the work of the ensuing morn." An exquisitely beautiful address to SLEEP, a theme on which Poets have ever delighted to dwell.

Somnia Pythagorea. Lat. HORACE.—"When parties were no longer kept together by the pressure of external danger, his *somnia Pythagorea* were rudely dispelled:" that is to say, his *dreams of private and public virtue* were, &c. [literally, his *Pythagorean dreams*]. N.B. Pythagoras was one of the ancient Greek philosophers, and a believer, or *pretended* believer, in the doctrine of the "*transmigration of souls.*"

Sortie. Fr.—"A sally." "A vigorous *sortie* was made from the town on the French works."

Sotto voce. Ital.—"In an under-tone, in a whisper."

Souvenir. Fr.—"A remembrance, memorial."

Souvent femme varie,
Bien fol est qui s'y fie. Fr. FRANCIS THE FIRST.—
"Everything at Chambord reminds us of FRANCIS THE FIRST. We still look with interest at the pane of glass on which with the diamond of one of his rings he scratched this memorable distich [*couplet of verses*]:—

'*Souvent femme varie,*
Bien fol est qui s'y fie.' "

Often does woman change, and very foolish is he who trusts her:—

"Oft does woman change her mind,—
Trust her not, thou foolish hind!"

Or,
"Oft does woman veer about,—
Trust her not, thou lumpish lout!"

Spargere voces in vulgum ambiguas. Lat. VIRGIL.—"To give utterance to words of dubious import, of doubtful meaning, among the crowd." To circulate deceptive rumors among the populace. This is an imputation frequently brought forward by one or the other of two contending parties.

———————**Spatio brevi**
Spem longam reseces. Dum loquimur, fugerit invida
Aetas. Carpe diem, quam minimum credula postero.
Lat. HORACE.—
"In consequence of the brief span of human existence, indulge not in

remote expectations. E'en whilst we are speaking, envious time, time, that grudges us our enjoyments, is rapidly passing away. Enjoy, then, the present day, trusting as little as possible to futurity."

"Thy lengthened hopes with prudence bound
Proportioned to the flying hour.
E'en while we chat in careless ease,
The envious moments wing their flight:
Instant the fleeting pleasure seize,
Nor trust to-morrow's doubtful light."

See "*Vitae summa brevis*," *&c.*

Spectas et tu spectabere. Lat.—"You see, and you shall be seen." You witness here the exhibition of character: but, if your faults deserve it, you shall be exhibited in your turn.

Spectatum admissi, risum teneatis, amici? Lat. HORACE.—"Can you, my friends, on being admitted to see (the picture), refrain from laughter?" Must not the risible muscles, even of partiality, give way at an exhibition so ridiculous?

Spectemur agendo. Lat.—"Let us be tried by our actions." Let us be examined by our conduct, be regarded according to our conduct.

Spem bonam certamque domum reporto. Lat.—"I bring home with me a good and certain hope." The prospect which opens on me is highly soothing and encouraging.

Spem pretio non emo. Lat. TERENCE.—"I do not buy hope with pounds, shillings, and pence." I do not annex any value to idle expectations.

Sperat infestis, metuit secundis
Alteram sortem bene praeparatum
Pectus. Lat. HORACE.—

"The mind which is well prepared hopes for a change of condition in adversity, and fears it in prosperity."

"Whoe'er enjoys th' untroubled breast,
With Virtue's tranquil wisdom blest,
With Hope the gloomy hour can cheer,
And temper Happiness with Fear."

The philosophic mind can buoy up distress by hope, and curb the insolence of success by reflecting on its instability.

Sperate, et vosmet rebus servate secundis. Lat. VIRGIL.—"Live in hope, and reserve yourselves for more prosperous times." An appeal, from the only source of consolation left, to companions in adversity.

Sperate miseri, cavete felices. Lat.—"Let the wretched live in hope, and the happy be on their guard." Such is the mutability of fortune that the lowest have something to expect, and the highest something to fear.

Speravimus ista dum fortuna fuit. Lat. VIRGIL.—"We hoped for such things when favored by fortune." We presumed so far in our better days.

Sperne voluptates,—nocet emta dolore voluptas. Lat. HORACE.—"Despise all vain enjoyment; pleasure, when purchased at the price of pain, is injurious." The pursuit of pleasure to excess not only takes away the faculty of enjoyment, but also leaves a sting behind.

Spero meliora. Lat. OVID.—"I hope for better times or things."

Spes incerta futuri. Lat. VIRGIL.—"The uncertain hope of the future: the hope reposed in the future [which, either for good or for evil, is altogether a matter of uncertainty]." The hopes and fears held in equal balance.

Spiritus intus alit, totamque infusa per artus
Mens agitat molem, et magno se corpore miscet.

Lat. VIRGIL.—
"The Spirit of GOD, the Divine Spirit, supports the vital principle, and, diffusing itself through every limb, sets in motion the entire bodily machine, and blends itself with the whole frame."

Splendide mendax. Lat. HORACE.—"Egregiously mendacious or false." "I did not dare to follow an example so *splendide mendax:*" that is, so "remarkably inaccurate." N.B. In the *original* passage the meaning is "*Gloriously false*," that is, "*False in a good cause.*"

Spretae injuria formae. Lat. VIRGIL.—"The insult offered to her despised beauty." This is spoken of the resentment of JUNO in consequence of the well-known judgment of PARIS. The intrigues of courts, where women bear sway, have made it a phrase of modern application.

Stans pede in uno. Lat. HORACE.—"Standing upon one leg, in a very short time." A work composed *stans pede in uno,*—with no more than an ordinary degree of exertion.

Stare decisis, et non quieta movere. Lat. Law maxim.—"To stand by things as decided, and not to disturb those that are tranquil, that are going on in the old jog-trot style."

Stare super vias antiquas. Lat.—"To stand to the old paths," and not to give way to any bold novelties.

Stat magni nominis umbra. Lat. LUCAN.—"He stands merely as the shadow of a mighty name." He exhibits only a faint shadow of his former greatness.

Stat mole sua. Lat.—"Firm in its impregnability, unmoved it stands." "To those who predict the ruin of England, an Englishman may say, *Stat mole sua.*"

Stat sua cuique dies; breve et irreparabile tempus
Omnibus est vitae; sed famam extendere factis,
Hoc virtutis opus. Lat. VIRGIL.—
"Every man has his appointed time allotted him; a short and irrecoverable term of existence is assigned to, bestowed on, all; but to extend our fame, our renown, to gain a glorious name by distinguished achievements, this is, in troth, true virtue's work." Superior genius or virtue can overleap the brief span of human life, and consecrate the name of their possessor to immortality.

Statim daret, ne differendo videretur negare. Lat. CORNELIUS NEPOS.—"He would give at once, lest, by delaying, he might seem to deny the favor." This language is used by the historian in speaking of Themistocles. It is in other words the proverb, *Bis dat,* &c., [which see].

Status Lat.—"Position." "His *status* in society."

Status in quo. Lat.—"He resolved to face at once the legion of interests pledged to the maintenance of the *status in quo*," that is, of the "*existing state of things*," of the "*state of things as they now are.*"

Status quo ante. Lat.—"Things returned into the *status quo ante*;" that is to say [in]to the *same state in which they were before the outbreak.* N.B. "*Status quo*," or "*status quo ante bellum*," are phrases used in speaking of belligerent powers when they agree, as a preliminary to peace, to restore their conquests, to return to that condition in which the parties respectively stood before the commencement of hostilities. The *opposite* of these phrases is "*Uti possidetis*,"—As you now possess, now are. [A maintenance for a time of the respective positions of two sovereigns.] A diplomatic phrase, used when two sovereigns, after sacrificing a number of human lives, &c., choose to make peace, "each retaining the possessions which he may have acquired."

Stavo bene, ma per star meglior sto qui. Ital.—"I was well, but by endeavoring to be better I am here." "I was well, would be better, took physic, and died." The epitaph on a hypochondriac, who, though well in health, was not easy until he had quacked himself into his grave. Used to mark the discontent of those who are dissatisfied when in an eligible situation.

Stellas inter Luna minores. Lat.—"However high may be our comparative rank, however we may shine by the force of contrast, *stellas inter Luna minores*,—there is still too fatal a scope for the benevolent exertions of the philosopher and the philanthropist to authorize the inactivity of either:" that is to say, as *the Moon* [shines] *among the smaller stars.* N.B. In the *original* passage in Horace the words are "*inter ignes Luna minores*," that is, as *the Moon* [shines] *among the feebler fires* [of the night],—the stars. The meaning, however, is the same.

Stemmata quid faciunt? Quid prodest, Pontice, longo
Sanguine censeri? Lat. Juvenal.—
"Of what avail are pedigrees, or to derive one's blood from a long line of ancestors?" Without virtue or genius, what are the boasted advantages of high birth?

Stimulos dedit aemula virtus. Lat. Lucan.—"He was spurred on by rival valor." An honorable emulation is the best incentive to acts of greatness.

Stimulus. Lat.—"A motive, spur, inducement, or incentive." "A moral *stimulus*."

Stratum super stratum. Lat.—"One layer upon another." Beds of matter ranged alternately one upon the other.

Strenua nos exercet inertia; navibus atque
Quadrigis petimus bene vivere: quod petis, hic est.
Lat. Horace.—
"A laborious idleness occupies us, engrosses all our attention; and with our ships and our carriages we seek for a spot in which to live happily. That which we seek is on the spot."

"Anxious through seas and lands to search for rest
Is but laborious idleness at best.

In any wretched spot the bliss you'll find,
If you preserve a firm and equal mind."

Again:—

"Active in indolence, abroad we roam,
In search of happiness, which dwells at home.
With vain pursuits fatigued at length you'll find
No place excludes it from an equal mind."

It is not in change of place to afford that happiness which is only to be found in the bosom of honest consciousness.

Studiosus emeritus. Lat.—"A student who has gone through or completed his academical, or collegiate, career."

Stultitiam patiuntur opes. Lat. Horace.—"Riches bear out folly." The rich fool is suffered to play such pranks with impunity, as, if played off by one in an inferior station, would meet, not only with derision, but also with punishment.

"Their folly pleads the privilege of wealth."

Stultitiam simulare in loco sapientia summa est. Lat. prov. —"To assume the garb of folly is, in certain situations, the most consummate wisdom." Such was the conduct of the first Brutus, who, by affecting to be mad, eluded the vengeance of Tarquin, and ultimately succeeded in expelling that tyrant.

Stultorum incurata pudor malus ulcera celat. Lat. Horace. —"The false shame of fools makes them hide their uncured sores." It is the height of folly to conceal our faults from those from whom we may derive amendment. This maxim applies both morally and physically.

Stultum est timere quod vitare non potes. Lat. Publius Syrus. —"It is idle to dread that which you cannot avoid." In such a case, instead of giving way to fear, we should summon up all our fortitude.

Stultus labor est ineptiarum. Lat. Martial.—"Silly is the labor that is bestowed on trifles."

Stultus, nisi quod ipse facit, nil rectum putat. Lat. prov.— "The fool thinks nothing well done but what is done by himself."

Style ampoulé. Fr.—"A high-flown, or bombastic style [of writing]."

Sua cuique voluptas. Lat. prov.—"Every man has his own peculiar pleasure." Every person has a taste for some particular enjoyment.

Sua quisque exempla debet aequo animo pati. Lat. Phaedrus. —"Every man is bound to tolerate the act of which he himself has set the example." No man can fairly complain of that as injustice, of which he himself has furnished a previous specimen.

Sua si bona norint. Lat. Virgil.—"If they did but appreciate the blessings they enjoy." "If these students duly reflected on their own privileges,—*sua si bona norint*,—they must feel their position to be one of great advantage."

Suave est ex magno tollere acervo. Lat. Horace.—"It is pleasant to take from a great heap." The poet speaks sarcastically of a miser, whose perverse delight it was to take from a large hoard the little that he ventured to use.

Suave, mari magno. Lat. Lucretius.—"They are amused with his manner of browbeating and badgering a witness. *Suave mari magno:* they are glad it is not they themselves; and they feel a prospective dread of ever undergoing the same ordeal." "*Suave mari magno*" is the commencement of an oft-quoted passage in Lucretius [a very celebrated Latin poet]. The lines, to which allusion is here made, are these:—

"*Suave, mari magno turbantibus aequora ventis,*
E terra magnum alterius spectare laborem:"

that is to say, *Sweet, pleasant,* or *agreeable is it, when the waves of the ocean are agitated by a storm* [when the sea runs high], *to view from the shore—land—the severe labors of others* [the distress in which others are plunged].

"When raging winds the ruffled deep deform,
We look at distance and enjoy the storm;
Tossed on the waves with pleasure others see,
Nor heed their danger, while ourselves are free."

Secure ourselves, we too often view with indifference the dangers of others.

Suaviter in modo, fortiter in re. Lat.—"We need men of experience, of firm and intelligent minds, who can blend the *suaviter in modo* in due proportion with the *fortiter in re:*" that is to say, who can blend *pleasing manners* in due . . . with the *vigorous discharge of their duties.* N.B. The *literal* meaning of "*suaviter in modo, fortiter in re*" is, *sweetly,* or *pleasantly, in manner,* but *vigorously,* or *firmly, in action, deed,* or *execution.*

Sub dio. Lat.—"In the open air."

Sub judice lis est. Lat. HORACE.—"The matter in question is before the judge, is undecided: the point is undecided."

Sub poena. Law Lat.—"Under a penalty." The name given to a writ for the summoning of witnesses.

Sub rosa. Lat.—"Under the rose." "I will, *sub rosa,* afford you my best assistance:" that is, I will, *privately, secretly, confidentially:* literally, *under the rose.* N.B. Much controversy has arisen about the expression "*under the rose,*" and two different origins have been assigned to it. Some assert that it ought to be spelled "under the *rows,*" inasmuch as in former days almost all towns were built with the second story projecting over the lower one, a sort of piazza or *row* as they termed it, and which may still be seen at Chester, and some other old English towns; so that, whilst the papas and mammas were sitting at the windows gravely enjoying the air, their sons and daughters were making love where they could not see them, "under the *rows.*" The other solution is much more elegant. Cupid, it is said, gave a rose to Harpocrates, the god of silence; and from this legend originated the practice, that prevailed among Northern nations, of suspending a rose from the ceiling over the upper end of the table when it was intended that the conversation was to be kept secret; and this it was, according to others, which gave rise to the phrase, "*under the rose.*"

Sub silentio. Lat.—"In silence." The matter passed *sub silentio,* without any notice being taken of it.

Sublata causa, tollitur effectus. Lat.—"When the cause is removed, the effect must cease." The efficient cause of a distemper in the human frame, for instance, being removed, its effects may be expected speedily to terminate.

Sublatam ex oculis quaerimus. Lat. HORACE.—"When taken

away from us, then do we know how to appreciate it, or them, and in vain regret the loss of it, or them." Said in reference to virtue, virtuous men meritorious men, men illustrious by their merits.

Sublimi feriam sidera vertice. Lat. HORACE.—"My lofty head shall strike the stars: I shall strike the stars or firmament with my exalted head." This flight of the poet is now employed as a commonplace pleasantry.

Substantia prior et dignior est accidente. Lat. Law maxim.—"The substance should be considered as prior to, and of more weight than, the accident." No judgment, it is held, shall be arrested in any court of record for any defect in point of *form*, or unless it be a matter of *substance* on which the judges of those courts are to decide.

Subterranea. Lat.—"The subterraneous or underground parts of the earth, the bowels of the earth."

Succedaneum. Lat.—"A substitute." "It is the best *succedaneum* for the genuine article." Impudence is frequently used as a *succedaneum* for argument.

Sufficit ad id, Natura quod poscit. Lat. SENECA.—"We have a sufficiency when we have what Nature requires." Her wants are but few, and the consciousness of this should teach us limitation and content.

Sufflamen. Lat.—"The cost usually proves a sufficient *sufflamen* in these days to the belligerent propensities of nations:" that is to say, a sufficient *drag-chain*, *stop*, *delay*, *choke-pear*, in these, &c. N.B. The *literal* meaning of "*sufflamen*" is *that which is put into the wheel to stop or stay it, lest the cart or carriage be overthrown, a trigger of a wheel.*

Suggestio falsi. Lat.—"The suggestion of a falsehood, or hint tc give utterance to a falsehood." This and the *suppressio veri*, or "sup pression or concealment of the truth," are the strongest charges whicl can be made against a public orator or writer.

Sui cuique mores fingunt fortunam. Lat. CORNELIUS NEPOS.—"His own morals (or manners) shape the fortune of every man." Thu the English proverb, "Manners make the man."

Sui generis. Lat.—"Of its own kind, of a kind peculiar to itself."

Suite. Fr.—"A sumptuous dinner was provided for His Excellency and *suite*," that is, and *retinue, attendants.*

Sumite materiam vestris, qui scribitis, aequam
Viribus. Lat. HORACE.—

"Do ye who compose literary works, fix on a subject adequate to your powers of mind, suited to your capacity, abilities." If in the labor of literature, as well as in the works of art, it is all-important to produce a complete and finished *whole*, and not to confine ourselves merely to certain individual parts that are more within our reach than others, it becomes equally important for us to be well acquainted with the nature and extent of our own talents, and to be careful to select such a subject as may in all its parts be proportioned to our strength and ability.

Summam nec metuas diem, nec optes. Lat. MARTIAL.—"Neither fear nor wish for your last day." The philosophic mind neither timidly shrinks from death, nor desperately wishes to accelerate its approach.

Summi honores medicinae. Lat.—"The highest honors in the faculty of medicine, in the medical profession."

Summum bonum. Lat.—"The chief good." The object the most desirable to be attained. N.B. Among the ancients, some philosophers held pleasure to be the "*Summum bonum*" of this life, while others preferred virtue.

Summum crede nefas animam praeferre pudori,
Et propter vitam vivendi perdere causas. Lat. JUVENAL.—"We do not think any Greek could have understood or sympathized with Juvenal. Is it possible to put into Greek such lines as these?—

'*Summum crede nefas animam praeferre pudori,*
Et propter vitam vivendi perdere causas:' "

that is to say, *Deem it the summit of impiety* [the very height of wickedness] *to prefer existence, life, to honor, and for the sake of life to sacrifice life's only end!*

"Think it a crime no tears can e'er efface,
To purchase safety with compliance base,—
At honor's cost a feverish span extend,
AND SACRIFICE FOR LIFE LIFE'S ONLY END!
[LIFE! I profane the word: can those be said
To live, who merit death? No! They are dead]."

Summum jus summa injuria. Lat.—"Strictness of law is sometimes the greatest injustice. Extreme justice is sometimes extreme injustice." A too rigorous interpretation of the law is not unfrequently productive of results which do not accord with equity.

Sunt bona, sunt quaedam mediocria, sunt mala plura. Lat. MARTIAL.—"Some are good, some but middling, and a decided majority bad." Said by the poet in speaking of the Epigrams he had written.

————————**Sunt certi** [denique] **fines,**
Quos ultra citraque nequit consistere rectum.
Lat. HORACE.—

"There are certain fixed limits, on either side of which what is right, or rectitude, cannot be found, cannot exist."

Sunt lacrymae rerum, et mentem mortalia tangunt. Lat. VIRGIL.—"Tears are due to human misery, and the woes of mortality affect the heart." Every virtuous mind, on hearing of such calamities, must be touched with sympathy.

Sunt superis sua jura. Lat. OVID.—"The gods or supreme powers have their own laws." This is sometimes quoted in political discussions, to intimate that the higher powers often overlook those duties and promises which are supposed to be binding on the lower orders of the community.

Suo Marte. Lat.—"By his own exertions." He performed it *suo Marte*, by his own unaided skill and ability.

Suo sibi gladio hunc jugulo. Lat. TERENCE.—"With his own sword do I stab this man." I defeat him figuratively, and in argument, with the weapons and the admissions which he himself has furnished.

Super subjectam materiam. Lat.—"On the matter submitted." A lawyer is not responsible for his opinion, when it is given *super subjectam materiam*,—on the circumstances as they are laid before him by his client.

Superanda omnis fortuna ferendo est. Lat. VIRGIL.—"Every misfortune is to be subdued by patience." See "*Tu ne cede,*" *&c.*

Supersedeas. Law Lat.—"You may remove or set aside." A writ to stay proceedings.

Suppressio veri. Lat.—See "*Suggestio falsi.*"

Surgit amari aliquid, &c. Lat. LUCRETIUS.—See "*Medio de fonte,*" *&c.*

Surplus. Compounded from the Latin.—See "*Bonus.*"

Surveillance. Fr.—"The officer has been placed under *surveillance:*" that is to say, under the *inspection or supervision* of the police. N.B. "*Surveillance*" is often used to signify *supervision, superintendence, watching over, or looking after*, without reference to the police.

Susceptibilités démocratiques. Fr.—"Democratic touchinesses, irritabilities;" leanings, tendencies, of a democratic cast or character.

Suspectum semper invisumque dominantibus qui proximus destinaretur. Lat. TACITUS.—"The next in succession is ever hated and suspected by those who are actually in possession of the supreme power." This can only apply to those governments where the persons in possession of absolute power fear that it may be wrested from them by violent means. In the language of our poet, they

"Bear, like the Turk, no brother near the throne."—POPE.

Suspendens omnia naso. Lat. HORACE.—"A man who makes a joke of every thing that passes, goes on, in the social circle, who turns every thing into ridicule for the purpose of exciting laughter."

Suum cuique. Lat.—"Let every one have his own." Let the laws of property be strictly observed. "Conversations on art are surely not inferior to conversations on the sports of the field,—*Suum cuique:*" that is, "*Let every one please himself.*"

Suum cuique incommodum ferendum est, potius quam de alterius commodis detrahendum. Lat. CICERO.—"Every man should bear his own grievances and inconveniences, rather than detract from or abridge the comforts of another."

Suus cuique mos. Lat. TERENCE.—"Every man has his particular habit." In opinions and habits there is a permanent diversity, and every person should in fairness be left to the free exercise of his own.

Symposium. From the Greek.—"A drinking-party, a banquet or feast."

T.

Table d'hôte. Fr.—"An ordinary, a dinner at which the landlord of an inn or tavern presides."

Tableau de genre. Fr.—A painting of any kind, except *history* and *landscape.* The *plural* is "*tableaux de genre.*"

Tabula rasa. Lat.—"A shaved (or smoothed) tablet." His mind is a *tabula rasa*, it is a mere blank. The idea is taken from the waxed tablets of the ancients, on which they wrote with a sharp instrument, called a *stilus*, with the other broad end of which they afterwards erased what they had written.

Tacent, satis laudant. Lat. TERENCE.—"Their silence is sufficient praise." It is ample proof of worth, when the censorious have nothing to allege.

Tacitum vivit sub pectore vulnus. Lat. VIRGIL.—"The secret wound still lives within the breast." The injury is not forgotten, but is treasured up for an opportunity of revenge.

Taedium vitae. Lat.—"A weariness of life, burden of existence." A disgust with existence. This, in France, is called *ennui;* but this does not amount to the full force of the Latin term.

Tam deest avaro quod habet quam quod non habet. Lat. PUBLIUS SYRUS.—"The miser is as much in want of that which he has as of that which he has not."

Tam Marte quam Mercurio. Lat.—"They have exhibited in the strongest light either the firmness which disdains to correct an error, or the cunning which rejoices to smuggle an enactment,—*Tam Marte quam Mercurio;*" that is to say, *As much by courage as by roguery.* N.B. By a figure of speech *Mars*, the heathen god of war, is here used for *courage*, and *Mercury*, the heathen god of thieves, for *roguery.*

Tam Marte quam Minerva. Lat.—"As much by MARS as by MINERVA." He has succeeded "*tam Marte quam Minerva,*" equally by his courage and his genius.

Tant mieux. Fr.—"So much the better."

Tant pis. Fr.—"So much the worse."

Tantae molis erat Romanam condere gentem. Lat. VIRGIL.—"Of the promised growth of British art we must still say, as was said of the greatest fabric of antiquity,—

Tantae molis erat Romanam condere gentem:"

that is to say, *A task of such difficulty was it to found the Roman nation,* or, *So difficult was it to found the Roman nation or state:*

"So vast the work, to build the mighty frame
And raise the glories of the Roman name."

Tantaene animis coelestibus irae. Lat. VIRGIL.—"Can heavenly minds such anger entertain?" Is it possible for exalted minds to descend to such low resentments?

Tanto buon che val niente. Ital. prov.—"So good that he is good for nothing." Applied to that weak good nature, which is injurious to the possessor, without being of advantage to any other person.

Tanto homini fidus, tantae virtutis amator. Lat.—"A faithful friend to so great a man, and a steady admirer of such distinguished excellence."

Tantum de medio sumtis accedit honoris. Lat. HORACE.—"So much honor is due to subjects taken from middle or common life: so much grace may be imparted to subjects taken from the common mass:" *in other words,* So capable are the meanest and plainest things of ornament and grace. This is a praise justly granted to authors of plays where the sentiments come home to every man's business and bosom, as contradistinguished from those where emperors, queens, and heroes fill the scene, and whose sorrows astound for the moment, but in a moment are forgotten.

Tantum se fortunae permittunt, etiam ut naturam dedis cant. Lat. QUINTUS CURTIUS.—"So much do they give themselves up to the pursuit of fortune as even to forget their nature, their natural disposition, the noble objects for which they were created."

Tantum series juncturaque pollet. Lat. HORACE.—"Of so much force are system and connection." A less perfect book, if stamped with these characters, will please more than one of superior quality, in which the principles are scattered and the reasoning disjointed.

Tarde, quae credita laedunt, credimus. Lat. OVID.—"We are slow to believe that which, if believed, would hurt our feelings."

Τη γνωμη ὑπηρετειν εθιστεον το σωμα. Gr. XENOPHON.—"We must accustom the body to obey the mind."

Te Deum. Lat.—The "*Te Deum*" is a hymn of the Romish Church, beginning with these Latin words, "*Te Deum Laudamus*"—We praise Thee, O GOD; *or rather*, We praise Thee, the LORD GOD Almighty—*or*, We give praises that Thou art the LORD GOD Almighty. This sublime hymn is sung on extraordinary occasions, in giving thanks to Almighty GOD for a victory, on any other propitious occurrence.

Tel brille au second rang qui s'éclipse au premier. Fr.—"A man may shine in the second rank who would be eclipsed in the first." Many, who conceive themselves fitted for first-rate characters in life, would in fact appear to more advantage in subordinate situations.

Tel en vous lisant admire chaque trait,
Qui dans le fond de l'âme et vous craint et vous hait.
Fr. BOILEAU.—"Such a one, on reading your work, admires every stroke, but from the bottom of his soul he both fears and hates you." The living satirist excites more fear than regard.

Tel est notre plaisir. Fr.—"Such is our pleasure." An expression much used by LEWIS THE FOURTEENTH of France.

Tel maître, tel valet. Fr. prov.—"Like master, like man.

Τελος ορᾶν μακρον βιου. Gr.—"To see the end of a long life." This was the wish of Chilias, one of the celebrated Seven Wise Men of Greece.

Τηλου ναιοντες φιλοι ουκ εισι φιλοι. Gr.—"Friends dwelling at a distance are no friends, can scarcely be called friends."

Telum imbelle sine ictu. Lat. VIRGIL.—"A feeble dart thrown without effect." Applied metaphorically to a weak, silly, or worthless argument.

Temperatae suaves sunt argutiae: immodicae offendunt. Lat. PHAEDRUS.—"Temperate witticisms, witticisms in season or well timed, are ever gratifying: improperly introduced they are offensive."

Tempestivus usus. Lat.—"The suitable or fitting time for using any thing, making use of any thing [administering remedies, for instance]."

Tempora mutantur, et nos mutamur in illis. Lat.—"The times are changed, are perpetually changing, and we ourselves change with the times." Naught is fixed or stable, either in situations or in opinions.

"Men change with fortune, manners change with climes,
Tenets with books, and principles with times."

Tempora si fuerint nubila, solus eris. Lat. Ovid.—"If storms set in, you will be alone, will be left entirely to yourself." Adversity finds but few companions or comforters. See "*Donec eris,*" *&c.*

Tempore ducetur longo fortasse cicatrix:
Horrent admotas vulnera cruda manus. Lat. Ovid.—
"In process of time the wound will, perhaps, be closed: it shrinks, however, from the touch, while it is yet recent, fresh." This is figuratively applied to sorrow, in the first burst of which it will reject the most friendly appeal: some time should, therefore, be suffered to elapse before any attempt is made to administer consolation.

Tempore felici multi numerantur amici
Si fortuna perit, nullus amicus erit. Lat. Ovid.—
"In the day of prosperity we may number many [so-called] friends: but, if riches take to themselves wings and fly off, we shall be left all alone, we may help ourselves as we can." See "*Donec eris,*" *&c.*, and "*Tempora si,*" *&c.*

Tempus edax rerum. Lat. Ovid.—"Time is the devourer, consumer, of all things."

Tempus omnia revelat. Lat. prov.—"Time reveals, brings to light, all things." Few things escape the disclosure of time.

Teneros animos aliena opprobria saepe absterrent vitiis. Lat. Horace.—"The disgrace that others fall into often deters the youthful mind, tender minds, from the practice of vice, from vicious propensities."

"Oft does another's shame the tender mind alarm."

Tenet insanabile multos scribendi cacoëthes. Lat. Juvenal.—"Many have an incurable itch for writing, an incurable propensity to become authors." Numerous in every age has been the race of those

——————"Who in despite
Of nature and their stars will never cease to write."

Tenez bonne table et soignez les femmes. Fr.—"*Tenez bonne table et soignez les femmes,* was the sum of Napoleon's instructions to the Abbé de Pradt, when dispatched to gain over Poland to his cause:" that is to say, *Keep a good table, give good dinners, good spreads, and pay attention to the ladies, don't forget or neglect the ladies,* was the sum, &c. N.B. The word "*Abbé*" properly means *Father;* it is the title or designation of every French Catholic clergyman.

——————**Tentanda via est, qua me quoque possim**
Tollere humo, victorque virum volitare per ora. Lat. Virgil.—"A course must be tried, by which I also may be enabled to rise from the earth, from obscurity, and triumphantly spread my fame." A quotation often applied sarcastically to literary adventurers, who, trying a new path, often mistake deviation for improvement.

Teres atque rotundus. Lat. Horace.—"A man smooth and round, polished and round." N.B. "*Teres atque rotundus*" means one who is conscious of his own rectitude, and sensible of the regularity and evenness of his dispositions and desires, and who, like a polished globe, rolls on without deviation, in his even course, keeps the noiseless tenor of his way.

Terra firma. Lat.—"He finally reached *terra firma* in safety:"

that is to say, reached *the ground*, &c. [said of a very pompous country squire alighting from his carriage]. "We soon made *terra firma*:" that is to say, We soon made *the land*, or soon reached *land*.

Terra incognita. Lat.—"An unknown land: a land to which any one is a perfect stranger."

Terra malos homines nunc educat atque pusillos. Lat. JUVENAL.—"This earth now maintains, as before, both bad and weak men." The condition of the human species in all ages is nearly the same.

Terrae filius. Lat.—"A son of the earth." An Oxford phrase, signifying a man of no birth.

Terrae motus. Lat.—"Truckling, as is the rule, when no immediate *terrae motus* is apprehended, he consented to produce the dispatches:" that is to say, when no immediate *hubbub, commotion*, is, &c. N.B. The *literal* meaning of "*terrae motus*" is an *earthquake*.

Terminus a quo and **Terminus ad quem.** Lat.—"My *terminus a quo*, as the lawyers call it, was Fleet Street, and my *terminus ad quem*, Charing Cross." "*Terminus a quo*" means "a starting-point." "*Terminus ad quem*," "the end of one's journey."

Tertium quid. Lat.—"A third something." Struck out by the collision of two opposite forces or principles.

Της φυσεως γραμματευς ην, τον καλαμον αποβρεξων εις νουν. Gr. SUIDAS.—"He was the writer (or interpreter) of nature, dipping his pen into mind."

Tête-à-tête. Fr.—"A private interview or conversation between two individuals." "And so terminated the *tête-à-tête*."

Tête-de-pont. Fr.—A military term. "The work that defends the head or entrance of a bridge."

Têtes montées. Fr.—"Over-excited persons, persons whose heads are turned."

Tiers-état. Fr.—*Literally*, "The third estate," that is, "The people of France as distinguished from the nobility and the higher clergy."

Timeo Danaos et dona ferentes. Lat. VIRGIL.—"I fear the Greeks, even when they offer presents." I am on my guard against an enemy, and particularly when he proffers kindness.

Timidus se vocat cautum: parcum, sordidus. Lat. PUBLIUS SYRUS.—"The coward says that he is cautious; the miser, that he is sparing." We have each an excuse, or palliation, for our respective faults.

Tirade. Fr.—"An invective, philippic," [which see].

Toga virilis. Lat.—"The manly robe." "The assumption of the *toga virilis* should take place before the young man's entrance into public life." N.B. "*Toga virilis*" signifies *the manly gown, or gown of manhood*, a garment worn by the Roman youth when they came of age. The assumption of the *manners, habits, appearance, and dress of a gentleman* should, &c.

Toilette. Fr.—"Dress and every thing connected with it."

Tolle ambitionem et fastuosos spiritus, nullos habebis nec Platones, nec Catones, nec Scaevolas, nec Scipiones, nec Fabricios. Lat. SENECA.—"Take away ambition and vanity, and where will be your heroes or patriots?" Compare ROCHEFOUCAULT. "Virtue would not go far, if vanity did not bear her company."

Tolle jocos: non est jocus esse malignum. Lat.—"Away with such jokes; there is no joke in being spiteful, malignant." Applied, and properly so, to that sarcastic merriment which wounds the peace or feelings of the individual, for the purpose of giving entertainment to the many.

Tolle moras: semper nocuit differre paratis. Lat. LUCAN.—"Away with all delays; it is even injurious to postpone, when you are in readiness." The application is in particular to war. When you are ready, you should allow the enemy no time for preparation.

——————————**Tolle periclum;**
Jam vaga prosiliet frenis natura remotis. Lat. HORACE.—"Take away the danger of detection in aught that is wrong, and soon will vagrant nature, nature that is so prone to deviate from the path of rectitude, go beyond all bounds when restraints are removed, when there is no check on it."

"But take the danger and the shame away,
And vagrant nature bounds upon her prey,
Spurning the reins."

Tolluntur in altum ut lapsu graviore ruant. Lat. CLAUDIAN.—"They are raised to such a height that they may tumble with a heavier fall." Some men seem to have been raised to the summit of their ambition only to aggravate the subsequent reverses which Providence has doomed them to experience. See "*Saevius ventis*," *&c.*

Tota hujus mundi concordia ex discordiis constat. Lat. SENECA.—"The only concord, in which the whole world agree, consists of discordant principles, or of principles altogether discordant."

Tota sua vita durante. Lat.—"During the whole of one's life."

Totidem verbis. Lat.—"In so many words, in just as many words." "The story is told *totidem verbis*."

Toties quoties. Lat. Law term.—"As often, so often: as many times as, then so often." A term frequently used in law proceedings: thus—if A. B. commit a certain offense, he shall be fined £10, and so on, *toties quoties;* namely, on every repetition of the offense he shall incur a similar penalty.

Totis viribus. Lat.—"With all his strength, with all the power of which one is master, in the strongest manner possible."

Toto coelo. Lat.—"By the whole heavens." The men differ *toto coelo*, their dispositions are as opposite as the poles.

Totum. Lat.—"The whole." "He objects to the *totum* as not including the *pars* [part]."

Totum hoc indictum volo. Lat.—"I wish the whole of such language to be unsaid: I could wish the whole," &c. [I recall, so far as I can, all such language.]

Totus his locus est contemnendus in nobis, non negligendus in nostris. Lat. CICERO.—"This place (the place of our sepulture) is wholly to be disregarded by us, but not to be neglected by our surviving friends."

Totus in toto, et totus in qualibet parte. Lat.—"Whole in itself, and whole in every part." This was the definition given by the ancient schoolmen of the human mind.

Totus mundus agit histrionem. Lat.—"All the world acts the player." All the world's a stage.

Tour d'adresse. Fr.—"A sleight-of-hand trick."

Tour d'impuissance. Fr.—"A feat displaying a signal want of capacity or ability."

Tour de force. Fr.—"A feat of strength."

Tourner casaque. Fr.—"To turn a man's coat." This in former times was regarded as a disgrace.

Tours de page. Fr.—"School-boys' tricks."

Tous frais faits. Fr.—"All expenses paid."

Tous les hommes sont fous, et malgré leurs soins
Ne diffèrent entr'eux que du plus ou du moins.

Fr. BOILEAU.—"All men are fools, and with every effort they differ only in the degree." There will only be the more foolish and the less foolish.

Tout éloge imposteur blesse une âme sincère. Fr. BOILEAU.—"Nothing wounds the feelings more than praise unjustly bestowed."

Tout ensemble. Fr.—"His *tout ensemble* conveys an impression of knowledge founded on experience:" that is, His *whole appearance* conveys, &c.

Tout est grand dans un grand siècle. Fr.—"The dispatches of Tallard, Harcourt, and Villars are hardly inferior in style to those of LEWIS XIV., yet they were all military men, and but scantily educated. May we not say, with Monsieur Cousin, *Tout est grand dans un grand siècle?*" that is to say, *Every thing is great in a great age.*

Tout le monde. Fr.—"Every one, everybody."

Tout le monde se plaint de sa mémoire, et personne ne plaint de son jugement. Fr. ROCHEFOUCAULT.—"Every man complains of his memory, but no man complains of his judgment." However great the cause may be, our pride will not suffer us to impeach the latter.

——————————Trahit ipse furoris
Impetus, et visum est lenti quaesisse nocentem.

Lat. LUCAN.—"They are borne away by the violence of their rage, and they think it a waste of time to inquire who are the guilty." A forcible description of popular and indiscriminate vengeance.

Trahit sua quemque voluptas. Lat. VIRGIL.—"Every man is led by his own peculiar taste or pleasure."

Transeat in exemplum. Lat.—"May it pass into an example." May an act so meritorious stand recorded as a precedent for others to follow.

Tria juncta in uno. Lat.—"Three joined in one." This is sometimes used in speaking of the Trinity: but more frequently in speaking of a political coalition consisting of three members.

Tribus Anticyris caput insanabile. Lat. HORACE.—"A head incurable even by three Anticyrae." There were two Anticyras in the ancient world, one in Thessaly and the other in Phocis. Both were celebrated for producing hellebore, a vegetable product, that was prescribed in cases of madness. The poet here speaks of a head so very insane as not to be cured by the produce of *three* Anticyras, were there even three places of the name, and not merely two. The phrase means an incurable madman.

Tritus, et e medio Fortunae ductus acervo. Lat. JUVENAL.—"[A case that is] worn thread-bare, and drawn from the middle of Fortune's heap."

"One that from casual heaps without design
Fortune drew forth, and bade the lot be thine."

"The motto prefixed to the work is a most judicious one, *Tritus, et e medio*," &c.

Tros Tyriusque mihi nullo discrimine agetur. Lat. VIRGIL.—"Trojan and Tyrian shall be treated by me with no difference, shall both be treated by me in the same way, exactly alike." The parties are equally indifferent to me, and I shall act impartially between them.

Trousseau. Fr.—"A lady's marriage outfit."

Trouvaille. Fr.—"A god-send."

Truditur dies die. Lat. HORACE.—"One day presses on the heels of another." The progress of time, however neglected by man, is silent and irresistible.

Truditur dies die
Novaeque pergunt interire Lunae:
Tu secanda marmora
Locas sub ipsum funus; et sepulcri
Immemor, struis domos. Lat. HORACE.—

"One day presses on the heels of another, and moons in succession hasten onward to their wane; and yet thou, though on the very brink of the grave, art bargaining to have marble cut for an abode, and utterly regardless of, unmindful of, death, thou art ever engaged in building and such like occupations."

"Day presses on the heels of day,
And moons increase to their decay:
But you, with thoughtless pride elate,
Unconscious of impending fate,
Command the pillared dome to rise,
When, lo! your tomb forgotten lies."

Tu ne cede malis, sed contra audentior ito. Lat. VIRGIL.—"Yield not to misfortunes, but, on the contrary, meet them with fortitude."

Tua res agitur, paries quum proximus ardet. Lat. HORACE.—"Your own property is at stake when the next house is on fire." We should remember that the calamity which afflicts our neighbor most seriously threatens ourselves.

Tuo tibi judicio est utendum. Virtutis et vitiorum grave ipsius conscientiae pondus est; qua sublata jacent omnia. Lat. CICERO.—"You must use your own judgment in the guidance of yourself. Great is the influence of conscience in deciding on your own virtues and vices: if that be taken away, all is lost."

Turpe est aliud loqui, aliud sentire; quanto turpius aliud scribeie, aliud sentire! Lat. SENECA.—"It is dishonorable to say one thing, and to think another; how much more base then is it to write that which is contrary to one's real sentiments!" The act of *writing* is of greater deliberation, and of broader tendency. An attempt to deceive in this way is, therefore, more highly criminal. Were this maxim properly felt by party-writers, the world would not be inundated by such a torrent of falsehoods.

Turpe est difficiles habere nugas, et stultus labor est ineptiarum. Lat. MARTIAL.—"It is shameful, disgraceful, to make difficulties of trifles, to make mountains of mole-hills; and labor bestowed on trifling matters is downright folly."

Turpe est in patria peregrinari, et in iis rebus quae ad patriam pertinent hospitem esse. Lat. MANUTIUS.—"It is shameful for a man to live as a stranger in his own country, and to be uninformed of her affairs and interests."

Turpe est laudari ab illaudatis. Lat.—"It is degrading to be commended by those who themselves are unworthy of praise."

Turpe est viro id, in quo quotidie versatur, ignorare. Lat.—"It is shameful for a man to be ignorant of that in which he is every day employed."

Turpe quidem dictu, sed si modo vera fatemur,
Vulgus amicitias utilitate probat. Lat. OVID.—
"It is shameful to say it, it is a humiliating acknowledgment, but, if we honestly confess the truth, the masses only value friendship from mere motives of advantage or interest."

Turpe reos emta miseros defendere lingua. Lat. OVID.—"It is a base, shameful, disgraceful, thing, to defend, by language that you have been paid for using, those wretched individuals who are accused of any crime or misdemeanor."

Turpia decipiunt caecum vitia. Lat. HORACE.—"The disagreeable blemishes of a beloved object escape the notice of a blinded admirer."

"So lovers, to their fair one fondly blind,
E'en on her ugliness with transport gaze."

Turpis et ridicula res est elementarius senex : juveni parandum, seni utendum est. Lat. SENECA.—"Nothing can be so ridiculous or absurd as to see an old man in his rudiments. It is for youth to acquire, and for age to make use of those acquirements."

Turpiter obticuit, sublato jure nocendi. Lat.—"He was shamefully silent when he had lost the power to injure."

Tuta est hominum tenuitas: magnae periclo sunt opes obnoxiae. Lat. PHAEDRUS.—"The poor, the obscure, those in a low condition, are safe, in a state of safety: whereas great riches [rich men] are at all times exposed to, liable to, danger."

Tuta timens. Lat. VIRGIL.—"Fearing even that which is safe." Men who are at the pinnacle of fortune should ever bear in mind that they are not out of the reach of its vicissitudes.

Tutor et ultor. Lat.—"The protector and the avenger." A compliment of but little meaning, but which is generally found on the medals inscribed to a successful prince or potentate.

U.

Ubi bene, ibi patria. Lat.—"Where one is well off, there is his country." The motto of unfeeling, heartless, and selfish individuals.

Ubi idem et maximus et honestissimus amor est, aliquando praestat morte jungi quam vita distrahi. Lat. VALERIUS MAXIMUS.—"Where there exists the greatest and most honorable love, it is sometimes better to be joined in death than separated in life."

Ubi jus incertum, ibi jus nullum. Lat. Law maxim.—"Where the law is uncertain, there is there no law." No legal decision can properly be made on vague and undefined enactments.

Ubi major pars est, ibi est totum. Lat. Law maxim.—"Where the greater part is, there by law is the whole." The only way of determining the acts of many is by the major part, or the majority; as the majority in parliament enact laws, &c.

Ubi mel, ibi apes. Lat. PLAUTUS.—"Where there is honey, there will there be bees." Wherever there is a pleasing attraction, there will be no want of followers.

Ubi plura nitent in carmine, non ego paucis
Offendar maculis, quas aut incuria fudit,
Aut humana parum cavit natura. Lat. HORACE.—
"Where there are many beauties in a work, I shall not cavil at a few faults, proceeding either from negligence, or from the imperfection of our nature." In a great work of general merit, candor requires that we should excuse any small or partial defect.

"Now where the beauties more in number shine,
I am not angry when a casual line
[That with some trivial faults unequal flows]
A careless hand, or human frailty, shows."

Ubi reddunt ova columbae. Lat. JUVENAL.—"Where the pigeons lay their eggs." This, at Rome, was in the interstices under the roofs of houses, in the garrets of which then, as now, poets had that honorable residence, which by some is called "the first floor down the chimney," and by others, "the roost of eminence," and still more generally, "the *Attic* story."

Ubi supra. Lat.—"Where above mentioned." "We stated [*ubi supra*] that it was not exactly known."

Ubicunque ars ostentatur, veritas abesse videtur. Lat.—"Wherever art is displayed, truth seems to be wanting." Seldom do we witness a laborious exertion to excite interest or to give pleasure, that we do not begin to doubt the reality of the interest or pleasure which is thus forced upon us.

Ubique patriam reminisci. Lat.—"Everywhere to remember your country." The motto of LORD MALMESBURY.

Udum et molle lutum es: nunc nunc properandus et acri
Fingendus sine fine rota. Lat. PERSIUS.—
"Thou art now merely soft and moist clay: and, therefore, instantly and incessantly to be formed by the glowing wheel." The allusion is to the

potter's wheel, and the application is to the mind of youth, which should be formed with assiduity, whilst it is tender, pliant, and susceptible.

Ultima ratio. Lat.—"The last resource or expedient."

Ultima ratio regum. Lat.—"The last or final reasoning, argument, of kings." The logic of kings. "Military reasoning [always excepting the *ultima ratio regum*] is not invariably convincing." An appeal to violence and hostility. Many pieces of ordnance still lie in British arsenals bearing this motto, said to have been engraved on his cannon by order of LEWIS THE FOURTEENTH.

——————————————**Ultima semper**
Exspectanda dies homini, dicique beatus
Ante obitum nemo supremaque funera debet. Lat. OVID.—"Man should ever look to his last day, and no man should be accounted happy before his decease and the performance of his funeral rites." Such is the instability of human affairs that no man should be considered as fortunate, until death has precluded any further possibility of change.

"For no frail man, however great or high,
Can be concluded blest before he die."

Ultima Thule. Lat. VIRGIL.—"At dinner-parties, I always dreaded the *Ultima Thule* of hostesses' elbows. Good places for cutting turkeys, but bad for cutting jokes." "*Thule*" was the most remote island in the northern parts either known to the Romans, or even described by the poets; hence the epithet of *ultima*, as applied to it. Camden takes it to be *Zetland* [Shetland], still called by seamen *Thylensel.* "*Ultima Thule*" is put for *the extremity of the earth.* In the above quotation it of course means *the extremity* or *very end of the dining-table.* The pseudo-gentleman, or mock-gentleman, is in appearance and manner the caricature of a fop, and may very properly be designated the *Ultima Thule* of extravagant frippery.

Ultimatum. Lat.—"A final proposition."

Ultimum remedium. Lat.—"A last resource, expedient, shift."

Ultra. Lat.—"Beyond." "An *ultra* kind of sympathy," that is, An *extreme*, &c. An *Ultra* is "one who goes BEYOND others in his views, ideas, and opinions."

Un air noble. Fr.—"A noble, distinguished, patrician, air or appearance."

Un enfant en ouvrant ses yeux doit voir la patrie, et jusqu'à la mort ne voir qu'elle. Fr. ROUSSEAU.—"The infant, on first opening his eyes, ought to see his country, and to the hour of his death never lose sight of it." The love of our country should be implanted early, and should be nourished through life.

Un grand destin commence, un grand destin s'achève. Fr.—"A mighty course doth now begin, a mighty course doth close." "Men cannot behold with indifference those memorable epochs, during which, in the fine language of CORNEILLE—'*Un grand destin,*' *&c.*"

Un homme d'esprit serait souvent bien embarrassé sans la compagnie des sots. Fr. ROCHEFOUCAULT.—"A man of wit would often be much embarrassed without the company of fools." He would be at a loss for a butt for his sarcasms.

Un sot trouve toujours un plus sot qui l'admire. Fr. BOILEAU.

—"A fool always finds a greater fool to admire him." Used in censuring a silly or adulatory commendation of an indifferent work.

Un ventre affamé n'a point d'oreilles. Fr. prov.—"A hungry belly has no ears." "Though gluttony is detestable, yet would I not preach forbearance to a starving man, for I know that *un ventre affamé n'a point d'oreilles.*" N.B. The above proverb is often quoted *incorrectly*, thus, *Un ventre affamé n'a point* des *oreilles.*

Una salus victis nullam sperare salutem. Lat. VIRGIL.—"The only safety for the conquered is to expect no safety." The resolute despair of the vanquished sometimes brings about a relief not to be effected by any other means.

Una voce. Lat.—"With one voice." Unanimously.

Unde habeas quaerit nemo; sed oportet habere. Lat. JUVENAL. —"No one inquires how or from what source you have gotten your wealth; have it, however, you must [if you would be looked up to, be thought any thing of]." All pay respect to riches, without inquiring very scrupulously into the means by which they have been obtained.

Unde tibi frontem libertatemque parentis,
Cum facias pejora senex? Lat. JUVENAL.—"Whence do you derive the power and privilege, the air and authority, of a parent, when you, though an old man, fall into greater errors?" How can you presume to chide your juniors, when you, though advanced in years, set the vicious example?

Unguibus et ore. Lat.—"With talons and mouth." With tooth and nail: with might and main. "This they dispute *unguibus et ore.*"

Unguibus et rostro. Lat.—"With talons and beak." "He fought it *unguibus et rostro.*" "Tooth and nail."

Unguis in ulcere. Lat. CICERO.—"A nail in the wound." This strong phrase was applied by the orator to CATILINE. "Your country," he would have said in a paraphrase, "has received a dangerous wound, into which you, vulture-like, infix your talons, for the purpose of irritating and keeping it open."

Uni aequus virtuti, atque ejus amicis. Lat. HORACE.—"Tolerant to, mindful of, friendly to, virtue alone, and to the friends of virtue."

"Ever to virtue and to virtue's friends,
And them alone, with reverence he bends."

The character of the truly good man.

Universus hic mundus una civitas hominum recte existimatur. Lat. CICERO.—"The whole of this world is rightly deemed, considered as, looked upon as, a single city of the human race."

Uno avulso, non deficit alter. Lat. VIRGIL.—"When one is removed, another will not be wanting." Used in a political sense: "Remove that man, and you will have his like for a successor."

Uno ictu. Lat.—"At one stroke, or blow." "We rarely came *uno ictu* to a decision:" that is, *at once* to a decision.

Uno impetu. Lat.—"At once, at one bout." "Whatever is attempted in that climate must be done *uno impetu,*" that is, *they must slash away without hesitation.*

Unoculus inter caecos. Lat.—"A one-eyed man among blind men."

"However low the level of education may be laid, he that profits most by it will acquire in practice as complete a social superiority, *unoculus inter caecos*, as if he had been educated at Oxford or Cambridge." *See "Au royaume des aveugles," &c.*

Unus homo nobis cunctando restituit rem;
Non ponebat enim rumores ante salutem.
Lat. Fragment of ENNIUS.—"One man by delay restored the state; for he preferred the public safety to idle report." This was applied to FABIUS, who, by prudently avoiding a battle, at length wasted away the army of HANNIBAL, the inveterate and sworn enemy of the Romans. It is now sometimes quoted when caution or delay is to be justified on the part of a general or a statesman.

Unus Pellaeo juveni non sufficit orbis:
Aestuat infelix angusto limite mundi. Lat. JUVENAL.—"One world was not sufficient for the youth of Pella [a city of Macedonia]; the unhappy young man fretted at, grieved at, the narrow limits of our globe." Said in reference to ALEXANDER THE GREAT, who, on being told that there were worlds innumerable, exclaimed, "Unhappy man that I am, in not having yet been able to become master even of one of them!"

Unus utrique error, sed variis illudit partibus. Lat. HORACE.—"The same error belongs to each, but it mocks them in different ways: each errs, but in a different way from the other." Several men may engage in a pursuit of the same folly, yet each travels by a different road.

Unusquisque valeat in arte sua. Lat.—"We must not suffer a great name to lead us astray, *Unusquisque valeat in arte sua.* CICERO was an admirable orator, yet a very ordinary writer of verse: and Sir Isaac Newton is pronounced by no mean authority to have been, out of his own province, but a common man:" that is to say, *Every man may be strong, mighty, or great in his own peculiar line or vocation, in his own peculiar department.*

Urbem lateritiam invenit, marmoream reliquit. Lat. SUETONIUS.—"He found a city of bricks, and he left it of marble." This was the boast of AUGUSTUS, with respect to the city of Rome. It is sometimes flatteringly applied to other princely suggesters, or promoters, of great improvements.

Urit enim fulgore suo, qui praegravat artes
Infra se positas: exstinctus amabitur idem. Lat. HORACE.—"The anecdote of the citizen, who asked Aristides [a noble Athenian, surnamed '*The Just*'] to write his own name on the sherd, wishing to have him banished, because he was sick of hearing any one called *The Just*, may, perhaps, not be literally true; but it embodies a great truth: *Urit enim fulgore suo, qui praegravat artes infra se positas:*" the only consolation is, *exstinctus amabitur idem*—"Athens *buried* Aristides:" that is to say, *for he who bears down by superior merit the arts placed beneath him, burns by his very splendor* [he, whose superiority is oppressive to inferior minds, excites envy by this very pre-eminence]; the only consolation is, *yet—he, the very same individual, will after his decease be loved, admired* [when the too powerful splendor is withdrawn, our natural veneration of it takes place]: The man of exalted genius throws by the splendor of his talents all inferior merits into the shade. He is ex-

posed, therefore, to all the shafts of contemporary jealousy. His death alone can deprive envy of her sting; then, those who were most forward to detract will be the first to do justice to his merits:—

"For he, who soars to an unusual height,
Oppressive dazzles with excess of light
The arts beneath him: yet, when dead, shall prove
An object worthy of esteem and love."

N.B. In the above brilliant passage "*artes*" is equivalent to [used for] "*artifices,*" artists, artificers, craftsmen [individuals, the community at large].

Usque ad aras. Lat.—"To the very altars." To the last extremity.

Usque ad nauseam. Lat.—"Even to sickness." "The same ideas reappear *usque ad nauseam;*" that is, "*till they are absolutely sickening or nauseating.*"

Usque adeone mori miserum est? Lat. VIRGIL.—"Is it then so very wretched a thing to die?" Are the thoughts of mortality so very dreadful?

Ut ager, quamvis fertilis, sine cultura fructuosus esse non potest, sic sine doctrina animus. Lat. SENECA.—"As land, though rich, cannot be productive or fruitful without due culture, in the same manner is it with the mind when without learning or education, when left uncultivated."

Ut ameris, amabilis esto. Lat. OVID.—"That you may be loved, show yourself deserving of love." To merit regard is the surest mode of obtaining it.

Ut desint vires, tamen est laudanda voluntas. Lat. OVID.—"Though the power [to do any thing of a benevolent or meritorious character] is wanting, yet the mere willingness or wish [to carry it out] is laudable, praiseworthy, deserving of commendation."

Ut homo est, ita morem geras. Lat. TERENCE.—"As the man is, so must you conduct yourself towards him." A practical maxim of the most useful kind. The man of tact, who has an object in view, a purpose to carry out, will be full of deference to the high and mighty, easy with the free, and of a complacent bearing towards the humble and lowly.

Ut jugulent homines surgunt de nocte latrones. Lat. HORACE.—"Robbers rise by night, that they may assassinate their fellow-creatures."

Ut metus ad omnes, poena ad paucos perveniret. Lat. Law maxim.—"That fear should reach all persons, and punishment be inflicted but on few." It is an ancient maxim of criminal justice, that the few might be punished, and the many be deterred, through fear of the consequences, from the commission of crime.

Ut nemo in sese tentat descendere; nemo:
Sed praecedenti spectatur mantica tergo! Lat. PERSIUS.—"How is it that no one tries to descend into, search into, himself, but looks at the wallet on the back of the man who is going before him!" The allusion is to the fable, in which men are represented as marching in a line, each with a wallet or bag on his chest, and another on his back; the one in front containing their neighbor's faults, whilst their own are slung unseen behind their backs. Compare PHAEDRUS:—

Peras imposuit Jupiter nobis duas:
Propriis repletam vitiis post tergum dedit,
Alienis ante pectus suspendit gravem.

'Jupiter has bestowed upon us two bags: the one he has placed behind our back, filled with our own vices or faults; the other on our chest, remarkably well filled or heavy with those of our neighbors, our fellowmen."

Hac re videre nostra mala non possumus;
Alii simul delinquunt, censores sumus.

"For this reason we are unable to see our own faults; but as soon as, whenever, others commit faults, are found tripping, then indeed are we quick enough in blaming or reproving them."

Ut pictura, poesis. Lat. HORACE.—"As is Painting, so is Poetry." There must always be an affinity between these sister arts.

Ut placeas debes immemor esse tui. Lat. OVID.—"Do you wish to please? be then regardless of self, throw self into the background."

Ut praeco, ad merces turbam qui cogit emendas,
Assentatores jubet ad lucrum ire poeta
Dives agris, dives positis in foenore nummis. Lat. HORACE.

"As artful criers, at a public fair,
Gather the passing crowd to buy their ware,
So wealthy poets, when they deign to write,
To all clear gains the flatterer invite."

Faithful friends are necessary in order to apprize poets of their errors. Such friends, however, are difficult to be obtained by rich and powerful bards. Horace very justly compares a wealthy poet to a public crier; the latter brings crowds together to buy up what is exposed for sale; the former is sure to collect around him a set of base and venal flatterers.

Ut quimus, quando ut volumus non licet. Lat. TERENCE.—"When we cannot act as we wish, we must act as we can." Every man should accommodate himself to circumstances, and particularly in suiting his aims to his powers.

Ut quisque suum vult esse, ita est. Lat. TERENCE.—"As every man wishes his (offspring) to be, so is he." The minds of children are of so plastic a nature that, if they do not answer the hopes of the parent, it is in the greater number of instances to be attributed to his neglect of their education.

Ut redeat miseris, abeat fortuna superbis. Lat. HORACE.—"That fortune may quit the proud, and return to the wretched."

"May Fortune with returning smiles now bless
Afflicted worth, and impious pride depress."

That something like the natural equality of condition may be restored.

Ut saepe summa ingenia in occulto latent! Lat. PLAUTUS.—"How often are men of the greatest genius buried in obscurity!" The exercise and the use of brilliant talents are frequently lost to the world through the want of protection and cultivation.

Ut sementem feceris, ita et metes. Lat. CICERO.—"As you have sown, so shall you reap." As your conduct has been, so shall be its fruits.

Ut silvae foliis pronos mutantur in annos,
Prima cadunt: ita verborum vetus interit aetas,
Et juvenum ritu florent modo nata vigentque.

Lat. HORACE.—

"As when the forest, with the bending year,
First sheds the leaves which earliest appear,
So an old race of words maturely dies,
And some new-born in youth and vigor rise."

Ut supra. Lat.—"As above-mentioned."

Utatur motu animi, qui uti ratione non potest. Lat.—"Let him be guided by his passions who can make no use of his reason." Fools may be impelled by their passions, but the man of reason is left without excuse.

Utendum est aetate; cito pede labitur aetas. Lat. OVID.—"We should make good use of our time, as time passes swiftly away."

Uti possidetis. Lat.—"As you possess." A diplomatic phrase, used when two sovereigns choose to make peace, "each retaining the possessions which he has acquired." Its opposite is the *status quo*, when both parties re-enter into the condition in which they stood before the war.

Utile dulci. Lat. HORACE.—"The useful with the agreeable, the pleasant." To say that he has combined the *utile dulci*, is to give the very highest praise to a writer.

Utinam tam facile vera invenire possem, quam falsa convincere. Lat. CICERO.—"I wish that I could as easily discover the truth as I can detect the falsehood." I have no clew to the former, but the latter betrays itself by its inconsistency.

Utitur in re non dubia testibus non necessariis. Lat. CICERO.—"He uses unnecessary proofs in a matter that is not called in question." Some affect to be very profound in arguing a clear case. Such persons contend without an opponent and triumph without a victory.

Utrum horum mavis accipe. Lat.—"Take whichever you prefer." A conclusion generally made in argument, after having offered your opponent a choice of difficulties.

V.

Vacuum. Lat.—"Between these two mighty realms we may conceive a *vacuum* to exist, so as to cut off all communication:" that is to say, we may conceive a *void, void place, common,* or *waste ground, neutral territory,* to exist, &c. N.B. The *literal* meaning of "*vacuum*" is *an empty thing, or emptiness.* Space not occupied by matter.

Vade mecum. Lat.—"Go with me." "The book is an indispensable *vade mecum:*" that is, an indispensable *pocket companion.*

Vae victis! Lat.—"Woe to the conquered! the vanquished!" If it should come to that point, *vae victis!* it will be a war of extermination.

Valde deflendum! Lat.—"Very much, or greatly, to be deplored, bewailed, lamented!" "In spite of the skill with which our power of deglutition has been enlarged by gastronomy, there is still a point, *valde* *deflendum!* beyond which the most intrepid *gourmand* [glutton, gastronomist, or gastrophilist] cannot proceed and live."

Vale! Lat.—"Farewell!"

Valeat quantum. Lat.—"The Scotch writers have so long held possession of the field of mental and moral science in this country, that it seems as if no man is to be tolerated who ventures a word in favor of the school of LOCKE and HARTLEY, and even contends for its superiority. But—*valeat quantum:*" that is to say, But—*let this feeling have full swing, go for what it is worth.* N.B. The *full* expression is "*valeat quantum valere potest.*"

——————Valet ima summis
Mutare, et insignem attenuat Deus,
Obscura promens. Lat. HORACE.—

"The Deity can change the lowest into the highest, extinguishing the proud, and bringing forward the humble and lowly." Compare Luke i. 52: "He hath put down the mighty from their seat, and hath exalted the humble and meek."—Prayer-Book Version. Every sublunary change is marked out by the finger of Providence.

Valete ac plaudite. Lat. TERENCE.—"Farewell, and give us your applause." This was the conclusion of the Latin comedy. It is now sometimes used in the way of triumphant irony at the conclusion of a political discourse.

Vana quoque ad veros accessit fama timores. Lat. LUCAN.—"Idle rumors were also added to well-founded fears, apprehensions." A quotation often made use of in every great crisis of national difficulty or danger, as the circumstance is of constant recurrence.

Variorum. Lat.—"It is time that *Variorum* editions of our standard works should issue from the press;" that is, "editions *with the notes of various editors.*"

Varium et mutabile semper femina. Lat. VIRGIL.—"A woman is at all times an inconstant, or fickle, and changeable thing, an ever-changeable creature." "When some sudden and somewhat violent changes of opinion were imputed to a learned judge, who was always jocosely termed Mrs. ——, '*Varium et mutabile semper femina*' was Sir William Scott's [*Lord Stowell's*] remark."

Vastus animus. Lat.—"A vast mind, an insatiable mind or disposition [an ambition that knows no bounds]." "Both CROMWELL and NAPOLEON had the *vastus animus:* both grasped at that which Fortune seemed to have placed far beyond their reach, and both were successful."

————Vatem egregium, cui non sit publica vena,
Qui nihil expositum soleat deducere, nec qui
Communi feriat carmen triviale moneta,—
Hunc, qualem nequeo monstrare, et sentio tantum.
Lat. JUVENAL.—

"The poet who is above his fellows, whose vein is not that of the common herd, who is accustomed to spin out no stale or vulgar subject, and stamps no hackneyed verse from a die, that all men may use,—him I cannot embody in words, but can feel only in my soul."

"The bard of every age and clime,
Of genius fruitful, ardent and sublime,
Who, from the glowing mint of fancy, pours
No spurious metal, fused from common ores,
But gold, to matchless purity refined,
And stamped with all the godhead in his mind,—
Him do I feel, but want the power to paint."

This is SHAKSPEARE.

"It is in the management of the character of LEAR more especially that SHAKSPEARE fills up that grand idea of a perfect poet, which we delight to image to ourselves, but despair of seeing realized. '*Vatem egregium,*'" *&c.* The qualifications of a good poet are here expressed figuratively under the classical metaphor of coin. The metal is the thought: the current stamp, the language: the mold is the poet's glowing fancy: *Vena, moneta, feriat.* In this passage JUVENAL means the same as HORACE:—

"*Ingenium cui sit, cui mens divinior, atque os*
Magna sonaturum, des nominis hujus honorem:"

[which see].

JUVENAL has improved his account by the subsequent line, "*Hunc, qualem,*" &c.: for here is the feeling of true taste [to which LONGINUS generally refers us], which is above all rule and all description.

Vaudeville. Fr.—"A ballad, popular song, and easy to sing: [requiring no great knowledge of music to sing]."

Vaurien. Fr.—"A worthless, good-for-nothing fellow."

Velim mehercule cum istis errare quam cum aliis recte sentire. Lat.—"Rather would I indeed be in error with those men than think aright with the others." So much do I approve of their general consistency that, though they may possibly be in error on this single point, they, nevertheless, shall have my concurrence with them.

Velis et remis. Lat.—"With sails and oars." With the utmost expedition. "He pushed forward *velis et remis;*" that is, "by every possible means."

Velle suum cuique est, nec voto vivitur uno. Lat. PERSIUS.—"Every one has his own peculiar fancy or whim, and there is in all a diversity of taste." Taste and opinions must, as a matter of course, differ both in men and in nations.

Vellem in amicitia sic erraremus, et isti
Errori nomen virtus posuisset honestum. Lat. HORACE.—

"Would that we erred in a similar way where our friends are concerned, and that virtue would give to this kind of weakness some honorable name."

"Oh! were our weakness to our friends the same,
And stamped by virtue with some honest name."

Would that, as the lover is blind to the imperfections of his fair one, so might we shut our eyes to the petty failings of a friend, and that they who teach the precepts of virtue would call this weakness on our part by some engaging name, so as to tempt more to indulge in it.

——————Velocius et citius nos
Corrumpunt vitiorum exempla domestica, magnis
Cum subeunt animos auctoribus. Lat. JUVENAL.—

"We are more speedily and fatally corrupted by domestic examples of vice, and particularly when they are impressed on our minds as it were from authority." Such is the effect, for instance, of bad example held forth by a father or mother to their children. N.B. "*Auctor legis*" is the mover or enactor of a law. This allusion, therefore, strongly shows that the example of parents is not only forcible, like law, but also lawful, venerable, irresistible: *magnis*. Its silence is language; its intimation, precept; its will, authority, especially in the more ductile parts of childhood and youth.

"Children, like tender osiers, take the bow,
And as they first are fashioned always grow."

Velox consilium sequitur poenitentia. Lat. LABERIUS.—"Hasty counsels are generally followed by repentance."

——————**Velut aegri somnia, vanae**
Finguntur species. Lat. HORACE.—

"Their ideas, like a sick man's dreams, are formed without any regard to sober reality." Their ideas are vague and confusedly jumbled together, like the dreams of a disordered brain. "Humorous they [madmen] are beyond all measure; sometimes profusely laughing, extraordinary merry, and then again weeping, without a cause; groaning, sighing, pensive, sad, almost distracted; restless in their thought and actions, continually meditating:—

——*Velut aegri somnia, vanae*
Finguntur species.

More like dreamers than men awake, they feign a company of antic fantastical conceits."

Venalis populus, venalis curia patrum. Lat.—"The people are venal, and the senate is equally venal." A description once given of Rome. It would not now be necessary to travel to Rome in order to make the application.

——————**Vendentem tus et odores,**
Et piper, et quidquid chartis amicitur ineptis. Lat. HORACE.—[A street] "where they sell frankincense, perfumes, and pepper, and things that are usually wrapped up in worthless paper [in waste paper]:"

"Where pepper, odors, frankincense, are sold,
And all small wares in wretched rhymes enrolled."

The allusion in "*chartis ineptis*" is to writings so foolish and unworthy of perusal as soon to find their way to the grocers, and subserve the humbler but more useful employment of wrappers for small purchases.

Vendidit hic auro patriam. Lat. VIRGIL.—"He sold his country for gold." He is nothing less than a venal traitor.

Venenum in auro bibitur. Lat. SENECA.—"Poison is generally drunk out of gold." Those who use less costly utensils are not so liable to such murderous attempts.

Veni, vidi, vici. Lat.—"I came, I saw, I conquered." This was the brief account transmitted by JULIUS CAESAR in reference to his victory over Pharnaces. It was gained at a place called Zela, in Asia Minor.

Venienti occurrite morbo. Lat. PERSIUS.—"Meet the approaching disease." Do not let the malady strike root, but seek the proper advice and remedy on its first approach. See "*Principiis obsta*," &c.

Venimus ad summam fortunae. Lat. HORACE.—"We have got to the top of the tree: we have attained the very height or summit of perfection." "Of all the improvements of civilization, there is nothing in life like a newspaper: and the newspapers of our times are the *ne plus ultra* [which see] of journals. *Venimus ad summam fortunae.*"

Venire facias. Law Lat.—"You shall cause or order to come." The judicial writ by which the sheriff is empowered to summon a jury.

Veniunt a dote sagittae. Lat. JUVENAL.—"The darts come from her dowry." Compare BUTLER in his *Hudibras:*—

"Now artful Cupid takes his stand
Upon a widow's jointure—land,
For he, in all his am'rous battles,
No 'dvantage finds like goods and chattels!"

Again:— "PLUTUS, not CUPID, touched his sordid heart,
And 'twas her dower that winged the unerring dart."

Ventis secundis. Lat.—"With prosperous winds." With uniform success.

Verba animi proferre, et vitam impendere vero. Lat. JUVENAL.—"To speak the words of the mind, to give utterance to one's real sentiments, and to stake one's life for the truth." To speak with honest frankness, and to prefer liberty to life. An admirable summary of the duties of a good citizen.

Verbatim. Lat.—"He was a *verbatim* and slavish reader of his sermons:" that is, He read his sermons *exactly as they appeared in his manuscript, without ever attempting to alter, improve, or elaborate.* N.B. *Verbatim* means *word for word.* "He made a *verbatim* report of the proceedings," that is to say, a report *word for word. A true and strictly accurate* report.

Verbiage. Fr.—"Wordiness, verbosity, verboseness." "His book is well written, and free from *verbiage.*"

Verborum multitudine supersedendum est. Lat. CICERO.—"We should avoid making use of too great a number of words, avoid being verbose." See "*Satis loquentiae,*" *&c.*

Verbum non amplius addam. Lat. HORACE.—"I will not add another word, one word more, a word more." "Then is it that the maker lays down his pen with the *dictum* [assertion or expression] of a master —*Verbum non amplius addam.*"

Verbum verbo reddere fidus interpres. Lat. HORACE.—"As a faithful interpreter to translate word for word." To give a translation strictly literal.

Veritas nihil veretur nisi abscondi. Lat. Law maxim.—"Truth is afraid of nothing but concealment." The characters of truth are plainness and frankness. It is in the nature of fraud, on the contrary, to be evasive and mysterious.

Veritas visu et mora, falsa festinatione et incertis valescunt. Lat. TACITUS.—"Truth is confirmed by inspection and delay: falsehood avails itself of haste and uncertainty." Falsehood relies on the first impressions; the truth comes haltingly behind, as wishing to meet the test of deliberation and circumspection.

Veritatis simplex oratio est. Lat. SENECA.—"The language of truth is simple." The orator, who is conscious of having truth on his side, should be careful neither to vail nor degrade her beauty by any meretricious decoration.

Vers de société. Fr.—"These stanzas are quite equal to any *vers de société* of our time:" that is to say, equal to any *society or company verses* of, &c. N.B. "*Vers de société*" are verses that have been composed for the amusement of a private party or assembly, without the slightest view to publication. Verses that are but "*so-so*," and those of the "*namby-pamby*" school, may very properly be designated "*vers de société;*"—at any rate, so said VOLTAIRE, a pretty good judge of such matters.

Versatile ingenium. Lat.—"A versatile genius, strong natural ability, that is suitable to, or competent to, every thing, that is able to grapple with every thing."

Versus. Lat.—"Against." "Counterpoise *versus* limitation."

Versus inopes rerum, nugaeque canorae. Lat. HORACE.—"Verses devoid of substance, and melodious trifles."

Verum illud est, vulgo quod dici solet,
Omnes sibi malle melius esse quam alteri. Lat. TERENCE.—"The common assertion is certainly true, that we all wish matters to go better with ourselves than with others." Whatever may be theoretically said of philanthropy and benevolence to others, self-love will generally be found to be the prevailing principle.

Verum putas haud aegre, quod valde expetis. Lat. TERENCE.—"You believe that easily, which you hope for earnestly." Men are led without difficulty into the belief of that which they ardently desire to find true.

Vestigia nulla retrorsum. Lat. HORACE.—"No going back." All the footsteps lead to the lion's den, but there are no marks of any returning. It is a danger from which there is no retreat. "It was this material change in the condition of the country that decided its future destinies, and preserved for the motto of the land, *Vestigia nulla retrorsum:*" that is, No going back [from a good position or state of things].

Vetera extollimus recentium incuriosi. Lat. TACITUS.—"We extol things that are ancient, things that have the recommendation of antiquity, regardless of those of later date." We are more ready to give praise to the deeds or writers of antiquity, than to do justice to contemporary merit.

Veto. Lat.—"I forbid, prohibit." "He admits of no *veto* on his scheme:" that is, of no *opposition* to, &c., of no *interference* with, &c.

Vetustas pro lege semper habetur. Lat. Law maxim.—"Ancient custom is always held or regarded as law." Where there is no positive law, the custom, if from time immemorial, may be pleaded.

Vexata quaestio. Lat.—"A disputed question." A question or point which has long been discussed without arriving at a satisfactory solution of its difficulties.

Vi et armis. Lat.—"By force and by arms." By main force.

Via. Lat.—"The 7th division entered *via* Perekop:" that is, *by way* of Perekop.

Via media. Lat.—"A middle course." "He advocates a *via media*."

Viam qui nescit, qua deveniat ad mare,
Eum oportet amnem quaerere comitem sibi.

Lat. Plautus.—

"He who knows not his way to the sea should take a river as his companion." A tedious, but certain, course to any given object is preferable to one which may possibly be more brief, but which is, at the same time, uncertain.

————————**Viamque insiste domandi,**
Dum faciles animi juvenum, dum mobilis aetas.

Lat. Virgil.—

"Take a course of strong rule or discipline, whilst the mind of youth is flexible, and capable of strong impressions." Vigorous methods, but devoid of harshness, should at an early period be called into use by those to whom the education of youth is committed.

Viaticum. Lat.—The word "*viaticum*" is often met with in Roman Catholic works on divinity, signifying the Eucharist [*the Holy Communion*], when administered to sick persons, whose lives are in danger, or to those who are disabled from going to church to receive it: it is so called from the Latin word "*via*," which means *a way, journey, voyage*, and because it gives spiritual strength to the dying, and prepares them for their last journey.

Vice versa. Lat.—"The terms being reversed, reversely, the reverse."

Vicissim. Lat.—"In turn, by turns, interchangeably."

Victor volentes per populos dat jura. Lat.—"A conqueror gives laws to a willing or submissive people." A compliment generally paid to a victorious leader.

Victrix causa diis placuit, sed victa Catoni. Lat. Lucan.—"The victorious cause was pleasing to the gods; that of the vanquished to Cato."

"The gods and Cato did in this divide,
They chose the conquering, he the conquered, side."

This extravagant flight of the poet is sometimes applied to a man who having wrestled, though unsuccessfully, against superior powers, has derived glory even from defeat.

Victrix fortunae sapientia. Lat. Juvenal.—"Wisdom frequently conquers fortune." A wise man will often parry or subdue the reverses of chance.

Victurus genium debet habere liber. Lat. Martial.—"One genius has made many clever artists; and some of their works, at least, would bid fair for life, if there were not one general rule in the world of imaginative literature, to which there is absolutely no exception: namely, in the words of Martial:—

Victurus GENIUM *debet habere liber:*"

that is to say, *The book that will make its way in the world, that will remain*, or *survive, as an imperishable monument*, or *memorial, must have the stamp of* GENIUS *upon it—must bear the impress of* GENIUS.

Vide. Lat.—"See." *Vide ut supra.* "See the preceding statement."

Vide et crede. Lat.—"See and believe." If any thing like incredulity remains, convince yourself by ocular demonstration.

Videlicet. Lat.—"Namely, to wit, that is to say." This compound word often appears in the hateful and most ugly form of VIZ.

Video meliora proboque, deteriora sequor. Lat. OVID.—"I see and approve of better things, but I follow those that are bad—worse." This is frequently used by the speaker or writer, as a sentence of self-condemnation. It may also be applied to a third person, where his conduct is directly opposite to his known sentiments. "A man may 'keep good and noble ideas before his mind, rejecting those that are the contrary,' and yet be a slave to his passions. How many

'Know the right, and yet the wrong pursue,'

and thus verify the words of the poet Ovid—

Video meliora proboque,
Deteriora sequor:"

that is to say, *I see better things, and approve of them, but* such is the infirmity of human nature that *I follow those that are bad:* in other words, *I see the right course, and approve of it, but,* in spite of my better judgment, *I follow the wrong.*

Vieux routier. Fr.—"An old stager—shrewd old fellow." N.B. A "*vieux routier*" is a man who has had very great experience in his business or profession—in the ways of the world—one who, in his peculiar vocation, is thoroughly "*up to the mark,*" an eminently *practical* man.

Vigilantibus, non dormientibus, servit lex. Lat. Law maxim.—"The law regards those only who watch, and not those who sleep." The law is only for the protection of those who take due care of their property. It notices not those who may suffer from their own neglect.

Vilius argentum est auro, virtutibus aurum. Lat. HORACE.—"Silver is of less value than gold, gold of less value than virtue, than the endowments of virtue."

Vincentem strepitus, et natum rebus agendis. Lat. HORACE.—"I was not armed," says GIBBON the historian, in reference to his habitual silence in Parliament, "by nature and education with the intrepid energy of mind and voice, *Vincentem strepitus, et natum rebus agendis.* Timidity was fortified by pride; and even the success of my pen discouraged the trial of my voice:" that is to say, the intrepid energy of mind and voice, *that at once bears down all noisy opposition and clamor, and displays a talent for business.*

Vir bonus dicendi peritus. Lat.—"A good man skilled in the art of speaking, of oratory." The ancient definition of an *orator.*

————————Vir bonus est quis?
Qui consulta patrum, qui leges juraque servat.

Lat. HORACE.—

"Who is a good man? He who respects the decrees of the legislature, and bows to, yields obedience to, every positive law and every moral obligation."

"Who then is good? Who carefully observes
The Senate's wise decrees, nor ever swerves
From the known rules of justice and the laws."

Vires acquirit eundo. Lat. VIRGIL.—"She acquires strength as she goes." Spoken by the poet in reference to Fame or Rumor. "*Vires acquirit eundo* is the motto which he might proudly, but justly, prefix to his Magazine:" that is, "It gains strength in its progress, increases in vigor as it progresses," &c.

"It gains new strength and vigor as it goes."

Viri infelicis procul amici. Lat. SENECA.—"Friends keep aloof from, fight shy of, a man who is unfortunate, is down in the world."

Viridantem floribus hastas. Lat.—"View me as one [in the words of a true and most impassioned poet] *viridantem floribus hastas*—things that express death in their origin [being made from dead substances, that once had lived in forests], things that express ruin in their use:" that is to say, *making verdant, and gay with the life of flowers, murder. ous spears and halberds.*

Virtuoso. Ital.—"One who has a talent or taste for the fine arts." The plural is *virtuosi.*

Virtus est medium vitiorum et utrinque reductum. Lat. HORACE.—"Virtue is the mean between two vices, and is equally removed from either extreme." Thus, generosity is the middle virtue, the extremes of which are avarice and prodigality.

Virtus est vitium fugere, et sapientia prima
Stultitia caruisse. Lat. HORACE.—
"It is a virtue to avoid vice, and the first step to wisdom is to be free from folly."

"E'en in our flight from vice some virtue lies,
And, free from folly, we to wisdom rise."

Virtus in actione consistit. Lat.—"Virtue consists in action." It does not rest on cold theory, but on positive exertion.

Virtus in arduis. Lat.—"Virtue (or valor) in difficulties."

Virtus incendit vires. Lat.—"Virtue kindles the strength."

Virtus, repulsae nescia sordidae,
Intaminatis fulget honoribus. Lat. HORACE.—
"That virtue which is unconscious of a base repulse shines with unstained or untarnished honors."

"With stainless luster virtue shines,
A base repulse nor knows nor fears."

N.B. The *correct,* though not generally received, reading is "*incontaminatis:*" the lines would then stand thus:—

"*Virtus, repulsae nescia sordidae, incontaminatis fulget honoribus.*"

"*Intaminatus*" means "*polluted,*" which is directly contrary to the poet's thought.

Virtutem incolumem odimus,
Sublatam ex oculis quaerimus, invidi. Lat. HORACE.-
"*Virtutem incolumen odimus* is a sentiment as old as HORACE, and we fear the application of it will never be obsolete. The feeling expressed in the latter part of the sentence, *sublatam ex oculis quaerimus,* is, we hope, no less natural to mankind:" that is to say, *We hate virtue when embodied in the human form; we hate merit, while it remains with us*

that is, *meritorious men—men illustrious by their merits, while they are alive*. The feeling . . . . . of the sentence, *but, when taken away from us, then do we know how to appreciate it*, or *them, and in vain regret the loss of it*, or *them*, is, we hope, &c.

"Though living virtue we despise,
We follow her, when dead, with envious eyes."

Virtutem videant, intabescantque relicta. Lat. PERSIUS.—"Let them [the wicked] see the beauty of virtue, and pine at having forsaken her." This is the greatest curse that can befall them.

Virtutibus obstat res angusta domi. Lat. JUVENAL.—"Straitened circumstances frequently stand in the way of rising virtue and ability."

"Rarely they rise by virtue's aid, who lie
Plunged in the depths of helpless poverty."

Vis inertiae. Lat.—"The power of inertness." In *physics*, this is applied to the power of a stationary body, resisting that which would set it in motion. In *morals*, it has a figurative application, and serves as another name for indolence.

Vis medicatrix naturae. Lat.—"The healing or curative power of nature."

Vis motrix. Lat.—"The motive or moving power."

Vis vitae. Lat.—"The vital powers or energy."

Vita mortuorum in memoria vivorum est posita. Lat. CICERO.—"The life of the dead is stored up in the memory of the living." They survive in remembrance, and still exist, as a biographer would say, in fair report.

Vitae est avidus, quisquis non vult
Mundo secum pereunte mori. Lat. SENECA.—
"He is greedy of life, who is not willing to die when the world is perishing around him." When he see that every thing is hastening to destruction and decay.

Vitae post scenia celant. Lat. LUCRETIUS.—"They conceal that part of their life which is passed behind the scenes." They throw a vail over their private life, and hide it from the world.

Vitae summa brevis spem nos vetat inchoare longam. Lat. HORACE.—"The short span of our lives forbids us to indulge in lengthened hope, remote expectations." Such is the brief term of our existence that he who looks to remote prospects is generally disappointed.

Vitam impendere vero. Lat. JUVENAL.—"To stake one's life for the truth." The best character of a good citizen.

Vitande est improba siren, Desidia. Lat.—"The destructive siren, Sloth, should ever be avoided." The indolent man may be considered as lost to himself and to society.

Vitavi culpam, non laudem merui. Lat. HORACE.—"I have avoided censure at any rate, even if I have not actually deserved commendation."

"Now though, perhaps, I may not merit fame,
I stand secure from censure and from shame."

Vitia otii negotio discutienda sunt. Lat. SENECA.—"The vices of sloth are only to be shaken off by business." The mind will rust and canker without employment.

Vitiant artus aegrae contagia mentis. Lat. OVID.—"When the mind is ill at ease, the body is to a certain degree affected." The converse of this proposition may with equal justice be asserted.

————**Vitiis nemo sine nascitur; optimus ille est,**
Qui minimis urgetur. Lat. HORACE.—
"No one is born without faults; the best man is he who has the smallest share of them."

"Now—we have all our vices, and the best
Is he who with the fewest is oppressed."

————————**Vitium commune omnium est**
Quod nimium ad rem in senecta attenti sumus.
Lat. TERENCE.—
"It is a fault that is common to all, that in advanced age, as we grow older, we are too much attached to our property." As prodigality is proverbially said to be the fault of youth, so is avarice that of later years.

Vitium fuit, nunc mos est, adsentatio. Lat. PUBLIUS SYRUS.—"Flattery, which was formerly a vice, is now grown into a custom." So familiar has it become that it no longer provokes our detestation.

Viva voce. Lat.—"By the living voice, by word of mouth." "A *viva voce* examination:" that is, an examination *by word of mouth,* an *oral* examination.

—————**Vivendi recte qui prorogat horam,**
Rusticus exspectat, dum defluat amnis. Lat. HORACE.—
"He who postpones the hour of living rightly is like the rustic who waits till the river shall have passed away." He defers his reformation to a period which can never arrive.

Vivendum recte, cum propter plurima, tum his
Praecipue causis; ut linguas mancipiorum
Contemnas—nam lingua mali pars pessima servi.
Lat. JUVENAL.
"You should live virtuously for many reasons, but particularly on this account, that you may be able to despise the tongues of your domestics. The tongue is the worst part of a bad servant."

Vivida vis animi. Lat.—"The strong force of the mind, vivid or glowing energy of mind, fervor of imagination." The lively *impetus* of genius.

Vivit post funera virtus. Lat.—"Virtue survives the grave."

Vivite felices, quibus est fortuna peracta
Jam sua. Lat. VIRGIL.—
"May those be happy whose fortunes are already completed." Though struggling through life, I can without envy see those whose efforts have experienced a successful termination.

Vivitur exiguo melius—natura beatis
Omnibus esse dedit, si quis cognoverit uti. Lat. CLAUDIAN.—

"Men live best upon a little. Nature has granted to all to be happy, if the use of her gifts were but properly known."

Vixere fortes ante Agamemnona
Multi; sed omnes illacrimabiles
Urguentur, ignotique longa
Nocte, carent quia vate sacro. Lat. HORACE.—
"Before great Agamemnon reigned,
Reigned kings as great as he, and brave,
Whose huge ambition's now contained
In the small compass of a grave;
In endless night they sleep, unwept, unknown:
No bard had they to make all time their own."

A beautiful illustration of the value of poetry, in consecrating and embalming the deeds of virtue and of valor.

Vocabula artis. Lat.—"Professional terms, words, or expressions: jaw-breaking words."

Volenti non fit injuria. Lat. Law maxim.—"To one who willingly embarks in any cause, or willingly gives his assent to any measure, no injury is done." No one can complain of wrong in a proceeding, when the measure had his previous assent.

Voluptates commendat rarior usus. Lat. JUVENAL.—"Our pleasures have a higher relish when they are but rarely used." The keenest sense of pleasure is blunted by a too frequent repetition.

Volventibus annis. Lat.—"In the course of years."

Vox et praeterea nihil. Lat.—"A voice and nothing more." An empty and unavailing sound; a fine speech without matter; a mere display of words; mere moonshine.

Vox faucibus haesit. Lat. VIRGIL.—"My voice stuck in my throat." Spoken by a person struck dumb with amazement.

Vox populi. Lat.—"The voice of the people, the popular voice."

Vox populi vox Dei. Lat.—"The voice of the people is the voice of GOD."

Vox Stellarum. Lat.—"The voice of the stars." "*Moore's Almanac*, the scandal of the respectable company of Stationers, is still sold by the Stationers at their Hall, with *Vox Stellarum* for the first words on the title-page."

Vraisemblance. Fr.—"Probability or likelihood." "There is a good deal of *vraisemblance* in the circumstances."

Vulnus alit venis, et caeco carpitur igni. Lat. VIRGIL.—"She [or he] nourishes the poison in the veins, and is consumed by the hidden fire." Applied very frequently to a secret passion, where, according to our immortal bard,—

"Concealment, like a worm i' th' bud,
Feeds on the damask cheek."

Vultus est index animi. Lat. prov.—"The countenance is the index or portraiture of the mind." So say the disciples of LAVATER; but, like other general rules, it is liable to many exceptions.

Vultus instantis tyranni. Lat. HORACE.—"The stern gaze or look of the threatening tyrant." In other words, the stern and ruthless tyrant himself. "One terrible presence, one active mischief, *vultus instantis tyranni,* is mercifully withdrawn from us."

Z.

Zollverein. German.—The Prusso-Germanic Customs League.

Zonam perdidit. Lat. HORACE.—"He has lost his purse." He is desperate through the want of money.

INDEX.

*** In this Index *only* the principal words, or those most likely to be remembered, in the several quotations, will be found, and the *initial* words are all omitted, as the quotations are arranged in alphabetical order.

Two (or more) words should always be looked out in the Index, when they occur in many pages of the work.

THE END.

www.ingramcontent.com/pod-product-compliance
Lightning Source LLC
LaVergne TN
LVHW021306110826
845150LV00003B/497